GEORGETOWN UNIVERSITY ROUND TABLE ON LANGUAGES AND LINGUISTICS 1995

*Linguistics and the Education
of Language Teachers:
Ethnolinguistic, Psycholinguistic,
and Sociolinguistic Aspects*

James E. Alatis,
Carolyn A. Straehle,
Brent Gallenberger,
and Maggie Ronkin, *Editors*

Georgetown University Press, Washington, D.C.

Bibliographic notice

Since this series has been variously and confusingly cited as *Georgetown University Monograph Series on Languages and Linguistics, Monograph Series on Languages and Linguistics, Reports of the Annual Round Table Meeting on Linguistics and Language Study,* etc., beginning with the 1973 volume the title of the series was changed.

The new title of the series includes the year of a Round Table and omits both the monograph number and the meeting number, thus: *Georgetown University Round Table on Languages and Linguistics 1995*, with the regular abbreviation *GURT '95*. Full bibliographic references should show the form:

Ferguson, Charles A. 1995. "Long-term commitment and lucky events." In James E. Alatis et al. (eds.), *Georgetown University Round Table on Languages and Linguistics 1995*. Washington, D.C.: Georgetown University Press. #–#.

Library of Congress Catalog Number:
ISBN 0-87840-130-X
ISSN 0186-7207

THIS VOLUME IS DEDICATED TO CHARLES A. FERGUSON, PH.D.,
PIONEER IN APPLIED LINGUISTICS AND SOCIOLINGUISTICS,
DEVOTEE OF THE "LESS COMMONLY TAUGHT" LANGUAGES,
PARTICIPANT IN THE FIRST G.U. ROUND TABLE, FRIEND OF GEORGETOWN,
AND INSPIRATION TO MANY OF THE CONTRIBUTORS TO THIS VOLUME.

Contents

Psycholinguistic approaches

Program development

Technology and language learning

Theoretical linguistic approaches

Trends, practices, and reflections

Linking theory and practice

Introduction to the volume

James E. Alatis, *Chair, GURT '95*
Carolyn A. Straehle, *Coordinator, GURT '95*
Brent Gallenberger, *GURT Associate*
and Maggie Ronkin, *GURT Associate*

This volume contains the published version of papers from the 1995 Georgetown University Round Table on Languages and Linguistics, also known as the Round Table, or GURT, for short. The theme of the 1995 conference, held March 6 through March 11, 1995, was "Linguistics and the education of second-language teachers: Ethnolinguistic, psycholinguistic, and sociolinguistic aspects."

The 1995 conference, which was the forty-sixth annual Round Table, was sponsored by Georgetown University's Center for International Language Programs and Research. Each year, the Round Table brings together college and university professors, program administrators, researchers, Government professional staff, elementary- and secondary-school teachers, authors, and students of languages and linguistics. Scholars and students from the United States and other countries—Egypt, Greece, Japan, Singapore, and Taiwan, to name a few—gathered to listen, discuss, and learn from one another.

The main sessions of the conference were opened by the conference Chair, James E. Alatis, the evening of Wednesday, March 8. Eugene Garcia, Director of the Office of Bilingual Education and Minority Languages Affairs, U.S. Department of Education, began the conference with some remarks on linguistic and cultural diversity in America's schools. Stephen Krashen, from the University of Southern California, followed by delivering the plenary address.

At the opening session, the proceedings of the 1995 Round Table were dedicated to Charles A. Ferguson of Stanford University. Since Professor Ferguson was unable to attend the conference, Thom Huebner of San José State University responded on his behalf. For the published proceedings, however, Professor Ferguson has contributed an article which reflects on his career and development as a linguist.

The conference featured forty-eight other speakers in three days of plenary and concurrent sessions. The first two plenary speakers, on Thursday, March 9, were Bessie Dendrinos of the University of Athens, Greece, and Kathleen Bailey of the Monterey Institute of International Studies. Friday's plenary sessions were presented by Leslie M. Beebe of Teachers College, Columbia University and Teresa Pica of the University of Pennsylvania. The plenary sessions on the closing day, Saturday, were offered by Marianne Celce-Murcia of the University of California, Los Angeles and Diane Larsen-Freeman of the School for International Training. Three days of presessions and preconference tutorials preceded the main conference.

The broad theme of the 1995 Round Table allowed the presenters the opportunity to look at language teaching from a variety of perspectives. As a result, the papers in this volume represent a range of research and reflection on the role of linguistics in the education of language teachers. Many of the articles are interdisciplinary in their approach to language teaching; still others look at what one discipline or subfield of linguistics has to offer language-teaching professionals. The articles in this volume are grouped into sections according to shared themes or approaches; within sections they are organized alphabetically by the last names of the authors.

Two sections highlight the ethnolinguistic and sociolinguistic research that informs language teaching. The articles in "Language, culture, and ideology" investigate how language learning and teaching are embedded in and shaped by larger societal and cultural contexts. The articles in "Discourse-based studies" present microanalyses of spoken and written discourse and connect findings to issues arising for teachers and learners of language, both in and beyond the classroom.

The "Psycholinguistic approaches" section presents psycholinguistic research that is teacher- and/or learner-oriented. The papers highlight topics ranging from learning strategies and learner-anxiety to how findings from psycholinguistic research can enhance teacher education and classroom practice.

The section on "Program development" presents articles focussing on the education of second-language teachers, from curriculum design and implementation to the role of linguistic research in a teacher-education program. Papers in the "Technology and language teaching" section discuss developments which integrate technology into the classroom, from instructional software to using the Internet.

The "Theoretical linguistic approaches" section features articles on phonology, morphology, and syntax that have implications for language teaching. "Trends, practices, and reflections" contains articles that consider practical and philosophical issues for learners and teachers in general, or that point to new directions for research. The final section, "Linking theory and practice," contains the papers from the two plenaries on Saturday, March 11. Both papers discuss in broader terms how the different approaches to linguistics —ethno-, psycho-, socio- and others—inform the education of second-language teachers, and thus capture the spirit of the conference.

In closing, the editors wish to thank the other members of the Round Table staff who were instrumental in the organization of the conference and the preparation of this volume, Mr. H.K. Kim and Dr. Deborah Fallows.

Greetings and remarks

Eugene E. Garcia
Office of Bilingual Education and Minority Languages Affairs
U.S. Department of Education

It is a pleasure to join you at the Round Table and address briefly the education of our linguistically and culturally diverse students. Critical leadership by many of you here has set the stage for a new direction in this arena throughout the nation. *This new direction builds upon the understanding that a child's "raíces"—roots—are important and implores us to build upon the strengths of diversity for all students and ensure that they achieve to high standards.*

As many of you have witnessed, the linguistic and cultural diversity in America's schools has increased dramatically over the past decade. One in three children nationwide is now from an ethnic or racial minority group, and one in seven children now speaks a language other than English at home. Educating children from diverse family backgrounds is—and should be—a major concern of school systems across the nation because for many of these children American education has not been a successful experience. We are urged to *do* something different in our national reform efforts; but more importantly, all educators need to *think* differently about these students. These students must be perceived as national resources, not as a national problem.

For many of you, not only are you familiar with this diversity, but you value it and welcome the challenge of educating linguistically and culturally diverse students to high academic standards. Your exemplary commitment to ensure that all students have a successful educational experience will help other educators and community members embrace the challenge of diversity. For educators who may be unfamiliar with our students' diversity, this can be a daunting personal and professional challenge of adapting, in adulthood, to a degree of diversity that did not exist during their own childhood or educational experiences.

The Improving America's School Act (IASA) embodies a new beginning in the education of our children where all resources are available to address the multiple educational needs of students in a comprehensive manner and where all children are expected to achieve to high standards. The entire legislative package in education, which includes Goals 2000, School-to-Work, and IASA, calls for the integration of educational services to meet the needs of today's students. This change is both a resource and challenge for all educators to find creative ways to implement reforms that will address the needs of students. For linguistically and culturally diverse students, several critical elements are:

- Title VII will continue to provide funds for the development of exemplary instructional programs for linguistically and culturally diverse students; the scope of grants has been increased to be a lever for broad-scale systemic reform.
- Title I, for the first time, provides for the inclusion of limited English proficiency (LEP) students who are too poor to receive educational services supported by this seven-billion-dollar investment of federal funds. Thus, Title I becomes a major source of continuing support for programs developed with Title VII funds.
- Title I requires high academic standards of *all* children and youth, including those who may have limited English proficiency; assessment of student achievement of Title I standards requires assessment that is valid and reliable—close interaction between Title I and Title VII on research, technical assistance, evaluation, and dissemination activities is encouraged for purposes of improving the quality and use of assessment.
- Title I and Title VII promote schoolwide programs—schools will be able to combine their Title VII funds with their Title I funds for comprehensive reform in schoolwide programs. This coordination enables schoolwide approaches to ensure that linguistically and culturally diverse students have access to the full mainstream curriculum.
- Parental involvement is a major component in both Title I and Title VII. Schools are expected to effectively communicate with and include the participation of parents of linguistically and culturally diverse students, and Title VII requires strong parental participation in program development, implementation, and evaluation.
- Both Title I and Title VII emphasize staff development to improve the quality of instruction; and
- Title II and Title VII provide strengthened professional development programs for individuals engaged in education. Title II funding is provided for professional development that is guided by challenging state content standards and is integrated into systemic educational reform efforts. Title VII makes a greater investment in professional development through four types of grants which allow for the training of new and existing educators to serve linguistically and culturally diverse children and youth.

Within the framework of Goals 2000, the Improving America's Schools Act provides programmatic support to help schools build their capacity to implement reform that will allow them to ensure that *all* their students achieve to high standards. As the Department of Education continues to seek ways to support you in your important work, your input will continue to be essential. As the field moves to implement reform efforts, your leadership and commitment will be vital. Allow me to ask of you five things:

(1) Take on the new educational challenge with resolve, commitment and "ganas" (gains),
(2) Be up-to-date on the new knowledge base,
(3) Share the knowledge with the education community,
(4) Accept the challenges of leadership and teamwork to effect reform, and
(5) Care and be an advocate for our culturally diverse children and families by nurturing, celebrating, and challenging them.

Together, we shall ensure that our linguistically and culturally diverse students, like all other students, reap the benefits of educational reform. A commitment of time and resources together with our creative spirit and leadership can enable the future for our linguistically and culturally diverse society.

Dedication of Round Table Proceedings to Charles A. Ferguson

James E. Alatis
Georgetown University

It is a Round Table tradition to recognize important scholars in the field of languages and linguistics—scholars whose achievements have been many and distinguished, and whose association with this conference has been vital and significant—by dedicating the published *Proceedings* in their honor. Among those we have honored in recent years are Professor Kenneth L. Pike, Robert J. Di Pietro, and Father Francis P. Dinneen.

To the roster of distinguished scholars whom the Round Table has recently recognized, tonight we shall add the name of Professor Charles A. Ferguson. Professor Emeritus at Stanford University, Charles A. Ferguson has been at the heart of linguistics for fifty years. His research spans the areas of South Asian linguistics, Arabic linguistics, child language, the language spoken to children and foreigners, language and religion, sociolinguistics, and language universals. Unfortunately, due to illness, Professor Ferguson cannot be here tonight to join me on this stage and speak before you; instead, allow me to give a brief introduction, followed by Thom Huebner, of San José State University, who has graciously agreed to say a few words in response.

Professor Ferguson received his Ph.D. from the University of Pennsylvania in 1945. He began his career as a linguist with the Foreign Service Institute of the U.S. Department of State, and in addition to his tenure at Stanford, has held prestigious university appointments around the world. Indeed, Georgetown itself was honored to count him among the faculty members of the Linguistics Department for several years. He is a respected author and editor in the fields of child language, child phonology, sociolinguistics, Arabic dialects, and Bengali grammar. His seminal article on diglossia is a classic, and his 1971 book, *Language Structure and Use: Essays by Charles A. Ferguson*, is one of his best-known works.

Professor Ferguson has always been generous with his time and with his talents. He was the first Director of the Center for Applied Linguistics, an organization formed in 1959 to serve as a clearinghouse of information for universities and others concerned with the application of linguistic science to practical language problems. During his career, he has served as President of the International Association for the Study of Language Acquisition, President of the Linguistic Society of America, and President of the Arabic Linguistics Society.

A scholar of extraordinary range, Professor Ferguson has integrated theoretical and applied concerns, demonstrating the intrinsic unity of scholarship. Accomplished and recognized in many of the subfields of linguistics, many consider him to be among this country's founders of sociolinguistics. So valued are his numerous accomplishments to the field of linguistics that, in 1991, Georgetown awarded him the degree of Doctor of Humane Letters, *honoris causa*.

The papers which Professor Ferguson has delivered at Round Table meetings in the past constitute some of this meeting's most important contributions to the field of linguistics. He prides himself in saying that he was present at the very first GURT. Over the years he has also been a close personal advisor and source of advice on Round Table matters. It is, therefore, with great pleasure that, in recognition of his distinguished achievements in the field—indeed, the many subfields—of linguistics, and in recognition of his faithful friendship to this University and to this Round Table Conference, we hereby dedicate the *Proceedings* of the 1995 conference in honor of Charles A. Ferguson.

Dedication to Charles A. Ferguson: A response

Thom Huebner
San José State University

When I learned I would be accepting this honor on Professor Ferguson's behalf, I asked him if there was anything in particular he would like me to say. In his typically humble way, he asked only that I relay his deep gratitude to Georgetown University and then, almost as an afterthought, added, "You could remind them that I was at the first GURT."

Since that first GURT, Ferguson's association with Georgetown University has run deeper than the frequent contributions he has made subsequently to this distinguished forum. He holds an honorary degree from Georgetown. He has taught classes here, both during the regular academic year, and during the Linguistic Society of America's Summer Linguistics Institutes held at this institution. And as anyone who talks to him for even the shortest period of time about his Georgetown connections soon learns, he was married to Shirley Brice Heath on this campus. He recalls with delight that he, a Lutheran, was married in a Jesuit chapel, with an Orthodox Jew (Joshua Fishman) singing the Blessing, followed by a reception held at the home of a Greek Orthodox couple (James and Penelope Alatis). It is because of these many professional and personal ties to Georgetown University that Professor Ferguson particularly regrets not being able to attend this evening.

The Fergusonian acceptance and inclusion of diversity so pervasive in his private life finds expression as well in every phase of his professional career, a career which has provided any number of models for all of us to follow. Not only did he attend the first GURT, he was among the first group of four linguists hired by the Foreign Service Institute; he was the first Director of the Center for Applied Linguistics; he was the first to Chair the Committee on Sociolinguistics of the Social Sciences Research Council; he is a charter member of TESOL; he taught the first course in the United States entitled "Sociolinguistics"; and he held the first chair in linguistics at Stanford University. In areas of study ranging from Arabic linguistics to applied linguistics, from child language acquisition to language planning, from language and religion to language universals, from Bengali syntax to American sports-announcer talk, seminal papers bear his authorship. He has held academic appointments at universities on five continents (North America, Asia, Europe, Australia, and South America). A festschrift on the occasion of his sixty-fifth birthday (Fishman et al. 1986) had editors from five continents and, as he has often pointed out with no small degree of satisfaction, from four different religious traditions.

Well into his retirement from Stanford University, Professor Ferguson's scholarship continues at a pace to which more junior researchers can only aspire. A collection of his papers in sociolinguistics, including several previously unpublished, is about to appear from Oxford University Press (Ferguson 1995), as is a collection of his papers on Arabic linguistics from E. J. Brill (Ferguson, to appear). At the same time, he is working on reviews in the areas of literacy and language planning. From his earliest through his most recent publications, his broad-ranging inquiries into the nature of language are united by his search for what of language is universal, what is subject to social conventionalization, and what is open to individual differences. Regardless of the direction his wide interest in language has taken him, his work has been characterized by uncommon diligence, breadth of knowledge, and intellectual integrity. Although he has never adhered steadfastly to a single theoretical framework, he consistently reminds us of the facts of language structure, acquisition, and use that a theory of linguistics must account for.

It has been a privilege for me to have had the opportunity to work with Charles Ferguson and to call him a friend. On behalf of both him and Shirley Brice Heath, I want to thank Georgetown University for honoring him here tonight.

REFERENCES

Ferguson, Charles A. 1995. *Perspectives in sociolinguistics: Papers on language and society by Charles A. Ferguson, 1959-95*. New York: Oxford University Press.
Ferguson, Charles A. (to appear). *Structuralist studies in Arabic linguistics*. Leiden, The Netherlands: E.J. Brill.
Fishman, Joshua, Andree Tabouret-Keller, Michael Clyne, Bh. Krishnamurti, and Mohamed Abdulaziz (eds.). 1986. *The Fergusonian impact: In honor of Charles A. Ferguson on the occasion of his sixty-fifth birthday*. Berlin: Mouton de Gruyter.

Long-term commitment and lucky events

Charles A. Ferguson
Stanford University

As I think about those aspects of my life that have most to do with understanding the history of American linguistics and the kind of individuals involved in it, I feel that the most important points to be considered are only two—how I came into linguistics, and the constructive tension between purely academic career activities and more "activist" or "applied" activities outside academe proper. This tension took permanent hold with my decision to take a job with the Foreign Service Institute in 1947. In this short autobiographical sketch I will speak to both these points and add a brief backward look at my whole long commitment to linguistics.

Early Interest in the Field. In my own mind there is no doubt when my interest in human language and different languages began. Like many linguists of my generation and perhaps of other generations, my interest in languages and/or linguistics was aroused in my early teens. At first, of course, I had no idea what linguistics was, but as soon as I reached some understanding of what linguistics was all about, I identified with it and ever since have felt that no matter what I was doing "for a living," I was in any case being a linguist in the sense of doing linguistics.

In my case the early interest came simply as a fascination with all foreign languages as well as with some of the phenomena of English. I was an avid reader as far back as I can remember, but the fascination with books in or about foreign languages did not begin until about junior high. My family (father, mother, mother's parents) were not great readers, but they tended to tolerate my reading, considering it at worst a peculiar way to waste time and at best a possible avenue to advanced education and professional status. None of them, for various reasons, had ever graduated from high school.

My mother was born in Philadelphia of German working class ancestry (all her grandparents were born in Germany), and she felt that her teachers and the other children had thought of her as "Dutchie" and made fun of her until she dropped out of school. My father was born in Terre Haute, Indiana, orphaned early in life, and was taken care of by various relatives and institutions in the Midwest. He was from a farming family of Scotch-Irish stock, came East during

World War I, found a job at the Philadelphia Navy Yard, met my mother and married her in 1920; I was born in Philadelphia in 1921. Later my father worked for the Pennsylvania Railroad. When I was in third grade the family moved to the West Philadelphia suburb of Upper Darby. My father died of pneumonia when I was twelve.

One of the sources of my interest in languages was the language situation in my family. My mother's mother, who lived with us until her death during my university years, could carry on a limited conversation in German, which she had learned in what must have been the bilingual German-English home of her childhood. This was a very marginal part of our family life, which was activated only whenever an elderly neighbor stopped by to talk in what for her was also a language remembered from childhood. I could listen to the two women talking. This aroused my curiosity about how the German language worked, and I bought a little German phrase book that provided a few pointers on pronunciation and grammar in addition to sets of contrived conversational phrases. I soon discovered that my grandmother's German did not correspond too well to the phrase-book German: she used American r's, replaced /ü/ and /ö/ with corresponding unrounded front vowels, and her inflectional endings were much reduced from the ones in the book. Some of these differences probably represented dialect variation in Germany; others came from the influence of contact with American English. In short, it was my first intimation that languages could have quite substantial dialect variation and could be drastically influenced by contact with other languages. I soon gave up trying to understand or speak my grandmother's brand of German—it seemed to be too far away from what I assumed "real" German must be like.

Another source of my interest in languages was the tie between religion and language. My parents had sent me to a Lutheran church, for the simple reason that it was the closest Protestant church in our neighborhood. The three boys I walked to school with and associated with after school through junior and senior high school were Tom Foltz, a Catholic, Bill Bernard, whose family attended a Reform Jewish temple in downtown Philadelphia, and Franklin Weeks, of an agnostic family with a Swedish step-father. At the Lutheran church, careful reading of the introductory material in the hymnal—I early acquired the habit of reading prefaces in books—showed that the Lutheran liturgy was translated (and simplified) from Latin to German, Swedish, and other modern languages at the time of the Reformation, and later into English in America. Bill had Hebrew lesson books with their exotic consonant letters and vowel signs, Tom had little helps for participation in the Latin mass at which he sometimes served, and Franklin offered a bit of counterpoint for our adolescent talk about religion and shared my fascination with languages (later we studied German and Russian together at an institute in Philadelphia).

Another source of the language interest—or better, a strengthening or reinforcement of it—was the knowledge of several adults I got to know, mostly teachers. In ninth grade I elected Latin in school and enjoyed the experience. The teacher was not particularly good, but he actually spoke fluent French, my first experience of a live speaker of a modern foreign language in its standard form. My teacher in Ancient History the same year was Wilda Shope, who was then a graduate student in Classics at the University of Pennsylvnia. She felt that teaching Latin and ancient history in a high school was a kind of *summum bonum*, and she told me stories about a Professor Roland Kent, author of books on the sounds and forms of Latin and Greek, and a grammar of Old Persian, and at that time Secretary of the Linguistic Society of America (LSA).

One person exerted a particular attraction for me. He was a young Methodist minister in Upper Darby whom I came to know because he exhanged pulpits with a Methodist minister in England. I learned of their exchange from a local newspaper and visited the local church one Sunday when the English preacher was there and then sometime later when the American was back home. He was James Pritchard, then a graduate student in Oriental Studies at Penn and he lived right across the street from our junior high school. I visited him often and undoubtedly made a nuisance of myself, but he was at that time studying ancient South Arabian inscriptions and we had fascinating discussions about details of the South Arabian alphabet. Much later he became a professor at Crozer Theological Seminary in Chester and author of a widely used book on ancient texts of biblical times. Here was a real scholar in action, not primarily a linguist of course, but very familiar with linguistic concepts. The other two individuals at the time who reinforced my interest in language—and incidentally also religion and language—were the Misses Helen and Vera Wagner, older sisters of the pastor of the Lutheran church I attended. I believe they were retired schoolteachers. In any case, they encouraged me to read the New Testament in the Latin Vulgate version. They assured me it would be easier reading than some of the authors I would read in school, which turned out to be true.

Finally, of course, there were books. In the little secondhand bookstore we had in our township I discovered a used copy of Cassell's Latin dictionary. Naturally I wanted it, but could not afford the couple of dollars it cost. I went back repeatedly to the shop to covet it and make sure it was still there. One day it was gone; as it turned out, my mother, who was well aware of my desire, had bought it and saved it to give to me on an occasion, I don't remember whether it was birthday or Christmas. I still have and use that old dictionary with my mother's inscription about 'having faith'. My chief source of language-related books was not school libraries or our municipal library but the public library on Logan Circle in downtown Philadelphia. That library had a surprising number of books on language, such as Henry Sweet's little *Primer of Phonetics* and *History of Language*, phonetics books by Wilhelm Vietor and Paul Passy (especially the latter's *Petite Phonétique Comparée*) and lots of other treasures.

During my years in junior and senior high school, I managed to complete four years of Latin, two of French, and one of German. The year of German was second year, since I was able to pass the exam for first-year German because of my study with Franklin Weeks and assorted phrase books and grammars. My teachers were good in various ways (e.g. French teacher excellent, but poor pronunciation; German teacher poor, but native-speaker pronunciation). One teacher, however, was important for my further development toward linguistics. Miss Nobel, who taught third and fourth year Latin, was not only a superb teacher, but she introduced us to traditional Latin grammatical terminology, figures of speech, Classical mythology, and some notion of literary history and criticism (we read not only the traditional Cicero and Vergil but short selections of various other Latin authors).

My graduation from high school was in 1939, and by a nice coincidence the annual meeting of the LSA was held at the University of Pennsylvania in Philadelphia in December of 1938. I attended that meeting, without of course trying to join the organization, and without much understanding of its purposes and practices. It was a great experience to see in person a number of linguists whose names were familiar to me from my reading.

University of Pennsylvania and the War Years. I don't remember the exact sequence of events, but at some point a cousin of my mother's called our attention to a competitive examination for awarding a four-year scholarship for the University of Pennsylvania to a dependent of an employee or former employee of the Pennsylvania Railroad. I took the exam and was fortunate enough to win the scholarship. We could certainly not have afforded the tuition fees of Penn without that award, so this was the first of a succession of lucky events in my life that influenced (or even determined?) important decisions in my career path.

Of Penn I will say little except that it was perfect for me at the time, even though there was no department of linguistics and no "major" in linguistics either undergraduate or graduate. I had an excellent set of instructors and courses from my freshman year through the Ph.D., with an undergraduate major in Philosophy (thesis on an axiom set for linguistics as a science) and a graduate major in Oriental Studies (master's thesis on Moroccan Arabic verbs, doctoral thesis on the phonology and morphology of Bengali). Penn had a wide range of course offerings and few constraints on the student's selection of courses. I wallowed in the academic diversity, choosing in my freshman year courses in psychology, English history, French language, elementary logic, Nicomachean ethics, history of the English language, and elementary Swedish among others. My undergraduate language study included courses in Latin, French, German, Greek, Modern Hebrew, and Old English.

Oriental Studies at Penn had a stellar group of scholars (including refugees from Nazism and Fascism such as Ranke and Levi della Vida): E. A. Speiser,

H. Ranke, G. Levi della Vida, W. Norman Brown, and of course Zellig Harris, who was my primary adviser throughout. During part of my graduate studies I had the valuable experience of close contact with Rulon Wells. He already had a Ph.D. in Philosophy (essentially logic and philosophy of language) and came to Penn to get some understanding of the linguistic approach to language, primarily by studying with Harris. We rented out a room in our home to him, which helped out our financial situation and gave the two of us a great deal of time to talk. We attended Brown's Sanskrit classes together, where Rulon began his interest in Indian philosophies of language. Henry Hoenigwald came to Penn at about that time too and enriched my understanding of historical linguistics.

During my university years, in addition to my education in linguistics (which was mostly but not exclusively in the structuralist descriptive approach of the period) and to my first acquaintance with Arabic and Bengali (which remained areas of research interest the rest of my life), I had two significant language-related formative experiences. One was involvement with second language acquisition as student, teacher, and researcher, and the other was interaction with Roman Jakobson, especially on his interest in the relationship between linguistic theory and language development in the child.

The Intensive Language Program. Beginning with fellowship support from the Intensive Language Program (ILP) of the American Council of Learned Societies (ACLS), I became thoroughly involved with the ILP. The fellowship support enabled me to work with native speakers of Moroccan Arabic living in New York, at first by regular trips to New York and finally by spending the whole summer of 1942 there. The ILP, whose history has been only partially written (Cowan 1975, 1991; Joos 1986; Hockett 1995), was an important feature of the American linguistic scene immediately before, during, and, for a while, after World War II. The Program, which engulfed many American linguists in language analysis, language teaching, and preparation of language teaching materials, was never the behaviorist, pattern-practice, narrow ideology it is often pictured as being, but the linguists *did* share a number of views that came from various sources and might now be modified or even repudiated by some of the linguists involved:

(1) Speech has primacy over writing and requires a corresponding emphasis on the analysis and teaching of spoken language.

(2) Practice, i.e. the actual *use* of a language, is more valuable for learning than the presentation of description, no matter how accurate.

(3) Description of the target language should always be with contemporary linguistic concepts, i.e. structuralism (though not necessarily with its technical terminology).

(4) One good teaching method is memorization of natural conversational material on useful topics ("dialogues"), then "freeing them up" by listening to

the same lexical, phonological, and grammatical material in new combinations and drilling on selected features to achieve fluency in particular aspects of the language.

(5) A trained linguist working with a native speaker of the target language can provide more helpful instruction than either one alone.

All these views have some validity and all of them have some weaknesses, but this is not the place to dissect the ILP. Suffice it to say that I came to admire the wisdom and foresight of Mortimer Graves, Executive Secretary of the ACLS and one of the architects of the ILP. He believed that American linguists, who were so excited by their recent progress in understanding the nature of human languages, should, in the national interest, become involved in improving the miserable American competence in foreign languages, especially ones not commonly taught. He also believed that every American, as part of his or her normal education, should acquire competence in one foreign language and that the process of acquisition should include learning how to go about learning a foreign language on one's own; this he thought because he assumed that there was no way to predict in advance which language or languages an American would find need for in the course of a lifetime and whether classroom instruction would be available. I also came to know and respect Milt Cowan, who coordinated the ILP and later became Secretary of the LSA and head of the Division of Modern Languages at Cornell.

My work with the Moroccans began my long association with Arabic studies. It also gave me the opportunity to prepare instructional materials based on the typical ILP views. I must note here that this first venture into fieldwork enabled me to make a great variety of mistakes in dealing with native speakers ("informants") to discover the structure of their language. The wife was completely illiterate in any language and completely secure in her knowledge of her brand of spoken Arabic; the husband was very slightly literate in French and English and quite literate in Arabic in the sense that he had memorized the Koran and could "read" appropriate passages of it from memory at funerals and other ceremonial occasions. I did learn a lot about the structure and use of human languages in general and Arabic in particular, much of it matters that could not easily be learned from textbooks of linguistics. I also had a little experience of teaching some Moroccan Arabic to Penn students.

During this period I became quite skillful in doing various kinds of linguistic analysis (particularly, as the fashion was, in phonology) and also in the strange setting of linguist-cum-native speaker as teaching team. In a succession of different projects and programs at Penn, much of it sponsored by the ILP, I found myself helping Army and Office of Strategic Services (OSS) personnel, with considerable success, to acquire competence in such languages as Moroccan Arabic, Japanese, and Bengali, in which I was far from adequately competent myself. I also experimented with similar patterns of language learning and teaching outside the university setting. For example, I studied a little Russian with Franklin Weeks at an institute in Philadelphia, and I aided American Friends Service Committee people to acquire Finnish in preparation for their going to Finland to help in relief work after the Russo-Finnish war. From my first observation of the process of second language acquisition, I was convinced that it offered a unique and valuable window on linguistic structure, a conviction that was explored in a series of publications of mine culminating in Huebner and Ferguson 1991.

On the linguistic analysis side, I began the traditional academic routine of reading papers at professional meetings and publishing articles. One of my first professional papers was " 'Short *a*' in Philadelphia English," which was read at a meeting of the LSA; it continued the work of George Trager on the phonemic split of short *a* in Newark English and made a useful contribution to a line of research that has since included publications by myself, William Labov, Paul Cohen, Paul Kiparsky, Roger Lass, and others. Also, one of my first published papers appeared during this period, "Chart of the Bengali verb" (*Journal of the American Oriental Society* 65:54-55 (1945)).

Contacts with Roman Jakobson. My interaction with Jakobson began with a visit he made to Penn, when he gave a lecture presenting some of his views on phonology and referred to his recent *Kindersprache* monograph. By a nice coincidence his visit came at a time when I was taking a course in the psychology of speech at Penn. I was impressed with how separate the psychological and linguistic streams of research were; I wrote a paper for the psych course that strongly recommended that the two streams should become connected and so benefit from each other. I decided at that time that I would some day try to do research on child phonology that would draw on both streams. As it happened, I had no opportunity to do so until 1967, when I offered courses on child language at Stanford University and at the Linguistic Institute that summer at the University of Michigan. That year I also initiated the Child Phonology Project at Stanford, which persisted with outside funding, mostly from the National Science Foundation, until 1991, and in some ways can be seen as culminating in Ferguson, Menn, and Stoel-Gammon 1992. My original exposure to Jakobson was so captivating that I arranged to commute one day a week over to New York to attend a course on phonetics and phonology which he was giving at Columbia University, and a decade later I profited from interaction with him at Harvard.

Tension between "pure" and "applied". In 1947 I accepted a position offered to me at the newly-established Foreign Service Institute (FSI) of the U.S. Department of State. My academic friends were displeased by this apparent betrayal of academic loyalties, but it was a wonderful opportunity for me and I never regretted the decision. It was the second point in my career where a lucky possibility opened up and I was able to respond. For the next twenty years I was constantly operating with a professional tension between solving practical language problems and doing academic linguistics. This was obviously the case with the FSI apppointment. The small language section of FSI, which eventually became the School of Languages, saw its role as improving the language competence of the Department of State and the U.S. Foreign Service in whatever way we could, within the constraints of the resources available and the policies in force.

As I remember, we started with a staff of four: my boss Henry Lee ("Haxie") Smith, often remembered for a radio program in which he identified the place of origin of American interviewees by their dialect characteristics, Carleton T. Hodge, a fellow Oriental Studies/Linguistics Ph.D. from Penn, myself, and Madeline Pignatelli, a career public servant who provided administrative and clerical support. The three linguists had all been infected by the ILP enthusiasms and transferred some of those views to the FSI task. Since many people considered the limited competence in Arabic and Middle Eastern studies a problem in the Foreign Service, it was soon decided that because of my exposure to Arabic I should be sent to set up an Arabic language school as an FSI branch in the Middle East. In fact, I spent the greater part of 1947-1948 operating a trial run in Beirut, and later, in 1953-1955 actually establishing an Arabic language school in Beirut, which continued for some years until conditions in Lebanon became too difficult. At that time it was shifted to Tunis, where I believe it is still in operation. The field branch was combined with various programs of Arabic instruction in Washington, and a corps of "Arabists" was gradually developed in the Foreign Service, which eventually included several well-known and highly respected ambassadors (a suggestive but sometimes inaccurate and misleading picture of this corps of "Arabists" was given to the public in Kaplan 1992).

In 1955 came my third lucky event. While I was in Beirut, Professor Edward Mason of Harvard, on his way back from consultations in Pakistan, stopped in to see me and expressed interest in having me join the faculty of the newly-established Middle East Center (MEC) to assist in Arabic instruction. The possibility was appealing to me as long as I could be affiliated with the linguistics program at Harvard. As a result of that initiative I became a Lecturer in Linguistics supported by the Middle East Center. This became a four-and-a-half year stint at Harvard, teaching linguistics under the direction of the somewhat idiosyncratic scholar Joshua Whatmough and teaching Arabic as part of the MEC program. Shortly after I came we had the good fortune to be joined by the prominent Arabist and scholar of Islamic studies, Sir Hamilton Gibb.

Several other scholars were at Harvard at the time who influenced my intellectual development, although the university structure did not encourage inter-departmental contacts. I have already mentioned Jakobson, who was then a Professor of Slavic studies there. Several social scientists helped reinforce my concept of linguistics as a social science, a branch of anthropology if it had to be placed more precisely. That view was quite common at the time: some of Harris's courses at Penn were listed under Anthropology. At any rate I had some interaction with Dell Hymes and Roger Brown of Social Relations and Jack Carroll of Psychology, partly directly and partly through shared students (e.g. Victor and Milla Ayoub, Jean Berko [later Gleason], Clifford and Hildreth Geertz). My interests in language acquisition and social attitudes toward language were strengthened and given more shape, and I developed some appreciation of the problems of measurement of language competence and behavior. Visiting scholars at the Middle East Center often contributed to my knowledge and philosophical outlook; in particular, I shared an office one year with Haim Blanc, the Israeli Arabist/linguist, from whom I learned a great deal.

Center for Applied Linguistics. The Ford Foundation had for several years been attempting to assist a number of developing nations with their language problems, especially by supplying linguists specializing in the teaching of English as a second language (Fox 1975). The Foundation had a hard time locating properly qualified and available persons, and they sponsored a meeting at the University of Michigan (Linguistic Institute 1955), bringing together specialists in linguistics, English, and national development to discuss the problems the Foundation was having. One outcome of that meeting was the formation of a committee sparked by Trusten ("Trux") Russell of the Conference Board of Associated Research Councils, who was faced with some of the same problems in administering Fulbright appointments to other countries. At some point I was invited to join in the deliberations of the committee, which included such people as Mel Fox of the Foundation staff, Trux Russell, Milt Cowan (then at Cornell), Arch Hill (Virginia), Al Markwardt (Michigan), and Freeman Twaddell (Brown). At one meeting of the committee, the discussions led to a recommendation that some kind of center be set up that would serve as a "clearinghouse and informal coordinating body" for the solution of practical language problems. I drafted a memo spelling out the committee's recommendation and suggested the name Center for Applied Linguistics. In due course CAL was established, with largely Ford Foundation support, at first under the aegis of the Modern Language Association, later as an independent organization. I was asked to be its first director; thus my Harvard academic interlude was interrupted by lucky event number four. The job seemed to be exactly appropriate for my interests and experience, and I served from February 1959 through December 1966.

Although my full-time professional position was again definitely "applied" in nature, I kept up my regular output of linguistic publications and linguistics teaching, the latter outside working hours (e.g. evening teaching at Georgetown University) and in the summers (e.g. Linguistic Institutes at Michigan, Indiana,

Georgetown, University of Washington at Seattle, and one summer at an Institute supported by the Rockefeller Foundation at the Deccan College in Poona, India). CAL started with a staff of three: myself, Raleigh Morgan (Ph.D. in Romance Linguistics, fluent in German, overseas experience in the U. S. Information Agency), and Nora Walker (a Syrian American with secretarial and administrative experience).

It was an ideal time to start such an organization: Congress had just passed the National Defense Education Act, which included provisions for strengthening the study of foreign languages in the U. S., and the U.S. Office of Education, the Ford Foundation, and various other government agencies and non-governmental funding sources were eager to support assorted projects helping to solve language problems. Within a relatively short time CAL was thriving to the extent of a million-dollar annual budget and a staff of about a hundred. The history of CAL has been only partially written (Fox 1975, Russell 1961), but it clearly has played, and continues to play, a significant role in the history of linguistics in America. It stimulated the establishment of similar institutions elsewhere, whether explicit imitations (e.g. Centres de Linguistique Appliquée in Dakar, Senegal, and Abidjan, Côte d'Ivoire) or more often simply similar in aims and methods (e.g. ETIC, the English Teaching Information Centre, London; BELC, the Bureau pour l'Étude et l'Enseignement de la Langue Française, Paris). CAL and AILA (Association Internationale de la Linguistique Appliquée) were probably the two institutions most responsible for the spread of the concept "applied linguistics" in the sense of solving practical language problems by applying principles from the language sciences, including linguistics.

In 1965 the fifth and presumably last lucky event took place. I had been looking for a university appointment, preferably far from my previous East coast experience. I had tried a year's leave of absence to teach at the University of Washington in Seattle, which I found very congenial, and I had some conversations with Berkeley, which did not work out. Stanford University invited me to examine their current situation with regard to linguistics and English for Foreign Students (EFS). I recommended that they strengthen their inter-departmental graduate program in linguistics by appointing at least one full-time linguist with primary loyalty to the program and that they keep EFS connected to linguistics as long as there was provision for research as well as teaching. They accepted the recommendations and offered me the linguistics position as a full professor, just matching my salary at CAL. I began my new job January 1, 1967 and taught courses in sociolinguistics and child language in addition to courses in linguistic analysis of more traditional kinds.

My interest in the role of language in society was actually of long standing. I had always viewed language as primarily a social phenomenon, and with the new Chomskyan emphasis on language as a matter of individual cognitive competence, I felt that one of the principal problems of linguistics was how to understand the relation between individual competence and socially shared competence, what I have since come to call the problem of conventionalization. My own contributions to sociolinguistic research had been quite varied: concern with different types of language situations and their possible outcomes over time, the processes of language standardization, language planning and public policy, in particular language problems of so-called "developing countries," and register variation, i.e. variation in linguistic structure correlating with different occasions of use.

I had been a member of the national Committee on Sociolinguistics of the Social Science Research Council (SSRC) since its establishment in 1963-64, chaired the national seminar on sociolinguistics sponsored by the Committee held in the summer of 1964 at Indiana University, and participated actively in a series of other national and international conferences sponsored by the Committee. When the journal *Language in Society* was instituted in 1972 I served on its editorial board from the beginning for the next twenty years. In fact I suppose some linguists think of me, with some justification, as primarily a sociolinguist.

From the time of the Indiana summer of 1964, my friendship with a number of active researchers in the field of language in society deepened and influenced my own thinking; in particular this was true of Joshua Fishman and his family with whom I have been closely associated professionally and socially. Other sociolinguistic researchers with whom I served on the SSRC Committee and in other settings over the years include: Bill Bright, Susan Ervin(-Tripp), Allen Grimshaw, John Gumperz, Einar Haugen, Dell Hymes, Wally Lambert, and Gillian Sankoff.

At Stanford I was able to shift my focus away from "applied" issues to more centrally linguistic concerns, although I maintained some connections with those other activities. Thus, the "constructive tension" between applied work and more purely academic responsibilities was at last resolved. Joseph Greenberg and I began a Language Universals Project, which continued for nine years with National Science Foundation funding. The purposes of the project, as I understood them, were threefold: (1) to build up a body of cross-linguistic generalizations that could stimulate various kinds of linguistic theory construction; (2) to broaden the range of theoretical perspectives from which linguistic research could proceed; and (3) to reinvigorate a more empiricist approach to the construction of linguistic theory, as a kind of counterpoise to the productive, but increasingly narrow, rationalist approach of the dominant generative model. We were particularly concerned with encouraging the investigation of many languages before making hypotheses about "linguistic universals" on the basis of one language or a handful of familiar languages.

The results of the project were disseminated by a series of twenty "Working Papers on Language Universals (WPLU)" and finally by the publication of a four-volume set *Universals of Human Language* (UHL) (Greenberg et al. 1978).

The papers that were published, either in the WPLU series or the UHL volumes, went a long way toward accomplishing our aims: they represented not a naive empiricism but a variety of different research perspectives, and they drew on a relatively large number of languages for data. Over the period of the Project, an increase in theoretical variety and investigation of a greater number of languages became apparent in the generative tradition. Although some of these changes doubtless came from other sources, including a natural maturing of the generative approach, some of the changes we feel were due to our project. Also, we probably helped to stimulate the new publications that began to appear in a typological-universalist approach, as in works by Comrie, Mallinson and Blake, Dahl, Croft, and others.

I also found that I personally had the opportunity to encourage research that pursued some of the same aims as the Universals Project itself, with the inclusion of the perspectives of language acquisition (both L1 and L2), and diachronic change. Examples include research on nasals and nasalization (Ferguson et al. 1975), conditional sentences (Traugott et al. 1986), and grammatical agreement (Barlow and Ferguson 1988). In short, I found the position at Stanford a delight, and I was enormously pleased to have a surprise two-volume Festschrift in my honor appear in 1988 (Fishman et al. 1988); I was especially gratified that the five co-editors of the Festschrift were from five different continents and four different religious traditions.

Envoi. In looking back over my fifty-plus years of commitment to linguistics, I notice several recurrent themes. One has been an abiding interest in analyzing the structure and use of languages and in describing language situations. In both aspects, languages and language situations, my interest has always been in diversity and comparison. Zellig Harris certainly refined my interest in description and analysis, and Joseph Greenberg convinced me of the importance of discovering universal characteristics of languages and language situations. I have always found comparison of a few exemplars the most congenial first step in arriving at "universals." Thus, my early monograph co-edited with John Gumperz, *Linguistic diversity in South Asia*, and my early article on "baby talk" (Ferguson 1964) are good indications of an approach that appears again and again in my research and publications.

A second recurrent theme has been the social nature of language, and several of my most original papers have been devoted to aspects of that undertaking: Diglossia (1959), Structure and use of politeness formulas (1976), and Sports announcer talk (1983) all have been reprinted as fundamental papers in sociolinguistic anthologies.

My interest in language acquisition, both the natural language development of the child and the learning of a second, third, or nth language as child or adult, goes back to the earliest days of my interest in language and has persisted to my most recent publications. My interest in acquisition differs somewhat from that of many linguists: I regard language learning as a special case of language change, i.e. diachronic change in language includes both change from one state of a language system to another—the usual focus of historical linguistics—and language change from zero in the direction of a full system—the usual focus of developmental psycholinguistics. This point of view was spelled out in Ferguson (1968), but its full implications have not been explored.

In this autobiographical sketch I have made a point of the tension in my career between activist or "applied" problem-solving on the one hand and "pure" linguistic analysis and theory building on the other. While I recognize some validity to this dichotomy, I have never been able to agree with the extreme valorization of either at the expense of the other. It has always seemed to me that a theory that has little or no practical problem-solving capacity is *ipso facto* less good than one that does and that one of the best places to look for clues to theory is in situations of "application." Sapir found that the investigation of "mistakes" in his informant's spelling yielded valuable insights into the nature of his phonological system, and it is this kind of interplay between applied and pure that I regard as the normal state of affairs in doing linguistics.

Interviewers often ask such questions as, What was the best (or worst) experience you have had in your career? If I ask myself which courses I have most enjoyed teaching, the answer is completely clear. On three occasions I have found a particular course unusually lively and stimulating. The first was in the summer of 1971 at Stanford, when I offered a course called "Urban language problems." The students must also have found it a good course, since at least two of them (Elaine Anderson and John Rickford) decided, largely on the basis of that course, to become linguists. The second was in the summer of 1973 at the University of Michigan, a course on "Language and religion." It was a large class, very diverse in interests and status—from beginning graduate students to post-Ph.D.-practicing anthropologists, sociologists, and linguists. From the first session when we talked about dialect variation based on religious affiliation to the last day when one of the students spoke in tongues (glossolalia), the course dealt with phenomena not usually discussed in linguistics classes. Several of the students later reported how they were "inspired" by the course. The third success was a seminar on so-called "simplified registers" held at Stanford, which was attended by a group of interested graduate students and faculty members and eventually was the basis for an article of mine (Ferguson 1982).

If asked which articles I most enjoyed producing, I would name four: (1) "The Arabic koine" (Ferguson 1959b), in which I offered argumentation for positing a more or less homogeneous, dialect-leveled koine in the early centuries of Islam which was the linguistic ancestor of most of the modern colloquial varieties of Arabic; this paper is often cited by Arabists, usually with disapproval. (2) "Words and sounds in early language acquisition" (Ferguson and Farwell 1975), in which we offered modifications to Jakobson's model, based on empirical studies of three children's early phonologies; the paper is often cited by child phonologists, usually with approval. (3) "Verbs of being in Bengali, with a note on Amharic" (Ferguson 1972), not often cited by anyone, but containing useful description and suggestive claims about verbs of being and verb-final languages. (4) "Variation and drift" (Ferguson forthcoming), a comparative study of the gradual loss of grammatical agreement in English and Swedish; it is due to appear in a Festschrift in honor of William Labov. It is interesting to note that all four have something to do with diachronic change, which is not typical of my linguistic research.

Not only have I had moderate success in my chosen field, even though I probably cannot be reckoned in the contemporary American mainstream of formal syntactic research, but I have had the good fortune to see a great improvement in the scholarship of those areas of linguistics of greatest interest to me: Arabic syntax (cf. the volumes of proceedings of the annual Arabic Linguistic Symposium), child phonology (cf. Ferguson, Menn, and Stoel-Gammon 1992), and sociolinguistics (cf. Hudson 1982, Fasold 1984.). I have also been fortunate to be "in on the ground floor" of a surprising number of new institutions and organizations in linguistics and related fields. As already mentioned, I was part of the beginnings of FSI and CAL, and I was present at the first meeting of the annual Georgetown University Round Table on Languages and Linguistics (1950). I was a charter member of the now large and flourishing Teachers of English to Speakers of Other Languages (TESOL) and of the American Association of Teachers of Arabic (AATA) and the Arabic Linguistic Society (ALS). Finally, I was the first fulltime appointment and later first chair of what became the Department of Linguistics at Stanford. Whether by long-term commitment or by lucky events, or some of both, I can with gratitude say in the words of the psalmist "The lines for me have fallen in pleasant places." (Psalms 16:6)

REFERENCES

Barlow, Michael and Charles A. Ferguson. 1988. *Agreement in natural language*. Stanford, California: Center for the Study of Language and Information; Chicago, Illinois: University of Chicago Press.
Butterwoth, Brian, Bernard Comrie and Osten Dahl (eds.) 1983. *Explanations of linguistic universals*. The Hague: Mouton.
Comrie, Bernard. 1981. *Language universals and linguistic typology:Syntax and morphology*. Chicago, Illinois: University of Chicago Press.
Cowan, J Milton. 1975. "Peace and war." *LSA Bulletin* 64: 28–34.
Cowan, J Milton. 1991. "American linguistics in peace and at war." In Konrad Koerner (ed.), *First person singular II*. Amsterdam and Philadelphia: John Benjamins.

Croft, William. 1990. *Typology and Universals*. Cambridge: Cambridge University Press.

Fasold, Ralph. 1984. *The Sociolinguistics of Society*. Oxford: Basil Blackwell.

Ferguson, Charles A. 1959a. "Diglossia." *Word* 15:325-340. (Reprinted in *Language in Culture and Society*, ed. by D. Hymes. New York: Harper and Row, 1964 and in *Language and Social Context*, ed. by P. P. Giglioli. Penguin Books, 1972.)

Ferguson, Charles A. 1959b. "The Arabic koine." *Language* 35. 616–630.

Ferguson, Charles A. 1968. "Contrastive analysis and language development." In James E. Alatis, (ed.), *Georgetown University Round Table, 1968*. Washington, D.C.: Georgetown University Press. 101–112.

Ferguson, Charles A. 1972. Verbs of being in Bengali, with a note on Amharic. In J. W. M. Verhaar (ed.), *The verb 'be' and its synonyms* (5). Dordrecht, Holland: D. Reidel.

Ferguson, Charles A. 1976. "The structure and use of politeness formulas." *Language in Society* 5:137-151.

Ferguson, Charles A. 1982. "Simplified registers and linguistic theory." In L. Obler and L. Menn (eds.), *Exceptional language and linguistics*. New York: Academic Press.

Ferguson, Charles A. 1983. "Sports announcer talk: Syntactic aspects of register variation." *Language in Society* 2:153–172.

Ferguson, Charles A. forthcoming. "Variation and drift: Loss of agreement in Germanic." To appear in a Festschrift in honor of William Labov.

Ferguson, Charles A., Lise Menn, and Carol Stoel-Gammon (eds.). 1992. *Phonological development: models, research, iImplications*. Timunium, Maryland: York Press.

Ferguson, Charles A. and Carol B. Farwell. 1975. "Words and sounds in early language acquisition." *Language* 51. 419–439.

Ferguson, Charles A., John Ohala, and Larry Hyman (eds.). 1975. "Nasalfest: Papers on nasals and nasality." Stanford University Department of Linguistics.

Fishman, Joshua A., Andree Tabouret-Keller, Michael Clyne, Bh. Krishnamurti, and Mohamed Abdulaziz (eds.). 1988. *The Fergusonian impact*. Berlin: Mouton de Gruyter.

Fox, Melvin J. 1975. *Language and development: A retrospective survey of Ford Foundation language projects 1952-1974*. New York: Ford Foundation.

Greenberg, Joseph H., Charles A. Ferguson, and Edith A. Moravcsik (eds.). 1978. *Universals of human language*. Stanford, California: Stanford University Press.

Hockett, Charles F. 1995. "J Milton Cowan." *Language* 72(2) 341–348.

Huebner, Thom and Charles A. Ferguson (eds.) 1991. *Cross-currents between linguistic theories and second language acquisition research*. Amsterdam and Philadelphia: John Benjamins.

Hudson, R. A. 1980. *Sociolinguistics*. Cambridge: Cambridge University Press.

Joos, Martin. 1986. *Notes on the development of the Linguistic Society of America, 1924 to 1950*, With a forward by J M. Cowan and C. F. Hockett. Ithaca, NY: Linguistica.

Kaplan, Robert D. 1992. "Tales from the bazaar." *The Atlantic*. 270: 2, August 1992:37-61.

Russell, Trusten W. 1961. "Fulbright programs in linguistics and the teaching of English." American Council of Learned Societies Newsletter. 17(9):8-12.

Traugott, Elizabeth C., Alice ter Meulen, Judy Snitzer Reilly, and Charles A. Ferguson (eds.) 1986. *On conditionals*. Cambridge: Cambridge University Press.

Standard versus nonstandard:
The intersection of sociolinguistics and language teaching

David R. Andrews
Georgetown University

Introduction. Sociolinguistics often takes a back seat in second-language teaching. Some instructors have little formal expertise in the area themselves, while others consider sociolinguistic competence secondary to linguistic proficiency in the strictest sense. In other instances the discussion is limited to lexical or morphological variation, for there is a widespread presumption that the sociolinguistic subtleties of pronunciational and intonational variation are inaccessible to the nonnative speaker. It is this final presumption which I seek to refute in this paper. Not only is sociolinguistic competence in language variation a vital component of cultural knowledge, but it also has a direct bearing on the ability of L2 speakers to function successfully in the foreign environment. Nonnative speakers without proper exposure to and sufficient mastery of the standard may suffer from distinct sociolinguistic disadvantages, of which they are often completely unaware.

American intonational patterns in Russian. Among Russian emigrés in the United States, intonation is often cited anecdotally as the most likely feature of their native language to undergo unconscious Americanization. Changes in intonation can occur after only a short period of residence in this country, and friends and relatives in Russia are especially quick to comment on them. Moreover, even well-educated emigrés who jealously guard the "purity" of their Russian and avoid the more overt instances of language interference, such as English lexical borrowings, often succumb to intonational shifts.

In "American intonational interference in emigré Russian" (Andrews 1993), it was my intention to examine the Russian intonational patterns most subject to American interference, as well as to describe the particular nature of each such instance, on the basis of recorded data. Using a series of prints depicting the same section of some mythical Germanic city at intervals from 1953 to 1976, I elicited structurally similar speech samples by conducting interviews with informants of three groups: (1) Russian emigrés who had left the Soviet Union as adults, (2) young-adult emigrés (between the ages of twenty-one and twenty-nine) who were born in the Soviet Union but came to the United States during childhood or early adolescence, and (3) college-educated Americans of non-

Russian heritage.[1] Subjects in the first two groups were recorded in Russian. The young-adult emigrés all continued to speak only Russian as their language of the home, but of course had become native or near-native speakers of English as well.[2] The Americans were recorded in English. All of the interviews were divided into the same four stages in order to facilitate subsequent comparisons. By showing the prints in the same order and asking similar questions about each of them, I was able to elicit thematically similar responses from all of the informants, regardless of language.

The three major instances of intonational interference were sporadic in the speech of the older adult emigrés, but widespread and generalized among the young adults. The most consistent example occurred in declarative utterances with falling tones. Like most languages, both Russian and English use some kind of fall in completed declaratives; the difference lies in the exact nature of the fall. In English, neutral declaratives are produced with a so-called "high fall," which has a slight rise or step-up on the tonic syllable before the downglide.[3] In standard Russian the step-up is lacking, and neutral declaratives contain a simple, or "low," fall on the tonic syllable. Although subtle, the difference has profound implications. English also has a low fall, but it usually adds some nonneutral coloration (disapproval, abruptness, boredom, etc.) to the utterance. Another potentially nonneutral fall is what Ladd (1978) calls the "stylized" fall —a step-down of two level tones, used in formulaic utterances like "Thank you" or "Excuse me" in ritualized situations. Like the low fall, it lacks a step-up on the tonic syllable. In my recorded speech samples, the emigré youngsters have almost completely adopted the English high-fall for declaratives. It seems clear that they are avoiding the standard-Russian low fall because they have internalized English patterns, where the lack of a step-up before the downglide denotes a marked contour.

Another nonstandard intonational feature occurs in yes–no questions. The standard-Russian construction, which in the Russian literature on this topic is called "intonation construction 3" or "IC-3" (Bryzgunova 1980), involves a sharp rise on the tonic syllable with an equally abrupt fall on an existing post-tonic syllable. This is markedly different from the most usual pattern in American English, where there is a gradual rise after the tonic syllable with a high-level continuation until the end of the utterance. Although it is strikingly

---

[1] These prints were first used by Schallert (1988,1990a, 1990b) in work conducted on standard-Russian intonation.

[2] The original experiment also included two American-born children raised in Russian-speaking families.

[3] Here and throughout, I use the classificatory system of "nuclear tones" proposed by Cruttenden (1986) in all descriptions of English intonation.

different from the standard-Russian contour, many of the young-adult informants substituted the English gradual rise for the Russian IC-3. Acoustically, this is an even greater deviation from the standard than the young adults' use of the high-fall in declaratives.

The final example of interference occurs in complex sentences. As Schallert (1990b) has demonstrated, standard Russian also uses IC-3 as a marker of connectedness in discourse. It is the preferred intonation for nonfinal phrases (i.e. the topic in topic-comment analysis) syntactically or semantically linked to a subsequent phrase or clause. Various commentators (Bolinger 1964, 1989; Leed 1965; Daneš 1967; Ladd 1977) have also proposed a special nexal intonation in English for the same situation, but the English contour is a fall–rise, very unlike the Russian. Among the young-adult emigrés, there is an almost wholesale abandonment of the Russian IC-3 for this usage in favor of the English-inspired fall–rise.

The sociolinguistic implications of this intonational interference are especially interesting. Many of the young-adult emigrés in my experiment complained that their parents often accused them of having adopted an Odessa accent, even if they had been born in Moscow or Leningrad and had had little or no exposure to Odessa speakers. In Russia there is a stereotypical Odessa accent, usually associated with but not limited to the Odessa Jews and perceived by standard speakers as a singsong. It may be the result of a former Yiddish substratum there. The Odessa accent is the object of ridicule and the subject of jokes and anecdotes in Russia even among other, more acculturated Jews. This is partly the result of the city's colorful and eccentric reputation in the popular imagination, a stereotype reinforced by Russian literature, and partly the result of the nonstandard nature of the Odessa accent itself.[4]

The most salient feature of Odessa intonation is a posttonic high rise in yes–no questions, very similar to that of American English. The older emigrés also hear the singsong in their children's use of the English-like high falls in declaratives. These are often produced in connection with diphthongized vowels, with the step-up on the first part of the diphthong and the downglide on the second. In standard Russian, vowels are generally nondiphthongal, and their incorporation by the young-adult emigrés signals an incipient American accent. Because of its similarities to the Odessa speech, however, the Americanized intonation of the young-adult emigrés may sound quite comical to standard-Russian speakers.

The implications for L2 American learners of Russian are obvious. American speakers of Russian are prone to the same types of English intonational interference if they have not been properly trained in Russian

---

[4] This stereotype has even entered American popular culture with the Hollywood dramatization of Il'f and Petrov's *The Twelve Chairs*.

intonation. As a result they will suffer not only from the general disadvantages of a foreign accent, but also from reproducing the intonational patterns of the Odessa accent. Their speech will therefore have comical overtones for many Russians, even if only on a subconscious level. The consequences can be even graver than simply being taken less seriously by native speakers. The gemination or drawling of Russian vowels by standard speakers occurs only in strongly marked complaints or appeals; it is the characteristic inflection of children trying to wheedle their parents into something. The English high-fall together with diphthongization of vowels therefore conveys a whiny, petulant tone to the Russian ear.

In the summer of 1993 I was the faculty group leader for an American exchange program in St. Petersburg. There were several instances when instructors misinterpreted the intent of student comments because of this type of intonational interference. Simple requests or comments by the American students were often interpreted by their Russian instructors as statements of extreme dissatisfaction or disappointment. Intonational interference in yes–no questions can also lead to sociolinguistic ambiguities. As Leed (1965) points out, the use of an English high-rise usually results in no outright misinterpretation. It can, however, turn a simple yes–no question into one with overtones of incredulity or amazement.

There is also the purely practical matter of the students' ability to function in the Russian classroom. For most Americans on their first study-abroad trip to Russia, it is difficult enough to follow and take notes on lengthy lectures in Russian. If L2 learners are not sufficiently aware that IC-3 is also the most frequent nexal intonation in connected discourse, it becomes almost impossible for them to develop the proper listening strategies.

Of course, everything in the above discussion can be applied in reverse to native speakers of Russian in an American setting. In fact, according to the experimental investigation of Holden and Hogan (1993), Russians who carry over their native intonation into English are at an even greater sociolinguistic disadvantage than their American counterparts. Similar difficulties in listening strategies may result from the differences in markers of connection in discourse.

Language attitudes in Russia and the United States. In the summer of 1993 in St. Petersburg, I conducted another experiment measuring the subjective reactions of standard-Russian speakers to nonstandard pronunciations.[5] The experiment used the two most familiar regional variants of Great Russian, both based primarily upon a single phonological feature. The first is called "okan'e" or, literally, "o-saying." It involves the retention of the vowel [o] in unstressed syllables, which in the standard language exists only under stress and otherwise

---

[5] The full treatment appears in Andrews (1995a).

reduces to [a] or schwa. Okan'e is spoken in a wide geographic area to the north and east of Moscow. The other regional variety involves the replacement of the voiced velar stop [g] with the voiced velar fricative [ɣ] or a laryngeal fricative nearly identical to English [h]. This pronunciation occurs throughout the southern third of European Russia and also predominates among the roughly 25% of the Ukrainian population that claims Russian as its mother tongue.

The methodology of the experiment was the matched-guise technique, pioneered by Lambert (1960, 1967) in his examinations of linguistic prejudices in Quebec. Homogeneously grouped subjects listen to a series of recorded voices, all reading the same text or word list. Some voices use the prestige variety in the particular language environment, others whatever stigmatized speech form is under investigation. Using a numerical scale, the subjects rate each speaker on a number of different attributes. They are unaware, however, that certain voices have been recorded at least twice, once in the prestige speech form and again in the stigmatized variety. If other voices are inserted between the two versions, subjects will generally not recognize a repeated voice, or so-called "matched guise." While the experimenter must record speakers who can be convincingly bilingual or bidialectal, the matched guises control for reactions to voice quality.

A total of fifty-four subjects participated in the experiment. They were all standard speakers of Russian, residents of St. Petersburg or Moscow, and university graduates. Subjects heard nine recordings of the same well-known passage from Lev Tolstoy's *War and Peace*, with the author and novel specifically identified each time. The passage was chosen so that the listeners would react only to differences in pronunciation and not to other linguistic variables. Nonstandard pronunciations, whether fairly or unfairly, are often associated with nonstandard morphology and syntax. It is certainly possible, however, to use a regional pronunciation while adhering to the standard in all other respects.

After each recorded version of the passage, subjects rated that speaker on a scale of one (lowest) to five (highest) in eighteen different categories. The subjects, of course, assumed that there were nine different voices on the tape, when in fact a total of only six people had been used. One woman was recorded in a southern-Russian guise as Person #3, in an okan'e guise as Person #6, and in a standard-Russian guise as Person #9. One male speaker was used in a standard-Russian guise as Person #1 and in an okan'e guise as Person #8. Four other voices, two male and two female, were recorded only once, in standard pronunciation, as foils for the repeated voices.

The experiment confirmed my suspicion that nonstandard pronunciations are indeed stigmatized in some domains. On the attribute "educated/intellectual," the female and male standard guises dramatically outscored their respective dialectal guises, with mean differences significant at < .0001 for this sample size.[6] In other prestige categories the standard was also rated above the dialectal guises. In addition to "educated/intellectual," the standard female guise was rated better looking, smarter, better able to express herself, and having a better sense of humor than both dialectal guises, with mean differences significant at < .01.[7]

A surprising result was that the female okan'e guise was rated significantly higher that the standard in four categories: "kind," "honest/sincere," "hard-working," and "hospitable." In the semantically related categories "dependable/trustworthy," "humble," and "pleasant/friendly," the female okan'e guise was also more highly rated, but the differences were not significant at < .01. The results for the male matched voice were identical, except that "reliable/trustworthy" was significant at < .01, while "hard-working" was not.[8] While clearly not a prestige dialect, it seems that okan'e elicits in many Russians the same positive stereotype—rustic charm and hospitality—that certain southern-American accents may elicit in the United States. For the southern-Russian speech, however, the latter results are totally lacking. In fact, this pronunciation is severely stigmatized in the same personal-worthiness categories where the okan'e is favored. As some subjects informed me after completing the experiment, this may partially result from the fact that a preponderance of Soviet-era political leaders were from the southern-dialect area.

I can best illustrate the profound implications of this data for L2 American speakers of Russian with a personal anecdote from my teaching experience at Georgetown. Two years ago an entering freshman placed into an upper-level conversation course I was teaching. He had just returned from spending his senior year of high school in Kiev, which despite its status as the Ukrainian capital is still a predominantly Russian-speaking city. Although his spoken Russian was virtually fluent, he had adopted the southern-Russian pronunciation characteristic of most Kiev speakers. For me it was quite an anomaly to hear this pronunciation from another American. The reactions of my native-Russian colleagues, however, were much more pronounced, alternating between amusement and consternation. In fact, the following semester this student's instructor was our visiting professor from St. Petersburg, and she was quick to speak with me about the matter. She considered it a real problem and spoke at

---

[6] The statistical procedure used was a two-tailed t-test for non-independent samples.

[7] The standard male guise also outscored the okan'e guise in the other prestige categories, but the differences were not significant at < .01 for this sample size.

[8] The upgrading of non-standard pronunciation by standard-speaking subjects is quite unusual in any culture and has been reported only sporadically. See Powesland and Giles (1975) and Edwards (1977, 1982) for evidence from the British Isles.

length about how detrimental it would be if this student ever decided to work or study in Moscow or St. Petersburg in the future.

This is not an isolated incident. Under socialism, there were very few opportunities for Americans to study anywhere in the Soviet Union except Moscow or Leningrad, but that has changed dramatically. There is a growing number of Americans, including high school students, studying in the southern-dialect area. If they adopt this pronunciation, they will be at a double sociolinguistic disadvantage. It is a stigmatized speech form not only for status effects but also for the personal attributes ascribed to its speakers. These students will simply not interact as effectively with standard-speaking Russians, who are likely to comprise the majority of their future professional contacts.

Of course, such prejudices against nonstandard pronunciations exist in many societies, including the United States. Inspired by the interesting Russian results and suspecting certain similarities between Great Russian and American English, I subsequently decided to conduct a matched-guise experiment in this country using two American regional pronunciations. The American experiment closely paralleled the Russian in procedure and methodology, and the two pronunciations tested were Brooklyn and rhotic southern-American. [9] There were indeed many similarities between the American and Russian results. If anything, the nonstandard pronunciations were even more downgraded in the prestige categories. In the personal-worthiness categories, the reactions to the Brooklyn male guise were especially negative and therefore reminiscent of the southern-Russian pronunciation in this regard. Therefore, the same sociolinguistic caveats that apply to L2 speakers of Russian may also apply to L2 speakers of American English.

Conclusion. It was not my intention in the above discussion to sound like an old-fashioned prescriptivist, for I am certainly not suggesting that the standard is inherently more worthy than any other speech variety. The elevation of one dialect to the standard is simply an accident of history and a matter of social convention, and there is no linguistic basis for equating "nonstandard" with "substandard." However, deeply ingrained prejudices against nonstandard speech varieties are a social fact. L2 speakers, while not being compelled to adopt any one type of pronunciation, should at least be made aware of the difficulties they may face by failing to do so.

---

[9] The full treatment of the experiment, including a comparison to the Russian, appears in Andrews (1995b).

REFERENCES

Andrews, David R. 1993. "American intonational interference in emigré Russian: A comparative analysis of elicited speech samples." *Slavic and East European Journal* 37(2): 162–177.

Andrews, David R. 1995a. "Subjective reactions to two regional pronunciations of Great Russian: A matched-guise study." To appear in *Canadian Slavonic Papers*.

Andrews, David R. 1995b. "Subjective reactions to non-standard pronunciations in Great Russian and American English: A comparison of two matched-guise studies." *Language Quarterly* 32(3/4): 149-164.

Bolinger, Dwight. 1964. "Around the edge of language: Intonation." *Harvard Educational Review* 34(2): 282–293.

Bolinger, Dwight. 1989. *Intonation and its uses: Melody in grammar and discourse.* Stanford, California: Stanford University Press.

Bryzgunova, E. A. 1980. "Intonacija." In N. Ju. Švedova (ed.), *Russkaja grammatika, Tom 1.* Moskva: Nauka. 96-122.

Cruttenden, Alan. 1986. *Intonation.* Cambridge, U.K.: Cambridge University Press.

Daneš, František. 1967. "Order of elements and sentence intonation." In *To honour Roman Jakobson: Essays on the occasion of his seventieth birthday.* The Hague: Mouton. 499–512.

Edwards, J. R. 1977. "Students' reactions to Irish regional accents." *Language and Speech* 20: 280–286.

Edwards, John R. 1982. "Language attitudes and their implications among English speakers." In Ellen Bouchard Ryan and Howard Giles (eds.), *Attitudes toward language variation: Social and applied contexts.* London: Edward Arnold. 20–33.

Holden, Kyril T. and John T. Hogan. 1993. "The emotive impact of foreign intonation: An experiment in switching English and Russian intonation." *Language and Speech* 36: 67–88.

Ladd, D. R. Jr. 1977. *The function of the A-rise accent in English.* Bloomington, Indiana: Indiana University Linguistics Club.

Ladd, D. Robert Jr. 1978. "Stylized intonation." *Language* 54(3): 517–540.

Lambert, W. E., R. C . Hodgson, R. C. Gardner, and S. Fillenbaum. 1960. "Evaluative reactions to spoken languages." *Journal of Abnormal Psychology* 60: 44–51.

Lambert, W. E. 1967. "A social psychology of bilingualism." *Journal of Social Issues* 23: 91–108.

Leed, Richard L. 1965. "A contrastive analysis of Russian and English intonation contours." *Slavic and East European Journal* 9(1): 62–75.

Powesland, Peter and Howard Giles. 1975. "Persuasiveness and accent-message incompatibility." *Human Relations* 28: 85–93.

Schallert, Jan Eames. 1988. "Intonational aspects of descriptive spontaneous speech." Paper presented at the national convention of the American Association of Teachers of Slavic and East European Languages, Washington, D.C., December 28, 1988.

Schallert, Jan Eames. 1990a. "Pragmatic uses of intonation in contemporary standard Russian." Paper presented at the national convention of the American Association for the Advancement of Slavic Studies, Washington, D.C., October 21, 1990.

Schallert, Jan Eames. 1990b. "Intonation beyond the utterance: A distributional analysis of rising and falling contours." In Margaret H. Mills (ed.), *Topics in colloquial Russian.* New York: Peter Lang. 51–65.

The use of Arabic in Egyptian T.V. commercials: A language simulator for the training of teachers of Arabic as a foreign language[1]

Elsaid M. Badawi
The American University of Cairo

Television service was inaugurated in Egypt in 1960. Today, nothing remains of the fascination, excitement, and wonder that the early viewing of great events (such as the first rush of waters from the High Dam at Aswan) brought to the then still raw and unseasoned public. Commercial jingles, in the early days associated with products such as Savo soap powder and Melamine plastic dishes, have met, however, a better fate. The slogan *Salam ?ashanu* ("hurrah for him") as a popular expression is still going strong in Egypt, even at a time when the product it used to "glorify" has almost disappeared from the market.

Since those early days, Egyptian T.V. commercials have grown more powerful, become increasingly more sophisticated and, as in the West, employed extraordinarily high-pressure selling techniques. In a country suffering from a great disparity in the levels of education among its almost sixty million inhabitants, T.V.-commercial copywriters—in their tireless efforts to sell anything from learned journals to plastic kitchenware—use a wide spectrum of language varieties. These range from the idiom of the illiterate on one extreme to the idiom of the highly educated on the other.

However, in spite of the countless language varieties (including French and English) employed in Egyptian T.V. ads from 1960 up to the present, we have yet to find a single commercial of any type that addresses any educational level of audience where spoken Modern Standard Arabic (MSA, known in Arab countries as *al Fusha*, "the correct, the pure Arabic") is used as the medium in a face-to-face situation, be it a dialogue between two persons or even a direct address to the viewers. In fact, the use of Spoken Modern Standard Arabic (SMSA) in T.V. commercials is severely restricted to out-of-sight delivery either

[1] A large number of the commercials upon which the basic research for this paper is based have been made available courtesy of Mr. Tarik Nour, Founder-Chairman of Americana Advertising, Cairo. I also thank Ms. Lisa White and Dr. Alaa Elgibali for reading a draft of the paper and making valuable suggestions.

as a final message at the end of a certain type of advertisement or as the mere narration of a message appearing in printed form on the screen.

The use of SMSA in this manner in T.V. commercials would seem to be in harmony with the language situation in Egypt and in other Arab countries. It is widely observed that SMSA is used in Egypt, and indeed other Arab countries, with varying degrees of success (but always with less than native proficiency) only in very restricted situations—e.g. delivering university lectures (particularly on Arabic language and Islamic subjects) with questions from students and answers from professors in educated colloquial Arabic. It is also used, haltingly, at conferences on similar subjects as a means of exchange between scholars from various Arab countries. Using SMSA for an exchange between two Arabs outside such restricted situations (no matter how "formal" or how highly educated they may be) would indeed be taken as jesting and never completely seriously. It is evident that MSA is primarily a written medium,[2] with the various types of colloquials, particularly the educated one, making up the rest of the four-skill package, as will be outlined below.

Yet pressure is mounting from curriculum planners engaged in teaching Arabic as a foreign language (TAFL), particularly in the U.S.A., to accord the speaking of MSA a status equal to the reading, writing, and comprehension of MSA without paying sufficient attention to the language situation in the Arab world. In this, the curriculum designers for TAFL are in complete agreement with their Arab counterparts who are responsible for designing curricula for teaching Arabic to Arab children. The motives and the degree of seriousness with which they pursue their respective goals, however, are different: Arab language planners are prompted by an urge to "reinstate" (This is how they describe their action) to universal usage in Pan Arab society the norms of a "pure" linguistic model which, they believe, was the language of the intelligentsia in Arabia up to the second century of the Islamic calendar.

On the other hand, TAFL planners, in their exasperation with the polyglossic language situation prevalent in every Arab country (with problematic implications for learners of the language), seem to ignore the question of authenticity and advocate teaching SMSA even though it is not a native tongue anywhere.

This is one example of the many contradictions between observable language phenomena in Arab society on the one hand, and time-honored dogmas about Arabic and the practices employed in teaching it on the other. These contradictions are largely caused by the distance that exists between theoretical studies and their applications, which is far greater in the case of Arabic than in the case of, among others, European languages. Another source of such contradictions is the scarcity of authentic materials representing what actually

---

[2] A good account of the position of SMSA in Arab societies can be found in Kaye (1994).

occurs in the various language varieties in real situations. This scarcity is caused inter alia by the practices, long established in Arab society, of editing out from written texts features not complying with the norms of the "pure" linguistic model codified some twelve centuries ago, and by generally treating the spoken media as merely sets of deviation from the correct language from which they must be set apart. This situation for a long time inhibited the field of teaching of Arabic to both native speakers and foreign learners.

The introduction of the genre of the T.V. commercial in Egypt (as a product originating in a non-Arab society) has, however, changed the picture. Under the pressure to sell as many goods as possible which, it seems, is greater than the pressure to adhere to traditionally prescriptive practices, T.V. commercials have brought about novel and complex life-like situations. In these situations, each of the various levels of the language (said to be five) plays a societal role which is not only different from the rest but, more significantly, is in complementary distribution with them.

Arranged on a descending scale reflecting the degree of education (not formality as some suggest) or *al Fusha* features, the five varieties or levels, as they have been termed, are:

Level I: *Fusha al-turath* (Classical Arabic);
Level II: *Fusha al-<asr* (Modern Standard Arabic);
Level III: *<aammiyyat al-muthaqqafiin* (Colloquial of the Educated);
Level IV: *<aammiyyat al-mutanawwiriin* (Standard Colloquial); and
Level V: *<aammiyyat al- 'ummiyyiin* (Colloquial of the Illiterate).

These levels are not segregated entities; a certain amount of overlap exists between them, thus blurring their lines of demarcation and creating a graded continuum of features in the area between Levels I and V. But the most characteristic property of this continuum is that phonological, morphological, and societal functions and other features peculiar to Level I are gradually eroded in the transition to Level V and, vice versa, features peculiar to Level V are gradually eroded as we move to Level I.

As it is the case with social phenomena, features distinguishing each of the five levels are numerous, but the feature utilized most in commercials is the degree of *intimacy* associated with each: MSA, as a basically written, not spoken, school medium is aloof, standing distinct from the inner being of even the most educated members of society. In spite of the fact that I am an educated Egyptian who is regarded as very conversant in Levels I to IV and who uses spoken MSA in the prescribed situations as described above, I do not remember ever having dreamt in MSA, not even once, even though I quite often dream in English in addition, of course, to educated colloquial Arabic. There is not one intimate nonjesting situation I can think of in which spoken MSA can be an element. On the other hand as native tongues, Levels V and IV can, of course, be intimate to any degree.

As foreign languages, English and French do not share in the intimate–nonintimate features. Instead they stand in contrast with the rest as associated with "things exotic" in the case of French and, in the case of English, with "things reliable."

Because each of the five levels is in fact a significantly proportionate mixture of features from Levels I and V as stated above, the use of the various levels in commercials, whether singly or in combination, follows a generalizable pattern in addressing certain sectors of the population or in trying to promote a particular service or a product. (Of course, in our less-than-perfect world, not every ad is a good one.) Used alone, each of the five levels functions in the following contexts:

Level I (Classical Arabic). Over the last ten years, I was able to find only one ad in this level. This ad was put out by the Water Board to promote water conservation. In it, a middle-aged man in native attire (*galabiyya*) performs the ritual ablution for the prayer under a strong jet of water issuing from a tap, with water flowing from the sink and running over a tiled floor. In the background, a male's deep low-toned voice is heard reciting from the Qur'an "... and of water we fashioned every living thing." The authoritative, stern, nonintimate message here is that whatever the reason, wasting water, even for the purpose of performing an essential religious ritual, is antisocial and indeed, antireligious. No intimacy whatsoever is indicated. In addition to the stern voice emanating from the void, the audience sees only the back of a man standing in a badly-lit large barn.

Level II (Modern Standard Arabic). Whereas the source of "authority" derives from divinity in Level I, in Level II its source lies in reasoning, science, technology, good organization, time-honored experience, etc. Banking, investment, construction, precision instruments, insurance companies, and the like are subjects readily associated with this level. The degree of intimacy expressed at this level is conveyed through the gestures and facial expressions of the participants who are seen, but never heard, in the commercial. The usually-male voice issuing from behind the screen is also less deep and slightly higher in pitch than in Level I.

Level III (Colloquial of the Educated). As the spoken medium of the educated this level represents a midpoint on the language continuum stretching between maximum education and maximum illiteracy. A balanced mixture of intimacy and nonintimacy characterizes this level. A family doctor giving advice is a typical situation where this level is used, either in the form of a dialog or as a direct address to the audience: The friendly doctor lectures on the quasi-scientific properties of a brand of toothpaste, the protective quality of a baby diaper, or the curative power of certain medicine. Another common situation at this level features a know-it-all neighbor who intimates, for example, the cleansing power of a new formula of soap powder.

Level IV (Standard Colloquial). With the high degree of intimacy associated with this level, ads about familiar subjects such as tasty foods, comfortable furniture, useful gadgets, nice clothes, and things generally connected with self-indulgence are expressed at this level. Not surprisingly, commercials employing this level, either singly or in combination with other levels, account for well over seventy percent of the ads appearing on Egyptian T.V.

Level V (Colloquial of the Illiterate). Like Level IV, this is a mother-tongue level, and the primary difference between commercials in these two levels is the type of goods promoted in each. Commercials in Level V are numerically few and are concerned with goods used by the lowest stratum in Egyptian society, e.g. types of soap powder useable for washing clothes by hand. In contrast, automatic-washing-machine powder is promoted in Levels III and IV, differing in the "argument" they present to the audience: "Washes whiter" would normally be the message in Level IV, whereas in Level III the message would be to demonstrate the action of "the secret scientific formula."

In combination, up to three levels, including French and English, are used in ads in which each of various participants plays a distinctive but complementary role. Toothpaste promoters quite often employ this type of ad, of which the following three-scene commercial is an example:

- Scene One: A family picnic. Two young parents with two good-looking children, a girl and a boy, sitting for lunch under a tree. The girl offers an apple to her mother saying in Level IV: "Mummy, take a bite." The mother, touching her mouth, answers, also in Level IV, "no, my gum is bleeding."
- Scene Two: A doctor's clinic with a doctor in a white coat sitting behind a desk. The doctor, in an alarmed voice and speaking in Level III, uses popularized scientific jargon to explain why this symptom should be taken seriously and recommends toothpastes with certain protective properties.
- Scene Three: A picture of a tube of a certain type of toothpaste. A male voice details in Level II the scientific properties of this brand (which happen to be similar to those enumerated in the doctor's talk) and ends by recommending, in a commanding tone, the use of this brand for protection of the gums.

Various contrastive combinations of levels are also employed for the promotion of different types of the same article or service. For example, luxury villas on an exclusive, quiet stretch of the Mediterranean coast west of Alexandria are advertised in a commercial employing Level II and English. Using Level II (in the final message of the ad) suggests "reliability" and using English (in the main text) suggests "class". But Levels V and IV are used in advertising the sale of small apartments in a huge condominium in a very crowded area of Alexandria itself. The people targeted there are the semi-literate nouveau riche who would feel secure in being addressed in the medium of their birth language, viz. Level V. The message in that ad is providing "a home-away-from-home" atmosphere (Level V) and having the chance of "rising one step higher on the social ladder" (Level IV).

Several conclusions can be drawn from the above. The basic difficulty inhibiting the field of teaching Arabic as a foreign language (TAFL) has been, and continues to be, the absence of a realistic assessment of the language situations prevalent in Arab societies, especially the sociolinguistic characteristics of Arabic, the degree of interaction between each of its varieties and localized, generalized Arab culture and, very importantly, *the language competence of the educated native speakers*, who—as Lado suggests (1964: 8)—should be the model for foreign learners. Clearly understanding such situations is a prerequisite for not only the successful training of TAFL teachers but also mainly for establishing a framework for learning and teaching the language with all its paraphernalia of curricula devising, materials writing, etc. However, attitudes, both in Arab societies and in the field of TAFL, as illustrated above by the position of spoken MSA in the curriculum, show that still more empirical research is needed before agreement on those prerequisites can be reached; these attitudes also reveal that it is very difficult to obtain authentic and nonedited language samples representing levels of Arabic which function in comparable or related-enough situations as to render empirical research feasible.

The situation is different, however, in the case of the T.V. commercials. Because they are regarded by the language watchdogs as too frivolous to be worthy of concern, T.V. commercials are allowed to continue to reflect the "real" language situation in Egypt, as much as the ability of the copywriter permits.

In order to combat the effect of the inhibited language situation in Arab society upon the TAFL field, it is suggested here that comprehensive sets of commercials should be used as language simulators for the linguistic training of TAFL teachers. Arabic T.V. commercials, with their employment of levels, such as those described above, alone or in combination, try to bring the audience a slice of the "real" world outside and offer a unique opportunity for the study in miniature of the dynamics of the language within one unified uninhibited context, viz. the context of selling. There is no single type of activity in Egyptian society where equal coverage through language of all strata of the society is the main objective as it is in T.V. commercials. Notwithstanding the somewhat contrived nature of the material itself, the benefits of T.V. commercials for both teachers and learners of TAFL for the study of a polyglossic, societally inhibited language like Arabic are plentiful.

REFERENCES

Kaye, Alan S. 1994. "Formal vs. informal." *Journal of Arabic Linguistics* 27: 47–66.
Lado, Robert. 1964. *Language teaching: A scientific approach.* New York: McGraw-Hill.

Boundary discourse and the authority of knowledge in the second-language classroom: A social-constructionist approach

Barbara A. Craig
Tunghai University, Taiwan

Introduction and contextualization of examples. Much of the second-language teacher-education (SLTE) literature discusses language teaching and teacher education at what Richards and Rodgers (1986) have called the levels of "design" and "procedure." These aspects of teaching—methods, materials, techniques, activities—can be thought of as the "tools" of teaching. They are increasingly being informed by linguistic research in second-language acquisition and pedagogy and are critically important in the second-language classroom. However, in this paper I would like to focus on teacher education at what Richards and Rodgers refer to as the level of "approach" by looking at how a teacher's philosophies of language and language learning influence the role and authority of the instructor in the second- or foreign-language classroom.

In 1992, I taught in an intensive English as a foreign language (EFL) program at National Taiwan University in Taipei, Taiwan. The program was jointly sponsored by the National Science Council of the Republic of China and the Institute of Applied Mechanics at National Taiwan University. A team of five American teachers of English as a foreign language designed the curriculum to prepare a group of young Chinese scientists from Taiwan's National Space Program Office for short-term technical training in the United States.

I will be using my experience in this program to illustrate several points in this paper. There are a number of reasons why the Taiwan program provides examples that are particularly illuminating for my purposes. First, it describes a typical foreign-language-learning scenario: Students in their home language environment who are attempting to learn a second language in a classroom situation. Second, the students have a well-defined, real-world motivation for learning the second language. They will be using the language in a foreign country, which most of them have not visited previously, in order to learn technical content material on which their future career success will depend. Third, and perhaps most importantly, the Chinese students' views of teaching and learning differ dramatically from those of their American teachers. These differing perceptions include: The students' role in the learning process, the teacher's authority in the classroom, and the appropriate and accepted ways in which a second language is taught and learned.

This paper will contrast traditional notions of the language teaching and learning process (represented by the Chinese students' perspective) with the social constructionist view (exemplified by the American teachers' approach) and explore some of the implications of the latter for the teacher's role as a source of authoritative knowledge in the second-language classroom. It will conclude with the provisional outline of a discourse-based, sociolinguistically grounded philosophy of second-language teaching and its implications for SLTE practice.

The role of the instructor in the second-language classroom. A good deal of research in applied linguistics has been devoted to the application of models of second-language acquisition to the teaching of foreign languages. Figuring prominently in the literature have been topics such as the use of a communicative syllabus (Savignon 1983; Widdowson 1978); the role of comprehensible input (Krashen and Terrell 1983; Krashen 1985) and the negotiation of meaning (Gass and Varonis 1985; Long 1983; Pica 1993; Varonis and Gass 1985); the teaching of language through disciplinary content (Snow, Met, and Genesee 1989; Brinton, Snow, and Wesche 1989); and the importance of learners' cognitive and metalinguistic strategies (O'Malley and Chamot 1990; Oxford 1990; Rubin and Thompson 1994; Wenden and Rubin 1987).

Recent research has paid increasing attention to classroom interaction (Cazden 1988; Wong Fillmore 1991); the need for learners to focus on linguistic form (Doughty 1991; Lightbown and Spada 1990, 1993); the development of pragmatic and crosscultural competence as essential components of communicative competence (Cohen and Olshtain 1993; Hatch 1992; Kramsch 1993; Paulston 1990; Scollon and Scollon 1995; Tyler 1993); the knowledge-base of language teachers (Freeman 1991; 1994); and how teachers make instructional decisions in the classroom (Richards 1994). Of central concern in many of these later studies is the question of the role of the teacher in the language classroom. As Widdowson (1993: 505) observes, "Over recent years there has been a good deal of persuasive advocacy of natural instinctive learning and a corresponding distrust of teacher authority. The traditional roles of the classroom protagonists have been called into question." It is this question of the role and authority of the classroom teacher that I want to explore in this paper.

Teacher as authoritative expert. Traditionally, the teacher's role has been seen as that of an authoritative expert. This view is based on the conception of knowledge as a quantifiable intellectual commodity. The teacher, as an expert in a field of inquiry or as an expert speaker of a language, has more of this knowledge than his or her students have. Because this knowledge has a separate existence outside of its knowers, it can be given, or taught, to the learners by the teacher-expert. Freire (1970: 58) uses a "banking" metaphor to describe this view of education, "in which students are the depositories and the teacher is the depositor ... Knowledge is a gift bestowed by those who consider themselves knowledgeable upon those whom they consider to know nothing." Thus the traditional view of knowledge leads to a "transmission model" of education in which knowledge is passed from teacher to learner.

The view of knowledge as a separately exisiting commodity has a parallel in the "conduit metaphor" of communication (Reddy 1979; see Donato 1994 for a critique of this model). Based on information-processing theory, this model defines communication as information transfer and privileges speaker intent over intersubjectivity. Because the identities of the interlocutors are separately defined as speaker or hearer, the speaker becomes the conveyor of information and the hearer becomes the passive recipient of it. Merging the transmission model of education with the conduit model of communication results in the identification of the speaker with the teacher-expert and the hearer with the learner.

In the foreign-language classroom, the transmission model of education and the conduit model of communication, combined with the structural view of language, gave rise to methods such as grammar-translation, the direct method, and audiolingualism (Richards and Rodgers 1986). Language learning was seen as correct mastery of the language subsystems of sound, form, and meaning. Authority resided in the models of speaking and writing provided by teacher and text, and learners were evaluated based on how closely their linguistic production approximated educated native-speaker norms.

This is the model of language learning most familiar to the Chinese students in the EFL program described at the beginning of this paper. As learners, these students were most comfortable *learning about* English rather than *learning how to use* the language. The traditional image many of these Chinese students held of themselves was that of an "empty vessel" into which the teacher-expert would "pour" knowledge (Freire 1970: 58) about the correct pronunciation and grammatical patterns of the English language.

Social interactionist approaches. By contrast, the learner-centered and peer-assisted approaches the American teachers used in class were foreign to the Chinese students' "ways of knowing" (Heath 1982). Because such communicative or interactional approaches are based on a functional view of language, learners are evaluated according to how well they can communicate in the second language about various topics and concepts. The satisfaction of the learners' sociocommunicative needs is seen as underlying their development of linguistic and communicative competence. In communicative classrooms then, the teacher's role is to structure the language-learning environment so that learners can participate in meaningful verbal interactions with each other in the target language. Kramsch (1993: 239) observes that "The success of communicative approaches to language teaching have been accounted for by their functional usefulness and universal characteristics, but their real potential may lie in their ability to engage the learner in the dialectic of meaning production."

Even though the responsibility for creating classroom communicative situations and the authority for specifying language functions resided with the teacher, our Chinese students quickly found that their customary passive-learner role was untenable in a communicative classroom. The central source of tension for these students was the fact that they were used to relying on the teacher as sole authoritative source of language input, while their teachers were allowing —in fact requiring—them to take more responsibility for their own learning. Thus it was not the transfer of knowledge about language, but the transfer of authority for learning—jointly creating their own linguistic knowledge—that the students experienced.

Authoritative discourse in the foreign-language classroom. In his writings on Soviet semiotics, Mikhail Bakhtin (1981: 341) distinguishes between two modes of verbal learning in school. The first is "transmission," often demonstrated when students "recite by heart" the teacher's words. Bakhtin uses the term "authoritative discourse" to identify the language that teachers use to convey "acknowledged scientific truth" to their students. According to Bakhtin, "The authoritative word demands that we acknowledge it, that we make it our own; it binds us, quite independent of any power it might have to persuade us internally; we encounter it with its authority already fused to it" (1981: 342). It is this kind of language, characterized by Bakhtin as distanced, inert, and inflexible, that students learn to recite by accepting their teacher as exclusive source of acceptable language input. And, in fact, it was this kind of language, delivered with authority by the teacher, that our Chinese students wanted to receive in their language classes.

Bakhtin distinguishes the second type of verbal learning as "appropriation," or "retelling in one's own words" (1981: 341). In this mode, the learner enters into an internal dialogue through "the process of selectively assimilating the words of others." By this double-voiced representation and interpretation of another's utterance, the speaker makes it his own, investing it with his own semantic intention and expressive purpose (Bakhtin 1981: 293).

Kramsch (1993: 239) points out in this regard that "there will always be a struggle between the teacher whose charge it is to make the students understand and eventually adopt foreign verbal behaviors and mindsets, and the learners who will continue to use transmitted knowledge for their own purposes, who will insist on making their own meanings and finding their own relevances." It is this second mode of language learning described by Bakhtin and elaborated by Kramsch—the ability to internalize and use the language—that the we American teachers wanted our Chinese students to adopt. Our challenge as language teachers then, was to replace the transfer of knowledge with a partial transfer of authority from teacher to students.

Teaching as language-acquisition planning. As linguists, we study language: The organized intersection of patterned subsystems of sound, form, and meaning. Outside the language classroom, we tend to view the various components of the system of language as the constituent parts of a unifed whole. But as Bahktin points out, "Language is never unitary. It is unitary only as an abstract grammatical system of normative forms, taken in isolation from the concrete, ideological conceptualizations that fill it, and in isolation from the uninterrupted process of historical becoming that is a characteristic of all living language" (1981: 288). As language teachers, our stock in trade is this "living language": the words and utterances produced by our students as they strive to become linguistically and communicatively competent in a second language. These language behaviors, how our students internalize and use the second language, are both the focus and the result of our teaching.

Experience and research has shown that effective classroom language instruction is not random. It is planned, orderly, sequenced, and—at its best—informed by principled decisions and choices on the part of the language teacher (Widdowson 1993: 505). While most language teachers would not consider themselves to be language planners, Cooper (1989: 35) defines language planning as "efforts to influence language behavior." Seen from this perspective, language teaching is a form of language planning, and in fact Cooper proposes the term "language-acquisition planning" to designate "organized efforts to promote the learning of a language" with the goal of increasing its number of users (1989: 157). As studies in both linguistics and education are increasingly illustrating, one of the teacher's most important tools in influencing language behavior is ordinary conversation: the shaping of students' utterances through dialogue (see Bayer 1990; Bruffee 1986, 1993; Bruner 1978, 1987; Cazden 1988, 1992; Cummins 1989; Hatch 1992; Kramsch 1993; Ochs and Schieffelin 1984; Tharp and Gallimore 1988, 1991; Wong Fillmore 1991).

"Boundary conversation" in the second-language classroom. The ongoing discourse among teachers and students is referred to by a number of terms: "teacher talk/student talk" (Flanders 1960, cited in Kramsch 1993: 6); "classroom interaction" (e.g. Cazden, John, and Hymes 1972; Cazden 1988); "participant structure" (Philips 1972: 377); or "instructional conversation" (Green and Wallet 1981: 161; Tharp and Gallimore 1988: 109; Shaw and Bailey 1990). I would like to focus on the teacher/learner dialogue by borrowing Kenneth Bruffee's (1993: 17) term "boundary conversation," which he defines as the resocializing of learners by their teachers into the discourse of a new knowledge or speech community.

Based on Soviet psychologist Lev Vygotsky's (1978) concept of the social origins of learning, Bruffee (1993:8) defines knowledge as "a socially constructed, sociolinguistic entity" and learning as "an interdependent, sociolinguistic process." His words echo Bakhtin's, who describes education as "the ideological becoming of a human being" and the acquisition of language as "the process of selectively assimilating the words of others" (Bakhtin 1981: 341). Bakhtin contrasts "the authoritative word (religious, political, moral; the word of a father, of adults, and of teachers, etc.)" with what he terms the "internally persuasive discourse" of the individual speaking consciousness: a "word that is denied all privilege, backed up by no authority at all." These two modes of discourse unite in the individual learner's discourse as "struggle and dialogic interrelationship" (1981: 342). It is this process of the interplay of authoritative and internally persuasive discourse that gives birth to what Bruffee calls "boundary conversation" in the second-language classroom.

Drawing once again on the example of Taiwanese students learning English, the process of linguistic resocialization into the community of speakers of English is exactly the task that their American teachers had undertaken. The point is that simply transferring knowledge *about* a language from teacher to learner will not make the learner a member of the teacher's speech community. However, by forming a learning community in which teacher and students collaboratively engage in boundary conversation between their two languages and cultures, together they construct what Kramsch (1993: 9) calls a linguistic and cultural "third place". Bakhtin would call the discourse of such a third place a "hybrid construction":

> an utterance that belongs, by its grammatical (syntactic) and compositional markers, to a single speaker, but that actually contains mixed within it two utterances, two speech manners, two styles, two 'languages', two semantic and axiological belief systems ... There is no formal—compositional and syntactic—boundary between these utterances, styles, languages, belief systems; the division of voices and languages takes place within the limits of a single syntactic whole, often within the limits of a simple sentence. (Bakhtin 1981: 304)

This description of boundary conversation will be immediately recognizable to second-language teachers and to linguists who study the phenomenon of code-switching in bilingual speakers.

In the social constructionist view then, the language teacher's goal is to assist learners to become members of a new sociolinguistic community by helping them appropriate words from the target language and use them for their own communicative purposes. In the second-language classroom, these conversations take place on the boundary between individual speakers at the intersection of two speech communities. As Bakhtin points out (1981: 293), "language, for the individual consciousness, lies on the borderline between oneself and the other." The dialogue between individual speakers takes place in hybrid utterances that are internally persuasive to the speaker, not in the formal authoritative discourse of teacher or text. As Bakhtin explains, this is because "authoritative discourse permits no play with the context framing it, no play with its borders, no gradual and flexible transitions, no spontaneously creative stylizing variants on it" (1981: 343). As most second-language teachers will attest, such hybrid utterances are characteristic of learners, especially at the lower levels of proficiency. Because she stands at the boundary between authoritative second-language discourse and the learners' hybrid utterances, the teacher acts as translator, encouraging learners to use the second language to "retell in their own words" thoughts and experiences from their individual personal and sociolinguistic histories.

Teacher as translator. To encourage these acts of translation, the second-language teacher begins by exercising control and authority over the communicative situations created in the classroom. The teacher initially directs the learners to participate in problem-solving and communicative activities with each other in pairs or small groups, giving corrective feedback as needed. Gradually, the teacher/expert withdraws authority, guiding the learners to rely instead on each other and to provide their own peer correction as they gain confidence in using the second language for the communicative purposes that they increasingly choose themselves. As the learners take more responsibility for their own learning, their need for an authoritative teacher/expert decreases.

An example from the EFL program in Taiwan will illustrate these successive stages in the learners' development. Over a period of three weeks, students in an intermediate academic speaking class first participated in structured exercises that encouraged them to develop group discussion skills. Next, they worked in small groups of three or four to brainstorm and develop topics for a three-minute oral class presentation. They worked consecutively with three different groups, rehearsing and refining the content they would present on their chosen topic. Finally, near the end of the three-week period, the students returned to their original groups where they practiced the revised talk that they would give the next day in front of the entire class. Through these successive peer interactions, the students were able to assist each other while using their English speaking skills to solve problems and talk about specific subject-matter content of interest to them. The teacher's role in this process, referred to as "scaffolding" (Wood, Bruner, and Ross 1976), was to break the speaking task down into a series of increasingly difficult but individually manageable tasks and structure them so that students could build their proficiency collaboratively. (For a discussion of peer/learner scaffolding in second-language acquisition, see Donato 1994).

Barnes (1973: 19, cited in Long 1990: 310) describes the type of language typically used in student small-group work, terming it "exploratory talk." Such talk is filled with hesitations, pauses, corrections, and other disfluencies, as students actively try to use language to communicate and to learn. This kind of speech is an excellent example of boundary conversation as it is engaged in in the second-language classroom. Long underscores the value of student small-group work in encouraging such talk, pointing out that in a full-class session "the 'audience effect' of the large class, the perception of the listening teacher as 'judge,' and the need to produce the short, polished 'finished article' would all serve to inhibit this kind of language" (Long 1990: 310). In the relative security of peer groups then, second-language learners feel more free to use hybrid constructions in their boundary conversations. At the same time, the more proficient students provide comprehensible input for the less proficient ones, while increasing their own proficiency through oral practice.

Moving through the "zone of proximal development." Vygotsky (1978) uses the term "zone of proximal development" (ZPD) to describe the difference between the level of learners' individual performances and the increased proficiency they demonstrate when working collaboratively with each other. In explaining the notion of the ZPD in learning theory, Vygotsky points out the boundaries of collaborative performance for any individual student, noting that "what collaboration contributes to ... performance is restricted to limits which are determined by the state of his development" (1987: 209). Thus while learners working together can always do more than any one of them could do independently, this does not mean that the learners no longer need the expert assistance of the teacher to guide them, individually and as a group, to even higher levels of performance. As Vygotsky reiterates, "What lies in the zone of proximal development at one stage is realized and moves to the level of actual development at a second. In other words, what the [learner] is able to do in collaboration today he will be able to do independently tomorrow" (1987: 211).

Applying Vygotsky's theory to the second-language classroom, learners acquire the language through interaction with more proficient speakers, both their teachers and "more competent peers" (Vygotsky 1987: 86). Through scaffolded instruction engendering cooperative dialogue, students in the second-language classroom help each other progress while increasing their own levels of proficiency. At the same time, the teacher has more time to assist the performance of individuals or small groups than she would in a more traditional teacher-centered situation.

In a second-language classroom organized around the principles of cooperative learning and communicative activity then, the teacher gradually cedes to the students more and more control over the learning process. Tharp and Gallimore (1988: 21) describe this mode of learning as "assisted performance." Assisted performance defines what the learner can do in his

ZPD, aided by the teacher or by other students, that he cannot do alone. As Cazden (1981) points out, this type of language-learning situation makes possible "performance before competence."

Through repeated instances of assisted performance, the language learner internalizes what has been practiced cooperatively in the group, ultimately converting that assisted performance into individual competence. In Bakhtin's terms, while the learner begins by "reciting by heart" the authoritative discourse of the teacher and others, he gradually becomes able to "retell in his own words" the utterances he has appropriated and translated and is now using as his own.

Teaching as assisting performance. If language learning can be defined as appropriating and using the words of others then the goal of language teaching becomes enabling learners to actively construct their own linguistic knowledge by assisting their communicative performance. The discourse-based, sociolinguistic approach to language teaching that this paper describes is based on the social constructionist notion that effective second-language teaching and learning are achieved through both expert/novice and peer interactions in the classroom.

Such an approach requires that teachers, acting as language-acquisition planners, create a classroom environment in which students can assist each others' performance through their zones of proximal development. As students move from "reciting by heart" to "retelling in their own words," the teacher gradually withdraws authority as the sole source of linguistic knowledge and shifts some of that authority to the learners. Through this process, teacher and students jointly create a new sociolinguistic classroom community on the boundary between the students' own language and the second language they are learning. Through conversations across this boundary with their teacher and with each other, the learners gradually become socialized into the sociolinguistic conventions of the second language and gain confidence in appropriating and using the authoritative words of teacher and text.

Implications for practice: Teacher education. Shulman (1986: 11) proposes that there are three types of propositional knowledge used in teaching: "principles" derived from empirical research; "norms" which are the basis of morality or ethics; and "maxims" representing the wisdom of practice. The truth-value of these maxims is built up over time through social interaction and is manifested as the joint construction and reconstruction of practical knowledge by generations of teachers, but is not necessarily confirmed or supported by empirical research.

One such maxim from teacher education is that "Teachers learn to teach the way they were taught." Many university professors, for example, teach primarily through lectures and class discussions. Chances are good that this is the way they learned their own disciplines. A teacher-education curriculum based on readings, lectures, and explanations presupposes the transmission model of education and is thus congruent with the goal of preparing teachers to become university lecturers.

By contrast, much has been written recently in the second-language teacher-education literature that supports the idea of incorporating cooperative learning, team teaching, and peer assistance into teacher-education programs (e.g. Bayer 1990; Nunan 1992; Shaw 1992; Tharp and Gallimore 1988). The general rationale for using a cooperative learning approach to teacher education is that the mode of novice teacher learning should reflect the philosophy underlying the teaching approach they are learning (Shaw 1992). The intuitive appeal of the maxim cited a moment ago supports this rationale: "Teachers learn to teach the way they were taught."

If it is true, however, that teachers teach the way they themselves were taught, this fact presents a real dilemma for contemporary language teachers attempting to implement a social-constructionist philosophy of language teaching. Many of today's second- and foreign-language teachers did not learn a second language in a communicative-classroom environment, nor were they trained, as novice teachers, in using interactive, peer-assisted activities in their classes. Team teaching with others schooled in communicative approaches, as well as teaching and learning along with their own students through boundary discourse in the second-language classroom, can provide alternative ways for seasoned teachers to incorporate social-constructionist notions into their teaching. In addition, current efforts to incorporate interactionist theories of learning and second-language acquisition into SLTE programs hold promise as another way to redirect second-language-teaching practice to reflect the philosophy of a discourse-based, sociolinguistic approach to second-language teaching.

Implications for practice: Learner resocialization. Perhaps more importantly, students' views of their roles as learners and of the accepted ways to learn a language must also change. In critiquing what this paper has called the transmission view of education as realized in the traditional second-language classroom, Long (1990: 309) uses the phrase "the classroom foreign language learning socialization package." He points out that teacher-student interactions in the traditional classroom often follow the "stimulus-response-evaluation" pattern (Long 1990: 308) and are often limited to short, one-utterance answers on the part of the student. Moreover, Long argues that this pattern of classroom management also reinforces several social norms in the second-language classroom, among them that the teacher is the initiator and evaluator and the student is the respondent, and that sentence form and phonological accuracy, based on adult, native speaker standards, are more important than utterance meaning (1990: 309).

How, then, can second-language teachers influence their students' views of appropriate language-learning behavior to bring them more in accord with social-constructionist views? Based again on our experience as American teachers teaching Chinese students in Taiwan, I would suggest three possible approaches. First, it seems both obvious and necessary to start where the students are by constructing a scaffold to guide both their language learning (content, or "what") and their attitudes towards that learning (process, or "how"). For example, the students in the academic speaking class described earlier were accustomed to reading or listening to lessons about how to use English correctly in oral presentations. It was necessary for the teacher to first take the role of expert and present some authoritative examples of topic selection, content organization, and delivery style for the students to imitate in order to move them along towards more communicative activities. Once the students had been presented with examples, they were less resistant to experimenting with their own forms using hybrid utterances in boundary discourse in small student groups, and ultimately before the entire class.

Secondly, in single first-language student populations, the teacher needs to be aware of, and build upon, native sociocultural norms and predispositions. For example, our Chinese students already held cooperation and group consensus as valued cultural norms, and were thus willing to work in small, student peer-groups. In this situation, the teacher's challenge was to encourage each student to participate actively in group discussions using the second language. When teaching in a native cultural environment where individualistic and competitive behaviors are more highly valued (such as in a class of North American students learning a foreign language, e.g. French or Japanese), it may be necessary to place greater emphasis on individual scores or contributions when designing the evaluation component of the program. In that way, even though students may be required to work together in learning the second language, they can still be assured that each will receive "credit" for his or her individual contribution to the group's effort or product. In mixed first-language groups, various configurations emphasizing group, team, and individual efforts may need to be employed.

Finally, the teacher needs to show that she is serious about giving the students more responsibility for their learning. One way to do this is to ask for regular written feedback from the students about the approach to language teaching that the teacher is implementing. By requiring the students to be self-reflective about their own learning processes, skills, and discomforts, the teacher enables them to make these aspects of language learning explicit and thus gain control over the possibility of changing them. In addition, by remaining open and sensitive to student difficulties with what may be a new and uncomfortable mode of learning for them, the teacher can modify her approach in order to remain within the students' zones of proximal development. Vygotsky points out that "instruction is maximally productive only when it occurs at a certain point in the zone of proximal development ... It is as fruitless to teach the [student] what he is not able to learn as it is to teach him what he can already do independently" (1987: 212–213). As students gain confidence in participating more interactively in language learning, they will jointly enable each other to build competence as they move through their ZPDs.

This paper has argued that both the teachers' and the students' perceptions of the teacher's authority and the student's role in the second-language-learning process are based on their underlying views of language and of language learning. Because students' views of the teacher's authority and of their own role in the learning process are often implicit, it is the teacher's responsibility as expert to accept that authority initially. By using teacher authority to influence the learners and redirect their teacher-dependence towards peer-group interaction and mutual support, the teacher can assist students' performance so that they ultimately achieve competence and learner autonomy. Thus, because both teacher and student views of learning influence their modes of verbal and social interaction in the classroom, it is only by using the teacher's implicit authority as expert to renegotiate student expectations that change is possible.

REFERENCES

Bakhtin, Mikhail M. [1975] 1981. "Discourse in the novel." In Michael Holquist (ed.), *The dialogic imagination*, trans. by Caryl Emerson and Michael Holquist. Austin: The University of Texas Press. 259–422.
Bayer, Ann Shea. 1990. *Collaborative-apprenticeship learning*. Mountain View, California: Mayfield Publishing Company.
Brinton, Donna M., Marguerite Ann Snow, and Marjorie Bingham Wesche. 1989. *Content-based second language instruction*. New York: Newbury House.
Bruffee, Kenneth A. 1986. "Social construction, language, and the authority of knowledge: A bibliographical essay." *College English* 48(8): 773–790.
Bruffee, Kenneth A. 1993. *Collaborative learning: Higher education, interdependence, and the authority of knowledge*. Baltimore: Johns Hopkins University Press.
Bruner, Jerome S. 1978. "The role of dialogue in language acquisition." In Anne Sinclair, et al. (eds.), *The child's concept of language*. New York: Springer-Verlag.
Bruner, Jerome S. 1987. *Making sense: The child's construction of the world*. London and New York: Methuen.
Cazden, Courtney B. 1981. "Performance before competence: Assistance to child discourse in the zone of proximal development." *Quarterly Newsletter of the Laboratory of Comparative Human Cognition*. 3(1): 5-8.
Cazden, Courtney B. 1988. *Classroom discourse: The language of teaching and learning*. Portsmouth, N.H.: Heinemann.
Cazden, Courtney B. 1992. *Whole language plus: Essays on literacy in the United States and New Zealand*. New York: Teachers College Press.
Cazden, Courtney, Vera John, and Dell Hymes (eds.). 1972. *Functions of language in the classroom*. New York: Teachers College Press.

Cohen, Andrew D. and Elite Olshtain. 1993. "The production of speech acts by EFL learners." *TESOL Quarterly* 27(1): 33–56.

Cooper, Robert. 1989. *Language planning and social change.* Cambridge, U.K.: Cambridge University Press.

Cummins, Jim. 1989. "Language and literacy acquisition in bilingual contexts." *Journal of Multilingual and Multicultural Development* 10(1): 17–31.

Donato, Richard. 1994. "Collective scaffolding in second language learning." In James P. Lantolf and Gabriela Appel (eds.), *Vygotskian approaches to second language research.* Norwood, N.J.: Ablex.

Doughty, Catherine. 1991. "Second language instruction does make a difference: Evidence from an empirical study of second language relativization." *Studies in Second Language Acquisition* 13(4): 431–469.

Freeman, Donald. 1991. "'Mistaken constructs': Re-examining the nature and assumptions of language teacher education". In James E. Alatis (ed.), *Georgetown University Round Table on Languages and Linguistics 1991.* Washington, D.C.: Georgetown University Press. 25–39.

Freeman, Donald. 1994. "Educational linguistics and the knowledge-base of language teaching". In James E. Alatis (ed.), *Georgetown University Round Table on Languages and Linguistics 1994.* Washington, D.C.: Georgetown University Press. 180–196.

Freire, Paulo. 1970. *Pedagogy of the oppressed,* trans. by Myra Bergman Ramos. New York: Continuum.

Gallimore, Ronald and Roland Tharp. 1990. "Teaching mind in society: Teaching, schooling, and literate discourse." In Luis Moll (ed.), *Vygotsky and education: Instructional implications.* 175–205.

Gass, Susan and Evangeline Varonis. 1985. "Task variation and NNS/NNS negotiation of meaning". In Susan Gass and Carolyn Madden (eds.), *Input in second language acquisition.* Rowley, Massachusetts: Newbury House. 149–161.

Hatch, Evelyn. 1992. *Discourse and language education.* Cambridge, U.K.: Cambridge University Press.

Heath, Shirley Brice. 1982. "What no bedtime story means: Narrative skills at home and school." *Language in Society* 11: 49–76.

Hymes, Dell. 1974. *Foundations in sociolinguistics: An ethnographic approach.* Philadelphia: University of Pennsylvania Press.

Kramsch, Claire. 1993. *Context and culture in language teaching.* Oxford: Oxford University Press.

Krashen, Stephen. 1985. *The input hypothesis: Issues and implications.* New York: Longman.

Krashen, Stephen and Tracy Terrell. 1983. *The natural approach.* Oxford: Pergamon Press.

Lightbown, Patsy and Nina Spada. 1990. "Focus-on-form and corrective feedback in communicative language teaching: Effects on second language learning. *Studies in Second Language Acquisition* 12(4): 429–448.

Lightbown, Patsy and Nina Spada. 1993. *How languages are learned.* Oxford: Oxford University Press.

Long, Michael H. 1983. "Linguistic and conversational adjustments to nonnative speakers". *Studies in Second Language Acquisition* 5(2): 177–194.

Long, Michael H. 1990. "Group work and communicative competence in the ESOL classroom." In Robin Scarcella, Elaine Andersen, and Stephen Krashen (eds.), *Developing communicative competence in a second language.* New York: Newbury House.

Nunan, David (ed.). 1992. *Collaborative language learning and teaching.* Cambridge, U.K.: Cambridge University Press.

Ochs, Elinor and Bambi Schieffelin. 1984. "Language acquisition and socialization: Three developmental stories and their implications." In R. Shweder and R. LeVine (eds.), *Culture theory: Essays on mind, self, and emotion.* Cambridge, U.K.: Cambridge University Press. 276–320.

O'Malley, J. Michael and Anna Uhl Chamot. 1990. *Learning strategies in second language acquisition*. Cambridge, U.K.: Cambridge University Press.

Oxford, Rebecca. 1990. *Language learning strategies: What every teacher should know*. New York: Newbury House.

Paulston, Christina Bratt. 1990. "Linguistic and communicative competence." In Robin Scarcella, Elaine Andersen, and Stephen Krashen (eds.), *Developing communicative competence in a second language*. New York: Newbury House. 287-301.

Philips, Susan. 1972. "Participant structure and communicative competence: Warm Springs children in community and classroom." In Courtney Cazden, Vera John, and Dell Hymes (eds.), *Functions of language in the classroom*. New York: Teachers College Press. 370-394.

Pica, Teresa. 1993. "Communication with second language learners: What does it reveal about the social and linguistic processes of second language learning?" In James E. Alatis (ed.), *Georgetown University Round Table on Languages and Linguistics 1992*. Washington, DC: Georgetown University Press. 435-464.

Reddy, Michael. 1979. "The conduit metaphor: A case of frame conflict in our language about language." In Andrew Ortony (ed.), *Metaphor and thought*. Cambridge, U.K.: Cambridge University Press. 284-324.

Richards, Jack C. 1994. "The sources of language teachers' instructional decisions". In James E. Alatis (ed.), *Georgetown University Round Table on Languages and Linguistics 1994*. Washington, DC: Georgetown University Press. 384-402.

Richards, Jack C. and Theodore S. Rodgers. 1986. *Approaches and methods in language teaching*. Cambridge, U.K.: Cambridge University Press.

Rubin, Joan and Irene Thompson. 1994. *How to be a more successful language learner: Toward learner autonomy*. Boston: Heinle and Heinle.

Savignon, Sandra. 1983. *Communicative competence: Theory and classroom practice*. Reading, Massachusetts: Addison-Wesley.

Scollon, Ron and Suzanne Scollon. 1995. *Intercultural communication: A discourse approach*. Oxford: Basil Blackwell.

Shaw, Peter A. 1992. "Cooperative learning in graduate programs for language teacher preparation". In Carolyn Kessler (ed.), *Cooperative language learning*. Englewood Cliffs, N.J.: Prentice Hall Regents. 175-202.

Shulman, Lee S. 1986. "Those who understand: Knowledge growth in teaching". *Educational Researcher* 15(2): 4-14.

Snow, Marguerite, Myriam Met, and Fred Genesee. 1989. "A conceptual framework for the integration of language and content in second/foreign language instruction". *TESOL Quarterly* 23(2): 201-217.

Tharp, Roland G. and Ronald Gallimore. 1988. *Rousing minds to life: Teaching, learning, and schooling in social context*. Cambridge, U.K.: Cambridge University Press.

Tharp, Roland G. and Ronald Gallimore. 1991. *The instructional conversation: Teaching and learning in social activity* (Research Report #2). Santa Cruz, California and Washington, D.C.: National Center for Research on Cultural Diversity and Second Language Learning.

Tyler, Andrea. 1993. "Discourse structure and the perception of incoherence in international teaching assistants' spoken discourse." *TESOL Quarterly* 26(4): 713-729.

Varonis, Evangeline and Susan Gass. 1985. "Miscommunication in native/non-native conversation." *Language in Society* 14(3): 327-343.

Vygotsky, Lev S. 1978. *Mind in society: The development of higher psychological processes*. In M. Cole, S. Scribner, V. John-Steiner, and E. Souberman (eds. and trans.). Cambridge, Massachusetts: Harvard University Press.

Vygotsky, Lev S. 1987. *The collected works of L.S. Vygotsky*, In Robert W. Rieber and Aaron S. Carton (eds.), trans. by Norris Minick. New York: Plenum Press.

Wenden, A.L. and Joan Rubin. 1987. *Learner strategies for language learning*. Englewood Cliffs, N.J.: Prentice-Hall.

Widdowson, Henry G. 1978. *Teaching language as communication*. Oxford: Oxford University Press.

Widdowson, Henry G. 1993. "Perspectives on communicative language teaching: Syllabus design and methodology". In James E. Alatis (ed.), *Georgetown University Round Table on Languages and Linguistics 1992*. Washington, D.C.: Georgetown University Press. 501–507.

Wood, D., Jerome Bruner, and G. Ross. 1976. "The role of tutoring in problem solving." *Journal of Child Psychology and Psychiatry* 17: 89–100.

Wong Fillmore, Lily. 1991. "Second-language learning in children: a model of language learning in social context." In Ellen Bialystok (ed.), *Language processing in bilingual children*. Cambridge, U.K.: Cambridge University Press. 49-69.

Foreign-language-textbook discourse
and the pedagogization of the learner

Bessie Dendrinos
University of Athens

Introduction. The thesis underlying this paper is that in learning a language people acquire a positioned approach to social reality and that in using the language they participate in this reality, maintaining and reproducing it. Language is understood here as social practice, which entails a view of language users as social actors, performing as subjects of social institutions. By performing as a subject of the educational institution, for example, one participates in a particular social reality that carries meanings and values which have developed on the basis of an asymmetrical relationship: between those who are given the power to order and those who must obey; and between those who are omniscient and those who are ignorant. By behaving in ways which are acceptable and approved by the institution, people uphold the existing social order. For instance, teachers who act as authority figures and address their students as objects of instruction maintain the asymmetrical power relationship.

Many examples could be provided from within or from outside the school context to show how, by using language in ways which are subject to social convention, people are in fact practicing dominant ideologies. The grammatical choices people make when they speak, for example, often match the dominant ideology concerning success and power, gender, class, status, etc. The grammar of a language is a "meaning potential," and so are other features of language which we use to load our texts ideologically. Of course, in taking this position, I am implying that there is an element of choice involved in how we construe our texts. This leads to an additional statement basic in this paper: In using language, people function as social subjects not only to maintain, but also to change, dominant ideologies. In fact, our texts are indeed the articulation of institutionally determined discourses, but they are also reflections of ideological conflict since social institutions are sites of ideological struggle. In producing texts we perform practices linked with social relations of domination, but also with struggles to alter these relations. This means that if we are aware of what our choices mean, we can try to change them.

For educators this awareness seems particularly pertinent. It is important that teachers are conscious about what social reality they are constructing, reconstructing and transmitting to their students by what they say because, through the status and role they are assigned by the educational institution, they affect students' perception of reality in significant ways. What teachers say and the way they say it ultimately pedagogizes students as learners, as social beings, and as social actors. Of course, students are also pedagogized through the written texts used in classes, not only because texts carry an authority which is partly related to the power of the written language, but also because they appear in the schoolbook: a cultural artifact that carries unique authority not by virtue of its ethereal origin, but by virtue of its having been authorized by an administrative source whose authority is in turn institutionally bound (Luke et al. 1983: 117). Actually, as many would agree, textbooks are increasingly designed to inscribe instructional practices and content, and in so doing inscribe particular forms of institutional authority. Indeed school textbooks constitute an authorized medium that conveys to students "legitimate" knowledge (de Castell and Luke 1989: 413–414). It is for this reason that I turn our attention to the textbook. I want to deal with some of the ways in which we can examine its texts critically because the ability to do so leads to an understanding as to what type of social practices are performed and reflected through its texts and how these position and ultimately pedagogize students as learners and as social beings.

We shall be concerned with the foreign-language textbook in particular, understanding that in the foreign-language class, more than in other classes, the textbook determines what is to be taught and how. We will focus on one particular category of texts from textbooks used for the teaching of English as a foreign language. Elsewhere (Dendrinos 1992) I have referred to the type of texts we will deal with as instructional texts, distinguishing them from other types of texts we find in EFL textbooks. Instructional texts are those which contain the object of instruction, i.e. the language elements that students are to learn. I will review a few texts from EFL textbooks, focusing on the pedagogical and social values practiced therein. In doing so, my aim is to present different approaches that can be used to analyze texts critically.

Positioning the student as learner. One way of critically analyzing instructional texts in the foreign-language textbook is by examining the narrative line developed in them to understand how this narrative positions students as readers or listeners. As an example, let us consider the story about a young man by the name of Sam Wagner, the main character in one unit from the elementary EFL textbook, *Task Way English 2*. The first bits of information about him are presented to learners through the conversation of two women. (See the text marked as [E.Tb] 1 in the Appendix.[1]) In this text we see that the informational input is provided to listeners through the two women's opposing views about

---

[1] All text examples for this paper found in the Appendix.

Sam's character. Students listen to this instructional text in order to respond to two tasks which require of them to be active listeners. (See the text marked as [E.Tb] 3.) However, it is also the instructional text itself which invites students to be an active listeners. In the way the text is structured, it poses a problem to the listeners, who are provided with some contextual clues but not with an answer as to which of the two speakers is right about Sam Wagner. Thus, it requires listeners to assess the information presented, to make hypotheses, evaluations and interpretations. The clues provided in the text function in a way so as to activate the listeners' "schematic repertoire," with which they are able to connect discourse schemata of the text that operate lexically and syntactically with their own experiential field.

As the narrative line about Sam is further developed in this unit of the textbook, students are provided with additional information about the young man with another instructional text (marked as [E.Tb] 2). This reading text does not provide evaluative information regarding Sam's character. It only provides clues about his actions. Readers, who will untimately make a value judgment about Sam, must use this information. They must relate it to the information they have extracted from another text, and make a series of inferences so as to reach a conclusion, and shape an opinion about Sam's personality. As such, readers are involved in the process of narrative development, and they continue being so when they are provided with additional bits of information through a third instructional text ([E.Tb] 4). With this text, containing notes for a recommendation letter to be written about Sam, readers are presented with his positive qualities. This input, added to previously acquired information, completes the narrative about the young man. It is a narrative which has been developed progressively, and students have taken an active part in its development.

The way the narrative line about Sam is constructed differs greatly from the narrative developed about the character from another elementary EFL textbook, *Building Strategies 2*. Rod is one of the main characters in this textbook in the sense that he appears in various situations presented in different lessons or units. However, students receive a clear picture of him through one reading text ([E.Tb] 5), which is full of factual statements. Readers are not challenged by the text in any way to make any interpretative choices, and they are not invited to participate in the development of the narrative. This text, like the previous ones, conveys a variety of messages which constitute ideological inscriptions of dominant culture reality. We shall not be concerned with these right now, however.

At this point, I would like to note that the decoding processes, in which the narrative lines of the two different textbooks involve students, reveal different ideologization processes, not simply because each narrative structure is a different ideological construction (and it is), but because each type of narrative line entails a different relationship between text and reader or listener, and ultimately a different pedagogical relationship. The narrative about Rod is developed in what Luke (1989) calls a "closed text," whereas the narrative line about Sam is developed through a series of "open texts."

Luke's concept of open and closed text is based on the semiotic approach to text by Eco (1976) and on his theory of the role of the reader (1979). Eco views the text as a total "syntactic-semantic-pragmatic device," the creation of which has to rely on a "series of codes," and claims that the text "creates the competence of its model reader" (Eco 1979: 7). In other words,

> the text takes existing knowledges and competences and can either enable an "opening"—an elaboration, rejuxtaposition, reconsideration, extrapolation or novel recombination of that which the reader knows prior to the reading —or it can enable a "closing"—a restriction, delimitation, simple reinforcement and confirmation of prior knowledge, conventions and ideological beliefs. (Luke 1989: 67–68)

According to Luke, insofar as its structure is concerned, the open text may operate within common or less common narrative conventions and will call, as will the closed text, for the cooperation of the reader. Unlike the closed text, however, the open text challenges the reader to make a series of interpretative choices which, although not infinite, are greater than one. In this manner, the open text engages the reader as an active "principal" and hence participant in the interaction. This may be achieved, Luke believes, because there is "flexibility" of the text grammar in validating the widest possible range of interpretative proposals. By contrast, the grammar of the closed text simply entails the matching and testing of hypotheses against the serially disclosed information of the text. To achieve this, it relies also on the consistency of the same narrative scheme throughout various texts. Through redundancy, writers like Agatha Christie, Ian Fleming, and the D.C. comics authors establish a pattern of intertextuality because the "iterative scheme" (from Eco, i.e. each event takes up again from a sort of virtual beginning, ignoring where the preceding event left off) is a familiar one, repeated throughout the particular genre (e.g., detective story, comic strip, basal reader narrative). Textual cues do not require construction of the response, but rather reinvoke a familiar response, which is facilitated by the fact that the iterative scheme entails high redundancy messages: a repetition of the text grammar and of the cognitive and schematic extensions that the unfolding of the events permits.

Based on the above, we could identify the cartoon series so frequently used in modern EFL publications as closed texts. They present repeated events in the linear fashion (i.e. Eco's "iterative scheme"). These texts are not unlike so many other episodic texts in the EFL textbooks which are addressed to and sold in an international market. Most of them rely on linearity and conventionality to present surface images of people and situations. All these are closed structures presenting unitary messages which aim at the obedient cooperation of the recipient. As such, they succeed in transforming reading into a process of recognition of the familiar because the generic format, the "serial disclosure" of information follows characteristic ideological patterns. They are the patterns of the "mythological" texts of popular culture, to use Eco's term, which appeal to the common opinions and emotions shared by the majority of readers through the use of elementary oppositions (such as good/bad, disloyal/trustworthy, love/hate), personification of "primitive universal forces," the normalization of ideology, and narrative redundancy. In fact, such texts rely on "ideological overcoding," and they are ideological not only in what they say, but in how they say it, and in what they do to reading and the role of the reader.

Actually, it is interesting to examine instructional texts from this perspective because, in understanding what role students are assigned as readers, we become aware of what role they are assigned as learners; that is, whether they are positioned as passive recipients of legitimate knowledge and information, or as active participants in an interaction which aims at learning through the negotiation of meaning.

Positioning the learner as social being. In the instructional texts of the foreign-language textbook one can also trace the social reality created for learners, the ideological constructs conveyed to them. For example, it is interesting to consider the text marked as [E.Tb] 5, referred to earlier, about the young man by the name of Rod. First we look at the title ("Making a new start") which conveys the overall message of the text, i.e. that people can make a fresh start in their lives when they wish to do so. Implied here is that individuals have total control over their lives and fates. A person can simply decide to change his or her life, and it is natural sever all ties with the present and past just because one is bored with seeing the same people and doing the same things everyday at work (lines 17–22). Further, one does not have to worry about or plan for the future because it will take care of itself (lines 49–51). The false reality presented in the text is transmitted through the narrative developed and specific language used. Here is a young, handsome man, whose qualifications are not really made clear, who manages to alter his life completely because he wants adventure (lines 20–22), and because he would like to live for a time by the sea—on account of his father having been a sea captain (lines 29–32). Adventure and a new job presented as related concepts, Rod miraculously finds a good job in an important company in another country, despite the unemployment problem there (lines 45–49). Moreover, the criterion on the basis of which he chooses this job is that the city in which the company is located is attractive! He finds this out by coming across some photographs that appear in a travel brochure issued by the British Tourist Association (lines 24–27). It is perhaps worth noting that the sociocultural reality of the city is established in terms of its age, castles, cathedrals, and other "things like that" (lines 27–29), including its location near the sea, and its kind, friendly people who have a sense of humor (lines 35–36). It is also interesting to mark the generic qualities attributed to people of a community and of specific countries. For example, England in comparison to Canada has a slower pace of life, and English food is marvelous (lines 40–43).

In more general terms, the text just discussed is a sample of many others appearing in EFL textbooks which portray a reality of the will and freedom of individuals who are alone in shaping their lives in any way they choose. These ideological meanings are articulated through the lexical and grammatical choices of the text, both of which present a narrow and intersubjective view of the world. They are the linguistic properties of a text which are not in any way coherently related to society as a unit of interdependent institutions and agencies, inhabited by people who are responsible for their maintenance. In such a text, the social construction of individuals is one-dimensional and their actions are socially meaningless.

Positioning the learner as social actor. The foreign-language textbook aims at helping students learn to act and interact using the language they are acquiring. Students must learn to understand and produce language that is both grammatically correct and socially appropriate. This necessarily involves the textbook writer(s) in creating instructional texts where language is used in particular social contexts, by "appropriate" users, expressing themselves in "appropriate" forms, to convey "appropriate" meanings. In doing so, foreign-language-textbook writers create models of social interaction; convey social norms concerning human relationships and individual behavior; present social institutions and social values; and select what counts as important in a society. Therefore, it seems particularly interesting to investigate instructional texts and the choices made in terms of which language elements are chosen as points to be taught and learned.

Consider, for example, the "language functions" that a textbook writer chooses as the object of instruction. We know that the selections, loosely connected to learners' terminal needs, are arbitrary. However, we are not actually conscious of the fact that these selections are ideologically bound and that their realizations are ideologically loaded. Yet, the language functions chosen and presented in a foreign-language textbook construct social realities about what can be said by whom, when, under what circumstances and for what purpose. A case in point is the language function of *complaining*. It is a language function included in only two out of a total of twenty EFL textbooks examined for the ideological inscriptions in their instructional texts. In eighteen of the textbooks, people are portrayed as social actors who ask for and give information, agree or disagree, make suggestions, describe, instruct, apologize, offer to do things, state intentions, preferences, etc., but who never complain.

The choice of the authors to exclude this language function from the syllabus of their textbook is ideologically bound, as is the choice of the two authors who include it. On the other hand, when we examine how complaining is presented in each of the two textbooks which include this language function in their syllabus, we may become aware of the ideological inscriptions therein.

In the early intermediate EFL textbook, *Break into English*, the act of complaining is presented as an act of *reprimanding*. In the text used to present the new language function to learners (marked as [E.Tb] 6), we see an employer authorized with the power to complain, in the form of reprimanding his employee. Also, in the texts that follow, we note that the act of complaining is always realized by a person who is dissatisfied with someone else's behavior, or with the condition of things, and that s/he conveys annoyance to her/his interlocutor who is in some way responsible for the things going wrong. Therefore, the language features that students are provided with as examples of language to be used for complaints in another text (marked as [E.Tb] 7) are features of coercive statements. They are either addressor-centered utterances (such as "I'm not satisfied with ... ;" "Look! I must really complain about ...") or addressee-centered (such as "You'll have to do something about ... ;" "What are you going to do abou t ... ; ") and action-centered utterances (such as "It can't go on like this ... ;" "It just isn't good enough ... "). The former category of utterances is associated with social acts during which actors use their prerogative to assert themselves and their dissatisfaction to their interlocutors. The latter category is associated with social acts during which actors demand that their interlocutors change the behavior which has caused them the displeasure. The coercive language presented to learners in this textbook is then to be used in situational contexts provided in another text (marked as [E.Tb] 8). Learners are required here to role-play according to the situations in order to practice the new language point: the function of complaining. The social act they are asked to perform, in the particular communicative instances, positions them as social subjects in such a way as to consider legitimate the asymmetrical relationships of power and control.

In another EFL textbook, *A Case for English*, the language function of complaining is not only framed within different situational contexts, but the act of complaining is quite dissimilar from the previous one. In examining the utterances presented to students examples of how someone complains (See [E. Tb] 9), we realize that none of them are reprimands like in the case of *Break into English*. They are utterances which someone uses to *whine about* or to *criticize* somebody, but they could not be characterized as coercive language. All six utterances are either modalized (e.g. "Personally, I think ... ") or formed as interrogatives (e.g. "What does he think he's doing ... ?"), and they are examples of someone complaining in the form of problem-posing to a friend, colleague, etc., about a third party who has been the cause of dissatisfaction.

The addressee is presented as sympathetic to the problem, and s/he makes suggestions in an attempt to solve it. This is why along with the language function of complaining, students are also introduced to suggestions, and on the same page of the textbooks there are expressions useful for the performance of this language function (See [E.Tb] 11). By examining this text, we are led to understand that in this EFL textbook the social reality constructed for learners is one of more cooperative relationships. And this conclusion is supported by the communication roles the students are asked to play in another text (marked as [E.Tb] 10), intended to offer learners the opportunity to practice the new language function. Unlike the role-play in *Break into English*, this one invites learners to carry out a communicative exchange which requires collaborative action to confront institutionalized power.

In examining the excerpts from the two textbooks the aim has been to show that different selections of language functions and choices as to how these operate in social contexts are ideologically bound and hence contribute to the development of different conceptions of social reality. In fact, they determine how the student as a social subject will interact with that reality. A critical assessment could be made of selections related to other language functions such as giving advice, agreeing/disagreeing, or apologizing. It is revealing to investigate ideological inscriptions in the kind of speech acts people are portrayed as making in specific situations. No less revealing is the investigation of other language features, because the textbook is a composite of ideological selections: Educational, cultural and linguistic. Lexical choices, for instance, are interesting features to focus upon. Consideration of the adjectives, adverbs, nouns, prepositional phrases, relative clauses, etc. used as premodifiers and postmodifiers to nouns and proper names in the instructional texts of textbooks may disclose the images of people developed therein.

Conclusion. Having examined some instructional texts in EFL textbooks, I hope I have contributed toward the understanding that linguistic and textual analysis of schoolbook texts can provide us with an awareness about ideological, and ultimately pedagogical, practices. Such understanding helps in constructing the social reality in which we feel students should be participating. Social reality is created by language use, which we understand as social practice. This leads us to acknowledge that its use and users are affected by social structure. However, acknowledging this means that we have to accept the reverse as also true. The way language is used and its users are positioned toward it may significantly affect the social order (as this is shaped by the ideological conflicts traversing social institutions)—contributing significantly to its maintenance or to its transformation. This thesis is also defended by Fairclough, who explains:

Linguistic phenomena are social in the sense that whenever people speak or listen, read or write, they do so in ways which are determined socially and have social effects. Even when people are most conscious of their own individuality and think of themselves to be most cut off from social influences ... they still use language in ways which are subject to social convention. And the ways in which people use language ... are not only socially determined by the social relationships ..., they also have social effects in the sense of helping to maintain (or, indeed, change) those relationships. (Fairclough 1989: 23)

Hence, in conclusion, we may say that language is not merely an instrument of ideological subjection but also an instrument for change of ideologies. Awareness of how it is used to convey social meanings may help us use this instrument to achieve our pedagogical goals. Language choice in the textbooks we use with our students to help them learn a language is significant in their pedagogization as learners, as social beings, and as social actors.

REFERENCES

De Castell, Susan and Allan Luke. 1989. *Language, authority and criticism: Readings on the school textbooks*. London: The Falmer.

Dendrinos, Bessie. 1992. *The EFL textbook and ideology*. Athens, Greece: N.C. Grivas Publications.

Eco, Umberto. 1976. *A theory of semiotics*. Bloomington, Indiana: Indiana University Press.

Eco, Umberto. 1979. *The role of the reader*. Bloomington, Indiana: Indiana University Press.

Fairclough, Norman. 1989. *Discourse and power*. London: Longman

Luke, Allan. 1989. "Open and closed texts: The ideological/semantic analysis of textbook narratives." *Journal of Pragmatics* 13: 53–80.

Luke, Carmen, Susan de Castell, and Allan Luke. 1983. "Beyond criticism: The authority of the school text." *Curriculum Inquiry* 13(2): 111–127.

EFL TEXTBOOKS

Abbs, Brian and Ingrid Freebairn. 1987. *Building strategies: Strategies 2*. London: Longman. ([E.Tb] 5)

Carrier, Michael and Simon Haines. 1987. *Break into English, Book 3*. London: Hodder and Stoughton. ([E.Tb] 6, 7 and 8)

Dendrinos, Bessie et al. 1987. *Task way English 2*. Athens: Organismos Ekdoseos Didaktikon Vivlion (Organization for Publication of Educational Books) ([E.Tb] 1, 2, 3 and 4)

Hicks, Diana et al. 1978. *A case for English*. Cambridge, U.K.: Cambridge University Press. ([E.Tb] 9, 10 and 11)

APPENDIX

[E.Tb] 1

Isadora	:	Hi, June... Long time no see...
June	:	Yea... I was studying for my Physics test last week.
Isadora	:	Have you got your project ready yet?
June	:	No, not yet Isadora. I plan to work with Sam but he had to fly back...
Isadora	:	Sam? You mean Sam Wagner, the guy who drives that old jeep?
June	:	Right. The one who gave you a lift to town last month, remember?
Isadora	:	Of course, I remember. But I never thought you'd want to work with someone like Sam!
June	:	And may I know why?
Isadora	:	He's the sort of guy who can't take college seriously.
June	:	You're wrong Isadora. On the contrary, Sam is the sort of student who works hard but who isn't interested in just grades.
Isadora	:	Are you sure we're talking about the same Sam Wagner - the one who used to go to McKinley High School?
June	:	I think so. I think he was star athlete there, wasn't he?
Isadora	:	That's right. He's the one who used to be good at sports and bad at everything else.
June	:	I don't know how he did in high school, but now he's doing very well. He's a hard worker, he's intelligent, he's creative... Besides, we work wonderfully together! He's cooperative, he's not at all selfish, he's...
Isadora	:	O.K.... O.K.! I guess you think Sam is great. I sure hope you're right.

[E.Tb] 9

When you want to complain use expressions like:

I don't know about you but ...
What does he think he's doing ...?
What does he think he's playing at ...?
What on earth is he ...? (+ing)
I think he's got a damned check ...
Personally, I think

[E.Tb] 2

3. BACK TO JUNE AND SAM

TASK 1

June and Sam haven't got their project ready yet, because Sam had to fly home. Read the newspaper article and find out why Sam went back to his home town.

STAR ATHLETE
DEFENDS
HIS OLD COACH

Ralph Kessler, basketball coach for 15 years at McKinley High, was accused yesterday for accepting a large sum of money to make his team lose the very important match with Lehman High School last Friday night.

We interviewed teachers and students at his school. Everyone seems to think highly of the coach. They say that "he's the sort of person who believes in ideals, the kind of coach who gives his team all he's got." His colleagues think that he is honest and trustworthy. Among his defenders is Sam Wagner, star athlete at McKinley two years ago. Now a top student at the University of Northern Iowa, Sam came back home to stand by his old coach. "I can't believe all these lies," Sam told our reporters. "Mr Kessler is a coach who cares about his players. He's sincere, sensible and wise. He's the kind of coach who spends all his free time with the team. I'm sure there's a misunderstanding, and that everything will clear up. And I am not leaving here until it does. All of us, his old and new athletes are here to defend him."

[E.Tb] 3

[E.Tb] 4

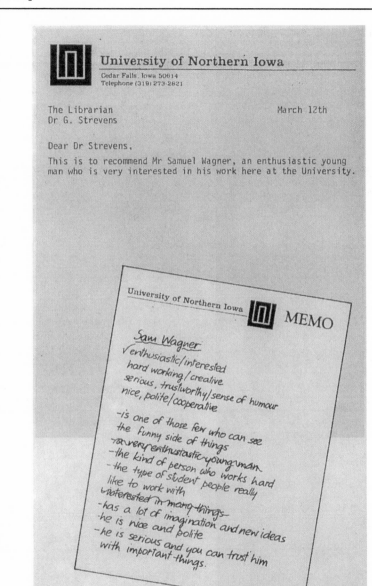

University of Northern Iowa

Cedar Falls, Iowa 50614
Telephone (319) 273-2821

The Librarian   March 12th
Dr G. Strevens

Dear Dr Strevens,

This is to recommend Mr Samuel Wagner, an enthusiastic young
man who is very interested in his work here at the University.

University of Northern Iowa   MEMO

Sam Wagner
✓ enthusiastic / interested
hard working / creative
serious, trustworthy / sense of humour
nice, polite / cooperative

- is one of those few who can see
the funny side of things
- a very enthusiastic young man
- the kind of person who works hard
- the type of student people really
like to work with
✓ interested in many things-
- has a lot of imagination and new ideas
- he is nice and polite
- he is serious and you can trust him
with important things.

[E.Tb] 5

Reading

MAKING A NEW START

Every week Mike Sanders meets people who are making a new start in life. This week he meets a young Canadian.

Rod Nelson is a young, good-looking Canadian, who is on his first visit to Bristol. He comes from Ottawa and is an electrical engineer. He first trained at a college of technology and then worked for the Canadian government. Last month he arrived in Britain to start a new job with Western Aeronautics, a company which produces electrical components for the aircraft industry here in Bristol.

Why did you leave Canada?
I was bored. I worked in the same office and saw the same people and did the same thing every day. I needed a change. I wanted adventure.

Why did you choose Bristol?
I saw some photographs of Bristol in a brochure which I got from the British Tourist Association. It looked attractive. Besides, I like old cities, castles, cathedrals — things like that. Also, I like being near the sea. You see, my father was a sea captain in Newfoundland. That's probably why I like the sea.

What do you think of Bristol?
Actually, I like the people very much. They're very kind and friendly. And they have a sense of humour. The way of life is very different from Canada. It's a bit slow here in Britain perhaps, but I like it. And I prefer the food here — the fresh cream, the marvellous cheeses, the bread and, of course, the roast beef!

Have you any plans for the future?
So far I'm enjoying working at Western. Anyway, as there's so much unemployment at the moment, it's going to be difficult to find another job — in the UK at least. To tell you the truth I'm not keen on making plans.

[E.Tb] 6

Jeremy Edwards works as a clerk for a large insurance company in London. He is 22 and this is his first job, but during the last three weeks he has been late for work several times. Mr Martin, Jeremy's boss, decides he must complain to Jeremy about his repeated lateness.
Listen to their conversation:

LISTENING 1

Mr Martin Mr Edwards! Can I have a word with you in my office immediately, please?

Jeremy Just coming, Frank.

Mr Martin Sit down, Jeremy. Look! I have to say that I'm not at all satisfied with your punctuality. . . .

VOCABULARY

insurance company *business which makes agreements with customers to pay money in case of accidents, death, loss, theft or damage to property.*

punctuality *arriving at the right time*

[E.Tb] 7

Language Focus

COMPLAINING

Formal Complaints:

I'm not satisfied with	the service in this shop (?)
What are you going to do about	your punctuality
You'll have to do something about	your appearance

I've got a complaint to make
Look! I really must complain (about ...)

NOTE
'Look' or 'Listen' are often used before a complaint.
They attract the other person's attention.

Informal expressions of complaint/dissatisfaction

It can't go on like this.
It just isn't good enough.
(I'm sorry, but) this can't go on.

[E.Tb] 8

Practice

How would you complain in these situations? Work out two or three expressions in case your first attempt does not succeed:

- **Situation 1:** a friend or acquaintance keeps borrowing things from you and forgetting to give them back. Now he/she has actually lost something that you need.
- **Situation 2:** you have a part-time job on two evenings a week. You have now been doing the job for three weeks and your employer has paid you nothing.
- **Situation 3:** the postman keeps putting the wrong letters through your door. You are getting your neighbour's mail and they are getting yours. This has been going on for a month.
- **Situation 4:** you keep getting letters from a mail-order company saying that you owe them money for something you did not order and have not received. You are going to telephone the company to complain.

[E.Tb] 10

Mini role play

Now work out with your partner similar dialogues using the following situations:

a) One colleague complains to another that the office coffee is undrinkable, the other suggests that they buy a new coffee-maker.

b) One commuter complains to another that there is never any heating on their train, the other suggests they boycott the train service.

c) One hotel guest complains to another over dinner that the soup is always cold, the other suggests that they complain to the management.

d) A subscriber complains to the telephone company that his line never works properly, the operator suggests that he contacts the Engineering Department.

[E.Tb] 11

When you want to make a suggestion, use expressions like:	
Why don't we ...?	Have you thought of ...? (+ing)
Why don't we suggest ...?	Don't you think that's a good idea ...?
How about ...? (+ing)	One way would be to ...
Wouldn't it be a good idea to ...?	Maybe the best thing would be to ...

Triangulations:
Converging insights from studies of "genre," "situated learning," and second-language acquisition

Aviva Freedman
Carleton University, Ottawa

Introduction. My research has focussed primarily on language learning in the mother tongue: More specifically on how adults or young adults "learn" or "acquire" the new written genres that are elicited from them as they proceed through their university years; as they move from the university to the work force; and as they move to different arenas or forums within the workplace. As my highlighted use of the terms "learn" and "acquire" indicates, in theorizing about my findings I have been influenced profoundly by work in Second Language Acquisition (SLA) (especially the work of Krashen 1981, 1984, 1985, 1992; Ellis 1990, 1994).

Thus it is only just that I attempt to return the favor by offering to SLA and English as a Second Language (ESL) scholars and educators insights from other areas of scholarship with which they may be less familiar and that may prove as useful in studying second language learning as it has been for understanding the acquisition of new written genres by novices. On the one hand, the theories I wish to discuss here are remarkably consonant with cognitively-based SLA theory, while on the other, they open up other perspectives on, and ways of thinking about, the facilitation of learning by focussing on the social dimensions of language and learning.

The two scholarly fields I will draw on here are, first, genre studies, as that field has developed within the North American rhetorical tradition; and second, situated learning, an approach to knowing and learning developed within the field of psychology, based largely on Russian work and with a radically social orientation.

Where relevant, I will be referring to research that I have conducted in the past (1990, 1993a, 1993b, in press), and that my colleagues and I (Freedman, Adam, and Smart 1994) are currently undertaking: specifically, research that focusses on the acquisition of genres at university and professional levels. Our current work includes longitudinal study into the acquisition of, and differences between, university and workplace genres in four fields: business, government, social work, and architecture.[1]

Genre studies. In recent years, there have been a number of scholarly publications, deriving from different disciplines, all directed towards redefining the term "genre." (See for example Miller 1984; Bakhtin 1986; Reid 1987; Swales 1990; Cope and Kalantzis 1993. Swales provides an overview of some of the contributing disciplines.) What is common to all this work is an expansion of the traditional definition of genre, according to which genres were seen as collocations of textual regularities, or text-types. More recent interpretations include such notions as recurrent communicative goals, social processes, or sociocultural actions. There are important differences in emphasis, however, in the way in which the term has been used in the North American rhetorical tradition, especially in contradistinction to the way it has been used in applied linguistics. It is these differences that I wish to highlight here.

One fundamental difference is captured by the contrast between the term "communication," which recurs in Swales's definitions, and terms relating to "knowledge creation," which recur in the work of rhetoricians and writing researchers, or composition specialists. (See for example Bazerman 1988; Berkenkotter and Huckin 1993; Schryer 1993.) Within the reinvented tradition of rhetoric, with its reinfusion of classical notions into composition theory and research, came the recognition of "invention"—the discovery and/or making of meaning—as the primary or central feature of rhetoric (Freedman and Pringle 1980; Freedman, Pringle, and Yalden 1983). Writing is not simply communication or translation of something already extant in the world or in the mind. The composing process itself is a way of making meaning.

With the shift in composition research and theory from the cognitive to the social in the 1980s, this emphasis on "invention" has remained equally prominent, although redefined: The difference is that social constructionists stress the degree to which meanings are *communally and collaboratively* constructed.

The notion of "genre" derives naturally from this emphasis, with its accompanying recognition that, in all aspects of our lives, we as humans interpret experience socially: We communally define sets of stock situations, which are social interpretations of, selections from, and reconstructions of the complex web of lived experience. Genres are typified responses to these

---

[1]This research has been funded by the Social Sciences and Humanities Research Council of Canada and is being undertaken by a team of researchers from the Department of Linguistics at Carleton University, Ottawa, and the Faculty of Education at McGill University, Montreal. In addition to myself, principal investigators include Patrick Dias, Peter Medway, and Anthony Pare.

recurrent situations—or at least to situations that are socially constructed as recurrent.[2]

All this is argued particularly cogently by Bakhtin, whose work has become influential recently in cultural, literary, and rhetorical studies. In his essay, "Speech Genres," Bakhtin (1986:78) writes: "All our utterances have definite and relatively stable *typical* forms of construction"; if "we speak only in definite speech genres", that is because these speech genres "correspond to typical situations of speech communication" (1986: 87).

In fact, it is the work of Bakhtin as well as that of the new rhetorician, Miller (1984), that has been the most influential in shaping the field of genre studies as it is instantiated in North American writing research circles. Thus it is significant that, in his monograph situating his definition of "genre" within various disciplinary fields, Swales omits the work of Bakhtin—an omission that he has more recently rectified (1992). That is itself telling, however, in light of the argument I am constructing here concerning the different conceptions of "genre" held by composition scholars as opposed to applied linguists.

The particular differences that I wish to emphasize are two. First, as alluded to above, there is the far greater recognition in composition theory and research of the meaning-making that exists at the heart of rhetorical creation. Second, there is the emphasis on the fact that rhetorical acts must be seen as ways of encompassing situations, or as strategies for responding to social or rhetorical exigencies (Burke 1941, 1966; Bitzer 1960; and Miller 1984), with genres representing typified ways of responding to recurrent social situations (i.e. to situations that are socially constructed as recurrent.)

It is true that Swales and scholars in the tradition of Halliday, i.e. the Sydney School, acknowledge, even insist on, the social dimensions of genre, but it is the nature and the degree of emphasis on the social that differs. As even the most cursory review of the relevant literature reveals, the rhetorical genre scholars probe far more deeply into the social and cultural contexts. (See for example the work of Bazerman 1988; Yates 1989; Doheny-Farina 1992; Berkenkotter and Huckin 1993; Devitt 1993; Schryer 1993.) In this work, the primary focus of the analysis is not so much on an explication of the rules governing textual features but rather on a highly nuanced and sophisticated discrimination of the range of sociocultural, historical, ideological, and political dimensions of the rhetorical exigencies which elicit the textual features characterizing the genres. Miller sees the work of genre scholars as ethnomethodological: specifically, explicating the knowledge that practice makes. And both the knowledge and the practice include, but subsume, linguistic and discourse rules. To put it another way, and to use Spielmann's (this volume)

---

[2]For a fuller discussion, see Carolyn Miller's seminal article, "Genre as Social Action," 1984, with its references to Schutz's notions of "situation-types."

distinction, there is less emphasis on features of "code" and more on the interaction among code, culture, context, and content (although rhetoricians might prefer different categorizations).

As a consequence of this kind of analysis, a different conception of genre emerges—different especially from that put forward by the Sydney School genre theorists. There is far greater recognition of the degree to which contexts and our interpretations of these contexts shift, and, because of this close attention to shifting sociocultural and historical contexts, these theorists share a relatively fragile, dynamic, and shifting sense of genre. Thus in Schryer's (1993) terms, genres are "stabilized-for-now" entities. Bakhtin (1986) describes genres as dynamic, plastic and free, and Miller (1984) reports that genres "evolve and decay, and that their number is indeterminate." At the same time, historical genre research provides the support for this conception: Examples include Bazerman's (1988) study of the development of the research article in response to changes in knowledge and knowledge construction and Yates's (1989) discussion of the evolution of the office memo, in response to technology and management philosophies of business enterprises.

Also central to this notion of genre, although not always made explicit, is the recognition of agency—the power of an individual to reshape, realign, or reaccentuate a genre. Genres are not seen as totally deterministic and determining (as is suggested in some of the work of the Sydney School scholars, as well as that of many post-structuralist cultural critics). This is not to say that there is no recognition of the shaping power of already extant genres; on the contrary, through Bakhtin's (1981) discussions of "dialogism," there is everywhere a recognition of the degree to which all utterances reflect, echo, respond to, and anticipate the utterances of others. In other words, there is a dialectical tension between the agent and the genre. Significantly, the sociologist of choice is Giddens (1984), for whom structure and agency exist in reciprocal relation.

Finally, and in particular contrast with the Sydney School genre work, the rhetorical genre tradition thus far has not had as a major focus an interest in direct application to pedagogy. (See Freedman 1993a, 1993b.) For one, explicit teaching about specific genres and their features, as recommended by the Sydney School scholars in Australia, hardly seems possible, since we can analyze with precision only those genres that arose in the past, in response to circumstances that undoubtedly no longer hold true. In addition, the complexity of the highly contextualized and interactive nature of specific genres also points to the futility of any kind of direct or explicit pedagogy.

Situated learning. How then are genres learned or acquired? The models from SLA proposed by Krashen and Ellis provide an answer—an answer that I have drawn on elsewhere. (See Freedman 1993a, 1993b.) A more socially-based explanation, however, and one that is consistent with the social orientation of genre studies themselves, is one that can be found in recent work on situated learning—a field which owes much itself to Russian scholarship, in this case in Activity Theory.

To say that the thinking by scholars in the field of situated learning is socially-oriented is to understate the case. For many key thinkers in this area, learning and knowing are social—not in the narrow sense of involving some cognitive analysis of audience, but rather in the broadest sense possible. Learning and knowing as activities are seen as extending beyond the cranium of the specific individual involved. Just as Bateson (1972) argued that the boundaries of self are extended to include tools, so do those involved in situated learning—which is sometimes referred to as socially-distributed cognition—recognize that meanings are intersocially created and that this creation is typically mediated by culturally-constructed, semiotic sign-systems such as language.

The field of situated learning, however, is far from unitary. While there is a common recognition of the importance of the social and of collaborative performance in learning, various scholars and researchers operate with different conceptions of many of the key notions.

The commonalities underlying this field are these: Learning and knowing are context-specific; learning is accomplished through processes of coparticipation; and cognition is socially shared. Given these commonalities, however, there are different streams within the literature. Lave (1991:66) has specified three different theories of "situated experience." The first she calls the "cognition plus view," in which researchers simply "extend the scope of their intraindividual theory to include everyday activity and social interaction ... social factors become conditions whose effects on individual cognition are then explored." This is the most limited and, for this discussion, least relevant model.

The second is the "interpretive view [which] locates situatedness in the use of language and/or social interaction" (Lave 1991: 63). Lave (1993) directs our attention to the intellectual forebear of this emerging understanding in the phenomenological tradition of social theory, with its emphasis on intensely interactive communal interpretation of experience. "Language use and, thus, meaning are situated in *interested*, intersubjectively negotiated social interaction" (Lave 1991: 67, italics mine). Individuals work together hermeneutically, through (largely verbal) interactions, towards a shared understanding, within contexts where they are each or all actively engaged.

Both the first and second view are limited, according to Lave, in that they "bracket off the social world" and thus "negate the possibility that subjects are fundamentally *constituted in* their relations with and activities in that world" (1991: 67). She adds thus to the interpretive position a third perspective, whose intellectual source is Russian Activity Theory, which itself derives broadly from the work of Vygotsky (1962, 1978). Fundamental to this work is the notion that knowing is social—not in the sense that one mind transmits knowledge to another, but rather in the Vygotskian sense that "higher mental functioning in the individual derives from social life" (Wertsch 1991a: 87). The third view, which Lave calls "situated social practice" or, where appropriate, "situated learning," includes, along with the interpretive perspective, an insistence that "learning, thinking, and knowing are relations among people engaged in activity *in, with, and arising from the socially and culturally structured world*" (Lave 1991: 67, italics mine). These emphases on activity, persons-in-activity, and mediation through sociocultural tools such as language become important in situated learning, but also evoke key elements in genre studies. It is a qualified version of this last perspective which informs our own analysis of the learning we observed, and which I report on here.

Consonance. Work in situated learning has particular congruence, and allows for powerful intermeshing, with the work on genre studies, as Gee (1984) has suggested. In his words, genres "are each instantiated in *situated meanings*. Both situated learning and genre studies place great emphasis on activity and action—doing things with words (Austin 1962), or knowing and learning through doing, rather than transmission. Central notions are performance, participation, and collaboration.

In addition, there is in both fields a recognition of the powerful role of context. All knowing and all learning are situated responses to specifically local contexts.[2] Of course, the definition of context, according to the activity theorists, is considerably extended, enriched, and complicated. Engestrom defines it thus:

> For activity theory, contexts are neither containers nor situationally created experiential spaces. Contexts are activity systems. An activity system integrates the subject, the object, and the instruments [material tools as well as signs and symbols] into a unified whole (1993:67).

Indeed, the role of context is deemed so powerful that the very possibility of portability has been raised persistently in the literature on situated and everyday cognition, questioning the blithe assumption in earlier work that skills learned in one context are easily carried over to others. (See for example Rogoff and Lave 1984; Lave 1988; and Petraglia n.d., who emphasize especially the lack

---

[3]Anthropology, in particular the work of Clifford Geertz (1983), has been influential here as well.

of carryover between performance in classroom situations and everyday experience.)[4]

Models of learning. The literature on situated learning has produced (at least) two analytic perspectives from which such learning can be viewed: the notion of "guided participation" in the work of Rogoff (1990) and the concept of "legitimate peripheral participation" as developed by Lave and Wenger (1991). While these two perspectives have not been developed as alternatives to each other, they do at least foreground different aspects of the learning process. My research associate, Christine Adam, and I have found that by highlighting these differences, we were able to develop two distinct but overlapping models that accounted for both the similarities and the differences in the contexts we observed: the university and the workplace. The terms we use are "facilitated performance" (FP) and "authentic attenuated participation" (AAP). The echo in the names is intended as an acknowledgement of their sources in Rogoff (1990) and Lave and Wenger's work (1991); the difference in wording is intended to reflect the fact that we are using these terms in more specialized and possibly narrower ways than those intended by the originators. (For a detailed theoretical discussion of the differences between FP and AAP, see Freedman and Adam 1994.)

Common features of all instances of situated learning are the following:

(1) Learning is *not* the acquisition of propositional knowledge;
(2) learning occurs through processes of coparticipation;
(3) the learner's role in the collaboration is "attenuated" and supervised by the guide; and
(4) learning is mediated through cultural tools.

These broad parameters include the variations represented by FP and AAP.

---

[4]The consonance of rhetorical genre scholarship and the work on situated learning is implicitly highlighted by Wertsch (1991a, 1991b) in his discussion of learning as mediated through tools. Beginning with Vygotsky's work, which stresses the degree to which human activity is mediated through tools, Wertsch goes on to emphasize the need to complement this analysis with Bakhtinian notions. Wertsch emphasizes in particular the way in which speakers "ventriloquate" portions or aspects of their ambient social languages in attempting to realize their own speech plans. All our words are filled with, and are echoes of and responses to, others' words. (As Bakhtin 1986:69 repeats, "No-one breaks the eternal silence of the universe.") Each person's utterances are dialogic responses to earlier utterances as well as anticipations of responses by their listeners. The relations are multiple, complex, shifting, and dynamic. They demand and reward engagement and attention—and involve notions of complex interplay between an individual's free speech plans and the speech genres available, and between an individual's own utterances and the ambient social languages.

Facilitated performance (FP). Rogoff develops the notion of "guided participation" from the Vygotskian discussion of the "zone of proximal development" and his often-quoted statement that what a child can do in collaboration with a skilled adult today, she will be able to do alone tomorrow; in other words, learning takes place through processes of co-participation with an adult. Rogoff explains as follows:

> Guided participation involves adults or children challenging, constraining, and supporting children in the process of posing and solving problems through material arrangements of children's activities and responsibilities as well as through interpersonal communication, with children observing and participating at a comfortable but slightly challenging level. The processes of communication and shared participation in activities inherently engage children and their caregivers and companions in stretching children's understanding and skill to apply to new problems. Practical considerations of culturally organized activities (such as avoiding damage or waste), along with young children's eagerness to be involved, lead to structuring of children's participation so that they handle manageable but comfortably challenging subgoals of the activity that increase in complexity with children's developing understanding. (1990:18)

From this model, we took two notions to be central: guidance or facilitation, and performance. While the notion of performance, or of learning through doing, is crucial, equal emphasis is placed on the need for very careful guidance, orchestration, and sophisticated nuanced environmental design and for supportive, sensitive back-up. It is not enough simply to place individuals within similar contexts and rely on their interpreting the contexts similarly. (Gee 1994 discusses how widely disparate different children's constructions of the same poem can be.) There must also be careful cueing, nudging, directing of attention, realignment, and outright correction—in other words, carefully controlled, collaboratively performed activity, in which one actor gives over more and more of the activity to the other, as the situation and ability of the learner permit.

We extend Rogoff's notions beyond the interactions of caretaker and children to formal learning contexts. To take the example of a university class, the professor not only designates the sociocultural context by requiring certain texts, suggesting others, and offering her own text in the lectures, but at the same time, she points to what parts of different texts are more or less relevant (by quoting, rephrasing, or reading from them, or by assigning specific tasks in relation to them). She reaccentuates parts of some texts with her own meanings, repeats certain themes, ignores others, recycles, and provides feedback in various ways when she sees students straying (through their questions, assignments, and body language). The interaction is subtle, fine-grained, multidimensional, and familiar to us all.

Attenuated authentic participation (AAP). Lave and Wenger (1991) introduce the term "legitimate peripheral participation" as an analytic perspective from which to look at a range of social practices that can be loosely referred to as apprenticeships—ranging from activities associated with processes of becoming midwives in Yucatán to processes of becoming members of Alcoholics Anonymous. In common with Rogoff's "guided participation" is a view of learning through co-participation, under attenuated conditions. In Hanks's (1991) formulation, Lave and Wenger situate learning within communities of practice, and view that learning is enabled not by transmitting knowledge or information from the head of the master to the head of the learner, but rather according to the master's "ability to manage effectively a division of participation that provides for growth on the part of the student" (1991: 21). In contrast to instances of guided participation, however, apprentices are initiated into communities of practice by *participating in authentic tasks which are not themselves invented or stage-managed as opportunities for getting newcomers to learn*.

Allied consequently to notions of learning through AAP are those of assuming new identities or full membership in communities of practice. Furthermore, "legitimate peripheral participation refers both to the development of knowledgably skilled identities in practice and to the reproduction and transformation of communities of practice" (Lave and Wegner 1991: 55).

The two models of situated learning point in the direction of two kinds of language learning contexts: one reminiscent of most formal educational settings (but similar as well in striking ways to middle-class learning crossculturally, as Rogoff 1994 has pointed out), and the other evocative of informal learning (or apprenticeship systems, as described by Lave and Wenger.)

While the literature on child language acquisition has tended to present a model akin to "guided participation," ethnographic research conducted in nonmainstream communities and cultures can be characterized more accurately by AAP. (See, for eaxmple, Heath's 1983 Trackton families.)

Furthermore, while the school seems to be particularly constituted to allow for FP, increasingly there are experiments in schools aiming at creating communities of practice, whereby learners become involved in authentic tasks to the degree to which they are able (see Gutierrez et al. 1994; Rogoff 1994). Many ESL teachers have been at the forefront of developing such cooperatively based kinds of learning.

Conclusions. It will be apparent to all those familiar with the literature on SLA that the models based on situated learning overlap with those developed by

Krashen and Ellis—despite the fact that the latter tend to be situated within psychological and cognitive frames and the former are socially oriented. From a theoretical perspective, this consonance is itself significant and lends power to both arguments.

Both theories lead to many of the same conclusions about the nature of learning (and of language learning as a specific instance): the need for relevant, rich exposure, and for performance on the part of the learner, appropriately attenuated and scaffolded by a guide (with the attendant questions about the role of direct and explicit instruction during the performance), and the recognition of the role of affective factors. Both denigrate the role of decontextualized explicit declarative instruction.

Implications for teaching. The implications for teaching are rich and have been discussed in considerable detail elsewhere (Freedman 1993a, 1993b, 1995). Many, in fact, are consistent with the kinds of practices that have evolved from the cognitively-based models put forward by Krashen (1981, 1984, 1985, 1992) and Ellis (1990, 1994).

A social and rhetorical theory of language learning, however, does cast doubt on some strategies currently in practice. I will focus here only on one, whose significance is made salient by the slightly different emphasis provided by the social perspective. Both genre studies and the discussions of situated learning considerably complicate the notions of exposure and context, stressing as they do both the richness of the social dynamic and the thickness of the texture of the context. They recognize the degree to which contexts or situations are socially constructed, and the degree to which communal social interpretation (and, consequently, cueing by the instructor) creates both situation-types and their respective genres (which exist in a dynamic interactive relationship).

Many writing studies have revealed the ways in which specific disciplinary classes elicit specialized genres, which can be differentiated according to complex syntactic, argumentative, and pragmatic rules (see Herrington 1985; McCarthy 1987; Freedman 1990, in press). For example, Giltrow and Valiquette (1994) reveal the different standards for what may count as shared knowledge in different university disciplines. Kaufer and Geisler (1989) explicate the complex rules for what counts as appropriate "novelty" in student composition writing. In all these instances, the precise rules are as unknown explicitly to the instructors who elicit them as they are to the students who realize them in their writing.

Furthermore, all these studies underscore the fragility of genres, and the highly interactive nature of genre and context. Subtle changes are likely to occur in response to changes in instructor, gradual evolution in the discipline, or as a consequence of the complex negotiation during the course of instruction among instructors and students. (Adam 1994 points to some of this complexity in her analysis of the reading protocols of instructors evaluating student writing.)

All this raises important questions about the possibility of portability—say, from the composition class, to Sociology, or indeed any discipline. For even in a Writing Across the Curriculum (WAC) or English for Academic Purposes (EAP) writing class, where readings from a range of disciplines are selected, the setting can hardly approach the richly textured and subtly nuanced quality of the actual disciplinary class. For one thing, the instructor herself is not likely to have access to the same degree and depth of disciplinary knowledge, nor to the time necessary, to create the appropriate context. Furthermore, as opposed to content-area specialists, instructors in EAP and WAC classes have a set of underlying and overriding pedagogic goals which shape their instruction, complicate the discursive context, and redefine the rhetorical exigence.

The genres of the L2 class are undoubtedly as idiosyncratic, specialized, and characterized by highly specific rhetorical and pragmatic rules as the content-area classes described by Herrington (1985), McCarthy (1987), Giltrow and Valiquette (1994), and Kaufer and Geisler (1989). And this is equally true of the EAP class where there is an attempt to bring in authentic disciplinary reading and writing tasks. Students in writing or speaking respond to and pick up on the linguistic/discourse cues highlighted for them in the EAP contexts. Insofar as students are being prepared for other academic writing, that caveat must be borne in mind.

Unless students are actually submitting their writing to another, disciplinary class (to whose context they are responding), students writing for the EAP classes will write EAP genres. Whether this is a good thing is something to be determined. It must first be acknowledged.

A social and rhetorical view of written-language learning—one derived from socially-based scholarship in genre studies and work on situated learning—in part reinforces psychologically-oriented theories of second-language learning, in part enriches this understanding, but in part complicates and problematizes this understanding and the pedagogic practices that have emerged. By seeing language use as intimately connected to, and affected by, a range of complex contextual forces, often invisible to the participants and especially to the most socialized among them (i.e. the experts or teachers), we are forced into a profound reconsideration of the institutional, ideological, sociocultural, and rhetorical forces brought to bear in the classroom, and consequently of the implications of our teaching for our students' learning.

REFERENCES

Adam, Christine. 1994. " Exploring the exigencies of institutional reading practices: A comparison of reader responses in two settings." M.A. thesis, Carleton University, Ottawa, Ontario, Canada.

Austin, John. 1962. *How to do things with words*. Oxford: Oxford University Press.

Bakhtin, Mikhail M. 1981. *The dialogic imagination*. Michael Holquist (ed.), Caryl Emerson and Michael Holquist (trans.). Austin, Texas: University of Texas Press.

Bakhtin, Mikhail M. 1986. "The problem of speech genres." In Caryl Emerson and Michael Holquist (eds.) and Vernon W. McGee (trans.), *Speech Genres and Other Late Essays*. Austin, Texas: University of Texas Press. 60–102.

Bateson, Gregory. 1972. *Steps towards an ecology of mind*. San Franciso, California: Chandler.

Bazerman, C. 1988. *Shaping written knowledge: The genre and activity of the experimental article in science*. Madison, Wisconsin: University of Wisconsin Press.

Berkenkotter, Carol and Thomas Huckin. 1993. "Rethinking genre from a sociocognitive perspective." *Written Communication* 10: 475–509.

Bitzer, Lloyd. 1960. "The rhetorical situation." *Philosophy and Rhetoric* 1: 1–14.

Burke, Kenneth. 1941. *The philosophy of literary form: Studies in symbolic action*. Berkeley, California: University of California Press.

Burke, Kenneth. 1966. *Language as symbolic action*. Berkeley, California: University of California Press.

Cope, William and Mary Kalantzis (eds.). 1993. *The literacies of power and the powers of literacy*. London: Falmer Press.

Devitt, Amy J. 1993. "Generalizing about genre: New conceptions of an old concept." *College Composition and Communication* 44: 573–586.

Doheny-Farina, Stephen. 1992. *Rhetoric, innovation, technology*. Cambridge, Massachusetts: M.I.T. Press.

Ellis, Rod. 1986. *Understanding second language acquisition*. Oxford: Oxford University Press.

Ellis, Rod. 1990. *Instructed second language acqusition: Learning in the classroom*. Oxford: Blackwell.

Ellis, Rod. 1994. *The study of second language acquisition*. Oxford: Oxford University Press.

Engestrom, Yrjo. 1993. "Developmental studies of work as a textbench of activity theory." In Jean Lave and Seth Chaiklin (eds.), *Understanding practice: Perspective on activity and context*. Cambridge, U.K.: Cambridge University Press.

Freedman, Aviva. 1990. "Reconceiving genre." *Text* 8/9: 279–292.

Freedman, Aviva. 1993a. "Show and tell? The role of explicit teaching in learning new genres." *Research in the teaching of English* 27: 222–251.

Freedman, Aviva. 1993b. "Situating genre: A Rejoinder." *Research in the teaching of English* 27: 272–281.

Freedman, Aviva. 1995. "The what, where, when, and why of school genres." In J. Petraglia (ed.). *Reconceiving writing. Reconceiving writing instruction*. Hillsdale, N.J.: Erlbaum Associates. 121–144.

Freedman, Aviva. (in press). "Argument as genre and genres of argument." In Deborah Berrill (ed.), *Perspectives on written argumentation*. Cresskill, N.J.: Hampton Press.

Freedman, Aviva and Christine Adam. 1994. "Simulations as Internships." Paper presented at the Annual Conference on College Composition and Communication, New Orleans.

Freedman, Aviva, Christine Adam, and Graham Smart. 1994. "Wearing suits to class: Simulating genres and simulations as genre." *Written communication* 11: 193–226.

Freedman, Aviva and Ian Pringle (eds.). 1980. *Reinventing the rhetorical tradition*. Ottawa, Ontario, Canada: CCTE Press.

Freedman, Aviva, Ian Pringle, and Janice Yalden (eds.). 1983. *Learning to write: First language/ second language*. London: Longman.

Gee, James P. 1994. "Genre in relation to a sociocultural view of mind, reading, and writing." Paper presented at the Discursive Practices in Workplace, School, and Academic Settings Symposium, Monash University, Melbourne, Australia. July 1994.

Geertz, Clifford. 1983. *Local knowledge*. New York: Basic Books.

Giddens, Anthony. 1984. *The constitution of society*. Berkeley, California: University of California Press.

Giltrow, Janet and Michele Valiquette. 1994. "Genres and knowledge: Students' writing in the disciplines." In Aviva Freedman and Peter Medway (eds.), *Learning and teaching genre*. Portsmouth, N.H.: Heinemann Boynton/Cook.

Gutierrez, Kris and Joanne Larson with Marc Pruyn and Claudia Ramirez. 1994. "Zones of possibility: Reconstituting classroom activity for Latino children." Paper presented at the annual meeting of the American Educational Research Association, New Orleans, Louisiana, April 1994.

Hanks, Thomas. 1991. "Foreword." In Jean Lave and Etienne Wegner (eds.), *Situated learning: Legitimate peripheral participation*. Cambridge, U.K.: Cambridge University Press. 11-21.

Heath, Shirley Brice. 1983. *Ways with words: Language, life, and work in communities and classrooms*. New York: Cambridge University Press.

Halliday, Michael A. K. 1978. *Language as a social semiotic*. London: Edward Arnold.

Herrington, Anne. 1985. "Writing in academic settings: A study of the contexts for writing in two college chemical engineering courses." *Research in the teaching of English* 19: 331-361.

Kaufer, David and Cheryl Geisler. 1989. "Novelty in academic writing." *Written Communication* 6(3): 286-311.

Krashen, Stephen D. 1981. *Second language acquisition and second language learning*. Oxford: Pergamon.

Krashen, Stephen D. 1984. *Writing: Research, theory, and applications*. Oxford: Pergamon.

Krashen, Stephen D. 1985. *The input hypothesis: Issues and implications*. New York: Longman.

Krashen, Stephen. D. 1992. "Another educator comments." *TESOL Quarterly* 26(2): 409-411.

Lave, Jean. 1988. *Cognition in practice: Mind, mathematics and culture in everyday life*. Cambridge, U.K.: Cambridge University Press.

Lave, Jean. 1991. "Situating learning in communities of practice." In Lauren Resnick, Joseph Levine, and Stephanie Teasley (eds.), *Perspectives on socially shared cognition*. Washington, D.C.: American Psychological Association. 63-83.

Lave, Jean. 1993. "The practice of learning." In Jean Lave and Seth Chaiklin (eds.), *Understanding practice: Perspective on activity and context*. Cambridge, U.K.: Cambridge University Press. 3-32.

Lave, Jean and Etienne Wegner. 1991. *Situated learning: Legitimate peripheral participation*. Cambridge, U.K.: Cambridge University Press.

McCarthy, Lucille M. 1987. "A Stranger in Strange Lands: A college student writing across the Curriculum." *Research in the teaching of English* 21: 233-265.

Miller, Carolyn. 1984. "Genre as social action." *Quarterly Journal of Speech* 70: 151-167.

Petraglia, Joseph. (n.d.) "The role of affect in situating rhetorical cognition." Unpublished ms.

Reid, Ian (ed.). 1987. *The place of genre in learning*. Geelong, Victoria, Australia: Deakin University.

Rogoff, Barbara. 1990. *Apprenticeship in thinking*. New York: Oxford University Press.

Rogoff, Barbara. 1994. "Understanding communities of learners." Scribner Award address, American Educational Research Association, New Orleans, April 1994.

Rogoff, Barbara and Jean Lave (eds.), 1984. *Everyday cognition: Its development in social context*. Cambridge, Massachusetts: Harvard University Press.

Schryer, Catherine F. 1993. "Records as genre." *Written communication* 10: 200-234.

Spielmann, Guy. This volume. "Multidisciplinary Integrated Language Education: New questions for second/foreign language teaching."

Swales, John M. 1990. *Genre analysis*. Cambridge, U.K.: Cambridge University Press.

Swales, John M. 1992. "Re-thinking genre: Another look at discourse community effects." Paper presented at the Rethinking Genre colloquium, Carleton University, Ottawa, Ontario, Canada.

Vygotsky, Lev S. 1962. *Thought and language*. E. Hanfmann and G. Vakar (trans.). Cambridge, Massachusetts: M.I.T. Press.

Vygotsky, Lev S. 1978. *Mind in society*. Cambridge, Massachusetts: Harvard University Press.

Wertsch, James V. 1991a. "A sociocultural approach to socially shared cognition." In Lauren Resnick, Joseph Levine, and Stephanie Teasley (eds.), *Perspectives on socially shared cognition*. Washington, D.C.: American Psychological Association. 85-99.

Wertsch, James V. 1991b. *Voices of the mind: A sociocultural approach to mediated action*. Cambridge, Massachusetts: Harvard University Press.

Willard, Charles A. (1982)."Argument fields." In James R. Cox and Charles A. Willard (eds.), *Advances in argumentation theory and research*. Carbondale, Illinois: Southern Illinois University Press.

Yates, JoAnne. 1989. *Control through communication*. Baltimore: Johns Hopkins University Press.

Teaching Chinese teachers what constitutes "Chinese"

William C. Hannas
Georgetown University

Today college teachers of Chinese enter the profession with native or native-like skills in the standard national language, with some knowledge of language pedagogy, and with advanced degrees in linguistics, Chinese literature, or both. This is a far cry from the situation twenty years ago, when many native Chinese teachers lacked academic credentials, when nonnative teachers with the credentials could not speak the language properly, and neither group knew much about how it should be taught. As interest in this less-commonly-taught and most-commonly-spoken language increases, however, students and college administrators are demanding—and getting—teachers who can speak the language, know how to make others speak and read it, and can communicate something of its essence and related culture.

Unfortunately, many Chinese teachers still are not giving their students an accurate account of the subject. Taught to be proficient in the Beijing dialect of the national standard, after four years of schooling students remain ignorant for the most part of what Chinese is, what it is not, and how it relates to other languages. This ignorance has practical implications. One is direct and immediate: Students finish a four-year program and discover what they should have been told earlier—that the Mandarin they learned in the classroom often is not what works in the Chinese world. Another effect is more subtle, but has devastating consequences for the way the non-Chinese world views China: Somewhere in the course of their studies it should have been pointed out that there is nothing unique, unfathomable, or otherwise "special" about Chinese that entitles the languages or its speakers to be viewed any differently from other languages and their speakers, or to be held to different standards.

Some students figure this out by themselves. Most, I dare say, manage to graduate with degrees in Chinese befuddled by one or more aspects of the Chinese Myth, confirming by their stature as degree-holders lay misconceptions about Chinese and China that eventually find their way into national policy. How do we let this happen? Part of the reason is the thrill of being different. Let's face it: It's *fun* to imagine that somewhere in this world there are people with a writing system so different that it enables them to access ideas "directly," or that there is a language in use which has been spoken for "5,000 years," or that an area larger than Europe really is host to a single "language." This is especially gratifying if the language and people are one's own.

Are there other reasons why our students may not be getting an honest picture of what Chinese is all about? Let us play devil's advocate for a moment, and suppose that it is not only fun pretending to be unique, but that it is also *useful*. Being different in strange and wonderful ways boosts one's status at the same time that it mystifies others. It buys respect, or at minimum keeps people from poking around and asking embarrassing questions which those who identify with the existing order in China would rather not answer. Domestically, the Chinese have a phrase for this kind of operation aimed at stifling inquiry before it materializes: It is the *yumin zhengce*—"the policy of keeping the people stupid." What can we call its foreign analog? I suggest we provisionally name it the *pianwai zhengce*, which can be fairly, if ungraciously, translated as "the policy of scamming the foreigner."

This latter phenomenon has several manifestations, but we shall confine our discussion of it to the linguistic. Why for Heaven's sake would a *language* teacher, of all people, be unable or unwilling to provide accurate information about one's subject? What is to be gained by passing on hocus-pocus about the Chinese language to young women and men with whose education we are entrusted? The short answer is: Our careers. When entry visas, publishing venues, access to research materials, funds, and peer acceptance are controlled by the Chinese government, or by people under its direct influence, or by people who for reasons of their own have a stake in obfuscating the reality of language in China, there is a strong incentive for buying into the Chinese Myth, or at least for not complaining about it too loudly.

The downside is that playing along leaves a bad taste in one's mouth, which I would like to spit out along with ten facts about Chinese that teachers of the language should be made aware of.

1. Chinese is *not* a "language," and all the wishful thinking in China will not make it one. Chinese is a *branch* of the Sino-Tibetan language *family* (Mair 1991). Within Chinese there are seven or eight major—or, depending on the criteria, as many as several hundred—languages. The best known Sinitic language today is Mandarin, the national standard, spoken natively by some 70% of China's Han population. It has three or four major *dialects*, whose differences compare with American, Australian, and British English. The remaining 30% of Han Chinese speak other Sinitic languages, such as Shanghainese with more than eighty million native speakers, Cantonese with nearly fifty million, etc. (Ramsey 1987: 87). The difference between the Sinitic languages is said to be roughly comparable to the differences between the modern Romance languages, although this seems like an understatement. China, an empire by its own standards, has always had difficulty maintaining its political integrity, and the myth that its people speak one language presumably makes the rulers' job easier. To a linguist, the claim is nonsense.

2. Chinese is not "the world's oldest living language" any more than the Germanic branch of Indo-European is. What was spoken in China 3,500 years ago had very little in common with what was used there 2,000 years ago, and shared almost nothing with the Chinese spoken in the sixth century A.D., from which point most of the modern Chinese languages began to develop (Forrest 1973: 220). Obviously, there are genetic links between modern Mandarin and *something* in the past as far back as one wishes to trace it. But to consider Mandarin and its antecedents any more than a few hundred years ago one "language" makes no sense at all. Ironically, nonstandard Chinese languages such as Cantonese and Min, which Han nationalists and most intellectuals usually sweep under the table, are much closer to what was used in China 1,400 years ago than is Mandarin.

3. Another point commonly confused by Chinese language teachers, including many with Ph.D.s in linguistics, is that the language is *not* the writing system. Chinese writing is a vehicle for *expressing* the language, and a poor one at that. I grant that the writing system has influenced the language just as the physical constraints of speech have. But I never spoke a Chinese character in my life, and I rather doubt anyone ever has. This misidentification of language with writing has had unfortunate consequences in the classroom, where teachers mistakenly assume that having students read texts will somehow translate into oral proficiency. Untenable in any language, the proposition is even less plausible here because of the haphazard way Chinese writing reflects speech sounds and the wide divergence of spoken and written styles.

4. Chinese teachers need to be reminded that the writing system does not *belong* to China any more than the alphabet that is used to write English belongs to Greece. We have no records of Chinese writing in its first stages. The earliest extant specimens on bones, tortoise shells, and bronze show a system already fairly well-developed. We hypothesize from the absence of contrary evidence that Chinese characters were an indigenous development, and we know for certain that they were *adapted* by Koreans, Japanese, and Vietnamese to write their own languages. But this was a long time ago—nearly two millennia. Now the characters have different shapes depending on the country in which they are used, many characters were created outside China and "borrowed" back in, some characters are used for some languages but not for others, they have different meanings in different languages, and the mapping relationships between characters and the different languages vary. Japanese and Koreans certainly do not think of their writing as exclusively Chinese property, and neither should we.

5. Teachers of Chinese should do their part to dispel what John DeFrancis (1984: 133) and others have called "The Ideographic Myth" which holds, absurdly, that Chinese characters deal directly with ideas. In fact, they do no such thing. Chinese characters in any language map onto the *morphemes* of that language, and are hence tied directly to *particular languages* both phonetically and semantically, in the same way that the written words of an alphabetically written Western language are, albeit on different levels. There is nothing "magical" about the system, and certainly nothing mysterious. It is, for the most part, an unprincipled phonological/semantic mess, whose practical value lies in its ability to untangle problems which its own use has created.

6. Similarly, the character writing system is in no sense "universal" either among the different East Asian languages that still use them, or even among the different Chinese languages. In the former case, we have already observed that the characters often have different meanings and nuances depending on the language, and that their shapes vary. Although isolated words written in characters can sometimes be understood by speakers of different East Asian languages, this is roughly on the order of what Europeans can manage by looking at each other's writing. For connected discourse, transitivity between Chinese and Japanese, or between Chinese and Korean, approaches zero. As for the Chinese languages, it is simply untrue that they vary only in pronunciation. The core vocabularies of the nonstandard languages differ markedly from standard Mandarin and from each other. Their morphemes use characters that are obsolete in Mandarin, or which are used in Mandarin with different meanings; often they have no character representation at all (Cheng 1978). There is no such thing as one written Chinese language any more than there is a single spoken Chinese language. When a nonstandard Chinese speaker reads a text in the standard language, he or she is exercising bilingualism, having learned enough Mandrin to make this possible.

7. Moreover, as just intimated, Chinese has no family or "genetic" relationship to the other major East Asian languages: Japanese, Korean, and Vietnamese. The link, as such, is through borrowed vocabulary, which is exactly analogous to the situation everywhere else in the world. Since writing is not language, but a means of *expressing* language, it makes no more sense to say, for example, that "the Chinese and Japanese spoken languages are different but their written languages are the same," than to make a comparable claim about, say, the relationship between English and Vietnamese, which also uses the Roman alphabet and a fair amount of borrowed English vocabulary.

8. Let us put to rest the notion that Chinese developed entirely independently, and was the sole creation of its speakers. Modern historical linguistics has identified hundreds of very early Sinitic terms that are cognate with—of all things—Indo-European. The list includes not just terms that may have been borrowed, but many items of basic vocabulary. More importantly, the phonetic correspondences have been shown to match in great detail (Chang 1988). This relates to the origins of Sinitic. The same is true of its relationship to Austro-Asiatic and, for later times, Altaic languages such as Turkic, Mongolian, and Manchu. In terms of its development, there was a lot more give and take between Chinese and other languages than many Chinese are willing to recognize. Sanskrit borrowings into Chinese were numerous. More recently, Chinese "repatriated" many hundreds of terms coined in Japan with Sinitic morphemes. Direct phonetic borrowing of English vocabulary into spoken Chinese is also increasing, and is finding its way into written Chinese despite the character writing system.

9. Teachers also tend to misrepresent Chinese as an "exotic" language. It's hard to imagine how any language spoken by a billion or more people can be "exotic"; it is about as common as a language can get. Structurally the language is not unique, either. Its use of tones as a phonemic feature is shared by many other languages, in that part of the world particularly. Morphologically, Chinese is no more "monosyllabic" than English, possibly less. In terms of syntax, it shares with English the same SVO structure and use of word order as the main indicator of grammatical class.

10. Finally, Chinese language teachers have a professional responsibility not to create the impression among their students that ethnic Chinese have a natural monopoly over the language, or that it cannot be learned well by a foreigner, as implied in the saying (which rhymes in Chinese): "I am not afraid of heaven, and I am not afraid of earth. The only thing I fear is a foreigner speaking Chinese." In fact, Chinese can be mastered by nonnative speakers with the same facility with which many Chinese have acquired English. I raise the point here because I have encountered many teachers, especially in China, who have not managed to shake their belief that Chinese is something that only comes out of Chinese mouths. I could cite many anecdotes to support this thesis, but would prefer merely to suggest that condescension should not be a part of a language teacher's—or any teacher's—repertoire.

Myths have their place in every culture, but not in our classrooms and certainly not when passed off as facts. It is not the duty of Chinese-language teachers to perpetuate Chinese myths, however fanciful, or to help Chinese governments achieve national goals, however laudable one might imagine them to be. Our responsibility to our students and profession is to accurately assess the linguistic reality, and model that reality as best we can in our scholarly work and in the way we conduct our language classes. This entails, at a minimum, answering students' questions *about* Chinese honestly, with facts culled from linguistics and not from mythology or politics. Furthermore, students should be made aware early on of the existence of different Sinitic languages, and for advanced students, some skills in one or more of the nonstandard varieties should be encouraged.

This means that we, as teachers, need to reassess our own preconceptions about Chinese in light of what linguistics teaches us about languages in general. Certainly linguistics has something to learn from the Chinese languages, but I'm afraid the opposite is even truer. Equally important, we must try to erase our prejudices and unscientific notions about the way things *ought* to be, and present China to our students as the multilingual, multicultural treasure house that it is.

REFERENCES

Chang, Tsung-tung. 1988. "Indo-European in Old Chinese." *Sino-Platonic Papers* 7 (January, 1988). 1–56.
Cheng, Robert L. 1978. "Taiwanese morphemes in search of Chinese characters." *Journal of Chinese Linguistics* 6(2): 306–313.
DeFrancis, John. 1984. *The Chinese language: Fact and fantasy*. Honolulu: University of Hawaii Press.
Forrest, R.A.D. 1948/1973. *The Chinese language*. London: Faber and Faber.
Mair, Victor. 1991. "What is a Chinese 'dialect/topolect?' Reflections on some key Sino-English linguistic terms." *Sino-Platonic Papers* 31 (September 1991). 1–31.
Ramsey, S. Robert. 1987. *The languages of China*. Princeton, N.J.: Princeton University Press.

Sociolinguistics and language pedagogy:
Are language teachers double agents?[1]

Mary McGroarty
Northern Arizona University and National Foreign Language Center

One of the themes prevalent in discussions of teaching and learning is the call for empowerment (Cummins 1989), for teachers, learners, parents, and others to assume the power to change and develop creative approaches to the difficulties and contradictions of their own situations. In this enterprise, language teachers are dual agents in at least two different ways: They are agents, or representatives, of the language they teach and the culture it represents yet, to be effective in this role, they must have a profound sense of how this language fits into the lives and experiences of the learners with whom they engage. Besides this, language teachers are the agents, or originators, of pedagogical activity; they are also, often perforce, agents in the sense of being advocates for the learners with whom they work.[2] As dual agents twice over then, language instructors must constantly balance the demands of their roles as teachers, their grasp of the language they teach, the learners they serve, and the social context in which they teach. In this talk paper, I want to lay out some of the dimensions of second-language teachers' dual agency with respect to language and learners; in these multiple loyalties lie some of the greatest challenges and rewards of second-language teaching. The pioneering sociolinguistic research and provocative insights exemplified in the work of Charles Ferguson, to whom these proceedings are dedicated, and others who have followed some of his

---

[1] An earlier version of this paper, "Language teachers as double agents," was presented as a plenary address at the ACTA/ATESOL Conference, Sydney, New South Wales, Australia in January 1995. ATESOL's permission to reproduce portions of that talk, which also appears in the conference proceedings edited by Beth Cavallari, is gratefully acknowledged.

[2] My thinking about second-language teachers as double agents has been much enhanced by conversations with my colleague Jim Bartell of Northern Arizona University, and I am grateful to him for sharing his views. He notes that teachers of literature, as compared with language, often have the additional responsibility of challenging students' notions of conventional structures and appropriate plot lines (i.e. challenging expectations for a happy ending) in addition to sensitizing them to the forms and uses of the language, making teachers of literature thus "triple agents." This challenge to conventional social interpretations has also begun to shape some second-language-teaching materials (Dendrinos 1995).

many productive directions have helped theorists, researchers, and teachers attain a clearer vision of their work and shape the areas of inquiry still central to the theory and practice of language teaching.

Teachers as agents of culture and curriculum.

Agents of the dominant culture. It is conventional to note that one of the general functions of education is the enculturation of the learner and the development in the learner of the skills needed to succeed in a given setting. Both of these goals demand careful definition: Enculturation according to whose vision of culture? Success in what, and according to whose definition? These areas are now noted to be contentious ones, as they should be (Said 1993; Takaki 1993). For too long now in institutional educational systems, typical definitions of appropriate culture, the nature of success, and the language needed to ensure these have been dominated by a single vision, that of a middle-class mainstream perspective (Apple 1993; Delpit 1988). Schools are institutions established by organized cultures to imbue younger members of the culture with the values and skills thought important for cultural membership; in their daily work, teachers are thus carrying out a cultural mandate as well as whatever developmental or disciplinary level they represent (McGroarty 1986). In the case of second-language teachers working with learners who may be new to a country, the cultural dimensions of activity are even more overt.[3]

Agents of pedagogy. It is also typical to regard teachers as the chief decision-makers in the classroom, at least with respect to choice of methods, and lesson formats, and often of materials, too. Thus teachers are agents of language policy, when it is defined (as it ought to be, in my view) to include acquisition planning or choices about who should acquire which forms of language and how the instruction should be implemented (Ferguson and Heath 1981; Cooper 1989).

---

[3] That they are overt does not mean that they are necessarily any less contentious. One of the most regrettable aspects of education for immigrant groups in the U.S. is the conflation of beliefs about educational fundamentals with those expressing nonessential cultural conventions of a certain era (often related to, say, particular activities well suited or proscribed for each gender, or links between language learning and patriotism; see McGroarty 1985). Adherence to the latter was accepted as a precondition for achieving the former. Such practices were by no means limited to immigrant education; they have affected educational approaches for all students to one degree or another. Probably their most dramatic manifestation in the U.S. was in the design of educational programs for indigenous groups from the period of 1870–1930, in which a militaristic and heavily regimented approach to education was promoted as the only way to integrate native groups into society and bring them into modern ways of life. Educational programs for native Americans still deal with the legacy of bitterness brought about by such coercive benevolence. The larger point is that cultural conventions of a specific time and place have been mistaken for educational essentials and then imposed with special force on groups in a relatively marginal position vis à vis the larger society.

Teachers make instructional decisions based on a variety of local possibilities and constraints, only one of which is professional training. Much ethnographic research has shown that teachers bring to teaching much more than their professional training, and that factors such as their beliefs about language socialization and about appropriate forms of activity are strongly shaped by personal history and unconscious cultural expectations as well as professional norms (Heath 1983). Such culturally-based expectations have sometimes blinded teachers to the realities of current classrooms, constricting their pedagogical choices unnecessarily. It is my hope that an exploration of past limitations, conscious or unconscious, will assist all of us connected with second-language teaching to develop a broader perspective on our work, a greater appreciation of teachers as key agents of language acquisition policy, and a wider repertoire of pedagogical alternatives.

What are some of the past limitations on the work of language teachers? Let us take the matter of the appropriate language for teachers to teach. Here I distinguish between language as medium and language as object of instruction. Second-language teachers are in the intriguing position of dealing with both to varying degrees, so each merits attention. I will discuss limitations that have affected our professional awareness of language as medium and language as object, summarize how sociolinguistic research has expanded professional understanding, and suggest avenues for future exploration.

Language as medium of instruction. Language as the medium of instruction in the second-language class poses particular challenges in the world of English as a second language, where teachers and students may not share any other language in which to communicate. How do teachers communicate with students when they do not speak the same language? How do they provide students with appropriate practice opportunities in a classroom setting? How do they convey subject matter other than language in understandable terms if their students are still achieving proficiency? All these questions bear on matters of language as the medium of instruction, and in all these areas, current research and practice indicate that the range of available alternatives is broader than it first appears.

Choice of language. The very choice of which languages to use or allow in a class for learners of English is not necessarily the obvious one, English. Teachers, even teachers who speak no language other than English, have found ways to use students' native languages as instructional resources in some settings where student numbers, skill levels, and tasks to be accomplished make this a productive part of instruction. In this area, at least in the U.S., the political and emotional symbolism of language choice often overrides considerations of the pedagogical suitability of bilingual instruction (McGroarty 1992), the approach preferred for optimal outcomes with bilingual students. However, even in the supposedly English-Only Special Alternative Instructional Programs (or SAIPs), which serve multilingual student groups where staff resources in native languages were limited, Lucas and Katz (1994) found frequent occasions of native-language use by students and school staff to accomplish various academic and interpersonal goals.

In the world of adult literacy instruction, too, English is not the only possible choice; native-language literacy instruction may sometimes be offered to precede or supplement instruction in English when circumstances warrant (Gillespie 1994). Moreover, the learners' first language can be an important way to gather information for needs analysis and program design (Roberts, Davies, and Jupp 1992). While there is very little evaluative data on adult programs that incorporate the first language for any purpose, the growing body of experience with adult learners suggests that choice of language for instruction ought not to be regarded as an all-or-nothing proposition, even for English as a second language teachers; there are various ways exploit the students' native languages to assist in the mastery of English and academic subject matter and to affirm the learners' own cultural foundations. In devising ways to promote effective learning, language teachers may thus need to examine the ways in which they can incorporate native-language skills where appropriate and encourage students to draw on such abilities as a part of their own learning processes.

Teacher speech and discourse patterns. In addition to drawing on native languages where appropriate, second-language teachers typically adjust aspects of their own speech, the classroom format, and the nature and design of lessons to learner levels. The kinds of linguistic adjustments to learner age, sophistication, and background are encapsulated in the term "teacherese," often thought, like motherese (Snow and Ferguson 1979), to be a variety particularly well adapted to learners still in the process of development. Research indicates clearly that teachers vary the length and complexity of their speech according to learner proficiency level in the second language (Chaudron 1988). Classroom discourse, too, has its own peculiar tripartite formula of teacher initiation, student response, and teacher evaluation (Cazden 1986a), a structure that consigns students to a subsidiary and relatively powerless role in the interaction.

While varying one's speech may well contribute to effective language instruction, equally important is judging how much exposure to controlled, simplified "teacher talk" is optimal in a given classroom setting, for specific learners completing a specific task (Wong Fillmore 1985), and what kinds of discourse patterns are both congenial and productive for doing so. Pedagogical decisions, even in language classes, cannot be based solely on learner language level; they must include understanding of the nature of access, if any, learners have to the second language outside the classroom, a grasp of the implications of learners' cultural preferences and levels of tolerance for different types of activity (Saville-Troike 1985; Wong Fillmore 1982), and a clear vision of the types of student outcomes expected as a result of classroom activity (Cohen 1994). For none of these is there a straightfoward recipe regarding the adjustment of teacher speech or other kinds of input; each is a contextually specific decision.

One of the most crucial questions for school-age second-language learners is the nature of the adjustments needed not only in teacher speech but in entire instructional settings to enable learners to develop control of both academic language and academic subject matter (Wong Fillmore 1994). This area includes both the kind of talk—the range of discourse patterns used in the classsroom —and the types of literacy work teachers must foster. How can teachers exploit language as a medium of instruction to give learners access to and practice with the full range of linguistic skills they need? Learners should not be limited to input from the teacher or from a text, if that is a variable; while both have a place, each is limited.

How then can teachers use language as medium of instruction in maximally useful ways and develop classroom settings that promote rather than inhibit learners in their path towards proficiency? Two areas of current investigation and innovative practice come to mind; both suggest that all language teachers, as well as teachers of other subjects, learn to use various formats for the presentation, collaborative construction, and practice of material to enhance both language and academic learning and draw students into the joint creation of knowledge through language.

Group work. The judicious use of different group structures and genre types is one way to expand students' and teachers' uses of language in the classroom. These two pedagogical developments have grown up independently out of different situations and different research traditions. I believe, however, that they show important commonalities in theory and in practice, and so merit consideration together here. I will discuss genre-based language instruction in the next section; here let me concentrate on the value of group work. Using student pairs, groups, or teams of different sizes in the classroom is a feature of many approaches to the acquisition of language and literacy skills (e.g. Tharp and Gallimore 1989; Brown 1994). In well-planned group work, students can take on roles that demand the creation and manipulation of knowledge through oral and written language (McGroarty 1993).

Yet putting students in groups is not enough to insure linguistic or academic progress in all areas. While peer work is extremely useful for developing fluency and confidence, it cannot always assist learners with fine-tuning particular formal aspects of language (Pica 1994), depending on the nature of the task to be completed by a group. A recent study of the efficacy of peer revision for improving college-level composition found that careful training, in the form of modeling by the instructor and of good revision strategies, improved both the quality of students' discussion of writing and student attitudes toward writing but did not make a significant difference in the overall quality of compositions (Zhu 1994). Indeed, the nature of appropriate tasks for group activity at different stages of student proficiency and for different settings is one of the most important areas of research activity in first- and second-language classrooms at present (Crookes and Gass 1993).[4]

Language as object.

Teachers as standard-bearers. Language as object of instruction is sometimes thought to be the purview of "English as a native language" teachers. Yet the occupational stereotypes of teachers generally—and of language teachers particularly—attest to the strength of social expectations related to the nature of the language a teacher is expected to teach (McGroarty forthcoming). Those who have institutional responsibility for language instruction— in English, in English as a second language, or in any other language—are often expected not only to know the language fluently (not an unreasonable expectation), but also to endorse and promote knowledge of standard forms and prescriptive rules. Language teachers are to be agents of the standard language and help students develop active abilities in standard forms and uses of language. This is not an unreasonable expectation either, unless it is reduced to the much narrower mandate to "teach grammar," where grammar is defined as a finite set of invariant rules, and ignore aspects of both the linguistic and structural factors that condition grammatical choices. We might call this the handbook mentality, the mind-set that holds teachers responsible for inculcating a certain set of rules presumed to be correct in all circumstances and contributes to the popular stereotype of the English-language teacher as a grammatical enforcer, with his or her red pen ever in hand.

Research on language variation. Teachers who understand the implications of current research are liberated from their quasi-punitive role. Current linguistic

---

[4] A crucial aspect affecting the appropriateness of group tasks for students in heterogeneous classrooms, those serving students of differing levels of academic ability and second-language proficiency, is the nature of skills required to complete the tasks. Cohen (1994) reminds us that, if group tasks depend on high-level literacy skills for completion, they are likely to reward students whose literacy skills are already high and may further disadvantage students, whether second-language speakers or others, whose levels of academic reading and writing are not as high, creating a further source of status differentials and tensions in a classroom. To counteract this, she recommends basing group tasks on a multiple-ability curriculum which requires and rewards many different types of abilities in group efforts (see Cohen 1994, especially chapters 3, 8, and 10). This is an area where careful descriptive research is urgently needed to help teachers make well-reasoned decisions regarding the types of group work to implement in their classrooms.

research tells us that there is no single standard form in any language. "Standardness" is a function of a certain set of co-occurring linguistic features used in a certain communicative circumstance. Understanding the regularities of language variation can thus assist teachers in making choices about the number and types of forms to which students are exposed and are expected to comprehend and produce. Thus pedagogical norms must reflect variation if they are to prepare learners to use language realistically (Valdman 1988).

Another area of sociolinguistics that contributes to a more differentiated understanding of language as object is the rapidly burgeoning specialty of corpus linguistics. Drawing on increasingly sophisticated computational knowledge and technological capability, corpus linguistics yields a more sophisticated grasp of language use. This can help language teachers make principled judgments about the forms that learners must be able to recognize and use, as Biber, Conrad, and Reppen (1994) argue. They show for example that many ESL grammar texts devote three to ten times more space to relative clauses and participial phrases than to prepositional phrases as postnominal modifiers, though the latter are far more common across a variety of registers of written English (Biber, Conrad, and Reppen 1994: 171–174). Such current research alerts all language teachers to new sources of direction about the varieties of language to be taught. Understanding findings on language variation can free teachers from the false obligation to teach a single form for a single function.

Some of the most interesting developments in language as object of instruction owe their genesis to work on genre-based language and literacy development, well-established in Australia (Derewianka 1990; Collerson 1989) and coming to be used more widely in the U.S. (Reppen 1995). Such work shows that even young children are quite capable of identifying and evaluating texts which represent different genres, and that doing so helps them engage in intelligent academic discourse and develop critical literacy skills. Genre-based instruction has great potential for application in several curricular areas; Reppen (1995) provides a fine example of its value in a fifth-grade class studying explorers in which students wrote narrative, descriptive, and persuasive pieces in response to the historical material. Both corpus linguistics and genre-based language instruction, then, speak directly to these issues and can help teachers make better pedagogical choices.

When considering language as object of instruction, though, we cannot neglect issues of language forms and uses which vary within subcultures and across cultures. Here considerations of language as social identity come into play, and here, it seems to me, language teachers as double agents face some of the contradictions and pressures of their roles most directly.

Developing linguistic range through drama. Forms and uses of language express social identity. Second-language teachers working with students from historically subordinated groups must find ways to help students develop the language abilities that will allow access to and mobility in the dominant culture, if that is desired. Doing so demands creativity and sensitivity in designing school experiences that give learners the freedom to experiment with different uses of language and, at the same time, lets them achieve accurate knowledge of how these uses will be evaluated by different audiences. In planning language instruction, teachers as agents of culture and of acquisition planning must make it possible for learners to try out various linguistic and cultural roles in ways that make sense given their own lives and social settings.

Drama is one technique that allows teachers and students to make the classroom into a rehearsal space for a variety of linguistic roles and styles (Heath 1993). Teachers who use drama effectively do not simply impose rote repetition of lines on learners; they allow learners to generate various approaches to presentation, practice and critique various ways to develop a character, and to see what happens when alternative approaches are used. Understanding the motivating power of performance, some community youth organizations also emphasize the aquisition of skills for the presentation of drama or dance events and give learners ample opportunity for practice, coaching, and experimentation with different performance styles and formats; in addition, in preparing for their performances, young people learn to evaluate themselves and their peers critically, just as they expect future audiences to do (Heath and McLaughlin 1993). Role-plays of typical work situations, including role reversals where participants take on parts they would not normally play, have also proven valuable in workplace communication programs (Roberts, Davies, and Jupp 1992: 355–358).

Opening up the world of language through drama demands that teachers acknowledge the difficulties and contradictions in learners' social situations and also acknowledge the perceptions of the learners as a part of any educational activity. If learners see a job literacy program as a way to exert social control over their already limited independence, they will be unlikely to participate enthusiastically (Gowen 1992). If they are to be advocates for the learners as well as the language, teachers must recognize these pressures, even when doing so puts them in the position of questioning the rationale or techniques of conventional language instruction.

Teachers as agents for learners and learning.

Can teachers be advocates? Cazden (1986b) has called for second-language teachers to be advocates for ESL children in three areas: (1) Avoiding reductionist approaches to language and curriculum; (2) insuring that differences between a child's language socialization and the teacher's expectations do not lead to misperception or negative labeling; and (3) promoting smooth and frequent communication among all adults who deal with the learners, both other teachers in a school and parents. Second-language teachers have particular responsibilities toward their students because of specialized training and the institutional positions they may hold. Here I would like to sketch out some of the additional dimensions of the role of language teacher as advocate, or agent for the best interests of students, that particularly interest me and apply to all levels of students, not only children. Much of the work described represents the influence the expanded understanding of sociolinguistics has had on educational research.

Creating a favorable learning environment. Teachers serve as advocates for students when they establish an environment that makes it possible for learners to make progress in developing language and literacy in school. I have already discussed changes in approaches to language as medium and as object of instruction that can promote mastery and confidence in the second language; these are a part of a teacher's professional charge. Also relevant here is the teacher's role as decisionmaker regarding teaching materials, including textbooks and technological aids. Like many others, I have been struck by the diversity in definitions of, for example, literacy which animate textbooks for adult learners of English. When a colleague and I surveyed texts widely used in the U.S. (McGroarty and Scott 1993), we found that they did not agree either on approaches to literacy or on the types of skills in which students received practice. These differences in approaches have pedagogical consequences; teachers need to be aware of gaps or infelicities in textbooks and alleviate them through appropriate classroom activities.

Fostering student autonomy. As the diffusion of technology such as closed-captioned T.V. and better computer-adapted language practice and testing increase, teachers will need to be able to advise students of effective ways to refine and continue their language learning. To help students become autonomous learners then, teachers need to know something about the possibilities of various methods, materials, and current technologies to enhance language learning. Concurrently, though, they must realize that the very goal of individual autonomy may be culturally conditioned (Roberts, Davies, and Jupp 1992). They must seek to understand how their students define and perceive progress in second-language learning and enable students to recognize their own progress.

Linking students with resources. Second-language teachers often know more about school and social-service agencies because of their training and experience with diverse populations. It is imperative that they share this knowledge with learners and with other professionals in the educational system. This is a constant challenge, for the levels and the location of resources of all kinds —information included—change. Yet without current information, neither teachers nor learners (or their parents, if this applies) can tap the support services that sometimes make the difference between educational survival and failure, particularly for students whose educational progress is at risk of being thwarted by financial pressures or family problems (Mehan et al. 1994). Further, educators who know learners individually and see them frequently can provide clearer direction and more personal monitoring of the learners' use of additional resources than an outside person who visits occasionally.

Cross-national comparisons of the sort long encouraged by Charles Ferguson illuminate this aspect of teacher advocacy further. The role of teacher as advocate is different in the U.S. than in such countries as Britain, where the educational system gives particular teachers the responsibility of addressing students' personal and social development apart from the academic concerns shared by all teachers; in the U.S., in contrast, institutional arrangements typically demand that teachers of academic subjects, including language teachers, serve as the first line of intelligence regarding the social psychological and personal issues faced by their students (Freedman 1994). Second-language teachers trained in sociolinguistics may be better able to recognize some of the social issues that affect language learning and use, in school and out.

Addressing sources of conflict. Second-language teachers and learners live in a world marked by conflicts among classes, races, generations, and genders. Sometimes these conflicts include overt or covert racism experienced by second-language learners; sometimes conflicts between learners and their parents or other community members affect educational participation. Further, in part because all educators have not had training related to culturally and linguistically diverse students, there may be staff conflicts within a school over issues of curriculum design or educational services to be provided. Teachers cannot ignore these conflicts but must take action to deal with them according to their circumstances. For school-age learners, they must strive to ensure smooth communication between home and school (Handscombe 1994). For adult learners, they must recognize the impact of prejudices on the learners' life experiences; teachers may also wish to explore training directed specifically at enhancing crosscultural communication (Roberts, Davies, and Jupp 1992) for themselves, colleagues, and other professionals who serve linguistically diverse groups.

Dispelling myths about language. Another source of social tension which bears on teachers' professional activities is the frequent mismatch between public understandings of language and the professional awareness of teachers trained in linguistics (Lo Bianco 1989). With sociolinguistic training, language teachers are better able to articulate the language history and contemporary language situation of the communities in which they teach; descriptive research in sociolinguistics (e.g. Ferguson and Heath 1981) assists them. Furthermore, contemporary research in psycholinguistics and sociolinguistics has provided language teachers with more accurate and detailed information about language itself and about language-learning processes (e.g. McLaughlin 1992). By sharing this information with colleagues, parents, and students, language teachers can help dispel the myths about language (Ferguson and Heath, 1981) which constrict or pervert good educational practice.

Shaping language policy. Individually and as members of professional organizations, language teachers can work to influence language policies. While the extent of teacher influence is a product of the complex interaction between national educational systems and local educational arrangements, it is still true that teachers can be active agents, not simply the passive recipients of directives from above. Individually and through professional organizations, teachers can raise public consciousness of language issues, share information about promising programs and practices, and work to contribute to the public discourse regarding language-policy decisions.

The perils and rewards of double agency. Double agents, typically, do not have a happy end, either in fiction or in history. I believe that second-language teachers, to the contrary, will be effective only to the extent they take their multiple loyalties to the teaching profession, the language they teach, and the learners seriously. Sociolinguistic research as embodied in the remarkable contributions of Professor Ferguson and his many fortunate collaborators and students help them do this. Good language teachers, like good intelligence agents (and like Charles Ferguson), use keen observation, professional training, detailed knowledge of changing contexts, skillful communication at a variety of levels, and insights into individual and group experience to be successful. The results of their work, like that of intelligence agents, shift the balance of power. For teachers, though, the rewards are not those of spy novels or newspaper headlines but the satisfaction of enabling themselves and the learners they serve to better achieve and exploit power and agency through language.

REFERENCES

Apple, Michael W. 1993. *Official knowledge: Democratic education in a conservative age*. New York: Routledge.
Biber, Douglas, Susan Conrad, and Randi Reppen. 1994. "Corpus-based approaches to issues in applied linguistics." *Applied Linguistics* 15(2): 169–189.
Brown, Anne Louise. 1994. "The advancement of learning." *Educational Researcher* 23(8): 4–12.
Cazden, Courtney. 1986a. *Classroom discourse: The language of teaching and learning*. Portsmouth, New Hampshire: Heinemann.

Cazden, Courtney. 1986b. " ESL teachers as language advocates for children." In Pat Rigg and D. Scott, and S. Enright (eds.), *Children and ESL: Integrating perspectives*. Washington, D.C.: Teachers of English to Speakers of Other Languages. 9–21.

Chaudron, Craig. 1988. *Second language classrooms*. Cambridge, U.K.: Cambridge University Press.

Cohen, Elizabeth G. 1994. *Designing groupwork: Strategies for the heterogeneous classroom, Second edition*. New York: Teachers College Press.

Collerson, J. (ed.) 1989. *Writing for life*. Rozelle, New South Wales, Australia: Primary English Teaching Association.

Cooper, Robert L. 1989. *Language planning and social change*. Cambridge, U.K.: Cambridge University Press.

Crookes, Graham and Susan M. Gass (eds.). 1993. *Tasks in a pedagogical context: Integrating theory and practice*. Clevedon, U.K.: Multilingual Matters.

Cummins, Jim. 1989. *Empowering minority students*. Sacramento, California: California Association for Bilingual Education.

Delpit, Lisa D. 1988. "The silenced dialogue: Power and pedagogy in educating other people's children." *Harvard Educational Review* 58(3): 280–298.

Dendrinos, Bessie. This volume.

Derewianka, B. 1990. *Exploring how texts work*. Rozelle, New South Wales, Australia: Primary English Teaching Association.

Ferguson, Charles A. and Shirley Brice Heath. 1981. "Introduction." In Charles A. Ferguson and Shirley Brice Heath (eds.), *Language in the U.S.A*. Cambridge, U.K.: Cambridge University Press.

Freedman, Sarah Warshauer. 1994. *Exchanging writing, exchanging cultures: Lessons in school reform from the United States and Great Britain*. Cambridge, Massachusetts: Harvard University Press.

Gillespie, Marilyn K. 1994. *Native language literacy instruction for adults: Patterns, issues, and promises*. Washington, D.C.: National Clearinghouse for ESL Literacy Education/Center for Applied Linguistics.

Gowen, Sheryl Greenwood. 1992. *The politics of workplace literacy*. New York: Teachers College Press.

Handscombe, Jean. 1994. "Putting it all together." In Fred Genessee (ed.), *Educating second language children*. Cambridge, U.K.: Cambridge University Press. 331–356.

Heath, Shirley Brice. 1983. *Ways with words*. Cambridge, U.K.: Cambridge University Press.

Heath, Shirley Brice. 1993. "Inner city life through drama: Imagining the language classroom." *TESOL Quarterly* 27(2): 177–192.

Heath, Shirley Brice and Milbrey McLaughlin (eds.). 1993. *Language and social identity: Beyond ethnicity and gender*. New York: Teachers College Press.

LoBianco, Joseph. 1989. "Science or values: The role of professionals in language policymaking." In Christopher N. Candlin and Timothy F. McNamara (eds.), *Language learning and community*. Sydney, New South Wales: National Centre for English Language Teaching and Research, Maquarie University.

Lucas, Tamara and Anne Katz. 1994. "Reframing the debate: The roles of native languages in English-Only programs for language minority students." *TESOL Quarterly* 28(3): 537–561.

McGroarty, Mary. 1985. "From citizen to consumer: Images of the learner in English language texts for adults." *Issues in Education* 3(1): 13–30.

McGroarty, Mary. 1986. "Educators' responses to sociocultural diversity." In *Beyond language: Social and cultural factors in schooling language minority students*. Los Angeles, California: Evaluation, Dissemination, and Assessment Center.

McGroarty, Mary. 1993. "Cooperative learning and second language acquisition." In Daniel Holt (ed.), *Cooperative learning: A response to linguistic and cultural diversity*. McHenry, Illinois: Delta Systems, 19-46.

McGroarty, Mary. (forthcoming). "Language attitudes, motivation, and standards." In Sandra Lee McKay and Nancy Hornberger (eds.), *Sociolinguistics and language teaching*. Cambridge, U.K.: Cambridge University Press.

McGroarty, Mary and Suzanne Scott. 1993. "Reading, writing, and roles in U.S. adult literacy textbooks." *TESOL Quarterly* 27(3): 563-573.

Mehan, Hugh, Lea Hubbard, Angela Lintz, and Irene Villanueva. 1994. *Tracking untracking: The consequences of placing low track students in high track classes*. Santa Cruz, CA: University of California at Santa Cruz, National Center for Research on Cultural Diversity and Second Language Learning.

Pica, Teresa. 1994. "Research on negotiation: What does it reveal about second-language learning conditions, processes, and outcomes?" *Language Learning* 44(3): 493-527.

Reppen, Randi. (1995). "A genre-based approach to content instruction." *TESOL Journal* 4(2):31-35.

Roberts, Celia, Evelyn Davies, and Tom Jupp. 1992. *Language and discrimination*. London: Longman.

Said, Edward. 1993. *Culture and imperialism*. New York: Alfred A. Knopf.

Saville-Troike, Muriel. 1985. "Cultural input in second language learning." In Susan M. Gass and Carolyn G. Madden (eds.), *Input in second language acquisition*. Rowley, Massachusetts: Newbury House. 51-58.

Snow, Catherine E. and Charles A. Ferguson. 1979. *Talking to children*. Cambridge, U.K.: Cambridge University Press.

Takaki, Ronald. 1993. *A different mirror*. Boston: Little, Brown.

Tharp, Roland and Ronald Gallimore. 1989. *Rousing minds to life*. Cambridge, U.K.: Cambridge University Press.

Valdman, Albert. 1988. "Classroom foreign language learning and language variation: The notion of pedagogical norms." *World Englishes* 7(2): 221-236.

Wong Fillmore, Lily. 1982. "Instructional language as linguistic input: Second language learning in classrooms." In Louise C. Wilkinson (ed.), *Communicating in the classroom*. New York: Academic Press.

Wong Fillmore, Lily. 1985. "When does teacher talk work as input?" In Susan M. Gass and Carolyn G. Madden (eds.), *Input in second language acquisition*. Rowley, Massachusetts: Newbury House. 17-50.

Wong Fillmore, Lily. 1994. "Learning a second language at school: Conditions and constraints. " Plenary address at Rocky Mountain Regional TESOL Conference, Tucson, Arizona, October 1994.

Zhu, Wei. 1994. *The effects of training for peer revision on college student writing*. Unpublished Ph.D. dissertation, Northern Arizona University.

Native cultural interference in Japanese English

Linju Ogasawara
Japanese Ministry of Education (Emeritus)

1. The need for foreign language (FL) teachers who can also teach culture. I sometimes ask my college students which type of Japanese teacher they like better—an English teacher who is competent in teaching techniques, or an English teacher who has a passable command of English but who knows about cultural aspects behind the language. My students answer that, even if their English teacher is not very competent in teaching techniques, they believe they can make up for it somehow, but it is very hard to find an English teacher who can teach culture, especially one who can teach aspects of culture that are often hard to find in books, preferably from the viewpoint of comparing Japanese culture and the culture or cultures behind English. A contrastive presentation of cultural differences tends to help students understand the two cultures, and even helps learners become introspective about their own culture, i.e. native Japanese culture.

Suppose we have a good English teacher who can adequately teach aspects of culture. Let us ask that teacher how and where he or she learned such cultural information. It comes from many sources, including the teacher's own observation of things and people's behavior, either by associating with native English speaker residents in Japan or through the teacher's own experiences in a country where English is spoken as a native language. But teachers usually admit they learned very little or practically no culture in preservice or inservice teacher-education courses. In Japan, against such complaints, some professors might say, "Well, I have taught student-teachers English or American literature. Isn't that enough?" My answer is, "No, not at all." Here I have to say the discussion depends upon the definition of the term "culture." However, I do not think that I have to go into details to precisely define "culture" here; I think I only have to point out that by culture many cultural anthropologists mean ways of doing things and ways of thinking, i.e. the value system that a people or a nation has acquired. This culture is an everyday thing. It does not have to be very sophisticated or highbrow. Interpreting literature may have something to do with studying a culture, but it only offers an indirect approach to cultural studies. And some literature reflects very little culture. I think there are better ways of learning culture than reading literary works.

2. Needs for crosscultural sociolinguistics. The inclusion of "everyday" culture in language research and language teaching is not a new idea. The idea has been with some of us for more than eighty years. Unlike generative grammarians, quite a few structural linguists, whether British or American, have included cultural elements within their research domain. Actually, it was by such American linguists in earlier years that terms like "ethnolinguistics," "anthropological linguistics," and "sociolinguistics" were created. The first person to coin the term "sociolinguistics" was a teacher in a provincial college somewhere in the South. He coined the term in the 1930s or 1940s, much ahead of linguists. I witnessed the dramatic moment when that teacher was brought onto the platform and was introduced to the audience by Professor Einar Haugen, if I remember the scene correctly. It was at the Sociolinguistics Conference here at Georgetown University in 1971 or 1972.

Terminological points are not very important. We have only to recall that Charles C. Fries and Robert Lado constantly preached about the necessity of systematically teaching the culture related to the language being taught, preferably in the form of "contrastive cultures." However, Fries's and Lado's published comparative examples were mainly about differences between American English and Latin American Spanish. In fact, Professor Fries had considerable interest in aspects of Japanese culture as well. When he stayed in Japan in 1956 for nearly six months to write an English corpus for English teaching in Japan, I was fortunately appointed a research assistant to him. By that time I had finished my first contrastive sketches of English and Japanese and related cultures. Somehow I was known for that and, I believe accordingly, was chosen to help Professor Fries. Anyway, the University of Michigan professor frequently and enthusiastically asked me about aspects of Japanese culture and language. He even expected that when the teachers' guide was prepared to accompany the course books produced from his English corpus, I would write English-Japanese crosscultural notes for Japanese English teachers to teach culture in class. I was happy to do that for Professor Fries, but this project was never realized because his advisory committee in Japan contained few language-teaching professionals.

Let me bring up another anecdotal point: I first came to the United States in 1970 when a three-year project was launched. It was organized as part of a Japan-U.S. Joint Government Project to promote sociolinguistic studies for improving crosscultural communication between the two nations. I was chosen as a Japanese member. The American members were Eleanor Jordan, William Labov, Roger Shuy, and John Asher, among others. All the Japanese members were fairly crosscultural in our outlook, but we discovered that our American counterparts were either specialists on variations of English within the American context, or were language pedagogists. We felt that most American sociolinguists stayed within the framework of their subcultural variations. I wonder how much crosscultural progress American sociolinguists have made since those days.

On the other hand, English-language classroom teachers in Japan have often been in the position to notice structural differences and, to some extent, cultural differences between the two languages. But, as I stated at the outset of my presentation, cultural differences should be taught to students in colleges of education or in similar courses in colleges. The problem is that professors who are teacher educators or teacher trainers are more interested in either literary studies or pure linguistics, i.e. theoretical linguistics.

Another problem I should point out here is that very few cultural-comparison studies have been published in usable form, although I have to admit that recently increasing numbers of researchers in pragmatics and discourse linguistics have been publishing—in academic or professional journals—results of their concrete comparative analyses. Yet, I feel that there should be some popularizers who will present and restate such results in forms accessible to language educators.

Thus, as an old time crosscultural linguist, I wish more American sociolinguists would be involved in crosscultural sociolinguistics.

3. Introducing "contrastive cultures" into English as a Foreign Language (EFL) in colleges of education. Influenced by Sapir, Whorf and Fries, I included contrastive linguistics, error analysis, and even "contrastive cultures" between Japanese and English in 1953 when I published my proposal for a new curriculum for English majors at colleges of education, and actually began to teach such courses. But ever since, very few colleges of education in Japan have offered such courses.

The Japanese Ministry of Education, which prescribes guidelines for types and kinds of courses in college education, revised the guidelines for courses in colleges of education in 1992, and has finally introduced "Contrastive Cultures" or "Cultural Comparisons" into the preservice English-teacher-education course list. The question is, who can teach this "new" discipline? Also, the faculty authority in the English departments of many colleges of education knows very little about what to do about it.

4. Examples of native-culture interference in Japanese English usage. In the rest of this paper, I would like to present samples of some cultural differences that cause either Japanese English expressions or Japanese English speech behavior.

4.1. Japanese are said to live in a vertically-structured society. Japanese are also said to have lived in a kind of closed society which must have had its origin in rice-paddy villages, where villagers knew each other extremely well and established very close personal relationships. In such a village or villages, villagers naturally developed many in-groups. Thus the Japanese are used to greeting a person in the same in-group, but are not used to greeting or showing a friendly smile to a person from another group.

Within the same in-group, Japanese people are constantly aware of who is in a senior position and who is in a junior position. Otherwise, they could not use honorifics properly. This consciousness is seen also in the situation where a person is introduced to or runs into another person. Both people wonder what the other person does and what occupational status the person has. The newly encountered person's name is not very important. They feel they can trace the person's name when necessary as long as they keep their exchanged name cards. Japanese name cards show the person's occupational status. If both people feel the other person's status is useful for future transactions, promotions, etc., they establish and maintain the relationship. From that time on, the other person's name will be meaningful.

All this explains why a Japanese cannot naturally greet another person in English and why the Japanese do not easily remember all their acquaintances' names.

4.2. In Japanese culture, a person within the same in-group does not often have to be addressed by his or her name. It is obvious who is talking to whom. Using the person's name in addressing him or her tends to imply that the person doing the addressing intends to bring the relationship to the point of intimate or personal relations.

Especially if a person's first name is used, the person takes it as an intentional approach and either feels uneasy or has a special feeling of expecting something. Thus the Western—especially North American— habit of using first names sounds odd or is an alien custom. The Japanese feel comfortable continuing to use each other's family names. Even in grade school or junior high school, teachers usually do not use students' first names. They use students' last names. Thus it is no wonder that a Japanese English speaker does not use or even cannot naturally use another person's first name in a conversation.

4.3. There are two types of Japanese people. One type looks into the other person's eyes during their conversation; the other does not frequently look into the eyes of a conversational partner. Many Japanese people do not habitually use eye-contact because, according to their psychology, they are afraid it would be rude to look into another person's eyes. This habit of less frequent eye-contact is transferred to the way Japanese people behave in English dialogs. Native English speakers, on the other hand, find such behavior rude or insincere. They even think the Japanese person they are talking to is not listening to or interested in what they are talking about.

4.4. Japanese people frequently nod while they are listening to their conversational partners. They do the nodding mainly to show that they are still listening. Thus, in a sense, nodding compensates for little eye-contact. Nodding by a Japanese person does not necessarily mean agreement with the speaker. The Japanese habit is often used when the Japanese converse with speakers of English. Native English speakers tend to take the nodding by Japanese listeners as a sign of agreement. Thus, occasionally there is misunderstanding, even of the serious kind.

4.5. Another aspect of nodding on the part of Japanese when they listen to the other person is that they nod to make the speaker believe that they understand what is being said. Japanese people have a peculiar idea that, if they stop nodding and tell the speaker that they cannot follow what is being said, it would disappoint the person. Therefore they just pretend to be following the conversation. This habit also happens when a Japanese person listens to an English speaker.

4.6. In a similar way, the Japanese are not often interested in making sense of exchanging questions and answers in a dialog. They do not care whether or not the question has been properly answered. They tend to be satisfied to only have exchanged words. A Westerner in a question and answer session often asks, "Did that answer your question?" The person who asked can say, "No, I'm sorry. It didn't." A Japanese speaker could not say such a thing in English in such a situation. Japanese people fear that they will sound demanding and will say "Yes, thank you." In this connection, although they may have questions or comments, the Japanese do not want to bring it up, because they consider presenting a question or making a comment in such a situation as a kind of trumpet-blowing,. The person would rather follow the wisdom of the Japanese saying, "A nail sticking out must be pounded down."

4.7. Another similar case is when the Japanese have a serious discussion. Although a Japanese speaker may have a different opinion, he or she will usually hesitate to bring it up out of fear that such frank behavior could hurt the other person's feelings or make that person lose face, especially in the presence of others. At a lecture conducted in English, Japanese participants rarely ask questions. That does not mean they do not have any questions. They just do not want to stand out in the audience. They would rather remain silent.

4.8. Japanese people have come to have the same type of mentality and feeling. They have a strong "we" mentality. In other words, they feel at ease as long as they belong to a dependable group or groups. Thus they tend to say, "We Japanese think so," or "Our country is proud of that."

4.9. Such a feeling as I have just described also reveals that "we" should be given priority or preference because "we" are the insiders. People from other countries are outsiders. They should not expect to be given the same kind of treatment Japanese people enjoy. A person from the outside is called *gaijin* or *gaikokujin*, which is somewhat equivalent to the English word "foreigner." Thus Japanese do not hesitate to use the word "foreigner" when they speak or write English.

4.10. One of the common Japanese greeting expressions is *Dochira-ni-o-dekakedsu-ka?* which literally means, "Where are you going?" This Japanese expression is not really a question. You do not have to give an exact answer. Japanese usually merely say, "Just around there," or "Just to a certain place." This is why some Japanese people say in English, "Hello, where are you going?" even to a friend or a neighbor, or to an acquaintance who is not very close.

We have an interesting reverse case. The English greeting, "How are you?" usually is not a serious question. But Japanese take it as a real question and sometimes answer it with, "I'm not very well," "I have a headache," "I'm feverish," "I'm tired," etc.

4.11. The concept of "privacy" may differ from culture to culture. In Japan, most employers use a salary scale determined by age. Thus an employee's salary is usually determined by what year he or she graduated from college or started working for the company. An employee's salary has nothing to do with his or her competence. So when someone tells other people he or she is paid only such and such an amount, they do not think the employee is incompetent. They think the company should know better. So Japanese people tend to ask English speakers about their salary, or mortgage, or rent.

4.12. Japanese people are not as interested in human beings as they are in relevant locations or things. Thus they often say "Mr. Takahashi lives next to my house," "I helped with his homework," "Go and ask at the front desk," "Pay at the cash register," or "This store is closed today."

4.13. Japanese people prefer to look or sound modest with other people. So when they give someone a gift or present, they use modest expressions, such as, "This is a humble present from me. I'm afraid you may not like it, but please accept it." A proverbial example, occurs when one is invited to dinner at a Japanese couple's home: When the wife says, "Dinner is ready," the host often says, "There's nothing to eat, but let's move to the other room. My stupid wife should know how to cook better." When the guest is shown in the other room, he or she will be surprised to see a variety of delicious food on the table.

When someone says to you, "You have a lovely wife," a Japanese man might say, "Oh, no, no. She is far from being lovely." Japanese people hesitate to accept a complimentary remark about their family members.

4.14. Japanese people are more interested in the process of an action or effort than in the result. Thus Japanese speakers tend to say, "I want to become a teacher," "You will become a good wife," "I will go there at three," or "How long does it take to go to the next town?"

4.15. In Japanese conversations and statements, much is left unsaid if understanding is presupposed because of the situation or people's common knowledge. If you ask a Japanese person, "I want to visit the Ise Shrine, the mecca of Shinto. How far is it from Tokyo?" he or she will say, "It takes about three hours." To Japanese people, such an answer is not puzzling. But to many native English speakers, the answer is incomplete. They say they want to know three hours by what type of transportation. To Japanese it is usually obvious that people go to Ise Shrine first by bullet train to Nagoya, where they change trains to get to the shrine, so they do not feel the need to mention the type of transporation. I have to add that, nowadays, many Japanese drive long distances, so we can no longer take the type of transportation for granted.

4.16. Generally, Japanese people are satisfied with vague general feelings about factual things like populations, heights, numbers or amounts of things, etc. Since they are not interested in exact figures, very few Japanese people are ready to answer English questions such as "What is the population of Tokyo?" "How many universities and colleges are there in Tokyo?" "How high is Mt. Fuji?" or "How far is it from Tokyo to Hiroshima?"

I could continue at length with examples of such crosscultural problems, but I think the foregoing examples are enough to show that EFL professors and teacher trainers as well as EFL teachers for Japanese English learners should have some knowledge and understanding of such differences and language–culture transfer.

Beginning at the end:
"Bilingual education for all" in Singapore and teacher education

Anne Pakir
National University of Singapore

Introduction. A basic tenet in multilingual Singapore is that bilingual education is "good for everybody" and should be made an end for all school children. Indeed, young Singaporeans are propelled by internal as well as external pressures to achieve moderate to high levels of bilingualism in English. This tenet has implications for teacher education in a country where English is the predominant home language for only one-fifth of the population and a widespread second language for the rest.

The issues raised in this paper touch on the quality, role, and discourse of language teachers and their sociolinguistic and pedagogical awareness vis-à-vis English as the main medium of education. The range of educational backgrounds and proficiencies of the teaching staff is examined here with a view to ascertaining the types of classroom models that they represent. It is suggested finally that four pillars of teacher education should be built for multilingual contexts like Singapore where English-knowing bilingualism is becoming the norm. The pillars are (1) grammatical grounding, (2) sociolinguistic sensitivity, (3) discourse discernment, and (4) pedagogic perception.

Background. A brief overview of the country, or "Singapore at a glance" sums up the challenges for education in a multilingual small nation:

- **Space:** 641.1 sq.km.; built-up: 316.5 sq.km.; non-built-up: about 300 sq.km.
- **People:** 2.87–3 million; Workforce: 1.6 million; Tertiary educated: 95,000; Primary 6 or lower educated: 850,000; Foreign workers: 300,000—77.7% Chinese, 14.1% Malay, 7.1% Indian, and 1.1% "Others."
- **Education:** Number of school teachers: 20,172; Enrollment figures for primary and secondary schools: 251,005 (primary)+196,791 (secondary and postsecondary)=447,796 students in 187 primary schools, 145 secondary schools, 6 full schools, and 14 junior colleges.

- **Languages:** Four official languages: English, Mandarin, Malay and Tamil. Malay is also the national language. There are at least twenty-two other languages in use.
- **Economy:** GNP: $90.2 billion.

The educational system keeps with the government's aim to "nurture talent and develop individual potential to the fullest," (*Education Statistics Digest* 1994: 3) providing for at least ten years of general education for all children. According to the Ministry of Education,

> pupils learn at least two languages, English and their mother tongue in school. The mother tongue, which could be Chinese, Malay, or Tamil, is given prominence, as is English, the medium of instruction and language of administration, commerce and technology in Singapore. In this way, pupils keep in touch with their cultural links whilst being equipped with skills to function in a modern, industrialized economy. (*Education Statistics Digest* 1994: 3)

"Bilingual education for all." Being a small country with only people as its resource, since 1966 Singapore has embarked on a bilingual-education policy which has English as its cornerstone. This focus on English has implications for Singapore's 20,000 school teachers, who mainly teach content subjects in English. Bilingual education in many countries of the world means teaching and learning in the medium of two languages. However, in Singapore, it is teaching and learning principally in the first school language, English, while a second language (chosen from the other three official languages of Singapore) is taught as a language to preserve Asian cultural values. In other words, the English language is considered to be a tool while the ethnic mother tongues are viewed as ties, languages which bind the different communities to their respective cultural traditions.

In the population of three million (1990 Census), 77.7% or 2,252,700 are Chinese, 14.1% or 408,000 are Malays, 7.1% or 229,500 are Indians, and 1.1% or 126,200 are labelled "others," which include Eurasians and Europeans. This multilingual population, speaking a diversity of tongues before independence in 1965—Chinese languages such as Mandarin, Hokkien, Teochew, Cantonese, Hainanese, Hakka, Shanghainese; several dialects of Malay; and several Indian languages such as Tamil, Telugu, Malayalam, Hindi, Punjabi, Bengali, Urdu, Gujerati—is rapidly becoming an English-knowing bilingual population (see Pakir 1991, 1992). However, only one-fifth of the population claim to use English as a predominant home language.

Because of its limited size, Singapore has had no choice but to make good the linguistic legacy left behind by the former British colonialists—the English language (Pakir 1994: 375-376). For pragmatic reasons, English is the working language of the country, even for a population which speaks several other languages in addition to English.

Some emerging trends. What are the emerging trends for the language situation in Singapore?[1] The promotion of English as the working language and the intergroup language of Singapore, and the promotion of Mandarin as the intragroup language for the Chinese, who make up 77.7% of the population, have led to language-acquisition and language-use patterns which show a major language shift taking place among the younger generations. To take just a brief measure of the orality and literacy patterns, we turn to two major sources of information, The Censuses of Population 1980 and 1990, and the data compiled annually by the Ministry of Education on the predominant household languages of six-year-old school children in Singapore.

The Censuses of Population indicate a trend of increasing English use and literacy. In 1990, English as the predominant language spoken in homes increased to 20.8% of households, compared to 11.6% in 1980.[2] At the same time, it should be noted that a shift to Mandarin from the other Chinese dialects also took place. Mandarin as the predominant household language rose to 23.7%, from 10.2% in 1980. (And while 20.8% of all households use English as the main household language, Ministry of Education figures reveal that in 1990 one-quarter (25.4%) of six-year-olds used English most frequently at home.)

In fact, data compiled annually from 1980 to 1993 by the Ministry of Education indicate that six-year-olds in the predominant ethnic group, the Chinese, are using more English and Mandarin as the main household languages. The trends seem set to continue (for example see Table 1 below, which shows the shift to English and Mandarin among Primary 1, or Grade 1, Chinese pupils).

From the data in Table 1 we note again that the young tend to use more English than the general population, attesting to the success of Singapore's bilingual-education policy. In the orality aspect, the statistics on the predominant language spoken in the homes by six-year-olds (1980–1993) indicate that the trends towards English and Mandarin as predominant household languages will increase.

---

[1] A recent book, *Language, society and education in Singapore: Trends and issues* (Gopinathan et al. 1994), covers most of the emerging trends vis-à-vis the use of English, Mandarin, Malay, and Tamil in the country.

[2] Many of these households are bilingual households, i.e. the residents speak more than one language.

Table 1. Distribution in percentages of Primary 1 Chinese pupils by first most-frequently-spoken language at home (1990–1993).

Year	Dialect*	Mandarin	English	Others
1980	64.4	25.9	9.3	0.3
1981	52.9	35.9	10.7	0.4
1982	42.7	44.7	12.0	0.5
1983	31.9	54.4	13.4	0.5
1984	26.9	58.7	13.9	0.4
1985	16.1	66.7	16.9	0.2
1986	16.1	67.1	16.5	0.3
1987	12.5	68.0	19.1	0.4
1988	9.5	69.0	21.0	0.5
1989	7.2	69.1	23.3	0.4
1990	5.6	67.9	26.3	0.2
1991	4.5	66.6	28.6	0.3
1992	3.6	28.6	31.1	0.6
1993	3.7	63.9	31.6	0.8

*In Singapore, "dialect" denotes the other Chinese dialects such as Hokkien, Teochew, Cantonese, etc. as opposed to Mandarin, which has the status of an official language.

In the Census of Population 1990, literacy was defined as "the ability to read a newspaper with understanding" (Lau 1993: 2). The overall literacy rate rose from 84% in 1980 to 90% in 1990. When we examine literacy rates by agegroup, we see that the rate in the younger age groups is higher than those in the older age groups. In 1990, the literacy rate for persons in the ten-to-nineteen-year-old age group was 99%, sliding down progressively to 64% for those in the fifty-years-and-older age group (Lau 1993: 3). The data on the proportion of children who are ten years old and over and who were literate by type of official language and ethnic group show clearly the preference for English literacy, a 10% increase since the 1980 Census.

Taking the Chinese group alone—the majority group—there was a 9% increase in English literacy but only a 3% increase in Chinese literacy (Lau 1990: 5). Among the literate population ten-years-old and over, literacy in English (English only or English and another language) increased from 56% in 1980 to 66% in 1990. The literacy rate in the Tamil language among the Indian community had also improved to 50% from 48% in 1980. Literacy in the Chinese language among the Chinese rose to 79% from 77% in 1980. However, in the Malay language among the Malays, the literacy rate remained unchanged at 96% (Lau 1993: 5).

These results have come about after a heavy investment in educational linguistics, that is, providing an acquisition environment based on findings in current research on first- and second-language learning and acquisition in the classroom, applying methodologically and theoretically sound practices, and providing innovative and coherent curricula. Better teachers, resources, and support from the home, as well as improved training and innovative curriculum planning have been provided to ensure that children had a good chance to learn two of the official languages.

However, with the population showing language shift, there exist unique sociolinguistic parameters and contexts which bear upon the teaching profession. For example, in many cases discourse in the home may not be in English at all and, when it is, many kinds of English are used.

The quality of teachers and their role, discourse, and sociolinguistic and pedagogic awareness are the focus of attention with regard to the questions of teacher education in this context.

The quality of teachers. In the context of the evolution of educational excellence in Singapore, teacher education is a vital component. Thirty years of teacher education targeted at the development of better-quality educational personnel, have meant teacher pre-service training and preparation, inservice training and upgrading, and post-training self-access learning. Professional growth is taking place continually.

The question of teacher competency is important, especially for English-language teaching in Singapore; consequently, the educational attainment of teachers is a key matter. The greater the number of years spent in English-medium schooling, the better the mastery of the English language and its subsequent teaching. However, because of two initial problems, it was not possible to ensure high educational levels of English language teachers so that Standard English would be found in the classroom,

First, historical developments in education had already planted the seeds of compromise with regard to "standards" in the teaching of English in the Singapore classroom. From 1965, the year that Singapore became independent, the government sought to make universal education readily available. A mass recruitment of teachers took place. During this period of responding to quantitative demands (1965-1972),[3] school enrollment peaked, causing in tandem a peak expansion in teacher demand. Because of the crash program, the quality of education was low, with selection and training at a level far below acceptable standards.

A period of qualitative consolidation then followed (1973-1981), with improving training conditions, followed by a phase of enhancing the profession's

Table 2. Changing educational levels of teachers.

Year	O level	A level	Graduate	Total
1979	65.3%	16.8%	17.9%	19,388
1988	47.4%	21.2%	31.3%	21,015
1994	35.4%	28.9%	35.5%	20,172

Figures include principals, vice-principals and teachers seconded to the Ministry.
Source: Personnel Division, Ministry of Education.

image (1982-1990). The picture now emerging (Table 2) shows teachers are smarter and better qualified (as reported in *The Straits Times*, September 1, 1988). The latest statistics (from the *Education Digest 1994*) also indicate an increasing percentage of teachers who have attained higher educational levels.

The fact remains that in Singapore one's degree of mastery over the language called Standard English is more often than not correlated with years spent in formal schooling. Thus, those teachers who have "O"-level qualifications had only ten years in the English medium of education before proceeding to teacher training. From Table 2, it is still evident that in 1994, 35.4% of the 20,172 teachers in Singapore schools had only "O" levels, although the trends indicate better qualifications among teachers as a whole. The situation can only improve with time, with more inservice courses and with increased sociolinguistic and pedagogical awareness on the part of the teachers.

Second, with the rapidly rising enrollments in English-medium schools in the 1960s and 1970s, an accelerated retraining and deployment of mainly Chinese-educated—plus some Tamil-educated and Malay-educated teachers— to teach in English had to take place. This brought on further problems in the practice of teaching in schools. Whether they were teaching Mathematics, Science, History, Geography, or Moral Education in English, these teachers,

---

[3] Yip and Sim (1990: 153-182) have an excellent chapter on twenty-five years of teacher education in Singapore from 1965 to 1990.

especially the Chinese-educated, were steeped in the tradition of learning by rote and class recitation. They were also accustomed to strict hierarchical control over the class, and expected full obedience and respect from their students. Besides their difficulty in being fluent and comfortable in teaching in the medium of English, these teachers had different communicative styles in terms of greetings, attention-getting, floor-holding, and other interactional exchanges.

With respect to the two "limitations," what we are really discussing is a matter of modeling. Gopinathan and Saravanan (1985:71), who are lecturers at the Institute of Education, believe that even teachers themselves, purportedly the norm carriers of Standard English, are not the clearest models for children in the classroom: "One cannot hope to use teachers as classroom models without being clear as to the type of models they represent and the direction in which they need to be moved."

The role of teachers, their discourse in the classroom, and their sociolinguistic and pedagogic awareness. Of some significance are the norms of interaction and norms of interpretation in the classroom setting as well as how teacher roles are realized in the developing contexts of English-language situations in Singapore. Some competence in the rules of using language in different sociolinguistic contexts is necessary.

The discourse of "English-knowing bilinguals" in the school domain must be seen in the light of the increasing trend towards learning English,[4] and the accompanying increase in the range and depth of its use. The discourse is explained with a model of "expanding triangles" formed by the English-speaking base population and two distinctive Singapore English speech clines, graded on formality and proficiency considerations.[5]

It is clear that the Singapore English speech continua are formed minimally along two dimensions. The first dimension is along the cline of formality from Singapore Standard English (SSE) on the upper end to Singapore Colloquial English (SCE)[6] on the lower end. SSE is used for formal contexts—in Parliament, the courts, administration and high finance, public speeches, high powered meetings, and classrooms, especially at the tertiary level. SCE is reserved for informal situations—among friends, with semi-strangers, in service encounters, the workplace, and at play.

---

[4] Since 1987, English-medium education became the mainstream or national norm of education in Singapore.

[5] Some of the discussion that follows and some of the data from a Singapore classroom have already been presented elsewhere (see Pakir 1991).

[6] A term used by Gupta (1989) to refer to the low (L) variety of English on the formality dimension.

The second dimension is along the cline of proficiency in English, a range which I have arbitrarily broken up into five graded series based on Joos's (1967) "Five Clocks": the highest is "advanced" (inter alia, educated, or standard variety), followed by "adept," "intermediate," "basic," and "rudimentary" or pidgin-like at the lowest level. These levels correlate with number of years of contact with English, usually in an institutional setting like school.

The near-universal use of English in Singapore today, in addition to the other languages, has produced a population that knows English, but with varying proficiency levels. Proficiency, in turn, determines the largest movement in terms of expanding triangles of English expression by English-knowing bilinguals in Singapore. Speakers of English low on the cline of the proficiency continuum remain pretty much at the lower end and cannot range in their formality dimension. In other words, they form small triangles, starting from the rudimentary end; whether the occasion is most formal or most intimate, their English subvariety remains essentially nonstandard. As proficiency increases, bigger triangles are possible with shifts made for corresponding formality levels, including greater varietal range (see Figure 1 below).

Highly educated users of English are found at the top ends of both speech clines. However, their movement along the clines is fluid and far-ranging as compared to others who are less proficient. They are capable of moving along the whole formality continuum using high (H) and low (L) varieties of English as the occasion calls for, matching the styles along the proficiency continuum, often remaining at the top end and occasionally stretching down to the intermediate level or even lower. In the most intimate situations, they are capable of producing very "basic" or "rudimentary"-like expressions such as "Always like that one," or a teacher's complaint made affectionately and couched in nonstandard usage: "How come no trouble for new teachers? Old

Figure 1. Expanding triangles of English expression by English-knowing bilinguals in Singapore.

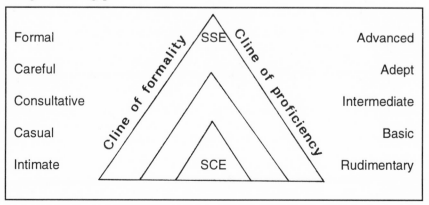

teachers only so much trouble, ah." (see data below, Example 5). However, at their most formal, the English that they use is identifiably Standard English, almost no different from the variety used by educated speakers of English elsewhere.

The sociolinguistic and pedagogic facets of teacher education can be helped by examining the discourse of English-language students and teachers in the context of expanding triangles of English expression in Singapore. The teachers' role is to orient toward this notion, and to engage in the discourses therein. This model of expanding triangles can be used to understand the range and diversity of the subvarieties of English—the kinds used at home and in school—spoken by English-knowing bilinguals in Singapore.

It is clear that the teaching of Standard English (the H variety) and proficiency in Standard English is "a primary responsibility of the school" (Gupta 1989: 36). Even in countries where native speakers of English are found, Standard English for some children is a variety that is school-acquired. "The teacher ultimately sets the standard of spoken and written English for Singapore's 500,000 students," according to Mr. Koh Kong Chia, English Language Specialist and Assistant Director of Examinations, Ministry of Education (as reported in *The Straits Times*, May 22, 1982). In Singapore, it is believed that in the home parents, brothers, and sisters may make "bad models"—and neighbors may be worse. So for a long time to come, our pupils cannot depend on their home environment to acquire Standard English.

With regard to non-Standard English used in Singapore (sometimes called "Singapore Colloquial English," sometimes "Singlish"), the schools should seek not to eradicate but to differentiate it for their students. If the L variety (SCE) cannot be made to serve the instrumental, the regulative, and the heuristic functions, then the school is on the right track if it orients itself to giving students the (H) variety (SSE). The non-Standard (L) variety will be caught, but the Standard (H) variety has to be taught.

Several teachers, teaching English as a first school language, are aware that children who come in with an L variety of English learned informally in the home and from neighbors are quite comfortable switching to the lower-lectal variety to communicate efficiently with other students.

School teachers are purportedly the norm-makers of English usage in Singapore and have to teach with exonormative standards (see Pakir 1994b: 174). Teachers have to proceed with the notion that standards exist and that they come from elsewhere. But sociolinguistic sensitivity on the part of teachers includes not just knowing how classroom discourse development can proceed with proper guidance in Standard English, but also knowing (1) that students find it too formal and irrelevant for natural discourse and (2) that teachers find it irksome to teach prescribed exonormative standards when they themselves may not be confident of their own standards.

However, the school offers several "contexts of situation" invoking several varieties of English along a generational level (less English, more Chinese —Mandarin or dialects—in the lower primary levels; increasingly more English in the upper primary and secondary levels). There is a plethora of English subvarieties that are used in the different subdomains in school, for example, the playground, the canteen, the school field, the staff common room, or the classroom (and this includes the factor of plus or minus the presence of the teacher). It is not uncommon that in subdomains where the teacher is not physically in front of the students in the class, much SCE is used and the lower cline of proficiency in English is evident.

Implications for teaching. Teachers will have to achieve, and then help their students achieve, larger triangles of English expression. Two implications for teaching can be seen in relation to "operacy" and "orientation" notions.

In terms of "operacy" (for both students and teachers), formal, explicit, and deliberate use of the language should be clearly distinguished and distinguishable from informal, implicit, and unconscious use of the language. The interpersonal function could be carried out in both forms, SSE and SCE, depending on the formality levels. In other words, proficiency in the language has to be attained in the first instance to allow this operational movement of switching between the two.

In terms of "orientation," which is an outlook adopted by the school authorities and carried out by the school, Standard English has to be imparted uniformly for all contexts. The regulative, heuristic, informative, and representative functions have to be carried out in higher end English (SSE), which is not completely dissimilar from international English, whether British, American, or Australian. Singaporean schools should not ignore the fact that international English is the ultimate goal, although the Singaporean variety has yet to gain recognition.

The model of expanding triangles may be useful in understanding how in classrooms—which are supposedly formal settings—a range of varieties of English can be expected. The receptivity of students to this fluidity of movement along the range, and their larger triangles, enables some comprehension of an otherwise haphazard and infinite array of linguistic diversity involving English use in Singapore, and enables one to understand English-knowing bilingualism in Singapore. English-knowing bilinguals range greatly on the clines of formality and proficiency, forming differently-sized triangles. Gaining proficiency is a process requiring instruction at the most formal level, and the schools really do need to have this orientation. Having gained proficiency in the language, the individuals are free to range from the highest levels of formality to the lowest, which includes forms that are representative of basilectal speech.

Some school practitioners may be alarmed at the level of informality (and, in tandem with that, the proficiency and fluency patterns used) in classroom discussions. On the positive side, we observe the remarkable ability of English-knowing students and teachers in ranging along the speech continua from high-level proficiency (as shown in the use of SSE) to low-level informality and the use of rudimentary or even pidgin-like proficiency (as represented in SCE). These varieties are used for any or all of these functions—instrumental, regulative, interpersonal, informative, imaginative and the innovative—within the same contexts of situation, involving the same interlocutors who have the same role-relationships in those contexts. Formal English which is expected in the staff rooms and classrooms when lessons are in session, alternates with intimate English as the need to signal casualness or intimacy arises. Standard English, which is expected in written work, is evident on wall charts, in exercise books, in creative writing, and in public oratorical contests.

The prognosis is that as the range and depth of English use increase, several levels of formality can be achieved with the same levelling up of proficiency in English. For this situation to evolve eventually, four pillars of pragmatic teacher education need to be built.

The four pillars of pragmatic teacher education in Singapore. It does seem then that for the unique circumstances found in Singapore, four important targets of teacher education are important.

Pillar 1: Grammatical grounding. Grammatical competence is a necessary foundation for communicative competence (cf. Canale 1983). Mastery of the language code is an important matter for any language program but even more so for second-language situations. To impart the standard in school, teachers should know the standard and be able to teach it well. To this end, several syllabuses—the structural, the notional, the functional, and the communicative—are to be used for different groups of students and for different levels of language attainment. Even for a communicative grammar, accuracy in the language code makes for effective and fluent communication.

Pillar 2: Sociolinguistic sensitivity. Powerful sociolinguistic concepts should be understood in a complex multilingual country such as Singapore. Correlations between social structure and linguistic structure, sociolinguistic explanations such as acts of identity, speech accommodation theory, the interplay between language, ideology and power, language management issues, and societal multilingualism are but some of the concerns. The issue of international intelligibility is important for a nation of traders. There should also be some awareness among teachers that the expanding triangles of English expression among English-knowing bilinguals can explain some of the sociocultural rules of discourse. With such a notion, teachers can concentrate on expanding their triangles, while continually recognizing the fact that the classroom is a special culture where rapport, solidarity, intimacy, and support are necessary for allowing students to change and grow.

Pillar 3: Discourse discernment. Discourse at home and discourse in school have to be understood in terms of congruency paradigms. In a population undergoing language shift to English for education, there are bound to be some match/mismatch problems in terms of acquisition of English at home (mostly an L variety) and in school (mostly an H variety) (see Pakir 1994b: 166–179). Many teachers are aware that discourse at home proceeds off the linear axis in terms of Standard English.

Parents, other grown-ups, and children in the home may not observe exonormative standards of English, in most cases because of limited proficiency levels and competence in the language, but in other cases for reasons of informality and solidarity.

Two main types of adult–child interaction are in focus here: Type-A homes where adults have mastery of the language but choose to drop the formal English code for the informal SCE in certain interactions (within the family, with close friends, and to small children); and Type-B homes where adults have limited proficiency levels and minimum competence in the English language either because they themselves were educated in some other medium of education or did not have the opportunity to complete their education. English is used for varying functions in these Type B homes, although it may not be the principal language.

Much of the interaction that goes on in Type-A homes takes place in SCE rather than Standard English. This kind of English is generally prevalent in Singapore society, and is used even by the highly educated and proficient in English. Examples are easily quoted:

A bank officer in the home: "Opposition still come in ah?"
A confidential secretary to her two-year-old: "You don't want, you don't move."

In Type-B homes, limited proficiency in English is a serious cause for concern when parents, thinking that they are helping their children to strike ahead of others by using with them the school language, English, are unwittingly hindering them in presenting non-Standard English linguistic models. In many of these homes, "tuition" sessions especially for language (English and/or Mandarin, Malay, Tamil) and the sciences (mathematics/sciences) are common. However, examining transcripts of interactions and negotiations in English between "tuition teachers" (as these home tutors are commonly referred to, a phrase which is a loan translation from the Chinese languages)[7] and their students, we find a variety of English which is closer to the lower ends of the Singapore English speech continua.

As mentioned earlier, the functions served by English in these newly developing contexts include the instrumental, regulative, interpersonal, and imaginative or innovative (see Kachru 1983: 52, footnote 6). What we see in Singapore is that the first three functions call for the subvariety of English found at the lower end of both the English speech continua in Singapore.[8] "Tuition teachers" and, I suspect, teachers in the school environment too, find it unnatural or difficult to use the H and/or advanced English varieties to serve regulatory, instrumental and interpersonal functions with their subordinates—for example, pupils in school—when they are not teaching English during the English period. For "tuition teachers," the context of the situation offers little scope for the use of formal English even though they are paid to teach it. The teaching situation calls for a formal H variety but the context of the home and speaking to children evokes an informal, and sometimes nonstandard, variety. In summary, we find that in the homes, and increasingly in the schools, changing "contexts of situation" militates against the use of Standard English.

Overlying this basic problem of English-language use in the home is a complicated linguistic-socialization phenomenon for the young. Spontaneous interaction processes in both types of homes (A and B) also include varying degrees of codemixing, codeswitching, and borrowing from several other languages. The pervasive influence of the contact languages and a great deal of what linguists term "interference" is seen, and this may reflect attitudinal reflexes of a population that rapidly is becoming English bilingual where once they were bilingual in other major languages or in the various minor languages in Singapore.[9]

Discourse discernment means that teachers need to understand fully the *interface* between discourse at home and discourse in the school. As sketched above, the language situation in Singapore is highly complex. Linguistic diversity and an evolving English-knowing bilingual society focuses our attention

---

[7] "Tuition teacher" is a direct translation of the Mandarin phrase *pu si lao shi*.

[8] Interestingly the fourth function, too, is increasingly being served by the lower end of the diglossic continuum in the recent flowering of "Made-in-Singapore" plays, books, and other creative productions.

[9] The distinction between major and minor languages was first made by Ferguson (1971), whose criteria were used by Kuo (1980: 45–46). Kuo's sociolinguistic profile of Singapore identifies five major languages (the four official languages plus Hokkien) and three minor languages (Teochew, Cantonese, Hainanese). My definition of minor languages would include all the other mother tongues in Singapore besides those identified by Kuo as major or minor.

on the complex home-to-school transfer that children in Singapore have to make in terms of language and linguistic socialization.

Mismatches occur all the time, not least of which is the discrepancy between precept and practice.[10] Children from homes where English is used as a principal language may encounter different accents, different norms, and different expectations in the school (this depends on the teachers they get—ones trained in some other official language; ones from abroad; local university graduates; holders of just "O" levls, etc.). Children from homes where English is hardly used have to make the adjustments from a non-English-knowing bilingual-home community to several kinds of English-knowing bilingual situations in school. For all these children, adaptation to speech styles occurs constantly as the child moves from home to classroom, to playground and canteen, and back again.

DATA FROM A SINGAPORE CLASSROOM. The following data from classroom observations show how large the triangles of expression work for English-knowing bilinguals in premier schools in Singapore. In the school, Mandarin is the usual mode for informal interaction among school girls. However, one group of sixteen-year-old students that were observed use English even for informal purposes, except for humorous effect, when they codeswitch to Mandarin and at times when communicative situations demand that they use another language, for example, when speaking to the school-bus driver who does not know English well enough. The class size in each case was relatively small, twenty in a class, rather than the norm of forty students in Singapore classrooms. The researcher was thus able to follow the students more closely while they engaged in the normal day-to-day lessons conducted in English, observing them in their English literature and English language lessons for a month.

This sample population was chosen precisely because they have a greater facility with the English language than their peers. English is their home language and school language, although all are proficient in and enjoy a good command of a second school language (viz. Mandarin/Malay in this group of students who are also obviously in the top percentile of their cohort). They display a tremendous ability in discussing issues such as surrogate motherhood, censorship in the media, and the use of emotive/subjective language by politicians and newsmagazine writers. They are equally versatile in analyzing events such as the biblical account of Saul's conversion (for example during a

---

[10] Tay and Gupta (1983: 187) recommended that "As part of the process of upgrading the teacher's English, data on two main aspects of Standard Singapore English must first be obtained: (1) a description of English spoken by primary and secondary teachers to determine how far short they fall of the expected standard so that remedial measures can be suggested for teacher training; and (2) a survey of textbooks and curricular material should be carried out to see if there are non-standard forms." Implicit in such a recommendation is the notion that there is a discrepancy between precept and practice.

pastoral care lesson) and the concept of the Great Chain of Being in *Macbeth* (for example during a literature lesson).

The girls were tape-recorded in naturalistic settings, viz. in the classroom and video-room, while engaging in groupwork, individual presentations, school lessons, and debates and discussion. As mentioned, schools in Singapore offer several contexts of situations, invoking subvarieties of English, as well as differentiated language use. In other words, schools offer different subdomains which invoke different subvarieties of English such as those used in the playground, the canteen, the school field (less formal and perhaps less standard), and those used in the staff common room and the classroom (more formal and more standard).

One finding from this study of classroom interaction (plus and minus the presence of the form teacher) is that once rapport, solidarity, and familiarity are established, the formality level drops and the proficiency (measured in terms of Standard English) exhibited by the same students goes along a wider range. Of interest is the way the teacher, familiar with the same girls over three years of constant interaction with them, uses English in class. Informality is preferred to formality, even though the teaching situation demands a formal use of English. Tapes 1–5 offer examples of teacher-use and student-use, with obvious ranges in degrees of standardness and formality (see Examples 1–8).

Example 1. On surrogate motherhood (Tape 1)
TR: What if the child is deformed? Will you carry on with the pregnancy? Can you reject the child?
ST: But it wasn't in the case of ...
TR: Never mind if it's not ... what would you do, how would you safeguard the whole thing?

This   segment (Example 1) demonstrates the kind of spoken Standard English that is in use for much of the time on the part of the teacher (TR) and her student/s (ST). However, later on in the same discussion, we see that one of the students drops comfortably to a less formal type of English, characterized by missing subjects (as indicated by the caret sign [^]) and the use of pragmatic/discourse particles such as *lah*[11] and *what*. (See Example 2.)

Example 2. On surrogate motherhood (Tape 1)
TR: But don't you want to safeguard it first by saying "You know, we should meet before we agree and for a longer period of time ... "
ST: ^Should meet before and during pregnancy lah.

---

[11] *lah* can serve serveral discourse functions: as an emphatic, solidarity, or assertive marker, among other things.

TR: You don't want to give the surrogate mother anything ... ?
ST: I mean it's better not to ...
Any breach of this contract is liable to attendance in prison (some sniggers heard).
^Can what!

In a group discussion with one student taking notes (Example 3), the girls (S1–S3) relate the circumstances surrounding Paul's conversion:

Example 3. On Paul's conversion (Tape 1)
S1: On the way to Damascus, ^saw bright lights, ^heard Jesus... Conversation with Jesus, Jesus gives him instructions...
S3: ^Got instructions. Can lah.
S1: OK, so what... Then Saul is blinded, right?
S2: He was instructed to go into the city; but he was going into the city anyway!
S1: Ya woh.
S3: Saul was baffled. Mystified. He heard the sound but did not see anyone.
S1: Did Saul see anyone?
S2: But "... did not see anyone" indicates that Saul must have seen something.
S3: He saw a bright light!
S2: Sorry, I'm sorry. So cheem.

Again, solidarity and familiarity markers are evident in the use of *lah*, *can* (with missing subjects) *ya* rather than "yes," and a borrowed Chinese lexical item, *cheem*. *Cheem* is a Hokkien-derived word which means "deep" or "having too much depth to be understood." In colloquial English elsewhere, it might mean something like "I'm out of my depth here." *Can lah*, *ya woh*, and *so cheem*, will only be understood by speakers in the Singapore context, and marks a kind of English discourse only slightly intelligible, if at all, to other speakers of English. Communicative particles, sometimes referred to as discourse particles or pragmatic particles, are found in situations where the interlocutors desire solidarity and/or informality.

In a discussion on *Macbeth*, TR uses Standard English and ST does too, except for the last part of this segment (Example 4):

Example 4. On *Macbeth* (Tape 2)
TR: Malcolm and Donalbain. What do you notice about them?

ST: They are perceptive .... because they realize that there's something
wrong with Macbeth lah ... because they said something like ... (to
her classmates): What did they say ah?

The student (ST) elicits the help of her friends by asking in typical SCE a
question with the *ah* particle. In non-Standard English, spoken by those less
proficient, it would normally be a statement, such as "They said what, ah?"
rather than "What did they say, ah?" In the first, *ah* is used as a question
marker, in place of a "proper" English construction with the initial interrogative
marker "What" and the subject–AUX inversion. In the second, the *ah* is used
as an intonational marker. The question is properly constructed, but in the
manner of a statement rather than a question. The final *ah* carries the
intonational marking for a question, rather than the expected rising intonation
expected in a question as in "What did they say?" It also marks the "friendly"
or "chummy" way to ask for cooperation from one's peers.

In the regulation of behavior (Example 5), the teacher again switches from
rather standard to a kind of informal English, recognizable in its non-standard
construction. The next segment is taken from a pastoral care lesson, emphasizing
the duties and responsibilities of the girls:

Example 5. On pastoral care (Tape 3)
TR: Handing in homework! Alright, people, handing in homework. What
rules? Has anyone not handed in homework? Do you think this chart
thing works?
ST: Yah!
TR: Can we have them all on one board? All the homework stuff will be
pinned there on that board, yah, OK? So reps (=representatives) for
the other homework... um... Biology?
ST: No trouble. New teacher.
TR: How come no trouble for new teachers? Old teachers only so much
trouble ah?

The same teacher, in giving a lesson on the use of emotive/subjective
language (Example 6), uses Standard Singapore English fluently and
competently:

Example 6. On the use of emotive/subjective language (Tape 3)
TR: Now, the whole idea of this exercise is not only to give you ideas
about how, what, to write for your composition when you want to
argue for or against surrogate motherhood or genetic engineering, but
more so, so that you know how to write either objectively or
subjectively.

The teacher does this again for another pastoral care lesson (Example 7):

Example 7. On pastoral care (Tape 4)
TR: All right! OK! We're talking about goal setting for 1990. OK girls, quiet. First you keep quiet, then you listen to me. The first thing you have to do is to reflect. What were your goals last year? Then you have to reflect on your achievements.

The students, like the their teacher, are capable of discourse using a variety which is expected of highly educated individuals speaking standard English (Example 8):

Example 8. From a class debate (Tape 5)
ST: OK, the motion today is that censorship of the mass media be abolished. Our definition of censorship is the elimination of elements detrimental, and possibly offensive, to the public in the mass media. What we are arguing for is that censorship in the mass media should not be abolished.

Thus we see that familiarity, rapport, and solidarity factors allow for an intimate level of discourse which invokes rapid switches from Standard to non-Standard English usage, even in classrooms where the formal variety is taught and expected.

Pillar 4: Pedagogic perception. Teachers should be in the forefront of curriculum or syllabus design, giving input from their teaching goals and objectives to the curriculum designers. The evolving syllabuses—structural, notional, functional, or communicative—would have to be used for different cohorts of students depending on their language-use backgrounds and their levels of proficiency. Obviously, knowledge-oriented and skill-oriented teaching and testing have to be distinguished. The standard of English in the teaching-learning situation can only be improved when teachers recognize the need to match student needs.

Conclusion. In summary, this paper looks at the unique sociocultural conditions that exist in Singapore and some of the historical developments that have led to the development of English-knowing bilinguals with expanding triangles of English expression. The implications for teacher education are also examined. In the context of second-language learning done in a language which is considered the school's first language, but which is not a real first language for the entire population, four pillars of pragmatic teacher education have been considered: grammatical grounding, sociolinguistic sensitivity, discourse discernment, and pedagogic perception.

Taken altogether, the curriculum-planning body of the central Ministry of Education, the Curriculum Development Institute of Singapore, and the external examination boards are relevant to teacher education. Equipping and enabling teachers in these four pillars would also be empowering. In order for teachers to become responsible for identifying their own problems and finding their own solutions—to have initial self-reliance— proper sequencing of the four pillars of pragmatic teacher education may perhaps be necessary.

In Singapore, language teachers need to develop their professional competence. They not only need to develop their own curriculum in regard to the nationally-controlled educational structure in Singapore, but they also need to carry out the central curriculum with a judicious selection of what is best within the complex nature of their school and classroom. Teachers will be best equipped and enabled for this task if their sociolinguistic and pedagogical awareness is raised through developments in the following four areas of teacher education in Singapore: grammatical grounding, sociolinguistic sensitivity, discourse discernment, and pedagogic perception.

REFERENCES

Canale, Michael. 1983. "From communicative competence to communicative language pedagogy." In Jack C. Richards and Richard Schmidt (eds.), *Language and communication*. London: Longman.
Education Statistics Digest. 1994. Singapore: Ministry of Education.
Ferguson, Charles. 1971. *Language structure and language use*. Stanford, California: Stanford University Press.
Gopinathan, Saravan and Vanithamani Saravanan. 1985. "Varieties of English and educational linguistics: An agenda for research." *Singapore Journal of Education* 7(1): 75-99.
Gopinathan, Saravan, Anne Pakir, Ho Wah-Kam, and Vanithamani Saravanan (eds.). 1994. *Language, society and education in Singapore: Issues and trends*. Singapore: Times Academic Press.
Gupta, Anthea F. 1989. "Singapore Colloquial English and Standard English." *Singapore Journal of Education* 10(2): 33-39.
Joos, Martin. 1967. *The five clocks*. New York: Harcourt, Brace, Jovanovich.
Kachru, Braj B. 1983. "Models for non-native Englishes." In Braj B. Kachru (ed.), *The other tongue: English across cultures*. Oxford, U.K.: Pergamon Press. 31-57.
Khoo, Chian-Kim . 1981. *Singapore census of population 1980: Languages spoken at home*. Release 8. Singapore: Department of Statistics.
Kuo, Eddie C.Y. 1980. "The sociolinguistic situation in Singapore: Unity in diversity." In E. A. Afendras and Eddie C.Y. Kuo (eds.), *Language and society in Singapore*. Singapore: Singapore University Press. 39-62.
Lau, Kak-En. 1993. *Singapore census of population 1990: Literacy, languages spoken, and education*. Statistical Release 3. Singapore: Department of Statistics.
Pakir, Anne. 1991. "The range and depth of English-knowing bilinguals in Singapore." *World Englishes* 10(2): 167-179.

Pakir, Anne. 1992. "English-knowing bilingualism in Singapore." In Kah-Choon Ban, Anne Pakir, and Chee-Kiong K. Tong (eds.), *Imagining Singapore*. Singapore: Times Academic Press. 234–262.

Pakir, Anne. 1994a. "Educational linguistics: Looking to the East." In James E. Alatis (ed.), *Georgetown University Round Table on Languages and Linguistics 1994*. Washington, D.C.: Georgetown University Press. 370–383.

Pakir, Anne. 1994b. "Education and invisible language planning." In Thiru Kandiah and John Kwan-Terry (eds.), *English and language planning: A Southeast Asian contribution*. Singapore: Times Academic Press.

Tay, Mary W.J. and Anthea F. Gupta. 1983. "Towards a description of Standard Singapore English." In Richard B. Noss (ed.), *Varieties of English in Southeast Asia*. Singapore: Regional English Language Centre. 173–189.

The Straits Times. 1980–1995. Various issues. Singapore: Singapore Press Holdings.

Yip, John S.K. and Wong-Kooi Sim (eds.). 1990. *Evolution of educational excellence: 25 years of education in the Republic of Singapore*. Singapore: Longman Singapore Publishers.

Culture and the teaching of foreign languages: A case study[1]

Sophia Papaefthymiou-Lytra
University of Athens, Greece

1. Introduction. In foreign-language learning there is a revived interest in teaching and learning about culture. In the 1970s and the 1980s, culture was seen primarily as an integral part of "social interaction." (See, for instance, Richards and Rodgers 1986, as well as Cook 1991, who surveyed the trends in language learning and teaching. The term culture is not even item-listed in the index of either publication.)

The overall goal of present-day interest, however, is to teach culture as "difference." Learners are expected to understand the "otherness" of target cultures not only in terms of products—i.e. as outputs or facts about cultures, but also as process that determines actions, beliefs, and ways of thinking. Cultural awareness will assist them to that end. (See McCarthy and Carter 1994: 150–171; Kramsch 1993a; Clark 1993; Valdes 1986; and also Fairclough 1989 for a discussion about critical language awareness and its meanings.)[2]

I would like to argue, however, that cultural awareness should have a coherent aim. It should aim at helping learners to develop a "working hypothesis" about the target culture. Thus L2 learners will be able to "interpret," "express," and "create" culture as participants in communicative events. This is only possible, however, if learners understand and interpret the processes, symbols, and meanings that constitute the otherness of the target culture.

In this paper I will report on research carried out to discover what the otherness of the target culture is from the learners' perspective with reference

---

[1] I would like to thank my colleagues, Walter Lohfert and Roland Dittrich of the Goethe Institute, Munich, as well as Maria Sifianou and Athina Apostolou-Panara—both of the University of Athens—who have discussed with me aspects of the research or have read earlier drafts of this paper. The shortcomings of this paper are, of course, all mine.

[2] For an interesting discussion about awareness and language learning, see Hulstijn and Schmid (1994). Contributors to this volume, however, hardly ever touch the issue of cultural awareness overtly.

to Greek as a foreign language.[3] The research was built around the concepts of "conflict" and "cultural misunderstanding." Learners' confrontation with the otherness of the target culture often results in conflict and cultural misunderstanding. Determining which aspects of the target culture may cause conflict and cultural misunderstanding can give us useful insights regarding a working hypothesis about the target culture. The findings can facilitate the selection-making process of syllabus designers, materials developers, textbook writers, teachers, and teacher trainers, etc. who, in designing learning/teaching materials which aim to develop the learners' working hypothesis about the target language through cultural awareness, must choose which cultural issues to incorporate.

2. Setting the scene.

2.1. Culture and conflict in FLT. Looking carefully at syllabuses such as *Threshold level '90* by van Ek and Trim (1991) of the Council of Europe—whose work has been very influential in Europe—one notices that cultural issues have permeated various sections of the syllabus. These issues appear, for instance, in the sections on sociocultural competence, compensation strategies, themes and topics referred to, etc. On examining the syllabus carefully, one realizes that, in reality, the learner is provided with fragmented information consisting of facts about culture as it relates to language in use. However, to paraphrase Seelye (1984:7), knowledge of linguistic structures and sociolinguistic rules does not automatically carry with it "any special insight into the political, social, religious, or economic system" of the target culture and country, a factor which usually shapes the processes operating in that culture. As a result, learners cannot easily develop a coherent understanding of the basic orientation of the culture and the most characteristic processes, symbols, and meanings operating in the target society. After all, cultural orientation and prevailing processes, symbols, and meanings determine the attitudes, and the beliefs, as well as the verbal and nonverbal behaviors, to which language users adhere. Consequently, language learners fail to develop a working hypothesis about the L2 culture for comprehension, production, interpretation and creative purposes. As Street (1991: 42–43) siding with Bloch (1991), states, "Now, not only is language as a model but also language as a vehicle or medium of culture being questioned"; he also adds that "anthropologists at least have overstated its

---

[3] On writing out a syllabus for Modern Greek, equivalent to *Threshold Level '90*, by the Council of Europe, it was decided to enrich the syllabus with a section about Greek culture. Relevant research was carried out in order to identify the major sociocultural issues that essentially define the otherness of Greek culture for L2 learners. The project was funded by the European Commission, Lingua Action-VB #93-03/0931/D-VB.

role and argue that the study of the storage and transmission of cultural knowledge should attend more to ... 'non-linguistic' procedures".

Similarly, Robinson (1985: 1) argues for the need to develop crosscultural understanding in the ESL/EFL/bilingual classroom. She defines this understanding as empathizing or feeling comfortable with another person, not merely as being able to decode someone else's verbal system or being aware of why someone is acting or feeling the way they do. Furthermore she claims that empathizing requires an understanding of the cultural orientation, processes, symbols, and meanings which the community adheres to and accepts at face value.

Kramsch (1993a) also states that, all things being equal, we could easily understand each other provided we shared the same code as a system. And this view, she argues, has been promoted by functional and pragmatic approaches to foreign-language learning. She maintains, however, that there are difficulties in understanding each other because culture comes into play, and culture is not as easily manageable as the code as a system. Culture, in fact, is omnipresent when the learner tries to use the L2 in real life. Thus perceptual mismatches in schemas, cues, values, and interpretations between people of different cultures—what learners consider to be dissimilar, distant, or puzzling in the L2 culture—may well result in cultural misunderstanding. Cultural misunderstanding usually results in conflict, which leads to a breakdown in communication (Kramsch 1993a).[4] Kramsch discusses the need to understand conflict, overcome conflict and develop crosscultural understanding in language teaching and learning. Thomas (1983) makes similar claims in her study on crosscultural pragmatic "failure."

Finally, McCarthy and Carter (1994) provide an interesting account of the importance of culture in language learning and of cultural awareness. They also provide specific definitions of culture as they are discerned in language teaching: namely, culture in art and literature, culture and the daily life of a group of people, and culture as social discourse. On exploring the curricular principles for the teaching of texts, they consider the contrastive principle (among others) important to develop learners' awareness. This is necessary for a variety of reasons. First, one's own cultural learning affects one's perception of other people. Different cultures assign different meanings to the "same" action and decipher these actions in different ways. Second, it seems that characteristics that are uncommon to the perceiver are often the most distinctive; therefore, perceptions of people from different cultures tend to reflect differences, even though these differences may not be the most representative of a person or

---

[4] For a discussion about conflict in communication and instructional language learning, see Papaefthymiou-Lytra (1989); on conflict and communication in the EFL classroom, see Papaefthymiou-Lytra (1990).

group. Furthermore, the very term culture itself changes its meaning and serves different, often competing, purposes at different times, since culture is an active process of meaning (Street 1993).

To my knowledge, however, no publication provides a working account of the cultural issues which may assist learners in developing a working hypothesis about a target language.

2.2. Culture, theoretical considerations, and FLT. In order to account for the diversity and complexity of culture, several definitions of culture have been put forward. Such definitions reflect different theoretical perspectives about what culture is and how it can be studied. Furthermore, they point the way to the methodology to be adopted in the foreign-language classroom (Robinson 1985).

"Behaviorist" and "functionalist" approaches to culture facilitate cultural description and awareness of why some people act the way they do. Behaviorist and functionalist views and concepts of culture assume that what is shared in the name of culture may be directly observed or inferred from observations. From a behaviorist point of view culture consists of discrete behaviors or sets of behaviors, e.g. traditions, habits, or customs. On the other hand, from a functionalist point of view culture is made up of discrete functional units. Some of these units are "static" and refer to men, women, and children, as well as a doctor, nurse, teacher, family, church, club, ideas, animals, etc. Other units designate "processes" as elements of culture for instance, to apologize, to direct, to rest, to study, to fish, to think, to die, to entertain, to flirt etc. Still other units designate "qualities" that are attributed to elements of culture, such as fast, slow, good, bad, gold, sleepy, cruel, etc. (Robinson 1985). In the language classroom, this concept of culture often leads to the study of discrete behavioral practices such as how to do X in the L2 (where X is replaced by specific functions, strategies, and appropriate linguistic realizations or nonverbal behaviors in specific situations), or what is Z like in the target culture (where Z is replaced by institutions such as the family, the town, entertainment, social structure, etc.). In other words, the functionalist concept of culture presents learners with societal and sociolinguistic facts about culture.[5] Moreover, both behavioralist and functionalist approaches to teaching culture may lead to stereotyping and inflexibility on the part of the language learner (Robinson 1985).

Culture, however, is characterized by *variation*. Within the same culture, groups differ from each other. After all, behaviors and functions are not static units. They change across time and across individuals; even the same individual may behave differently in different situations. Culture, as Isaacs (1975: 44)

---

[5] For practical applications of these views, see, for instance, Tomalin and Stempleski (1993). See also Seelye (1984) and Valdes (1986).

argues, does not look "like a set of neat boxes," but "more like a cell of living matter with a sprawlingly irregular shape." Often there may be some discrepancy between what people say they would do and what they actually do. In fact, people are often unaware of the reasons for their behaviors. Language users do not only act upon accepted cultural behaviors, but they also *create* culture. With regard to some dimensions, cultures do "have recognizable if irregular shapes" which distinguish them from each other, Isaacs (1975) argues. And it is on these recognizable shapes that language users base the judgment and assumptions with which they create culture. To gain a better understanding of how language users create culture, Robinson (1985) argues, we can turn for help to cognitive and symbolic views of culture.

The cognitive definition of culture shifts attention from the observable aspects of what is shared to what is shared as a means of organizing and interpreting the world, of creating order out of inputs. In other words, culture itself is a process through which experience is mapped out, categorized, and interpreted. In the words of Goodenough (1964), reported in Robinson:

> ... culture does not consist of things, people, behavior, or emotions. It is the forms of things people have in mind, their models for perceiving, relating and otherwise interpreting them. (1985:10)

In other words, culture is not simply a material phenomenon, a mere enumeration of facts about culture, but a process through which experience is mapped out, categorized, and interpreted. This is in accord with Moerman's (1988:4) claim that culture is "a set—perhaps a system—of principles of interpretation, together with the products of that system."

On the other hand, the symbolic definition of culture focuses on the product of processing, i.e. on the meanings and symbols derived. Culture is not only a matter of accumulation of a clearly defined body of facts, but also of historical experience, and attitudes and processes that have shaped a culture over the years. In this regard, Street (1993: 25) very rightly claims that there is not much point in trying to say what culture is. It is better to say what culture does. For what culture does is precisely the work of "defining words, ideas, things and groups"; afterall, he adds, we all live our lives "in terms of definitions, names and categories that culture creates." In this context, culture is concerned with the dynamic interrelationship between meaning, experience, and reality. Culture—the product of this interrelationship—is a dynamic system, an ongoing, dialectic process giving rise to symbols which may be viewed historically. Past experience influences meaning which, in turn, affects future experience which, in turn, affects subsequent meaning, and so on. The concept of culture as a creative, historical system of symbols and meaning has the potential to fill in the theoretical gaps left by behaviorist, functionalist and cognitive theories, Robinson (1985) argues, providing a detailed account of this view.

In this context, it is important to consider how cultural messages are transmitted. They are passed on from individual to individual and from generation to generation through language, sound or rhythm itself, space, time, body movement, touch, smell, and sight. Of course, perceptions of space, time, body movement, etc. differ from culture to culture. Cultural learning is, therefore, conveyed through learning modes that are analytical, emotional, kinesthetic, tactile, temporal, physiological, and aesthetic (Robinson 1985: 26–35; also Street 1991: 42–43).

In foreign-language learning and teaching, it can be very useful to know what processes, meanings, and symbols operate behind language users' expression of behaviors, actions, beliefs, attitudes, and likes and dislikes. And, it is also useful to know how, if they are not observed, they contribute to conflict, cultural misunderstanding, and frustration.[6] In the context of foreign-language learning, therefore, the job of studying culture is not simply to find and accept its definitions, but to discover "how and what definitions are made, under what circumstances and for what reasons" (Street 1993: 25).

Robinson (1985) argues that the potential implications of cognitive and symbolic theory have not been applied to a pedagogy for developing cultural understanding in second/foreign-language learning. However, they seem to offer very fruitful insights for using language in context appropriately.

3. Data collection: Methodological considerations. In an attempt to specify those aspects of Greek culture that are different from other cultures and can lead learners to conflict, cultural misunderstanding, and frustration, it was decided to carry out relevant research. In this section, I shall briefly describe how the data were collected and refer to some general methodological considerations that guided this process.

3.1. Data collection. The interview method was used to collect the data. Twenty-four interviews were conducted, taped, and analyzed. Trained research assistants interviewed European Union citizens living, working, or studying in Greece. The interviewees were asked to refer to experiences from their contact and acquaintance with Greek people—friends or relatives, employers or

---

[6] It has been argued that cultures can be placed on a continuum ranging from similarity to dissimilarity, or familiarity to distance. In the context of foreign-language learning, it is maintained that similarity and familiarity allow learners to cope easily with a foreign culture and develop positive attitudes towards the country and the people who speak the language. Of course, this is not always the case because easily recognizable or similar features of the C1 and C2 can very well be false friends. Specific elements of cultures may also have the same form and same meaning, but a different distribution (Seelye 1984).

employees, pubic services, etc.—that have led to conflict, cultural misunder-standing, and frustration.

The interviews were conducted in Greek with those subjects who felt competent enough to communicate their views in Greek. Otherwise, English, French, or German was used.

3.2. The subjects. Half of the subjects were men; the other half were women. Eight of them had settled peermanently in Greece after marrying Greeks. Eight more subjects had been in Athens for more than a year working in various organizations, institutions, or multinational companies. Finally, the remaining eight had been exchange students from various E.U. member states at the University of Athens for less than six months. The nationalities represented in the research were British, Belgian, German, Dutch, Italian, and Spanish.

The research subjects were limited to citizens of the European Union for the following reasons:

(1) Citizens of the European Union are thought to share a common cultural background stemming, to a great extent, from their Greek and Roman heritage; and
(2) Time limitations did not allow us to extend the research to subjects coming from other countries. (We hope to do so, however, in the near future.)

4. Analysis of the data
4.1. The categories of analysis. In a descriptive and evaluative study, a critical step is the selection of a framework within which the data can be viewed. In the present study the framework for classifying and categorizing the data comprises categories of analysis from various perspectives. The categories of analysis are redefined, where need be, to suit the data and the context in question.

Following the rational of the short discussion in Section 2 and the work of Triandis and Vassiliou (1972), Schumann (1978), Brown and Levinson (1987), Cowan (1990; 1991), Papaefthymiou-Lytra (1990), Sifianou (1992) and Jin et al. (1993), among others, I will attempt to construct a taxonomy of the basic factors in Greek society which shape and determine the way people act and behave. Knowledge and understanding of these factors will help learners to develop cultural awareness and a working hypothesis about the culture.

An ethnographic perspective is adopted to describe the target culture. This method can bring to the fore the conceptual framework that native speakers use to make sense of their construction of reality. This construction makes up their particular cultural identity and distinguishes them from one another (Cowan

Table 1. Categories of analysis.

Historical and geographical factors	Experience and reality
Processes	Preservation, positive culture orientation, in-/inter-/out-group attitudes, group dependency, hegemony, superiority, reaction to autocratic rulers, competition, and excessiveness
Macrocultural issues National/public domains	Class, status, ethnicity, public spheres, power and control, authority and antiauthoritarianism, social rights, and opportunities
Microcultural issues Private/interpersonal domains	School, neighborhood, church, work, private spheres, etc.
Role specifications and relationships	Men, women, children, fathers, mothers, doctors, taxi drivers, administrators, etc.
Input factors	Type of interlocutor, complexity of language and context of situation, and complexity of task
Contact factors	Goals, duration, intensity, and quality

1990, 1991). Wider cultural issues deriving from the symbolic and cognitive approaches to culture are incorporated into the proposed taxonomy of factors against which the data was analyzed (Table 1). These issues can demonstrate why people think or act the way they do.

Historical and geographical factors also seem to play an important role in determining the experiences and reality of a people (Triandis and Vassiliou 1972). It is from these experiences and reality that cultures derive the myths, symbols, and meanings which comprise the symbolic perspective (Cowan 1990, 1991; Street 1993). The symbolic perspective can be particularly instrumental in explaining the processes that seem to operate in the target culture. Such processes influence the ways human beings cognize the world around them and play an important role in setting up cultural frameworks for interpreting human action, as well as verbal and nonverbal behavior (cf. Seelye 1984; Robinson 1985; Brown and Levinson 1987; Sifianou 1992).

However, the symbolic and cognitive perspective is not enough to describe, categorize and analyze the data in question. In the suggested framework, I have also included the functionalist and behavioralist perspectives which can be very useful in describing and categorizing elements of culture in terms of domains, role specifications, and culturally conditioned relationships, input factors, and contact factors. The functionalist and behavioralist perspectives may further contribute to a better understanding of how culture operates in specific situational and pragmatic contexts.

4.2. Factors contributing to the development of a working hypothesis about culture. Triandis and Vassiliou (1972: 302) argue that the Greek character and culture are consistent with analyses of the ecology and history of that country—mountainous country, scarce resources, small isolated communities, and a long occupation by the Ottomans.[7] They maintain that geography and history suggest that modern Greek culture was influenced by six important factors: "a) scarce resources and keen competition for them, b) reaction to autocratic rulers, c) dependence on the 'male hero' for survival of the cultural values, d) increased dangers for boys resulting in increased protectiveness by mothers, e) unadapted importation of foreign institutions, and f) low control over the environment." These six factors, in turn, have led Greeks to "develop exceedingly effective procedures for meeting crises but have neglected skills for long-term planning" (Triandis and Vassiliou 1972: 304). Furthermore, these six factors have probably been instrumental in the development of an important concept in Greek culture, that of the "ingroup." Triandis and Vassiliou maintain that this important concept has evolved in opposition to the indigenous concept of the "outgroup."

The definition of the ingroup, Triandis and Vassiliou (1972: 305) argue, is somewhat different for Greeks than it is for Western Europeans or Americans. The ingroup is defined by the Greeks as "my family, relatives, friends and friends of friends." It provides protection, security, support, and a relaxing environment: "a haven from the larger world." Guests or people who are "showing concern for me" are seen as members of the ingroup. In contrast to the ingroup, the outgroup concept is defined to incorporate all those who are not concerned with one's welfare. Due to the operation of this basic dichotomizing process in Greek culture, Greeks seem to be very intimate, friendly, and ready

---

[7] In their short historical account, Triandis and Vassiliou (1972) refer to two periods of Greek history, the Byzantine period and the post-Byzantine or Ottoman period. They omit two earlier periods corresponding to Ancient Greece and the Hellenistic period. The latest period of Greek history corresponds to the present-day State of Greece. However, a close examination of symbols, values, beliefs, and ideas across time reveals some striking similarities and evolutionary tendencies in processes operating in Greek culture (cf. Konstantellou 1993 and Kerameus and Kozyris (1993), especially Chapter 1).

for all sorts of sacrifices towards the ingroup, while suspicious of strangers, very competitive, and ready to exhibit treachery toward the outgroup (Triandis and Vassiliou 1972: 305). Moreover, the ingroup/outgroup distinction seems to play an important role in determining behaviors and choices which concern microcultural issues in the private and interpersonal domains in particular.

The data furnish a good example how the ingroup process operates and may lead to cultural misunderstandings. Subjects state that family decisions are often made after consulting the members of the extended family, i.e. grandparents, uncles, aunts etc. who, in turn, are expected to provide financial and moral help. The extended family is always there to assist, comfort, intervene, interfere, or meddle in joy and sorrow, thus, subjects claim, depriving members (men, women, and children; young and old) of their rights to personal freedom and decision making.

In a broader context incorporating macrocultural issues, ingroup processes give rise to "preservation" as a basic process operating in society. Preservation is defined in terms of "loyalty and cohesion to the group as representatives of a particular social and ethnic milieu who share the same values, conventions, beliefs and thought patterns" (Schumann 1978, as reported in Papaefthymiou-Lytra 1990: 186). Preservation aims to maintain intragroup cohesion, solidarity, and cultural identity in the broader context of multiple ingroups. Such preservation processes strongly characterize small groups or isolated societies, i.e. rural societies. They also seem to play an important role pertaining to macrocultural issues in the national/public domain, in particular. As a result, Greeks have developed strong attachments to the villages and regions from which they come, keeping in touch through organized associations. Furthermore, Greeks are very proud of their past. Ingroup identification and preservation processes can help to explain certain aspects of the practices pursued in politics centering on local and/or national interests, for instance, or the phenomenon of the Greek Diaspora (cf. Holmes et al. 1993).[8]

Furthermore, humor exemplifies the phenomena of ingroup solidarity and group dependency which characterize the culture. In discussing Greek humor, Orso (1979; cited in Papaefthymiou-Lytra 1986) argues that the Greeks do not laugh at themselves as individuals but as a group. In this sense, they are trained in group dependency. Furthermore, Greeks prefer exoteric humor that displays Greek superiority rather than esoteric humor that demonstrates individual failings and shortcomings (Orso 1979). Taking a broader perspective, it appears to be true that, as Triandis (1990) claims, people in every culture draw on both individualist and collectivist tendencies, but the relative emphasis placed on each

---

[8] Holmes et al. (1993) discuss several factors which seem to inhibit language shift and support maintenance in the Greek community in New Zealand. Their findings strongly support the views in this paper.

varies. There is a tendency toward individualism in the West, and toward collectivism and group dependency in the East. Greek culture seems to be oriented toward the latter rather than the former (Triandis and Vassiliou 1972; Sifianou 1992).

A representative example of this attitude in the Greek culture—and as a source of cultural misunderstanding—is the subjects' claim that Greek education in general has an orientation toward conformity rather than helping young people to become independent. In their opinion, it emphasizes deductive approaches, and de-emphasizes individual learner activity and collaborative learning through processes such as group work (cf. Richards and Lockhart 1994: 107).

Here I would like to suggest that for preservation processes and group dependencies to operate smoothly, it seems necessary to postulate an in-between transitional stage, that of the "intergroup." This suggestion is in accord with Cowan's (1990: 11) argument—reported in Street—who writes:

> Although what culture is and how it works remains among the most vexed questions within anthropology, the concept of culture retains traces of its functionalist origins. It continues to be understood as the articulations of moral consensus and of shared symbols, beliefs, values, ideas. The problem is *not* that the claims are spurious and that nothing is shared. The problem, rather, is that when culture is defined as that which is shared, questions about sharedness—Is it actually shared? To what extent? By whom? How does it come to be shared—disappear by definition. (1993: 35)

It seems that polarized categories of analysis such as now/then, here/there, and ingroup/outgroup, may not effectively capture stages and processes that determine them, nor can they answer some of the questions posed by Cowan (1990) in the quoted extract.

This view is also supported by Triandis and Vassiliou (1972), who claim that "acquaintances are somewhat ambiguously classified more frequently in the ingroup than in the outgroup," as well as by Jin et al. (1993: 86), who discuss cultural misunderstandings among Chinese students studying in Britain. They seem to feel that the conceptualization of outgroup and ingroup boundaries needs some reconsideration.

The present research also suggests the need to conceptualize an in-between category. It seems that unless acquaintances have passed the test and are classified either as ingroup or outgroup members, they are in limbo concerning their relations to the group. Subjects claim that sometimes they feel welcome; other times they feel rejected by their Greek friends, which is not easy for them to understand. As an example, some subjects mentioned the practices Greek friends of theirs follow when they come across other Greek friends. Greek friends rarely introduce their foreign friends to their Greek friends; on the contrary, they tend to ignore foreign friends while conversing with Greek friends in Greek. And, as Sifianou (1992: 91) argues, when meeting people, one expects to be greeted, since this practice is common in Greek and Anglo culture. Lack of such behavior is interpreted as indifference, perhaps signalling a problem in the relationship. "Indifference is a real insult" for the Greeks "and is somewhat related to the notion ... that most Greek social relations are characterized by greater intimacy" (Triandis and Vassiliou 1972: 315). Still, some Greeks tend to overlook those much-appreciated practices when their intergroup relationships are involved.

This factor may also account for the notion of Greek hospitality, which has been widespread in the country for centuries. It may condition the practices often employed by locals in their kind treatment of foreigners living, working, or studying in Greece enjoy by the locals.[9]

The next important factor is the positive-politeness orientation of the Greek culture. Brown and Levinson (1987) suggest a distinction between societies with a positive politeness orientation and societies with a negative politeness orientation; in other words, between familiar, friendly, "solidarity politeness," and formal "deference politeness" (Sifianou 1992: 214). Brown and Levinson (1987: 134) actually define this dichotomy between positive and negative politeness as one in which " positive politeness is free-ranging," but "negative politeness is specific and focused."

Following Brown and Levinson (1987), Sifianou (1992), in her seminal work on politeness phenomena in England and Greece, argues that Greek culture has a positive-politeness orientation. She goes on to say that:

> negative politeness is narrower in that it addresses a specific act, whereas positive politeness is broader and considers the overall relationship between interactants. Thus, it appears that by definition negative politeness is more restricted than positive politeness in that the former reflects consideration for one of the addressee's basic needs—to be independent—whereas the latter reflects consideration for the addressee's perennial needs to be liked, approved of, admired, and so on. (1992: 87)

Consequently, use of the singular or friendly informal language, as well as questions indicating "intensive curiosity," or probing into private matters, such as income, marital status, and children are, in reality, an expression of concern and interest, a friendly way to approach others (Sifianou 1992: 93); much to the dismay of many subjects, however, who consider such practices a violation of privacy and personal rights.

---

[9] Zeus, the father of gods and men in Greek mythology, was also the god of hospitality. Hence, he was also called *ksenios Dias* ("Zeus god of hospitality ").

Politeness, however, is not only a matter of verbal behavior but also of nonverbal behavior. Body contact, such as kissing, embracing, patting on the shoulder, hand shaking and body posture, even the distance between interactants, enact and exemplify politeness practices in different cultures. Generally speaking, people from high-contact cultures, such as Arabs, Latin Americans, and Greeks, feel more comfortable at shorter distances when interacting than people from low-contact cultures, such as Americans and North Europeans (Morain 1986: 72, reported in Sifianou 1992: 75).

As Sifianou (1992) argues, the Greek positive-politeness orientation derives from the ingroup concept prevailing in the culture. The ingroup/outgroup distinction, she further claims, is so deeply ingrained in the society that it actually determines individual behavior, and this process is unconscious (Sifianou 1992: 93). People see each other in terms of relationships, cooperation, and mutual reciprocity. Positive politeness orientation indicates group dependency tendencies, whereas negative politeness orientation indicates individual tendencies in the culture (Triandis 1990). The Greek positive-politeness orientation has been a constant source of cultural misunderstanding for many of the subjects in this study. Body contact and asking personal questions, for instance, which may appear to violate privacy or status rights, are but a few of the potential sources of conflict and cultural misunderstanding.

Another interesting dichotomy that seems to operate in the Greek culture is that the concept of "hegemony" (Cowan 1990) opposes the concept of "reaction" to "autocratic rulers" (Triandis and Vassiliou 1972). The concept of hegemony is defined by Cowan (1990: 12) as "predominance obtained by consent rather than [the] force of one class or group over other classes or groups." She claims that hegemony is not necessarily an oppressive process; it "entails not a dismissal of 'culture' but a reformulation of it." Moreover, hegemony is characterized by 'internal control' in contrast with the external control of the state's repressive apparatus, for instance.

One may argue that a good part of Greek political and party life can be explained in terms of these two concepts. Furthermore, public behaviors such as pushing, using the car horn unnecessarily, or showing disrespect toward pedestrians crossing the street—which are but a few examples mentioned as sources of cultural conflict by subjects—can be attributed to those conflicting processes. In short, it is unclear who is superior and has precedence. On this issue, Sifianou (1992: 92–93) maintains that the major source of such behavior is the ingroup/outgroup distinction. She claims that people one does not know, such as pedestrians in the street or customers in a shop, belong to the outgroup. This difference of opinion clearly indicates that processes interrelate. It is not always easy to disassociate one from the other.

Another interesting pair of processes that seem to operate in Greek culture are "competition" and "excessiveness." "Scarce resources and keen competition for them" (Triandis and Vassiliou 1972: 302) make Greeks very competitive while at the same time they seem to do everything in excess. This excessiveness may be interpreted as an aspect of pride or *egoismos*, the male competitive expression of self-regard, as Sutton (1994) argues. A good example of this excessiveness, reported by subjects, appears in the shopping and consumption habits. Subjects often wonder why their friends and relatives have to buy things in bulk, when unconsumed and unused items may eventually be wasted.

The next two categories deal with the situational and pragmatic contexts. They can be divided into two major categories, depending on their function in society. One category comprises macrocultural issues pertaining to national/public domains; the other category comprises microcultural issues appropriate to private/interpersonal domains. Fishman (1972) defines "domains" sociologically in terms of institutional contexts or socioecological co-occurrences. They are recognizable units within a community that share their own norms of interaction and interpretation. Domains, Fishman argues, enable us to understand how language and culture are related to sociocultural norms and expectations (Papaefthymiou-Lytra 1981/1987: 60–61). Macrocultural issues in the realm of the national/public domains pertain to such categories as class, status, ethnicity, power, and control. On the other hand, microcultural issues in the realm of the private/interpersonal domains comprise such categories as school, family, neighborhood, church, and work. Of course, macro- and microcultural issues are not unrelated; they may influence each other. For instance, it was quite puzzling for many of the subjects—especially those from member states where church and state are separate—to discover how closely religion and church are interwoven into the Greek culture and life. It seems that they have played an important role in strengthening ingroup, intergroup, and preservation processes in the culture, as well as in further defining some role specifications (Hart 1992).

The next important category of analysis refers to role specifications and the relationships encountered among representatives of various roles. The role specifications of women, fathers, mothers, and children and their function in society are determined by macro-cultural issues. Other roles such as taxi driver, administrator, and teacher and their function in society are usually delimited by micro-cultural categories. (Loizos and Papataxiarchis 1991). In this context, it is also important to consider the relationships that are expected or allowed to develop among various role representatives in society, and how far they are culturally conditioned (Cowan 1991).

Issues concerning men and women, as well as family relations, have become sources of cultural misunderstanding. Subjects state that there are puzzling contradictions in attitudes toward women. Professional women seem to enjoy a better status at work than at home. At home there is still a male-dominated culture, which seems to be in accord with Triandis's and Vassiliou's (1972) important factor "dependence on the 'male hero' for survival of cultural values." Women are expected to assume the roles of mothers and housewives and perform them well. Further evidence of this male-dominated culture, the subjects claim, is the local coffee shop frequented by men and from which women have long been excluded. Family relations and child-rearing are also a source of conflict and cultural misunderstanding. Family ties are very close. Children are overprotected. The mother is the central figure and the strong personality around which the household evolves. She is responsible for rearing the children and often the grandchildren.

The next two categories comprise the input and the contact factors. Most of Hymes's (1972) suggested framework, "S.P.E.A.K.I.N.G.," which refers to setting, participants, purpose, key, channel, message content, and genre of discourse, has been incorporated in the categories pertaining to input and contact factors. The factors incorporated in these categories, in particular, can help us determine with whom, when, and where learners will use the L2 they are learning. In this connection, it is important that we limit our search for culture to "fields" pertaining to the interest, needs, and purposes of learners.

"Input factors" incorporate three components: type of interlocutor, complexity of language in relation to the context of situation, and complexity of task. "Type of interlocutor" refers to who a subject's interlocutor is. He/she can be a friend, a stranger, or an administrator. "Complexity of language" refers to the language used by the interlocutor and how difficult the subjects think it is to interpret in relation to the context of situation (Hymes 1972; Halliday and Hasan 1985). Complexity of language and type of interlocutor may become sources of conflict and cultural misunderstanding. Subjects, for instance, claim that the use of the singular—which indicates informality and friendliness—by taxi drivers, shop assistants, or office clerks, among others, is very confusing and unprofessional.

"Complexity of task" refers to how difficult a task seems to be for subjects, especially when they make comparisons with their own experiences. Here are two examples from the data. In reference to the public sphere, for instance, the subjects stressed the fact that in their contact with public services such as ministries, public corporations, hospitals, and banks, they have encountered a system of organization and management quite different from the one they are used to. In short, they consider things very slow-moving, quite bureaucratic and, from their point of view, not very efficient. As for the private sphere, on the other hand, subjects claim that when they invite friends and acquaintances home they are never sure who is coming since invitations are not accepted or rejected promptly. Such practices, they maintain, make life difficult.

"Contact factors" comprise the next category of analysis. The constituents of factors are goals, duration, intensity, and quality. "Goals" refer to the objectives subjects have in wanting to carry out a specific task. "Duration" refers to the time available to subjects to carry out a specific task. "Intensity" has to do with the demands that a task may impose on subjects in relation to the complexity of the task itself and the time available to carry it out. Finally, "quality" has to do with the expected outcome of the task undertaken. It refers to whether the outcome satisfies their expectations or not.

Time planning can be a source of cultural misunderstanding in relation to input and contact factors. Subjects maintain that social and business activities are not always planned well in advance. This is in accord with Triandis's and Vassiliou's (1972) claim that the Greeks "have neglected long-term skills." Often even important business activities, they claim, can be left unspecified until the last minute. As a result, input and contact factors suffer, leading to cultural misunderstandings. Michaelis and Coram (1984) discuss similar problems which are encountered in Mexican culture.

The six foregoing factors suggested by Triandis and Vassiliou (1972), the processes deriving from them, and the way they have influenced the other categories of analysis primarily reflect the culture of a people still very closely linked to the symbols, beliefs, values, and ideas of rural societies. Inevitable changes, due to factors such as urbanization, education, tourism, and the spread of mass media (among others), have started to make an impact on Greek society and culture. Cowan (1991: 200), for instance, in discussing gender and identity in a town in Northern Greece, stresses the fact that young female subjects of her research want to be treated as individuals with their own preferences. They reject culturally conditioned gender identities and the restrictions imposed on them. Similarly, Henze (1992: 53) who describes the function of literacy shifts in rural Greece, states that literacy in the past was closely related to the needs of the family. At present, the younger generation is learning to read and write "for communicative purposes that take them outside the family or inner circle. While they can and do assist less literate family members, the primary function is no longer service to the family" but their own advancement. Still, successful members are a pride to the family. The changes anthropologists have encountered in Greek society are reflected in concepts concerning processes, domains, and role specifications. How far these changes will eventually influence Greek culture toward more individualistic tendencies remains to be seen.

The categories and the factors that comprise them are not arranged in any hierarchical order. They are both constraints and resources for language users. Knowledge and understanding of the constituent parts of these categories will help learners to develop a working hypothesis about the target culture and cultural awareness. Thus, language learners are expected not only to express and interpret culture, but also to create culture as participants in communicative events. These factors are to be found across cultures, and are realized in different and very often contradictory ways (Halliday and Hasan 1985).

5. Discussion of findings. The data indicate that the subjects have encountered all kinds of cultural misunderstandings due to their unawareness of the processes operating in Greek society and of the historical and geographical factors that shape those processes and concepts over time. Many subjects clearly stated that, in order to have avoided conflict and cultural misunderstanding, they would like to know more about Greek culture and the ways past experiences have influenced meaning which, in turn, affects future experiences. Afterall, one group of people understands its past as a system of symbols and meanings in quite a different way from another. Consequently, the subjects claim, it is very difficult for language learners to comprehend the processes and outputs operating in decision making, the negotiation patterns employed, and the arguments developed by their interlocutors or found in texts, newspaper articles, advertisements, etc. Learning about "the beaches, the sun, the islands and the archeological sights" is not enough, they maintain. Learners need more than this, indeed.

For learners to develop a working hypothesis of the target culture, however, it is *not* enough "to explore the ways in which forms of language, from individual words to complete discourse structures, encode something of the beliefs and values held by the language user" (McCarthy and Carter 1994: 150). Culture is a reality that is historical, social, political, and ideological, and the difficulty of understanding cultural codes stems from the difficulty of viewing the world from another perspective, not simply of grasping another lexical or grammatical code and the encoded values, beliefs, and meanings (Kramsch 1993a: 188). Cultural awareness in the context of critical language awareness may contribute substantially to this end (Kramsch 1993a, 1993b; Clark 1993; Fairclough 1989).

Consequently, aspects of culture from such diverse sources as the following are especially welcome in learning materials (McCarthy and Carter 1994: 151):

(1) **Culture with capital "C"**—this refers to art, music, theater and, especially, literature;
(2) **Culture with small "c"**—this refers to habits, customs, social behaviors, and assumptions about the world of a group of people; and
(3) **Culture as social discourse**—this refers to the social knowledge and interactive skills which are required in addition to knowledge of the language system.

Such materials can really help learners to develop a working hypothesis about the target culture, provided that historical and geographical factors, as well as processes and concepts influencing culture dynamics, are there for presentation purposes. Otherwise, a rather fragmented view of culture is presented.

It has been difficult for subjects, for instance, to understand and interpret the adherence of their friends and relatives to traditions and customs and their resistance to change. This is true even if change concerns such simple things, they claim, as food and cooking. Here again, preservation and ingroup concepts permeate views and attitudes which, unless they are understood, become sources of conflict for outsiders. On the other hand, TV programs are not always representative specimens of Greek reality; rather, they exemplify the factor referred to as "unadapted importation of foreign institutions" (Triandis and Vassiliou 1972). Television discourse is hyperbolic, sensational, and commercial. It is characterized by typical mannerisms, such as the stress on initial syllables, which violates normal Greek prosody. This practice is very similar to French television practices as reported by Kramsch (1993a: 190).

These observations about attitudes and beliefs are supported by the results of a study by Tumposky (1991) reported in Richards and Lockhart (1994: 57). In this study, college students from the U.S. and the former U.S.S.R. were asked whether it was necessary to know about English-, Spanish-, or French-speaking cultures in order to speak English, Spanish, or French. The results are in Table 2.

Table 2. Results from Tumposky (1991), as reported in Richards and Lockhart (1994).

	Agree [%]	Neutral [%]	Disagree [%]
U.S.	58	22	19
U.S.S.R.	78	20	2

It seems that the more remote the L2 (language and) culture is from the learners' culture, the more they feel the need for cultural orientation. The reader should bear in mind that an important factor which facilitates language learning is knowledge of the world at large. Labov (1972) has defined this knowledge of the world at large as knowledge that is not part of any linguistic rule. It refers to learners' general cultural and pragmatic knowledge as substantive information about their society and of the world at large (Papaefthymiou-Lytra 1987: 83-90; Widdowson 1989). One thus expects learners of commonly taught languages, such as English, to have a substantial knowledge of the world at large concerning English or American culture in comparison to the knowledge of learners of less commonly taught languages like Modern Greek. Consequently, I may extend this argument and claim that the less commonly taught and known a language and culture is—in our case, Modern Greek—the more learners need a working hypothesis about the culture to rely on. Understanding the target culture will help language learners to interpret it correctly and avoid stereotypes and misconceptions. It is hoped that cultural awareness and a working hypothesis about the target culture will eventually lead learners to tolerance and understanding.

Classroom practice has shown that experiencing difference does not automatically come with learning a foreign language. The potential of foreign-language learning for the discovery of alternate realities is there, but it must be actualized, texts must be authenticated, and cultural contexts must be created (Kramsch 1993b: 357). By observing, documenting, interpreting, comparing and contrasting, reflecting, and experiencing, learners can understand and appreciate the difference and the otherness of the target culture. By incorporating such practices into learning materials, learners can develop a working hypothesis about the L2 culture, its orientation, values and beliefs, an awareness of the existing differences between the L1 and the L2 culture as processes, symbols, and meanings, as well as facts and social discourse. Finally, learners can develop sensitivity to and understanding in dealing with cultural conflict and misunderstanding by relying on self-learning strategies and conflict-solving practices.

6. Conclusions. In this paper, I have shown that cultural awareness in foreign-language learning should have a goal. It should aim to develop in learners a working hypothesis about the target culture in learners. Knowledge and understanding of the processes, meanings, and symbols that underlie cultural facts and behaviors will allow L2 learners to interpret and express language in context in a meaningful way and with sensitivity and understanding of cultural variation and pluralism. Such an approach, I believe, is particularly important for less commonly taught languages for which language learners quite often lack substantial knowledge of the world at large, an important factor for successful motivation and language learning.

REFERENCES

Barro, Ana et al. 1993 "Cultural studies for advanced language learners." In David Graddol, et al. (eds.), *Language and Culture*. Clevedon, U.K.: BAAL and Multilingual Matters, Ltd. 55–69.
Bloch, Maurice. 1991. "Language, anthropology and cognitive science." *Man* 26: 183–197.
Brown, Penelope and Stephen Levinson. 1987. *Politeness: Some universals in language usage. Studies in Interactional Sociolinguistics 4*. Cambridge, U.K.: Cambridge University Press.
Clark, Romy J. 1993. "Developing practices of resistance: Critical reading for students of politics." In David Graddol et al. (eds.), *Language and Culture*. Clevedon, U.K.: BAAL and Multilingual Matters, Ltd. 113–122.
Cook, Vivian. 1991. *Second language learning and language teaching*. London: Edward Arnold.
Cowan, Jane. 1990. *Dance and the body politic in Northern Greece*. Princeton, N.J.: Princeton University Press.
Cowan, Jane. 1991. "Going out for coffee? Contesting the grounds of gendered pleasures in everyday sociability." In Peter Loizos and Evthymios Papataxiarchis (eds.), *Contested identities: Gender and kinship in modern Greece*. Princeton, N.J.: Princeton University Press. 180–201.
Dubin, Frieda and Natalie A. Kuhlman (eds.). 1992. *Cross-cultural literacy: Global perspectives on reading and writing*. Englewood Cliffs, N.J.: Regents/Prentice Hall.

Dubisch, Jill. 1991. "Gender, kinship and religion: Reconstructing the anthropology of Greece." In Peter Loizos and Evthymios Papataxiarchis (eds.), *Contested identities: Gender and kinship in modern Greece*. Princeton, N.J.: Princeton University Press. 29–46.

Fairclough, Norman. 1989. *Language and power*. London: Longman.

Fishman, Joshua A. (ed.). 1972. *Advances in the Sociology of language, Volume II*. The Hague: Mouton.

Fishman, Joshua A. 1974. "The relationship between micro- and macro-sociolinguistics in the study who speaks what language to whom and where." In J. B. Pride and Jane Holmes (eds.), *Sociolinguistics*. London: Penguin. 15–32.

Goodenough, Ward H. 1964. *Explorations in cultural anthropology*. New York: McGraw-Hill.

Graddol, David, Linda Thompson, and Mike Byram (eds.). 1993. *Language and culture*. Clevendon, U.K.: BAAL and Multilingual Matters, Ltd.

Gumperz, John and Dell Hymes (eds.). 1972. *Directions in sociolinguistics: The ethnography of communication*. New York: Holt, Rinehart and Winston, Inc.

Halliday, M.A.K. and Ruqaiya Hasan. 1985. *Language, context and next: Aspects of language in a social-semiotic perspective*. Oxford: Oxford University Press.

Hart, Laurie K. 1992. *Time, religion and social experience in rural Greece*. Lanham, Maryland: Rowman and Littlefield.

Henze, Rosemary. 1992. "Literacy in rural Greece: From family to individual." In Frieda Dubin and Natalie A. Kuhlman (eds.), *Cross-cultural literacy: Global perspectives on reading and writing*. Englewood Cliffs, N.J.: Regents/Prentice Hall. 47–62.

Holmes, Janet, Mary Roberts, Maria Verivaki, and Anahina Aipolo. 1993. "Language maintenance and shift in three New Zealand speech communities." *Applied Linguistics* 14(1): 1–24.

Hulstijn, Jan H. and Richard Schmidt (eds.). 1994. "Consciousness in second language learning." *AILA-Review* 11.

Hymes, Dell 1972. "Models of interaction and social life." In John Gumperz and Dell Hymes (eds.), *Directions in sociolinguistics: The ethnography of communication*. New York: Holt, Rinehart and Winston, Inc. 35–37.

Isaacs, Harold R. 1975. *Idols of the tribe: Group identity and political change*. New York: Harper and Row.

Jin, Lixian and Martin Cortazzi. 1993. "Cultural orientation and academic language use." In David Graddol et al (eds.), Language and culture. Clevedon, U.K.: BAAL and Multilingual Matters. 84–97.

Kerameus, Konstantinos D. and Phaedon J. Kozyris (eds.). 1993. *Introduction to Greek Law, Second revised edition*. Deventer, The Netherlands: Kluwer/ Sakkoulas.

Konstantellou, Demetrius. 1993. *Ethniki taftotita kai thriskeftiki idiaiterotita tou Ellinismou*. Athens: Damascos Publications.

Kramsch, Claire. 1993a. *Context and culture in language teaching*. Oxford: Oxford University Press.

Kramsch, Claire. 1993b. "Language study as border study: Experiencing difference." *European Journal of Education* 28(3): 349–358.

Labov, William. 1972. *Sociolinguistic patterns*. Philadelphia: University of Pennsylvania Press.

Loizos, Peter and Evthymios Papataxiarchis (eds.). 1991. *Contested identities:Gender and kinship in modern Greece*. Princeton, N.J.: Princeton University Press.

McCarthy, Michael and Ronald Carter. 1994. *Language as discourse: Perspectives for language teaching*. London: Longman.

Michaelis, Joyce and Colleen Coram. 1984. "Doing business in Mexico: A step beyond language." In P. B. Westphal et al. (eds.), *Strategies for foreign language teaching: Communication–technology–culture*. Lincolnwood, Illinois: National Textbook Company. 105–117.

Moerman, Michael. 1988. *Talking culture: Ethnography and conversation analysis.* Philadelphia: University of Pennsylvania Press.

Morain, Genelle G. 1986. "Kinesics and cross-cultural understanding." In Joyce M. Valdes (ed.), *Culture Bound: Bridging the cultural gap in language teaching.* New York: Cambridge University Press. 64–76.

Orso, Ethelyn O. 1979. *Modern Greek humor: A collection of jokes and ribald tales.* Bloomington, Indiana: University of Indiana Press.

Papaefthymiou-Lytra, Sophia. 1986. "Humor and laughter in the EFL classroom." *G.A.L.A—Proceedings 4.* Thessaloniki, Greece: University Studio Press. 76–88.

Papaefthymiou-Lytra, Sophia. 1981/1987. *Communicating and learning strategies in English as a foreign language with particular reference to the Greek learner of English.* S. Saripolos' Library No. 65. Athens, Greece: The University of Athens.

Papaefthymiou-Lytra, Sophia. 1987. *Language, language awareness and foreign language learning.* Athens, Greece: The University of Athens.

Papaefthymiou-Lytra. 1989. "Conflict in communication vis a vis repairing in the foreign language classroom." *Journal of Applied Linguistics* 4: 43–67.

Papaefthymiou-Lytra, Sophia. 1990. *Explorations in foreign language classroom discourse.* Parousia Monograph Series No 11. Athens, Greece: The University of Athens.

Richards, Jack C. and Charles Lockhart. 1994. *Reflective teaching in the second language classrooms.* New York: Cambridge University Press.

Richards, Jack C. and Theodore S. Rodgers. 1986. *Approaches and methods in language teaching: A description and analysis.* New York: Cambridge University Press.

Robinson, Gail L. 1985. *Crosscultural understanding: Processes and approaches for foreign language, English as a second language and bilingual eduators.* New York: Pergamon Press.

Schumann, John H. 1978. "The acculturation model for second language acquisition," In Rosario Gingras (ed.), *Second language acquisition and foreign language teaching.* Arlington, Virginia: Center for Applied Linguistics.

Sifianou, Maria. 1992. *Politeness phenomena in England and in Greece: A cross-cultural perspective.* Oxford: Clarendon Press.

Sifianou, Maria. 1993. "Off-record indirectness and the notion of imposition." *Multilingua* 12(1): 69–73.

Street, Brian V. 1993. "Culture is a verb: Anthropological aspects of language and culture." In David Graddol et al. (eds.), *Language and Culture.* Clevedon, U.K.: BAAL and Multilingual Matters, Ltd. 23–43.

Seelye, H. Ned. 1984. *Teaching culture: Strategies for intercultural communication.* Lincolnwood, Illinois: National Textbook Company.

Sutton, David. 1994. "'Tradition and modernity': Kalymnian constructions of identity and otherness." *Journal of Modern Greek Studies* 12(2): 239–260.

Thomas, Jenny. 1983. "Cross-cultural pragmatic failure." *Applied Linguistics* 4: 91–112.

Tomalin, Barry and Susan Stempleski. 1993. *Cultural awareness.* Oxford: Oxford University Press.

Triandis, Harry C. (ed.). 1972. *The analysis of subjective culture.* New York: Wiley.

Triandis, Harry C. 1990. "Theoretical concepts that are applicable to the analysis of ethnocentricism." In Richard W. Brislin (ed.), *Applied cross-cultural psychology.* Newbury Park, California: Sage.

Triandis, Harry C. and Vasso Vassiliou. 1972. "A comparative analysis of subjective culture." In Harry C. Triandis (ed.). *The analysis of subjective culture.* New York: Wiley. 299–335.

Tumposky, N. 1991. "Students beliefs about language learning: A cross-cultural study." *Carleton Papers in Applied Language Studies* 8: 50–65.

Valdes, Joyce M. (ed.). 1986. *Culture bound: Bridging the cultural gap in language teaching.* New York: Cambridge University Press.

van Ek, Jan A. and John L. M. Trim. 1991. *Threshold Level 1990*. Strasbourg: Council of Europe Press.

Westphal, Patricia B., Maurice W. Conner, and Norman Choat (eds.). 1984. *Strategies for foreign language teaching: Communication-technology-culture*. Lincolnwood, Illinois: National Texbook Company.

Widdowson, Henry G. 1989. "Knowledge of language and ability for use." *Applied Linguistics* 10(2): 124-137.

Woodworth, D. E. (ed.). 1961. *Report on a conference on the meaning and role of culture in foreign language teaching*. Washington, D.C.: Institute of Languages and Linguistics, Edmund A. Walsh School of Foreign Service, Georgetown University.

Polite fictions:
Instrumental rudeness as pragmatic competence

Leslie M. Beebe
Teachers College, Columbia University

Introduction. In the field of pragmatics, the myth has persisted that rudeness is merely pragmatic failure at politeness. But this is a polite fiction. In reality, rudeness can also be a reflection of pragmatic competence. In this paper it is argued that native-speaker rudeness is usually instrumental—i.e. functional. It serves two functions: to get power and to vent negative feelings. The purpose of this paper is to use natural data to support the argument that rudeness is frequently instrumental and is not merely pragmatic failure. Two examples from the data illustrate situations where it is difficult to imagine that the speakers intended to be polite. It does not seem as if they miscalculated as they attempted politeness and were inadvertently rude. Rather, it appears as if they were using rudeness to serve some instrumental goal.

A man in a compact red car was trying to maneuver into a parking spot right next to a crosswalk at a corner in New York City. A woman was crossing the street with her two children as the man attempted to park. She was very thin. He had a big "beer belly." The two were arguing over whether she, the pedestrian, or he, the driver, had the right of way. Finally, the woman yelled:

Woman: Oh shut up you fat pig!
Man: Go fuck yourself.
Woman: Go on a diet!
Man: Go fuck yourself!

[source: Wendy Gavis, field notes]

It is hard to imagine how these words could possibly be intended as politeness.

In another example from the data, a young bicyclist came cycling down Central Park West in New York City and was clearly unhappy that a taxi driver had decided to slow down to let a pedestrian cross. If he kept riding straight, he would have to ride in front of the taxi who was turning right, and being reluctant to do that, he yelled,

Bicyclist: "Hey! Hey! Hey! You fuck!"

It is difficult to imagine how he might have had politeness as his goal. It seems farfetched to analyze this encounter as perception of rudeness due to clashing conversational styles. It also appears unlikely that this is crosscultural pragmatic failure. More probably, the bicyclist wanted to be instrumentally rude.

Background. The linguistic literature has traditionally emphasized research on politeness rather than rudeness (e.g. Lakoff 1973; Grice 1975; Brown and Levinson 1978, 1987; Ide 1982; Leech 1983). Although it is not within the scope of this paper to review the politeness literature, significant reviews of the literature exist (e.g. Fraser 1990; Kasper 1990) as well as important anthologies (e.g. Walters 1981; Watts et al. 1992;).

Lakoff (1973: 296) claims there are two rules of pragmatic competence:

(1) Be clear.
(2) Be polite.

Grice (1975: 45–47) posits that interlocutors operate according to "The Cooperative Principle," which is defined in terms of four conversational maxims. He believes that interlocutors can interpret each others' speech by assuming the Cooperative Principle or by viewing their conversational behavior as violations of the maxims of Quantity, Quality, Relation, and Manner. Lakoff (1973: 298) adds to Grice's maxims her own three:

(1) Don't impose.
(2) Give options.
(3) Make A feel good—be friendly.

Underlying this early work of Lakoff and Grice is the assumption that being polite, informative, truthful, relevant, succinct, and clear are the norms of conversation and, in addition, that these norms are universal.

Later, Lakoff (1989) specifically says that language may be classified as:

(1) Polite
(2) Nonpolite and
(3) Rude

Lakoff (1989, 1990) has written about settings, such as the courtroom (See also Beebe 1994b.) or the therapist's office, where the social rules and conventions of language are different from in everyday life and where there are limits to politeness as we know it in daily conversation. Lakoff (1989) discusses strategic rudeness—rudeness to fulfill a purpose. Still, she is only skirting the edges of instrumental rudeness, as she explores it in professional settings. In the present research, we look at instrumental rudeness in everyday conversation where we use rudeness and conflict talk to get or do what we want.

Building on the work of Lakoff (1989), Kochman (1984), and Leech (1983), Kasper (1990) includes a section on rudeness when she reviews the literature on politeness. Kasper (1990) divides rudeness into:

(1) Motivated rudeness and
(2) Unmotivated rudeness.

She further subdivides motivated rudeness into three categories:

(1) Lack of affect control (Kochman 1984),
(2) Strategic rudeness (Lakoff 1989), and
(3) Irony (Leech 1983).

We might therefore say that Kasper (1990) and Lakoff (1989) have done a great deal to dispel the myth that politeness is the norm, and rudeness is merely pragmatic failure at achieving that norm. Still, that myth permeates both the field of pragmatics (native-language pragmatics, interlanguage pragmatics, and crosscultural pragmatics) as well as the field of ESL teaching. Until recently, very little data have been collected on rudeness in everyday conversation, although related research exists, for example, on argument/dispute/conflict talk (e.g. Grimshaw 1990) and ritual insult (e.g. Labov 1972).

Beebe (1993a, 1993b, 1994a) outlines four areas of rudeness:

(1) Instrumental rudeness,
(2) Volcanic rudeness,
(3) No frills rudeness, and
(4) Conversational management rudeness.

Beebe (1993b) explains how these categories coincide with and add to categories existing in the literature and how they are subdivided.

Instrumental rudeness (Beebe 1993a, 1993b, 1994a) is similar to Lakoff's strategic rudeness (1989). It refers to rudeness intended to achieve a goal—an instrumental purpose. Leech's ironic rudeness (1983) is viewed as part of instrumental rudeness.

Volcanic rudeness (Beebe 1993a, 1993b, 1994a) is similar to Kochman's "loss of affect control" (1984) but this kind of rudeness is referred to as "volcanic" in order to rule out such affective responses as weeping with joy, seething with envy, or gushing with pride. Rudeness in the data collected seemed to relate to loss of one's temper. There were violent, explosive expressions of anger, as well as more minor outbursts of impatience and expressions of contempt. But hostility seemed to pervade the data.

The third category, no frills rudeness (Beebe 1993a, 1993b, 1994), was coined as a term for "blunt unsoftened rudeness," rude silences, and situations where brevity was used to the point of rudeness. There is no parallel category in Kasper's (1990) taxonomy.

Finally, conversational management rudeness (Beebe 1993a, 1993b, 1994) was added to characterize the rudeness perceived when people try to get the floor, hold the floor, make the interlocutor talk, or make the interlocutor stop talking. This category, like no frills rudeness, is not included in Kasper's (1990) taxonomy.

Tannen (1984, 1990) has shown that differing conversational styles can lead to the perception of rudeness, but her work has emphasized that speakers generally have good intentions, and it is primarily the cultural differences in conversational style that cause the problem. Tannen discusses "interruptions" versus "cooperative overlap," where a "high involvement" speaker may intend to overlap cooperatively with the talk of another. Yet the "high involvement" speaker may be perceived as rude by a "high considerate-ness" speaker who views any overlap as disruptive. In Beebe (1993b, 1994a), however, twenty-two strategies for managing conversation are illustrated with spontaneous natural data. The data provide illustrations of speakers who were viewed as rude while trying to get the floor, hold the floor, get the interlocutor to talk, or get the interlocutor to stop talking.

In the current paper, the rudeness categories are reorganized and reinterpreted, and new data are used as the basis for the taxonomy. But before outlining the new taxonomy of rudeness developed in this paper, we need to consider how the data were collected and what counts as rudeness (i.e. how rudeness is defined).

Methodology. This section of the paper briefly summarizes the data collection and the data analysis procedures. For a fuller explanation of the "notebook data" approach, see Beebe (1992, 1994c).

Data collection procedures. The data in this paper are based on approximately six hundred examples of perceived rudeness. All of the data were collected in New York City, and all but a few pieces of data were collected by the researcher. The other examples were collected by graduate students in applied linguistics and TESOL at Teachers College, Columbia University who were trained by the researcher. The data were collected between Spring 1991 and Spring 1995.

The data in this paper include only examples from spontaneous speech. No examples were elicited, and, with only one exception, the data are not taperecorded. Instead, data are recorded in notebooks, using "immediate facilitated recall" (Beebe 1994c). Beebe (1994c) discusses this approach, which entails immediate transcription of memorized segments. Notes are kept on which pieces of a conversation are exact word-for-word transcription and which are reconstructed later. If there is a delay in transcribing the data, the example is called "reconstructed dialog." For this study, no restrictions are placed on the examples in terms of the role relationships of the participants, the socioeconomic status of the speakers, or their age, ethnicity, race, or gender. We record sociolinguistic information, but this study is aimed at a taxonomy of all rudeness, so all data are relevant for this paper.

There are important methodological consequences to the use of this kind of "ethnographic" data (Wolfson 1983, 1989)—what I call "notebook data." Beebe (1994c) discusses the dramatic strengths and serious weaknesses of notebook data and presents a taxonomy of different kinds of these data. Most of the stengths relate to the spontaneity of the data and their rich variety of sources. Most of the weaknesses relate to the inability to acquire complete and accurate information and to the bias involved in collecting a corpus without formal constraints on setting and participants. Hence, there are legitimate concerns about limitations on determining the background of the speakers and getting an accurate transcript when examples get long. There are also concerns about the bias of collecting too many examples from one's own acquaintances, friends, family, and colleagues, not to mention bias in the strangers we observe. Still, the gain from removing limits on subjects and settings is tremendous in a study which is aimed at taxonomy—especially classification of a behavior which is stigmatized and therefore likely to be edited and distorted if elicited and likely to be absent in many formal settings conducive to traditional scientific data collection.

These data collection procedures are necessary due to Labov's Observer's Paradox (1970). Formal contexts which the scientist can observe and record most accurately are the ones where rudeness data are most likely to be absent or distorted. Interestingly, studying rudeness has led me to a new Observer's Paradox. "Beebe's Observer's Paradox" involves the unconscious avoidance of the very places where good data are available. The omnipresence of rudeness in New York City led me to realize its importance in the field of pragmatics, but the knowledge of where to find it led to the ability to avoid it. For example, the observer began taking taxis to avoid the rich data source of the subways. She also began guessing at postage to avoid the Post Office—another rich source of data. Beebe's Observer's Paradox comes into play when the data are found in an unpleasant setting.

Data analysis procedures.

DEFINITION OF RUDENESS. The greatest challenge to this research is deciding what constitutes rudeness. Rudeness is perceived differently by members of different cultures and speakers of different conversational styles (Tannen 1984, 1990). Consequently, this paper draws data from a corpus of perceived rudeness examples. Nevertheless, drawing only on examples which the researcher considers rude does not preclude bias; it only makes the bias consistent. And it does not exempt the researcher from the need to define the conversational phenomenon under investigation.

In this study, rudeness is defined as a face threatening act (FTA)—or feature of an FTA such as intonation—which violates a socially sanctioned norm of interaction for the social context in which it occurs. It is only rudeness if it receives insufficient redressive action to mitigate its force or, of course, if it does not occur in a context, such as intimacy or emergency, that would negate the need for redressive action. Consequently, it causes antagonism, discomfort, or conflict and results in some disruption to the social harmony. The idea that socially sanctioned norms of interaction are violated is central to the perception of rudeness. Another point about rudeness is that it can be verbal or nonverbal, explicit or implicit, intentional or unintentional, conscious or unconscious. Kasper (1990:208), drawing on Lakoff (1989), writes, "Rudeness ... is consituted by deviation from whatever counts as politic in a given social context, is inherently confrontational and disruptive to social equilibrium." Lakoff (1989) emphasizes that rudeness is confrontational behavior.

TAXONOMY OF RUDENESS. In this paper, the taxonomy proposed in Beebe (1993a, 1993b, 1994a) is reorganized. Instead of classifying rudeness into four descriptive categories and many subcategories, it is argued that there are two main functions of rudeness:

(1) To get power
(2) To vent negative feelings

Both of these functions of rudeness are seen as instrumental. In other words, in the earlier taxonomy there were problems of overlap in categories and problems of nonparallelism. Overlap is still possible with the new taxonomy, but the new system highlights that most rudeness is instrumental on some level, and rudeness can be summarized as serving two main purposes: Getting power and venting negative feelings.

Findings.
Rudeness to get power. Rudeness to get power consists of rudeness for several alternative purposes:

(1) To appear superior
(2) To get power over actions
   • to get someone else to do something
   • to avoid doing something yourself
(3) To get power in conversation (i.e. to do conversational management)

- to make the interlocutor talk
- to make the interlocutor stop talking
- to get the floor
- to shape what the interlocutor tells you (or how)

Some examples of rudeness also seem to be aimed at saving time, and others seem to convey intimacy. If the interlocutor perceives a time crunch and in situations where intimacy is considered sufficient, rudeness will not be perceived, or it will be excused. Efficiency rudeness, emergency rudeness, and intimate rudeness are beyond the scope of this paper.

To APPEAR SUPERIOR. One of the primary reasons why people are rude to get power is to make themselves appear superior to the interlocutor. One of the main ways this was accomplished in the New York data was to use what I call "YASI" (/yaesiy/)—an acronym for the "You Are Stupid Intonation." YASI can create rudeness on its own, but the intonation assists words in conveying the message. For example, a thirty-five-year-old woman called a receptionist for an appointment and inquired as to when the person she wanted to see was free. The receptionist said, "You're an adult. YOU pick a time."

Another example was coded under "insults" and "putdowns" in Beebe (1993a, 1994a). Of course, "putdowns" are a verbal way of saying that the speaker is superior. In one example, a professor asks another professor a question. Neither one can figure out the answer, so one of them asks a third professor who is running the meeting. The response: "You really AREN'T good at this. Even I knew THAT!"

To GET POWER OVER ACTIONS.
Power to get someone else to do something. One way to impose one's will is to use sarcasm. For example, a thirty-five-year-old woman was standing in the aisle of a drugstore at 96th Street and Columbus Avenue in Manhattan, contemplating different kinds of shampoo and conditioner. A woman appearing to be in her late seventies tried to pass, going in one direction (1) and then about five minutes later tried to pass going in the opposite direction (2).

(1) Elderly woman: Excuse me (gives the younger woman a "look").

(2) Elderly woman: Excuse me (mumbing audibly). What are you here for, the day?
                                              [source: Wendy Gavis, field notes]

Another example from the data might be called "pushy politeness." The increasing tendency of waiters to come up to a table every couple of minutes and ask (supposedly politely), "Would you care to order?" is considered by some to be rude and intrusive. The perception of rudeness depends on many variables—the price of the restaurant, the perceived intention of the waiter, the presence or absence of a waiting line, the response of the patrons, and many other factors, such as the restaurant's clientele and the type of service advertized. In one very expensive restaurant in Manhattan which caters to people in publishing—an industry that relies on the lengthy business lunch—a team of waiters traded off asking if the customers would like to order, even though the restaurant was not full, no one was waiting, and the customers made it clear they wanted to have a discussion during lunch.

> Waiter 1: Would you care to order?
> Customers: (indicate no)
> Waiter 2: Would you like to order?
> Customers: (indicate no)
> Waiter 1: Are you ready to order?
> Customers: (indicate no):
> Waiter 3: Have you selected? (standing over the table as if to say that he is not leaving until they order)

This seemed to reflect a desire on the part of the waiters to get it over with, not a policy regarding length of stay, a lack of communication among waiters, or a problem with crowding, so it was viewed as rude.

Power to avoid doing something. In order to get power, we sometimes use rudeness to get someone to do something, but we also use rudeness to avoid doing something for someone. We try to get them to go away or leave us alone or finish their business more quickly. We simply want to avoid something annoying or unpleasant, or perhaps to reduce our work load.

In one example from the data, a middle-aged garage attendant was asked by a young woman in her twenties from out of town how to drive north out of New York City. He rattled off quick directions as one would to someone who knows the area and knows the names of all the highways, bridges, and landmarks. The young woman kept asking questions to be sure she knew the way.

> Garage attendant: Lady, what do you want me to do, draw you a map?
> Young woman: Oh, thank you (with a big smile of relief, knowing full well it hadn't been a serious offer).
> Garage attendant: (softened, draws map)

The garage attendant's job is not to give directions, so he found it an imposition to be asked for such detail. He was busy. Although he was perceived as rude, he could also be partially excused because giving directions is not his job, and he was busy.

In another instance in the data, a bookstore saleswoman was viewed as very rude because she appeared to be unwilling to do what was in fact her job. At this bookstore, all books were displayed behind a counter.

> Saleswoman: If you want to browse, go to the library over there (pointing across the street). I can't show you everything in the store.

This example was interpreted as the saleswoman's attempt to get power —probably to reduce her work load. She was alone. She apparently had no work to do. There were no other customers in the store. Her job is to sell books.

One of the most common linguistic strategies used to get power to avoid dealing with someone is repetition. Two women went to Penn Station in Manhattan to catch a train to Princeton. They thought that the train did not go directly to the university campus, but they were not sure. The older woman asked the man at the ticket window for two roundtrip tickets to Princeton.

> Older woman: Does this train go to Princeton?
> Ticket seller: Take the Dinky.
> Older woman: Does it let you off in front of the university?
> Ticket seller: Take the Dinky.

This repetition seemed to be a power play. It was a refusal to clarify—a refusal to help in the way requested.

The data contain several examples of exact repetition as a strategy to avoid dealing with someone. Noticing that the school cafeteria is offering cottage cheese in its salad bar, but the container is now empty, a professor notifies an employee that the cottage cheese has run out. The employee says, "The salad bar is being replenished," giving no indication as to when. It is crowded, and the professor is having lunch with a colleague who has gone on ahead, so she says with a big smile, "So what does that mean for my salad?" She basically calls him on the "canned" way in which he responds without giving the needed information. The employee repeats his exact words, "The salad bar is being replenished." The use of repetition here is a kind of refusal to inform further or to apologize for not knowing the information that the customer needs.

To get power in conversation. Beebe (1993b, 1994a) called this conversational management rudeness. This category deals with turn-taking, interruption, overlap, getting the floor, and holding the floor. These papers outline twenty-two categories of conversational management rudeness. In this paper, however, I am lumping them into four broad categories of perceived rudeness:

(1) Rudeness to make the interlocutor talk,
(2) Rudeness to make the interlocutor stop talking,
(3) Rudeness to get the floor, and
(4) Rudeness to shape what the speaker tells the listener (or how).

Rudeness to make the interlocutor talk is exemplified by saying in a drawn out impatient tone, "Hellloooo!"—especially if the person hesitates while speaking. Rudeness to make the interlocutor stop talking is exemplified by instances in the data where someone says, "Shush!" during the interlocutor's turn—usually because the person wants to redirect the conversation and is impatient with the line of talk. In one instance, the person responded in anger, "Don't shush me!" This shushing is different from the one in the movies when nearby patrons are talking. Rudeness to get the floor consists of rude interruptions—not cooperative overlaps (Tannen 1990), but overbearing interruption to cut someone off (e.g. Zimmerman and West 1975). Rudeness to shape what the interlocutor tells you (or how) consists of interjections like, "What's your point?" In New York City, about forty percent of the people informally interviewed at a conference did not consider this rude—or at least not very rude. Some think it is rude only if there is overlap or interruption. Some think the attempt to get the interlocutor to get to the point and say what the listener wants to hear is inherently intrusive and rude. This underscores Tannen's (1990) point that there are crosscultural differences in perception, but the view of this paper is that we should also take an interest in what a majority of people find offensive, even if they are offended because of cultural differences. Only then can we understand reactions to language.

Rudeness to vent negative feelings.
TO EXPRESS ANGER. The two examples given at the beginning of this paper are examples of rudeness to express anger. In both instances it appears that the speaker senses a loss of control and is afraid. Going from fear to anger is a small step, and angry rudeness results. In the first case, the woman crossing the street yells, "Go on a diet" to the heavy set man who threatens her by trying to park his car where she and her children are crossing. In the second example, the bicyclist yells, "Hey! Hey! Hey! You fuck!" to the taxi driver. Most probably, he too was afraid that he would get hit, because the taxi driver's courtesy to a pedestrian meant that the bicyclist had to ride in front of the car or move into the line of traffic to go behind him. In neither case did the perpetrator of the rudeness have much chance of becoming safe by using rudeness. Both could only be safe by stopping their movement forward—unthinkable in New York. So we can infer (we obviously cannot know for sure) that the rude remarks were because the speakers were expressing anger.

The most extended example of blind anger that we found was transcribed verbatim by a student at Teachers College (Emily Ellis) who happened to witness a fight at a Korean grocery store in Harlem. Two women, who are strangers, get into a spontaneous argument over who is first in line to pay.

> Yolanda: Just take you (unintelligible) and get out-a-here, a'right?
> Maria: //What you think I'm doing, what you think I'm doing?
> Yolanda: Good Thank you. And just shut up.
> Maria: Why don't you make me shut up?

The fight continues:

> Maria: //Don't underestimate me, baby. Don't underestimate me, baby.
> Yolanda: //I'm the one underestimated.
> Maria: //I will shoot your brain off.
> Yolanda: (screaming) SHOOT YOUR GUN OUT, THEN, AND SHOOT ME. COME ON! //PULL YOUR GUN AND SHOOT ME.
> Maria: //That's all I tell you.//
> Yolanda: (still screaming) //PULL IT OUT//AND SHOOT ME ... (thirteen turns cut out here) ...
> Maria: Don't come (unintelligible) in my face. [command] DON'T COME IN MY FACE! [command]
> Yolanda: (screaming and bending in towards Maria's face)
> Maria: DON'T COME IN MY FUCKING FACE! //DON'T COME IN MY FUCKING FACE! [command]
> Yolanda: //PULL OUT YOUR GUN AND SHOOT ME! (voice starting to come down from screaming)
> Man (1): //Okay...Okay. ENOUGH! ENOUGH! ENOUGH!

> (source: Emily Ellis, transcript]

A frequent strategy for showing anger is name calling. In one example, an Indian proprietor of a magazine store recognizes a thief and starts calling him names as he steals a magazine.

> Thief: (male, possibly homeless) Excuse me (acting as if he is proprietor of the store, while stealing the $3.95 double issue of *People Magazine*)
> Proprietor: Give me back! (grabs the magazine back)
> Female customer: Oh God! (fearing violence)
> Thief: (comes back and throws the magazine on the snow)
> Proprietor: Motherfucker!
> Female customer: (steps back in fear of gun violence)
> Proprietor: (gets bat from behind the counter)

Female customer: Can I get out of here before we all get killed?
Proprietor: Asshole! (yelling after the thief)
Female customer: Is it okay if I leave?

TO EXPRESS IMPATIENCE. An example of impatience or frustration expressed in a rude way occurred when a Chinese graduate student called an American woman in New York by mistake twice and got a rude put-down as a repayment.

Chinese woman: May I please speak to Hui-mei Yang?
American woman: You've got the wrong number.
Chinese woman: I'm sorry (thinking she dialed wrong, she dials again)
American woman: What number do you want?
Chinese woman: (tells her the number)
American woman: You've got the right number, but there's no one here by that name.
Chinese woman: I'm sorry.
American woman: You SHOULD be! (hangs up)

[source: anonymous, reconstructed dialog]

In another example of impatience, a woman used spelling out a response as a strategy to show impatience.

Female professor 1: (suggests hiring someone they both know is a cheat and a thief as a program assistant)
Female professor 2: N—O! NO!

TO EXPRESS CONTEMPT. Some of the rudeness examples seem to be an expression of contempt—often a seemingly gratuitous expression of contempt, perhaps reflecting a generalized anger rather than a specifically provoked rudeness. Contemptuous rudeness is often accompanied by YASI—the "You Are Stupid Intonation." They frequently involve what appears to be a deliberate misinterpretation and employ sarcasm as a linguistic device to put down the interlocutor and express contempt. At Everyone's drugstore a customer is buying lots of little inexpensive things, so the total price is not obvious.

Customer: Is that good enough? (handing cashier a $20 bill, but not sure if $20 will be sufficient)
Cashier: It's money, isn't it? (with a look of contempt)

Another kind of contemptuous rudeness is seen in an example which was probably intended New York humor that was not well received. A woman who held a high-powered job in New York City says to a colleague that she has quit her job, moved West, and found a quieter, more relaxing and fulfilling life. She is happy to be out of the "rat race." A second colleague, a New Yorker, walks up at a party, and the woman tells her, too, that she has moved, but this time she meets up with the attitude that New York is the only place in the country a thinking person would choose to live.

> Ex-New Yorker: I moved to Reno.
> Dyed-in-the-wool New Yorker: On purpose?

The deadpan humor was not appreciated.

Beebe (1993a, 1994a) discusses rudeness which consists of criticism and/or lecturing as an expression of hostility. One of the examples involves a woman yelling at a Food Emporium manager, "YOU SHOULD LEARN TO MANAGE YOUR STORE!" as she starts walking out the door [source: Wendy Gavis, field notes]. Another example of rudeness to express contempt occurred at the New York County Criminal Court. The male judge interviews prospective jurors privately to determine schedule conflicts, and when told of a conflict, says:

> Judge: What do you want ME to do about it? (sneering)

Clearly, his job was to listen and to determine what, if anything, he should do about any potential schedule problems or ideological conflicts.

Conclusion. In conclusion, the purpose of this paper is to provide evidence that rudeness is instrumental and performs two major functions:

(1) Getting power and
(2) Expressing negative feelings.

In the linguistic literature, the emphasis has been on the intention of politeness and the accidental failure to convey politeness. What a beautiful world! But is it the world we live in? What the data in this paper show is that people use rudeness instrumentally—to serve needed functions in language and in life. We must also, therefore, turn the tables on our more traditional concerns and look at the intention of rudeness. This paper has attempted to look at rudeness that was perhaps not intentional in the sense that it was consciously planned in advance, but that was intentional in the sense that it fulfilled a function that the speaker intended, and it was not failed politeness. The speakers in these examples use instrumental rudeness to display pragmatic competence. It is high time we focused on rudeness. It is the language that ESL and native-speaking students have to deal with in the real world. They have to learn to get power/control and express negative feelings—but in appropriate ways. This is the neglected side of communicative competence.

ACKNOWLEDGEMENTS

The author gratefully acknowledges all the anonymous rude people in the city of New York who have provided her with a wealth of free data—including herself and her dearest friends! I also appreciate the assistance of the students in applied linguistics and TESOL at Columbia University Teachers College who participated in the data collection and offered many invaluable insights into the definition, classification, and analysis of rudeness. Students in TL5588 "Trends in SLA Research" (a course on politeness and rudeness) and TL6587 "Seminar in Second Language Acquisition" (a course on crosscultural pragmatics) participated in the data collection along with other research assistants and colleagues. I would like to acknowledge the following people in alphabetical order: Toshihiko Ashikaga, Elpida Bairaktari, Huimei Chu, Elite Deutsch, Emily Ellis, Naomi Fujita, Wendy Gavis, Peter Hoffman, Laura Holland, Paula Korsko, Rong Rong Le, Guillermo McLean-Herrera, Keiichi Nakabachi, Yoshihiko Nakazato, Bruce Nussbaum, Merce Pujol, James Purpura, H. Kuribara Shea, and Kayoko Shiomi, Tomoko Takahashi, Sarah Towle, and Hansun Zhang. Of course, the majority of field notes are my own, and the analysis, while influenced by the ideas of many others, remains completely my responsibility and does not necessarily reflect the ideas of those who participated in the seminar on politeness and rudeness in language.

REFERENCES

Beebe, Leslie M. 1992. "Questionable questions." Paper presented at TESOL Convention, Vancouver, BC, 1992.
Beebe, Leslie M. 1993a. "The pragmatics of rudeness." Paper presented at AAAL Convention, Atlanta, 1993.
Beebe, Leslie M. 1993b. "Rudeness: The undervalued skill in communicative competence." Paper presented at TESOL Convention, Atlanta, 1993.
Beebe, Leslie M. 1994a. "Rudeness: The neglected side of communicative competence." Plenary address at ALSIG Winter Conference, Mercy College, NY, 1994.
Beebe, Leslie M. 1994b. "Court-related rudeness and trumped up language to boot." Paper presented at AAAL Convention, Baltimore, 1994.
Beebe, Leslie M. 1994c. "Notebook data on power and the power of notebook data." Paper presented at TESOL Convention, Baltimore, 1994.
Brown, Penelope and Stephen Levinson. 1978. "Universals of language usage: Politeness phenomena." In Esther Goody (ed.), *Questions and politeness*. Cambridge, U.K.: Cambridge University Press. 54–301.
Brown, Penelope and Stephen Levinson. 1987. *Politeness: Some universals in language usage*. Cambridge, U.K.: Cambridge University Press.
Fraser, Bruce. 1990. "Perspectives on politeness." *Journal of Pragmatics* 14: 219–236.
Grice, H.P. 1975. "Logic and conversation." In Peter Cole and Jerry Morgan (eds.), *Syntax and semantics: Speech acts, Volume 3*. New York: Academic Press. 41–53.

Grimshaw, Allen D. (ed.). 1990. *Conflict talk: Sociolinguistic investigations of arguments in conversations*. Cambridge, U.K.: Cambridge University Press.

Kasper, Gabriele. 1990. "Linguistic politeness: Current research issues." *Journal of Pragmatics* 14: 193-218.

Kochman, Thomas. 1984. "The politics of politeness: Social warrants in mainstream American public etiquette." In Deborah Schiffrin (ed.), *Georgetown University Round Table on Languages and Linguistics 1984*. Washington, D.C.: Georgetown University Press. 200-209.

Labov, William. 1970. "The study of language in its social context." *Studium Generale* 23: 30-87.

Labov, William. 1972. *Language in the inner city: Studies in the Black English Vernacular*. Philadelphia: University of Pennsylvania Press.

Lakoff, Robin. 1973. "The logic of politeness; or, minding your p's and q's." In *Papers from the ninth regional meeting of the Chicago Linguistic Society*. Chicago: University of Chicago Press. 292-305.

Lakoff, Robin. 1989. "The limits of politeness: Therapeutic and courtroom discourse." *Multilingua* 8 (2/3): 101-129.

Lakoff, Robin. 1990. *Talking power: The politics of language*. New York: Basic Books.

Leech, Geoffrey. 1983. *Principles of pragmatics*. London: Longman.

Tannen, Deborah. 1984. *Conversational style: Analyzing talk among friends*. Norwood, N.J.: Ablex.

Tannen, Deborah. 1990. *You just don't understand: Women and men in conversation*. New York: William Morrow.

Walters, Joel.(ed.) 1981. "The sociolinguistics of deference and politeness." *International Journal of the Sociology of Language* 27: 77-92.

Watts, Richard J., Sachiko Ide, and Konrad Ehlich. (eds.). 1992. *Politeness in language*. Berlin and New York: Mouton de Gruyter.

Wolfson, Nessa. 1983. "Rules of speaking." In Jack C. Richards and Richard W. Schmidt (eds.), *Language and communication*. London: Longman. 61-87.

Wolfson, Nessa. 1989. *Perspectives: Sociolinguistics and TESOL*. New York: Newbury House Publishers.

Zimmerman, Don H. and Candace West. 1975. "Sex roles, interruptions and silences in conversation." In Barrie Thorne and Nancy Henley (eds.), *Language and sex: Difference and dominance*. Rowley, Massachusetts: Newbury House. 105-129.

Multilevel analysis of two-way immersion classroom discourse

Isolda Carranza
Georgetown University

1. Introduction. This study builds on the insights provided by Shuy's (1988) and Mehan's (1979, 1985) pioneering work on classroom discourse, and Christian's (1991, 1992, 1994) and Lindholm's (1990, 1992) ongoing research on two-way bilingual education. The perspective adopted is informed by research in interactional sociolinguistics, linguistic anthropology, and critical discourse analysis. Ethnographic observations in a two-way bilingual context provide the empirical basis. Such data are of value in their own right, since the two-way bilingual classroom is a type of setting that is becoming increasingly common.

This paper presents a close analysis of school practices and the interaction of teachers and students. The research scope comprises the levels of the conversational exchange (Section 4), the speech event (Section 5), and the language economy (Section 6). At each of these levels, the focus will be, respectively, on frames signalled by the language used, characteristics of the lesson as a speech event, and other instances of language use in the school in light of the broader historical and societal context. Educational implications (Section 7) are derived with a view toward making the most of opportunities to use the second language and granting equal respect to the majority and the minority language.

The findings suggest three modifications of school practices. First, there is a need to encourage students, during the time of the school day for the minority language, to use that language for various frames within interactions, in a wide range of speech registers, and for diverse interpersonal relations. Second, constant modeling and feedback on linguistic forms as well as attention to forms (in classroom posters, class lists, etc.) written in the minority language, project an attitude of respect for that language, and contribute to building the same attitude in students. Finally, quality instruction requires ongoing teacher training that includes availability of reading materials and courses to keep up the teachers' proficiency in that language.

2. Two-way immersion. What distinguishes two-way immersion programs from other immersion programs is the inclusion, in balanced numbers, of

English-speaking students who are learning a second language and students who are native speakers of a language other than English.

In addition, the academic curriculum is taught in the two languages in order to realize a basic tenet of the immersion approach to second-language acquisition, which "involves emphasizing the communication of meaningful content material through the L2, rather than focusing on teaching of the second language itself" (Swain and Lapkin 1983: 9).

Finally, the two languages are not used concurrently but are kept separate for instruction in a ratio that may vary from 50–50% to 90 (English)–10% (non-English language) (Lindholm 1990).

A growing number of papers by educators and linguists deal with the goals of functional bilingualism and intercultural understanding; the details of implementing two-way bilingual programs (Baecher 1986, 1991; Christian and Mahrer 1992, 1993; Christian and Montone 1994; Genesee 1987; Lindholm 1992); the levels of first- and second-language development and academic achievement attained through this type of program (Christian 1994; Genesee 1985; Lindholm 1991); and its advantages for majority- and minority-language students (Lindholm 1990).

3. Data. The three programs observed for this study are located in the Washington, D.C. metropolitan area. The languages of immersion are Spanish and English, each used for fifty percent of the instructional periods.

Students' interactional patterns with peers, teachers, and other school staff were observed in various physical settings: classrooms, halls, and the library. On the other hand, lessons are examined here for features and markers characteristic of the bilingual lesson as a speech event, and the findings I report refer to teachers' participation in establishing the norms of interaction, punctuating stages of the lesson, or dealing specifically with language form. Use of the non-English language of immersion—in this case, Spanish—was also observed in the general school environment.[1]

4. The conversational exchange. The present study finds a direct antecedent in McCollum's (1993) work, which was an attempt to determine what influenced students' language choice in a bilingual-school environment. McCollum studied a middle school which offered a two-way bilingual program. In this paper, I specify in detail the various levels of social interaction at which

[1] I must thank the Center for Applied Linguistics in Washington, D.C. for granting me permission to use some of the data collected at one of the three observation sites for a research project directed by Donna Christian (U.S. Department of Education Grant #R117G10022; National Center of Research on Cultural Diversity and Second Language Learning, University of California at Santa Cruz). The field workers for that study, Chris Montone and myself, compiled field notes and made audiotapes of lessons.

language use should be interpreted, and I describe the forces at play in the students' language choice.

It is crucial for educators in an immersion setting to know what factors they should try to influence in order to encourage students' use of the L2. It is easy to see the potential for controlling and influencing what language is used when the teacher initiates the interactional sequence. Less is known of the factors determining the choice of language when students volunteer the beginning of a sequence. In order to rectify this imbalance, only student-initiated exchanges are described in what follows.[2]

4.1. Frames and Code Choice. Following Bateson (1972), Goffman (1974) uses the concept of "frame" to refer to the terms in which social actors perceive experience to be organized. Participants come to an understanding of what is going on, what the situation is, and act accordingly (Goffman 1974:2). In Goffman's words, "definitions of a situation are built up in accordance with principles of organization which govern events—at least social ones—and our subjective involvement in them" (Goffman 1974: 10).

Interactional sociolinguistics makes use of the concept of "frame" because verbal interaction is a social event and because talk is interpreted according to the frame it occurs in and, at the same time, can be employed as one of the signals indicating what the current frame is. It is this latter function as a signal that concerns us here.

I distinguish between the official and the unofficial frame for students' conversational activity. The official frame is evoked by all talk produced in or about "doing school" (for example, talk about lesson topics or school topics, or talk that builds the coordination necessary for the performance of a task). The unofficial frame is evoked by talk unrelated to academic topics.

On the basis of these broad analytical categories, it is possible to make further distinctions and look for linguistic cues marking them. An examination of interactional frames shows that code choice is such a cue. Code choice and codeswitching[3] during the Spanish part of the school day were mainly observed to mark the frames outlined below.

4.1.1. OFFICIAL FRAME. An official frame manifests itself in two varieties. One variety is talk that is itself a classroom task (e.g. an oral presentation in front of the class) or an inherent part of the performance of a classroom task (e.g. students' talk about what they find in the textbook as answers to write on

---

[2] For a description of other aspects of the interactional dynamics in the two-way bilingual classroom, see Christian, Carranza, and Montone (forthcoming).

[3] Intrasentential switches or codemixing are left out of this analysis.

their worksheets). The utterances are produced aloud for the whole class to hear. Spanish was most often used for this interactional frame, as in Example 1.

Example 1. Fifth grade.
During the Spanish time of the school day, a Spanish-background child asked the teacher a vocabulary question, but another student intervened.

> S1: *¿Qué es "choza"?*
> What is "hut"?
> S2: *Una cabaña. Como una–*
> A cabin. Like a–
> S1: *Oh.*

Another variety of official frame is talk that is instrumental to the performance of a classroom task (e.g. asking for instructions), as in Example 2.

Example 2. First grade.
During a letter-writing activity in the English time of the school day, two Spanish-background children, Joshua (the letter writer) and Angelo (the addressee of the letter) held a long conversation about the spelling of "Angelo." They consistently used English.

Finally, within the official frame we can also find talk which is off-task but on a school topic or "doing school" (e.g. buying school lunch that day).

Example 3. Second grade.
S1: You're copying me, Rachel!
S2: No, I'm not!

Example 4. Fourth grade.
S (to the teacher): Can I sharpen my pencil?

Example 4 shows an instance of the prevalence of English—despite the fact that the Spanish teacher is being addressed—when the official frame defines the talk as oriented to a practical outcome but not a lesson task itself.

4.1.2. UNOFFICIAL FRAME. Unoffical frames mainfest as non-academic and non-school talk, as in the following examples.

Example 5. First grade.
When the students played a Spanish-reading competition game, they read the Spanish word on the flashcard, but conducted all interaction in English with utterances such as "I said it first" and "You already went."

Example 6. First grade.
Two Spanish-background children sitting with other students in a circle during Spanish time carried out this exchange:
S1: Do you have a girlfriend?
S2: No. (pause) My girlfriend married somebody else.

Example 7. Fifth grade.
During Spanish math all spontaneous, nonacademic speech by students was in English. For example, "Isn't that cool?" and "Oh my Gosh!"

Students can be observed to go back and forth from official to unofficial frames, just as interactants in a conversation make swift changes of frames. Goffman remarks on the ephemeral nature of interactional frames, noticing that "talk appears as a rapidly shifting stream of differently framed strips" (Goffman 1974: 544). Another characteristic of frames is that they are co-constructed in that the interlocutor may confirm the task, the metatask, or the nonacademic talk.

Code choice is applied to do the conversational work of marking the current frame. This is a sequential unmarked choice, i.e. as situational factors change, the balance of rights and obligations changes. In these cases, the "culture" of the bilingual classroom may well be summarized as "we all know that we can say it in two languages," the codeswitch is merely an attention-getter for a switch in the current frame.

4.2. Factors influencing code choice. The analysis of the data indicates that factors influencing language choice by students are:

(1) The students' proficiency level in L2,
(2) addressee, and
(3) classroom rules.[4]

There is also an interplay with another social dimension, since the effect of these factors varies according to the students' relationship to their interlocutor. This social relationship can be asymmetrical (child—adult) or symmetrical

---

[4] These factors do not coincide with those which, according to Bean (1994), are at work in a transitional-bilingual classroom.

(among peers). For example, an adult perceived as a native speaker of Spanish (and whose social role is not associated with the use of English) would be addressed in Spanish. The choice is different among peers. Pairs of Spanish-background children and pairs made up of one Spanish-background and one English–background child both show a similar tendency to speak in English even in the Spanish portion of the day.

4.2.1. THE INFLUENCE OF STUDENTS' PROFICIENCY LEVEL, ADDRESSEE, AND CLASSROOM RULES ON CODE CHOICE IN ASYMMETRICAL INTERACTIONS. Let us consider how factors (1)–(3) play out when the participants have asymmetrical relationships (child–adult). With regard to the first factor, if students' L2 proficiency level does not allow them to express their intended content, they will tend to use their L1.

The effect of the second factor influencing code choice can be described as "addressee design." This term helps us denote that the influencing factor is not just who the addressee is because the student may not know the addressee's social identity or language background; rather, the student's expectations and hypothesis about the addressee are critical. This initial decision is an "exploratory choice" (Myers-Scotton 1989, 1993) in the sense that the child tentatively addresses the adult in one of the two languages until a decision is negotiated as to what the language of the interaction will be. The adult may ratify the initial choice and respond in the same language used by the student.

Spanish-speaking fifth-graders spoke English to a visitor who looked Anglo-American. There is a feeling of "pretense" when two people communicate in one language, knowing that both can be more effective in another language. Students expected the Anglo-American–looking visitor to communicate better in English than in Spanish. Those same children spoke Spanish to me. In the various physical settings that exist within the school and during the various times of the school day (recesses, lessons, and transitions) students interact with different "types" of adults and the set of expectations also varies. For example, there need not be an "exploratory choice" in selecting the language to address the grade teacher (who the students know well) in the classroom (where the expectations are clearly determined).

The third factor at play in code choice in asymmetrical interactions is classroom rules. When the adult is the Spanish-section teacher and the exchange takes place during the Spanish lesson, the choice of language depends on either unexpected elements of the situation (e.g. in an emergency, students use the language they are more comfortable with) or, more commonly, on how strictly teachers and other adults enforce the rule "English for English time, Spanish for Spanish time."

Rules for language use in the classroom may be the same for the entire program, but their application varies with interesting effects. Here are some examples:

Example 8. Fifth grade.
Although the students have a good level of Spanish proficiency, they addressed the Spanish-section teacher in both Spanish and English. That teacher is, in addition, a native Spanish speaker.

Example 9. Third grade.
Students always addressed the teacher in Spanish during Spanish time and in English during English time, although (exceptionally) the same teacher was in charge of both sections.

4.2.2. THE INFLUENCE OF STUDENTS' PROFICIENCY LEVEL, ADDRESSEE, AND CLASSROOM RULES ON CODE CHOICE IN SYMMETRICAL INTERACTIONS. Let us now consider the interactions where the participants have symmetrical relationships (child–child). Proficiency level in the L2 is a factor determining language choice on some occasions. For example, two pairs of English-background students in the same third-grade class differed in the language they chose for the same type of unsupervised talk. The pair with a very high proficiency level in Spanish used Spanish, while the other pair talked in English.

Second, when level of proficiency cannot account for code choice, the addressee's social identity as a peer can determine it. Thus a Spanish-background pair and a pair of one Spanish-background child and one English-background child in the same grade would tend to speak English regardless of whether it was the English or Spanish time of the day. When proficiency is not a factor and, as mentioned before, students "know" they can express themselves in two languages, the "peerness" of the addressee determines the choice of English. This is, then, a case in which "English may encode solidarity even though it is a second language" (Myers-Scotton 1989: 338).

Among peers, including Spanish-background peers, a switch to English can be a choice of the ingroup variety. Therefore, what needs to be explored is not so much the indexing of group membership through choice of code, but other elements of the social context also indexed by codeswitching and choice: the frame to which it belongs (Goffman 1974: 2).

Third, "language rules" can regulate code choice among peers. The degree to which they are enforced accounts for differences between instances of unsupervised talk in Examples 10 and 11:

Example 10. Third grade.
The teacher enforces the rule of using Spanish during Spanish time so strictly that students use that language for all kinds of conversations. For example, two English-background children spent some time examining and talking about the teacher's seal in Spanish while the teacher was away from her desk.

Example 11. Fifth grade.
During pair-work in the Spanish math lesson, the students explained the activity to each other in English. The low level of rule enforcement allowed this choice.

The effect of the rules about what language to use must also be examined in association with physical setting and instructor's vigilance. For instance, talk in the classroom tends to follow the rules, while talk in the library does not.

Rules for classroom behavior, a factor in code choice for the microlevel of social interaction, are part of what makes a lesson a lesson. Therefore, contingencies in exchanges are sensitive to conditions imposed by a higher-order reality: the speech event. This is the level to be dealt with next.

5. The Speech Event. Ethnographic observations inform us about the two-way bilingual lesson as a unit of interaction. The search for the norms of interaction and the role of language in this speech event led me to concentrate on the following issues:

(1) The ritual aspects of classroom management;
(2) indirectness and metatalk in the students' and the teachers' speech; and
(3) the degree of saliency of form in the teachers' instructional talk.

The specific manifestations of these aspects and their instructional significance for the goals of two-way immersion are discussed below.

5.1. The ritual aspects of classroom management. The most ritualized components of classroom management are turn-taking and turn-allocation on the one hand, and the marking of transitions on the other. Ritualized management of the right to speak is illustrated by Example 12:

Example 12. First grade.
The teacher would say a child's name and indicate with a gesture that the child was to stop calling her. A nonverbal signal, the teacher's snapping her fingers, indicated that the class should be quiet. For this class, turn-taking was also strictly controlled: The next speaker could be designated only by the teacher. When a student called out an answer, that child was sent to stand at the back of the classroom.

There is a further dimension to having the floor to speak. Given that student participation not only have an effect on the learning of content, but also constitute opportunities to use, practice, and learn the second language, allocations of turns to talk take on an added significance in a bilingual classroom. To use an economic metaphor, in this bilingual context, time is a valuable "commodity" that should be made available to students and made available in equal shares.

Transition markers between activities accomplish their signaling function by virtue of being recognized as a communicative convention. Variation in the transition markers observed is wide: While one teacher would be verbose and unclear, another would use the ritual repetition of these lines:

If you are listening, put your hands on your nose,
If you are listening, put your hands on your eyebrows,
If you are listening, put your hands on your hair, etc.

5.2. Indirectness and Metatalk. The second element that characterizes the lesson as a speech event is its use of metatalk and indirect language. Teachers' metatalk, i.e. talk about talk and about rules, is fairly common. Furthermore, a striking case is illustrated by a teacher who, in addition to her own talk, made students speak at great length on what the rules were and why they were important, or what strategies they had to apply for each activity and why they were important.

Two typical instances of indirectness were: (1) The teacher's referring to herself by her name instead of using "I" and the teacher's referring to herself with the pronoun "we"; (See Shuy 1988 on these aspects.) and (2) indirect commands. Interestingly, the most indirect, subtle, and complex forms were observed in the earlier grades.

Example 13. First grade.
"I like Edward's hands."
"I'm seeing some superduper listening there."

This stands in stark contrast with the direct commands frequent in the higher grades:

Example 14. Fifth grade.
"Jim. Stop."

5.3. Degree of saliency of form. Recent research (e.g. Long 1991) indicates that the best pedagogical results seem to be obtained through focus on form within a communicative-teaching approach. Although school administrators are aware of these issues, they must deal with practical limitations such as the availability of personnel qualified in both elementary education and bilingual education.

The varying degree to which different teachers make language form salient may relate to differences in training and experience in bilingual education.

At the same grade level, one teacher with ten years of experience in bilingual schools focused on form much more than her less-experienced English-section counterpart. When the former used the word *carro* (car) she drew attention to the sound /r/ which is difficult for English speakers. Similar behavior was rarely seen in the other teacher. And while one teacher gave students several opportunities to repeat utterances and to produce form correctly, explicitly saying *Mike, trata* (Mike, try), in the other class, students seemed geared only to show knowledge of content.

During dictation, the teacher with more experience exaggerated the phonological form of some words to aid correct spelling, for example, *marzo* /márso/ (March) dictated as /má:r:só/. The other teacher did not use such exaggerations.

One teacher took every opportunity to correct forms implicitly through modeling:

Example 15. Fifth grade.
S: *Tiene hilejas.*
     It has [rows].
T: *Sí, tiene hileras.*
     Yes, it has rows.

The question arose whether in the other class there was less need to model, or whether the students with a lower level of language proficiency were not taking any risks.

This contrasts with Example 16, which shows how important it is for teachers of both program sections to have the specific qualification of being acquainted with immersion students' needs.

Example 16. Fifth grade.
The following exchanges took place after the students were instructed to write a comparison-and-contrast paragraph:
S1: Similarities?
T: *Sí, y las diferencias.*
     Yes, and the differences.
(Later)
S2: *¿Cómo se dice* similarities?
     How do you say "similarities"?
T: *Se dice "iguales." Se dice "similitudes."*
     You say "same." You say "similitudes."

Although this teacher did not take the first opportunity to teach a new vocabulary item, the students later asked for it.

The lesson's characteristics described above as well as others (its being two-way immersion, aiming at the use of only one language in a lesson, etc.) are sensitive to the existence of values in a language economy. This broader context is the aspect I will address next.

6. The language economy. The format of bilingual-education programs is undeniably influenced by the sociopolitical situation they are in. In Spain, for example, Catalan- and Basque-immersion programs are designed for Spanish-speaking students, i.e. the students' home language and culture are the dominant ones in the society. All teachers use Catalan or Basque at school but are, of course, Spanish speakers (Artigal 1993).

The analysis of discourse must attend to its location in a sociohistorical context.[5] In the U.S., foreign-language teaching is included at some stages of the educational system. At the same time, however, attitudes toward some languages are more negative than toward others, non-English languages do not enjoy the prestigious status of English, and many people oppose bilingual education. The latter tendencies have become manifest in the English Only movement, among others.[6]

---

[5] This a basic tenet of the current critical approach to discourse analysis. It is also implicit in past work in educational anthropology: Lutz (1983) describes the limitations of microethnography and supports the view that "the search for important and recurrent variables [...] must go beyond the narrow focus of a classroom or school" (1983: 29).

[6] Some have argued that language has become a banner used by right-wing groups because it is easier to enlist support for the "survival" of English than for banning foreigners.

The Official English movement rallied some public hostility against bilingual education on the basis of xenophobic fears of disintegration and a view of linguistic diversity only as a problem. For example, in March 1994, the Maryland Senate and House of Delegates passed a bill to make English the state's official language. Later, Gov. Donald Schaefer vetoed it. The measured had been supported by the group, English Inc., which has helped to enact similar proposals in nineteen states.

Prioritizing lower costs and fast mainstreaming are normally presented under the cover of concern for harmonious coexistence. For example, "A common language can only provide a better basis for understanding and tolerance" (Patricia Whitelaw-Hill, Institute for Research in English Acquisition and Development, as quoted in *The Washington Post*, November 10, 199, A24). The field observations made for this study as well as those reported by McCollum (1993) make it clear that, for U.S.-born and foreign-born Spanish-background children alike, English is already a common language shared with their English-background peers. Therefore, fears that immigrant children are not learning English in bilingual programs are completely unfounded. In response to a badly informed, critical article in the newspaper with the highest circulation in Washington, D.C., Eugene García, Director of the Office of Bilingual Education and Minority Languages Affairs, U.S. Department of Education, cites studies that show that bilingual education produces both high English language and content mastery (*The Washington Post*, November 10, 1994, A24). (See also Lindholm 1991.)

The aspects described at the language-economy level touch upon issues that are at the core of diversity in the population. Ethnographic observations show concrete ways in which situations outside schools are translated into practices of the social actors inside schools.

6.1. Minority-language background students. In the area of the schools observed, an increasing number of Spanish-background students and teachers do not use Spanish in the home environment. (This situation is likely to be very different in other areas in the U.S.) In the particular programs observed, for some students, their L1 is not necessarily their "home language." English may be the language chosen by the adults in the home, one parent may be an English-speaker, or the students' care-givers may be relatives who are long-term residents of the U.S. or older siblings who have lost fluency in Spanish. As a result, the concepts "school language" and "home language" are not so useful as descriptive terms to differentiate English and Spanish in the students' repertoire. The terms "majority language" and "minority language," denoting instead the relative status of languages and their speakers in the society, are more appropriate. Instruction that aims to achieve high levels of communicative competence in both languages cannot assume that students are already proficient in one. Both languages of immersion, then, need to be equally developed.

Spanish-background second graders mostly from low-income, poorly educated families at one school produced instances of interference from English. At the syntactic level, *El bebé silla quebró* mirrored "The baby's chair broke" as opposed to *La silla del bebé se quebró.*[7] At the morphological level, the English lack of gender marking was mirrored in one student's speech. This child said *gordo* (fat masc.) instead of *gorda* (fem.) in reference to a girl, and *frío* (cold masc.) instead of *fría* (cold fem.) in reference to *avena* (oatmeal), a feminine noun. A few students said *sentar* (sit down) which is reflexive in Spanish, instead of *sentarse.* As regards phonology, one student, for example, pronounced *tierra* with an aspirated /t/ and an approximant /r/, while another one pronounced /b/ as a stop where it is a fricative (in word-initial and intervocalic positions). The characteristics described here are significant because they are not expected in language development that occurs in a monolingual environment.

6.2. The minority language in the school. Teachers need to be supported in their efforts to keep up the non-English language of immersion. Indications that they need this support come from the written form of the minority language used at school, in this case, Spanish. Classroom posters seen in the sites visited often

---

[7] For more attested cases of this borrowed genitive construction, see Silva-Corvalán (1990, 1991).

had spelling mistakes. The hand-written class list provided by an immersion teacher at one school contained misspelled last names, with no accents or dieresis. This absence may not cause a difference in pronunciation, for example, in *Chavez* instead of *Chávez*, but in most cases, as in the names on that list, it does (for example, *Agüeda* /awéda/ vs. *Agueda* /agéda/, and *Mancía* /mansía/ vs. *Mancia* /mánsia/). Such inaccuracies in the spellings of students' names do not send a message of respect for the minority language.

The language spoken in the school also provides some examples of majority-language interference. A child's first name *Germán* /xermán/ was pronounced "German," even in the Spanish classes. Co-occurrences of some forms of address (for example, *Sra. López*) and the second-person-singular pronoun or verb form (*tú* or V + second-person-singular morpheme) were register-inconsistent since, calling people by their titles and last names is formal, while using the second-person-singular pronoun or verb form is informal.

In the Spanish section of the programs, some teachers are balanced or English-dominant bilinguals; others are simply native speakers of English with good commands of Spanish. However, in addition to the shortage of bilingual teachers and the increasing need for them (Freeman and Freeman 1993), schools are increasingly finding bilingual teachers who are second- or third-generation bilinguals. This suggests that schools need support to maintain standards of minority-language teaching.

7. Implications for instructional and institutional practice.
7.1. Implications at the conversational-exchange level. The central tenet of immersion programs is that the L2 not be treated exclusively as an academic subject, but as a medium of instruction and of social relations.

> in accordance with the idea that the L2 is learned by being used, [...] the basic goal of immersion programmes is to make the school into a "large and natural L2 use/acquisition context." (Artigal 1993: 34)

If we accept the premise that habitual use of an L2 in spontaneous, naturally occurring social contexts and events promotes the acquisition of the new language, we can conclude that the more varied the social contexts and events in which the student uses the second language, the richer the L2 repertoire he or she will develop.

Hence, it is important to facilitate the use of an L2 across frames and addressees. A school could become closer to a natural L2 context if the multiple layers of social encounters were exploited for their potential for L2 use.

Myers-Scotton (1989: 334) explains that the code that a speaker associates with a particular exchange becomes, for that speaker, the unmarked choice to index the expected interactional rights and obligations in that particular exchange.

> Through the weight of frequency a code becomes associated with encoding that [interpersonal] balance [...] Speakers abstract this [social] information through exposure to use. (Myers-Scotton 1989: 334)

Along these lines, the above-mentioned goal of immersion programs can be stated in the following terms: Get students to associate both languages of immersion with the interpersonal balance existing in multiple situations.

I propose that the variety of interactions that take place during the school day and the variety of exchanges within those interactions are a *resource* that must be made use of fully. Acquisition, maintenance, and development of the minority language would be strengthened by constantly encouraging students in all grades to use the minority language (during the corresponding times of the day) in unofficial interactions and for various frames within interactions.

The particular reality of the schools observed poses a paradox for sociolinguistic studies. It is often stated that through this kind of bilingual education the dichotomy "school language"/"home language" is broken in that the home language is given the status of a language fit for serious academic business, and it is valued as one of the languages of instruction. But for the population observed for this study, which differs greatly from those in other areas of the U.S., there is another danger: The minority language be restricted to academic business without extending to the management of social events, e.g. to the occasions when teachers switch to English to discipline children or give homework.

If the minutiae of verbal interaction and its importance in language learning go unheeded, the mere "weight of frequency" of use may make the majority language become permanently associated with ("unmarked" in) a wider range of interpersonal relations (e.g. peer as well as child–adult) and speech registers (e.g. informal conversation as well as classroom talk and formal announcements and ceremonies) than the range of interpersonal relations and speech registers the minority language is associated with.

In the observed programs, where languages are separated by time, teachers are aware of the importance of consistency and enforcement of the English-time and Spanish-time rules and achieve it to different degrees in their classrooms, according to the specific contingencies they have to deal with. In addition, teachers correctly accept codeswitching by the students. However, their efforts to achieve functional proficiency in both languages can be enhanced with strategies to manipulate the mechanics of verbal interaction. Teachers can foster minority-language use in every frame by modelling immediately after the separation-by-time violation to show students how to express what they have said in English in Spanish, allowing time for the student to repeat and, finally, proceeding to make the next interactional move. This will provide the minority-language form that is appropriate for the current frame. The net result will be that more minority-language forms will be available for the performance of language functions in an increased range of frames.

7.2. Implications at the speech-event level. One major implication of the observations at the speech-event level is the advantage of giving feedback on both content and language primarily because it draws attention to, and thereby stimulates, the acquisition of the language being used, which is always an L2 for fifty percent of the class. In addition, in the case of the minority language, it sends the message that the language is important and valued.

There is also another important aspect to this "focus on form" (Long 1990). English-section teachers should be very sensitive to the comprehension needs of the Spanish-background half of the class. Since we acquire languages only by receiving comprehensible input (Krashen 1985), the benefit of mere exposure is lost if the child cannot process what she/he cannot understand. As Snow has noted:

> Effective immersion teachers often use teacher talk, modifying their input to make it more comprehensible. They may talk at a slower rate of speech and attempt clearer enunciation. In the early years, they may purposefully use shorter, less complex sentences and recycle their vocabulary as much as possible. (Snow 1989: 41)

A further point at the level of the lesson questions the need for rigid turn-taking rules. Students' self-selection to speak is not necessarily disruptive. It often confirms the interactional frame established by the teacher. In addition, it is an opportunity to check the child's language-proficiency level in spontaneous, voluntary conversational contributions.

7.3. Implications at the language-economy level. The majority of the Spanish-background students in the middle-school program observed by McCollum (1993) used English during classroom instruction and in social interactions. The values of the school were reproduced within peer-group culture where students gained status and popularity by speaking English. McCollum warns of the danger that structural features, such as the misuse of minority languages, may become cultural features internalized by the peer group and eventually have very deleterious effects on the maintenance of the minority language and culture.

Expanding English-background students' repertoire of applications of Spanish to various frames, and expanding Spanish-background students' association of Spanish with peer culture and popularity are feasible objectives.

For both groups, Spanish should not be the language for some lessons, but the language of the "real" business of everyday school organization, rules, and communication with staff about all matters. Only by acknowledging the power of institutional practices can we make them serve the goal of valuing all students' cultural capital.

The programs observed differ in the importance given to the two-way immersion program within the school, the regard for and attention to those involved with the program, and the involvement of ethnic community members in decision-making positions. The difference is even greater in the proportion of administrative staff that can understand Spanish. Inevitably, these institutional aspects have consequences for the position granted to the minority language and may eventually have consequences for minority-language use, since attitude-forming practices affect future language choice and maintenance.[8]

For the English section of the program, teachers with a knowledge of the non-English language of immersion are a most valuable asset. In the early grades, with English teachers who have learned Spanish, minority-language students can express themselves in their L1 and be understood. The teacher can acknowledge what the student has communicated and respond in English, thus maintaining the consistent separation of languages (by teacher and by time of day, i.e. Spanish time vs. English time). Furthermore, teachers who have themselves gone through the process of learning a second language are sensitive to the difficulties posed to the learner by features such as rapid rate of delivery or careless articulation. They also are sensitive to opportunities for vocabulary expansion using, in addition to usual vocabulary-teaching techniques, other techniques specific for second-language teaching to exploit similarities between the two languages, point out differences, contrast meanings, or show derivations, compounds and collocations. In sum, teachers for the English section of the program who have second-language-learning experience are in a position to predict what areas of language structure need to be simplified, and at what point, to ensure comprehension by L2 learners. Such teachers will know what structural contrasts are relevant and will make them salient, thus facilitating students' awareness of form in both languages.

For the Spanish section of the programs, two essential elements must be made available: reading materials for teachers as well as for students, and teacher-training courses on Spanish language, not just on teaching methodology. Thus teachers and students will able to keep up or improve their Spanish, and compensate somewhat the absence of a "native" context.

---

[8] Maintenance of Spanish proficiency among middle-school children has been found to be principally associated with students' attitudes towards bilingualism (Villar, Aguilar, and McLaughlin 1994).

8. Closing remarks. Because learning a second language takes more time than is commonly realized, emphasis on conversational proficiency as well as academic proficiency should continue into the higher grades. For those from the minority-language background, we need to provide opportunities to *continue* to acquire a repertoire of linguistic styles appropriate for various occasions, along with complex grammatical structures, vocabulary, and literacy. To cite Snow again:

> students need to learn the functional language they need for "managing" communication and miscommunication. [...] Helping students *extend* and *refine* their communication skills is the third role of the immersion teacher. [...] immersion students need to be "pushed" to produce comprehensible output throughout *all* levels of instruction. Only through extended opportunities to use the language productively will immersion students continue to grow linguistically across all skill areas. (Snow 1989: 43–44, emphasis mine)

Two-way immersion programs should be strengthened because they are an effective way for children to learn a second language and appreciate the richness of linguistic diversity, and because the educational system benefits by helping all students maintain their bilingualism through high school, instead of having to learn a "foreign" language later in their academic or professional lives.

Bilingual citizens are a valuable national resource. More and more jobs require proficiency in languages other than English; those who already know two languages should be allowed to develop and refine both, to compete in tomorrow's labor market. Teacher education should include awareness of issues like this, since, as we have seen, macrolevel institutional and societal forces influence microlevel social interaction.[9]

Awareness of these issues should also orient research efforts so that research-based proposals serve the communities in which the research is conducted. Reflecting on the usefulness of sociolinguistic research, Mehan reminds us:

> If it can be said that schooling facilitates mobility or reproduces the existing status and class arrangements in society, then sociolinguistic studies are important for showing *how* these activities are carried out. (Mehan 1987)

---

[9] Zeichner (1993) also argues in favor of raising teacher trainees' awareness of these social issues.

To paraphrase Mehan, classroom and school discourse have the potential to facilitate social change, and discourse studies can make contributions to that enterprise.

REFERENCES

Artigal, Josep. 1993. "Catalan and Basque immersion programmes." In Hugo Baetens Beardsmore, (ed.). *European models of bilingual education*. Clevedon, U.K.: Multilingual Matters.
Bateson, Gregory. 1972. *Steps to an ecology of mind*. New York: Chandler.
Baecher, Richard E. and Charles D. Coletti. 1986. "Two-way bilingual programs: Implementation of an educational innovation." *SABE Journal* 2(1).
Baecher, Richard E. 1991. "Language learning for success: The promise and practice of two-way bilingual programs." In Angela L. Carrasquillo (ed.), *Bilingual education: Using languages for success*. New York: New York State Association for Bilingual Education.
Bean, Martha. 1994. "Language choice among Spanish-English bilingual learners." Presentation at the American Association for Applied Linguistics Annual Meeting. Baltimore, Maryland.
Christian, Donna. 1991. "Two-way bilingual education: English plus for students." *EPIC Events* 4(5): 1–2.
Christian, Donna. 1992. "The other program down the hall: A call for cooperation among language educators." *NABE News* (November, 1992): 6–7.
Christian, Donna. 1994. *Two-way bilingual education: Students learning through two languages*. Educational Practice Report No 12. Santa Cruz, California: National Center for Research on Cultural Diversity and Second Language Learning.
Christian, Donna and Cindy Mahrer. 1992. *Two-way bilingual programs in the U.S. 1991–92*. Washington, D.C.: National Center for Research on Cultural Diversity and Second Language Learning.
Christian, Donna and Cindy Mahrer. 1993. *Two-way bilingual programs in the U.S. 1991–92*. Washington, D.C.: National Center for Research on Cultural Diversity and Second Language Learning.
Christian, Donna and Chris Montone. 1994. *Two-way bilingual programs in the U.S. 1991–92*. Washington, D.C.: National Center for Research on Cultural Diversity and Second Language Learning.
Christian, Donna, Isolda Carranza, and Chris Montone. (forthcoming). "Two-way bilingual education: Theory and practice." In *Teaching for success: Reforming schools for children from culturally and linguistically diverse backgrounds*. Washington, D.C.: National Center for Cultural Diversity and Second Language Learning.
Freeman, David and Yvonne Freeman. 1993. "Strategies for promoting the primary languages of all students." *The Reading Teacher* 46(7): 552–558.
Genesee, Fred. 1985. "Second language learning through immersion: A review of U.S. programs." *Review of Educational Research* 55(4): 541–561.
Genesee, Fred. 1987. *Learning through two languages: Studies of immersion and bilingual education*. Cambridge, Massachusetts: Newbury House.
Goffman, Erving. 1974. *Frame analysis: An essay on the organization of experience*. New York: Harper and Row.
Krashen, Stephen. 1985. *The Input Hypothesis: Issues and implications*. London: Longman.
Lindholm, Kathryn. 1990. "Bilingual immersion education: Criteria for program development." In Amado M. Padilla, Hatford H. Fairchild, and Concepión M. Valadez (eds.), *Bilingual education: Issues and strategies*. Newbury Park, California and London: Sage.

Lindholm, Kathryn J. 1991. "Theoretical assumptions and empirical evidence for academic achievement in two languages." *Hispanic Journal of Behavioral Science* 13: 3–17.

Lindholm, Kathryn J. 1992. "Two-way bilingual education: Theory, conceptual issues and pedagogical implications." In R. V. Padilla and A. Benavides (eds.), *Critical perspectives on bilingual education research*. Tucson, Arizona: Bilingual Review.

Long, Michael. 1991. "Focus on form: a design feature in language teaching methodology." In Kees de Bot, D. Coste, Claire Kramsch, and R. Ginsberg (eds.), *Foreign language research in crosscultural perspective*. Amsterdam and Philadelphia: John Benjamins.

Lutz, Frank W. 1981. "Ethnography—The holistic approach to understanding schooling." In Judith L. Green and Cynthia Wallat (eds.), *Ethnography and language of educational settings*. Norwood, N.J.: Ablex.

McCollum, Pamela A. 1993. "Learning to value English: Cultural capital in a two-way bilingual program." Paper presented at the American Educational Researchers Association Annual meeting, Atlanta, Georgia.

Mc Houl, Alexander. 1978. "The organization of turns at formal talk in the classroom." *Language in Society* 7: 183–213.

McLaughlin, Barry. 1994. "Linguistic, psychological and contextual factors in language shift." *Linguistic Minority Research Iinstitute Report* 3(4): 1–3.

Mehan, Hugh. 1979. *Learning lessons*. Cambridge, Massachusetts: Harvard University Press.

Mehan, Hugh. 1985. "The structure of classroom discourse." In Teun van Dijk (ed.), *Handbook of discourse analysis. Volume 3: Discourse and dialogue*. New York: Academic Press.

Mehan, Hugh. 1987. "Language and schooling." In George Spindler and Louise Spindler (eds.), *Interpretive ethnography of education: At home and abroad*. London: Lawrence Erlbaum Associates, Publishers.

Myers-Scotton, Carol. 1989. "Code-switching with English: Types of switching, types of communities." *World Englishes* 8(3): 333–346.

Myers-Scotton, Carol. 1993. "Common and uncommon ground: Social and structural factors in codeswitching." *Language in Society* 22: 475–503.

Salinas Sosa, Alicia. 1992. "Bilingual Education—Heading into the 1990s." *The Journal of Educational Issues of Language Minority Students* 10: 203–216.

Shuy, Roger. 1988. "Identifying Dimensions of Classroom Language." In Judith Green and Judith Harker (eds.), *Multiple perspective analyses of classroom discourse*. Norwood, N.J.: Ablex.

Silva-Corvalán, Carmen. 1990. "Current issues in studies of language contact" *Hispania* 73: 162–176.

Silva-Corvalán, Carmen. 1991. "Lexico-syntactic modeling across the bilingual continuum." Presentation at NWAVE annual meeting, Georgetown University, Washington, D.C.

Snow, Marguerite Ann. 1989. *Negotiation of meaning: Teacher's activity manual*. Rockville, Maryland: Division of Academic Skills, Office of Instruction and Program Development, Montgomery County Public Schools.

Swain, Merrill and Sharon Lapkin. 1983. *Evaluating bilingual education: A Canadian case study*. Clevedon, U.K.: Multilingual Matters.

van Dijk, Teun. 1993. "Principles of critical discourse analysis." *Discourse and Society* 4(2): 249–283.

van Dijk, Teun. 1994. Editorial. *Discourse and Society* 5(4): 435–436.

Villar, Anthony, Edward Aguilar, and Barry McLaughlin. 1994. *Language choice, use and attitudes: The Pájaro Middle School study*. Linguistic Minority Research Institute Research Report. Santa Barbara: Linguistics Minority Research Institute, University of California.

The Washington Post. November 10, 1994. Letters to the Editor. A24.

Zeichner, Kenneth. 1993. "Educating teachers for cultural diversity." *NCRTL Special Report*. East Langsing, Michigan: National Center for Research on Teacher Learning.

Using native speech
to formulate past-tense rules in French

Nadine O'Connor Di Vito
University of Chicago

1. Introduction. Few, if any, French grammar points are more difficult to describe, teach, or acquire than the functional distinctions between the *passé composé* (PC) and the *imparfait* (IMP) (Bourgeacq 1969, Conner 1992, Dansereau 1987). Although one might assume that degree of exposure to these past tenses is in some way related to one's success in acquiring them, some researchers have suggested that there is actually no correlation between the number of years of formal study of French and one's ability to appropriately use the PC and IMP (Conner 1992). Thus, not suprisingly, even at the very advanced levels of study, French teachers typically are required to devote a considerable amount of time reviewing PC and IMP rules of use. Confronted with this state of affairs, one must begin to wonder if the problem is not the feebleness of language learner's brains but rather our characterization of past-tense use in French. How accurate are contemporary descriptions of the PC and the IMP, which have changed little over the past few hundred years? And where does the *passé simple* (PS) fit into the picture? Is this tense, as some would claim (Barthes 1965), a mere remnant from the past which is no longer productive and, consequently, worth little consideration in the foreign-language classroom?

2. The corpus. This paper reports preliminary findings of French native speaker use of the PC, PS, and IMP in a spoken and written corpus of 53,265 clauses; the final version of this study will appear in the book *Linguistic patterns across spoken and written French: Empirical research, linguistic theory, and pedagogy* to be published by D.C. Heath. The spoken corpus for this study consists of television news broadcasts, academic presentations, televised interviews with renowned French intellectuals, and taped conversations between university-educated, native-speaker French teachers. The written corpus consists of excerpts from literary prose and plays from the eighteenth to the twentieth century, folklore, detective novels, travel guides, magazines, and formal correspondence. Thus the speech in this corpus represents a wide variety of the spoken and written genres which constitute the linguistic life of typical, university-educated native French speakers. These are types of discourse, therefore, which even the most conservative French teacher would view as part of a language learner's acquisitional goals and which should be targeted in the French language classroom.

3. Traditional explanations of uses of the PC, PS, and IMP. Numerous prescriptive grammars and theoretical studies of French indicate that the primary difference between the PC and the IMP is temporal specificity. The PC is said to highlight the beginning or end of an event or condition, a change in state, or the fact that some past event or condition is completed. The IMP, on the other hand, is typically said to describe a past action in progress, a habitual or repeated past action, and a past action or condition which lacks explicit temporal boundaries (Abrate 1983, Dansereau 1987, Terry 1986). Often mentioned is the correspondence between the IMP and the English past progressive and expression "used to." In keeping with these distinctions, many French-language textbooks often present lists of verbs and adverbs which one might associate with either the IMP or the PC because of their inherent semantic quality (Figure 1).

Figure 1. Lexical elements commonly considered linked to use of the IMP or PC

	Verb	Adverb
IMP	*être* (to be)	*souvent* (often)
	penser (to think)	*d'habitude* (generally)
PC	*commencer* (to begin)	*soudain* (suddenly)
	dire (say)	*puis* (then)

Thus stative verbs, verbs of thinking and feeling, and adverbs like *souvent* (often) and *d'habitude* (generally) are typically presented as triggers for use of the IMP, while more dynamic verbs and adverbs such as *soudain* (suddenly) and *puis* (then, next) are typically presented as triggers for use of the PC. Finally, of the textbooks which present the PS in any detail, most indicate little more than its use as a purely literary tense, overlooking the possible interplay between the PC and the PS in such texts and, perhaps even more importantly, how one defines "literary text" and in which types of literary texts the PS is found. Such, then, are the traditional explanations of past-tense use presented in prescriptive French grammars. The following empirical study of native-speaker use of the PC, PS, and IMP will evaluate the descriptive accuracy and explanatory power of these explanations.

4. Analysis of native speaker use of the PC, PS, and IMP.

General tense frequencies. In examining the 63,265-clause database, one is first struck by the overall frequency of PC, PS, and IMP forms (Table 1). There are 18,360 occurrences of these three tenses, or 19% of the spoken corpus and 43% of the written corpus. In individual written text samples, the percentage of past-tense forms borders on the incredible; for example, these three tenses comprise 91% of the 1,045 clauses examined in Flaubert's *La légende de St. Julien hospitalier* and 69% of the 1,410 clauses examined in Zola's *Attaque du moulin.*

Table 1. Relative frequency of IMP, PC, and PS.

	IMP	PC	PS	N/Total N	%
SPOKEN DATA					
Conversations	53%	47%	0%	484/3,045	16%
Conferences	43%	57%	0%	564/4,050	14%
Interviews	41%	59%	0%	1,432/7,601	19%
News Broadcasts	32%	68%	.5%	402/1,540	26%
WRITTEN DATA					
20th C. Prose	65%	10%	25%	4,130/7,960	52%
19th C. Prose	55%	4%	41%	5,036/7,970	63%
Detective Novels	58%	7%	35%	1,613/2,564	63%
18th C. Prose	47%	13%	42%	1,819/5,059	36%
Magazines	37%	61%	3%	327/1,661	20%
Theater (18th-20th C.)	35%	63%	3%	1,072/7,543	14%
Folklore	33%	9%	58%	1,431/2,662	54%
Travel Guides	32%	61%	7%	226/1,084	21%
Correspondence	17%	83%	0%	94/526	18%

In general, these past tenses are more frequent in prose than in theater texts, which we will find to be in many ways more similar to the spoken texts than to the discourse found in either literary or nonliterary prose fiction.

With respect to the relative frequency of different tenses within genres, immediately noticeable is the relative absence of the PS in all spoken genres as well as in the magazine, travel guide, and theater discourse. On the other hand, the PS is more frequent than the PC in several of the written texts, including detective novels, folklore, and some of the literary prose texts (Flaubert's *La légend de St. Julien hospitalier* again is noteworthy in that there was not one example of the PC in this third-person-narrative-fiction excerpt). In other words, the division between use of the PS and use of the PC does not seem to be based in a traditional literary-nonliterary distinction, since the PS is very infrequent in some of the literary prose, such as *Jacques le fataliste* by Rousseau, and *Le désert* by Le Clézio, as well as in all of the theater texts. The theatrical pieces by Beaumarchais, Marivaux, Vigny, Musset, Giraudoux, and Claudel are, of course, typically considered model examples of fine French literature despite the fact that they contain primarily PC forms rather than PS forms. On the other hand, the PS is frequently used in such popular prose as detective novels and folklore.

In sum, given the distribution of PS and PC forms, the division appears to be less a question of whether a work is literary or nonliterary and more a question of whether the text could be characterized as third-person-narrative fiction (or *récit*) or first-person prose (or *discours*). Of course, many researchers have suggested that the PS is primarily a third-person tense, restricted to the domain of the narrative, or *récit*. Examination of tense distribution with respect to person and number is, however, necessary to support or reject this hypothesis.

Frequency and distribution of person and number across past tenses. A look solely at third-person use of these three tenses, however, evidences a more complex picture of tense use than is typically indicated in descriptive or prescriptive grammars (Table 2). First of all, it is clear that genre is as much a factor in number and person frequencies as tense type. In travel guides and magazines, for example, not only third-person PS forms but also third-person PC and IMP forms are virtually the only forms found. As for the spoken genres, third-person forms also predominate in the two noninteractive discourse types: news broadcasts and conference speech. This is not surprising, of course, given the emphasis placed on objectivity in these particular genres.

In written genres such as folklore and literary prose, third-person forms predominate in both the PS and IMP, with much lower frequencies in PC forms. In these texts, PC forms are typically restricted to personal dialogic exchanges between characters.

Finally, in detective novels and theater, third-person forms are frequent but are certainly not exclusively used. Use of the PS in these data, therefore, appears to be not just the mark of a third-person narrative, but also a way to fictionalize a first-person recounting or to create psychological distance between the reader and the text. As for third-person tense links, perhaps surprisingly, the data suggest some association between the IMP and third-person forms; in some genres, such as detective novels, this link appears even stronger than the PS–third-person association.

A closer examination of IMP forms in detective novels and other prose indicates their frequent use in relative-clause constructions, as in example (1). Such constructions often serve to elaborate on particular characteristics of people, places, and things central to the story. In many cases, stative verbs (such as *être*) are used to convey this supplementary descriptive information, which suggests that the semantic nature of the verbs and other lexical items may play some role in determining tense choice.

(1) *Il connaissait toutes les étoiles, il leur donnait parfois des noms étranges, **qui étaient comme des commencements d'histoires**.*
He knew all the stars, he sometimes gave them strange names, **which were like beginnings of stories.**

Frequency of lexical triggers for particular past tenses. As indicated previously, many prescriptive grammars suggest that certain types of verbs and adverbs trigger use of the IMP and the PC. Stative verbs and verbs of thinking and believing are typically linked to use of the IMP, while the more dynamic verbs are linked to use of the PC. In the same way, adverbs such as *soudain* (all of a sudden) or *tout de suite* (immediately) are often presented as triggers for the PC while the adverbs *souvent* (often) and *d'habitude* (generally) signal use of the IMP.

Examination of the tenses used with various types of verbs and adverbs does not, however, resoundingly support this semantically-based lexical-trigger hypothesis. If one looks at the degree to which some very common non-momentary verbs (*être* = to be, *avoir* = to have, *penser* = to think, *aimer* = to like/love, *connaître* = to know) appear in the IMP, the percentages vary tremendously across particular verbs and discourse types (Spoken data: 33%-100%; Written data: 0%-100%). As for common momentary verbs (*commencer* = to begin, *demander* = to ask, *entrer* = to enter, *dire* = to say), use in the PC or PS is also far from categorical in many genres (Spoken data: 0%-100%; Written data: 29%-100%).

Some researchers have suggested that one should think of these verb-tense associations not as necessarily categorical rules but rather as "tendencies" which can be overridden by the existence of particular elements in the discourse,

Table 3. Relationships between adverbs and past-tense use.

	souvent		puis		avant/après	
	%IMP	N =	%PC/PS	N =	%PC/PS	N =
SPOKEN DATA	57%	7	72%	18	48%	23
WRITTEN DATA	60%	40	75%	132	67%	149

termed as "contrary indications" by Abrate (1983:549). Such a hypothesis could explain, for example, the use of the PC with the verb *avoir* in (2).

(2) *Soudain, j'ai eu peur.*
Suddenly, I **became** afraid.

Although one might expect the stative verb *avoir* to be conjugated in the IMP, one could argue that the presence of the adverb *soudain* serves to counteract the semantic nature of the verb and to prompt use of the PC. Examination of a few of the most common of these adverbs demonstrates to what extent these anecdotal, intuitive examples of tense–lexical-trigger links are empirically justified (Table 3). While there is some evidence of a link between *puis* and the PC or PS, there is little to suggest that *souvent* in some way triggers use of the IMP or that the presence of *avant* or *après* guarantees use of the PC or PS.

Finally, what is a language learner to do with these frequencies when deciding when to use a particular past tense? The inconsistent patterns seen in the association of tense with these verbs and adverbs only confirm the inadequacy of a sentence-level approach to understanding past-tense use in French. The reason why one cannot count on these lexical prompts to determine which tense is appropriate is that the temporal and aspectual nuances created by particular tenses primarily operate on the discourse level rather than on the sentence level.

5. The IMP in spoken and written French discourse.
There is reason to believe that the IMP, long considered associated with temporal indefiniteness, has been expanding its domains of use over the centuries to include a wide variety of discourse contexts in which temporal or chronological fuzziness is desired. As functions of the PS rapidly disintegrated in the sixteenth and seventeenth centuries, temporal distinctions became increasingly less clear between the PC and the IMP. As early as the nineteenth century, grammarians had begun to bemoan the fact that the IMP and the historical present were commonly found in traditionally PC/PS contexts. These

and other "nontraditional" uses of the IMP (i.e., uses which contradict the standard rule) have become so numerous that what we now find in many descriptive grammars is a traditional explanation for IMP use followed by a lengthy list of "special functions" or exceptions to the rule. Many of these nontraditional functions are found in discourse contexts in which narrative recountings are quite common and often involve story elaborations or even stories within stories. While some well-developed spoken narratives contain such features, these types of narratives are more frequent in written prose, both literary and nonliterary. Therefore, let us turn now to some examples of non-traditional uses of the IMP in order to formulate a more descriptively accurate characterization of the IMP, PC, and PS.

In (3) we see the protagonist of a detective novel, lost in reverie in a bar. As events unfold around him, he sits in a daze. The author even states explicitly that time has stopped. The way in which these chronologically-ordered events are portrayed as frozen in time is through their representation in the IMP. Use of the IMP here cannot be said to indicate temporal indefiniteness at the sentence level but, rather, atemporality within the larger narrative context.

(3) *Timar avait-il déjà bu toute une bouteille? On la lui changeait. On remplissait son verre. Il apercevait une partie de la cuisine et, à ce moment précis, la patronne frappait de son poing fermé le visage de Thomas...Un temps d'arrêt. Un coup d'oeil. Une phrase: «Qu' attends-tu pour faire danser la femme de ton patron?» Il suivit la direction du menton et vit une grosse ménagère en robe rose, à côté du gérant de la Sacova.*

Had Timar already drunk a whole bottle? He was given a new one/new ones. His glass was filled up/kept being filled up again. He noticed/could see a part of the kitchen and, at that precise moment, the proprietor struck/was striking Thomas's face with her closed fist...Time stopped. A blink of an eye. A sentence: "What are you waiting for? You should invite your boss's wife to dance!" He followed the direction of her chin and saw a fat housewife in a pink dress, next to the manager of the Sacova. (Detective Novels: Simenon: 18–19)

This narrative atemporality is also evident in (4), where the main protagonist of a twentieth-century literary novel, in the midst of his travel across the desert, stops at a tomb to pray. Again, a series of events unfold while Nour is at the tomb, but since this whole episode is a narrative detour, all of the events are recounted in the IMP.

(4) *C'était comme si le monde s'était arrêté de bouger et de parler, s'était transformé en pierre...« Je suis venu », disait l'homme à genoux sur la*

*terre battue...Il se penchait en avant, **prenait de la poussière rouge
dans le creux de ses mains et la laissait couler sur son visage, sur son
front, sur ses paupières, sur ses lèvres...** Puis il se **levait et marchait**
jusqu'à la porte...**Puis, quand tout fut fini, l'homme se releva
lentement et fit sortir son fils.***

It was as if the world had stopped moving and speaking, had been
transformed into stone... "I have come," the man kneeling on the
beaten earth was saying...He leaned forward, took red dust in the
hollow of his hands and let it run over his face, over his forehead, over
his eyelids, over his lips...Then he got up and walked over to the
door...Then, when everything was finished, the man got up slowly and
led his son out. (Twentieth Century Prose: Le Clézio: 13–14)

Examples abound in the database which illustrate use of the IMP in contexts
traditionally requiring the PC or PS. The unifying characteristic of these
examples is that they are events which are meant to be understood as outside of
the main development of the story line. Thus, while perhaps temporally-bounded
and chronologically-ordered, these events recounted in the IMP are presented as
background information. Such backgrounded events are not necessarily self-
contained subnarratives. They can be as few as one or two clauses long, such
as in (5).

(5) *ETIENNE posa la valise dans le vestibule, ouvrit la porte de la salle à
manger et dit: « Je t'ai préparé un petit souper froid, à tout hasard.»
« Je te remercie, mon chéri, dit Marion. Mais je n'ai pas faim. J'ai
déjà mangé dans le wagon-restaurant.»
Debout devant la glace de l'entrée, elle **retirait** son chapeau, ses gants,
ébouriffait ses cheveux sur ses tempes. Une douce lassitude marquait
son visage. Elle paraissait heureuse et rompue.
« Que c'est bon de se retrouver chez soi!» dit-elle encore, en étirant ses
bras devant elle.*

Etienne placed the suitcase in the vestibule, opened the door of the
dining room, and said: " I prepared a little cold dinner snack for you,
just in case."
"Thank you, my dear," said Marion. "But I'm not hungry. I already
ate in the dining car of the train."
Standing in front of the entrance mirror, she took off her hat, her
gloves, ruffled her hair over her temples. Soft lassitude lined her face.
She seemed happy and tired.
"How good to be back home!" she said again, stretching her arms in
front of her. (Twentieth Century Prose: Troyat: 44)

In these and numerous other instances, the IMP serves to indicate temporal indefiniteness at the discourse level as opposed to the PC or PS, which advance the development of the main narrative. Thus even if the traditional IMP and PC rules, which distinguish the two tenses by their temporal specificity at the sentence level, work in certain limited examples, it is clear that the primary distinction between the IMP and the PC is that the IMP serves to background events or conditions by emphasizing their imprecise temporal nature or by merely setting them against other events represented by the PC or IMP. On the other hand the PC and PS foreground events or conditions, making them possible stages in the advancement of past narrative. Finally, distinctions between the PC and the PS have also evolved from sentence-level aspectual and temporal differences to differences in use at the discourse level, with the PS now signalling the fictionalization of first-person as well as third-person narratives and creating not just temporal distance but also psychological distance between the reader and the text.

6. Conclusion. In conclusion, these data demonstrate that there is no lexical or grammatical formula which defines use of the IMP, PC, and PS. Tense use depends on whether one is talking about the spoken or the written language, on the nature of the genre, and on the nature and function of the clause with respect to the larger discourse context. Granted, such an explanation of past-tense use is less clear-cut than lists of temporal and aspectual rules and lexical triggers. But then again, talking about the PC and PS as different types of techniques to foreground events and advance the storyline, and talking about the IMP as a means to background events and expand on various aspects of the story without moving it along is really nothing more than a question of perspective.

REFERENCES

Abrate, Jayne. 1983. "An approach to teaching the past tenses in French." *The French Review* 56(4): 546–553.
Barthes, Roland. 1965. *Le degré zéro d'écriture*. Paris: Gonthier.
Bourgeacq, Jacques A. 1969. "L'Emploi de quelques temps du passé: Une méthode." *The French Review* 42(6): 874–881.
Conner, M. 1992. "A Processing strategy using visual representation to convey the *passé composé/imparfait* distinction in French." *International Review of Applied Linguistics* 30: 321–328.
Dansereau, Diane. 1987. "A Discussion of techniques used in the teaching of the *passé composé/imparfait* distinction in French." *The French Review* 61(1): 33–38.
Di Vito, Nadine O'Connor. (In press). *Patterns across spoken and written French: The interaction among forms, functions and genres*. Lexington, Massachussettes: DC Heath.

Flaubert, Gustave. 1965. "La légende de St. Julien Hospitalier." In J. D. Gunthier, and S. J. and L. A. M. Sumberg (eds.), *Les grandes scrivains Français*. New York: Holt, Rinehart, and Winston. 604–618.

Le Clézio, Jean Marie Gustave. 1980. *Le désert*. Paris: Gallimard.

Rousseau, Jean-Jacques. 1966. *Emile ou de l'éducation*. Paris: Garnier-Flammarion.

Simenon, Georges. 1960. *Le coup de lune*. Paris: A. Fayard.

Terry, Robert. 1986. *Let Cinderella and Luke Skywalker help you teach the passé composé and imperfect*. Hastings-on-Hudson, N.Y.: ACTFL Materials Center.

Troyat, Henri. 1951. *La tête sur les épaules*. Paris: Plon.

Discourse analysis of classroom interaction and the training of classroom teachers

Caroline M. El-Kadi
Old Dominion University

Introduction. In the often hectic environment of the typical ESL program, experienced teachers and student teachers alike rarely have time to examine their own or others' teaching with a view to reflecting on the effectiveness of teaching methods and practices. In contrast, one of the main emphases of many linguists working at the discourse level has been the examination of classroom interaction. Much of the research into discourse structure has been conducted in classrooms because classrooms have such well-defined boundaries and easily defined "rules"; that is, classroom discourse is in general much neater and thus easier to examine and segment than the largely indefinable discourse of everyday life. The easily definable limits of the classroom provide a useful "laboratory" for research into the often difficult-to-define elements of language above the sentence level. The systems that have arisen out of such research are ways of defining what is going on at the discourse level, as well as ways of setting parameters and establishing rules of discourse similar to the rules of syntax.

The primary impetus for most of these systems has not been to provide help to the practitioner but rather to reach a deeper theoretical understanding of language at the discourse level. But since the language of the classroom is so integral to the primary aim of the ESL teacher, deeper insight into how interaction between the teacher and the students works is likely to be of great utility in teacher enrichment, to both beginning and experienced teachers. If these systems of analysis developed by linguists illuminate aspects of classroom interaction similar to those focused on by experienced ESL practitioners, then at least the systems could be used in teacher-training programs as a means of focusing novice teachers' attention on pertinent aspects of the language in the classroom.

Although classroom observation has long been regarded as a useful tool in teacher training, one of its drawbacks is that inexperienced teachers do not necessarily know what they are looking at or looking for. It would be short-sighted to believe that any one system of linguistic analysis shows the "reality" of the classroom, whatever that is. However, the descriptive systems devised by discourse analysts are undoubtedly less biased and more fruitful than coding systems or checklists that ask observers to concentrate on predetermined criteria such as "speaks clearly and distinctly" or "uses illustrations effectively."

To investigate the feasibility of using such systems for pedagogical purposes, I conducted an ethnographic study in an urban university that has both an intensive ESL program and a graduate program for training new ESL teachers (El-Kadi 1994). In an article called "Ethnography in ESL: Defining the essentials," Watson-Gegeo discusses how qualitative research in the ESL classroom can "directly serve practice" (1988: 587). As she says, ethnographic techniques can be used for feedback "whether in initial teacher training or in staff development" (Watson-Gegeo 1988: 588). Through ethnographic studies, "teachers can gain new awareness of classroom organization, teaching and learning strategies, and interactional patterns in their own classrooms." A combination of "intensive ethnographic research" and teachers' "ethnographic observations of their own practice" can help produce a "multilevel understanding of good teaching" (Watson-Gegeo 1988: 588).

I gathered classroom data by audio– and videotaping one teacher's classroom in a seven-week advanced speaking/listening course that met three times weekly. I recorded and transcribed twelve hours of data, capturing a broad range of teacher-student and student-student interaction. I then gathered reactions on a selection of the transcripts and videos from the teacher himself and from two student teachers. Finally, I analyzed segments of the transcripts using methods devised by discourse analysts. I compared the results of my analyses to the observations of the experienced and novice teachers.

To varying degrees, I found that the linguistic analyses did indeed illuminate the discourse in ways which could prove fruitful for helping novice teachers see pertinent elements in the classroom more clearly. I also found that the research experience as a whole was a valuable one. The data gathering, the close observation of the classroom discourse, and particularly the detailed and yet wide-ranging discussions with the teacher of the class demonstrated the intrinsic value of action research and teacher-researcher collaboration.

Recording the classroom discourse. Transcribing the data was both time-consuming and tedious. Those who have made transcripts know this; those who have not, however linguistically sophisticated they may be, have no idea what problems arise. It is important to point this out because so many research studies suggest that teachers can or should collect their own data and observe or analyze their own or others' teaching. Transcribing recorded speech, particularly of non-native speakers, is an enormously slow process. Numerous decisions must be made, such as degree of detail to be included, where sentence breaks and line breaks should appear, and whether and where pauses should be inserted. Transcribing thus involved an expenditure of time and effort that is unlikely to be readily available to those working in a typical ESL program. It also required a wide familiarity with ESL and linguistics, which suggests that it was not a task that could not have been done satisfactorily by an inexperienced clerical worker or a student. And yet the process was a valuable one. I concluded that, in spite of the difficulties, the process of data collection leads to useful insights. Like the deconstruction of a text, it enables the researcher to understand the whole better once it is put back together again.

When the transcripts were ready, I gave them to the teacher (Roger), along with some of the videos, and he made extensive written comments. He and I then embarked on a series of free-ranging discussions about what the videos and transcripts showed and to what extent they illuminated his overall goals and specific teaching techniques. I then worked with two students in the TESOL program, one (Kate) a woman in her late forties with no teaching experience at all, and the other (Chris) a much younger woman who had just completed a TESOL methods class and had done some tutoring. They examined one of the transcripts in detail and watched parts of two of the videos, while I took notes on their reactions and discussed with them what they felt was happening in the classroom.

Analyzing the observers' insights. Roger's reactions overall were noticeably different from those of the two student teachers. The experience that Roger brought to the classroom enabled him to "see" in a way that was quite different from the "seeing" of the novices. He used the transcripts to get a composite picture of the classroom, noting the overall flow of the classes rather than specific segments. He saw the class as a social event, as a community, and every piece of it was integral to the whole. Moreover, Roger viewed the record of his teaching both as a broad overview of his teaching style and as a way of zeroing in on specific segments of the interaction that demonstrated particular techniques or propensities. He noted the flow of classes and the means he used to ensure that his classes were always student centered, for instance in topic shifting, questioning techniques, and the amount of teacher talk versus student talk. Finally, he also noted episodes showing the class as a social event, emphasizing, for instance, the difference between classroom talk and "real" talk.

In contrast, both student teachers focused on conventional notions of "lessons," with definite divisions and segments. The class that Chris and Kate examined in detail, for example, started with a fairly long guided conversation, which was closely coordinated by Roger, but gave all the students a chance to speak freely (six pages of transcript). This was followed by a pronunciation exercise focusing on reductions (just over four pages of transcript). Both Kate and Chris said that the lesson consisted of the pronunciation exercise. They regarded the conversation as "just chatting."

I was struck by the difference between the ways Chris and Kate approached the task. Kate commented on the classroom in narrative fashion, with very few comments on how Roger taught. She assumed that there was a right and a wrong way of looking at the transcript, and did not know which was which. Chris, on the other hand, approached the task fresh from her Methods class. She was actively looking for things to criticize. Part of this difference might have had to do with both personality and age. Kate was old enough to be wary; Chris was young enough to be overconfident. Regardless of these initial differences, their discussion quickly became a criticism of Roger's style of teaching rather than an objective examination of the classroom dialog. The focus shifted from examining teaching techniques to judging the teacher.

Both Roger and the student teachers noted the significance of the amount of teacher talk and student talk. But Roger's interest in this aspect of the classroom lay in noting how, or whether, he succeeded in making the classroom student–centered. Kate and Chris, on the other hand, were interested in teacher talk versus student talk for what it showed about control of the classroom. Their comment on one section of the conversation was that Roger was "showing them who was in control." Roger's comment on the same section of dialog had been about the extent to which he was able to keep the students central. The "control" he exerted, in fact, was a means of keeping the focus away from himself and placing it on the students. Chris and Kate did not see this.

Both Roger and the student teachers noted the treatment of individual students. But Roger's purpose was once again to monitor his success in making the class student-centered. Chris wanted to count utterances simply to support her contention that Roger talked more to one student than another and to note that in her view one student was permitted to dominate the others. In the case of one particularly reticent student, Graciella, whom Roger frequently encouraged to speak, both Chris and Kate perceived Roger as cutting her off and interrupting her. Here is a typical segment of dialog, in which Roger tries to persuade Graciella to tell the class about the game called Clue:

Roger:	You like that one? (pause) It's fun.
Graciella:	Yes.
Roger:	What kind of game? Explain for Koji and Yoshi.
Yoshi:	What is Clue?
	(long pause)
Yoshi:	What do you use?
	(pause)
Yoshi:	Cards? Or coins?
	(long pause)
Graciella:	We use cards. (pause) But they have pictures.
	(long pause)
Graciella:	We didn't—um—someone get kill?
Roger:	Killed.
Graciella:	Another one. And you need to solve who was the murder?
Roger:	Uhu.

Yoshi: Solve?
Graciella: And what the murderer used.
                (pause)
Roger: It's like the game we played in class, remember?

There are seven pauses in this short exchange that were long enough to have been noted on the transcript. All mark points where either Roger or one of the other students leaves space for Graciella to speak. They clearly show Roger's propensity for giving students room to respond. They also show him responding immediately to Graciella only when she asks him a usage question ("kill" versus "killed") and a specific question about the game. Both Roger and the student teachers noted pauses in their discussion; however, it was evident that the novice observers reached conclusions quite different from those of the experienced teacher. Graciella would typically answer an open-ended question with one or two words and then stop. Roger always deliberately waited to give her time to continue. Neither student teacher noticed that he did this. Both Roger and the student teachers noted the use of questions; however, once again, their observations were quite different. As an experienced teacher, Roger was interested in types of questions, sequencing of questions, and the pedagogical purpose of questioning techniques. The student teachers, on the other hand, noted questions only to consider who asked more or who was asked more. In the excerpt above, for instance, Roger's concern was with whether he allowed enough space for student response and whether he avoided simple yes/no questions. The student teachers, on the other hand, took this sequence and others like it simply as proof that Roger dominated the questioning, even though in the excerpt above he is clearly giving room for another student, Yoshi, to do the asking, and deliberately does not participate except to help Graciella with usage or real-life information.

Overall, Roger was interested in looking at his own teaching in order to note propensities and techniques—i.e. what worked and what did not. The student teachers, on the other hand, quickly became critical, to an extent that surprised me, it had been clearly stated that the intention of the exercise was simply to examine what was happening in the classroom.

Experienced observers versus novices. These differences between Roger's observations and those of the student teachers mirror differences between expert and novice reactions that have been extensively documented in educational research. A 1994 article by Willis Copeland et al. illustrates this research. Copeland and his fellow researchers examined the results of an experiment in which twenty-eight participants reacted to a videotaped vignette of classroom life. The participants were divided into neophytes, apprentices, and masters, depending on the level of their experience and expertise in education. The researchers found that the most experienced participants "tended to focus on a consideration of educational purpose which casts learning as an interactive process of discovery and creative thinking." Those with the least experience, on the other hand, "expressed their understanding of educational purpose as a concern for teacher control of students and for eliciting students' correct answers" (Copeland et al. 1994: 177).

These findings are in accord with the differences between Roger's perception of the class and the observations of Chris and Kate. While Roger focused on ways in which the classroom discourse showed cooperative interaction between teacher and learner, both Chris and Kate quickly focused on the issue of teacher control. Both said they saw Roger constantly asserting control, and yet at the same time Chris saw lack of control as an issue, expressing her irritation at Roger's extreme informality and (apparent) lack of order.

It seems that without some guidelines about what to look for, the students' observations had a focus quite different from Roger's or from mine in my discussions with Roger. The student with no teaching experience and no theoretical background was both too anxious and too diffident. The student with some background, on the other hand, was all too ready to make hasty judgments. Both became very evaluative and were not able to look objectively at the transcripts or the videos. They needed some sort of measuring instrument, a method of analysis that could be used as an aid to their seeing as much as possible, as clearly and objectively as possible. I felt that systems of analysis developed by linguists could be used for such a purpose. I therefore examined parts of my data using such systems, with a view to discovering whether what I saw through these systems would be congruent with the teacher's insights and might illuminate aspects of the discourse that the students had either not noticed or misinterpreted.

Choosing systems of analysis. With the plethora of systems available for analyzing language at the level of discourse, deciding which ones to use was an interesting exercise. I found at least three major groupings or types: The comprehensive, hierarchical type; the multiple perspective type; and the holistic, larger-dimension type. Ultimately, I chose the following three systems, each representing a major framework type: (1) Sinclair and Coulthard's system first described in *Towards an analysis of discourse* (1975) and later in Coulthard's *Introduction to discourse analysis* (1977); (2) John Fanselow's FOCUS, described in his book *Breaking rules* (1987); and (3) a system devised by Roger Shuy to analyze classroom discourse holistically, described in "Identifying dimensions of classroom language" a chapter in *Multiple perspective analyses of classroom discourse* (Green and Harker 1988).

Sinclair and Coulthard developed a comprehensive, hierarchical system, purporting to describe every aspect of classroom language, much as a system of grammar describes language at the syntax level. They were influenced by earlier systems devised by researchers such as Bellack and Flanders (Bellack 1966; Flanders 1970). Thoroughly grounded in discourse theory, theirs is a seminal approach, which has been frequently used and adapted for a variety of different circumstances.

Fanselow's system relies heavily on both Bellack and Sinclair and Coulthard. Like these earlier systems, Fanselow's is comprehensive in that it sets out to describe all of classroom discourse. Unlike the earlier systems, however, Fanselow's is meant to be used on an everyday level, by teachers, as a tool for discovering more about their own teaching styles and techniques. He describes it as "an observation system to generate and explore alternatives in language teaching" (Fanselow 1987: 19). His system is multidimensional, describing diverse, coexisting aspects of the discourse. It typifies the many systems that emphasize the complexity of classroom interaction.

Shuy's system contrasts with these comprehensive, descriptive types of analysis. It is not a grammar of discourse but rather a system that can take a holistic glance at one, or several, or many dimensions of the classroom language. It is geared specifically toward language classrooms, although the classrooms examined in his study were not second-language classes; and it focuses on the larger dimensions of the classroom and several specific techniques of language teaching. Unlike the other two methods, Shuy's is evaluative. He specifically says that the chapter "discusses where the talk takes place and how the talk takes place, and suggests some bases for evaluating the effectiveness of classroom discourse" (Shuy 1988: 115).

These three choices are by no means comprehensive, even though they do broadly represent particular trends. Obviously, researchers or teachers might be interested in other systems for a variety of reasons. However, I felt that choosing three such different systems would produce results that could be extrapolated to fit the needs or interests of researchers examining very different classrooms or teaching styles. The kinds of difficulties I encountered, and the kinds of issues which arose, would be relevant for choosing any type of analysis framework for the analysis of language in different classroom settings.

Sinclair and Coulthard's method. Analyzing a segment of the discourse using Sinclair and Coulthard's method was an interesting exercise. Their system seemed very complex at first but proved easy to reduce to a basic framework and express in simple, easily understood terms. In this form, it was relatively easy to apply to a segment of discourse, yet because the system was developed in a classroom quite different from the one I had, much of my data did not fit neatly. The very untidy and incomplete nature of the analysis, however, was in itself interesting.

Sinclair and Coulthard's system can be summarized fairly simply. They identify five levels of classroom discourse from top to bottom: lesson, transaction, exchange, move, and act. The lesson is made up of transactions, which in turn consist of exchanges. Exchanges are made up of moves, and moves comprise acts, the lowest level. Their system is a rank scale, the basic assumption of which is that a unit of any rank consists of one or more units of the rank below it. For instance, an exchange consists of one or more moves, and a move consists of one or more acts. The main element of this hierarchy seems to be the exchange, the most important type of which is the teaching exchange, consisting of moves which play the functional roles of initiation, response, and feedback. This is the basic pattern, which occurs repeatedly in their data. The initiation consists of an opening move, the response consists of an answering move, and the feedback consists of a follow-up move. Sinclair and Coulthard identify five types of move: Opening, answering, follow-up, framing, and focusing. They also identify twenty-two acts in their data, the most prevalent of which seem to be those that play the functional roles of elicitation, directive, and informative act (parts of an opening move); reply, reaction, and acknowledgement (parts of an answering move); and acceptance, evaluation, and comment (parts of a follow-up move).

Many significant elements of Roger's teaching style came to the fore through the analysis, and in several instances, points where the student teachers had misread the interaction were clarified. Both Kate and Chris, for instance, had seen Roger as an interrupter. The lesson they had examined clearly showed the opposite when it was analyzed using Sinclair and Coulthard's system. It showed Roger standing back giving plenty of space for the students to initiate and sustain conversation, and it showed the many occasions on which Graciella in particular did not pick up on these opportunities.

Consider this short dialog between Graciella and Koji:

Graciella:	Sunday is the day that you worship the Lord.
Koji:	Something.
Graciella:	Sunday.
Koji:	You can learn something about which one?
Graciella:	Huh?
Koji:	Excuse me, I don't know.
	(pause)
Graciella:	Sunday is the day that you—worship?
Roger:	Uhu.
Graciella:	—the Lord.
Koji:	Oh, OK.

In this segment, Koji clearly does not understand anything Graciella has said. The analysis highlights Roger's deviation here from the "typical" classroom pattern of teacher initiation, student response, and teacher feedback. Where a beginning teacher would almost surely have attempted to clarify the situation, Roger gives Koji the opportunity to struggle through the communication himself, dealing in English with Graciella's reticence and finally producing the real-life (non-classroom) utterance of "Excuse me, I don't know." Roger's only contribution is "Uhu" when Graciella asks about the word "worship." This deviates completely from the typical pattern, since it consists of student initiation and teacher response, rather than the reverse. The system thus enabled the observer to "see" in a way that corresponded closely with the insights of the teacher himself. The points that the system made clear were invariably ones which interested Roger, or which he had commented on.

Simply dissecting the classroom discourse hierarchically and thus putting order onto it was a valuable exercise in itself. And since Sinclair and Coulthard's system can be presented fairly succinctly, I concluded that it could easily be used as part of an exercise in a TESOL methods class, to enable student teachers to look clearly at the interaction and better understand classroom interaction.

Fanselow's method. In comparison with Sinclair and Coulthard's system, Fanselow's was more difficult to understand and to apply. His system distinguishes among five different characteristics of communication, answering two main questions: What is being done? and How is it being done? The first two characteristics, answering *what*, are source/target, and move type. The three characteristics that answer *how* are medium, use, and content. Unlike Sinclair and Coulthard's system, Fanselow's is not hierarchical. All five characteristics are seen as working together and can be considered either separately or in unison. Each of the five characteristics is divided into subcategories: Source/target may be teacher, student, or other. Moves are classified as structure, solicit, respond, react, and bear. Medium may be linguistic, nonlinguistic, paralinguistic, or silence. Use may be to attend, characterize, set, reproduce, relate, or present. And finally, content is either study, life, procedure, or unspecified.

I did a close analysis of two long segments, working with all of Fanselow's categories. Although the exercise was an interesting one, it turned out to be primarily a means to better understand Fanselow's system. The questions that arose had more to do with Fanselow's categories than with understanding the classroom discourse. Unlike Sinclair and Coulthard's system, Fanselow's is quite difficult to grasp and synthesize. The complexity of this framework can, of course, be seen as one of its merits, since the rationale behind such a system is to demonstrate the multidimensional, complex nature of discourse.

Despite the difficulties, I found Fanselow's method to be useful for dissecting small pieces of discourse. For example, one aspect of Roger's teaching style in which both he and I were interested was his use of "fillers," words or phrases like "OK" and "That's good." A piece of dialog containing such a sequence of apparently empty words occurred towards the end of a segment in which the students were reviewing a pronunciation exercise they had just completed. Roger called on one student to say the answer he had written down and then asked another student to respond with either "I agree" or "I disagree." Here is the sequence:

1.	Roger:	Do you agree with that, Besant?
2.	Besant:	I'm not sure.
3.	Roger:	You're not sure.
4.		Graciella?
5.	Besant:	I didn't get it.
6.	Graciella:	Me either.
7.	Roger:	You're not sure either.
8.		OK.
9.		I agree.
10.		That's good.
11.		OK.

At first glance, the last four lines seem to be nothing but a string of reassuring murmurs. However, with an analysis of the surrounding dialog, they take on more clarity. Move 8, "OK," is what Fanselow calls a *bearing* move, which is an idiosyncratic communication people make such as scratching their heads or touching their ears. It acts as a transition. Move 9, "I agree," is a *react* move, and its use is to *reproduce*, since what Roger is doing here is affirming the response made by the student in the pronunciation exercise. He tried to get this response from both Besant and Graciella, but when both said they were not sure, Roger supplied the response himself. With this interpretation, the next move, "That's good," can be seen as a *react* to the original answer, already affirmed by the previous line, "I agree." The final "OK," in move 11, can then be categorized as a *bearing* move, covering the content of the whole exercise and preparing the students to move on to the next section of the lesson. I checked this sequence against what Roger himself had noted when he looked through the transcripts. These were his comments:

"OK."	transition
"I agree."	affirmation
"That's good."	praise
"OK."	transition

My analysis of the sequence using Fanselow's method was confirmed by Roger's own interpretation.

Besides its usefulness in such close analysis, I also found Fanselow's system insightful for examining very large pieces of discourse in a more selective way, for instance, skimming the transcript for examples of a previously chosen dimension. However, for a comprehensive view of a large piece of dialog such as a whole class, Fanselow's system would be impractical because it would require an enormous outlay of time. The diagraming and rediagraming needed as each new dimension is added would be unwieldy and time consuming. But it could be useful for quick discussions of specific teaching techniques or discourse questions.

To be fair, Fanselow himself does not suggest using the system so comprehensively. Instead he looks at pieces of dialog in a more selective way, picking out certain moves or certain aspects of the content with a view to answering particular questions. For example, one of his *content* subcategories, *life*, is a useful one because with it one can ask whether or to what extent a teacher brings in "real-life" language, useful outside the classroom. This could be achieved without a comprehensive, minute examination of every dimension of the dialog.

The difficulties I experienced with Fanselow's system were probably exacerbated by the unconventional layout of his book *Breaking Rules*. The book is meant to be used as a workbook, not as a reference, and thus it is quite hard to comprehend his system fully without practicing its use extensively. In fact, Fanselow himself says that the book "requires activity and action on the part of readers" and that "the generation and exploration of alternatives that I am advocating is a multi-year undertaking" (Fanselow 1987: 14). It would be quite difficult—and unfair, I think—to use his method for student teachers in anything less than a full course because of the initial difficulty in figuring it out and working with it.

Shuy's method. In contrast to Fanselow's, I found Shuy's method of analysis of classroom discourse particularly amenable to illuminating the aspects of the classroom that were most important to Roger himself. Shuy's system identifies six main dimensions of classroom discourse: question-asking strategies, use of language for management of the classroom, topic manipulation, self-referencing, suprasegmentals, and naturalness of language use.

I found the system valuable for its illumination of the techniques inherent in Roger's manipulation of apparently loose conversation. The analysis of question-asking strategies could be a useful exercise for student teachers, particularly for analysis of a listening-speaking class. A particularly interesting sequence in this respect was the one already discussed above, which occurred between Roger and Graciella in the segment of dialog that both student teachers had dismissed as "just chatting." Here is the sequence, with omissions of some of the dialog indicated by square brackets:

Roger:	What are you going to do on Sunday?
Graciella:	We go to church on Sunday—um—Sunday morning.
Roger:	Excuse me, you go where?
Graciella:	To church [...] I take a nap [...]
Roger:	You like to sleep during the day.
Graciella:	Yeah.
Roger:	And you can't during the week.
Graciella:	No.
Roger:	So Sunday's a good day.
	(pause)
Graciella:	I play with them games, you know, table games.
Roger:	For example?
Graciella:	Um—um—they have Clue. Clue?
	[...]
Roger:	You like that one?
	(pause)
Roger:	It's fun.
Graciella:	Yes.
Roger:	What kind of game? Explain it for Koji and Yoshi.
	[...]
Roger:	It's a detective game, right?

This sequence shows Roger grappling with Graciella's tendency to answer in monosyllables and not pick up on conversation topics. An examination of his questioning strategy shows how he deals with this. He begins with an open-ended question, then works down to an information (wh-) question. From there he tries several openings in statement form, to get her to respond at least with a yes or no. When she finally mentions a game, he uses the opportunity to return to an open-ended question: "For example?" When, after a significant pause, she answers his yes/no question (You like that one?) simply with a yes, he tries another open-ended question: "What kind of game? Explain it." The whole topic, which Graciella apparently does not want to pursue, ends with a tag question: "It's a detective game, right?" The patterning in this segment of the class shows Roger's technique of using open-ended questions to get a topic started. He then moves to wh- questions and yes/no questions when they are needed to help a student along. And, when possible, he seizes opportunities to go back to open-ended questions.

As already mentioned, neither novice teacher saw anything of interest in this opening conversation. With Shuy's system to guide them, they could have been directed to look at how Roger sequenced questions and what types of questions he asked. They would then have realized that, in the classroom of an experienced teacher, "just chatting" is usually much more sophisticated than it appears to an inexperienced observer.

Because Roger was interested in classroom style as a whole, in methods rather than techniques, the broad brush style of this method of analysis was very useful. While the other two types direct the researcher or student teacher to concentrate on detailed aspects of classroom language, Shuy's method allows one to get a broad overview of the classroom quite quickly. It uses few, if any, technical terms and thus is easy to grasp. For these reasons, it would be ideal for class discussion of particular teaching techniques such as a particular teacher's questioning strategies. One drawback, perhaps, is that it is overtly evaluative. I found it difficult to stop myself from making judgments about how "well" or how "badly" Roger was performing on each of the dimensions. It is easier to jump to conclusions, and perhaps for that reason, one is likely to be more subjective. Novice teachers, who are likely to jump to conclusions anyway, might find the very ease of this system a drawback. Experienced practitioners, on the other hand, are likely to find it more readily useful than a more complex or technical system.

Conclusions. I found that the results of all three methods of analysis bore out the intuitions and insights of the experienced teacher. Each one allowed the researcher to concentrate on different aspects of the classroom, and all three illuminated aspects of the interaction that the student teachers either had not noticed or had misunderstood. I felt that each system has the potential to be used as a teaching tool, although the more complex a system is, the less useful it would be because of time and resource constraints. But any of the three systems I examined would enable teacher trainers to replace vague or irrelevant questions about what is happening in a classroom with specific suggestions about what to look for and how to discuss the relevance of certain types of interaction or dimensions of language.

In spite of the many practical drawbacks, particularly the time constraints, I concluded that analysis of classroom discourse is an insightful and valuable exercise for teachers and students. Simply looking at the interaction and examining it in detail was valuable. However, undirected analysis has its disadvantages: It is useful only if the person doing the looking has the kind of experience and insight needed to make the exercise worthwhile. An experienced teacher can analyze a transcript of his or her own classroom or that of another teacher and notice interesting aspects of the discourse and examples of valuable teaching techniques. Inexperienced students or teachers might look at the same interaction and fail to see or understand what the teacher is really doing. For this reason, directed looking can be a valuable tool. My study showed that systems of analysis developed by linguists can provide such a tool. The analyses that I did, to varying degrees, illuminated what Roger himself found pertinent and what the novice teachers had either misunderstood or failed to notice.

The main implication of the study is that theory is very pertinent to practice. The growing trend toward collaboration between teacher and researcher is a useful one. As this study showed, such collaboration is both practical and insightful. In particular, the collaboration between teacher and researcher proved to be very worthwhile. The discussions Roger and I had as a result of our looking at the lesson transcripts together were wide-ranging. We discussed not only the particular lessons we examined but also teaching methods in general, how to deal with particular classroom problems, insights into teaching gained by both of us over the years, and a variety of other pedagogical subjects. Such free-ranging discussions were the inevitable result of collaboration in a study such as this one. Their effect is unquantifiable but real, for example, in terms of increasing both one's self-awareness when teaching and one's alertness in planning and executing particular lessons.

Looking at and discussing a particular classroom, whether one's own or someone else's, is a way of working on teacher enrichment without resorting to criticism. It is a way for colleagues to cooperate rather than for practitioners to be judged by observers. As Fanselow puts it, "As we explore our craft ... rules are broken that say we teachers must seek alternatives from those in charge, rather than ourselves or our peers, and that we must work alone within our autonomous but isolated and lonely classrooms, rather than with colleagues" (Fanselow 1987: 7). Action research ought to become a priority. Teaching practices can be investigated through analyses of classroom discourse that direct the viewer's observation toward elements of pedagogical value. Analyzing another teacher's classroom or one's own can raise one's level of awareness of the effect of various techniques and assumptions.

I recommend that graduate courses in TESOL incorporate some data-gathering activities. Gathering the amounts of data used in this study would not be feasible; however, the analysis of even small amounts of real classroom data would be a useful exercise for beginning teachers. Looking at discourse that has already been transcribed is valuable, but it does not replace producing one's own. The decision about how to divide the discourse on the page—the pauses, for example—leads the researcher to think carefully about what decisions are being made by the teacher. Over time, materials such as videotapes, transcripts, and exercises in guided observation can be gathered for the libraries of Intensive English programs or graduate programs in TESOL. Such collaborative data gathering and analysis could further close the gap between theory and practice and provide materials to help raise the level of expertise among ESL practitioners.

REFERENCES

Bellack, Arno, Herbert Kliebard, Ronald Hyman, and Frank Smith, Jr. 1966. *The language of the classroom.* New York: Teachers College Press.
Copeland, Willis D., Carrie Birmingham, Lisa DeMeulle, Marianne D'Emidio-Caston, and Dottie Natal. 1994. "Making meaning in classrooms: An investigation of cognitive processes in aspiring teachers, experienced teachers, and their peers." *American Educational Research Journal* 31(1): 166-96.
Coulthard, Malcolm. 1977. *An introduction to discourse structure.* London: Longman.
El-Kadi, Caroline M. 1994. "Linguistic theory applied to teaching practice: Looking through linguists' eyes at an urban ESL classroom." Unpublished Ph.D. dissertation, Old Dominion University.
Fanselow, John. 1987. *Breaking rules: Generating and exploring alternatives in language teaching.* New York: Longman.
Flanders, Ned A. 1970. *Analyzing teacher behavior.* Reading, Massachusetts: Addison-Wesley.
Shuy, Roger. 1988. "Identifying dimensions of classroom language." In Judith L. Green and Judith O. Harker (eds.), *Multiple perspective analyses of classroom discourse.* Roy O. Freedle (ed.), *Advances in discourse processes*, No. 28. Norwood N.J.: Ablex. 115-134.
Sinclair, John and Malcolm Coulthard. 1975. *Towards an analysis of discourse: The language used by teachers and pupils.* Oxford: Oxford University Press.
Watson-Gegeo, Karen Ann. 1988. "Ethnography in ESL: Defining the essentials." *TESOL Quarterly* 22(4): 575-592.

Language awareness in applied-linguistics students: Evidence from "linguistic- and cultural-heritage essays"[1]

Adam Jaworski
University of Wales Cardiff

1. Introduction. This paper investigates the level of language awareness (LA) among applied-linguistics students, who may be deemed potential future teachers of mother-tongue English, English as a second language, and of modern foreign languages (MFL). The research tradition from which this paper derives is that of predominantly British work associated with the LA movement (see e.g. James and Garrett 1991a), and adds a new perspective to the discussion of LA in a teacher-centered context (cf. Chandler, Robinson, and Noyes 1988; Mitchell and Hooper 1991; Merchant 1991; Mitchell, Hooper, and Brumfit 1994).

The objective of the present study clearly follows that of Mitchell and Hooper's (1991) work investigating language teachers' LA, although there are some important methodological differences between the two studies. Mitchell and Hooper interviewed language teachers (of English as a mother tongue and of modern languages) in several secondary schools in the south of England. The informants in the present study were undergraduate students who had not yet (and indeed might not) become language teachers. Mitchell and Hooper conducted hour-long interviews, whereas written essays form the data in this study. The role of explicit knowledge about language (KAL) in the teachers' work was the main focus of the Mitchell and Hooper research, while the students in the present study were asked to write about their linguistic and cultural awareness as one of the several areas which they addressed in their essays.

Mitchell and Hooper found that the English teachers and the MFL teachers differed somewhat from each other in their conceptions of language and in their foci with regard to introducing explicit linguistic knowledge to their pupils. The English teachers' views on language in their work were centered around teaching effective oral and written communication. The other group of teachers viewed KAL as a useful tool in developing productive competence in a target language, although only with regard to the "more able students." The "less able" ones,

---

[1] I am grateful to Peter Garrett for his careful reading and useful comments on earlier drafts of this paper. He is no way responsible for the remaining mistakes and inadequacies.

Mitchell and Hooper's subjects said, would probably be only confused by explicit talk about language.

Among the MFL teachers, the prevailing view of language was that of a morphosyntactic structure conceptualized in terms of parts of speech, sentence structure, verb tenses, and gender. English teachers manifested a greater diversification of their KAL and conceptualized language in four general categories:

(1) Syntax (parts of speech, sentence and phrase structure, morphology, and lexis);
(2) Language variation (stylistic and genre variation in writing, and standard/nonstandard English);
(3) The writing system (punctuation, paragraphing, and the alphabet); and
(4) Literary analysis ("figures of speech" and poetic forms, e.g. rhyme and meter).

From the above list, the structural aspects of language (traditional grammar) and the literary aspects of language were among the most frequent topics discussed by the English teachers with their pupils in the classroom. Other topics, which reflect more recent developments in linguistics, included stylistic and register variation in written language and dialectal variation in spoken language. These topics, however, were found to be introduced by the teachers in the classroom with varying degrees of "normativism" (i.e. they included guidelines for correct usage).

Mitchell and Hooper mention the conspicuous absence of several topics from the English teachers' interviews: Analysis of spoken language, analysis of texts above the level of sentence (except for "paragraphing"), and language acquisition and development.

Some English teachers expressed a belief that explicit teaching about language would be beneficial to their pupils' improvement of (native) language skills, though most of the respondents did not see KAL as a prerequisite for this or any other "useful" end. On the other hand the MFL teachers, with their strict view of language as "structure," insisted that the explicit teaching of formal aspects of language was necessary for the pupils to move beyond the phrase-book stage of learning of any second language (L2).

The teachers in the Mitchell and Hooper study had little or no linguistic training in their educational backgrounds. Most of them came to the teaching profession through literature/education-based undergraduate studies with subsequent teacher training which concentrated on teaching methodology. Most of the linguistic awareness demonstrated in the interviews had been acquired by the teachers at inservice training sessions, through their own readings, and through informal contacts.

If this picture of LA among British language teachers seems rather bleak, a somewhat more optimistic picture emerges from a study by Merchant (1991).

This study focused on a different dimension of LA. Merchant presented the responses of one hundred and thirty-eight teachers to the question "What do you understand by the term 'linguistic diversity'?" asked as part of a pre-course questionnaire distributed prior to the teachers' participation in programs of the E.C.-funded Linguistic Diversity in the Primary School Projects. It appears from Merchant's report that although, as he observes, many of the teachers' responses were somewhat narrow in scope and even simplistic, most teachers felt that linguistic diversity was an important aspect of the educational (and more generally, social) reality. The fact that these teachers chose to take part in LA courses, however, suggests that their interest in the linguistic issues was already greater than average. (See below on a related research finding reported by Leets and Giles 1993).

In the Merchant study the teachers' definitions of linguistic diversity fell into five general categories (from the most to least frequent):

(1) Community languages and different languages spoken in society;
(2) Accentual and dialectal variation in a language;
(3) Different languages and language forms used in the classroom;
(4) Showing respect and valuing community languages; and
(5) Language-related problems with education among minority and working-class children.

Merchant also expressed concern that some definitions were downright wrong and confusing. However, after the courses, many teachers expressed very positive responses to the LA work in which they had been involved and showed much more understanding of the issues of linguistic diversity, such as:

(1) The significance of linguistic variation beyond the school setting;
(2) Class-, ethnic- and gender-related variation; and
(3) Linguistic variation and its significance in construing power, status, identity, and self-esteem.

In sum, the Mitchell and Hooper study demonstrates that the LA of British language teachers is relatively low and that it can be attributed to the lack of explicit linguistic training of teachers at the undergraduate and postgraduate levels (although see Chandler, Robinson, and Noyes 1988 for a less pessimistic picture of student teachers' LA). The Merchant study shows clearly that explicit linguistic training increases the LA of teachers dramatically, and that this LA bears direct relevance to the teachers' practice in the classroom.

The consequences of the findings of both studies summarized above have immediate relevance to the main tenet of this paper, i.e. that formal language studies are a necessary element in building the LA of future, as well as present, language teachers.

2. Aims and data. The studies reported in the previous section lead to the conclusion that if teacher training does not include a substantial element of language studies, it is very hard for the teachers to think about language beyond the level of "structure" (or "grammar"); in addition, the notion of linguistic variation can be a hazy one and tinged with large doses of normativism. On the other hand, where inservice training or other means of raising LA are available, new and broader sociolinguistic issues are willingly taken on board and seem to make a difference in the teachers' outlook on the teaching and learning process, on the language of their pupils, and on society in general. This view finds further support in the recent work on perceptual dialectology carried out among school teachers in Wales (see Coupland, Williams, and Garrett 1994; Garrett, Coupland, and Williams 1994; Williams, Garrett, and Coupland submitted).

The study reported here is based on self-reflective essays on "linguistic and cultural heritage" written by undergraduate students of applied linguistics enrolled in B.A. programs in communication, language and communication, and Modern English studies at the School of English Studies, Communication, and Philosophy at the University of Wales Cardiff. These students, who were mostly British and of varying ages (several of them being "mature" students), were taking a course in "Intercultural communication" taught by the author in the 1993–1994 academic year. However, neither age nor gender has been considered in the subsequent analysis of the students' essays. It is important to note, however, that only the British students' essays (twenty-four in total) were analyzed for the purpose of this paper.

The essays, the average length of which was 1500–2000 words, were in fact assessed, but assessment was based mainly on their stylistic/academic writing merit. They counted towards 10% of the students' final assessment in this particular lecture course. At the time the essays were written, the students were in the middle of their second or third (final) year of their degree schemes and had taken a significant part of their lecture courses in linguistics, sociolinguistics, pragmatics, discourse analysis, and other related subjects.

There are several goals to be accomplished in asking the students to write these "heritage" essays. For example, the essays reveal the students' own awareness of the role of language and culture in the shaping of their personal and group identities (see e.g. Schwerdtfeger 1993). The essays also help students develop skills in academic writing while dealing with relatively familiar topics (personal and family histories, experiences, anecdotes from the past, etc.) (see for example Ivanic 1988; Clark and Ivanic 1991; Ivanic and Roach 1990). However, this paper is directed at another aspect of the essays: *The identification of the students' areas of linguistic and cultural awareness.*

3. Results and discussion. The categories of LA to be discussed in the following subsections, are ranked from the most to the least frequent. The study is based on an impressionistic, qualitative content-analysis of the type employed by Mitchell and Hooper (1991) in their investigation of language teachers' LA. This method is an imperfect one. For example, one weakness is the possible unreliability of "coding" the informants' responses, and another is the impossibility of detailed comparisons of results between different studies. However, in view of a lack of any *explicit* framework for the study of LA (although see James and Garrett 1991b for suggestions), it allows for an initial categorization of the subjects' responses/writings. The categories which emerged from this procedure (especially sections 3.1–3.4 below) show some overlap but may be regarded as a preliminary, functional taxonomy before a more rigid framework is applied.

Passages[2] classified as referring to the students' LA resulting from their language studies depended on the explicit statement in the essay that a given idea or conceptualization of language had come about due to the students' degree course. As always, there was a degree of fuzziness involved: Sometimes it was not possible to decide very easily if an instance of reported LA was a verbalization of ideas which had occurred to students prior to their university studies, or whether they emerged as a result of those studies:

1 One of the effects that my varied social background has had on me is that I find many linguistic forms "acceptable," viewing none as a "standard." Indeed, the whole concept of a standard linguistic form seems to me to be a very subjective one (PS93/94).

Such doubtful cases of self-reported LA were left out from the discussion as not related to the students' language studies. However, it seems that even though certain manifestations of LA were not attributed to their study of language, the students' ability to use relatively sophisticated metalanguage in expressing their LA acquired prior to their language studies must be seen as one very important aspect of their linguistic/professional training.

3.1. Personal growth and reinforcement of one's own views on language ("therapeutic" and "revelatory" functions of LA). By far the most common aspect of LA mentioned in the students' essays was that of personal under-standing, development, and verification of one's own feelings in relation to language. Fourteen students suggested different ways in which their personal outlook on language had been altered or reinforced by their language studies. They stated that language studies had been "interesting," especially where they had prior experience meeting members of other speech communities in the UK and elsewhere.

---

[2]*Editors' note*: Passages from student essays appear in their original form.

2 My language studies course has enabled me to think about my own language use in a completely new way and I find it very interesting (ST93/94).

3 I did not realise/acknowledge aspects of my linguistic and cultural heritage until they were presented to me by my language studies (LS93/94).

4 Having studied Language and Society and Intercultural Communication as well as some communication courses earlier, I have become more aware of speech styles and different linguistic traits. Having a lot of contacts with Sweden as well as with other countries which I have communication with through people I met at the International College I went to, I find linguistic differences very interesting (AW93/94).

Language studies reportedly broadened their horizons, allowing them to gain an ability to observe critically everyday linguistic interaction (e.g. at home, in service encounters, in talk during travel, and so on). As a consequence, students feel that they can approach different facets of communication with a better understanding for others, which will lead to avoidance of miscommunication:

5 My language studies have been very interesting in the sense that they have validated feelings I may have had about my linguistic and cultural heritage. Whereas before I may have had vague notions of the way I felt, my studies have shown me that these are genuine ways to feel and explained why people feel them. Especially interesting in this respect have been the theories of social identity, ethnicity, code mixing and switching and accent convergence and divergence. Similarly the politeness theory gives you a great understanding of why you say the things you do and when. Although I have little opportunity at home of observing different cultures interacting, the study of it has been interesting. It allows you to comprehend the difficulties and misunderstanding that can arise in these circumstances. This hopefully gives a far greater tolerance and makes you aware of when prejudice and stereotyping occur and that they are not only bad but misleading and wrong assumptions (LK93/94).

Several students emphasized that their language studies had "validated" their previous feelings about their linguistic and cultural heritage: They discussed the connections between what they learned and their own experiences with social and ethnic identity, codemixing, codeswitching, and the mechanisms of convergence and divergence when interacting with different speakers (here the students almost invariably cited Communication Accommodation Theory as one of the most influential topics in their lectures and readings):

6   I think one of the reasons I have found my language studies so interesting is that I can see a direct link between certain topics we have discussed on the course and my own experiences. I found Communication Accommodation Theory and Bilingualism especially relevant (LM93/94).

7   Language studies is very useful in clarifying the oddities of one's own linguistic and cultural heritage. With the academic armoury of this subject I find it increasingly rewarding to apply what I see and hear to the enormous range of methodologies I've learnt. This is especially useful when I observe at home, when talking amongst friends, listening to local people talking during bus journeys, interaction in shops and so forth (TLD93/94).

In addition, the students reported a better understanding of their own accents and individual language variation. LA gains of this nature can be called therapeutic: The students acquire self-confidence and the conviction that what they had often intuitively believed to be true of language variation and the parity of different accents about language was adequate.

8   Today, I make a conscious effort to maintain my Welsh accent because I am proud to be Welsh. My Welsh cultural heritage will continue to be important to me because it is an essential part of my personal and social identity. To be born Welsh, is to be born privileged, with music in your heart and verse in your soul. I for one, certainly do not intend to loose my Welsh identity simply because of the prejudiced views of others (HDL93/94).

Several Welsh students reported that they had gained an awareness (sometimes "painful") about their language (Welsh) being under the threat of extinction and a realization that this fact posed a threat to their and their nation's sense of identity and even existence.

9   Theories and concepts set forward during my "language studies" course reinforced a sudden and acutely painful awareness that my language— the lifeblood of my cultural heritage was under a very real and imminent threat. As this awareness grew, so did the importance that I attached to the Welsh language and as this growth took place so my sense of cultural identity strengthened (ND93/94).

3.2. Prejudice versus tolerance. The second most frequently mentioned aspect of the students' self-reported LA was an awareness of the prejudice, intolerance, and racism that exists and of their own heightened tolerance of other people's different accents and languages. This aspect of LA was mentioned by eight students, and some even made this topic the focus of their essays. Given the geographical location of the College, not surprisingly the most frequent examples of negatively stereotyped language and accent were the Welsh language and Welsh English, respectively.

10   Where I live most people, including myself, speak with a strong South
      Wales accent. As you would expect whether it is standard or
      non-standard depends on other factors such as age, sex and
      socio-economic status. However, the Welsh language and Welsh
      accents change considerably depending on where you live. Like my
      parents I have a standard Welsh accent. It could be considered to be
      quite a prestigious form as it is used by Welsh news presenters and in
      the Welsh media in general. However, you can still face prejudice as
      there are marked differences between a Welsh standard accent and an
      English RP accent (LM93/94).

However, some students also reported the existence of Welsh people's negative attitudes towards the English. One student described those negative feelings, although she attempted to redefine them in positive terms of asserting in-group solidarity:

11   In my local community some inhabitants view English people or others
      they see as outsiders, with distrust. I have witnessed scenes in shops
      and pubs for example, when the locals diverge from the "outsider."
      They may even switch the language code from English to Welsh. By
      accentuating their vocal and linguistic differences they are excluding the
      other person and making it known that they are not welcome. Also the
      Welsh interactants may define the encounter in ingroup terms. They
      may want to promote a positive ingroup identity. Therefore by
      accentuating their "Welshness" they are promoting their solidarity and
      distinguishing themselves from people with different accents
      (LM93/94).

Several students expressed the belief that an awareness of language leads to the abandonment of negative stereotyping and prejudice, while eliminating the possibilities of linguistically-motivated misunderstanding and conflict. They also stated a view that although learning foreign languages fosters tolerance and international understanding, harmonious relations between different speech communities (countries) depend on their members' acceptance of the others' cultural values. They also felt that in a multilingual, pluricultural society it was necessary to accept the right of minorities to speak their languages (e.g. Welsh in Wales). It is worth mentioning that this view is shared by many practitioners in LA (see James and Garrett 1991a).

12 Language is then an important tool which is used in a variety of contexts. It not only acts as a means of communicating messages, but also, it determines our position in the domain of social stratification. Its function as a marker of identity can also create fear and suspicion. On a personal level I have again through my linguistic studies been made aware of the danger of such sentiments. Derisory attitudes towards not only language variation, but also minority languages, have no place in a multilingual society. And to this extent I applaud my sister for placing my nephew in a Welsh medium school where he may just re-capture a language and culture once prominent in our family (JPJ93/94).

13 As a monolingual speaker I am acutely aware of the prevalence of the Welsh language in Cardiff. At first it appeared strange to see signs and posters in Welsh but as I began to understand more about the community in which I lived, the importance of the Welsh language became clear. Being a language studies student living in Wales has, I feel, added a different dimension to my course than if I had been studying in England. It is only through my degree course that I have taken an interest in the languages that surround me and I hope that now perhaps with greater understanding I am more tolerant of accent, dialect and language differences (ST93/94).

3.3. Solidarity and identity. Just as frequently, the students emphasized their realization that language was a powerful marker of in-group identity, solidarity, and acceptance.

14 Studying in Cardiff I have found that in some lectures, there is an emphasis on certain aspects of language in Wales which can be related to my linguistic and cultural heritage. The Cardiff dialect has been closely studied along with the language attitudes of Welsh people and bilingualism in Wales. I can also relate my technical knowledge of linguistics to living in different speech communities. For example, I now know that language variety contributes to group identity. Therefore the dialect that I used in Cardiff strengthened my in-group solidarity with other people from Cardiff, but because my dialect was different to the people of Berkshire, I found it harder to adjust to living there.

The distance was increased between us due to our linguistic differences. Also, I now understand that vernacular and non-standard forms were used in the area of Cardiff I lived in to show allegiance to the local community. Here, local bond values override the prestige values that are of importance in the speech community I belonged to in Berkshire (SS93/94).

Some students also reported that their language studies helped them develop a greater resistance to being stigmatized due to their use of nonstandard accents:

15 In my first year at university, I was largely surrounded by standard English speakers. I have always spoken with a strong, Welsh regional accent. I refrain from using the terms "less prestigious" or "inferior" accent because I do not believe that to be true. Certainly, there were many times in those first months of university life that I was made to feel that I spoke a subordinate variety of English. Comments like, "Speak English" were often said in so called "harmless fun" by many English students. On particular occasions, I have been regarded as somehow less intelligent simply because of my Welsh accent. Of course this type of prejudices has always existed and continues to exist against regional accents. Today, I disregard such unnecessary condescending remarks about my Welsh identity. To me, these remarks only reflect the arrogant and ignorant attitudes of the minority (HDL93/94).

3.4. Situational and regional variation. The last of the relatively common aspects of LA (discussed in six essays) was that of the students' recognition of the universality and significance of linguistic variation. The most prominent issues discussed in this category were the social stratification of linguistic variation and the recognition of situational variation as well as the more established regional variation. Several students related aspects of their new knowledge about linguistic variation to their own usage of English (see Section 3.1); some commented on the growing acceptance of nonstandard and foreign English accents in the U.K.

16 Language variation then is a strong indication of social group membership or social stratification, and can be seen as a quality which influences both positive and negative attitudes within its interactants. Positive attributes such as loyalty and compatibility to one's social ordering can be undermined by negative opinions formulated by linguistic features which represent a divergence not only of class, but also of race, age, sex, and religion. Such aspects can be instrumental in provoking an individual to be guilty of social stereotyping and

prejudice. From a personal point of view these negative features have manifested themselves as attitudes towards a speakers accent variety of language. For instance "Received Pronunciation" or that language of the English public schools represented an elitist class which was an anathema to my working class traditions. Therefore, individuals who used this accent were stereotyped as being prosperous and educated. Prejudicial new points were also levelled towards ethnic minorities. People who I believed "misused" the English language were regarded as uneducated and lacking respect towards a nation's culture. Such judgements are purely social but nevertheless reflect attitudes towards language variation. (JPJ93/94).

3.5. Other manifestations of LA. The remaining issues of LA resulting from the students' language studies were discussed in only a few individual essays.

Three students picked up the issue of foreign learners of English and their possible problems in a British academic environment. One of them wrote:

17 I am also more aware of foreign students that are taking the same lectures as myself and I wonder how they understand lecturer's accents let alone the lecture content. Having listened to some of these students in tutorials it appears that they do often have trouble with the English language [and that this] must make studying for their degree even more difficult than [it is for] native English speakers. I think it is only as a language student that I have become aware of this and sympathetic toward language differences (ST93/94).

Two students commented on their understanding of gender-related language use (male and female conversational styles), and expressed their conviction of the significance of gender-related studies to their own experiences, e.g. in recalling how their parents communicate with each other:

18 During my second year we looked at Fishman's (1983) work on verbal interaction between men and women. "The Work Women Do" is an apt way to describe the interaction between my parents. I could draw parallels between the strategies my mother uses and the strategies the women in the study used. For example she asks more questions than my father, initiates more topics and uses more attention beginnings. However this is isn't going to be specific only to my linguistic and cultural heritage (LM93/94).

One student wrote how she understood the nature of manipulative language use in advertising and news coverage in the mass media, as well as how sexist and racist language can perpetuate social and political inequality; then she concluded:

19 My studies have led to an increased awareness of language's power and manipulative possibilities (AH93/94).

The above example attests to an important aspect of the students' LA (related to the *power* dimension of LA as formulated by James and Garrett 1991a) which extends beyond classroom practice. One might suggest that this form of LA has a role to play in shaping an individual's new civic ethos.

3.6. Conceptualization of language. Only two students stated explicitly that their language studies had made them aware that language was more than a code used to exchange information. They came to view language as a system for transmitting cultural values and organizing society:

20 A language has to be studied within its own culture because the culture of a language is inherent to the understanding of the language itself. Communicative competence is an important part of this [...] Communicative competence involves not only knowing the language but also what to say to whom and how to say it appropriately in any given situation. [...] To study language for me is a chance to gain some understanding of other cultures. French and Welsh are subsidiary to my English competence and use, but they are an important factor in my existence as a communicative being (HM93/94).

Although explicit ways of conceptualizing language as "communication" and "culture" were relatively infrequent in the essays, the implied view of language was, in most cases, congruent with the one in the above example. This suggests that the students in this study radically depart from the traditional "school" view of language as code as reported earlier in the work of Mitchell and Hooper (1991) (see Section 1), and that they conceptualize language not only as "speech action" but also as "social action" (see Dendrinos, this volume).

4. Conclusion. The students' self-reported LA affected by their language studies has been found to cluster around the following main areas:

(1) Understanding of one's own language practices, confirmation of one's own beliefs about language, and broadening of one's horizons ("language studies are interesting");
(2) Acceptance of linguistic diversity and heightened tolerance of the linguistic and communicative practices of other communities;

(3) Understanding of the relational function of language, i.e. its role in shaping one's relations with others (power and solidarity);

(4) Grasping the complexities of linguistic variation—regional, social, ethnic, stylistic (situational), etc.—and clarification of the relationship between standard and nonstandard accents; and

(5) Appreciation of interpersonal and intergroup differences in communication, which may potentially lead to misunderstanding and conflict, and of the manipulative uses of language.

The topics in LA discussed by the students in their essays reflect a wide range of problems and concerns. Sometimes it is not entirely clear if a student's example of his/her LA comes from frequent contacts with members of other communities, or whether it is a *post hoc* formulation prompted by the requirement to write a "heritage" essay. For example, one of the students mentions his varied social background, living in different parts of Britain and meeting people from different backgrounds, as the factor which had led him to find "many linguistic forms 'acceptable'." He also stated that these experiences had made him realize that the idea of a standard linguistic form was a "very subjective one." This instance of self-reported LA was not attributed to this student's language studies, although it would be unwise to underestimate the role of language studies in enabling the students to voice an opinion like this with confidence.

It is obviously possible to claim that one's LA need not depend on the formal study of (socio)linguistics. Nicholas (1991), for example, points out that second-language learners possess a level of language awareness which they cannot always state explicitly. However, in the light of the studies quoted above (Mitchell and Hooper 1991, and Merchant 1991), it becomes quite clear that no or little linguistic education tends to limit language teachers' LA. Furthermore, as Merchant points out, courses in LA (or, more broadly, in sociolinguistics) are very effective methods of consciousness-raising among teachers. Thus even if the students in their heritage essays relate their LA to informal contacts with linguistically diverse speakers and situations, it seems safe to assume the following:

(1) Language studies can enable students to reflect on their own linguistic histories in order to assess them in depth—otherwise it is difficult for linguistically untrained individuals to go beyond the level of stereotype and anecdote in assessing their own and others' language use; and

(2) Language studies can provide students with the metalanguage which is indispensable in discussing language-related topics. This skill has given the students a "voice" to report their personal and linguistic histories in their heritage essays, and it is only through this metalanguage that

their LA can be further disseminated in their future work as language teachers.

In practical terms, the above points lead to a suggestion to include (socio)linguistic teaching in educational courses for future teachers of English (as first and second language) and MFL. Although exposure to linguistic diversity is not in itself an unimportant aspect of gaining LA, it does not seem to be sufficient to guarantee the understanding, tolerance, and promotion of LA. Language is a highly abstract construct and needs formal explanation. It is important that some of it reaches the students who have not made it the main object of their studies. In this respect this author shares Bloor's (1986: 157) conviction that "people ought to know about language in general and be able to talk and write about it."

In fact, many students themselves stated explicitly that language-related issues are socially, politically, and culturally important, and expressed a need for the dissemination of sociolinguistic ideas among the general public. The most prominent outcome of the students' applied-linguistic studies which they thought merited promotion was increasing tolerance of linguistic diversity, eliminating negative stereotyping and prejudice, and granting minorities their language rights.

Leets and Giles (1993) caution us that the general link between education and the fostering of tolerance, or the specific one between LA and intergroup or crosscultural understanding and acceptance can be deceptive. They cite several examples of research where education did not change the existing values in individuals prejudiced against specific others. Leets and Giles' own research has also suggested that the link between LA and tolerance is not a straightforward one. Likewise, relating LA to teaching practice, Chandler, Robinson, and Noyes (1988: 172) state that "Knowing about language is quite separate from using this knowledge appropriately and effectively in the classroom."

If indeed, as Leets and Giles say, LA does not uniformly lead to greater tolerance and intergroup or crosscultural understanding, then it does seem to provide students with tools for critical reflection on their own communicative behavior and the communicative behavior of others. Intolerance and prejudice may not completely disappear from the value systems of linguistics students, but at least such students demonstrate a considerable amount of knowledge about the mechanisms of their own intolerance. As one student ended his essay:

21　[O]ne major consequence of my language studies to date has been to reduce if not eliminate any excuses I may have had for making evaluative, and frequently pejorative declarations about accent, dialect and language use (BN93/94).

It may be too ambitious to expect applied-linguistics programs to eliminate prejudice. Nevertheless, if they can at any rate "eliminate excuses" for it, then raising the LA of students, who in turn will raise the LA of their own students in the future, has to be viewed as an important goal of applied-linguistics programs. Taking the above quote as a realistic representation of linguists' goals as teachers and of our students' achievements, there is certainly room for modest satisfaction and optimism in the linguistics profession.

REFERENCES

Bloor, Thomas. 1986. "What do language students know about grammar?" *British Journal of Language Teaching* 24(3): 157–160.

Chandler, P.W., P. Robinson, and P. Noyes. 1988. "The level of linguistic knowledge and awareness amongst students training to be primary teachers." *Language and Education* 2(3): 161–173.

Clark, Romy and Roz Ivanic. 1991. "Consciousness-raising about the writing process." In Carl James and Peter Garrett (eds.), *Language awareness in the classroom.* London: Longman. 168–185.

Coupland, Nikolas, Angie Williams, and Peter Garrett. 1994. "The social meanings of Welsh English: Teachers' stereotyped judgements." *Journal of Multilingual and Multicultural Development.* 15(6):471–489.

Dendrinos, Bessie. This volume. "Foreign-language textbook discourse and pedagogization of the learner."

Garrett, Peter, Nikolas Coupland, and Angie Williams. 1994. In press. "'City Harsh' and 'The Welsh version of RP': Some ways in which teachers view dialects of Welsh English." *Language Awareness 4(2).*

Ivanic, Roz. 1988. "Critical language awareness in action." *Language Issues* 2(2): 2–7.

Ivanic, Roz and Denise Roach. 1990. "Academic writing, power and disguise". In Romy Clark, Norman Fairclough, Roz Ivanic, Nicki McLeod, Jenny Thomas, and Paul Meara (eds.), *Language and power: Papers from the Twenty-Second Annual Meeting of the British Association for Applied Linguistics held at Lancaster University, September 1989.* London: Centre for Information on Language Teaching and Research. 103–121.

James, Carl and Peter Garrett (eds.). 1991a. *Language awareness in the classroom.* London: Longman.

James, Carl and Peter Garrett. 1991b. "The scope of Language Awareness." In Carl James and Peter Garrett (eds.), *Language awareness in the classroom.* London: Longman. 3–20.

Leets, Laura and Howard Giles. 1993. "Does language awareness foster social tolerance?" *Language Awareness* 2(3): 159–168.

Merchant, Guy. 1991. "Linguistic diversity and language awareness: The views of primary school teachers." In Carl James and Peter Garrett (eds.), *Language awareness in the classroom.* London: Longman. 51–61.

Mitchell, Rosamond and Janet Hooper. 1991. "Teachers' views of language knowledge." In Carl James and Peter Garrett (eds.), *Language awareness in the classroom.* London: Longman. 40–50.

Mitchell, Rosamond, Janet Hooper, and Christopher Brumfit. 1994. "'Final report about language': Language learning and the National Curriculum." *Occasional Papers* 19. Southampton, U.K.: Centre for Language in Education, University of Southampton.

Nicholas, Howard. 1991. "Language awareness and second language development." In Carl James and Peter Garrett (eds.). *Language awareness in the classroom*. London: Longman. 78–95.

Schwerdtfeger, Inge C. 1993. "A phenomenological approach to the teaching of culture: An assent to the teaching of language awareness." *Language Awareness* 2(1): 35–46.

Williams, Angie, Peter Garrett, and Nikolas Coupland. In press. "Perceptual dialectology, folklinguistics and regional stereotypes: Teachers' perceptions of variation in Welsh English. *Multilingua*.

Wright, Tony, Rod Bolitho. 1993. "Language awareness: A missing link in language teacher education." *ELT Journal* 47(4): 292–304.

Directness and indirectness in professor–student interactions: The intersection of contextual and cultural constraints

Christina Kakavá[1]
Mary Washington College

Introduction. The notion of directness or indirectness in different types of discourses has been the focus of voluminous studies. Some researchers have claimed that directness or indirectness is a strategy that typifies a cultural group as a whole. For example, Scollon and Scollon (1995) discuss research that considers Asian groups to fall on the indirect end of a continuum when compared to western groups, which fall on the direct end. Katriel (1986) has described the *dugri* "straight talk" speech of Sabra Israelis, whose characteristic is directness, and contrasted it with the Arabic intercultural ethos of *musayra*, which is realized as indirectness. In an early study by Tannen (1981), Greeks and Greek-Americans were found to concentrate on the indirect message or metamessage of a statement more than their American counterparts. This finding is further corroborated by Sifianou (1992), who found that both Greeks and British speakers focused more on the indirect message of an utterance.[2] Some other researchers have focused on certain groups within a culture (for instance in terms of gender) as more direct or indirect, and have accounted for this difference in terms of politeness, interactional goals, or communicative norms. Lakoff (1990), for example, lists indirectness as one of the linguistic traits of American women's talk, which can be viewed as women's politeness. In

---

[1] I want to thank Dean James E. Alatis for giving me the opportunity to participate in the Georgetown University Round Table. This year's theme is especially dear to my heart. Despite the fact that I am a sociolinguist, and a discourse analyst in particular, I was first an EFL teacher in Greece and then an ESL lecturer in the U.S., and I therefore feel very much at home. This Round Table is also important to me for another reason. I decided to pursue graduate studies in sociolinguistics partly because one of the best professors I had as an undergraduate student at the Department of English Studies, University of Athens, urged and encouraged me to do so. She is Bessie Dendrinos, one of our plenary speakers, and I am thrilled to see her after eight years.

[2] More recently, Carmen Silva-Corval, a professor at the University of Southern California, described the Salvadoran culture as more indirect, whereas she characterized Anglo patterns as "more direct, almost rude, with fewer hedges." This comment was in reference to the testimony of Rosa Lopez, a Salvadoran native and key witness in the O.J. Simpson trial (see Lindlaw 1995).

contrast, Keenan (1974) finds that Malagasy men employ an indirect mode of speech which is indexical to a noncommittal behavioral norm. As Keenan puts it, "One is noncommittal for fear that an action openly advocated might have consequences that would have to be borne alone" (1974:130).

Recent studies and discussions of the notion of directness and indirectness have pointed out some of the problems that arise from a blanket generalization of a particular cultural group or subgroup as direct or indirect. Both Tannen (1993, 1994) and Scollon and Scollon (1995) argue that directness or indirectness should not be viewed as a bipolar division. They have suggested that a cultural group or an individual may not use directness or indirectness exclusively, and even the same individual may use different degrees of indirectness depending on the context of the situation and the sociocultural norms of interaction. In addition, one needs to consider specific speech acts within a particular situational context.[3] Are we describing directness or indirectness regarding requests for information, orders, or disagreements? We may find that certain speech acts and not others may be conveyed with different degrees of directness, depending on the potential imposition they cause to the addressees, and other contextual parameters. For instance, in some of my prior research regarding disagreement (Kakavá 1994a, 1994b, 1994c, forthcoming), I found that personal involvement with the topic discussed triggered more direct types of disagreement in the casual conversations of both Greek men and women.

For this reason, to properly examine the contextual and cultural constraints of directness and indirectness, I focus in this paper on a particular speech act, disagreement, which I define here as an oppositional stance taken in response to a prior position. Building on my previous work on undergraduate classroom discourse (Kakavá 1993c), I examine two contextual parameters: institutional and knowledge-based power—that is, the power that one has over other people by knowing more than they do about the subject of talk. The analysis is based on forty hours of tape-recorded classroom interactions between a Greek male student and his American male professor, focusing on their disagreement sequences. The undergraduate classroom provides a good example of a nonreciprocal relationship between professors and students since professors possess institutional power. By that I mean that the professor is the one who normally orchestrates the turns, changes topics, and in general regulates the flow of discussion. The professor is also the one who evaluates what the students say and write, and ultimately the one who grades them. Usually, it is the professor who possesses more knowledge of the subject matter and provides relevant information, which creates another asymmetrical relationship as a result. In

---

[3] Research reported in Blum-Kulka (1989) and in Sifianou (1992) is an example of this type of approach, in which specific types of speech acts are compared cross-culturally.

addition, the classroom provides a forum that is guided by implied distancing norms of politeness, for example Lakoff's (1979, 1990) "Don't impose" rule, since professors are supposed to avoid direct confrontations with students, which would jeopardize classroom harmony.

I found that the student's rather direct disagreement strategies correlated with the amount of factual knowledge he possessed, and, as I have suggested elsewhere (Kakavá 1993a, 1993b), with his conversational style, which may be indexed to his Greek cultural style. The more knowledge he possessed about the subject matter, the more direct his disagreements were. Amount of information for the professor, however, did not correlate with different degrees of directness in his disagreement strategies: The professor did not use direct disagreement strategies in his interactions with the student. Instead, in some cases he opted to ask another student's opinion about a contested point, thus expressing his disagreement through another person. Even in the cases where the professor expressed his disagreement with the student's position without an intermediary, he opted to use what I have called "strong-yet-mitigated" disagreements (Kakavá 1993a, 1993c), for example, ironic statements, and "mitigated types" of disagreement such as accounts. I suggest that the reason the professor did not engage in direct confrontation with the student is because the professor is expected to encourage rather than deter students to participate and voice their opinions. In other words, his tendency to opt for more indirect types of disagreement could be viewed as his effort to create symbolic distance between himself and the student, which is a distancing norm of politeness.

From these findings, I conclude that (1) institutional power does not correlate with direct forms of disagreement; (2) power over one's realm of expertise does not necessarily correlate with the directness of a disagreement strategy; and (3) context-specific politeness norms may "lead" to and reflect different degrees of directness (or indirectness) in the speakers' disagreement discursive strategies.

I start by giving an overview of some relevant research in the area of directness/indirectness as it pertains to issues of power, politeness, and disagreement. I then move to the analysis of data. Based on the findings, I draw conclusions, and finally I discuss the application of this study to the teaching of English as a second or foreign language.

Directness/indirectness, power, politeness, and disagreement. As is well established, speakers may choose a variety of forms to express the same message. In the case of the speech act of disagreement, speakers may decide to use an explicit performative "I disagree," a direct form of disagreement; alternatively, speakers may provide a counter-claim or assessment to a prior claim, for example, speaker A: "She's bright." Speaker B: "No, she's not," where the explicit negative and the counter-claim highlight the polarity between the two statements. According to Lakoff (1990: 30), "One should be honest, direct, and straight from the shoulder". But as she suggests, people live by a "more complex precept" (1990: 30):

> Try to be honest and direct and make your point clearly; but when doing so would infringe on manners or taste, or be actually or potentially hurtful to one or both participants, mitigate your utterance make it harder to understand in order to make it gentler and kinder. (1990:30)

When this second precept is in effect, people may use indirectness, which discourse analysts refer to as the invitation of background or contextual knowledge to interpret the meaning of an utterance. As a result, indirect forms of disagreement will be used, such as, "Wouldn't you say that X is also possible?"

It is not surprising that indirectness has been considered the language of the powerless, since by being indirect, people do not assume the responsibility that a direct speech act entails, thereby avoiding the danger of being held accountable for an action. Lakoff (1990) argues that for the powerless, being indirect is equally dangerous, since their indirectness can be easily misunderstood. This is something, she claims, the powerful need not have to fear because, as she puts it, "Who cares what underlings think of them?" (1990: 32). Furthermore, as Tannen (1994) has illustrated in her book, *Talking from 9 to 5*, being indirect does not exclude power, and both women and men use indirectness in different situations and in different ways. Finally, Scollon and Scollon (1995), in illustrating the relationship that exists between rhetorical patterns, directness, and hierarchical order, argue that deductive rhetorical patterns can be viewed as an involvement politeness strategy, since common ground between the speaker and hearer is assumed. They are both interested in hearing each other's position. In contrast, inductive rhetorical strategies are viewed as an independence politeness strategy in that the speaker does not assume that the listener would "automatically" agree with a position. Scollon and Scollon even go one step further and suggest that in asymmetrical relationships, the person occupying the higher social position is expected to use the deductive approach to bring up a topic, whereas the lower socially ranked person would use the inductive approach.

Regarding the speech act of disagreement, I have shown that disagreement forms can be placed along a continuum that ranges from strong to mitigated (Kakavá 1993a, 1993b); onto this which I now superimpose a direct-indirect continuum (Figure 1).

Based on the variability of forms I found in my data, I have suggested that the oppositional stance that a person takes reflects and constitutes his or her

Figure 1. Continua of disagreement types and degree of directness

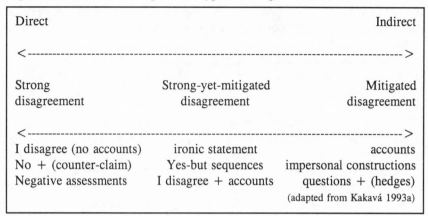

Direct		Indirect
< -- >		
Strong	Strong-yet-mitigated	Mitigated
disagreement	disagreement	disagreement
< -- >		
I disagree (no accounts)	ironic statement	accounts
No + (counter-claim)	Yes-but sequences	impersonal constructions
Negative assessments	I disagree + accounts	questions + (hedges)
		(adapted from Kakavá 1993a)

conversational style along with other contextual parameters such as status, age, gender, communicative norms, and personal involvement with the topic discussed (Kakavá 1993a). In this paper, I will examine two of these factors, namely institutional power and knowledge-based power, and show how they correlate with the degree of directness expressed in disagreement in the hierarchical setting of the undergraduate classroom.

Data analysis. The examples I will discuss come from a forty-hour corpus of audiotaped classroom discourse of an undergraduate Southern European history course.[4] The class took place at an American university for one semester, during which I did participant observation, took field notes, and audio-taped all the sessions with permission. The class consisted of eighteen students representing various ethnic backgrounds such as American, Greek, Greek-American, Italian, and Spanish. Their professor was a white American in his early forties. From the forty recorded hours, I extracted and transcribed two hours which were composed of different excerpts containing disagreement. In this paper, I limit my analysis to disagreement turns taken between the professor and one of the Greek students.

The first two examples will illustrate how the professor expresses his disagreement with a position taken by Minas, a Greek student. At the time the data were collected, Minas, born and raised in Greece, was twenty-two. He had been in the U.S. for four years. His father is Greek and a surgeon, while his mother, a housewife, was born in the U.S. but is of Greek nationality. In the first example, the professor uses a strong-yet-mitigated disagreement strategy,

---

[4] For more information on the data see Kakavá (1993a, 1993b).

an ironic statement. In the second, the professor uses accounts followed by his counter-position. The professor seems to possess more factual information related to the contested point in both examples, which illustrate different instances of the same topic.

The professor had elicited different opinions from the students about two authors, Carlo Levi, and Edward Banfield, who had written books about Italy. The discussion divided the class into two camps. The professor and some American students had pointed out that both authors presented the same picture of southern Italy but differed in their ways of presenting it. On the other hand, the Italian–Greek alliance had a different point of view. They thought that Banfield "seemed to be more negative," whereas Levi was more "appreciative" of the Italians and "more objective." Let us now examine how the professor indirectly disagrees with Minas, the Greek student, who has been an ardent supporter of Carlo Levi. The transcript starts with the concluding statement of an American student who supports the professor's position.

Example 1. Professor–student exchange
(This is the conclusion of a lengthy argument made by Jeff.)

297	Jeff	he [Banfield] did make some valuable observations.
298		Nevertheless, that in some cases,
299		[p] we have seen /??/
300		it might be in some cases a little less dramatic,
301		but nevertheless honest.
302	Prof. →	Minas prefers to throw the baby out with the bathwater.

The professor, by saying that "Minas prefers to throw the baby out with the bathwater," indicates that he sides with the American students and that he does not agree with Minas's position, but he does so in an indirect way, employing a negative politeness strategy (Brown and Levinson 1987), that is, an ironic statement.

Let us now examine another example that follows the previous exchange in which the professor again employs an indirect type of disagreement. Minas had just presented some further evidence against Banfield, arguing that he portrayed the Italians as "doomed," especially since he believed that no economic effort could save the south. The example starts in the midst of Minas's argument and continues with the professor's response.

Example 2. Professor–student exchange

313	Minas	But the fact that he does not claim,
314		specifically, and Banfield does,
315		that any type of solution, any type of investment,
316		or economic effort, or economic development in the south

317		will be doomed,
318		it might be the difference.
319	Prof.	Mhm.
320		Now what does-
321	→	is- this is a very interesting uh way to approach the question,
322		and I haven't thought of it in these terms before.
323		What does Levi propose,
324		as the solution to the problem to the south?
325		He has about ten pages,
326		where he goes into the problems of the south,
327		and tells you what was necessary.
328		You follow that concept?
329		Lucy?
330	Lucy	Uh he opposes autonomous ki- time
331		that the individual to the state prior, by the um,
332		the autonomous communities,
333		and rural communities,
334		and having the peasants being controlled of the schools
335		and the hospitals,
336		and getting rid of this intermediary, of the middle class,
337		uh well, having them control it,
338		control their own communities,
339		instead of these middle class people,
340	Prof.	Mhm.
341	Lucy	to be controlled.
342	Prof.	Mhm.
343		He, he calls for, effectively,
344		the- the liquidation of these doctors and chemists,
345		and druggists or lawyers and mayors,
346		those who represent the state in Galiano,
347		and he says,
348		this is not a precise quotation,
349		but I think it's fair to his meaning,
350		he says,
351	→	nothing short of a peasant revolution,
352		*will* suffice....to solve the problems of the south.
353	→	That means.....Minas,
354	→	that *he's* got no faith in the- in the- in the state,
355		if the state we- were to put all the investment of the south,
356		and try to....build roads and dams and bridges.
357	Minas	I was not aware of the fact that he said that.
358	Prof. →	It's in here, somewhere, guaranteed.

| 359 | Andy | What did he think of the peasants? |
| 360 | Prof. | He does have faith in the peasants. |

Note that in the beginning the professor assesses Minas's point about Banfield positively (line 321) and he even acknowledges that he had not thought of this issue in these terms. At the same time, however, he tries to elicit from the students Carlo Levi's solution for southern Italy by asking them to consider specific pages from the book. After Lucy presents some facts, the professor takes a turn and, by alluding to a specific point made by Carlo Levi (lines 351–352), he points out that Carlo Levi was not optimistic about the south either. At this point he addresses Minas (line 353) and provides the claim that makes Carlo Levi no different from Banfield. Recall that Minas had presented Banfield as not having any faith in the south. The professor, by pointing out that Carlo Levi is no different from Banfield, disagrees with Minas's assessment. What is interesting to note here is that the professor chooses to allude to a specific point in the text that proves that he is right and Minas is wrong in his estimation of the two authors' perspectives, but he does not directly disagree with Minas. He employs an inductive type of reasoning (accounts followed by position), reaching his conclusion at the end, rather than stating his disagreement and then providing the reasons (position followed by account), which is a form of deductive reasoning. So what we have seen in this case is that despite the fact that the professor has both the institutional and the knowledge-based power, he opts not to confront his student directly. (Note, for example, that the professor "guarantees" the piece of information he provided when Minas states that he did not know that Carlo Levi had made such as statement about the future of the south [lines 357–358], which indicates that the professor has a greater knowledge base of the topic).

Let us now turn to examine two examples that illustrate the range of disagreement types that Minas expressed. In the first example, he does not seem to have substantive evidence for his position and his disagreement is rather mitigated. In this case, Minas argues with the professor over the significance of the fascist movement in Italy and its effect on the Italian people. Before the section that I analyze here, the professor had given a lengthy account of the fascist movement. He had mentioned that fascism gave a positive direction to certain groups of people (e.g. to those who were dissatisfied with their life and those resentful of societal changes), since it offered them a program which they found appealing. Minas disagrees with the professor's account:

Example 3. Student–professor
17	Professor	...OK, those are the loose ends that..
18		Any questions about any of those?
19		OK, uh, oh, sorry Minas.

[The professor apologized because he hadn't seen Minas's hand]

20	Minas →	Just, I don't know,
21		uh, I think it's relevant with what you said,
22	→	but, wouldn't it be fair to say
23		that there was more of a reactionary movement
24		rather than a movement that proposed-
25		that had a particular set of policies
26		and a particular direction?
27		I mean it was-
28		But- but in a very in a very concise and- and exact manner.
29		It was more of a reaction to socialists,
30		it was more appealing to the psyche of the individual,
31		the action-oriented movement,
32		this is the /??/ et cetera,
33		but it was not, it was not a movement
34		that really had a set,
35		other than maybe the restoration of Roman imperialism
36		but that had other set goals.
37	→	Maybe, I'm wrong, I don't know,
38	→	but wouldn't it be fair to say that?
39		For example, in governing Italy,
40		it seems that they were doing things,
41		where they found the holes,
42		they were trying to use the old institutions,
43		and trying-
44		they did not have a vision of uh
45		they had a /broad/ vision,
46	→	but they did not have an exact program,
47	→	I guess is what I want to say, beforehand.
48		But they sort of managed the economy,→ all the government the institutions, etc.
49		as they went to /long/ l??l change power.
50	→	Maybe I'm wrong, I don't know.

First note that Minas's turn is marked with some reluctance markers (in line 20 he uses hedges such as "just" and "I don't know"). In the course of his monologic argument, Minas uses two yes/no questions (the second is a repetition of the first). In line 22, the question "wouldn't it be fair to say..." is positioned between the contrastive marker "but" and the upcoming talk, which is Minas's counterclaim: "there was more of a reactionary movement..." (line 23). The second question in line 38 "but wouldn't it be fair to say that?" brackets his preceding contentious position (that fascism did not have a set of goals and a specific direction) and the ensuing example which supports his position. Therefore, we can claim that his support-seeking or confirmation-seeking questions act as "buffers," mitigating either the preceding or subsequent opposition to the professor's position.

Toward the end of his turn (line 46), Minas reiterates his contentious position towards fascism and its supporters: "They did not have an exact program." Although Minas reasserts his point, he brackets his opposition to the professor's point with a mitigating statement: "Maybe I'm wrong, I don't know" (line 50). Despite the fact that Minas expresses a counterposition to the one held by the professor, he makes an effort to mitigate it with support-seeking yes/no questions, hedges, and even acknowledging that "he may be wrong."

Let us compare this example to the following one. In this example, Minas seems to possess more factual information than the professor. The type of disagreement that he uses this time is more direct.

Although the example is rather lengthy, I provide it almost in its entirety to properly contextualize it and show the textual structure of Minas's disagreement strategies. Petros, another Greek student, had asked the professor a question regarding a politician named Karamanlis, who is now the President of Greece. In 1974, after the junta fell, Karamanlis came to Greece from France, was welcomed as a savior, won the elections, and became the Prime Minister. Petros' question was whether the fact that Karamanlis was an "outsider," because he had come from France, had any effect on his acceptance by the Greek people.

Example 4. Student–professor

675	Prof.	Your question makes sense,
676		in the other cases,
677		those who were put in power after juntas,
678		I believe they did not come back from exile,
679		they've been there all along.
680		Although somewhere Alfonsin did come /??/.
681		uh, what difference does that make?
682	→	I'm not sure.]
683	Petros	[I mean when the people who see him
684		and then view his- his newly found policies,
		did they trust him more,
686		do they
687	Prof. →	I don't [know
688	Petros	[Because he's [a
689	Prof.	[Karamanlis had a-
690		had a long track record in- in Greece,
691		he'd been away for most of the uh junta years,

692		but he was a great politician,
693		as you've just told us,
694		and everybody knew who he was,
695		and uh where he stood.
696	→	So.. I guess it's plausible,
697	→	I'm not sure about this,
698	→	plausible that– that,
699		because he had chosen exile,
700		chosen not to..associate himself
		in any way possible he could,
702		with the colonels,
703	→	this uhm lent him a certain um moral authority
704	→	that he otherwise probably would not have had.
705		And that he could cash in on this,
706		exploit this in late '74,
707		but I should think,
708		it would very quickly wear away,
709		as soon as political decisions had to be made.
710	→	So that if it provided him with any extra good will,
711	→	I think it would have had a very short half-life.
712	→	But I-that's just one opinion and maybe we can get some more.
713		Minas and then Amalia.
714	Minas→	I– I disagree with this.
715	→	First of all, he wanted self exile,
716		when the junta came in.
717		He went to self exile
718		four years prior to the junta /?/.
719	Prof.	/??/
720	Minas→	[And it was *not* because of the junta. [increased speed+tempo]
721	→	It was because basically he had lost the elections,
722		and there were a lot accusations
723		about his rigging the elections,
724	→	uh, uh there was a clash
725		that he personally had with the- uh with the monarchy,
726		uh and he left.
727	→	So he didn't leave Greece,
728	→	because of the- because of the junta.
729		Now *this* was something
730		that was viewed toward- by the right,
731		in negative terms.
732		Because he basically abandoned his party.

733		I mean he lost power
734		and he left.
735		He fled.
736		He went to France.
737	→	So it's not that he left
738		because of the junta.
739		But it was– it was–
740		he– he left
741		because he was basically losing the political game.
742		Four years prior to the junta coming into power.
743		And that was a negative factor within his party.
744	→	Now, why was he the one
745		that was– that was viewed like that,
746		like, you know, the- the- the restorer of democracy,
747	→	because he was the smartest guy.
748	Prof.	(laughs)
749	Minas	He was he was a great statesman.
750		And he was the most devious and /had/.
751		Now I don't want to use the expression
752		that he could do it.
753		And– and basically everyone knew that.
754		That he could–
755		that he could pull–
756	→	he could pull the right together,
757		and um– and start the gradual pro– process of– of dejuntification.
758		Clearly, if you look at the politicians
759		that had remained in Athens,
760		and who the political world was at that time,
761		he was the only one
762		who could undertake such a task.
763		uh, and at that point anyone who had,
764		in '74, any politician,
765		who was sort of boosted by the others,
766		to take over,
767		would have been recei- received by the same,
768		uh vigor and happiness by the people.
769	→	So his self exiling was a negative fact,
770		because- because of the circumstances,
771		that were- [under which he went to /see/
772	Prof. →	[He was in France from '63?]
773	Minas	[Yes.]

774   Prof.   [Through'74?
775   Minas   Yes.

In response to Petros' question (lines 683–686), the professor indicates several times that it is possible that Karamanlis's coming from France rather than from Greece could have played a factor in his being more easily accepted by the Greeks, but he also seems to be reluctant to accept this as a valid account. For instance, in line 682 he says "I'm not sure," in line 687 "I don't know," and in lines 696–698 "So...I guess it's plausible, I'm not sure about this, plausible that- that." However, he also does not reject the possibility that this could be a reason, especially when, in lines 703–704, he states that Karamanlis could have gained "a certain moral authority that he otherwise probably would not have had" because he had "chosen not to ... associate himself" with the junta leaders (lines 700–702). But then again in lines 710–711 he mitigates his assessment by claiming that this type of "good will" would have had a "very short half-life." It is important to note at this point that the professor's assessment is a speculation, an opinion, as he characterizes it, at the end of his turn: "But I-that's just one opinion and maybe we can get some more ... " (line 712).

Let us examine how Minas responded to this assessment. Minas expresses his disagreement with the professor's assessment using a strong-yet-mitigated type of disagreement, that is, on-record disagreement followed by accounts that provide counter-evidence to what the professor had seen as plausible scenarios. Minas lists as his first reason that Karamanlis wanted the exile (line 715), and then states that Karamanlis did not go to France because of the junta (line 720), which is the professor's suggested reason for Karamanlis' acceptance. Then he offers more reasons why he believes that the professor's point is wrong, namely that Karamanlis went to France because he had lost the elections (line 721) and because he had a "clash with the monarchy" (line 724–725). I find it interesting that Minas not only disagrees with the professor's suggestion, but also underscores his disagreement by repeating his key contested point three times ("And it was *not* because of the junta," with marked stress in line 720; "so he didn't leave Greece because of the junta" in lines 727–728; and "So it's not that he left because of the junta" in lines 737–738). Then Minas gives his own reasons why Karamanlis was successful: (1) because he was "the smartest guy" (line 747), and (2) because he was the only politician "that could pull the right together" (line 756).

I want to suggest that this type of relatively strong and direct disagreement reflects not only Minas's conversational and cultural style, as I have argued elsewhere (Kakavá 1993c), but also the amount of information he has. Note for example that the professor does not disagree with Minas's assessment, but instead verifies with him the year that Karamanlis left from Greece.[5] Since he asks the clarification questions and Minas answers them, the professor changes the participation structure of the teacher-student relationship. (The lines are provided below for ease of reference.)

772	Prof. →	[He was in France from '63?]	
773	Minas	[Yes.]	
774	Prof. →		[Through'74?
775	Minas	Yes.	

Conclusion. To summarize the findings, I have shown how the professor opts not to disagree directly with his student, but instead employs more indirect means to express his disagreement. On the other hand, I have illustrated that the student's types of disagreement ranged from strong-yet-mitigated to mitigated and correlated with the amount of information he possessed. From these findings, I can conclude that in this setting, for the professor, power (whether institutional or knowledge-based) does not correlate with the degree of directness expressed in his disagreements. Consequently, I suggest that the professor's speech actions were susceptible to a norm of distancing politeness or independence; that is, "Don't impose" (see Figure 2).

As for the student's disagreement types, it became evident that the more knowledge he possesses over the subject matter, the stronger and more direct they became. Therefore, we can conclude that the institutional power differential that existed between him and the professor did not seem to hinder him from expressing his disagreement with the professor rather vehemently, especially when he possessed factual information. It seems that the student's stances could be viewed as subscribing to involvement politeness rules, in other words, those which lead us to "Assume common ground." This interpretation is suggested by Scollon and Scollon (1995) for the deductive rhetorical patterns one uses to raise a topic. In this case, I extend their interpretation to cover the disagreement that the speaker used, since these strategies follow the deductive versus inductive mode.

These two different types of politeness were reflected in the two different disagreement discourse patterns these speakers used. The professor would usually use an inductive discourse pattern (accounts followed by position) when in disagreement with the student, whereas the student employed a rather

---

[5] The junta took over in Greece in 1967. Karamanlis' departure to France in 1963 was prior to the junta and thus not the reason Karamanlis left Greece.

Figure 2. Continuum of disagreement discursive strategies (DDSs)

	Directness	Indirectness
	< -- >	
• Politeness strategy	Involvement	Independence
• DDSs:	Deductive	Inductive
	(Position + accounts)	(Accounts + position)
	(Greek student)	(American professor)

(Modified from Scollon and Scollon's 1995 rhetorical strategies)

deductive discourse pattern (position followed by accounts).[6] It is important to note that this finding is counter to what Scollon and Scollon (1995) predict regarding the use of deductive and inductive discourse patterns in Western cultures in general. They suggest that we would normally expect the person in a higher social position to use the deductive pattern (a more direct discursive strategy) and the person in a lower social position to use the inductive one (a more indirect discursive strategy). I have shown that social position or hierarchical power does not correlate neatly with the type of disagreement discourse pattern used; this illustrates the need for context-specific investigations of notions such as directness/indirectness and disagreement.

It is a given that a professor has institutional power, and yet we found he did not use direct types of disagreement. That does not mean, however, that the professor relinquished or lost his power, or that he is not able to engage in direct disagreement in other cases. As I have argued, particular contexts such as the undergraduate classroom may be guided by implied norms of politeness which some speakers adhere to but others resist, irrespective of their status within a hierarchy. I have also demonstrated how the amount of information one possesses (a form of power) can affect the type of disagreement a person may use, and also how this particular parameter is subject to different norms of

---

[6] In the discussion period after my oral presentation, Sofia Papaefthymiou-Lytra suggested that the Greek student's deductive strategy is influenced by his cultural style and the explicit training that Greek students get in deductive forms of reasoning. Although I agree with her point, I believe that Americans students (and, in this case, American professors) also get trained to follow a deductive form of reasoning in their expository writing (having taught academic writing in the U.S. myself, I can testify to that). And, as a matter of fact, in other, non-contentious cases, the professor did follow a deductive form of reasoning. What I want to point out through my study is that although the professor had at his disposal both a deductive and an inductive form of argument, he opted to use an inductive discursive pattern, possibly because this form is less confrontational than the deductive one and, consequently, more polite and "expected" from a professor.

politeness which are *context-specific*. I think this is very important because other studies have shown that many American men tend to view direct engagement in conflict as a form of involvement and status negotiation (Tannen 1990), while studies on disagreement in electronic newsgroups (e.g. Herring 1995) find that more men than women engage in direct confrontations, called "flaming." This study validates Tannen's (1994) claim that people may use different types of strategies depending on the context, and also my claim that disagreement as a speech action is context-dependent and affected by several interactional and non-interactional forces (Kakavá 1993a).

If we accept that the professor's and student's exchanges were an extension of an "adversative round"[7] during which both the professor and the student were negotiating status (Tannen 1990), it becomes apparent that the professor uses less-direct-disagreement discursive strategies to negotiate it, whereas the student uses more direct ones, especially when he seems to possess more factual information. I consider the professor's move to be pedagogical rather than indicative of his lack of power or inability to express disagreement directly.

Let me conclude by referring to some practical applications this study has for the teaching of ESL or EFL.

Applications. This study has a direct application to the ESL (or EFL) classroom, because it highlights the intricacies of language use as it intersects with several contextual and cultural constraints. Furthermore, it underscores the importance of establishing a "speech act set" as Olshtain and Cohen (1983, 1989) suggest. In other words, in the case of disagreement, ESL/EFL students would benefit from being exposed to different means of expressing disagreement within a language system, for example strong-yet-mitigated and mitigated types. Equally important is the students' exposure to the linguistic, textual, and paralinguistic means of expressing disagreement. These include the conventional forms of expressing disagreement (such as "I don't agree," "It doesn't seem to be right," etc.), the sequential organization of these structures (e.g. disagreement followed by accounts or stories, or accounts followed by disagreement), and their prosodic features of disagreement (accelerated tempo, marked stress, or prosodic features associated with irony, which is a means of expressing disagreement).[8] The next step would be to discuss parameters such

---

[7] In Kakavá (1993a:87), I define adversative rounds as "sustained disagreement for a minimum of two consecutive argumentative turns marked by structural repetition, substitution, and competitive overlaps."

[8] Equally important would be the kinesics involved in the expression of disagreement such as body posture and gestures. Since my study was based on audio-taped data, however, I cannot offer any concrete examples of these types of oppositional stances. Readers are referred to Goodwin's (forthcoming) study for a discussion of this type of oppositional stance.

as the type of relation, i.e. symmetrical/asymmetrical, or the amount of information possessed by the participants. The final step would be to discuss notions such as involvement and independence, or positive and negative politeness, as they pertain to a particular context and culture, and how these different strategies (linguistic, textual, and prosodic) could convey different meanings. This way students would not only achieve a better command of the diverse means to express disagreement, but they would also communicate more effectively in the target language. This would help them avoid potential false characterizations of their personality because of participants' different expectations regarding appropriate and context-specific disagreement discursive strategies.

REFERENCES

Blum-Kulka, Shoshana. 1989. "Playing it safe: The role of conventionality in indirectness." In Shoshana Blum-Kulka, Juliane House, and Gabriele Kasper (eds.), *Crosscultural pragmatics: Requests and apologies*. Norwood, N.J.: Ablex. 37–70.

Brown, Penelope and Stephen C. Levinson. 1987. *Politeness: Some universals in language usage*. Cambridge, U.K.: Cambridge University Press.

Herring, Susan. 1995. "Negotiating gendered faces: Requests and disagreements among computer professionals on the Internet." Paper presented at the Georgetown University Round Table Presession on Computer-Mediated Discourse Analysis, March 8, 1995, Washington, D.C.

Goodwin, Candace. (forthcoming). "Co-construction in girls' hop scotch." In Mary Bucholtz, Anita Liang, and Laura Sutton (eds.), *Communication in, through, and across cultures*. Proceedings of the Third Berkeley Women and Language Conference. Berkeley, California: Berkeley Women and Language Group.

Kakavá, Christina. 1993a. "Negotiation of disagreement by Greeks in conversations and classroom discourse." Unpublished Ph.D. dissertation, Georgetown University.

Kakavá, Christina. 1993b. "Aggravated corrections as disagreement in casual Greek conversations." *Texas Linguistic Forum* 33: 187–195.

Kakavá, Christina. 1993c. "Conflicting argumentative strategies in the classroom." In James E. Alatis (ed.), *Georgetown University Round Table 1993*. Washington, D.C.: Georgetown University Press. 395–414.

Kakavá, Christina. 1994a. "Stylistic variation and macrovariables: Testing Bell's hypothesis." Paper presented at the Linguistic Society of America Annual Meeting, Boston, Massachusetts, January 8, 1994.

Kakavá, Christina. 1994b. "Topic, involvement, and stance as stylistic variables." Paper presented at the American Association of Applied Linguistics Annual Meeting, Baltimore, Maryland, March 8, 1994.

Kakavá, Christina. 1994c. "'If it was your sister...': Personalization in arguments." In Irene Philippaki-Warburton, Katerina Nicolaidis, and Maria Sifianou (eds). *Themes in Greek linguistics: Current issues in linguistic theory, Volume 117*. Amsterdam: John Benjamins. 261–268.

Kakavá, Christina. (forthcoming). "'Do you want to get engaged, baby?': The cultural construction of gender through talk." In Mary Bucholtz, Anita Liang, and Laura Sutton (eds.), *Communication in, through, and across cultures.* Proceedings of the Third Berkeley Women and Language Conference. Berkeley, California: Berkeley Women and Language Group.

Katriel, Tamar. 1986. *Talking straight: Dugri speech in Israeli Sabra culture.* Cambridge, Massachusetts: Cambridge University Press.

Keenan (Ochs), Elinor. 1974. "Norm-makers, norm-breakers: Uses of speech by men and women in a Malagasy community." In Richard Bauman and Joel Sherzer (eds.) *Explorations in the ethnography of speaking.* Cambridge, U.K.: Cambridge University Press. 125–143.

Lakoff, Robin Tolmach. 1979. "Stylistic strategies within a grammar of style." In Judith Orasanu, Mariam Slater, and Leonore Loeb Adler (eds.), *Language, sex, and gender: Annals of the New York Academy of Science* 327: 53–78.

Lakoff, Robin Tolmach. 1990. *Talking power: The politics of language.* New York: Basic Books.

Lindlaw, Scott. 1995. "Poor memory or just culture gap?" *Fredericksburg Free Lance Star*, March 4, 1995. p. A14.

Olshtain, Elite and Andrew Cohen. 1983. "Sociolinguistics and language acquisition." In Nessa Wolfson and Elliot Judd (eds.), *TESOL and sociolinguistic research.* Rowley, Massachusetts: Newbury House. 18–35.

Olshtain, Elite and Andrew Cohen. 1989. "Speech act behavior across languages." In Hans W. Dechert and Manfred Raupach (eds.). *Transfer in language production.* Norwood, N.J.: Ablex. 53–67.

Scollon, Ron and Suzanne Wong Scollon. 1995. *Intercultural communication: A discourse approach.* Cambridge, Massachusetts: Blackwell.

Sifianou, Maria. 1992. *Politeness phenomena in England and Greece: A cross-cultural perspective.* Oxford: Clarendon Press.

Tannen, Deborah. 1981. "Indirectness in discourse: Ethnicity as conversational style." *Discourse Processes* 4: 221–438.

Tannen, Deborah. 1990. *You just don't understand: Women and men in conversation.* New York: William Morrow.

Tannen, Deborah. 1993. "The relativity of linguistic strategies: Rethinking power and solidarity in language in gender and dominance." In Deborah Tannen (ed.). *Gender and conversational interaction.* New York: Oxford University Press. 165–188.

Tannen, Deborah. 1994. *Talking from 9 to 5: How women's and men's conversational styles affect who gets heard, who gets credit, and what gets done at work.* New York: William Morrow.

Addressee, setting, and verbal behavior: How relevant are they in foreign-language teaching?

Yuling Pan
Georgetown University

Introduction. Sociolinguistic studies provide an understanding of how language is situated in social and cultural life (e.g. Goffman 1959, 1967; Gumperz 1982a), and how language, culture, and society are grounded in verbal interaction (e.g. Schiffrin 1994). But the application of findings from sociolinguistic research to foreign-language teaching still lags behind. For example, what specific role does a particular socio-cultural factor play in a given language? Do the factors that influence our verbal behavior share the same weight across cultures? To what extent does a particular social factor—e.g. the setting or the addressee's or speaker's social attributes—call for special attention in teaching a certain foreign language?

This paper explores answers to the above questions with special reference to the Chinese language, and tries to apply findings of sociolinguistic studies to teaching Chinese as a foreign language. Following Brown and Levinson's ([1978] 1987) politeness model, I investigated Chinese politeness behavior in different social settings. This study, based on qualitative and quantitative analyses of audio- and videotaped, naturally occurring conversations and interactions in Chinese, focuses on the use of politeness strategies in Chinese verbal interaction. I argue that there are two fundamental motivations for politeness behavior in Chinese society: One is the acknowledgment of social differences between the speaker and the hearer; the other is the recognition of the addressee's external power associated with situational conditions. In other words, politeness considerations in language use are addressee-oriented as well as setting-sensitive. As a result, the hierarchical level of interaction is given greater emphasis than the interpersonal needs in face work (Goffman 1967; Brown and Levinson 1978, 1987).

I also argue that the setting and the addressee's social attributes are interrelated: One cannot function without the other, because not all social factors play an equal role in different settings. In each setting, there is a tendency for a certain social factor to be recognized as the source of power. For instance, institutionalized power overrides power based on age and gender in the official setting. But gender overwhelms institutionalized power in the family setting. And deference is usually shown to the person with the most power (whether it comes from official rank, gender, or age) in a given setting. Politeness strategies are aspects of language, whereas the addressee's status and setting are social aspects. Because of the inability to separate language from the world in which it resides (Schiffrin 1994), to understand which politeness strategies should be applied in a certain situation, we have to know the dominant factor in that particular setting.

The data for this study were collected using an ethnographic approach in Foshan City, in the Guangdong Province of the People's Republic of China over a period of one year.[1] All taped conversations and interactions occurred in natural settings which included official meetings, family dinner-table conversations, and service encounters. Both Mandarin Chinese and Cantonese Chinese were used in these conversations and interactions. In the next section, I will look at the role of the addressee in verbal interaction. In the section following that, I will examine the role of setting. Then I will conclude with a discussion of the application of the study to teaching Chinese as a foreign language.

The role of the addressee. Brown and Levinson (1987: 62), in their politeness model (1978, 1987), presuppose that human beings possess two kinds of face: positive face—the want that one's own wants be desirable to others; and negative face—the want that one's own actions not be impinged upon by others. Brown and Levinson claim that these face wants are universal and are the basic elements in politeness behavior. Politeness is a face-saving need with different strategies (bald-on-record, positive politeness, negative politeness, and off-record politeness) to address these face wants.

Brown and Levinson's claim regarding face wants in politeness is true in an individualistic society like the United States, where interactants' territory, privacy, and freedom of action are highly valued, and the individual's positive and negative face wants tend to carry more weight than the power associated with the setting and addressee (external factors).

In a society in which hierarchy is strictly observed and collectivism is emphasized, however, group membership can be regarded as the basis for interaction. (See also Ide 1989 for a study of Japanese politeness behavior.) As Scollon and Scollon (1991: 118) point out, "the Asian world is divided into inside (*nei*) and outside (*wai*) relations." Inside relations are those of close regular contact, such as family members, friends, co-workers, or schoolmates. Outside relations are those temporary contacts one has with taxi drivers or clerks in service encounters. This distinction between inside and outside relations is very important in understanding Chinese politeness behavior toward different addressees, because it is these relationships that govern speaking rights and

---

[1] Most conversations were taped by the researcher in various settings. Some were taped by friends and family members.

one's use of different politeness strategies. In an inside relation in Chinese society, there is a culturally established hierarchical relationship between the interlocutors, such as father–son or boss–employee. These social roles also determine who speaks first and who should be deferential. In an outside relation, a service encounter for instance, the positions of the parties are tightly fixed within a role relationship. It is then impossible to develop any relationship other than the business role each party assumes; therefore, no facework is required.

Findings in my study echo Scollon and Scollon's observation. I found that Chinese speakers tend to focus attention on their relative position vis-á-vis the addressee's when choosing politeness strategies. This is because Chinese are "inclined to be socially or psychologically dependent on others, for this situation-centered individual is tied closer to his world and his fellowmen" (Hsu 1981: 13). And for this reason, the sociocultural conditions in which the speech activity takes place assume a larger role than those in the English-speaking world where speech activities are basically speaker-based. It is of vital importance that Chinese speakers take into consideration the external power that is associated with the addressee's social position in verbal interaction. When choosing politeness strategies, the question that the speaker considers here is: "What would be the appropriate thing to say to him/her?" Alternatively phrased, speakers decide what to say and how to say it based on their knowledge of the addressee's age, gender, and social status (especially official rank). Speakers have to recognize the power that comes from the presence of such factors, and follow the cultural norms for different social settings.

Let us consider two pairs of examples. The first pair is two service encounters taking place in a state-run stamp store with the same clerk talking to different customers. The second pair of examples comes from an official setting. Each pair shows how the same speaker talks to different addressees and how social relations between the speaker and hearer affect the use of politeness strategies.

Example 1. In a state-run stamp store.
[C#13 (customer #13) is a male in his twenties. The clerk is a female in her thirties. The interaction is in Cantonese.]
(C#13 approaches the counter.)
→ (1) C#13: *Beih leng zeng godi mingsenpin.*
("give two CL² those postcards")
Give me two of those postcards.
(2) Clerk: *Yed tou dinghei leng zeng?*
("one set or two CL")
One set or just two postcards?

---

² CL denotes a classifier.

(3) C#13: *Yed tou.*
            ("one set")
            One set.
(4) Clerk: *Yed tou sam hou.*
            ("one set three dime")
            Thirty cents for one set.
(5) C#13: *Sam hou.*
            ("three dime")
            Thirty cents.
(C#13 pays the money, and the clerk gives him the postcards.)

In this interaction, the relationship between the clerk and her customer is assumed to be an outside one, in which there is no established hierarchical order because the marked social status of each interlocutor is not revealed. Thus the relationship involves no more than the business roles of buyer and seller. Also, since this is a state-run business, the clerk does not have to worry about pleasing customers;[3] therefore, no facework is required. In this encounter, verbal exchanges are brief and terse without politeness strategies. The customer initiates the interaction by a direct request (line 1, "Give me two of those postcards"), which is a task-oriented bald-on-record strategy. The clerk contributes two turns to this interaction: One is a question to clarify the customer's request (line 2, "One set or just two postcards?"); in the other, she tells the total price. At the closing of this interaction, there is no verbal exchange or formal ending to the service encounter, in contrast to American English where both servers and customers are expected to say "Thank you" and maybe "Goodbye" to close encounters. We may well say that in a Chinese outside relationship, the interpersonal relationship is minimized and no facework is expected.

Let us look at another interaction, this time between interlocutors in an inside relation. The excerpt in Example 2 is the first part of an interaction between the same clerk and her superior (the chairman of the labor union). We notice that the interaction is much longer, with small talk before and after the transaction itself. Small talk, as Brown and Levinson put it, is "where the subject of talk is not as important as the fact of carrying on a conversation" (1987: 109). Also, it is a way to claim common ground between the speaker and the addressee—the articulation of common concerns and common attitudes towards interesting events (1987: 117–118). Small talk aims at creating sociability, which, as Simmel (1961: 158) described it, "in its pure form has no ulterior end, no content and no result outside itself." This type of interaction

---

[3] In a state-run business, the employee gets a fixed salary regardless of sales volume and, once hired, he/she is not likely to be fired. This affects the employee's attitude toward work.

style focuses on the interpersonal relationship and is certainly different from the style found in Example 1.

Example 2. In a state-run store.
[Customer #24 is a male in his fifties and chairman of the labor union of the stamp company. The interaction is in Cantonese.]
(C#24 walks into the store.)

(1) Clerk: *Wai, neihge zei fanlei la?*
             ("hi your son return TW[4]")
             Hi, is your son back?

(2) C#24:   *Fan la.*
             ("back TW")
             Yes.

(3) Clerk: *Ah?*
             ("ah")
             What?

(4) C#24:   *Fan la.*
             ("back TW")
             Yes, he's back.

(5) Clerk: *Ah? fugyun la?*
             ("ah get out of (army) TW")
             Oh, out of the army?

(6) C#24:   *Fanlei.*
             ("return")
             He's back.

(7) Clerk: *Hei m hei fugyun la?*
             ("be not be get out of (army) TW")
             Did he get out of the army?

(8) C#24:   *Hei ya. A Wu gemyed mou fan?*
             ("yes TW ah Wu today not back")
             Yes. Is Ah Wu back today?

(9) Clerk: *A Wu gemyed sengzeo gindou keur.*
             ("Ah Wu today morning see him")
             Yes, I saw him this morning.

(There are eight more exchanges of small talk about Ah Wu and somebody else.)

(10) C#24:   *Souyedfung dou zo mei?*
             ("F.D.C. arrive ASPECT not")
             Have you got the F.D.C. (stamps) yet?

---

[4] TW denotes a tone word.

The relationship between C#24 and the clerk is considered an inside one within a superior–subordinate hierarchy. Thus the clerk, as the one in the lower position, greets the chairman first by asking about the Chairman's son (line 1), in contrast with Example 1, where the customer makes the initial move. The chairman asks about another person (Ah Wu) whom they both know. This small talk goes on for a few seconds before the chairman makes his request to buy stamps (line 10). As Scollon and Scollon (1991) observe, in Chinese culture, the subordinate is expected to greet his/her superior in a structured answer to a subtle, but clear, nonverbal signal from the superior that he/she is open to a greeting. This observation applies to this case because the chairman walks in and makes eye contact with the clerk, who then responds to this signal with a verbal greeting. Even though both the clerk and the chairman know quite well the expected goal of their encounter—to sell or buy stamps—they are engaged in small talk before the customer brings up the topic of wanting to see some F.D.C. stamps. This strategy of deferring the introduction of the topic until after a considerable period of small talk serves the purpose of extended facework.

The second pair of examples is from an official meeting. These examples show how the addressee's official rank affects the use of politeness strategies. In Example 3, Fan, a deputy secretary of the Municipal Youth League Committee,[5] is talking to one of his subordinates.

Example 3. Fan is talking to a subordinate
(1) Fan: *Xingkeih geih? Wei, lo go go*
("week what-day hey get that CL")
yedlig lei.
("calendar come")
What day is today? Hey, hand me that calendar.

Fan occupies a higher position than the addressee in terms of rank. This institutional constraint of rank hierarchy gives Fan the power to deliver an order without using any politeness strategies to reduce the imposition. He does not use any address form, but just utters the word "Hey" to get the addressee's attention, and directly issues the order. This direct style, however, does not offend the addressee, since their relationship is acknowledged as that of a superior and a subordinate, and no linguistic devices are needed to modify this face-threatening act (FTA).

Nevertheless, in another situation when a subordinate talks to a superior, the subordinate modifies his speech by showing deference to the addressee who has

---

[5] The Municipal Youth League Committee is a government organization in charge of political education and activities for young people under twenty-eight.

a higher position. Example 4 is an excerpt of a discussion at a meeting on working out a New Year plan for the Municipal Youth League Committee. In this example, we will see how subordinates show support to Leo, the person of highest rank in the group, by using the rhetorical devices of repetition and providing details.

Example 4. Discussing the New Year plan.
[The conversation is in Cantonese. The participants, presented in rank order, are: Leo (male, secretary, age 34), Fan (male, deputy secretary, age 28), Tai (male, department head, age 30), and Rong (male, department head, age 30).]

(1) Leo: *Ngo ding go yed-ji.*
("I set CL date")
I'll set a date.

→ (2) Tai: *Ding go yed-ji la.*
("set CL date TW")
Set a date.

→ (3) Rong: *Ding go xi-gan. Lo-dou co-bou yi-gin,*
("set CL time get primary opinion")

(4) *fan-heur qu-leih, hou m hou?*
("go-back handle good not good")
Set a date. (We'll) get some ideas and can go back to handle it, right?

→ (5) Tai: *M hei, yeo go xi-gan hou zou xi.*
("not be have CL time good do things")

(6) *Mou go xi-gan, m ji geih xi.*
("have-not CL time, not know what time")
No, it's easier to do things if we have a set date, otherwise (we) don't know our schedule.

(7) Fan: *Ngo tei gem-yengr hou m hou?*
("I see this-way good not good")

(8) *Teo-xin Leo xu-geih gong zo hou do.*
("just-now Leo secretary talk TENSE a lot")

(9) *zeo hei ni go yedji yiu ming-nin,*
("just be this CL date need next-year")

(10) *yi-ceh yiu hei ngo-deih ni go ...*
("moreover must at we this CL ...")
How about this. Secretary Leo talked a lot just now. The date should be set for sometime next year. What's more, it must be at our ...

(11) Leo: *Qun-wei wui qin*
("committee meeting before")

        Before the committee meeting.
→   (12) Fan: *Qun-wei wui qin. Qun-wei wui qin.*
        ("committee meeting before, committee meeting before")
    (13)   *Qun-wei wui qin.*
        ("committee meeting before")
        Before the committee meeting, before the committee meeting,
        before the committee meeting ...

In the above example, when Leo, the secretary of the committee and highest in rank of the group, makes a suggestion of setting a deadline for the work plan (line 1, "I'll set a date"), all other members show deference by giving assent. Tai repeats Leo's suggestion (line 2, "Set a date") to show that he is listening to and supports Leo. (For the function of repetition in discourse see Tannen 1989: 51.) Then both Rong and Tai provide further reasons for setting up a schedule (so that they will know what to do, lines 3–6). Fan also repeats three times what Leo suggests (lines 12–13, "Before the committee meeting, before the committee meeting, before the committee meeting"). All these repetitions and supporting details show each speaker's deference to the one in a higher position.

These examples suggest that speakers tend to modify their speech based on their knowledge of the addressee's social status. When there is an established hierarchical order between the interlocutors, deference is expected from the one in the lower position to the one in the higher position. This deference can be seen as a matter of social code (conventional norms) and a social fact reflecting the relative statuses of the participants in the hierarchy (cf. Hwang 1990). In the Chinese context, it is also a politeness consideration.

The role of setting. So far, I have discussed how the addressee's power (or lack of it) can affect a speaker's choice of politeness strategies. But does an addressee's power come from age, gender, or social status? And are these factors of equal importance in all verbal interactions? Does one override the other, and under what circumstances? This is where the role of setting comes in.

In Chinese culture, if the interaction takes place in a setting where no hierarchical relationship is established, it is difficult for interlocutors to speak with deferential politeness. This is the reason why Westerners find that in service encounters "the customary deferential politeness of the Chinese seems to be thrown to the winds" (Scollon and Scollon 1991: 118).

In an inside relationship, however, who is up and who is down depends on the circumstances of the interaction. There are different factors at play in different settings. As I show elsewhere (Pan 1994a, 1994b), rank is the determinant factor in the official setting, whereas in the service encounter, it is the relationship established prior to the business one that matters. For instance, if the server and the customer are acquainted, solidarity is sought after, therefore positive-politeness strategies are applied. In a situation where there is no prior relationship between the server and the customer, the use of strategies for face-saving is very limited. But in the family environment, gender overrides rank and age in crossgender interaction, and age takes precedence in the same gender group.

Consider the following example of a family dinner-table conversation with four participants: the mother (Liping, who is in her late fifties), the son (Fan, who is in his twenties), the daughter (Lanlan, who is in her thirties), and her husband (Dahua, who is also in his thirties). This excerpt shows how participants position themselves in relation to others, highlighting the fact that the impact of gender overwhelms age differences in crossgender interaction.

Example 5. Family dinner-table conversation in Mandarin.
Lanlan (female, 30's, daughter); Dahua (male, 30's, husband of Lanlan)

(1) Fan: *Houtian hai yao qu ci*
              ("the-day-after-tomorrow again need go once

(2)   *Sanshui, Houtian qu ci*
              ("Sanshui. the-day-after-tomorrow go once

(3)   *Sanshui,*
              ("Sanshui")
              I have to go to Sanshui (town) again the day after tomorrow.
              I'm going to Sanshui the day after tomorrow.

→ (4) Lanlan: *Shi bu shi ni gei wo mai bao?*
              ("be not be you for me buy bag")
              Would you buy me a bag?

→ (5) Fan: *Bu gei ni mai. Ni bu zhi yao mai*
              ("not for you buy you not know want buy

(6)   *shenme yang de bao.*
              what kind TW bag")
              No, I won't. You don't know what kind of bag you want.

(7) Liping: *Shenme bao, shoutibao ah?*
              ("what bag handbag TW")
              What kind of bag? Is it a handbag?

(8) Dahua: *Shenme dongxi dou keyi bang ni mai,*
              ("what thing all can help you buy

(9)   *shoutibao shi mei na yige bang ni mai.*
              handbag be no which one help you buy")
              He could buy anything else for you. But nobody can help
              you buy a handbag.

→ (10) Fan: *Meiyou banfa bang ni mai.*

("no way help you buy")
There is no way I can help you buy it.
→ (11) Dahua: *Eh, shoutibao yiding yao ziji mai.*
("TW handbag definitely need self buy")
Yeah, you definitely have to buy a handbag yourself.

In this excerpt, Lanlan makes a request asking her younger brother, Fan, to buy her a handbag. Her request is structured in the form of a question (line 4, "Would you buy me a bag?") which reduces the imposition of the request and thus makes it more polite (Brown and Levinson 1987: 135). Yet Fan not only refuses her bluntly without any face-redressive device (line 5, "No, I won't"), but also implies that Lanlan is the one that is to blame since she does not know what she wants (lines 5–6). He repeats his refusal in line 10, leaving Lanlan no space to negotiate. What is interesting is that Dahua, her husband, joins Fan, reaffirming and giving an explanation for Fan's refusal (lines 8–9, line 11) rather than teaming up with his wife. Here deference is shown to men and the factor of age is not so important in crossgender interaction.

The role of setting in Chinese politeness behavior can be explained in Schiffrin's argument that

> language and context co-constitute one another: language contextualizes and is contextualized, such that language does not just function *in* context, language also forms and provides context ... Language, culture, and society are grounded in interaction: they stand in reflexive relationship with the self, the other, and the self-other relationship. (1994:134)

In Chinese culture, the setting contextualizes verbal behavior and the hierarchical order among interlocutors. It is within a particular setting that a particular social factor becomes the source of power for the interlocutors' relationship.

It can never be overemphasized, however, that almost all sociocultural factors are present in all cultures. To understand why people speak the way they do, we have to know how much consideration they give to each factor and where their starting point is. Knowledge of this kind is indispensable in decoding the messages that speakers intend to convey by the language that they use.

Implications of this study. In this study, I emphasize the importance of the addressee's social attributes and setting in Chinese language use. I argue that Chinese politeness is hierarchical in nature and that the hierarchical order is different in different settings. This study can be applied to the following areas:

(1) *Teaching-material preparation.* Many textbooks use formal, polite expressions which may not occur in real life situations. If students are

taught only the formal and polite way of expressing themselves, it is easy for them to misunderstand the situation and people in real-life situations. For instance, they will think that the Chinese are very rude or they do not like foreigners when they encounter Chinese who do not use the polite, formulaic expressions found in textbooks. I suggest that data collected for sociolinguistic research can also be a relevant source for material development.

(2) *Teacher training*. For those who teach Chinese as a foreign language, knowledge of how people actually interact with one another is indispensable in guiding students toward appropriate use of Chinese, not just usage which is grammatically correct. If the ability to communicate effectively and appropriately is the final goal of our teaching, findings from the present study will help Chinese-language teachers realize the importance of the addressee's status in verbal interaction, and the constraints of a particular social setting on the interlocutors. Such findings will also provide reasons for people's verbal behavior, and reveal links between language use and larger sociolinguistic contexts.

(3) *Classroom activities*. If we understand the varieties of strategies used in real-life situations, classroom activities can be designed to include different settings, and the genders, ages, and social statuses of speakers.

Conclusion. Sociolinguistic findings do have applications for foreign-language teaching. Goffman (e.g. 1959, 1967) maintains that language is situated in particular circumstances of social life, and it reflects and adds meaning and structure in those circumstances. In this study I have shown that the cultural significance of the roles of the addressee and the setting is encoded in Chinese language in that uses of politeness strategies reflect speakers' concerns for addressees' social attributes and the particular settings of interactions. If we understand the relationship between language and social life, and the cultural constraints that affect Chinese-language use, we can certainly better cultivate our students' sensitivity to these issues.

REFERENCES

Brown, Penelope and Levinson, Stephen. [1978] 1987. *Politeness: Some universals in language usage*. Cambridge, U.K.: Cambridge University Press.
Goffman, Erving. 1959. *The presentation of self in everyday life*. New York: Anchor Books.
Goffman, Erving. 1967. *Interaction ritual: Essays on face to face behavior*. Garden City, N.Y.: Doubleday.

Gu, Yueguo. 1990. "Politeness phenomena in modern China." *Journal of Pragmatics* 14(2): 237-257.

Gumperz, John (ed.). 1982a. *Language and social identity*. Cambridge, U.K.: Cambridge University Press.

Gumperz, John. 1982b. *Discourse strategies*. Cambridge, U.K.: Cambridge University Press.

Hsu, Francis L.K. 1981. *American and Chinese: Passage to differences*. Honolulu: University of Hawaii Press.

Ide, Sachiko. 1982. "Japanese sociolinguistics: Politeness and women's language". *Lingua* 57: 357-387.

Ide, Sachiko. 1989. "Formal forms and discernment: Two neglected aspects of universals of linguistic politeness." *Multilingual* 8(2-3): 223-248.

Li, Charles and Sandra A. Thompson. 1981. *Mandarin Chinese*. Berkeley, California: University of California Press.

Lii-Shih, Yu-hwei E. 1986. *Conversational politeness and foreign language teaching*. Taipei: The Crane Publishing Co., Ltd.

Lii-Shih, Yu-hwei E. 1994. "What do *yes* and *no* really mean in Chinese?" In James E. Alatis (ed.), *Georgetown University Round Table on Languages and Linguistics 1994*. Washington, D.C.: Georgetown University Press. 128-149.

Liu, Zaifu and Gang Lin. 1988. *Chuantong yu zhongguoren* ("Tradition and Chinese"). Hong Kong: Joint publishing (H.K.) Co., LTD.

Matsumoto, Yoshiko. 1988. "Reexamination of the universality of face: Politeness phenomena in Japanese." *Journal of Pragmatics*. 12: 403-426.

Matsumoto, Yoshiko. 1989. "Politeness and conversational universals—observations from Japanese." *Multilingual*. 8(2-3): 207-221.

Pan, Yuling. 1993. "Chinese directives and politeness strategies." Paper presented at the Presession on Linguistic, Cultural, Pedagogical Issues in Chinese Acquisition, at the Georgetown University Round Table on Languages and Linguistics 1994, Washington, D.C.

Pan, Yuling. 1994a. "Politeness strategies in Chinese verbal interaction:a sociolinguistic analysis of spoken data in official, business and family settings." Unpublished Ph.D. dissertation, Georgetown University.

Pan, Yuling. 1994b. "Language use in Chinese official settings." Paper presented at the Fifth International Conference on Language and Social Psychology, University of Queensland, Brisbane, Australia.

Schiffrin, Deborah. 1994. *Approaches to discourse*. Cambridge, Massachusetts: Blackwell.

Scollon, Ron and Suzanne B.K. Scollon. 1981. *Narrative, literacy and face in interethnic communication*. Norwood, N.J.: Ablex.

Scollon, Ron and Suzanne B.K. Scollon. 1991. "Topic confusion in English-Asian discourse." *World Englishes* 10(2): 113-125.

Scollon, Ron and Suzanne Wong Scollon. 1994. *Intercultural Communication*. Cambridge, Massachusetts: Blackwell Publishers.

Tannen, Deborah. 1989. *Talking Voices*. Cambridge, U.K.: Cambridge University Press.

Zhao, Guangyuan and Wendshe Gao (eds.). 1990. *Minzu yu wenhua* ("Nationality and culture"). Nannin, China: Guangxi People's Publishing House.

Zheng, Dekun. 1987. *Zhonghua minzu wenhua shi lun*. ("Introduction to the history of Chinese nationality and culture"). Hong Kong: Joint Publishing (H.K.) Co., LTD.

Talk in mature L2 adult-learner classroom discourse

John J. Staczek
Georgetown University

Introduction. Classroom interaction research (Bailey 1980, 1990; Day 1990; Nunan 1989) has focused on teacher-learner and learner-learner interaction in the foreign language to identify what actually happens in the classroom in the foreign language. Much of the same classroom interaction research is interested in learner talk for what it reveals about stages of interlanguage or is interested in teacher talk for what it reveals about input and instruction. Another level of interaction is the learner comment, the learner "speak-out," "speak-up," "talk-out," or "act-out," followed sometimes by a teacher comment, and sometimes by subsequent learner-teacher negotiation in the L1 or in a combination of the L1 and the L2 that forms part of the negotiation of meaning about forms, structures, and usage. More often than not, the speak-out is intended for the learner or learner peer in the classroom and is thus not clearly audible to the teacher. Often it is one of the subtexts of the learner interaction. Its richness may provide some clues about the acquisition of linguistic knowledge and the process of dealing with the knowledge.

Purpose. In examining the data on classroom interaction subtexts, I am attempting to do the following: (1) to categorize the content of classroom metalinguistic social interaction (though not all the interaction is metalinguistic), (2) to determine the functions of the learner and teacher talk, (3) to define the contributions of casual interaction (style-shifting and code-mixing) to learner interlanguage, and (4) to explore created involvement by learner and teacher.

Data collection. The data for this paper were collected between 1991 and 1993 in formal instructional settings in Polish second-language acquisition. I was originally a participant in the class, and like many mature adult learners I audiotaped the sessions. After the second class in 1990 I began to realize that there was more than the usual learner-learner, teacher-learner interaction—that is, there was more talk than just instructional talk for input and output purposes. My attention was interrupted by the occasional "under the breath" talk in which participants or learners engage more for themselves and their peers than usually for their teachers. In my view, if it were intended for their teachers, their teachers would hear more of it more often. As the talk grew in frequency and intensity I realized I was becoming part of another level of instruction and comprehension in the second-language classroom. I recalled in my own language-teaching experiences over some twenty years that I had never really heard all that same talk or the detail of it because I was managing learning through the activities I had planned for instruction and learning. Thus I began earnestly listening more to the audience talk, the learner talk, and I began to take notes to remind myself what was going on when the talk turned away from systematic practice of forms, from teacher modeling, and from learner production. I thus became the participant-observer in the classroom interaction and, because I considered myself more advanced than most other learners with regard to experience with the phonology, the lexicon, listening comprehension, and linguistic descriptions of Polish, I eventually observed myself changing my role to that of observer while still trying to maintain my cover as a participant. In some ways, I was learning to split my attention, so to speak, in my language learning, between focus on form and focus on talk. The other learners, at least some of them, were also splitting their attention between learning and comment.

Description of learners and setting. Over the period of two courses (Introductory and Intermediate) offered through the School for Summer and Continuing Education at Georgetown University, I managed to collect about eighteen hours of tape-recorded material. The courses met for three hours each Saturday morning for approximately twenty-two weeks. The nineteen learner-participants had the following characteristics: An age range of nineteen to seventy-two, with a majority between twenty-seven and fifty-four; most had minimal exposure to Polish either through other courses, self-instruction, or immersion through personal relationships or through travel; the majority were highly motivated professionals, from graduate students to physicians to government bureaucrats to accountants; sixteen were women, eight were men. One was a retired professional writer. The oldest member of the group was perhaps the most outspoken in her talk-outs. None was a professional language learner; all seemed to be instrumentally motivated as many were planning job-related travel. One was married to an L1 speaker of Polish. Three were of Polish-American descent who had been exposed to Polish in early childhood.

The two teachers were both L1 speakers of Polish with professional degrees from Poland in Polish philology or applied linguistics. The data can be attributed to about nine of the total number of participants.

Categories of data. Turning to a categorization of the data by content, I find that there are at least two categories of talk: (1) Talk in which meaning about the grammar is negotiated through focus on form; and (2) talk which reveals affect on the part of the learner, affect that expresses anxiety, intolerance, indifference, discomfort, frustration, misunderstanding, solidarity with other learners, sarcasm, cynicism, perception, or attitude.

Forms of language data. A first category is the negotiation of meaning about the grammar, about the forms of the language. It is perhaps best exemplified by some of the research on focusing on form in which the learners talk explicitly about language forms. The interaction occurs mostly in English and not infrequently with Polish lexical items, most often in uninflected form. The learners are listening to the teacher-centered or other learner-centered modeling based on dialog repetition, story-telling, or other forms of practice based on oral and written exercises. They also seem to be attuned to learner-produced forms which the teacher evaluates positively with such reinforcing language as *dobrze, bardzo dobrze, świetnie,* and *pięknie,* the English equivalents of "good," "excellent," "great," and "nice"—the last being perhaps a bit more informal. Comments in the interactions or simple responses from the learners contain language about language in the learners' efforts to understand certain principles of the grammar, whether phonological, morphological, lexical, syntactic, or even pragmatic. The learners' comments underscore their emerging, often incomplete, knowledge of forms and their inability to inflect them.

For example, in response to the teacher's modeling of the word-final cluster *-tr* in *jesiotr* ("sturgeon"), the learner responds with:

(1)   S: Are we hearing that *r* in *jesiotr*?

The teacher responds with an exaggerated reproduction of the word-final cluster.

In the next three sequences, the learners indicate their level of knowledge about inflection and functions of forms, which often amounts to gaps in form-related knowledge:

(2)   S: Does English have an instrumental case?
(3)   S1: That [reference to a nominal form] would decline?
        T: Yes.
        S2: Yeah, you bet.
(4)   S: I know the *pana/pani*, but don't know the case.

In asking the following question, the learner allows us to see how she understands gendered forms of address and the singular/plural distinction, but fails on the choice of metalinguistic form for the morphological process:

(5)   S: Can *pana, pani, panstwo* conjugate?

In (6), the teacher focuses on a form produced by a learner and asks about its gender. The learner replies with different, but related, information:

(6)   T: Is it masculine, feminine, or neuter?
        S: It's plural.

The learner comment in (7) is a learner justification of a repair:

(7)   S: I did the singular so I had to change it.

In (8), the learner identifies a gap in his knowledge of forms by code-switching:

(8)   S: *To jest* ... I can't say it in Polish.

And in (9), the learner appears to admit to an ostensible lack of knowledge about certain forms, while at the same time even signaling an unwillingness to try to produce a form:

(9)   S: I don't know the pronouns.

In the turns of interaction between learner and teacher in (10), we have a negotiation about an adverb that is recognized as being related to an adjective, an awareness of gaps in form-related knowledge, a request for more information and a resolution/comment, mostly in desperation, even sarcasm. In the exchange in (10) between learner and teacher about the adverbial intensifier *bardzo* ("very") before an adjective that inflects for gender, the learner expresses some confusion:

(10)   S: Doesn't it change it?
        T: Why should it change it?
        S: I don't know.
        T: No, the adverb doesn't change.
        S: It doesn't change? Of *course* not.

I comment later on turn three and turn five in (10), for what they reveal about affect.

Within this category of talk the learner also lexically mixes English and Polish, in most cases calling attention to gaps in forms or classes, as shown in:

(11)   S: I only learned *lubić* "to like, love."
(12)   S: I think she's lying to us [re *wabić się* "to be named, called, lure"]. How can "call" and "lure" be related? [after checking a dictionary entry]

The first part of the turn in (12) also reveals something about learner affect and anxiety.

In (13), the learner, in focusing on form, reveals lexical knowledge and accompanying gaps in knowledge, not at all unlike what we notice in other language learning environments.

(13)   S: *Słucha* "she listens" and she's *śpiewa*ing "sing-"

Some related work done recently by Boyson, Jourdenais, Ota, and Stauffer (1994) at Georgetown discusses a similar kind of explicit mention of verb forms among second-language learners of Spanish, in such examples as (14) through (17):

(14)   S: *Entonces, la policia, u, corre,* nn now we're back in the present.
(15)   S: I think it's *pensó*, I don't know if the stem changes.
(16)   S: Um, I have no idea how to say that in the preterit.
(17)   S: It's irregular.

The comments in (18) and (19), while they come from the Polish class data, exhibit an undeniable universality, when compared to (14) through (17). They also exhibit the learner's ability to verify comprehension through minimal talk.

(18)   S: I didn't use the singular so I had to change it.
(19)   S: I don't need any ending, right?

In item (20), another attempt by the same learner which occurred during an exercise on telling time, the learner managed, via talk, to indicate confusion about how to say "twelve thirty," given such choices as "thirty minutes after twelve" or "thirty minutes before one" (in Polish *o wpól do pierwszej* or *dwunasta trzyjdziesci*).

(20)   S: I thought you had to do the backward thing (with reference to telling time on the half-hour).

The code-switched or code-shifted phrase is not unusual in the comments and is well represented in a comment such as (21), with a redundancy that literally translates as "in in Polish":

(21)   S: What's that in *po polsku*?

Affective data. On the phonological level, in (22) the learner is corrected by the teacher for nasalizing the final vowel. Since the final nasal does exist in several social varieties of Polish, the learner's response is defensive:

(22) S: *Będę* "I will" (final *ę* nasalized).
      T: *Będę* "I will" (non-nasalized final *ę*).
      S: That's how I was taught.

It is at this point, the third turn, in the interaction in (22), that we arrive at the second category of the interaction data that is perhaps best characterized by calling it affective comment, in which talk reveals affect on the part of the learner, affect that expresses anxiety, intolerance, indifference, discomfort, frustration, misunderstanding, solidarity, sarcasm, cynicism, resignation, perception, and attitude. These expressions of affect appear to be triggered by the focus on form in which gaps in learner knowledge are revealed. The teacher correction is acknowledged but not fully accepted, as indicated by the somewhat defensive tone in the turn.

In (23) the teacher comments on the forms of some *-ać* verbs, the response to which is a further comment from the learner about *-eć* verbs. The learner's comment is followed by a comment, meant humorously or sarcastically, from a second learner on the overall complexity in the verb morphology.

(23) T: Not all *-ać* verbs conjugate in the same way. There are some
         stem changes.
      S1: Think of what happens to the stem with *-eć* verbs. [re
          irregularity]
      S2: Terrible things.

In (24) the learner makes an attempt to refocus the activity for the teacher and the class.

(24) S: OK, honey, let's get back to *ptak* "bird."

The teacher was unfazed by the comment and the form of address.

On the phonological level, in an effort to assist the learner by providing some metalinguistic talk in the interaction in (25), the learner rebuffs the teacher for even mentioning "hard" versus "soft" sounds, or nonpalatals versus palatals.

(25) T: It's a hard sound.
      S: I don't know what's hard or soft.

Revisiting some of the examples cited earlier, the third turn in (3), rude as it may seem, conveys more affect:

(3)   S1: That [reference to a nominal form] would decline?
        T: Yes.
        S2: Yeah, you bet.

In (10), referred to earlier for its sequence of turns about metalinguistic knowledge, the learner conveys some level of resignation in unconsciously admitting to gaps in knowledge:

(10)   S: Doesn't it change it?
        T: Why should it change it?
        S: I don't know.
        T: No, the adverb doesn't change.
        S: It doesn't change? Of *course* not.

The rudeness depicted in (12), not overheard by the teacher, may be an attempt to create solidarity with another learner, or even to seek validation for shortcomings in her learning:

(12)   S: I think she's lying to us [re *wabić się* "to be named, called, lure"]. How can "call" and "lure" be related? [after checking a dictionary entry]

In an attempt at face-saving in (26), the learner responds with some embarrassment about his imperfect, gapped, or even absent knowledge about numbers in Polish:

(26)   T: (repeating question in English?) How long did you live in _____ ?
        S: I don't know my numbers.

This second category is replete with talk that reveals affect on the part of the learner, affect that is expressed as discomfort, frustration, misunderstanding, solidarity, sarcasm, cynicism, resignation, or attitude. Of course, not all affect is negative, as some of the most humorous examples demonstrate. In (27) through (31), the learners appear self-deprecating, seeking sympathy for their plight, creating solidarity in their endeavor, and finally showing their metalinguistic mastery.

(27)   S: Yeah, we're trying to demonstrate that we're totally retarded.
(28)   S: I forgot everything.

(29)   S1: I'm embarrassed to ask.
        S2: I'm glad you did.
(30)   S: I guess we're being told, *pan Henryk.*
(31)   S: Help me out here.

Through talk, the learner demonstrates some progressive knowledge about the learning, about forms, and about language use. The learner also demonstrates an eagerness to try, even if it is on his own terms, how he can cope. The efforts are all so human, so reminiscent of talk for bonding, for building relations, and for understanding.

In the talk, the learner opens a window on himself to reveal an organization of knowledge through negotiating talk. Referring to the teacher in (32), the learner did in fact respond to the teacher; and in (33) the learner sought the approval of her peers.

(32)   S: She said "try." I made a mistake, but I tried.
(33)   S: I'm going to miss these Saturdays. I'm going to miss the tension.

Conclusion. It was my intention to bring to your attention another level of classroom talk, of classroom chatter, that reveals in its richness another kind of discourse that is not often heard by the teacher or, if heard, exploited in any way by the teacher or the learner to understand the events of learning a foreign language. If I might take it a step further, it is revealing talk that the learner engages in to reach understanding. It is reactive talk during anxious moments by more mature learners. As talk it helps the learner become more aware of cognitive adjustments in the learning process. As preliminary as my analysis and description may be, and as the data relate to focus on form and management thereof, the talk suggests, as we are all no doubt aware, that there is more to learning language and acquiring knowledge than simply being exposed to input. The talk creates involvement and contributes to the negotiation of meaning and the acquisition of knowledge in the foreign-language classroom.

REFERENCES

Bailey, Kathleen M. 1980. "An introspective analysis of an individual's language learning experience." In Robin C. Scarcella and Stephen D. Krashen (eds.), *Research in second language acquisition.* Rowley, Massachusetts: Newbury House. 58–65.
Bloor, Thomas. 1994. "What do language students know about grammar?" *The British Journal of Language Teaching* 24(13):157–160.

Boyson, Beverly, Renée Jourdenais, Mitsuhito Ota, and Stephanie Stauffer. 1994. "Problems for focus on form: Does textual enhancement promote noticing? A think-aloud protocol analysis." Unpublished ms. Georgetown University.

Coupland, Nikolas, John M. Wiemann, and Howard Giles. 1991. "Talk as 'problem' and communication as 'miscommunication': An integrative analysis." In Nikolas Coupland, Howard Giles, and John M. Wiemann (eds.), *"Miscommunication" and problematic talk.* Newbury Park, California: Sage Publications.

Coupland, Nikolas, Howard Giles, and John M. Wiemann (eds.). 1991. *"Miscommunication" and problematic talk.* Newbury Park, California: Sage Publications.

Nunan, David. 1989. *Understanding language classrooms: A guide for teacher-initiated action.* New York: Prentice-Hall.

Scarcella, Robin C. and Stephen D. Krashen (eds.). 1980. *Research in second language acquisition.* Rowley, Massachusetts: Newbury House.

Selinker, Larry. 1992. *Rediscovering interlanguage.* London: Longman.

Patterns of lexis:
How much can repetition tell us about discourse coherence?

Andrea Tyler
Georgetown University

Introduction. Understanding what makes one English text seem more coherent to native listeners than another is a persistent issue in discourse analysis and a central one for language teachers concerned with the development of their students' discourse competence. One popular set of models argues that coherence ultimately has to do with the presence of certain patterns in the text, in particular patterns of lexical repetition. Perhaps the most well-known model within this camp is that of "lexical cohesion" (Halliday and Hasan 1976).[1] Under this model, the presence of lexical repetition and related semantic items contributes to text coherence by creating cohesive ties within the text. By this argument, discourse which is perceived as being more coherent should contain significantly more lexical repetition than discourse which is perceived as less coherent (assuming that both sets of discourse are on the same topic and aimed at roughly the same audience).

A second group of scholars have argued that a model which derives coherence primarily from features of the text, such as repetition, is misguided (e.g. Blakemore 1992; Brown and Yule 1983; Carrell 1982; Green 1989; Green and Morgan 1981; Morgan and Sellner 1980). They criticize such models for being static rather than dynamic, ignoring principles of pragmatic interpretation, and ultimately confusing symptom with source. By this argument, the perception of coherence has to do with the ease with which a listener can integrate the speaker's utterances into a reasonable, consistent interpretation of the discourse. The present paper takes up this debate by examining the claims of one of the newest models of lexical cohesion, that of Hoey (1991).

Hoey's basic claims. Hoey starts with Halliday's and Hasan's premise that patterns of lexical repetition, including synonyms and hyponyms, are key to

---

[1] Work by Tannen (1989) and others (e.g. Koch 1983; Norrick 1987) has established the importance of repetition in creating emotional effects, building rapport, and providing prefabricated chunks of discourse which allow smoother online production and processing. These functions of repetition are not under discussion here.

building text. However, in contrast to Hasan (1985), who sees all lexical repetitions as participating in the creation of text-building cohesive chains, Hoey argues that the crucial, coherence-creating repetitions are those which occur across sentence boundaries. He argues that sentences link to each other in some important, text-building way when they contain three overlapping lexical items. In Hoey's terms, such sentences are "bonded" (1991: 91). Sentences containing less than three overlapping lexical items are not so linked or bonded.

Hoey argues that lexical cohesion "contribute[s] to coherence" (1991: 26), and that "sentences linked by repetition [will] be more closely related than those not so linked even if they are separated by a number of sentences. Some sentences [will] be seen to be linked to a variety of other sentences, while others [will] be linked to few or none; the former [will] be central to the text, the latter marginal" (1991: 34). In expanding upon his theory of centrality and marginality, Hoey hypothesizes that "[w]e would expect a marginal sentence (i.e. one with low levels of lexical repetition) to have low information value, to be metalinguistic in nature or to offer information that is not directly needed or made much use of within the text" (1991: 43).

I argue that in spite of Hoey's attempts to extend the basic model of lexical cohesion, the analysis remains fundamentally flawed. First, I examine one of Hoey's central examples which reveals that textual material which his model labels as extraneous is, in fact, key to establishing a reasonable interpretation of the text. Second, I show that Hoey's framework makes the wrong predictions concerning two naturally-occurring English texts which were judged to differ in terms of coherence. Finally, I offer an alternative analysis of the role of repetition, based in an interpretative-pragmatic orientation.

Critique of Hoey. Let us consider a central example from Hoey's 1991 book, *Patterns of lexis in text*:

1 A drug known to produce violent reactions in humans has been used for sedating grizzly bears URSUS ARCTORS in Montana, USA, according to a report in the NY Times.
2 After one bear, known to be a peaceable animal, killed and ate a camper in an unprovoked attack, scientists discovered it had been tranquilized 11 times with phencyclidine [PCC], or 'angel dust', which causes hallucinations and sometimes gives the user an irrational feeling of destructive power.
3 Many wild bears have become 'garbage junkies' feeding from dumps around human developments.
4 To avoid potentially dangerous clashes between them and humans, scientists are trying to rehabilitate the animals by drugging them and releasing them in uninhabited areas.

5 Although some biologists deny that the mind-altering drug was responsible for the uncharacteristic behavior of this particular bear, no research has been done into the effects of giving grizzly bears or other mammals repeated doses of phencyclidine [PCC]. (1991: 35)

Figure 1a represents Hoey's analysis of all the simple lexical repetitions between sentence 1 and other sentences. Figure 1b represents Hoey's analysis of which sentences are linked by three or more lexical repetitions.

Figure 1a. Hoey 1991: 37

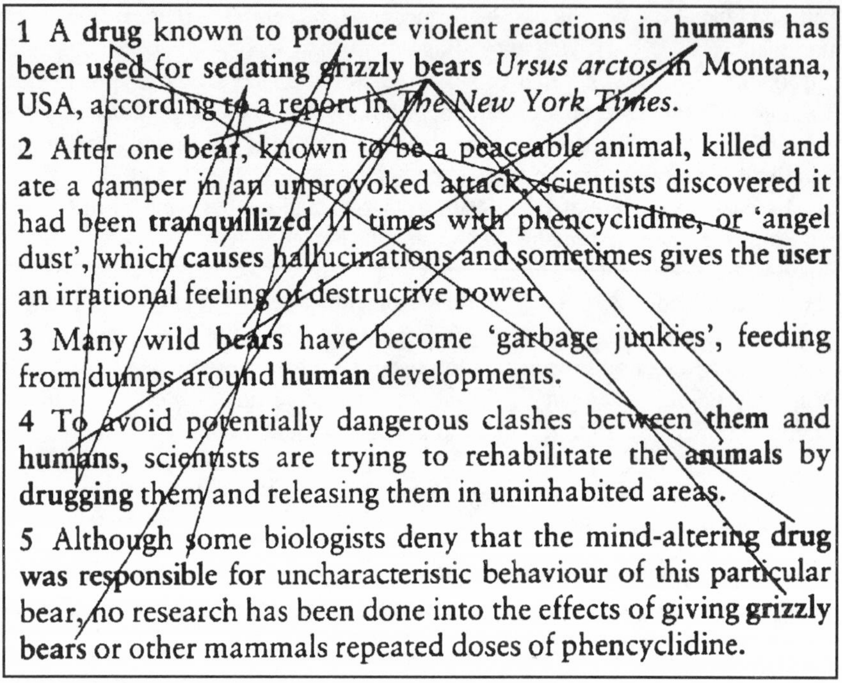

1 A **drug** known to **produce** violent reactions in **humans** has been u**s**e**d** for sedating **g**rizzly **bears** *Ursus arctos* **in** Montana, USA, according to a report in *The New York Times*.

2 After one be**a**r, known to be a peaceable animal, killed and ate a **c**amper in an unprovoked attack, scientists discovered it had been **tranquillized** 11 times with phencyclidine, or 'angel dust', which **causes** hallucinations and sometimes gives the **user** an irrational feeling of destructive power.

3 M**a**ny wild bears have become 'garbage junkies', feeding from dumps around **human** developments.

4 T**o** avoid potentially dangerous clashes between **them** and **hum**a**ns**, scientists are trying to rehabilitate the animals by **drugging** them and releasing them in uninhabited areas.

5 Although some biologists deny that the mind-alteri**n**g **drug** was re**s**ponsible for uncharacteristic behaviour of this particular bear, no research has been done into the effects of giving **grizzly** **bears** or other mammals repeated doses of phencyclidine.

Under Hoey's analysis, sentence 3 lacks sufficient lexical connection with all other sentences and is thus "marginal" to the discourse. In fact, Hoey argues that the text makes perfect sense without the sentence. In addition, he explicitly argues that, because of lexical linking or bonding, sentences 1 and 4 form a coherent text in a way that sentences 3 and 4 do not; moreover, "[s]entence 4 provides an explanation for the situation described in sentence 1, answering the question 'what for'? with regard to the use of the drug on bears. Thus there is as strong a relation between these two sentences as between any two adjacent sentences in the text" (1991: 46).

Figure 1b. Hoey 1991: 44

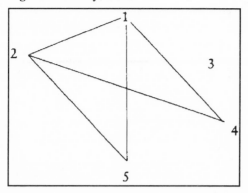

Let us look more closely at the text formed by sentences 1 and 4:

1 A drug known to produce violent reactions in humans has been used for sedating grizzly bears URSUS ARCTORS in Montana, USA, ...
4 To avoid potentially dangerous clashes between them and humans, scientists are trying to rehabilitate the animals by drugging them and releasing them in uninhabited areas.

In this minitext, sentence 4 appears to be saying that any and potentially all grizzlies in Montana are being drugged. I would venture to say that this message strikes most readers as bizarre. In addition, the phrase "trying to rehabilitate the animals by drugging them and releasing them" is, at best, puzzling. Contrary to Hoey's claim that sentence 4 provides the explanation for the use of PCC on bears, the reason for drugging the bears remains obscure. The reader has no idea in what undesirable behavior the bears have been engaging that would give rise to a need for rehabilitation.[2]

Now let us consider the interpretation of sentence 4 as it occurs in its original, natural context:

3 Many wild bears have become 'garbage junkies' feeding from dumps around human developments.
4 To avoid potentially dangerous clashes between them and humans, scientists are trying to rehabilitate the animals by drugging them and releasing them in uninhabited areas.

---

[2] We can perhaps infer that these bears have been in areas inhabited by humans, since they are being released into uninhabited areas; but nowhere in the text is location mentioned as part of the problem. *Moreover, it is the inference which creates coherence.*

Sentence 3 provides the crucial information that a certain subset of bears show problematic behavior—these bears like human food, which attracts them to dumps, where they inevitably have increased contact with humans. It is this subset of bears which scientists have been trying to rehabilitate—that is, wean from garbage. Thus sentence 3 provides two important pieces of information for establishing a reasonable interpretation of the text: (1) It provides an appropriate subset of bears with problematic behavior (which, in turn, provides an appropriate antecedent for both the pronoun "them" in the first clause of sentence 4 and the full NP "the animals" in the second clause); and (2) it provides the only explanation for why scientists are drugging the bears in the first place.

The point is that even though sentence 3 has few lexical links to other sentences, it articulates concepts which are central to a reader's ability to create a reasonable interpretation of the text. I would argue that the articulation of relevant concepts is the property that makes a sentence central or peripheral to a text, not the number of lexical repetitions or links it contains.

Hoey argues that his framework is a useful tool for teaching L2 reading. He suggests having students create synopses of texts by searching for and then marking out sentences linked with other sentences by three or more repetitions. He claims these linked sentences will provide a reasonable summary of a text.

But given the problems with his key example, we have no reason to believe that such a synopsis would consistently provide a reasonable representation of a text. If sentences containing key concepts happen not to articulate those concepts through lexical repetitions, important gaps will exist in the synopsis. To make sense out of the passage, readers will be forced to engage in increased inferencing, relying more heavily on their schema and background knowledge and less on the text. Current cognitive, interactive models of reading, such as Carpenter and Just (1987) and Perfetti (1988), suggest that overreliance on schema and underreliance on the actual text is precisely the reading behavior adapted by poorer readers. Thus close examination of the application of Hoey's framework raises serious questions about the model and its usefulness for L2 reading instruction.

A second potential use of Hoey's model is as a framework for evaluating the coherence of student-produced text or monologic discourse.[3] In this section,

---

[3] Hoey explicitly states that his framework was developed to analyze written nonfiction and thus might argue that extension to lecture discourse is an inappropriate application of his model. However, work by Biber (1986), among others, has shown that a simple dichotomy between spoken and written discourse is insupportable empirically. After examining over forty textual features such as sentence length, syntactic complexity, and use of specific lexical items, Biber found that planned spoken discourse, including academic lectures, shared more features with formal written nonfiction than many types of written texts (e.g. personal letters). In light of these findings, extending Hoey's model to planned spoken academic discourse would seem reasonable and appropriate.

I apply Hoey's framework to naturally occurring university math lectures. One lecture was given by a native speaker of English; the other by a native speaker of Chinese. In the segments of the discourse we will be considering, the instructors are explaining the same problem; therefore, the lectures clearly represent discourse on the same topic and addressed to highly similar audiences. Both instructors were observed by a math supervisor who gave the native speaker of English high marks on clarity of instruction and the native speaker of Chinese low marks. Since the supervisor's rating could have been influenced by the speakers' accents or knowledge of their native speaker (NS) status, two additional math professors, who were not familiar with these instructors and who were not informed that one was a nonnative speaker (NNS), reviewed transcripts of this portion of their lectures. These professors also judged the NNS's version as less focused and harder to follow than the NS's. The transcripts appear in Figures 2a and 2b.

By Hoey's account, repetition should play an important role in the perceived differences in coherence. The loops in Figures 2a and 2b represent the sentential bonds based on the guidelines set forth in Hoey. These patterns are quantified in Table 1. As figures 2a and 2b and Table 1 show, the NNS's discourse contains considerably more sentential linking than the NS's. Thus Hoey's analysis represents the NNS's discourse as being more coherent.

This finding, along with the problems of analysis illustrated in the grizzly-bear passage, raise serious doubts about the efficacy of a framework which assigns repetition a primary role in creating coherence.

Table 1. Results of analysis of NS and NNS lecture texts

No. of S	No. of links	No. linked S	% linked S	Ratio of links to sentences
NS 34	14	17	50%	1:2.5
NNS 58	35	35	65%	1:1.6

As with the grizzly-bear passage, I believe that the perception of coherence in the math lectures rests in how the utterances contribute to the listener's attempt to construct a consistent interpretation of the discourse rather than the amount of lexical linking the utterances contain.

Figure 2a. Native speaker of U.S. English

```
7a) Native Speaker of US English

Begins by writing P=2500e^{kt} on the board

1) OK now t is the time or year
2) This is the population of the city corresponding to the year 1990
   when t equals zero
3) So we're starting in 1990
4) Now in 1960 the population was 125,000
5) So the population was 125,000 when t is? Negative 30
6) Because we started the year at 1990 and go back to 1960 so it
   must be negative
7) Everybody see how we get negative 30?
8) That that's the big trick here   OK
9) We have 125,000 is equal to 140,500e to the k times negative thirty
10) Do you see what I'm doing here?
11) When t was negative our population was 125,000
12) Now I've got to find out what k is cuz I have no idea what k is
13) And I can't do much with this when I have two variables that I
    have no idea what they are
14) OK I can plug in t all I want
15) But if I don't have a k it's not going to get me anywhere
16) So your first step is to find k
17) You'll find that in a lot of these problems your first step is
    finding k
18) So how are we going to find our k?
19) Do you see the pattern? Same thing
20) Divide both sides
21) Get rid of the constant
22) Then we have this big number--which when you do it on your
    calculator you can simplify it but for now we can't--is equal
    to e to the negative 30 k
23) And then I? Take the natural log of both sides
24) Equals the natural log of e to the negative 30 k which is the
    same thing as negative 30 k
25) Because the natural log of e to the k ... [inaudible]
26) And then the way to solve for k is divide this whole humongous
    number by negative 30
27) So k is this big number which actually ends up being very small
    negative .0013
28) So now I have my k
29) Now I have k equal to 0.0013
30) So now my equation looks like this 140.500e to the .0013t
31) Now you can give me any t
32) You can give me 10, 20, 30, 40, 50, 60
33) And I can tell you p
34) Not off the top of my head but you can calculate it
```

I believe that a number of interacting problems involving contextualization cues, frame, and schema give rise to the perception that the NNS's discourse is unfocused. Because of space limitations, I will limit my remarks to one difference concerning schema. Rounds (1987: 656) notes in her study of university math instructors, "An accurate estimation by the teacher of how much the student can be expected to fill in is one factor affecting communicative competence in the classroom." I believe the math lectures reflect underlying differences in the instructors' schemas concerning just what information students can be expected to fill in.

Figure 2b. Native speaker of Chinese

```
7b) Native Speaker of Chinese

 1) Problem 30 OK is about [the] population of a city
 2) The formula is given by p=2500e ᵏᵗ
 3) And also we know when t is 0 it corresponds to the year 1990
 4) The t corresponds to the year 1990 + t
 5) Let's take a look at the book to see what we know  OK
 6) In 1960 and p the population is let's see 125,000
 7) What [do] we want?
 8) We want to find k and use this result to predict the population in
    the year 2000
 9) Also when t is 2000 find p
10) That's the problem
11) OK  Let's take a look at this year 1960
12) Which corresponds to t?
13) What is the t?
14) In this formula you see we have to know t and k then we can find p
15) As I said here (referring to earlier discussion)
16) In this formula we have three variables  three variables
17) If we know p and t we can find k
18) We can find k
19) If we know t and k we can find p
20) This is the first part of this problem
21) This is the second part of this problem
22) Now think about this problem
23) In 1960 which t which corresponds to this year?
24) t corresponds to this year 1990 + t
25) So that means 1990 is the year plus t equals to 1960
26) This implies t equals minus 30
27) For the first part of this problem t is minus thirty
28) And p is 125,000
29) You see  we know two things of this three variables
30) We can find the last one k
31) So how do we do that?
32) Just plug in these two things in this formula
33) What we get here is 140,500
34) And t equals minus 30
35) Divide both side by this number
36) Why do we do that?
37) Why I want to divide both side by this number 2500?
38) The reason for this is we want to solve the equation
39) This equation is an exponential equation with exponential function
40) To solve an equation, the first we want to do is to isolate the
    exponential part
41) This is an exponential part of this equation
42) We want to isolate this part
43) This is why we have to divide both sides by 2500
44) What we get here is k....
45) And this is a number
46) Then how do we find k?
47) This time we have to take natural log of both sides of this
    equation
48) Just take a look at the left side of this equation
49) So the left side of this equation is k multiply minus 30
50) So what['s] the k
51) To find k, it is so easy, we can just divide both side by minus 30
52) k equals...
53) So this is the first part of the problem
54) Now let's go back to this formula  PXT
55) We have three variables
56) By the assumption we know we know p and we have t
57) We want to find k
58) That is the process you can follow
```

Consider the two math lectures again (Figures 3a and 3b). An analysis of the content reveals that approximately one-quarter of the NNS's utterances are devoted to a very general level of information concerning the formula and general concepts not explicitly linked to the particulars of the problem. This material is underlined and is exemplified by statements such as "In this formula, we have to know t and p, then we can find k" (line 14). The amount of talk devoted to this level of explanation suggests the NNS instructor believes the students are having difficulty with very general concepts such as that two of the three variables must be known in order to solve an equation. This level of information is missing from the NS's discourse. Its absence suggests that the NS believes that this is information which can be assumed as established, background knowledge. Additional support for this analysis comes from the three consulting math professors who all stated that most students were likely to have learned this general level of information in high school and that it seemed off the point to emphasize it. Thus the NNS devotes a large amount of his discourse to already known information; from the listeners' perspective emphasizing this general information would not seem to be very useful in solving the problem and would hence contribute to making the discourse seem unfocused.

Moreover the placement of this abstract level of information seems to intensify its digressive effect. In two instances it occurs immediately after the NNS has focused the students' attention on a discrete step in the solution by asking a question. The first occurrence is in lines 14 through 19, immediately after the NNS asks "Which corresponds to t? What is the t?" The instructor's move to the very general level of information strikes the listener as disconnected from the question. The NNS does not articulate the particulars of how to solve for t until line 25, making the explanation of this step somewhat disjointed at best. This is in clear contrast to the NS's straight-forward, uninterrupted explanation (in lines 1–8) which explicitly states the notion that 1990 represents the starting time—time zero—and focuses the students' attention on the logical step needed to determine the value for t in 1960.

The second instance of this pattern occurs in lines 36 through 40, where the NNS instructor focuses the students' attention on the step of isolating the exponential function, and then moves to very general remarks ("The reason for this is we want to solve the equation," line 38). As one of the math consultants characterized the NNS's lecture, "You can't say his explanation is really wrong. He eventually gets to the point, but by the longest path possible" (M. Thompson, personal communication).

External support for the analysis that the two instructors differ in their assumptions about the students' background knowledge comes from comments made by the NNS during a video-playback session. He noted that he spent considerable time on the notion that it is necessary to know two of the three variables in order to solve an equation because the students had not been able work problems which involved this concept on the previous quiz. When I pointed out that it was possible that they understood this very general level of

Figure 3a. Transcript of native speaker of English

Begins by writing P=2500e^{kt} on the board

(1) OK now t is the time or year
(2) This is the population of the city corresponding to the year 1990 when t equals zero
(3) So we're starting in 1990
(4) Now in 1960 the population was 125,000
(5) So the population was 125,000 when t is? Negative 30
(6) Because we started the year at 1990 and go back to 1960 so it must be negative
(7) Everybody see how we get negative 30?
(8) That that's the big trick here OK
(9) We have 125,000 is equal to 140,500e to the k times negative thirty
(10) Do you see what I'm doing here?
(11) When t was negative our population was 125,000
(12) Now I've got to find out what k is cuz I have no idea what k is
(13) and I can't do mcuh with this when I have two variables that I have no idea what they are
(14) OK I can plug in t all I want
(15) But if I don't have a k it's not going to get me anywhere
(16) So your first step is to find k
(17) You'll find that in a lot of these problems your first step is finding k
(18) So how are we going to find our k?
(19) Do you see the pattern? Same thing
(20) Divide both sides
(21) Get rid of the constant
(22) Then we have this big number—which when you do it on your calculator you can simplify it but for now we can't—is equal to e to the negative of 30 k
(23) And then I? Take the natural log of both sides
(24) Equals the natural log of e to the negative of 30 k which is the same thing as negative 30 k
(25) Because the natural log of e to the k … [inaudible]
(26) And then the way to solve for k is divide this whole humungous number by negative 30
(27) So k is this big number which actually ends up being very small negative .0013
(28) So now I have my k
(29) Now I have k equal to 0.0013
(30) So now my equation looks like this 140,500e to the .0013t
(31) Now you can give me any t
(32) You can give me 10, 20, 30, 40, 50, 60
(33) And I can tell you p
(34) Not off the top of my head but you can calculate it

Figure 3b. Transcript of native speaker of Chinese

```
(1)   The problem 30 OK is about [the] population of a city
(2)   The formula is given by p=2500e^{kt}
(3)   And also we know when t is 0 it corresponds to the year 1990
(4)   The t corresponds to the year 1990 + t
(5)   Let's take a look at the book to see what we know OK
(6)   In 1960 and p the population is let's see 125,000
(7)   What [do] we want?
(8)   We want to find k and use this result to predict the
      population in the year 2000
(9)   Also when t is 2000 find p
(10)  That's the problem
(11)  OK Let's take a look at this year 1960
(12)  Which corresponds to t?
(13)  What is the t?
(14)  In this formula you see we have to know t and k then we can
      find                p
(15)  As I said here [referring to an earlier discussion]
(16)  In this formula we have three variables three variables
(17)  If we know p and t we can find k
(18)  We can find k
(19)  If we know t and k we can find p
(20)  This is the first part of this problem
(21)  This is the second part of this problem
(22)  Now think about this problem
(23)  In 1960 which t which corresponds to this year?
(24)  t corresponds to this year 1990 + t
(25)  So that means 1990 is the year plus t equals to 1960
(26)  This implies t equals minus 30
(27)  For the first part of this problem t is minus thirty
(28)  And p is 125,000
(29)  You see we know two things of this three variables
(30)  We can find the last one k
(31)  So how do we do that?
(32)  Just plug in these two things in this formula
(33)  What we get here is 140,500
(34)  And t equals minus 30
(35)  Divide both side by this number
(36)  Why do we do that?
(37)  Why I want to divide both side by this number 2500?
(38)  The reason for this is we want to solve the equation
(39)  This equation is an exponential equation with exponential
      function
(40)  To solve an equation, the first we want to do is to isolate
      the exponential part
(41)  This is an exponential part of this equation
(42)  We want to isolate this part
(43)  This is why we have to divide both sides by 2500
(44)  What we get here is k....
(45)  And this is a number
(46)  Then how do we find k?
(47)  This time we have to take natural log of both sides of this
      equation
(48)  Just take a look at the left side of this equation
(49)  So the left side of this equation is k multiply minus 30
(50)  So what['s] k
(51)  To find k, it is so easy, we can just divide both side by
      minus 30
(52)  k equals...
(53)  So this is the first part of the problem
(54)  Now let's go back to this formula PKT
(55)  We have three variables
(56)  By the assumption we know we know p and we have t
(57)  We want to find k
```

information but not the intermediate steps which would lead to the correct answer, he acknowledged that he assumed they would be able to figure out automatically how the data plugged into the formula once they understood the significance of the general principles.

The argument is that an important contributing factor to the divergent perceptions of coherence is that the instructors have rather different schemas concerning what background information can be assumed. This situation represents the inverse of the grizzly-bear passage where the concepts were relevant and central to creating a reasonable interpretation of the discourse, even though the words used to articulate those concepts did not participate in patterns of lexical repetition. Here the concepts that the NNS instructor is emphasizing are so well known and obvious that their mention is irrelevant to the students' difficulty in solving the problem. Despite the fact that these concepts are packaged in sentences containing a good deal of lexical repetition across sentence boundaries, the listener still has difficulty integrating them into a consistent, meaningful interpretation.

Conclusion. It is a fact that coherent English monologic discourse often contains patterns of lexical repetition. However, since we find coherent text with low levels of lexical repetition, lexical repetition cannot be a necessary condition for coherence. Conversely, since we find less coherent text with relatively high levels of repetition, neither can lexical repetition be a sufficient condition for coherence. This indicates that repetition is simply an attending reflex or epiphenomenon which often occurs with coherent text.

If a speaker or a writer is going to develop a discourse beyond one sentence, in order to stay on topic, she will have to make repeated reference to established discourse entities and concepts. Since words are, to paraphrase Nagy and Herman (1987), conventionally agreed-upon labels for concepts, the repetition of concepts and discourse entities is likely to be reflected in repetition of related lexical items from sentence to sentence. From this perspective, lexical repetition in monologic discourse is largely a result of staying on topic; repetition is a common symptom of coherence, but not its source. Models of discourse which give repetition a primary role in creating coherence, in Green and Morgan's (1981:176) words, "confuse symptom with source." Confusion over this relationship results in flawed analyses, as witnessed in the grizzly-bear example, and inaccurate predictions, as witnessed in the analysis of the math lectures. Ultimately they are not likely to provide reliable tools for either students trying to decipher a difficult English text or teachers trying to locate the sources of incoherence in their NNS students' texts.

REFERENCES

Blakemore, Diana. 1992. *Understanding utterances: An introduction to pragmatics.* Oxford: Blackwell.
Biber, William. 1986. "Spoken and written textual dimensions in English: Resolving the contradictory findings." *Language* 62: 384–414.
Brown, Gillian and George Yule. 1983. *Discourse analysis.* Cambridge, U.K.: Cambridge University Press.
Carpenter, Patricia and Maral Just. 1986. "Cognitive processes in reading." In Joyce Oranasu (ed.), *Reading comprehension: From research to practice.* Hillsdale, N.J.: Lawrence Erlbaum Associates. 11–29.
Carrell, Patricia L. 1982. "Cohesion is not coherence." *TESOL Quarterly* 16(4): 479–487.
Green, Georgia. 1989. *Pragmatics and natural language understanding.* Hillsdale, N.J.: Lawrence Erlbaum Associates.
Green, Georgia and Jerry Morgan. 1981. "Pragmatics, grammar and discourse." In Peter Cole (ed.), *Radical pragmatics.* New York: Academic Press. 167–181.
Halliday, M.A.K. and Ruqaiya Hasan. 1976. *Cohesion in English.* London: Longman.
Halliday, M.A.K. and Ruqaiya Hasan. 1985. *Language, context, and text: Aspects of language in a social-semeiotic perspective.* Oxford: Oxford University Press.
Hoey, Michael. 1991. *Patterns of lexis in text.* Oxford: Oxford University Press.
Koch, Barbara Johnstone. 1983. "Parataxis in Arabic: modification as a model for persuasion." Paper presented at the Linguistic Society of America Annual Meeting. December 1983.
Morgan, Jerry and M. Sellner. 1980. "Discourse and linguistic theory." In Rand Spiro, Bertram Bruce, and William Brewer (eds.), *Theoretical issues in reading comprehension.* Hillsdale, N.J.: Lawrence Erlbaum Associates. 165–200.
Nagy, William and Patricia Herman. 1987. "Breadth and depth of vocabulary knowledge: Implications for acquisition and instruction." In Margaret McKeown and M. Curtis (eds.), *The nature of vocabulary acquisition.* Hillsdale, N.J.: Lawrence Erlbaum Associates. 19–35.
Norrick, Neal. 1987. "Functions of repetition in conversation." *Text* 7: 245–264.
Perfetti, Charlie. 1988. "Verbal efficiency in reading ability." In M. Daneman (ed.), *Reading research: Advances in theory and practice, Volume 6.* New York: Academic Press. 109–143.
Rounds, Patricia L. 1987. "Characterizing successful classroom discourse for NNS teaching assistant training." *TESOL Quarterly* 21(4): 643–671.
Tannen, Deborah. 1988. *Talking voices: Repetition, dialogue, and imagery in conversational discourse.* Cambridge, U.K.: Cambridge University Press.

Toward a theory of second-language teaching: Ideas from classroom research on language teaching and learning

Kathleen M. Bailey
Monterey Institute of International Studies

Introduction. In the 1990 collection of papers from the Georgetown University Round Table, Diane Larsen-Freeman called for a theory of language teaching (as contrasted with a theory of language learning or acquisition). She said that second-language-teaching research "should be concerned with understanding how and why classroom interactions or features contribute to learning opportunities" (1990: 263). In discussing the need for a theory of second-language teaching, Larsen-Freeman listed three traits that such a theory would exhibit:

(1) It would need to be grounded in classroom data;
(2) It would be dynamic, since a particular teaching practice is likely to be manifest in different ways depending on the teacher's level of experience; and
(3) It would motivate research not only of what a teacher does, but also what a teacher thinks (1990: 267).

She added, "Research of this sort is likely to result in a theory which views the teacher as having a more central role in the processes of teaching and learning than in previous process-product research. It also suggests an active role for teachers in the research process itself" (1990: 268). Larsen-Freeman asserted that teachers are necessary partners in such research because "access to their thinking would be essential to the process of understanding why they make the decisions that they do" (1990: 268).

These two parallel roles—(1) the teacher's central role in the processes of teaching and learning, and (2) the teacher's active role in research—are relevant to second-language-teacher education, the theme of the 1995 Georgetown Universty Round Table. And, in fact, they provide the broad structure for this paper. We will first consider research results about the teacher's role in second-language learning, with a particular focus on teachers' decision-making. We will then consider methodological developments which promote teachers taking active roles in the processes of research.

Rationale for a theory of second-language teaching. In addition to Larsen-Freeman, several authors in second-language-teacher education have discussed the need for research into teaching processes in building a theory of teaching. Tony Wright has observed that "there are theories of language and theories of learning, but a theory of teaching can be drawn only from classroom experience, or at least can be informed only by that experience" (1990: 82). Richards and Nunan (1990) have also argued that research is needed on teachers' thought processes during language instruction in order to build a theory of second-language teaching. Furthermore, Richards states that the goal of language teacher education "must be to provide opportunities for the novice to acquire the skills and competencies of effective teachers and to discover the working rules that effective teachers use" (1987: 223). Discovering teachers' "working rules" is thus one legitimate pursuit of language classroom research, which should inform language teacher education. But Freeman and Richards note that "to date, however, there has been virtually no organized examination of the conceptions of teaching which undergird the field of second-language instruction and influence the various areas of endeavor within it" (1993: 193). And they add that "such scrutiny is both critical and overdue" (1993: 193).

As late as 1990, Gitlin stated that "educational research is still a process that for the most part silences those studied, ignores their personal knowledge, and strengthens the assumption that researchers are *the* producers of knowledge" (1990: 444). Donald Freeman elaborates on this idea as follows:

> To achieve a discipline of teaching ... the knowledge that teachers articulate through the process of disciplined inquiry must become public. It cannot dissipate in the recesses of private conversations, staff rooms, or even schools. The interpretations which teachers develop through research need to enter the wider community, to compete with other disciplines as ways of understanding education and of shaping public policy and debate. (in press)

Again, Donald Freeman (in press) has noted "In this process of teachers articulating, in their own voices, their understandings of what they know lies the start of a redefinition of the relationship of teaching and research."

In this same vein, Leo van Lier has described what he calls a "theory of practice" (1994a: 7). He looks at the role of teachers in building such a theory:

> Theorists as well as practitioners have a strong tendency to believe that research is part of theory and that theorizing is an essentially separate activity from practicing. Researchers build theories and need not be involved in practical affairs. Practitioners, on the other hand, need not theorize, though perhaps they should search existing theories for findings (i.e. things "found" by theoretical researchers) relevant to their work. This

separation must be broken down and a new dynamic interrelationship between theory, practice, and research established. Practice must be seen as an opportunity to do research, and as a source of theory. A practitioner must be a theorist, and a theorist must also be a practitioner. (1994a: 7)

In other words, van Lier would agree with Larsen-Freeman's concern that a theory of teaching should investigate teachers' central role in the processes of teaching and learning, and that teachers should be actively involved, as more than informants, in such research.

Returning to Larsen-Freeman's call for a theory of second-language teaching, we encounter the notion that "a number of hypotheses germane to second-language teaching will arise out of systematic attention to the classroom teaching/learning process itself, as has been the case so far with second language classroom research" (1990: 264). In addressing this point I will first briefly discuss what is meant by second-language-classroom research and then return to the issue of a theory of second-language teaching—particularly to Larsen-Freeman's suggestions that such a theory would need to be grounded in classroom data and that it would motivate research on what teachers think (1990: 267).

Language classroom research and a theory of second-language teaching. Language classroom research was defined by Long as "research, all or part of whose data are derived from the observation or measurement of the classroom performance of teachers and students" (1980: 2, 1983: 4). Allwright took this definition a step further when he wrote, "classroom-centered research is in fact research that treats the language classroom not just as the setting for investigation but, more importantly, as the object of investigation. Classroom processes become the central focus" (1983: 191). After nearly thirty years of language classroom research, numerous summaries of its procedures and findings are available in both articles (Allwright 1983; Bailey 1985; Gaies 1983; van Lier 1984, 1988, 1989) and books (Allwright and Bailey 1991; Brumfit and Mitchell 1990; Chaudron 1988; Edge and Richards 1993; Ellis 1990; Seliger and Long 1983). In this chapter I will consider some recent additions to this body of literature and the potential contributions of such language classroom research to a theory of second-language teaching.

What teachers think: The case of decision-making. Johnson (1992a: 507-508) shares Larsen-Freeman's concern that we have no theory of second-language teaching and sees the investigation of teacher cognition as a likely starting place. In 1992 she wrote, "Recent concern over the status of teacher education in the field of second-language teaching has focused on the lack of a theoretical framework to serve as a basis for second-language-teacher preparation programs." While acknowledging widescale agreement among teacher educators that teacher preparation programs should enable "preservice teachers to learn the skills and competencies of effective second language teaching," Johnson points out that, as a profession, we lack full understanding of what constitutes effective language teaching and how language teachers learn to teach.

Citing Chaudron's (1988) review of language classroom research, Johnson summarizes its early foci as being on "effective teaching behaviors, positive learner outcomes, and teacher–student interactions that are believed to lead to successful second language learning" (Johnson 1992a: 508). She notes that "only recently have researchers begun to recognize the importance of exploring the cognitive dimensions of how second language teachers' thoughts, judgments, and decisions influence the nature of second language instruction" (1992a: 508).

This concern for a research emphasis on teacher cognition is a repeated theme among researchers who examine second-language-teacher development. Freeman and Richards, for example, have written, "To understand teaching, we must look at how it is conceived, at the thinking on which it is based ... We argue that comparing classroom practices provides only partial information at best; one must first establish the conceptual basis of the teaching involved" (1993: 209). In order to establish this conceptual basis, they say, "It is critical that we shift the focus of discussions of teaching from behavior and activity to the thinking and reasoning which organize and motivate these external practices" (1993: 213).

Findings from L1 research on teacher cognition. Johnson further asserts that "Given the concern over the current status of teacher education in second language teaching, research on teachers' decision-making from L1 educational literature becomes an important starting point for explorations into the cognitive dimensions of second language teaching" (1992a: 509). In summarizing research on teacher cognition in general education (see e.g. Clark and Peterson 1986), Freeman states:

> ... teachers did not naturally think about planning in the organized formats which they had been taught to use in their professional training. Further, when they did plan lessons according to these formats, they often did not teach them according to plan. Teachers were much more likely to visualize lessons as clusters or sequences of activity; they would blend content with activity and they would generally focus on their particular students. In other words, teachers tended to plan lessons as ways of doing things for given groups of students rather than to meet particular objectives. (in press)

What we must keep in mind is that, as Shavelson has pointed out (1973: 18), "Any teaching act is the result of a decision, whether conscious or unconscious, that the teacher makes after the complex cognitive processing of available information." He further notes that this reasoning leads to the hypothesis that "the basic teaching skill is decision-making" (1973: 18; see also Freeman 1989: 31).

Teacher decision-making is usually viewed as being either preactive (in the planning stages, prior to classroom action) or interactive (taking place during instruction). There is a potential for confusion, however: The term interactive decision-making does not refer to making decisions interactively, i.e. with the students' input, but rather to decisions made by the teacher while the classroom interaction proceeds.

Leinhardt and Greeno describe teaching as a "complex cognitive skill" which "requires the construction of plans and the making of rapid on-line decisions" (1986: 75). They note that "skilled teachers have a large repertoire of activities that they perform fluently" (1986: 76). Leinhardt and Greeno were concerned with the dynamic tension that exists between preactive decisions and interactive decisions: "The conscious planning activity of teachers reflects only a small fraction of the planfulness that actually characterizes skilled teaching" (1986: 76).

Peterson and Clark (1978) investigated teachers' reports of their own cognitive processes as they were teaching. Videotaped segments of junior high school social studies lessons were used in the *stimulated recall procedure*, in which the teachers viewed the videos as they described what they had been thinking during the original interaction. In the data, Peterson and Clark identified four possible "paths" through a lesson: (1) "Business as Usual," in which case everything proceeds well and there is no need for the teacher to diverge from the plan; (2) the teacher sees problems, but has no alternatives and so continues with the plan in spite of evidence that it is not working; (3) the teacher perceives problems, has alternatives available, but stays with the plan or previous behavior; and (4) the teacher has alternatives available when problems are perceived and is thus able to change the teaching behavior. In the analysis, the choice of Path 3 correlated negatively with the students' achievement and with their attitudes (i.e. regarding the teacher, the methodology, and the subject matter). Path 1 was associated with the learning of facts, while Path 4 was associated with students' learning of higher order ideas. Thus, Peterson and Clark's analysis suggests that when teachers have options for altering lessons in progress, students' learning is enhanced.

Westerman's (1991) research, also conducted in a general education setting, yielded two models, one representing expert teachers' decision-making and one depicting novice teachers' decision-making. Compared to novices, expert teachers' decision-making included more awareness of the students in the preactive phases (before lessons), and more monitoring for student cues (behavior and/or learning) during the lesson itself (the interactive phase).

Findings from L2 research on language teachers' decision-making. Overall the L1 literature suggests that in the case of experienced teachers, interactive decisions to depart from the lesson plan are often smoothed by the ability to reach into the mental "bag of tricks" and pull out an appropriate, previously used idea—thereby recycling a strategy judged to have been successful in the past. The use of such strategies, or routines, allows the teacher to depart from the plan as needed, but minimizes the risk and the cognitive load in doing so. This is one important part of what it means to be an "experienced" teacher—to have a mental lexicon of resources, of teaching strategies, which can be called up as needed, skillfully, quickly, and with confidence (Leinhardt and Greeno's "large repertoire of activities" [1986: 76]).

The opposite, of course, can also occur. Johnson concluded that, given her cohort of six inexperienced ESL teachers, "Overall, the patterns of instructional actions and decisions found in this study suggest that these preservice ESL teachers did not possess a clearly defined cognitive schema for interpreting unexpected student responses" (1992a: 529). Furthermore, they had no "repertoire of instructional routines" for dealing with such unexpected responses when they arose. When this occurred, according to Johnson, the teachers would "repeat an often ineffectual cycle of instructional actions in response to unexpected student responses until concerns over instructional management took precedence" (1992a: 529).

In recent years, as Johnson's (1992a, 1992b) work illustrates, L2 researchers have begun to study teachers' decision-making during language instruction as well. For example, Donald Freeman (1989: 31) describes teaching as a dynamic decision-making process based on "knowledge, skills, attitude, and awareness." He notes that teachers are faced with both macrodecisions and microdecisions, but "the decision as a unit of teaching remains constant, even though its content is continually shifting" (1989: 31). His observation is consistent with Shavelson's point from the L1 literature that "the basic teaching skill is decision-making" (1973: 18).

Devon Woods (1989, 1993) has also conducted research on second-language teachers' decision-making. He proposed a different sort of model which incorporates two types of decisions: Sequential decisions occur when one decision follows another in a sequence but isn't part of the previous decision. Hierarchical decisions occur when decisions are carried out as a means of achieving a previous decision.

David Nunan (1992: 135) posed the research question, "What is the nature of the professional decisions made by teachers in planning and implementing their language programs?" In that study, Nunan observed nine Australian ESL teachers in the mid-range of experience. In the debriefing immediately after each lesson, he asked the teachers to comment on those areas where they had deviated from their lesson plans. He found that 30% of the teachers' decisions involved management and the organization of the class. Their interactive decisions regarding language most often involved vocabulary, followed by pronunciation and grammar.

Ian Malcolm investigated language teachers' interactive decision-making in one hundred classes of Aboriginal students in West Australian primary schools. Malcolm identified three macro tasks (the management of content, the management of participants, and the management of face) which teachers accomplished through the strategies he investigated. The paper (which is entitled "All right then, if you don't want to do that") documents several "abrupt and verbalized changes of strategy" (1991: 1) that reveal teachers' interactive decisions to abandon their plans in the face of non-cooperation from the learners.

Stimulated recall research. Some recent classroom research on language teaching and learning has utilized the stimulated recall procedure to elicit teachers' ideas about teaching. As noted above, in the review of related L1 literature, stimulated recall involves having informants (in our case teachers or learners) retrospect with the prompting of data drawn from the event they are recalling. In language classroom research, such data are typically audio or video recordings of lessons, transcripts made from the recordings, or observers' fieldnotes. For example, Johnson (1992a, 1992b) used the stimulated recall procedure to examine the interactive decision-making of six preservice ESL teachers. She incorporated Peterson and Clark's (1986) categories to generate frequency counts of student performance cues, the instructional actions the teachers implemented in response to those cues, teachers' interactive decisions, and their use of prior knowledge during lessons. Building on L1 work by Calderhead (1983), Johnson concluded that preservice teachers "rely on a limited number of instructional routines and are overwhelmingly concerned with inappropriate student responses and maintaining the flow of instructional activity" (1992b: 129). She suggested that preservice teachers need to recognize the "routines and patterns which experienced ESL teachers rely on to lessen the number of conscious decisions necessary during instruction" (1992b: 129). As Johnson points out, "Utilizing stimulus recall data from experienced ESL teachers may be one way of providing opportunities for preservice ESL teachers to trace the instructional decisions of experienced ESL teachers" (1992a: 129).

Nunan's most recent research (in press) on language teachers' decision-making also involved the stimulated recall procedure. In this study, using the data collected in Nunan (1992), he asked teachers to explain the reasoning behind their interactive decision-making. He found that teachers had very sensible reasons for making choices—reasons which were not always clear or even readily apparent to the outside observer. Typically their logic depended on complex, contextual factors and situational knowledge which were not accessible to the researcher until he sought the teachers' input.

In Bailey (in press), I also used the stimulated recall procedure to access information from six experienced teachers in an intensive ESL program. I had several prior end-of-session students' evaluations of these six teachers which confirmed that they were skilled as well as experienced. In collecting the data, I requested a copy of the teacher's regular lesson plan, made an audio cassette recording of the class, and took observational fieldnotes during the lesson. The audiotapes were transcribed, and the transcripts and fieldnotes were used as the basis for the stimulated recall procedure in the post-observation conference with each teacher, which was also audio recorded. When the teacher identified an unexpected event recorded in the fieldnotes, or when there was an apparent discrepancy between the lesson plan and the actual lesson, I asked the teacher to explain how and why she had decided to proceed. Finally I asked each teacher to articulate the principles which had guided her decisions, as if she were explaining those principles to a novice teacher (see Bailey, in press). My intent was to document the factors which guided these experienced teachers' interactive decision-making. Thus, I attempted to make explicit some of the things that experienced teachers know—knowledge which should contribute to a theory of language teaching.

Larsen-Freeman pointed out in her Georgetown paper five years ago that "there is only scant research looking at what teachers believe—and yet this is what teachers act upon" (1990: 266). I am happy to report that this situation has changed somewhat. There is now an emerging body of L2 research which addresses this concern. All of this information on teachers' thought processes, whether it is from first- or second-language studies, illustrates the complexity of interactive decision-making in instructional settings. This information begins to respond to Larsen-Freeman's notion that a theory of second-language teaching "would motivate research not only on what a teacher does, but also what a teacher thinks" (1990: 267). And, likewise, a theory of second-language teaching would be motivated by such research.

Methodological development in language classroom research. My second main point has to do with teachers taking active roles in the research process. Stimulated recall, described above, is one procedure for eliciting data, but it restricts teachers to the role of informants. Recently second-language-classroom research has incorporated teachers' points of view more frequently and more equitably than it did in the past. This trend is a result of many developments in the field, two of which will be discussed here. The first is the advent of the action research model in second-language studies, and the second is the increasing influence of ethnography as an approach to second-language classroom research.

The influence of action research. Action research is a model of participatory research which is broadly intended to bring about improvement in any given social setting. Action researchers do this by systematically using an iterative cycle of steps to develop "local understanding" of targeted issues. Various models of action research exist. (See e.g. Crookes 1993; Henry and Kemmis 1985; Kemmis and McTaggart 1982; Nunan 1989, 1990, 1993; van Lier 1994b.) But they all involve the cyclic procedures of planning, acting, reflecting, and replanning. Some have called for the dissemination of action research findings to be added to the cycle. (See van Lier 1994b.)

By definition, action research involves the participants in investigations of their own situations "in order to improve the rationality and justice of their own social or educational practices, as well as their understanding of these practices and the situations in which these practices are carried out" (Henry and Kemmis 1985: 1). For language education, this approach means that teachers (and learners) have not just an important role, but rather the central role to play in action research on language teaching and learning.

An example is Amy Tsui's report (in press) of an action research project carried out by thirty-eight secondary school EFL teachers in Hong Kong. These teachers collaborated in investigating the patterns of participation in their own classrooms. The objective was to discover what factors inhibited the students' oral participation in class and to develop strategies for increasing their participation. The teachers used the action research approach for four weeks, keeping journals and transcribing their own tape recorded lessons. What they discovered was somewhat surprising to them. The factors they identified as contributing to the learners' general reticence included the students' low English proficiency, and their fear of making mistakes and being ridiculed for it. These findings were predictable. But what the teachers also discovered was that they themselves were contributing to the problem by their intolerance of silence, by their uneven allocation of turns, and by providing input which was incomprehensible to the learners. The strategies they used to increase students' oral participation included lengthening their wait-time, improving their questioning techniques, accepting a variety of answers from students (instead of only the narrowly focused answers they had expected), using peer support and group work, focusing on content (instead of just form), and establishing good relationships with the students.

Tsui's report provides a readable account of how one group of teachers, working together, used the action research model to improve their teaching by first working to understand it better. Coming to understand our own practice as teachers is essentially what Dick Allwright and I have called exploratory teaching (Allwright and Bailey 1991).

The action research model has proven to be very productive in general education (see e.g. Nixon 1981) though it has not yet been widely used in language research. Two recently published examples in language education are

Bacon's (1992) investigation of cooperative learning with her secondary school Spanish students, and Kebir's (1994) paper on adult ESL learners' use of communication strategies.

The influence of ethnography. Increased incorporation of teachers' and learners' viewpoints as viable data is partially due to the the enhanced status of ethnography as an approach to language education research. Ethnography is defined as the "study of people's behavior in naturally occurring, ongoing settings, with a focus on the cultural interpretation of behavior" (Watson-Gegeo 1988: 576). Ethnography emphasizes triangulation, the importance of context, and the development of the emic perspective in research. Let us examine these three concepts.

First, triangulation is both a stance and a series of procedural safeguards which qualitative researchers use to challenge and confirm the interpretation of observed phenomena. Triangulation involves employing a variety of data and research methods to bring multiple data sets and research procedures to bear on the investigation of any issue (see Denzin 1970, 1978; van Lier 1988).

An example of triangulation in language classroom research is found in Block's study (in press) of an English course in Barcelona. Instead of describing his "subjects" Block writes:

> My main research partners were six MBA candidates (all aged 25–32) who were completing an obligatory English requirement, and their teacher, an English instructor who was interested in classroom research and above all in finding out more about what her students thought. (in press)

Block's study contrasts the teacher's intent in planning and executing the lessons with the students' interpretation of the lesson's purposes. The teacher and six learners kept "oral diaries" (tape recorded retrospections following class sessions). Seven other students agreed to be interviewed but did not keep diaries. Block also observed and audiotaped additional class meetings, after which he interviewed all thirteen students in the course. He writes:

> I organized my data in this manner because my chief aim was to triangulate, gathering as many points of view as possible. By the end of these days, I had my notes, [the teacher's] comments, the comments of those students who were keeping a diary, as well as the records of two of the three classes which I observed. (In one observation the tape recording did not work.) (in press)

The question addressed by all the participants in Block's research was, "What do you think was the purpose of the activities?" Of particular note is Block's data from Alex, a student who was especially unhappy with the course, primarily because he thought many of the activities were pointless. However, examination of the diary and interview data revealed that he did not understand the purpose or the end goal of most classroom activities. Reading Block's juxtaposition of Alex's complaints and the teacher's concerns will trigger a "déjà vu" feeling for any experienced teacher who has dealt with a dissatisfied student. This account will also offer insights to less experienced teachers and provide them with strategies for dealing with the Alexes of this world. As Block notes, it is important that teachers make their classroom intentions explicit to students: "The analysis of pedagogical purpose is not solely the domain of teachers" (in press).

Another example of triangulation at work in second-language-classroom research comes from Shaw's (in press) ethnographic study of a curricular innovation (content-based instruction) in a foreign-language department which had previously based its curriculum on four-skills courses, literature seminars, and language for specific purposes courses. In order to document the implementation of content-based instruction in this program, Shaw attended and recorded classes, interviewed both students and teachers, and read the journals they kept. He also utilized students' scores on oral interviews and cloze passages in their target languages. His conclusions are thus directly supported by language assessment data, as well as by multiple data sets provided by the participants themselves, and his own fieldnotes and transcripts of classroom interactions.

The importance of context is another central tenet which is codified as the "holistic principle" in ethnographic research. Watson-Gegeo (1988: 577) summarizes the holistic principle as the idea that "any aspect of a culture or a behavior has to be described and explained in relation to the whole system of which it is a part." Here again we see a connection with what language classroom research can contribute to a theory of second-language teaching. Larsen-Freeman notes that, "While SLA researchers are attempting to construct a causal-process theory which explains the process of SLA for all learners in general, a [second-language] teacher's knowledge arises from the need to comprehend the complexities of a given context" (1990: 265, citing Bolster 1983).

An example of the researcher-teacher's understanding of context and its role in language teaching and learning is found in Cummings's (in press) moving account of her experience teaching a community college composition course for "repeaters." The class was made up of twenty adult ESL learners who had all failed the course twice before. If they failed it a third time they would be dropped from the school. Cummings writes:

Passing the course would allow them to enter Basic Writing in the English Department. After two quarters of Basic Writing, they would be eligible to take Freshman Composition and begin taking courses in their major ... A class of twenty repeaters at a community college in urban America. One of many community colleges that has broken its promise (a career in two years) to its students who have immigrated to the United States hoping for new lives. (in press)

But new lives will be very hard for these students to attain. Cummings describes them as mostly women, half of them over the age of thirty, who have been in the U.S. and out of school for an average of eight years. Some have the equivalent of a high school diploma. Cummings's understanding of her students' context is apparent in how she writes and how she deals with their attempts to cut corners. She writes:

Jaime had his pocket picked on vacation. He gives his composition the title, "A Bad Vacation" and I recognize it as too-familiar, one that he probably wrote in a previous semester for another teacher. This happens a lot with repeaters. The effort to start again where they failed before is so colossal that they will do anything to avoid it. I understand this. I ask him to rewrite it anyway. (in press)

Another student gives Cummings a composition about the death of her boyfriend, with no grammatical errors, which Cummings is sure she has seen before. The day's topic is "How to Raise a Difficult Child," but the student doesn't have children and wants to write instead about the effects of drugs and alcohol during pregnancy. Cummings says no. "I am not usually so strict," she writes:

but she has her diskette from last quarter in the computer ... I am certain that the [composition] about the effects of drugs and alcohol on unborn children will be there. Instead I tell her that it doesn't matter if she has children or not. She was a child once herself, wasn't she? She slaps her head, as if she had forgotten. (in press)

Cummings encourages the students to write about what they know. The result? "They are stories of defeat. Reading and writing skills have little to do with the problems these students face. But I am here to teach them about reading and writing. I continue". (in press)

Thinking about a single parent among her students, Cummings says,

She can't concentrate. She has too many worries. She is always on her way to the doctor's or to the dentist, for herself or for her sons. There is no time to relax. She wears glasses with heavy black frames, the kind you buy from a rack at the drugstore ... What does any of this have to do with reading and writing? How can I interrupt all of this to talk about verbs? (in press).

The financial imperative is a fact of life for Cummings's students. When the class is practicing the conditional, she says:

We write sentences full of hopes and dreams, what we would do if we were mayor of the city, president of the United States, queen/king of the world. Many of them want to feed and shelter the hungry. All of them want to buy houses for their mothers. (in press)

Financial well being (or the lack thereof) looms large in the class discussions, the students' essays, and behind the scenes:

A lot of buying and selling goes on in these classes. Many of the students are Avon ladies, or some Latina equivalent, on the side. And who can blame them? More than verbs, they need money. When I turn my back to write on the blackboard, I can hear the crackling of a plastic bag as they try to tempt each other with costume jewelry and cut-rate cosmetics. There are days when I don't even try to stop them. I sympathize with these people who cannot get what they want, who are always struggling, who have dreams but cannot achieve them, who could achieve them if they could unload their cares, but whose cares will always be there. (in press)

Cummings's paper explains how she teaches writing in this class. And in the end, miraculously, something goes right. Eighteen of the twenty "repeaters" write end-of-term compositions which are judged to be successful by Cummings's colleagues who score the final exam. Her understanding of the students' context has helped her to help them to succeed. What we have here is a poignant portrayal of a group of students and an ESL teacher/researcher who fully understands the contextual constraints they face, and who reaches beyond those constraints to help the students improve their writing.

The emphasis on developing the emic perspective is also a central principle in ethnography (van Lier 1988, 1989; Watson-Gegeo 1988). Emic characteristics "refer to the rules, concepts, beliefs and meanings of the people themselves, functioning within their own group" (van Lier 1990: 43). The emic principle holds that "each situation investigated by an ethnographer must be understood from the perspective of the participants in that situation" (Watson-Gegeo 1988: 579). The participants' views often contrast with the researcher's etic (outsider's) framework.

An outstanding example is Freeman's study of how a high school French teacher, Maggie, and her students constructed "shared understandings" — specifically, "how authority and control were distributed through pedagogy and interaction, to build a shared understanding of French" (1992: 58). Freeman discusses the extent to which the notion of energy appears as a recurrent theme in Maggie's teaching. He writes:

> What is striking in our collaboration is that Maggie is largely unaware of the central role that the concept of energy plays in her teaching. As I identify it as a theme in the data, she responds immediately almost as if it were something she had known and yet forgotten. In an almost classic interplay of my view as an outsider and hers as an insider, we fashion a shared understanding of this central aspect of her teaching. In a sense, the understanding is as clear as it is unnecessary. Our collaboration only serves to articulate what is intuitive for Maggie; she can certainly operate without it. (1992: 58)

Here Freeman is commenting on the interpretive balance between the insider's emic perspective and the outsider's etic perspective. The views are often different. He continues:

> As I isolated segments with similar patterns of talk and activity, I tried to articulate to Maggie how I saw them as similar. Often she would see the segments in terms of the point of the activity; comparability was not her concern. Like standing too close to a pointilliste painting, she saw the discrete dots, patterns of color, and how they were put together; I saw the image which they represented, yet was often unclear how or why she did what she did: (1992: 66)

Freeman describes the "phases" he discovers in Maggie's teaching and shows how the students' understanding of French develops. He and Maggie would interpret the transcripts together, and—like the image of the students developing a shared understanding—the teacher and researcher developed their own shared meta-understanding:

> Teaching is a phenomenon she lived and I described; she did it and I tried to find words for what I saw and heard... Within this framework, the interplay of our points of view helped to move something which was private, intuitive, and unreflected into the public forum of writing and talking, the construction of our shared understanding expressing what she had done and I had found in her classroom. (1992: 78)

The kind of collaboration Freeman describes used to be infrequent: In order to maintain their objectivity, researchers working in the experimental tradition would keep their distance from the teachers and learners they studied. Nowadays, however, that attitude is changing. For example, Koenig and Zuengler (1994) have written a brief account about their collaboration as partners (in the primary roles of teacher and researcher, respectively) in conducting a study of teachers' and learners' goals during oral instructional activities. They enjoyed both predictable and unpredictable benefits from the collaboration. Koenig writes:

> At the very beginning of our collaboration, I viewed Jane [Zuengler] as more of a mentor because of her past research experience. However, my perspective changed quickly, as all of our decisions were mutual and our research questions and design evolved while we worked together. It has been exciting to analyze the transcripts and tapes together. We each bring different perspectives to the data, mine from immersion in my classroom and Jane's from a perspective outside the class. (1994: 41)

Zuengler, on the other hand, discusses how working with Koenig transformed her approach to conducting research. Her comments illustrate Larsen-Freeman's point that a theory of second-language teaching should be grounded in classroom data. She began her study with the typical academic strategy of reviewing the literature for key terms, "trying to find a conceptual framework for understanding goals in talk" (1994: 41–42). But then she writes:

> While I was still immersed in thinking about goals in learners' discourse from this kind of academic perspective, Jane [Koenig] came with a more practical concern about goals. What developed, as our conversations became a collaboration, was that I stopped my foray into the the academic literature for the time being. Our conversations about goals began with a focus on Jane's classroom. So we began by collecting data from her setting, and then going on to collect data from other teachers and another class. In other words, our study became what the research texts term data-driven. (in contrast to theory-driven; See Allwright and Bailey 1991)

The examples from Koenig and Zuengler and from Freeman's collaboration with Maggie suggest that further research partnerships of teachers and researchers will contribute richly to an emerging theory of second-language teaching.

Conclusions. In this paper we have considered the call by Larsen-Freeman (as well as others) for a theory of second-language teaching, focusing specifically on her ideas that such a theory would be grounded in classroom data, and would motivate research on teachers' thinking. We saw several examples of recent language classroom research which have examined teacher cognition as a central focus, and involved teachers in the research process more fully than heretofore.

We have seen that teacher decision-making is very complex (perhaps even more so in L2 classrooms where the choice of linguistic code may be an issue), and that skilled teachers' interactive decision-making often takes place instantaneously and invisibly. There is some evidence from L1 studies that teachers' decision-making is related to student achievement and that it develops as teachers gain experience. In the L1 context, Shavelson (1973: 18) has called decision-making the "basic teaching skill," and (as we saw above) in L2 research, Donald Freeman has said that "the decision as a unit of teaching remains constant, even though its contents are continually shifting" (1989: 31). We have also discussed a few empirical studies in L2 research on teachers' decision-making, some of which used the stimulated recall procedure.

We then examined two methodological developments which are giving teachers a more central role in language classroom research. The first, action research, although well established in other countries and in first-language educational research, is just beginning to bear fruit in the U.S. (at least in a widely accessible, published form). The second, the rise of ethnography as an approach to L2 classroom research, is a powerful and well respected avenue for developing a theory of second-language teaching. In particular, the ethnographic emphases on triangulation, contextual interpretation, and developing the emic perspective will stimulate language teachers' involvement in classroom research—as informants, partners in research, and investigators in their own right. While this paper has not itself articulated a theory per se, I hope it has shown that L2 classroom research in the past five years has moved us further towards a theory of second-language teaching.

REFERENCES

Allwright, Dick. 1983. "Classroom-centered research on language teaching and learning: A brief historical overview." *TESOL Quarterly* 17(2): 191–204.

Allwright, Dick and Kathleen M. Bailey. 1991. *Focus on the language classroom: An introduction to classroom research for language teachers.* New York: Cambridge University Press.

Bacon, Susan M. 1992. "Phases of listening to authentic input in Spanish. A descriptive study." *Foreign Language Annals* 25(4): 317–334.

Bailey, Kathleen M. 1985. "Classroom-centered research on language teaching and learning." In Marianne Celce-Murcia (ed.), *Beyond basics: Issues and research in TESOL.* Rowley, Massachusetts: Newbury House. 96–121.

Bailey, Kathleen M. (in press). "The best laid plans: Teachers' inclass decisions to depart from their lesson plans." In Kathleen M. Bailey and David Nunan (eds.), *Voices from the language classroom: Qualitative research in language education.* New York: Cambridge University Press.

Block, David. (in press). "A window on the classroom: Classroom events viewed from different angles." In Kathleen M. Bailey and David Nunan (eds.), *Voices from the language classroom: Qualitative research in language education.* New York: Cambridge University Press.

Bolster, Arthur. 1983. "Toward a more effective model of research on teaching." *Harvard Educational Review* 53(3): 294–308.

Brumfit, Chris and Rosamond Mitchell (eds.). 1990. *Research in the language classroom.* ELT Documents 133. London: Modern English Publications and the British Council.

Calderhead, James. 1981. "A psychological approach to research on teachers' classroom decision-making." *British Educational Research Journal* 7(1): 51–57.

Chaudron, Craig. 1988. *Second language classrooms: Research on teaching and learning.* Cambridge, U.K.: Cambridge University Press.

Clark, Christopher M. and Penelope L. Peterson. 1986. "Teachers' thought processes." In Michael Wittrock (ed.), *Handbook of research on teaching, Third edition.* New York: Macmillan Publishing Co. 255–296.

Crookes, Graham. 1993. "Action research for second language teaching: Going beyond teacher research." *Applied Linguistics* 14(2): 130–142.

Cummings, Martha Clark. (in press). "Sardo revisited: Voice, faith and multiple repeaters." In Kathleen M. Bailey and David Nunan (eds.), *Voices from the language classroom: Qualitative research in language education.* New York: Cambridge University Press.

Denzin, Norman K. 1970. *Sociological methods: A source book.* Chicago: Aldine.

Denzin, Norman K. 1978. *The research act: A theoretical introduction to sociological methods, Second edition.* New York: McGraw Hill.

Edge, Julian and Keith Richards (eds.). 1993. *Teachers develop teachers research: Papers on classroom research and teacher development.* Oxford: Heinemann International.

Ellis, Rod. 1990. *Learning through instruction: The study of classroom language acquisition.* Oxford: Blackwells.

Freeman, Donald. 1989. "Teacher training, development, and decision-making: A model of teaching and related strategies for language teacher education." *TESOL Quarterly* 23(1): 27–45.

Freeman, Donald. 1992. "Collaboration: Constructing shared understandings in a second language classroom." In David Nunan (ed.), *Collaborative language learning and teaching.* Cambridge, U.K.: Cambridge University Press. 56–80.

Freeman, Donald. (in press). "Redefining the relationship between research and what teachers know." In Kathleen M. Bailey and David Nunan (eds.), *Voices from the language classroom: Qualitative research in language education.* New York: Cambridge University Press.

Freeman, Donald and Jack C. Richards. 1993. "Conceptions of teaching and the education of second language teachers." *TESOL Quarterly* 27(2): 193–216.

Gaies, Stephen J. 1983. "The investigation of language classroom processes." *TESOL Quarterly* 17 (2): 205–217.

Gitlin, Andrew D. 1990. "Educative research, voice, and school change." *Harvard Educational Review* 60(4): 443–466.

Henry, Colin and Stephen Kemmis. 1985. "A point-by-point guide to action research for teachers." *The Australian Administrator* 6(4): 1–4.

Johnson, Karen. 1992a. "Learning to teach: Instructional actions and decisions of preservice ESL teachers." *TESOL Quarterly* 26(3): 507–533.

Johnson, Karen. 1992b. "The instructional decisions of preservice ESL teachers: New directions for teacher preparation programs." In John Flowerdew, Mark Brock and Sophie Hsia (eds.), *Perspectives on second language teacher education.* Hong Kong: City Polytechnic of Hong Kong. 115–134.

Kebir, Catherine. 1994. "An action research look at the communication strategies for adult learners." *TESOL Journal* 4: 28–31.

Kemmis, Steven and Robin McTaggart. 1982. *The action research planner*. Victoria, Australia: Deakin University.

Koenig, Jane and Jane Zuengler. 1994. "Teacher/researcher collaboration: Studying student and teacher goals in oral classroom activities." *TESOL Journal* 4(1): 40–43.

Larsen-Freeman, Diane. 1990. "On the need for a theory of language teaching." In James Alatis (ed.), *Georgetown University Round Table 1990*. Washington, D.C.: Georgetown University Press. 261–270.

Leinhardt, Gaea and James G. Greeno. 1986. "The cognitive skill of teaching." *Journal of Educational Psychology* 78(2): 75–95.

Long, Michael H. 1980. "Inside the 'black box': Methodological issues in research on language teaching and learning." *Language Learning* 30(1): 1–42; reprinted in Herbert W. Seliger and Michael H. Long (eds.) 1983. *Classroom oriented research on second language acquisition*. Rowley, Massachusetts: Newbury House. 3–35.

Malcolm, Ian G. 1991. "'All right then, if you don't want to do that...': Strategy and counter-strategy in classroom discourse management." *Guidelines: A Periodical for Classroom Language Teachers* 13(2): 1–17.

Nixon, John (ed.). 1982. *A teacher's guide to action research*. London: Grant McIntyre.

Nunan, David. 1989. *Understanding language classrooms: A guide for teacher-initiated action*. New York: Prentice-Hall International.

Nunan, David. 1990. "Action research in the language classroom." In Jack C. Richards and David Nunan (eds.), *Second language teacher education*. Cambridge, U.K.: Cambridge University Press. 62–81.

Nunan, David. 1992. "The teacher as decision-maker." In John Flowerdew, Mark Brock, and Sophie Hsia (eds.), *Perspectives on second language teacher education*. Hong Kong: City Polytechnic of Hong Kong. 135–165.

Nunan, David. 1993. "Action research in language education." In Julian Edge and Keith Richards (eds.), *Teachers develop teachers research: Papers on classroom research and teacher development*. Oxford: Heinemann International. 39–50.

Nunan, David. (in press). "Hidden voices: Insiders' perspectives on classroom interaction." In Kathleen M. Bailey and David Nunan (eds.), *Voices from the language classroom: Qualitative research in language education*. New York: Cambridge University Press.

Peterson, Penelope L. and Christopher M. Clark. 1978. "Teachers' reports of their cognitive processes." *American Educational Research Journal* 15(4): 555–565.

Richards, Jack. 1987. "The dilemma of teacher education in TESOL." *TESOL Quarterly* 21(2): 209–226.

Richards, Jack C. and David Nunan (eds.). 1990. *Second language teacher education*. Cambridge, U.K.: Cambridge University Press.

Seliger, Herbert W. and Michael H. Long (eds.). 1983. *Classroom oriented research on second language acquisition*. Rowley, Massachusetts: Newbury House.

Shavelson, Richard J. 1973. "The basic teaching skill: Decision-making." R & D Memorandum No. 104, Stanford, California: Center for Research and Development in Teaching, School of Education, Stanford University.

Shaw, Peter A. (in press). "Voices for improved learning: The ethnographer as co-agent of pedagogic change." In Kathleen M. Bailey and David Nunan (eds.), *Voices from the language classroom: Qualitative research in language education*. New York: Cambridge University Press.

Tsui, Amy B.M. (in press). "Reticence and anxiety in second language learning." In Kathleen M. Bailey and David Nunan (eds.), *Voices from the language classroom: Qualitative research in language education*. New York: Cambridge University Press.

van Lier, Leo A.W. 1984. "Discourse analysis and classroom research: A methodological perspective." *International Journal of the Sociology of Language* 49: 111–133.

van Lier, Leo. 1988. *The classroom and the language learner: Ethnography and second-language classroom research*. London: Longman.

van Lier, Leo. 1989. "Classroom research in second language acquisition." *Annual Review of Applied Linguistics* 10: 173–186.

van Lier, Leo. 1990. "Ethnography: Bandaid, bandwagon, or contraband?" In Christopher Brumfit and Rosamund Mitchell (eds.), *Research in the language classroom*. ELT Documents, 133. London: Modern English Publications and the British Council. 33–53.

van Lier, Leo. 1994a. "Some features of a theory of practice." *TESOL Journal* 4(1): 6–10.

van Lier, Leo. 1994b. "Action research." *Sintagma* 6: 31–37.

Watson-Gegeo, Karen A. 1988. "Ethnography in ESL: Defining the essentials." *TESOL Quarterly* 22(4): 575–592.

Westerman, D. 1991. "Expert and novice teacher decision-making." *Journal of Teacher Education* 42(4): 292–305.

Woods, Devon. 1989. "Studying ESL teachers' decision-making: Rationale, methodological issues and initial results." *Carleton Papers in Applied Language Studies* 6. Ottawa: Carleton University.

Woods, Devon. 1993." Processes in ESL Teaching: A study of the role of planning and interpretive processes in the practice of teaching English as a second language." *Carleton Papers in Applied Language Studies*. Ottawa: Carleton University.

Wright, Tony. 1990. "Understanding classroom role relationships." In Jack C. Richards and David Nunan (eds.), *Second language teacher education*. Cambridge, U.K.: Cambridge University Press. 82–97.

Learning strategies of elementary foreign-language-immersion students

Anna Uhl Chamot
Georgetown University

Introduction. This paper reports on the first year of a study being conducted by Georgetown University's Language Research Projects.[1] The study is investigating the learning strategies of elementary school children learning a foreign language in an immersion setting.

Language-immersion programs are characterized by a focus on learning school subjects through the medium of a second language, rather than an exclusive focus on the language being learned. Children in immersion programs typically begin in kindergarten or first grade and continue through the elementary years. In partial-immersion programs, some subjects are taught in the target language and others in English, while total-immersion programs teach initial literacy and mathematical skills as well as other subjects through the second language. In total-immersion programs, literacy in the children's native language is typically introduced in second grade or later, and the curriculum may gradually shift to a balance of foreign- and native-language instruction (Curtain and Pesola 1988; Met and Galloway 1992).

Immersion programs in French were initiated in Canada in the 1960s, and in Spanish in the United States in the early 1970s (Campbell 1984; Lambert and Tucker 1972). More than two decades of research indicate that this approach is highly effective in developing an impressive level of foreign-language proficiency in English-speaking children and grade-level or above achievement in English skills and content subjects (Curtain and Pesola 1988; Genesee 1987; Swain 1984). The thrust of this research has been on the linguistic and academic products of immersion education rather than on the teaching and learning processes involved (Bernhardt 1992). Thus while we know the levels of achievement attained by children in language-immersion programs, we have little knowledge about how they reach those achievement levels. In particular, the

[1] This research is conducted by the Georgetown University/Center for Applied Linguistics National Foreign Language Resource Center and through an additional grant from the International Research and Studies Program of the U.S. Department of Education. The views, opinions, and findings reported are those of the author and should not be construed as an official Department of Education position, policy, or decision unless so designated by other official documentation.

learning strategies used by children in foreign-language-immersion settings and the effects of learning-strategies instruction in such settings remain largely unexamined.

In contrast, the role of learning strategies has been extensively studied with children learning in native-language contexts and, to a lesser degree, with older language learners. Considerable success has been achieved in teaching elementary school children to use learning strategies in first-language contexts (Pressley and Associates 1990), but research in second-language elementary-school contexts has focused on the description of learning strategies used in English by bilingual students (Padron and Waxman 1988). Research with older students, however, has shown that effective language learners use strategies more appropriately than less effective language learners, and that learning strategies can be taught to both secondary- and college-level second-language students (Chamot 1993; Chamot and Küpper 1989; Cohen and Aphek 1981; O'Malley and Chamot 1990; Rubin, Quinn, and Enos 1988; Thompson and Rubin 1993). The application of this research to younger students in language-immersion programs holds promise for developing an understanding of their learning processes and ways for helping them learn even more effectively.

The study reported here builds on previous work conducted by the research team at the Georgetown University/Center for Applied Linguistics National Foreign Language Resource Center that has investigated learning strategies in high-school Japanese, Russian, and Spanish classrooms (Chamot, Barnhardt, El-Dinary, Carbonaro, and Robbins 1993; Chamot, Robbins, and El-Dinary 1993).

Research questions addressed over the three years of the investigation include the following: (1) Which learning strategies are used by more effective and less effective learners in elementary foreign-language-immersion programs? (2) Do these strategies change over time and, if so, how? (3) Do students who use learning strategies more frequently perceive themselves as more effective language learners? (4) Are students who use learning strategies more frequently also rated higher in language proficiency? (5) What are the differences in strategy use across the languages studied? (6) Do immersion teachers believe that strategies instruction improves their students' language learning?

The first year of the project addressed the first research question by identifying the learning strategies used by elementary school foreign-language-immersion students and comparing the strategies used by more and less effective language learners. Professional development for teachers began at the end of the first year and is continuing throughout the project. In the second and third years of the project, students will be explicitly taught strategies for language tasks.

Study participants and context. Three immersion programs in the Washington, D.C. suburbs are participating in the study and include five French-immersion classrooms, three Spanish-immersion classrooms, and six Japanese-immersion classrooms. The grade levels range from kindergarten through grade six, though not every level is included for each of the three languages, since teachers participate on a voluntary basis. The French and Spanish programs are total-immersion programs, in which all subjects are taught in the target language for most of the school day. The Japanese program is a partial-immersion program in which students receive instruction in mathematics, science, and health for half of each day, and then spend the remainder of the day in English instruction for subjects such as language arts and social studies.

Most of the students in these programs come from native English-speaking families. Only a very few children in the Japanese program have a Japanese-speaking parent. In the Spanish program, a somewhat larger number of children have a Spanish-speaking parent or parents. In the French program the majority of students also have native English-speaking backgrounds, but a number of francophone African and Haitian students are enrolled in this program as well.

Twelve of the fourteen participating immersion teachers are native speakers of the target language, and the two remaining are near-native speakers. All hold either permanent or provisional elementary-teaching certificates for the states in which they teach, and many also have teaching credentials and experience from their native countries. Participating teachers have all received considerable preparation and professional development in immersion philosophy and methodology through inservice workshops and/or university coursework. The teachers express enthusiasm for immersion education, are rigorous in providing instruction virtually exclusively in the target language, and devote considerable efforts to developing appropriate materials and techniques to assist their students to learn subject matter through the medium of a foreign language.

The curriculum in each of the immersion programs closely follows the school district's approved curriculum and standards. Rendering a curriculum designed for instruction through English into a content-based foreign-language curriculum has entailed the continuing identification and development of instructional materials. These include books and other materials from French- and Spanish-speaking countries and from Japan. Teacher-developed materials have been needed to meet curriculum objectives that are not represented at the relevant grade level in imported books. For example, the elementary science curriculum in one school district uses locally-developed science kits with materials for experiments and student workbooks. The immersion teachers use the same science kits, but have had to translate the workbooks and other student materials into Japanese. Similarly, the sixth-grade social-studies curriculum studies ancient history, so the French-immersion teachers have collected books and other materials in French on early and classical civilizations at the appropriate reading level. The Spanish-immersion program probably has easiest access to materials, given the availability of Spanish materials published in the United States.

Procedures. In the first year of the project a descriptive study was conducted to document the instructional practices of participating immersion teachers, to explore with teachers the feasibility of introducing or expanding instruction in learning strategies, and to identify the learning strategies already used by both more and less effective language learners.

To this end, regular observations of the fourteen immersion classrooms were conducted. These observations were open-ended and aimed at providing a rich description of the instructional context. They provided information about the teaching approaches of participating teachers and focused on the relationship of these practices to learning-strategies instruction.

Professional development was provided through meetings and discussions with the teachers and through workshops on teaching learning strategies. Researchers also worked with the teachers to develop criteria for rating their students' language proficiency and achievement levels. These rating scales were used to identify a random sample of highly effective and less effective learners in each classroom. In the spring of the project's first year, think-aloud interviews were conducted with the sample of students thus identified. A minimum of three high-achievement and three low-achievement students in each classroom participated in the think-aloud interviews. Where possible, oversampling took place as a precaution against the possible attrition of the students who would be followed in the longitudinal aspect of the study.

Teachers were asked to provide three tasks for the think-aloud interviews of students in their classrooms, one for mathematics, one for reading, and one for writing. These tasks were to contain new and somewhat challenging content, but were to be familiar in format. Typical tasks included a brief mathematical story problem, a narrative or expository reading text, and a writing prompt.

Individual interviews of approximately twenty minutes each were conducted with each student in the sample. The interviews were conducted in the target language, but interviewers switched to English if students had difficulty understanding the directions. This switching occurred almost exclusively with the younger children, as the older ones were sufficiently proficient in the target language to understand the interviewer. Students were assured that they could respond in the target language, in English, or in a mixture of the two languages. The researcher explained the purpose of the interview, and students were instructed to describe their thoughts as they worked on the three tasks. A preliminary warm-up task involving mathematical computation provided the students with practice in thinking aloud. Prompts provided by the researcher included comments such as: What are you thinking right now? How did you figure that out? Before you begin/go on, can you tell me what you're thinking?

Results and discussion. The interviews were tape-recorded and later transcribed verbatim. The transcripts were then translated into English, and analyzed for evidence of learning strategies. This analysis was used to develop a coding scheme for classifying types of learning strategies for the three tasks (mathematical problem-solving, reading, and writing). A team of researchers developed the coding schemes by analyzing sample think-aloud transcripts, developing classifications, comparing their classifications, and resolving differences. This process resulted in a consistent coding scheme that was then applied to the remaining think-aloud transcripts.

Descriptive profiles are being developed in order to capture the most prominent and consistent features of each student's think-aloud interview. These descriptive profiles are focusing on the reading and writing tasks, since these tasks elicited the greatest variety of language-learning strategies.

The preliminary analysis of the transcripts reveal a variety of strategies used in different ways by immersion students. Different patterns of strategy use characterize differences between more strategic and less strategic students. Based on the data analyzed so far, the following conclusions are emerging:

- many immersion students can describe their thinking processes,
- a few students experience difficulty in thinking aloud,
- some children exhibit metacognitive awareness of their own learning,
- some children can describe and use the strategies they have been taught, and
- more effective students selected more appropriate strategies for a task and used strategies more flexibly than less effective students.

The tables on the following pages contain some examples (translated into English for interviews conducted in target language) from the think-aloud transcripts and the descriptive profiles that illustrate these five conclusions. The classification of examples is tentative, since many of the examples illustrate more than one of the conclusions.

Conclusion. The findings to date on the study of learning strategies used by language-immersion students provide insights into the language-learning processes of elementary-school students when they use a foreign language as the medium for acquiring new information and skills. The degree to which many of these young learners could describe their own thinking and learning processes seems to indicate that metacognitive awareness begins at quite an early age. Analyses of the data collected from the second and third years of the study will provide additional information about (1) how children's strategies change over time, (2) the relationship between children's use of strategies and their perceptions of efficacy as language learners, (3) any differences in strategy use across the languages studied, and (4) the immersion teachers' evaluation of the effectiveness of explicit learning-strategies instruction.

Table 1. Description of thinking processes

Language	Grade	Examples	Comments
French	6	I: Are you thinking in French or in English right now? S: I think in both ... because I have like a picture in my head, but I think in French, but I take...when I...my vocabulary was born in English, so...that's why I translate into English.	The student describes what appears to be bilingual processing based on mental imagery. The student realizes that his initial vocabulary developed in English, and gives this as a reason for translating French words into English.
Japanese	5	I: Are you thinking in Japanese or in English? S: I'm not thinking in either way, because I'm not saying anything, so...only pictures.	The student is aware of his/her own use of mental imagery while thinking, and indicates that this imagery is language-independent.
Spanish	2	I: When you read, are you thinking completely in Spanish or a little bit in English, too? S: A lot in Spanish...just a little bit in English. I: When, do you realize when you think in English? S: When it said [referring to the story], "I heard a cheep cheep nearby," I thought a little bit in English...and all the rest in Spanish.	The student can make an estimate of how much thinking is done in each language and can identify the point in the story where thinking in English intruded.

Table 2. Difficulty in thinking aloud

Language	Grade	Examples	Comments
French	3	When D. (the less effective learner who used the word-by-word strategy) was given the text, he didn't look at the picture. I asked him what he was thinking before he started the text, and he just started reading.	The student did not use cues from the illustration to predict the story, and ignored the interviewer's request to describe his thinking.
Japanese	3	The student reads the text aloud, self-correcting occasionally. However, when it comes to reporting about his thoughts while reading, he mostly keeps silent or replies, "I don't know." During the writing task, the student also either keeps silent or says "I don't know" when asked what he is thinking.	These two students were uncommunicative when the interviewer asked them what they were thinking. Their standard response was "I don't know" or "No."
	5	The student reads the text aloud, but says nothing voluntarily about her thoughts while reading. In response to the interviewer's questions such as, "Did you think about anything here?" she keeps saying, "No."	
Spanish	1–3	Low-strategy users were less articulate than high-strategy users. The former were frequently silent when asked what they were thinking of or what they usually did to solve a reading/writing problem.	Students seemed to be unable to respond to questions about their thinking processes.

Table 3. Metacognitive awareness of students' own learning

Language	Grade	Examples	Comments
French	5	I: And what do you need to do when you see an exercise like this that you need to fill out? S: Me, I think that I need to think about what we did at the beginning of the school year, because this was the first thing that we did in social studies, and then I'm going to look at all the sentences and try to recall what it is. Since there are many that help me, and I only need to fill in a word in one place or another, it will be quite easy.	This student has a clear plan for proceeding with the task. The plan is based on her prior knowledge about similar tasks, her analysis of the requirements of the present task, and her confidence that she has the strategies which will make the task easy.
Japanese	1	The student listened to the first part of a story and used the illustration to guess what the story was about, since there were so many unfamiliar words. Then the interviewer read a portion of the story without showing the illustration and asked the student to tell what he was thinking. S: I was … I thought of the same thing. I: Okay. You remember the pictures? Okay, is there anything else you were thinking? S: Uh, just a couple of math problems. I: Math problems? You were thinking of math while you listened? S: Uh-huh. I: Oh, that's amazing! S: I know. I have one half of my brain that does thinking of stories and the other half does math problems.	Even without the story's illustration, the student relied on mental imagery while listening to part of the story. However, the student was also reflecting on the math problems completed before the reading task. The student believes that his brain is divided into compartments that either understand stories or process math problems.
Spanish	2	I: First, before reading, what are you thinking about at this moment, before starting to read? S: [Student examines the picture] That this story could be a fantasy. I: It could be a fantasy? Why do you say that? S: Because I think [still looking at the picture] that the story is going to be very funny and things are going to happen that can't happen.	This is an example of planning before reading. The student gets ready to read the story by using the illustration to make predictions about what the story will be about.

Table 4. Description/use of the strategies taught

Language	Grade	Examples	Comments
Japanese	1	The student notices that the first story includes lots of *ka-ki-ku-ke-ko* (the sequence of the Japanese alphabet/syllabary), and that the first part of each sentence starts with one of these syllables in order. She further mentions that each sentence in the second story starts with a Japanese vowel in sequence (*a-i-u-e-o*).	The teacher uses a large chart of the *hiragana* syllabary to teach the syllables in order, and students are taught to recognize different *hiragana* by going through the sequence.
Spanish	2	I: *[Shows student a math word problem to solve]* When you see a math problem, what do you think about? S: Mm ... that first you need to read the problem and then you think what strategy is easiest to use. Then you solve the problem, using whichever strategy. I: What are your favorite strategies? S: Mm ... drawing ... complete sentence, or a number sentence.	The teacher provides explicit instruction in a process for mathematical problem-solving strategies which include understanding the problem, deciding on a plan for solving the problem, carrying out the plan, and checking the answer. This student is focusing on the initial steps in the problem-solving process.

Table 5. Appropriateness and flexibility of strategies of more effective students

Language	Grade	Examples	Comments
French	5	(Student did not recognize the word "pastures" in French, and explained what she does when she doesn't know a word in French.) S: ...That depends, if I think that this word is important enough, I look it up in the dictionary, but if I can maybe understand the sentence and it's clear enough, I don't look it up in the dictionary and I deliberately forget about it.	The student makes a judgment about the importance of an unfamiliar word and then chooses which strategy to use.
Japanese	5	The student starts by asking questions about the (writing) task. Before writing, she generates content to be written by describing the picture in Japanese. She asks a question about how to say an item in the picture in Japanese. The student writes as she says what she is writing. When asked, she reports that she first constructs what she would write in her head and then writes it. She later reports that there were things that she thought about writing, but she didn't because she couldn't construct them in her head. She reports that when this happens in class, she usually looks the word up in the dictionary. Finally, she indicates metacognitive awareness by saying, "I know a lot of words in English, but unless I know them in Japanese, I cannot do it."	The student appears to have developed useful prewriting strategies, including imagery, brainstorming, prior knowledge, questioning for clarification, mental rehearsal, deletion of unknown words or phrases from the plan or use of a dictionary, and an assessment of her own knowledge.
Spanish	2	The student is asked what he does when he encounters a new word while reading in Spanish. S: Yes, and when I don't understand a word, I have a paper and I can write what page it's on and what sentence, and write the word—and the teacher can tell (me). I: Very good. And if there's no teacher, for example at home, if you're talking with your family and you don't want to use English, what do you do to find a word? S: Like when I want to talk in Spanish? And I don't know a word? I: If there's a word you don't know or can't remember.	This student has a series of strategies for dealing with gaps in his knowledge of the target language. He can describe the circumstances in which each particular strategy can be helpful for him.

ACKNOWLEDGMENTS

Members of the research team at the Georgetown University/Center for Applied Linguistics National Foreign Language Resource Center are making this research effort possible. I would like to express my thanks and admiration for the expertise, insights, and dedication of Sarah Barnhardt, Pamela B. El-Dinary, Catherine Keatley, Koichi Nagano, and Christine Newman.

REFERENCES

Bernhardt, Elizabeth B. (ed.) 1992. *Life in language immersion classrooms*. Bristol, Pennsylvania: Multilingual Matters.
Campbell, Russell N. 1984. "The immersion approach to foreign language teaching." In *Studies on immersion education: A collection for United States educators*. Sacramento, California: California State Department of Education. 114–143.
Chamot, Anna Uhl. 1993. "Student responses to learning strategy instruction in the foreign language classroom." *Foreign Language Annals* 26(3): 308–321.
Chamot, Anna Uhl and Lisa Küpper. 1989. "Learning strategies in foreign language instruction." *Foreign Language Annals* 22(1): 13–24.
Chamot, Anna Uhl, Sarah Barnhardt, Pamela B. El-Dinary, Gilda Carbonaro, and Jill Robbins. 1993. *Methods for teaching learning strategies in the foreign language classroom and assessment of language skills for instruction: Final report*. Washington, D.C.: ERIC Clearinghouse on Languages and Linguistics.
Chamot, Anna Uhl, Jill Robbins, and Pamela B. El-Dinary. 1993. *Learning strategies in Japanese foreign language instruction: Final Report*. Washington, D.C.: ERIC Clearinghouse on Languages and Linguistics.
Cohen, Andrew D. and Edna Aphek. 1981. "Easifying second language learning." *Studies in Second Language Learning* 3: 221–236.
Curtain, Helena Anderson and Carol Ann Pesola. 1988. *Languages and children—Making the match*. Reading, Massachusetts: Addison-Wesley.
Genesee, Fred. 1987. *Learning through two languages*. Rowley, Massachusetts: Newbury House.
Lambert, Wallace E. and G. Richard Tucker. 1972. *Bilingual education of children: The St. Lambert experiment*. Rowley, Massachusetts: Newbury House.
Met, Mimi and Vicky Galloway. 1992. "Research in foreign language curriculum." In Philip Jackson (ed.), *Handbook of research on curriculum*. New York: Macmillan. 852–890.
O'Malley, J. Michael and Anna Uhl Chamot. 1990. *Learning strategies in second language acquisition*. Cambridge, U.K.: Cambridge University Press.
Padron, Yolanda N. and Hershon C. Waxman. 1988. "The effects of ESL students' perceptions of their cognitive strategies on reading achievement. " *TESOL Quarterly* 22(1): 146–150.
Pressley, Michael and associates. 1990. *Cognitive strategy instruction that really improves children's academic performance*. Cambridge, Massachusetts: Brookline Books.
Rubin, Joan, Joanna Quinn, and John Enos. 1988. *Improving foreign language listening comprehension*. Report to the International Research and Studies Program, U.S. Department of Education, Washington, D.C.
Swain, Merrill. 1984. "A review of immersion education in Canada: Research and evaluation studies." In *Studies on immersion education: A collection for United States Educators*. Sacramento, California: California State Department of Education. 114–143.
Thompson, Irene and Joan Rubin. 1993. *Improving listening comprehension in Russian*. Report to the International Research and Studies Program, U.S. Department of Education, Washington, D.C.

Second-language acquisition for school:
Academic, cognitive, sociocultural,
and linguistic processes

Virginia P. Collier
George Mason University

Ever since I began studying linguistics in the early 1970s, I have been intrigued with the unnecessary artificial distance often created between researchers in education and linguistics, feeling that both fields of inquiry have much to say to each other. As I have watched the field of second-language acquisition deepen its knowledge base over the past twenty-five years, I have worked on synthesizing this important research into information useful for educators. When training public-school superintendents, administrators, counselors and teachers, as well as university faculty, I am continually amazed at the misinformation that persists about second-language acquisition. At the same time, I find that too many linguists maintain a dangerously narrow focus on their chosen specialization in linguistics, without keeping up with the deepening and informative knowledge base in education and social science research on second-language acquisition.

For these reasons, I have chosen in this paper to present a new theoretical perspective on second-language acquisition that addresses both audiences —educators and linguists—who are the focus of this Georgetown University Round Table. My proposed conceptual model on second-language acquisition for school is based on the work of many researchers in linguistics, education, and the social sciences, as well as my own work with co-researcher Wayne Thomas. For the past ten years we have been exploring the length of time needed for students attending school where instruction is conducted through their second language to reach deep enough levels of proficiency in the second language to compete on an equal footing with native speakers of that language. In this research, we have also worked on identifying the variables that seem to influence most strongly the process of second-language acquisition for school contexts. The conceptual model which has emerged from our research, is still in the initial stages of development and will continue to be refined in response to additional research findings. I hope this paper can at least stimulate dialogue among linguistics and education researchers and practitioners, as we continue to search for understanding and assist the process of second-language acquisition.

I am purposely choosing to delimit the context of second-language acquisition for this conceptual model to a formal-schooling context. In other words, I am asking the question, "How does second-language acquisition happen within a school context? What processes occur and what factors make a difference?" By focusing on formal schooling as the context of second-language use, I am not referring to learning a foreign language in the formal classroom as contrasted with natural second-language acquisition outside of school. Rather, this model focuses on *how students acquire a second language when it is used in school for instructional purposes across the curriculum.* While the examples in this paper focus on the language-minority student (who comes from a home where a language other than the dominant language of the society is spoken) being schooled in a second language for at least part or perhaps all of the school day, the conceptual model may also be applied to the language-majority student who speaks the dominant language and is being schooled in a bilingual classroom.

Second-language acquisition for school: A conceptual model. First, I will introduce the components of the model; then, through discussion of the strong research base that informs the model, I will illustrate its usefulness, with examples that speak to education practitioners. The model has four major components: academic, cognitive, sociocultural, and linguistic processes. To understand the interrelationships among these four components of second-language acquisition for school, I have created a figure to symbolize the developmental second-language-acquisition process (Figure 1 below). While this figure looks simple on paper, it is important to imagine that this is a multifaceted prism with many dimensions. The four major components—sociocultural, linguistic, academic, and cognitive processes—are interdependent and complex.

Sociocultural processes. At the heart of the figure is the individual student going through the process of acquiring a second language in school. Central to that student's acquisition of language are all of the surrounding social and cultural processes occurring in everyday life with family and community and expanding to school, the region, and the society—in the student's past, present, and future. Examples of sociocultural processes at work in second-language acquisition include individual student variables such as self-esteem or anxiety and other affective factors; classroom variables such as a competitive versus a collaborative instructional environment; school variables such as majority-minority relations or administrative structures that create social and psychological distance between groups; community or regional variables such as prejudice and discrimination expressed through personal and professional

Figure 1. Second-language acquisition for school. (©Virginia P. Collier)

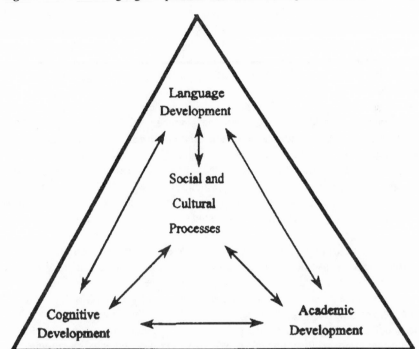

contexts; and societal variables such as the subordinate status of a minority group or patterns of acculturation versus forces of assimilation.

Language development. For second-language acquisition in school contexts, linguistic processes, a second component of the model, consist of the subconscious aspects of language development (an innate ability all humans possess for the acquisition of oral language), as well as the metalinguistic, conscious, formal teaching of language in school, *and* acquisition of the written system of language. This includes the acquisition of the oral and written systems of the student's second language across all language domains, such as phonology, vocabulary, morphology, syntax, semantics, pragmatics, paralinguistics, and discourse. Furthermore, to assure cognitive and academic success in the second language, a student's *first* language system, oral *and* written, must be developed to a high cognitive level across all these language domains at least through the elementary-school years. Thus, linguistic processes encompass the development of both first and second languages to a high degree of academic proficiency.

Academic development. A third component of the model, academic development, includes all schoolwork in language arts, mathematics, the sciences, and social studies for each grade level, kindergarten through twelfth grade and beyond. With each succeeding grade, academic work gets cognitively more complex, expanding vocabulary and the sociolinguistic and discourse dimensions of language to increasingly higher levels of development. Academic knowledge and conceptual development transfer from first language to second language; thus it is most efficient to develop academic work through students' first language, while teaching the second language during other periods of the school day through meaningful academic content. In earlier decades in the U.S., we emphasized teaching the second language as the first step, and postponed the teaching of academics. Research has shown us that postponing or interrupting academic development in first and second languages is likely to promote academic failure. In an information-driven society that demands more knowledge processing with each succeeding year, students cannot afford the lost time.

Cognitive development. The fourth component of this model, cognitive development, is also deeply interconnected to the other three components. The cognitive dimension had been mostly neglected by second-language educators in the U.S. until the past decade. In language teaching, we simplified, structured, and sequenced language curricula during the 1970s, and when we added academic content into our language lessons in the 1980s, we watered academics down into cognitively simple tasks. We also too often neglected the crucial role of cognitive development in the first language. Now we know from our growing research base that we must address all of these components equally if we are to succeed in developing deep academic proficiency in the second language.

Interdependence of the four components. All of these four compo- nents—sociocultural, academic, cognitive, and linguistic—are interdependent. If one is developed to the neglect of another, it may be detrimental to a student's overall growth and future success. The academic, cognitive, and linguistic components must be viewed as developmental, and for the child, adolescent, and young adult still going through the process of formal schooling, development of any one of these three components depends critically on simultaneous development of the other two, through both first and second languages. Sociocultural processes strongly influence, in both positive and negative ways, the students' access to cognitive, academic, and language development. It is crucial that educators provide a socioculturally supportive school environment that allows natural language, academic, and cognitive development to flourish.

Research evidence to support the model. Given the short format of GURT presentations, I have limited my discussion of the research evidence here to syntheses of some important factors that have emerged in the Thomas and Collier research (1995). For those who want a more detailed discussion of the extensive research base for this conceptual model, see Collier (1995).

First- and second-language acquisition: A lifelong process. To understand what occurs in first- and second-language acquisition for school, it is important to recognize the complex, lifelong process that we go through in acquiring our first language and the parallels in second-language acquisition. Development of a complex oral-language system from birth to age five is universal, given no physical disabilities and no isolation from humans. But the most gifted five-year-old entering kindergarten is not yet halfway through the process of first-language development. Children from ages six to twelve continue to acquire subtle phonological distinctions, vocabulary, semantics, syntax, formal discourse patterns, and complex aspects of pragmatics in the oral system of their first language (Berko Gleason 1993; de Villiers and de Villiers 1978; Goodluck 1991; McLaughlin 1984, 1985). In addition, children being formally schooled during these years add reading and writing skills to those of listening and speaking, across all the domains of language, with each age and grade level increasing the cognitive level of language use within each academic subject. An adolescent entering college must acquire an enormous vocabulary in every discipline of study and continue to acquire complex writing skills. These processes continue through adulthood as we add new contexts of language use to our life experience. As adults we acquire new subtleties in pragmatics, as well as the constantly changing patterns in language use that affect our everyday oral and written communication with others. Thus first-language acquisition is an unending, lifelong process (Berko Gleason 1993; Collier 1992a; Harley, Allen, Cummins and Swain, 1990; McLaughlin 1985).

Second-language acquisition is an equally complex phenomenon, paralleling first-language acquisition in many ways. As in acquiring our first language, we move through developmental stages, relying on sources of input to provide modified speech that we can at least partially comprehend (Ellis 1985; Hakuta 1986). However, second-language acquisition is more subject to influence by other factors than is oral development in our first language. When the context of second-language use is school, where a deep level of proficiency is required, it is necessary to examine the role of a student's first language in relation to the second language, the type of input and interaction needed for the second language to flourish, and the sociocultural context of schooling.

Academic second-language proficiency: How long? Cummins (1979, 1981, 1986b, 1989a, 1991) popularized for educators the concept that different levels of language proficiency are needed, depending on the context of language use, basing his theories on the work of many other researchers before him. Given the complex definition of language required in an academic context, provided in the previous section, my co-researcher, Wayne Thomas, and I have been exploring the "how long" question for the past ten years, following Cummins's initial examination (1981) of long-term academic achievement by immigrants to Canada. In the Thomas and Collier series of studies (Collier 1987, 1988, 1989c, 1992a, 1992b; Collier and Thomas 1988, 1989; Thomas and Collier 1995), we have carefully controlled for a wide variety of student-background variables and instructional treatments to examine student performance on many different types of outcome measures across time. The measures we use are the academic-achievement measures employed by school systems to monitor students' progress in school, including standardized tests and performance-assessment measures in language arts, reading, mathematics, science, and social studies. In contrast to a typical language-proficiency test, these are not static measures. Instead, they change with each succeeding grade level, because the academic and cognitive work expected with each additional year of schooling becomes increasingly more complex. Therefore, the results on these tests are very different from those on a language-proficiency instrument that uses the same form each time it is administered. We chose these tests because they are the ultimate measures of academic proficiency in a second language. When students being schooled in a second language reach proficiency levels in the second language deep enough to compete at the typical level of native-speaker performance (expressed on a standardized test as fiftieth percentile or normal curve equivalent [NCE]), it is a major achievement, because native speakers do not sit around waiting for nonnative speakers to catch up with them. During the school years, native speakers' first-language development continues at a rapid rate. Thus for nonnative speakers the goal of proficiency equal to that of a native speaker is a moving target (Thomas 1992).

In our studies we have found that in U.S. schools where all instruction is given through the second language (English), nonnative speakers of English with no schooling in their first language take seven to ten years or more to reach age- and grade-level norms of their native-English-speaking peers. Immigrant students who have had two to three years of first-language schooling in their home country before they come to the U.S. take at least five to seven years to reach typical native-speaker performance (similar to what Cummins 1981 found). This pattern exists across many groups, regardless of the particular home language that students speak, country of origin, socioeconomic status, and other student-background variables. In our examination of large datasets across many different research sites, we have found that the most significant student-background variable is the amount of formal schooling students have received in their first language. Across all program treatments, we have found that nonnative speakers being schooled in the second language for part or all of the school day typically do reasonably well in the early years of schooling (kindergarten through second or third grade). But from the fourth grade through middle school and high school, when the academic and cognitive demands of the curriculum increase rapidly with each succeeding year, students with little or no academic and cognitive development in their first language do increasingly less well as they move into the upper grades.

What about students schooled bilingually in the U.S.? It still takes a long time to demonstrate academic proficiency in the second language comparable to a native speaker. But the difference in student performance in a bilingual program, in contrast to an all-English program, is that students typically score at or above grade level in their first language in all subject areas, while they are building academic development of their second language. When students are tested in their second language, they typically reach and surpass native speakers' performance across all subject areas after four to seven years in a quality bilingual program. Because they have not fallen behind in cognitive and academic growth during the four to seven years that it takes to build academic proficiency in a second language, bilingually schooled students typically sustain this level of academic achievement and outperform monolingually schooled students in the upper grades (Collier 1992b; Thomas and Collier 1995). Remarkably, these findings apply to students of many different backgrounds, including language-majority students in a bilingual program. For example, in Canada, English-speaking students who receive all their schooling bilingually, typically begin to reach native-speaker norms on academic tests given in their second language (French) around fifth or sixth grade, and when tested in their first language, they outperform monolingually schooled students (California Department of Education 1984; Collier 1992a; Cummins and Swain 1986; Genesee 1987; Harley, Allen, Cummins, and Swain 1990; Swain and Lapkin 1981).

Role of first language. Many studies have found that cognitive and academic development in the first language has an extremely important and positive effect on second-language schooling (Baker 1988; Bialystok 1991; Collier 1989,1992c; Cummins 1991; Cummins and Swain, 1986; Díaz and Klingler 1991; Dolson 1985; Freeman and Freeman 1992; García 1993, 1994; Genesee 1987, 1994; Hakuta 1986; Lessow-Hurley 1990; Lindholm 1991; McLaughlin 1992; Snow 1990; Thomas and Collier, 1995; Tinajero and Ada 1993; Wong Fillmore and Valadez 1986). Academic skills, literacy development, concept formation, subject knowledge, and learning strategies developed in the first language will all transfer to the second language. As students expand their vocabulary and their oral and written communication skills in the second language, they can increasingly demonstrate their knowledge-base developed in their first language. Many literacy skills developed in any first language not only are easily transferred but also are crucial to academic success in a second language (Au 1993; Bialystok 1991; Cummins 1989a, 1989b, 1991; Cummins and Swain 1986; Freeman and Freeman 1992; Genesee 1987, 1994; Hudelson 1994;

Johnson and Roen 1989; Lessow-Hurley 1990; Lindholm 1991; Snow 1990; Tinajero and Ada 1993; Wong Fillmore and Valadez 1986).

Furthermore, some studies indicate that if students do not reach a certain threshold in their first language, including literacy, they may experience cognitive difficulties in their second language (Collier 1987; Collier and Thomas 1989; Cummins 1976, 1981, 1991; Dulay and Burt 1980; Duncan and De Avila 1979; Skutnabb-Kangas 1981; Thomas and Collier 1995). The key to understanding the role of first language in the academic development of second language is to understand the function of uninterrupted cognitive development. When students switch to second-language use at school, and teachers encourage parents to speak in the second language at home, both students and parents function at a level cognitively far below their age. In contrast, when parents and children speak the language that they know best, they are working at their actual level of cognitive maturity. Cognitive development can occur at home even with nonformally-schooled parents through asking questions, solving problems together, building or fixing something, cooking together, and talking about life experiences. Once parents understand the importance of cognitive development in the first language, they are usually overjoyed to realize that the language that they know best will further their children's growth (Arnberg 1987; Caplan, Choy, and Whitmore 1992; Collier 1981, 1986; Delgado-Gaitán 1990; Dolson 1985; Genesee 1994; Moll, Vélez-Ibáñez, Greenberg, and Rivera 1990; Saunders 1988; Skutnabb-Kangas and Cummins 1988; Wong Fillmore 1991a).

Role of input and interaction in language development. In our current research (Thomas and Collier 1995) we have also found that classes in school that are highly interactive, emphasizing student problem-solving and discovery learning through thematic experiences across the curriculum, are likely to provide the kind of social setting for natural language acquisition to take place simultaneously with academic and cognitive development. For school contexts, this applies to both first- *and* second-language acquisition since both are still developing throughout the school years. Krashen's work (1981, 1982, 1985) on the optimal conditions for oral and written input to foster natural language acquisition provides insight here, along with Ellis's research (1985, 1990) on the supportive but not central role that formal language instruction plays in the acquisition process. Swain (1985) emphasizes the importance of developing students' speaking and writing skills in first and second languages through interactive classes. From a comprehensive model developed through dialogs with Swain and many other linguists, Wong Fillmore (1991b: 52–53) warns us that three conditions are essential to second-language acquisition: "(1) *Learners* who realize that they need to learn the target language and are motivated to do so; (2) *speakers of the target language* who know it well enough to provide the learners with access to the language and the help they need for learning it; and

(3) a *social setting* which brings learners and target language speakers into frequent enough contact to make language learning possible." Collaborative interaction in which meaning is negotiated with peers is central to the language-acquisition process, both for oral- and written-language development (Allwright and Bailey 1991; Chaudron 1988; Ellis 1985, 1990; Enright and McCloskey 1988; Freeman and Freeman 1992; Gass and Madden 1985; Goodman and Wilde 1992; Hatch 1983; Johnson and Roen 1989; Swain 1985; Wong Fillmore 1989, 1991b).

Sociocultural context of schooling. Research from anthropology, sociology, sociolinguistics, psycholinguistics, and education has provided insights into the powerful influence that sociocultural processes have on language acquisition. This brief section can only provide a glimpse of a few of these very complex issues.

External social factors that students bring to the classroom from their past experiences represent one category of sociocultural influences. For example, among our new arrivals to the U.S. are undocumented as well as legal refugees escaping war, political oppression, or severe economic conditions. These students bring to our classes special social, emotional, and academic needs, often having experienced interrupted schooling in their home countries. Students seeking refuge from war may exhibit symptoms of posttraumatic stress disorder, including depression, withdrawal, hyperactivity, aggression, and intense anxiety in response to situations that recall traumatic events in their lives (Coelho 1994). Studies of these refugees' adaptation to life in the U.S. and success in school have emphasized the importance of a bicultural schooling context, integrating first language, culture, and community knowledge into the curriculum, as well as the importance of parents' maintenance of the home language and cultural traditions (Caplan, Choy, and Whitmore 1992; Tharp and Gallimore 1988; Trueba, Jacobs, and Kirton 1990).

Another powerful student-background variable that has been cited extensively in education research is socioeconomic status, although changes in instructional practices and school contexts can lessen its influence. Research on effective schools for language-minority students has found that schools that provide a strong bilingual/bicultural, academically rich context for instruction can lessen or eliminate the influence of family income level or parents' lack of formal schooling (Collier 1992b; Cummins 1989a; Krashen and Biber 1988; Lucas, Henze, and Donato 1990; Ramírez 1992; Rothman 1991; Thomas and Collier 1995; Valdez Pierce 1991).

External societal factors are another major influence on language acquisition for school. These include social and psychological distance created between first- and second-language speakers, perceptions of each group in interethnic comparisons, cultural stereotyping, intergroup hostility, the subordinate status of a minority group, or societal patterns of acculturation versus assimilation forces at work (Brown 1994; McLaughlin 1985; Schumann 1978). Majority–minority and interethnic relations, as well as social-class differences, are at the heart of these factors influencing second-language acquisition and success in school. Researchers such as Ogbu (1974, 1978, 1987, 1992, 1993), Oakes (1985, 1992), and Minicucci and Olsen (1992) have found extensive evidence of institutionalized structures in U.S. schools—tracking, ability grouping, and special programs that segregate language-minority students—that deny access to the core curriculum. Segregated transitional bilingual classes and English as a second language (ESL) classes can sometimes heighten the social inequities and subconsciously maintain the status quo in majority–minority relations (Hernández-Chávez 1977, 1984; Spener 1988). The negative social perception of these classes that both English-speaking and language-minority students have often developed in U.S. schools has led to the social isolation of second-language students, which denies them the critical conditions that Wong Fillmore (1991b) says must be present for second-language acquisition to take place. To break the perception of special classes as remedial in nature, they must be a permanent, desired, integral part of the curriculum, taught through quality instruction that encourages interactive, problem-solving, experiential learning through a multicultural, global perspective (Cummins 1986a, 1989a, 1989b; Frederickson 1995; Walsh 1991). In our current research (Thomas and Collier 1995), we have found that the school program most conducive to language-minority students' academic success in a second language is two-way bilingual education. This program model integrates majority- and minority-language speakers and stimulates the academic success of both groups in two languages. Thus schools can serve as agents of change, or places where teachers, students, and staff of many varied backgrounds join together and transform tensions between groups that currently exist in the broader society.

Research-based recommendations for linguistic theory-building and for educators. Now let us revisit my conceptual model of second-language acquisition for school. While the model has emerged from the multiple variables we are analyzing in our current research (Thomas and Collier 1995), it has strong connections to the work of many linguists. Larsen-Freeman (1985), in an overview of theories in second-language acquisition, found linguistic, social, and cognitive factors to be major categorical dimensions of the second-language-acquisition process. Some theorists consider only one of these dimensions to play the central role; others make reference to at least some aspects of the three dimensions. For example, Wong Fillmore (1985, 1991b) refers to linguistic, social, and cognitive processes as equally important in the language acquisition process. In this paper, I have expanded Wong Fillmore's conceptions of these three dimensions and applied them to a schooling context. In Larsen-Freeman's latest synthesis (1993) of second-language-acquisition research, she challenges those of us in the field to broaden our perspective, to take both learning and learner factors into account, as well as to answer questions about teaching. This conceptual model is an attempt to move the field of second-language acquisition towards a broader perspective.

Based on this model, our current research also leads to recommendations for educators (Thomas and Collier 1995). When examining interactions among student-background variables and instructional treatments and their influence on student outcomes, we have found that two-way bilingual education at the elementary-school level is the most promising program model for the long-term academic success of language-minority students. As a group, students in this program maintain grade-level skills in their first language at least through sixth grade and reach the fiftieth percentile or NCE in their second language generally after four to five years of schooling in both languages. They also generally sustain the gains they have made when they reach secondary education, unlike the students in programs that provide little or no academic support in their first language. Program characteristics include: (1) integrated schooling, with English speakers and language-minority students learning academically through each others' languages; (2) perceptions among staff, students, and parents that it is a "gifted and talented" program, leading to high expectations for student performance; (3) equal status of the two languages achieved, to a large extent, creating self-confidence among language-minority students; (4) healthy parent involvement among both language-minority and language-majority parents, for closer home–school cooperation; and (5) continuous support for staff development, emphasizing whole-language approaches, natural language acquisition through all content areas, cooperative learning, interactive and discovery learning, and cognitive complexity for all proficiency levels.

In our research, we have also found significant differences between "traditional" versus "current" approaches to language teaching for students schooled in the U.S. for kindergarten through twelfth grade. In the long term, students do less well in programs that focus on discrete units of language taught in a structured, sequenced curriculum in which the learner is treated as a passive recipient of knowledge. Students achieve significantly better in programs that teach language through cognitively complex content, taught through problem-solving and discovery learning in highly interactive classroom activities. ESL pullout in the early grades, when taught using a more traditional approach, is the least successful program model for students' long-term academic success. During Grades K–3, there is little difference among programs, but significant differences appear as students continue in the mainstream at secondary level.

For students entering U.S. schools at the secondary level, when first-language instructional support cannot be provided, the following program characteristics can make a significant difference in academic achievement for entering English language learners: (1) The second language taught through academic content; (2) a conscious focus on teaching learning strategies to help develop thinking skills and problem-solving abilities; and (3) continuous support for staff development which emphasizes activation of students' prior knowledge, respect for students' home language and culture, cooperative learning, interactive and discovery learning, intense and meaningful cognitive and academic development, and ongoing assessment using multiple measures.

In summary, in this research we have begun a complex process of attempting to identify the variables that most strongly seem to influence the process of second-language acquisition for school contexts. While it is clear that the process of acquiring a second language is extremely complex and variable from one acquirer to another, we have been able to find patterns in large school databases that inform educators and linguists. When examining the factors that play an important role, we find that they form an interwoven complexity that schools need to understand to provide an appropriate context for second-language acquisition to occur.

We have found that for young children and adolescents in Grades K–12, uninterrupted cognitive, academic, and linguistic development is essential to school success, and the neglect or overemphasis of one of these three components may affect students' long-term growth. Our data show that extensive cognitive and academic development in the students' first language is crucial to second-language academic success. Furthermore, the sociocultural context in which students are schooled is equally important to students' long-term success in second-language schooling. Contrary to the popular idea that it takes a motivated student a short time to acquire a second language, our studies examining immigrants and language-minority students in many different regions of the U.S. and with many different background characteristics have found that four to twelve years of second-language development are needed for the most advantaged students to reach deep academic proficiency and compete successfully with native speakers. Given this extensive length of time, educators must understand the complex variables influencing the second-language process and provide a sociocultural context that is supportive, and yet academically and cognitively challenging.

REFERENCES

Allwright, Dick and Kathleen M. Bailey. 1991. *Focus on the language classroom: An introduction to classroom research for language teachers.* Cambridge, U.K.: Cambridge University Press.

Arnberg, Lenore. 1987. *Raising children bilingually: The pre-school years.* Clevedon, U.K.: Multilingual Matters.

Au, Kathryn H. 1993. *Literacy instruction in multicultural settings.* Fort Worth, Texas: Harcourt Brace Jovanovich.

Baker, Colin. 1988. *Key issues in bilingualism and bilingual education.* Clevedon, U.K.: Multilingual Matters.

Berko-Gleason, Jean. 1993. *The development of language, Third edition.* New York: Macmillan.

Bialystok, Ellen (ed.). 1991. *Language processing in bilingual children.* Cambridge, U.K.: Cambridge University Press.

Brown, H. Douglas. 1994. *Principles of language learning and teaching, Third edition.* Englewood Cliffs, N.J.: Prentice Hall Regents.

California Department of Education. 1984. *Studies on immersion education: A collection for United States educators.* Sacramento, California: California Department of Education.

Caplan, Nathan, Marcella H. Choy, and Kathryn Faye Whitmore. 1992. "Indochinese refugee families and academic achievement." *Scientific American* 266(2): 36–42.

Chaudron, Craig. 1988. *Second language classrooms: Research on teaching and learning.* Cambridge, U.K.: Cambridge University Press.

Coelho, Elizabeth. 1994. "Social integration of immigrant and refugee children." In Fred Genesee (ed.), *Educating second language children.* Cambridge, U.K.: Cambridge University Press. 301–327.

Collier, Virginia P. 1981. "A sociological case study of bilingual education and its effects on the schools and the community." *Outstanding dissertations in bilingual education: Recognized by the National Advisory Council on Bilingual Education.* Washington, D.C.: National Clearinghouse for Bilingual Education. (Doctoral dissertation available from University of Southern California, 304 pp.)

Collier, Virginia P. 1986. "Cross-cultural policy issues in minority and majority parent involvement." *Issues of parent involvement and literacy.* Washington, D.C.: National Clearinghouse for Bilingual Education. 73–78.

Collier, Virginia P. 1987. "Age and rate of acquisition of second language for academic purposes." *TESOL Quarterly* 21(4): 617–641.

Collier, Virginia P. 1988. *The effect of age on acquisition of a second language for school.* Washington, DC: National Clearinghouse for Bilingual Education.

Collier, Virginia P. 1989. "How long? A synthesis of research on academic achievement in second language." *TESOL Quarterly* 23(3): 509–531.

Collier, Virginia P. 1992a. "The Canadian bilingual immersion debate: A synthesis of research findings." *Studies in Second Language Acquisition* 14: 87–97.

Collier, Virginia P. 1992b. "A synthesis of studies examining long-term language minority student data on academic achievement." *Bilingual Research Journal* 16(1–2): 187–212.

Collier, Virginia P. 1995. *Promoting academic success for ESL students: Understanding second language acquisition for school.* Trenton, N.J.: New Jersey Teachers of English to Speakers of Other Languages-Bilingual Educators.

Collier, Virginia P. and Wayne P. Thomas. 1988. "Acquisition of cognitive–academic second language proficiency: A six-year study." Paper presented at the annual meeting of the American Educational Research Association, New Orleans, Louisiana, April 1988.

Collier, Virginia P. and Wayne P. Thomas. 1989. "How quickly can immigrants become proficient in school English?" *Journal of Educational Issues of Language Minority Students* 5: 26–38.

Cummins, Jim. 1976. "The influence of bilingualism on cognitive growth: A synthesis of research findings and explanatory hypotheses." *Working Papers on Bilingualism* 9: 1–43.

Cummins, Jim. 1979. "Cognitive/academic language proficiency, linguistic interdependence, the optimal age question, and some other matters." *Working Papers on Bilingualism* 19: 197–205.

Cummins, Jim. 1981. "The role of primary language development in promoting educational success for language minority students." *Schooling and language minority students.* Sacramento, California: California Department of Education. 3–49.

Cummins, Jim. 1986a. "Empowering minority students: A framework for intervention." *Harvard Education Review* 56: 18–36.

Cummins, Jim. 1986b. "Language proficiency and academic achievement." In Jim Cummins and Merrill Swain (eds.), *Bilingualism in education.* New York: Longman. 138–161.

Cummins, Jim. 1989a. *Empowering minority students.* Sacramento, California: California Association for Bilingual Education.

Cummins, Jim. 1989b. "The sanitized curriculum: Educational disempowerment in a nation at risk." In Donna M. Johnson and Duane H. Roen (eds.), *Richness in writing: Empowering ESL students.* New York: Longman. 19–38.

Cummins, Jim. 1991. "Interdependence of first- and second-language proficiency in bilingual children." In Ellen Bialystok (ed.), *Language processing in bilingual children.* Cambridge, U.K.: Cambridge University Press. 70–89.

Cummins, Jim and Merrill Swain. 1986. *Bilingualism in education.* New York: Longman.

Delgado-Gaitán, Concha. 1990. *Literacy for empowerment: The role of parents in children's education.* New York: Falmer Press.

de Villiers, Jill G. and Peter A. de Villiers. (1978). *Language acquisition.* Cambridge, Massachusetts: Harvard University Press.

Díaz, Rafael M. and Cynthia Klingler. 1991. "Towards an explanatory model of the interaction between bilingualism and cognitive development." In Ellen Bialystok (ed.), *Language processing in bilingual children.* Cambridge, U.K.: Cambridge University Press. 167–192.

Dolson, David P. 1985. "The effects of Spanish home language use on the scholastic performance of Hispanic pupils." *Journal of Multilingual Multicultural Development* 6: 135–155.

Dulay, Heidi and Marina Burt. 1980. "The relative proficiency of limited English proficient students." In James E. Alatis (ed.), *Georgetown University Round Table on Languages and Linguistics 1980.* Washington, D.C.: Georgetown University Press. 181–200.

Duncan, Sharon E. and Edward A. De Avila. 1979. "Bilingualism and cognition: Some recent findings." *NABE Journal* 4(1): 15–20.

Ellis, Rod. 1985. *Understanding second language acquisition.* Oxford: Oxford University Press.

Ellis, Rod. 1990. *Instructed second language acquisition.* Oxford: Blackwell.

Enright, D.Scott and Mary L. McCloskey. 1988. *Integrating English: Developing English language and literacy in the multilingual classroom.* Reading, Massachusetts: Addison-Wesley.

Frederickson, Jean. (ed.). 1995. *Reclaiming our voices: Bilingual education critical pedagogy and praxis.* Ontario, California: California Association for Bilingual Education.

Freeman, Yvonne S. and David E. Freeman. 1992. *Whole language for second language learners.* Portsmouth, N.H.: Heinemann.

García, Eugene. 1993. "Language, culture, and education." In Linda Darling-Hammond (ed.), *Review of research in education* 19: 51–98.

García, Eugene. 1994. *Understanding and meeting the challenge of student cultural diversity.* Boston: Houghton Mifflin.

Gass, Susan and Carolyn Madden (eds.). 1985. *Input in second language acquisition.* Cambridge, Massachusetts: Newbury House.

Genesee, Fred. 1987. *Learning through two languages: Studies of immersion and bilingual education.* Cambridge, Massachusetts: Newbury House.

Genesee, Fred (ed.). 1994. *Educating second language children: The whole child, the whole curriculum, the whole community.* Cambridge, U.K.: Cambridge University Press.

Goodluck, Helen. 1991. *Language acquisition.* Oxford: Blackwell.

Goodman, Yetta M. and Sandra Wilde (eds.). 1992. *Literacy events in a community of young writers.* New York: Teachers College Press.

Hakuta, Kenji. 1986. *Mirror of language: The debate on bilingualism.* New York: Basic Books.

Harley, Birgit, Patrick Allen, Jim Cummins, and Merrill Swain. (eds.). 1990. *The development of second language proficiency.* Cambridge, U.K.: Cambridge University Press.

Hatch, Evelyn. 1983. *Psycholinguistics: A second language perspective.* Cambridge, Massachusetts: Newbury House.

Hernández-Chávez, Eduardo. 1977. "Meaningful bilingual-bicultural education: A fairytale." *NABE Journal* 1(3): 49–54.

Hernández-Chávez, Eduardo. 1984. "The inadequacy of English immersion education as an educational approach for language minority students in the United States." *Studies on immersion education: A collection for United States educators.* Sacramento, California: California Department of Education. 144–183.

Hudelson, Sarah. 1994. "Literacy development of second language children." In Fred Genesee (ed.), *Educating second language children.* Cambridge, U.K.: Cambridge University Press. 129–158.

Johnson, Donna M. and Donna H. Roen (eds.). 1989. *Richness in writing: Empowering ESL students.* New York: Longman.

Krashen, Stephen D. 1981. *Second language acquisition and second language learning.* Oxford: Pergamon.

Krashen, Stephen D. 1982. *Principles and practices in second language acquisition.* Oxford: Pergamon.

Krashen, Stephen D. 1985. *The input hypothesis: Issues and implications.* New York: Longman.

Krashen, Stephen D. and Douglas Biber. 1988. *On course: Bilingual education's success in California.* Sacramento, California: California Association for Bilingual Education.

Larsen–Freeman, Diane. 1985. "Overview of theories of language learning and acquisition." *Issues in English language development.* Washington, D.C.: National Clearinghouse for Bilingual Education. 7–13.

Larsen–Freeman, Diane. 1993. "Second language acquisition research: Staking out the territory." In Sandra Silberstein (ed), *State of the art TESOL essays: Celebrating 25 years of the discipline.* Alexandria, Virginia: Teachers of English to Speakers of Other Languages. 133–168.

Lessow-Hurley, Judith. 1990. *The foundations of dual language instruction.* New York: Longman.

Lindholm, Kathryn J. 1991. "Theoretical assumptions and empirical evidence for academic achievement in two languages." *Hispanic Journal of Behavioral Sciences* 13: 3–17.

Lucas, Tamara, Rosemary Henze, and Ruben Donato. 1990. "Promoting the success of latino language-minority students: An exploratory study of six high schools." *Harvard Educational Review* 60: 315–340.

McLaughlin, Barry. 1984. *Second language acquisition in childhood: Vol. 1. Preschool children, Second edition.* Hillsdale, N.J.: Lawrence Erlbaum.

McLaughlin, Barry. 1985. *Second language acquisition in childhood: Vol. 2. School-age children, Second edition.* Hillsdale, N.J.: Lawrence Erlbaum.

McLaughlin, Barry. 1992. *Myths and misconceptions about second language learning: What every teacher needs to unlearn.* Santa Cruz, California: National Center for Research on Cultural Diversity and Second Language Learning.

Minicucci, Catherine and Laurie Olsen. 1992. *Programs for secondary limited English proficient students: A California study.* Washington, D.C.: National Clearinghouse for Bilingual Education.

Moll, Luis C., Carlos Vélez–Ibáñez, James Greenberg, and Charlene Rivera. 1990. *Community knowledge and classroom practice: Combining resources for literacy instruction.* Arlington, Virginia: Development Associates.

Oakes, Jeanie. 1985. *Keeping track: How schools structure inequality.* New Haven, Connecticut: Yale University Press.

Oakes, Jeanie. 1992. "Can tracking research inform practice? Technical, normative, and political considerations." *Educational Researcher* 21(4): 12–21.

Ogbu, John. 1974. *The next generation: An ethnography of education in an urban neighborhood.* New York: Academic Press.

Ogbu, John. 1978. *Minority education and caste: The American system in cross-cultural perspective.* New York: Academic Press.

Ogbu, John. 1987. "*Opportunity structure, cultural boundaries, and literacy*" In J. Langer (ed.), *Language, literacy, and culture: Issues of society and schooling*. Norwood, N.J.: Ablex.

Ogbu, John. 1992. "Understanding cultural diversity." *Educational Researcher* 21(8): 5-24.

Ogbu, John. 1993. "Variability in minority school performance: A problem in search of an explanation." In Evelyn Jacob and Cathie Jordan (eds.), *Minority education: Anthropological perspectives*. Norwood, N.J.: Ablex. 83-111.

Ramírez, J. David. 1992 . "Executive summary." *Bilingual Research Journal*, 16(1-2): 1-62.

Rothman, R. 1991. " Schools stress speeding up, not slowing down." *Education Week* 11(9): 14-15.

Saunders, George. 1988. *Bilingual children: From birth to teens*. Clevedon, U.K.: Multilingual Matters.

Schumann, John. 1978. " The acculturation model for second language acquisition." In Rosario Gingras (ed.), *Second language acquisition and foreign language teaching*. Washington, D.C.: Center for Applied Linguistics. 27-50.

Skutnabb-Kangas, Tove. 1981. *Bilingualism or not: The education of minorities*. Philadelphia: Multilingual Matters.

Skutnabb-Kangas, Tove and Jim Cummins (eds.). 1988. *Minority education: From shame to struggle*. Clevedon, U.K.: Multilingual Matters.

Snow, Catherine E. 1990. "Rationales for native language instruction: Evidence from research." In Arnado M. Padilla, Halford H. Fairchild, and Concepcíon M. Valadez (eds.), *Bilingual education: Issues and strategies*. Newbury Park, California: Sage.

Spener, David. 1988. "Transitional bilingual education and the socialization of immigrants." *Harvard Educational Review* 58: 133-153.

Swain, Merrill. 1985. "Communicative competence: Some roles of comprehensible input and comprehensible output in its development." In Susan Gass and Carolyn Madden (eds.), *Input in second language acquisition*. Cambridge, Massachusetts: Newbury House. 235-253.

Swain, Merrill and Sharon Lapkin. 1981. *Bilingual education in Ontario: A decade of research*. Toronto: Ontario Institute for Studies in Education.

Tharp, Roland G. and Ronald Gallimore. 1988. *Rousing minds to life: Teaching, learning, and schooling in social context*. Cambridge, U.K.: Cambridge University Press.

Thomas, Wayne P. 1992. "An analysis of the research methodology of the Ramírez study." *Bilingual Research Journal* 16(1-2): 213-245.

Thomas, Wayne P. and Virginia P. Collier. 1995. *Language minority student achievement and program effectiveness*. Washington, D.C.: National Clearinghouse for Bilingual Education.

Tinajero, Josefina V. and Alma F. Ada (eds.). 1993. *The power of two languages: Literacy and biliteracy for Spanish-speaking students*. New York: Macmillan/McGraw-Hill.

Trueba, Henry T., Lila Jacobs, and Elizabeth Kirton. 1990. *Cultural conflict and adaptation: The case of Hmong children in American society*. New York: Falmer Press.

Valdez Pierce, Lorraine. 1991. *Effective schools for language minority students*. Washington, D.C.: The Mid-Atlantic Equity Center.

Walsh, Catherine E. 1991. *Pedagogy and the struggle for voice: Issues of language, power and schooling for Puerto Ricans*. New York: Bergin and Garvey.

Wong Fillmore, Lily. 1985. "Second language learning in children: A proposed model." In *Issues in English language development*. Washington, D.C.: National Clearinghouse for Bilingual Education. 33-42.

Wong Fillmore, Lily. 1989. "Teachability and second language acquisition." In Mabel Rice and Richard L. Schiefelbusch (eds.), *The teachability of language*. Baltimore: Paul Brookes. 311-332.

Wong Fillmore, Lily. 1991a. "A question for early-childhood programs: English first or families first?" *Education Week*, June 19, 1991.

Wong Fillmore, Lily. 1991b. " Second language learning in children: A model of language learning in social context." In Ellen Bialystok (ed.), *Language processing in bilingual children.* Cambridge, U.K.: Cambridge University Press. 49-69.

Wong Fillmore, Lily and Concepcíon Valadez. 1986. "Teaching bilingual learners." In Merlin C. Wittrock (ed.), *Handbook of research on teaching, Third edition.* New York: Macmillan. 648-685.

Personality, language-learning aptitude, and program structure

Madeline E. Ehrman
Foreign Service Institute

Introduction. For several years, I have been collecting and analyzing data on individual differences among foreign-language learners at the Foreign Service Institute (FSI), the training branch of the U.S. Department of State. The participants in the research project are all adults whose average age is nearly forty, and about two-thirds of them are between thirty and fifty. They are employees of the State Department (or other foreign affairs agencies) or members of family, and they come to training with a work-related purpose for language learning. Most are preparing for overseas assignments. They tend to be well-educated: their median level of education is between bachelor's and master's degrees. Slightly over half are male. More details about the sample can be found in Ehrman (in press) and in Ehrman and Oxford (in press).

I have been finding a fairly consistent pattern of characteristics that seem to relate to success in FSI classrooms, but I have also become increasingly aware of the degree to which these findings may be related to a specific classroom setting. This topic is addressed in several of my recent papers (Ehrman 1994, in press), in particular as it relates to the generalizability of my findings from the selected, mature, well-educated FSI sample to other populations.

Individual-difference findings comprise only one of the many factors that affect language learning. At least as important is the setting in which the learning takes place. This involves not only the purpose of the learning and the style of the teacher, but also the kinds of learning activities in which the student is expected to invest energy. This paper explores some aspects of the question of the relationship between sets of learner characteristics and curricular aspects of learning environments. In other words, it asks and seeks a partial answer to the question: How can learners, settings, task demands, and the interaction of these variables be described so that studies can be compared across settings and student populations? This paper attempts to introduce a framework to help with this task, making use of an extended metaphor comparing learning task types to ground transportation. It represents work in progress and therefore presents hypotheses for testing, not only clear research findings.

Review of relevant literature.

Language-learning aptitude. Efforts to predict language-learning success have a long history during the twentieth century. The Modern Language Aptitude Test (MLAT; Carroll and Sapon 1959) was perhaps the culmination of the tradition of psychometric test development; and it achieved a fairly respectable level of success in the audio-lingual and grammar-translation classrooms of its time (Spolsky 1994). Other important language aptitude tests include the Pimsleur Language Aptitude Battery (Pimsleur 1966) the Defense Language Aptitude Battery (DLAB; Petersen and Al-Haik 1976), and VORD (Parry and Child 1990). These tests appear to have similar predictive validity (Parry and Child 1990).

A desire for better prediction and the ability to exploit aptitude testing further has led to recent research efforts, including at least two major projects which have examined the role of individual differences in addition to strictly cognitive aptitude in language learning: the Defense Language Institute's Language Skill Change Project (Lett and O'Mara 1990) and the Foreign Service Institute's Language Learning Profiles Project, on which this paper is a partial report (Ehrman 1993, 1994; Ehrman and Oxford 1995). These projects are investigating variables such as biographic factors, personality, motivation, anxiety, and learning strategies, along with general intelligence (DLI only). The Defense Language Institute is also engaged in a large-scale effort to improve the DLAB (Thain 1992).

Much research addresses the use of the MLAT (and other aptitude measures) for predicting learning success, and indeed this is an important consideration for assignment to intensive and long-term language training at taxpayer expense. However, a measure like the MLAT also has potential utility for placement in a program (Wesche 1981) and for diagnosing learning difficulties, counseling students and tailoring programs to their needs (Demuth & Smith 1987; Ganschow et al. 1989). These applications have received far less attention in the literature, although the MLAT has been most successfully used for them. (Lefrancois and Sibiga 1986; Wesche 1981).

Other individual variables. Work on individual differences in the realms of learning styles, learning strategies, personality, and affective factors is covered quite thoroughly in the literature review sections of Ehrman (1993; 1994; in press), Ehrman and Oxford (1995), and in Oxford and Ehrman (1993). In particular, Ehrman 1993 provides a detailed description of the model of tolerance for ambiguity to which I refer in this paper. In short, the model has three components, all of which are necessary for a learner to manage ambiguity: (a) the ability to take in new information; (b) the ability to hold contradictory or incomplete information without either rejecting one of the contradictory elements or coming to premature closure; and (c) the ability to adapt one's existing cognitive, affective, and social schemata in the light of the new material (Ehrman 1993: 331).

Course-design factors. Untold numbers of books and articles have been written about language teaching methods and curricula. Some focus on the philosophies that underlie the choices teachers make: Among the best of these continues to be Stevick's classic *Teaching languages: A way and ways* (1980). Particularly common are the works that address curriculum variations in terms of categories such as "structural," "notional-functional," etc. Typical of this genre are Krahnke (1987) and Stern (1992). Another approach concentrates on the relationship between language skills and tasks; Yalden's 1987 work on course design is a good example of this approach. Dubin and Olshtain (1986) address course design from the point of view of pedagogical goals: For instance, they address sociocultural, cognitive, and personal growth objectives (for both teachers and learners).

Other works focus more directly on the interaction of learner variables and classroom factors. For instance, Nunan (1989), with his interest in learner-centered instruction, describes program design in terms of student and teacher roles and provides a detailed breakdown of learning strategies that should influence lesson design. Another very interesting book is Peck's *Language teachers at work* (1988), in which various language teacher cases are presented; each brings into focus a pair of bipolar teaching style dimensions, with a discussion of the effects of each pole of the program. None of these works, however, aims at building a model of the relationship between individual-difference variables and a learning-activity typology.

A typology of learning situations. In designing teacher training to enhance learner independence, it has been useful to employ a model that treats teacher directiveness as a continuum from the most closely structured to the most open. The operative dimension is learner need for external support. At the leftmost end, the learner needs a great deal of support, and the amount of external structure is very high, whereas the amount of learner freedom and independence is very low. At the rightmost end, the proportions of external structure and learner freedom are reversed. At various points on the continuum, the amounts of external support and learner freedom vary proportionally.

A similar continuum seems to apply to program design. In order to achieve the kind of simplification that is often inherent in model-building, however, I propose to divide the continuum into four ranked levels, a hierarchy of learning situations that takes into account the amount of supportive structure given to the student at one end of the continuum and the freedom available to the student at the other. In general, the cognitive demands made on the student will tend to increase as the amount of support is reduced and the amount of freedom increases.

I have found it helpful to apply a metaphor to the categories of learning situations, in which elements of the situations are compared to ground transportation routes:

(1) *Railroad* (or an urban subway system). On these, the traveler gets on at one end and needs to do nothing until reaching the destination. In very few cases is it possible to get from door to door by rail alone—other means of transportation must also be used.

(2) *Road network*, especially major highway systems. These have more options and choice points. On the other hand, maps are available for navigation, and one does not build a new road but must follow those that have already been built.

(3) *Walkways and trails*. One must find one's way in a network of paths, which are clearly delineated. However, ordinarily there is no map, so it is necessary to do some exploration. It is possible for an individual to start a new trail. Note that trails differ from roadways in that an individual can establish a new trail, but individuals can seldom establish new roadways, which are pre-set.

(4) *Open country*. Here there are no guidelines other than natural signs, which the traveler must learn to read and recognize. One must blaze one's own trail, find one's own way.

Here is a starter list of classroom elements that might characterize each "level" of the learning situations model:

Railroads: Defined dialogues for memorization; mechanical and some meaningful drilling; reading and listening matter designed to use lesson material.

Major Roadways: Oral interaction closely linked to lesson material. Some meaningful but largely communicative drilling; controlled conversation; edited texts and listening passages that may be based on authentic material.

Trails: "Free" conversation, heavily guided by the teacher to include repetition of previously learned material but with room for student initiative especially in subject matter. Generally authentic reading and listening material but with considerable teacher or curricular guidance in the form of advance organizers, outlines, and other guides.

Open country: Open-ended conversation, topics nominated and with branches by both student and teacher; authentic material for reading and listening. Student develops own strategies for coping.

Every class will have a different mix of these different kinds of activities. For instance, FSI classes vary widely, but a typical class is probably 33% railroad, 16% roadways, 16% trails, and 33% open country. Fifteen or twenty years ago, the mix was more like 55% railroad, 25% roadways, 10% trails, and (at most) 10% open country. This typology can also be applied to testing, where testing activities range from various kinds of discrete-point testing to interviews and beyond. The FSI oral interview test, for instance, is mostly open country in that language and topics are unpredictable, and examinees' coping strategies are as important as the structure and lexicon available to them. On the other hand, there is a standard format, and the testers are clearly in control, so to that degree there is a substantial proportion of trailway-level to the test.

Types of learner. Learners vary by in their preferences (learning styles) for coping with each kind of activity that appears in language training. They also vary in their abilities to cope with the various demands of learning (learning aptitudes). They have different kinds and levels of motivation, emotional arousal, and anxiety about learning. These affective variables moderate the quantity (and perhaps the quality) of coping available.

Learning styles. Most learning-style dimensions are bipolar. They usually represent a continuum of preference, but individual learners will often indicate a strong enough comfort zone that they may be quite inflexible in their ability to adapt to demands made by learning situations that do not match their preferences. Extreme inflexibility in either direction of a learning style dimension (e.g. rigidly sequential or rigidly random processing) can be so debilitating to learners that it may be considered something of a learning disability.

Figure 1 shows how a given style dimension can be expressed variously among different individuals. For instance, the first person, labeled "Preference for X," has a clear preference for the X pole of the X–Y learning style dimension. That is, he or she is most comfortable in activities that reflect the X approach to processing most of the time. However, this person can also make use of strategies and activities that are usually more comfortable for people who prefer the Y pole, and when circumstances encourage it, makes use of Y strategies. The fourth person, labeled "Rigid Preference for Y," in contrast, always operates in the Y mode and is not only somewhat uncomfortable using X strategies (as a person who simply has a preference for Y is) but actually cannot achieve access to X strategies. Figure 1 shows several of the almost infinite variations on this theme. Classification into X style or Y style is a convenient artifact for model builders, researchers, teachers, and program designers; it is a useful oversimplification of complex reality.

Figure 1. Some of the many possible variations on a given bipolar learning-style dimension.

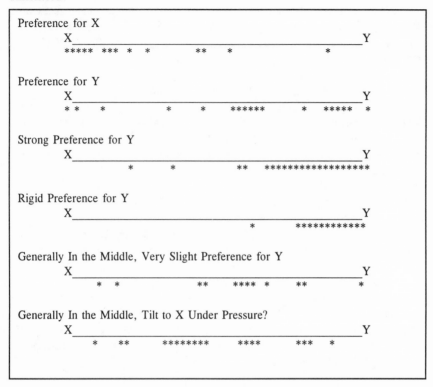

The following represent some important learning styles dimensions:

1. SENSORY CHANNELS. Visual, auditory, and kinesthetic/hands-on processing. Although these categories are very important in individualizing instruction, I have been unable to find much connection between sensory-channel preferences and learning success. I therefore do not address them further in this paper.

2. SEQUENTIAL VS. RANDOM PROCESSING. Sequential indicates one step at a time, begin at the beginning and go straight through to the end. Random is something like random-access memory, where the processing or retrieval path is unpredictable to the outsider, though it may be based on a system that is clear to the individual processor. This has proved to be an important dimension.

3. ANALYTIC VS. GLOBAL PROCESSING. There is considerable overlap with Sequential vs. Random, but they are not exactly the same. The analytic learner,

as the name suggests, wants to break units apart in order to understand them, is likely to find grammar appealing, and may have poor fluency because of emphasis on accuracy. The global learner likes to deal with language as a whole entity, rejects analytic strategies, often likes to make associations with culture and other non-linguistic factors, and may be "abominably fluent" (but inaccurate).

4. FIELD INDEPENDENT VS. FIELD SENSITIVE. This category has been widely researched (Brown 1994). Field independence (the ability to distinguish parts from the whole) often correlates with success at a variety of language-learning tasks, whereas Brown (1994) suggests that field sensitivity may provide an advantage in learning outside the classroom. This dimension probably overlaps substantially with Analytic vs. Global.

5. CONCRETE VS. ABSTRACT PROCESSING. As the names suggest, concrete learners like to deal with real-world, tangible matters in a hands-on way, whereas abstract processors are interested in a more conceptual world and may be more comfortable with deducing or inducing linguistic regularities.

6. THICK EGO BOUNDARIES VS. THIN EGO BOUNDARIES. This dimension is described in detail in Ehrman (1993) and Hartmann (1991). Within an individual, it represents the permeability between states of mind and to outside influences. A factor of thin external boundaries (permeability to outside influences) was shown to correlate somewhat with FSI end-of-training proficiency (Ehrman 1993).

Naturally there are numerous other dimensions, many of which overlap with each other. Learning-style models like the Kolb (Kolb 1985), 4Mat (McCarthy 1980), Gregorc (Gregorc 1982), and the Myers-Briggs Type Indicator (MBTI; Myers and McCaulley 1985) often combine these and other dimensions into composites. For instance, the MBTI Sensing-Intuition dimension includes concrete-abstract, sequential-random, and a degree of analytic-global.

Aptitude. There are various ways to look at learning aptitude. The most general is what is measured by intelligence or scholastic aptitude tests. These tests are not available for use with FSI students. There are also specialized aptitudes. Language learning has been considered such an aptitude, and several measurement instruments have been designed for it, as described above. (At least one study, Wesche et al. (1982), has shown that there is a general intelligence component in language-learning aptitude measurement.)

Figure 2. MLAT subscales.

Part I: Number Learning. This test appears to measure parts of memory and "auditory alertness" which play a part in auditory comprehension (showing how well one understands what one hears) of a foreign language.

Part II: Phonetic Script. This test deals with the ability to associate a sound with a particular symbol. It also measures how well one can remember speech sounds. In addition, it tends to correlate with the ability to mimic speech sounds and sound combinations in a foreign language.

Part III: Spelling Clues. Scores on this part depend largely on how extensive a student's English vocabulary is. As in Part II, it measures the ability to make sound-symbol associations, but to a lesser degree.

Part IV: Words in Sentences. This part deals with one's sensitivity to grammatical structure and thus can be expected to provide information about the ability to handle grammar in a foreign language. It is not clear to what degree scores reflect grammatical training; however, no grammatical terminology is used, so scores do not depend on specific memory for grammatical terms.

Part V: Paired Associates. This part measures one's ability to memorize by rote—a useful skill in learning new vocabulary in a foreign language.

Raw Score Total: Total of all five subscales. At FSI, a scaled score conversion of the Total is used; this is called:

Index Score: A scaled score for which the original mean was 50, with a standard deviation of 10. (These norms are now out of date; the Index is now simply a conversion of the raw Total into a scale ranging between 20 and 80.)

Descriptions of Parts I–V are based on those provided in the MLAT Manual (Carroll and Sapon 1959).

At FSI, the MLAT has been used for over 30 years. The MLAT is based on a factor analysis that yielded four main categories: phonetic coding ability (distinguishing sounds and representing them graphically), grammatical sensitivity (recognizing and using syntactic relationships), memory (rote and contextualized), and inductive language learning. All but the last of these four categories are directly addressed in the five parts of the MLAT (see Figure 2). Other components listed by scholars of language aptitude include motivation and knowledge of vocabulary in the native language (Pimsleur 1968), the ability to hear under conditions of interference (Carroll 1990), the ability to "handle decontextualized language" (Skehan 1989), and the ability to shift mental set and cope with the unfamiliar (Ehrman 1993).

Overall total score on the MLAT gives a crude measure useful at the extremes: A very low score indicates weakness in all the factors; a very high score suggests strength in all the factors. In the middle, it becomes useful to examine the "scatter" of the subscale scores.

Tested aptitude and learning style. Scatter analysis of the MLAT was done using correlations with other variables of learning style, preferred learning activities, and tested end-of-training proficiency in speaking (including interactive comprehension) and reading. Results suggest links between some of the MLAT parts and learning style variables My working hypotheses based on these findings are listed in Figure 3. I am currently testing these hypotheses in

Figure 3. Scatter analysis of the MLAT part scores.

Part I Number Learning: No clear associations so far, and no diagnostic hypothesis.

Part II Phonetic Script: Global processing (perhaps because of need to integrate auditory input and visual stimuli).

Part III Spelling Clues: Analytic processing (crossword puzzle relationship, shifting mental set, pattern analysis)

Part IV Words In Sentences: Analytic processing (sensitivity to syntax and grammatical categories, pattern analysis and matching).

Part V Paired Associates: Weakness may indicate poor mnemonic strategies, and possibly deficiencies in metacognitive strategies, because coping with the paired associates task requires some planning of the whole task.

---

student interviews, and the results so far are promising.

Other affective, personality, and cognitive aptitude relationships. A study of extremes in the FSI language-learner sample (Ehrman in press) included the top and bottom 4–5%, accounting for length of training and relative difficulty of target language for English speakers. Some of the findings for this study were quite dramatic and clarified results from correlational studies of the multiple variables in the study (Ehrman and Oxford 1995). Together, these analyses indicate certain patterns for strong and weak performers in FSI classes.

The main findings are shown in Figure 4. It may be helpful to remember that FSI classes in general are now roughly 50% "trails" and "open country."

Figure 4. Characteristics of weak and strong FSI learners.

WEAKER LEARNERS	STRONGER LEARNERS
	Younger (but M=40; SD 10; and many older learners are highly successful)
Less language-learning experience	More language-learning experience
	Higher education level (hence more use of learning strategies?)
Thick ego boundaries (inferred as low tolerance of ambiguity)	Rejection of neatness and order (thin ego-boundary direction) May indicate somewhat higher tolerance of ambiguity and be manifest in:
MBTI Sensing preference, i.e. sequential, pre-organized, concrete, and discrete-point learning	MBTI weak preferences for imaginative and emergent learning, i.e. more random, unplanned, or ambiguous learning
(Tolerance for ambiguity as defined through the HBQ and the MBTI may be less an advantage to the strongest students than its lack is a disadvantage to the weakest.)	
	Extremely strong students are less affectively aroused (motivation, anxiety), but there is a correlation overall between extrinsic and intrinsic motivation and desire to use TL with native speakers and learning success.
	Less negative about learning
	(Subsignificant anxiety about speaking in the classroom)
Substantially lower cognitive aptitude (Extremes 2 SD) as measured on the MLAT	More cognitive aptitude (Extremes ca. .6-.7 SD) as measured on the MLAT
	Tend to use mnemonic strategies
N too low, no significant statistics, but activities that limit input or restrict language use to already mastered material tend to correlate negatively with learning success)	Less time spent on study activities in general; use resources (feedback, explanations) but do not want to be routinized; tend to be independent learners and use deep-processing of new material; activities involving unrestricted input or language use tend to correlate positively with learning success.
(Based on correlations and ANOVAs)	

The clearest finding is that weak students have very significantly lower performance on the MLAT and tend to be highly intolerant of ambiguity. They tend to endorse the utility of classroom activities that limit input and output to material that has already been mastered (more like railroads than open country). They tend to be sequential learners.

Conversely, stronger learners have previous language-learning experience, generally higher MLAT performance, and indications of tolerance of ambiguity. Motivation does not directly distinguish the weak and strong learners, but weak learners tend to endorse motivation items that are negatively phrased (e.g., "I would rather study some subject other than language X"). The extremely strong learners, while highly motivated, indicated a somewhat lower intensity of motivation than the middle and weak students; I have interpreted this finding as a kind of emotional stability that avoids extremes of feeling, either high or low. This is consistent with my anecdotal observations that very good language learners are usually adept at affective self-management, including management of their expectations. Endorsement of relatively open-ended, authentic materials-based activities tends to correlate with higher end-of-training proficiency scores in both speaking and reading.

The goal of FSI language training is to enable our students to use language in a situation that is largely "open country" when they go overseas, so there is usually an increasing proportion of "open country" activities as the language course progresses over time. Thus, the ability to cope with less structured work becomes increasingly important as students attempt to reach the S-3 R-3 level. At the same time, diplomatic work requires a considerable level of accuracy of usage, so analytic skills remain important. Coping with "open country" and effective use of grammar rules requires all three levels of the tolerance for ambiguity model described above in the literature review; indeed, effective "random" processing calls for substantial command of all levels of tolerance for ambiguity. It is thus reasonable that students who achieve high levels of proficiency in training are largely those who can cope readily with "open country" and its demands for flexibility and tolerance of ambiguity.

Furthermore, FSI end-of-training testing can probably be characterized as 90% "open country" in nature and as 10% "trailways" (in that topics, level of language, and reading passages are selected by the examiner relative to ongoing estimates of examinee capacity). Thus the kinds of dispositions and abilities I have described are not only important for language learning, but necessary for showing others what one has learned in a test situation.

Individual differences and classroom activity types. Certain kinds of classroom activity can be expected to be compatible to greater or lesser degrees with various individual difference variables. A starter list of my suggestions for some of these relationships is shown in Figure 5. In general, the "railroad" level

Figure 5. Learning levels and individual-difference variables.

SKILL	LEARNING CHARACTERISTIC	INDIVIDUAL DIFFERENCE VARIABLE
	1. Railroad	
Defined dialogues for memorization, mechanical and some meaningful drilling; reading and listening matter designed to use lesson material.		
All	Motivation	Affective Survey Items
	Affective self-management	?
	Good study habits, Self-discipline	MBTI Judging
	Tolerance for closed-ended learning activities	
	Lack of ethnocentricity	Class Activity Survey Items HBQ Ethnic Group Factor?
	Ability to memorize	MLAT V
Conversation	Phonetic decoding	MLAT I, II, III
Reading	Sound-symbol decoding	MLAT II, III
Listening	Phonetic decoding	MLAT I, II, III
	2. Roadway System	
Oral interaction closely linked to lesson material. Some meaningful but largely communicative drilling; controlled conversation, edited texts, and listening passages that may be based on authentic material.		
All	Abstractions	MBTI Intuition
	Metacognitive skills (planning, evaluation)	MBTI Thinking, Judging
	Analytic skills	MLAT III, IV
	Deep processing strategies	SILL Cognitive Strategies
	Acceptance of external guidance	MBTI Sensing, Judging

Figure 5. (continued).

3. Trail Network

"Free" conversation, heavily guided by the teacher to include repetition of previously learned material but with room for considerable student initiative especially in subject matter. Generally authentic reading and listening material but with considerable teacher or curricular guidance in the form of advance organizers, outlines, and other guides.

All	Global/Simultaneous processing	MLAT II (sound and symbol)
	Random processing	MBTI Intuition and Perceiving
	Combination of cognitive abilities	MLAT Total or Index
	Recombination of old material	Yale-FSI Test?
Conversation	Coping with information gaps	SILL Compensation Strats.
Reading	Gisting skills	
Listening	Gisting skills	

4. Open Country

Open-ended conversation, topics nominated and branched by both S and T; authentic material for reading and listening; student develops own strategies for coping.

All	Tolerance of ambiguity	HBQ Total, External Boundaries
	Flexible shift of mental set	MLAT III, Yale-FSI Test
	Preference for open-ended earning	CLASSACT Items
	Independence (high-level metacognition and affective self-regulation)	
	Management of expectations	
	Moderation of affective arousal	Affective Survey

Note: Yale-FSI Test refers to a test of ability to cope with the unfamiliar that is under joint development by Yale University and FSI.

is hypothesized to advantage sequential and bottom-up processing activities. At the other extreme, "open country" is hypothesized to relate to open-ended activities with no control of linguistic or topical content. An effort is made to distribute activities and various individual dimensions in the two middle levels, although again this is a somewhat artificial endeavor, since the middle levels really represent somewhat arbitrary points on a continuum.

The following general principles apply to Figure 5:

(1) Each level includes those that precede it;
(2) Probably no classroom programs operate entirely at any of these levels;
(3) Affective factors (especially motivation, anxiety) moderate access to abilities, skills, and available "processing" capacity; and
(4) Interpersonal skill enhances performance at every level but especially 2–4 and, most especially, out-of-classroom, in-country language use.

Various learning styles predict comfort with activities at each level. For instance, looking at the poles of the sequential–random dimension, a very sequential learner is likely to be comfortable in a classroom with many "railroad" activities and will have to "stretch" him- or herself to do more open-ended activities. A strongly random learner will probably gravitate to "trailway" or "open-country" activities and have to work to contain some impatience during very "railroad"-type activities. On the other hand, learners of both "types" usually welcome activities outside their comfort zone. For example, many sequential learners have told me that working with texts that contain substantial unknown material is difficult and uncomfortable but necessary for them. Conversely, many FSI students who prefer random learning will include drilling and memorizing activities in their study repertoires and even welcome some of this kind of work in class. (More often they want to decide when and how to use these "railroad" activities and will often prefer to do them on their own rather than in class so they can use class time for more realistic practice.)

Outside the classroom. A nagging and very important question that persists in this kind of study is how individual differences (and situational variables) apply to non-classroom settings. These settings can be considered almost entirely "open country." Do they differ substantially from classrooms in which most or all of the work is at the "open country" level? Certainly one important difference is that there is likely to be no teacher to provide guidance and adjust the level of structure and difficulty in response to the learner's need. Much more is required of the learner in orchestrating his or her own learning "program."

I recently had the opportunity to learn an entirely new language for a specific purpose. I was invited to provide training in learning styles to Egyptian teachers of English under the auspices of USIA/Cairo. For about three weeks before my departure, I arranged to spend about an hour a day with one of the FSI Egyptian Arabic teachers.

Although I did not have the time to learn Arabic to a high level of proficiency, I did note some of the characteristics of my learning. I went into the experience knowing that my learning style is very "random" and includes many analytic/field-independent techniques along with global/field-sensitive ones. I tend to seek "trailways" and "open country" very rapidly and do the more structured work on my own. Figure 6 presents some of the things I did before my trip to Egypt and during the two and a half weeks I was there.

Coping with this completely "open country" environment required me to do more negotiation of social roles than is ordinarily required in a classroom, thus making the need for interpersonal skill especially clear. At the same time, I found my analytic skills invaluable, because they made me aware of the regularities in what I was being exposed to, and I could then use the regularities to try out new communication. Effective management of my expectations and feelings was vital. Above all, however, I felt that the true driving force for my learning was my motivation to communicate and relate, and this is more important in country than in the classroom, where the context provides so much of the motivation. For an English speaker on a short-term trip with a purpose that required that most interaction be in English, it would have been easy to avoid continued language learning and to rationalize this avoidance. It was the motivation that made the avoidance unthinkable.

In conclusion. There seems to be a kind of aptitude-personality nexus that consists of cognitive flexibility, tolerance of ambiguity (including ability to impose structure on input), and ability to make use of random access strategies.

The MLAT is the most powerful of the predictive variables used, even in programs that are very different from those in vogue when it was designed. It may be that the ability to manage unfamiliar and contradictory input leads both to success in communicative classrooms and to high scores on the MLAT. The MLAT may gain its relative power because it requires examinees to cope with the unfamiliar on tasks that at least partially simulate language-learning tasks, whereas personality inventories ask about general life preferences, and strategy inventories do not address how strategies are used but only whether students are aware of using them. The significant correlations between the MLAT and the personality measures, although not strong (between .21 and .33), are consistent across HBQ, MBTI, and MLAT subscales (Ehrman 1993, 1994). In both cases, MLAT scores are linked with variables that suggest tolerance for ambiguity.

The links between the MLAT and personality variables suggest a role for the disposition to use one's cognitive resources in ways that go beneath the surface and establish elaborated knowledge structures. Those who are open

Figure 6. Some learning activities to cope with "open country."

While Still In the US
- I let the teachers know in advance about my learning style. They were skeptical at first about whether the approach I recommended for myself would work but were quickly convinced of its effectiveness (for me).
- Because I knew that I could learn only a small subset of Arabic, I selected a focus of learning for my classroom work that I knew would be of use to me on my trip: small talk and social interaction.
- I negotiated activities and topics actively with the teachers.
- In order to make the best use of my limited contact time with teachers, I took the initiative in grammar learning, which I pursued largely on my own, asking questions in class when I felt a generalization was important. Questions were usually of the "how do you say X" or "can you say X" type for grammar as well as communication.
- From the very beginning, I went out of my way to learn to read and write the Arabic script.
- Although much of this had to be in English, I spent considerable class time on culture and how it affected me. This was time very well spent.

Both in the US and in Egypt
- I was strongly motivated to achieve acceptance by Egyptians (assimilative motivation).
- It was impossible for me to avoid awareness of my own limitations. At the 0+ level, I had not reached the point of critical language mass, so I became quickly fatigued. Acceptance of this fact and frequent rests from the intense effort required by language use were important aspects of my staying with the learning.
- A very important part of my learning was substantial affective self-management, especially in what I expected of myself as a learner. I tended to see the glass as half-full and to feel optimistic about my learning potential (though regretful that the opportunity was so short).

While in Egypt
- In social encounters I was at somewhat of a linguistic and cultural disadvantage. One of the ways I managed this was to arrange for a role shift, where I could become a language and culture student and my interlocutors became teachers, a role they enjoyed.
- Somehow I was able to convey my willingness to be corrected and taught even to casual acquaintances, despite pre-travel warnings that the Egyptians would be unlikely to correct me and would probably prefer to use English.
- I turned casual contacts, such as shopping and interactions with hotel personnel, into practice opportunities. In fact, I used all input or interaction contexts to practice.
- Throughout, I used conversation management and compensation strategies intensively.
- Whenever I could, I listened, especially to fluent foreigners conversing with Egyptians, because I could follow more, especially if I knew what they were talking about.
- I made a point of listening for and picking up culturally important social "lubricant" expressions such as "thanks be to God."
- From time to time, I reviewed lesson materials that I had brought with me, a good phrasebook, and my notes. I used an English-Egyptian colloquial dictionary when really stuck.
- Finally, I tried to read signs and other text in context, looking for relationships and classical Arabic variants.

to new material, tolerant of contradictions, able to establish hypotheses to be tested and focus on meaning, and can find ways to link the new with previous knowledge structures seem to have an advantage in managing the complex demands of language and culture learning.

The weakest students appear to be overwhelmed by the chaos they encounter; the strongest meet it head on and even embrace it to a degree. The strongest learners are indeed differentiated by this nexus of personality and tested aptitude, but the weakest ones are much more clearly delineated (Ehrman in press); that is, cognitive rigidity seems to disadvantage the weakest students more than cognitive flexibility advantages the strongest ones. Although this paper has suggested that concrete sequential learning preferences may be associated with learning situations that provide more structural support, a concrete-sequential learning preference need not mean poor learning, as long as the student is flexible and able to make use of strategies for coping with "open country." Furthermore, the need to tolerate ambiguity and cope with "open country" may imply an enhanced importance for affective self-management strategies, especially for those for whom this is a learning styles "stretch."

REFERENCES

Brown, H. Douglas. 1994. *Principles of language learning and teaching, Third edition.* Englewood Cliffs, N. J.: Prentice-Hall Regents.
Carroll, John. 1990. "Cognitive abilities and foreign language aptitude: Then and now." In Thomas Parry and Charles W. Stansfield (eds.), *Language aptitude reconsidered.* Englewood Cliffs, N.J.: Prentice Hall. 11-29.
Carroll, John and Stanley M. Sapon. 1958. *Modern Language Aptitude Test.* New York: Psychological Corporation.
Demuth, Katherine A. and Nathaniel B. Smith. 1987. "The foreign language requirement: An alternative program." *Foreign Language Annals* 20:67-77.
Dubin, Fraida and Elite Olshtain. 1986. *Course design: Developing programs and materials for language learning.* New York: Cambridge University Press.
Ehrman, Madeline E. 1993, "Ego boundaries revisited: Toward a model of personality and learning." In James E. Alatis (ed.), *Georgetown University Roundtable on Languages and Linguistics 1993.* Washington, D.C.: Georgetown University Press. 331-362.
Ehrman, Madeline E. 1994. "The Type Differentiation Indicator and adult language learning success." *Journal of Psychological Type* 30:1-29.
Ehrman, Madeline E. In press. "Weakest and strongest learners in intensive language training: A study of extremes." In Carol Klee (ed.), *Faces in a crowd: Individual learners in multisection programs.* Boston, MA.: Heinle and Heinle.
Ehrman, Madeline E., and Rebecca L. Oxford. 1995. "Cognition plus: Correlates of language learning success." *Modern Language Journal* 79(1): 67-89.

Ganschow, Leonore, Bettye Myer, and Kathy Roeger. 1989. "Foreign language policies and procedures for students with specific learning disabilities." *Learning Disabilities Focus* 5(1): 50–58.

Gregorc, Anthony F. 1982. *An adult's guide to style*. Maynard, MA.: Gabriel Systems, Inc.

Hartmann, Ernest. 1991. *Boundaries in the mind: A new psychology of personality*. New York: Basic Books.

Kolb, David. 1985. *Learning Styles Inventory*. Boston, MA.: McBer and Co.

Krahnke, Karl. 1987. *Approaches to syllabus design for foreign language teaching*. Englewood Cliffs, N.J.: Prentice-Hall.

Lefrancois, Jeanne and Therese Couillard Sibiga. June, 1986. "Use of the Modern Language Aptitude Test (MLAT) as a diagnostic tool." Unpublished paper.

Lett, John A. and Francis E. O'Mara. 1990. "Predictors of success in an intensive foreign language learning context: Correlates of language learning at the Defense Language Institute Foreign Language Center." In Thomas Parry and Charles W. Stansfield (eds.), *Language aptitude reconsidered*. Englewood Cliffs, N.J.: Prentice Hall: 220–260.

McCarthy, Bernice. 1980. *The 4Mat system: Teaching to learning styles with right/left mode techniques*. Barrington, IL.: Excel, Inc.

Myers, Isabel B. and Mary H. McCaulley. 1985. *Manual: A guide to the development and use of the Myers-Briggs Type Indicator*. Palo Alto, CA.: Consulting Psychologists Press.

Oxford, Rebecca L. and Madeline E. Ehrman. 1993. "Second language research on individual differences." In Grabe, William (ed.), *Annual Review of Applied Linguistics XIII, Issues in Second Language Teaching and Learning*, 188–205.

Nunan, David. 1989. *Designing tasks for the communicative classroom*. New York: Cambridge University Press.

Parry, Thomas and Charles W. Stansfield (eds.). 1990. *Language aptitude reconsidered*. Englewood Cliffs, N.J.: Prentice Hall.

Peck, Antony. 1988. *Language teachers at work: A description of methods*. New York: Prentice Hall.

Petersen, Calvin R. and Antoine R. Al-Haik. 1976. "The development of the Defense Language Aptitude Battery (DLAB)." *Educational and psychological measurement* 6: 369–380.

Pimsleur, Paul. 1966. *The Pimsleur language aptitude battery*. New York: Harcourt, Brace, Jovanovich.

Skehan, Peter. 1989. *Individual differences in second language learning*. London: Edward Arnold.

Spolsky, Bernard. 1994. "Prognostication and language aptitude testing: 1925-1962." Plenary address at the 1994 Language Aptitude Invitational Symposium. September, 1994. Arlington, VA.

Stern, H. H. (David). 1992. *Issues and options in language teaching*. New York: Oxford University Press.

Stevick, Earl W. 1989. *Teaching languages: A way and ways*. New York: Newbury House.

Thain, John. 1992. "DLAB II prototype development: Status report and CY92 plan." Technical report. Monterey, CA.: Defense Language Institute.

Wesche, Marjorie B. 1981. "Language aptitude measures in streaming, matching students with methods, and diagnosis of learning problems." In K.C. Diller (ed.), *Individual differences and universals in language learning aptitude*. Rowley, MA.: Newbury House: 119–153.

Wesche, Marjorie B., Henry Edwards, and Winston Wells. 1982. "Foreign language aptitude and intelligence." *Applied Psycholinguistics* 3: 127–140.

Yalden, Janice. 1987. *Principles of course design for language teaching*. New York: Cambridge University Press.

The cause–effect fallacy and the time fallacy

Stephen D. Krashen
University of Southern California

There are two profound misunderstandings in education, misunderstandings that are causing a great deal of suffering. To understand these fallacies, we first need to discuss how language acquisition and cognitive development take place.

The two fundamental principles.

Language acquisition: The input hypothesis. The input hypothesis claims that we acquire language by understanding messages, both aural and written. Evidence for the input hypothesis has been reviewed in previous GURT papers and elsewhere (e.g. Krashen 1991, 1994a, 1994b). Briefly,

(1) Those who obtain more comprehensible input consistently show more language and literacy development, both outside of school and inside school; and

(2) Rival hypotheses fail: The rival "instruction hypothesis" (a combination of the more basic skill-building and output plus correction hypotheses; see Krashen 1991) fails for several reasons: (a) the systems to be mastered are much too complex to be consciously learned; (b) many people have attained high levels of competence without instruction; (c) efforts to show the efficacy of direct teaching have not been successful (Krashen 1991, 1994a, 1994b); and (d) correction, an element considered crucial to instruction and conscious learning, occurs much too rarely to help language acquisition, and research on its efficacy yields disappointing results (Krashen 1991, 1994a, 1994b).

The rival "output" hypothesis (for literacy, the writing hypothesis) appears in several versions, including the simple output hypothesis (we acquire language by producing it, with or without feedback), and the comprehensible-output hypothesis (we acquire language by adjusting our output to make it comprehensible (Swain 1985)). The writing hypothesis runs into severe difficulty because (1) increasing student writing does not result in improved writing, and (2) writing occurs too infrequently, in school and outside of school, to account for literacy development. In addition, the successful adjustments demanded by the comprehensible-output hypothesis are not frequent, and more such adjustments do not result in more language acquisition (Krashen 1991, 1994b).

The problem-solving hypothesis. There are two competing hypotheses that attempt to explain how we learn new facts and concepts. What I will call the "study hypothesis" asserts that we learn new facts and concepts by deliberate study, by trying to learn. The problem-solving hypothesis claims that we learn new facts and concepts as a by-product of trying to solve problems.

I have argued that the study hypothesis is false and that the problem-solving hypothesis is true (Krashen 1991). Evidence for the problem-solving hypothesis includes laboratory studies showing the superiority of incidental learning over intentional learning when the task is of interest (reviewed in Krashen 1991). More impressive are informal observations of how much and how effortlessly people learn in daily problem-solving and how little and how inefficiently they learn by study. We have encyclopedic knowledge of the important details of our lives, many of which we learned in a single "trial." Consider the following poem:

> Do you love me?
> Or do you not?
> You told me once,
> But I forgot.

It is amusing because no one forgets things like that.

On the other hand, we forget, as soon as we leave the examination room, what we have studied.[1] In fact, it is probably true that accomplished people

---

[1] Semb and Ellis (1994) provide apparent counterevidence to the generalization that "school learning" is rapidly forgotten, claiming that "contrary to popular belief, students retain much of the knowledge taught in the classroom" (p. 279). Their results, however, are not at all inconsistent with the problem-solving hypothesis. Semb and Ellis reported that in general the use of instructional strategies involving "increases in responding, different types of responses, or more exposure to content" (p. 275) had no effect on learning or retention. (In some cases, the use of these kinds of strategies resulted in better learning, but "there were usually no interactions" (p. 275), that is, one could not attribute the differences in retention to the strategies used. Rather, the superior scores on the retention exam were due to the higher scores on the end-of-semester test.)

There were, however, a few studies in which the use of certain instructional strategies did influence retention, and it is clear that in each case problem-solving was centrally involved. In one study, for example (MacKenzie and White 1982, cited in Semb and Ellis), traditional learning of geography was compared with a treatment in which students "were given a worksheet with tasks to complete: Observing, sketching, recording and answering questions ... students participated in events such as walking through the mud of a mangrove shore, tasting foliage for salinity and wading in the sea" (p.276). This experimental group lost only 10% from the end-of-course exam after 12 weeks, while two traditionally taught groups lost 41% and 48%.

Another example is Sturges, Ellis, and Wulfeck (1981, cited in Semb and Ellis), who compared "topic-oriented" and "job-oriented" texts in learning about metal fasteners: The "job-oriented" text presented the information in the context of a job-like situation, while the topic-oriented text contained few references to how the information could be used on the job" (p. 277). Both never study; as we shall see later, they spend their time doing other things that are far more beneficial. In Smith's terms, study is not "what the brain does well."

Affect. In support of the input hypothesis, the pleasure hypothesis claims that activities that are good for language acquisition are perceived to be pleasant, while activities that are not good for language acquisition are often perceived to be unpleasant. There is, for example, strong evidence that free reading and hearing stories, which are very good for language acquisition, are enjoyable, while "forced speech," having to produce language containing elements that may be learned, but are not yet acquired, is perceived to be unpleasant by foreign-language students (Krashen 1994b).

The pleasure hypothesis can be extended to cognitive development as well: Activities that involve us in relevant problems are enjoyable, while study is not. We spent hours on projects that interest us, entering what Csikszentmihalyi (1991) calls "flow," a state in which one is so deeply involved in an activity that time seems to stand still, and one's sense of the self can disappear. Flow, Csikszentmihalyi suggests, occurs when our abilities and challenges are appropriately matched, and it produces true enjoyment: "In observing how supposedly creative people go about setting up a problem and solving it, I noticed the tremendous emotional involvement, even ecstacy, they seemed to experience ..." (Csikszentmihalyi, in Sobel 1995: 76).

Flow appears to be involved in language and literacy development as well. The acquirer, according to the input hypothesis, must be completely focussed on the message, "forgetting" that the goal is language acquisition.

Smith (1988) notes that we can be in only one of the following three states at any time: Boredom, confusion, or learning. (Here, of course, I use the term "learning" in the more general sense.) Learning, he proposes, is the natural state of the brain: It is what the brain does. It may also be the case that we are "designed to want to be in flow" (Sobel 1995: 90). If real learning and flow are both natural to the brain and are both enjoyable, and if flow occurs when we are involved in a problem that challenges our abilities appropriately, *it may be the case that problem-solving that results in flow is a necessary condition for cognitive development to take place.*

---

groups learned the material to 90% criterion, but the job-oriented group had less loss when retested six months later.

In addition, Semb and Ellis conclude that certain characteristics of the educational situation appear to improve retention, such as spaced, as contrasted to massed, study, and the degree of "coherence" in the content. These conditions are met naturally in real problem-solving. In real problem-solving, participants naturally encounter data as spaced, rather than massed, and the activity itself is an effort to make sense of something, that is, to make data more coherent.

Enterprises. Smith (1988) has introduced an extremely useful term: "enterprise." An enterprise is a problem to be solved, a task, or a project that naturally entails reading, writing, and discussion. According to the input hypothesis and problem-solving hypothesis, enterprises will result in both language and cognitive development.

Smith's view is that school should consist of enterprises. This is a model that is widely accepted for graduate school: Graduate students typically engage in projects, and do less traditional study-oriented work than do students at lower levels. In doing projects, they read, write, discuss, and grow intellectually and, in many cases, linguistically.

At a minimum, enterprises should be interesting and comprehensible, so interesting that the problem-solver is in a state of flow. These requirements are not easy to meet at the same time. The real world is full of projects that are interesting, but they are not always comprehensible for students. School is full of activities that are comprehensible, but not always interesting.

Enterprises should also provide students with competence and knowledge that is of use to them. An enterprise may be interesting and comprehensible, but be of little benefit. And ideally, an enterprise should help society, that is, it should be meaningful (Kohn 1993: 191).

We can easily classify enterprises according to these characteristics. Some games, for example, meet only the first two conditions. They may be interesting and comprehensible, but do not result in any useful abilities (from society's point of view, at least), nor do they contribute to society. Some games, however, such as certain role-playing games, do result in valuable cognitive and language development (Krashen 1992).

Research done by graduate students in Ph.D. programs are, ideally, examples of enterprises having all four characteristics. Such research is meant to make a genuine contribution to knowledge and thus serves society. In addition, the knowledge and abilities gained are of great use to the student, and projects selected are (or should be) of interest to the student and within his or her competence.

The cause and effect fallacy. The cause and effect fallacy was clearly stated by Smith (1986): Traditional schemes of learning "represent the world turned upside down" (Smith 1986: 75).

According to the input hypothesis our language ability, our ability to spell, our vocabulary, our grammatical competence, etc. is a *result* of comprehensible input. According to the problem-solving hypothesis, our knowledge of concepts and facts is a *result* of problem-solving. School often makes the opposite assumption: We first learn vocabulary, learn to spell, learn grammar, etc. and practice in contrived, classroom situations to "automatize" them. Only after these "basics" are mastered are we allowed to actually use language for real communication.

Similarly, school has traditionally assumed that we learn concepts and facts, that third graders should learn "what every third grader should know," and practice them in contrived classroom situations in order to "automatize" them. Only after these basics are mastered are we allowed to engage in real enterprises.

Clearly, tests are a major force in promoting activities that go in the wrong direction: When a language test focusses students on form, the effect is for teachers to teach form directly. If, for example, the final test focusses on vocabulary, instruction will emphasize vocabulary lists. We know, however, that reading is much more efficient in terms of words acquired per minute (Nagy, Herman, and Anderson 1985). In other words, those who do it in the right direction do well on tests, even tests that focus on form, a conclusion supported by the superior test performance of students who do sustained silent reading (Krashen 1993). (Exceptions are language tests that focus on late-acquired items that even fairly advanced language students will typically not acquire without extensive reading and/or residence in the country.)

The public has assumed that some things must first be "learned," that a lot of hard work is necessary before students can go on to more interesting activities. The problem-solving and input hypotheses do not require delayed gratification. When students engage in real problem-solving and are exposed to interesting stories and texts immediately, they acquire language and learn concepts and facts much more easily.

Kohn (1993) has recognized this: "For all our talk about motivation, I think we often fail to recognize a truth that is staring us in the face: If educators are able to create the conditions under which children can become engaged with academic tasks, the acquisition of intellectual skills will probably follow" (Kohn 1993: 146).

The time fallacy. School success is usually measured in terms of rate of attainment, not ultimate attainment. Grades for example are based on how much is learned in a given amount of time, often in relation to other students. (Foreign language "aptitude," in fact, is specifically defined as the speed of grammatical and vocabulary learning (Krashen 1981).) There is, in addition, great concern about children being at grade level and being able to "compete" in school. (Note that often grades are a measure of speed of learning arbitrary information unrelated to any problem-solving. They are, in other words, a measure of speed of learning of what students perceive to be nonsense.)

Both language acquisition and cognitive development demand, however, that the student be completely involved in the activity, that he or she be in a state of flow. Recall that when one is in flow, in a sense time stops—only the task exists, and even the sense of self can disappear. A focus on trying to get done quickly and on how one will be evaluated disturbs flow, disturbs learning, and makes life harder and less enjoyable. As Kohn (1993) expresses it, " ... the more the student is focused on how well he's doing, the less he is absorbed in the task itself. That absorption facilitates learning, so anything that undermines it is educationally disruptive" (Kohn 1993: 156).

Evidence consistent with this position comes from Csikszentmihalyi (in Sobel 1995), who reported on a study involving high-school students "who had many flow experiences" and those who did not, who were asked to participate in a "standard learning situation where they responded to questions presented on a computer screen" (Sobel 1995: 77). Evoked response data showed that the first group did better on the test and spent much less effort on the task with less cortical activity; in other words, they didn't work as hard. In addition, "those often in flow turned out to feel much less self-conscious in the test situation" (1995: 77). Those not in flow, according to Csikszentmihalyi, "make a greater mental effort because they not only respond to the problem on the screen, but also monitor themselves and wonder, 'Will I do it right?' 'What does the experimenter think?' Their self-consciousness puts an extra burden on their mental effort" (1995: 77).

Workaphiles. The purpose of time pressure and grades is to get students to "work hard" and put in more time on a task. But those who are in flow do this without this extrinsic motivation. There is good evidence that those who have achieved eminence and expert status have typically devoted a great deal of time to their work or activity. Simonton (1988) has reviewed this research: "... one study [Simon] found that distinguished researchers in the physical and social sciences worked 60-70 hours per week for virtually the entire year ... Herbert Simon admitted that he spent 100 hours per week doing the things that eventually earned him a Nobel Prize ..." (p. 139). Simonton quotes hair stylist Vidal Sasson: "The only place where success comes before work is a dictionary" (p. 238) and Lehman: "As compared with the average individual ... distinguished creative thinkers have usually possessed, among other things, an astonishing capacity for hard patient work" (Simonton 1988: 57).

Such effort is not, I suggest, painful study. Rather, it is attempts at problem-solving. It is not the confusion and boredom associated with school, but real learning that results in both accomplishment and the enjoyment of flow: As Simonton notes, "Anne Roe concluded from her intensive interviews with 64 illustrious scientists that all exhibited a 'driving absorption in their work.' 'They have worked long hours for many years, frequently with no vacations to speak of, because they would rather be doing their work than anything else.'" (1988: 238).

In a recent interview with David Frost, Ralph Nader revealed that he worked long hours, but was in flow:

> David Frost: ... your work schedule is what? Eighty hours a week I read somewhere, at least?
>
> Ralph Nader: Well, it's pretty much all the time except, you know, eight hours to eat and sleep. But I enjoy it so much. You see the definition of work tends to imply a drag, a chore, something you'd rather not be doing but it's important to do. I don't see it that way. It's a joy.

Jim Trelease (personal communication) has suggested that such people should be called "workaphiles" rather than "workaholics."

The time paradox The time paradox is well stated in the following zen story: The student goes to the Zen master and asks, "Master, if I study with you, how long will it take me to be enlightened?" The master responds, "Ten years." The student, eager to get the job done, then asks, "What if I work very hard, then how long will it take?" To this the master responds, "Twenty years." Surprised, the student then asks, "What if I become your best student, if I do the practices faithfully, morning, noon, and night, then how long?" Predictably, the master replies, "In that case, thirty years." "Why," the student asks, "should it take longer if I work harder?" The master responds, "If you have one eye on your goal, you will only have one eye for your work, and your work will suffer."

Overconcern with time takes our minds off the task, immobilizes us, and prevents us from entering flow. It thus actually has the effect of slowing us down. Concern with the activity itself, however, results in real accomplishment and, ironically, completion in a shorter time. We have all seen this phenomenon in our own lives: Rigid deadlines only result in excessive worry about meeting the deadline. But with no deadline, we are free to get really involved in the work, to get into a state of flow.

Deadlines and schedules also interfere with the creative process. Csikszentmihalyi and Sawyer (1995) interviewed a number of highly creative people, and concluded that "incubation is facilitated by periods of idling (and) leisure" (1995: 359). After a great deal of hard work on a problem, good thinkers report that solutions typically come while alone and idle. This idle time could be a fairly long vacation (according to one informant, "You have to do six months of very hard work first and get all the components bumping around in your head, and then you have to be idle for a couple of weeks, and then— ping—it suddenly falls into place ..." (Csikszentmihalyi and Sawyer 1995: 350)), or could consist of short breaks during the day (Piaget claimed that his ideas came to him while writing, but "after he worked for a few hours he would go for a walk, not think about it very much, and when he went back to his desk his ideas would be clearer ..." (Gruber 1995: 426)).

Wallas (1970) noted that "the stage of incubation should include a large amount of actual mental relaxation ... A.R. Wallace, for instance, hit upon the theory of evolution by natural selection in his berth during an attack of malarial fever at sea; and Darwin was compelled by ill health to spend the greater part of his waking hours in physical and mental relaxation" (p. 95).

In my work, I never set deadlines for myself ("Today I will write three pages"). Rather, I find I am much more efficient if I simply try to involve myself in the work without any time pressure. If I lose myself in the sentence or paragraph, or the data analysis, and allow the idle time that Wallas and others recommend, the work is done in surprisingly short time.

The result is also much more enjoyment and less fatigue. Interestingly, those destined to make notable contributions often get through their schooling quickly. Simonton (1994) reports, for example, that eminent psychologists finished their graduate education when they were five years younger than the average Ph.D. in their field. This was not, I suggest, because they studied harder, but because they were more involved in problem-solving.

Formal education. Research on the effect of formal education is consistent with the fundamental principles presented earlier. Simonton (1984) reviewed the literature on school success and eventual accomplishment and concluded that "There is little evidence to suggest that scholastic success has any impact whatsoever on long-term achievement ... scholastic honors do not predict occupational success" (p. 73). Cases of those who did not do especially well in school but who accomplished great things are common knowledge. Simonton comments on Einstein:

> According to one of Einstein's most distinguished professors at the Zurich Polytechnic Institute, Hermann Minkowski, "in his student days Einstein had been a lazy dog. He never bothered about mathematics at all." (Simonton 184: 74).

In addition, Simonton notes that in a sample of three-hundred eminent people studied by Goertzel, Goertzel and Goertzel, only twenty percent were honor students and eight percent were failures in school.

If they aren't studying, what do accomplished people do? They work. As noted earlier, they put in enormous amounts of time on enterprises.

Of course, not all successes in life do poorly in school. Simonton notes that some accomplished people were excellent students:

> Marie Curie was a couple of years ahead of her elementary school classmates in all subjects and received a gold medal at sixteen upon graduation from the Russian lycee. Sigmund Freud was at the head of his class at the gymnasium and graduated summa cum laude. J. Robert

Oppenheimer graduated summa cum laude from Harvard with the highest honors ever awarded an undergraduate. Clearly, academic and extracurricular knowledge acquisition are not necessarily inconsistent. (Simonton 1984: 75)

My hypothesis is that those who did well in school, and who also went on to become eminent in their fields, did not do it by deliberate study alone. Rather, their interest in certain topics stimulated their participation in enterprises, in personal reading and investigation: This resulted in a great deal of knowledge of subject matter, which fortunately coincided with the subject matter in classes. Classes were simply a test that they passed. As Roe phrased it (cited in Simonton 1994), "Once a student has learned that he can find things out for himself, bad pedagogy is probably only an irritant" (p. 161).

Simonton (1988) concluded that "gifted children and adolescents do seem dedicated to the independent pursuit of knowledge, as evinced by extensive independent reading and numerous intellectual hobbies ..." (p. 124). Maybe this behavior has something to do with how they got to be "gifted" and survived school.

Of course, some people probably succeed in school through "hard study" alone. My prediction is that those who did so did not go on to make important contributions. And they certainly didn't have a good time in school.

Table 1 summarizes the possibilities for the relationship between school success and life success and relates them to the way the student gained knowledge. Those who relied on solving problems of interest to them may or may not have succeeded in school, but typically do well in life. Supporting evidence comes from Bloom (1963), who reported that former graduate students at the University of Chicago who went on to successful research careers did not necessarily have the best grades, but consistently exhibited as students "a preoccupation with problems rather than with the subject matter of courses ... the relatively complete acceptance of the role of research worker and scholar (rather than the role of student)" (Bloom 1963: 257–258).

Those who studied hard may or may not have done well in school; hard study will not be enough for those who come to school without the background the curriculum assumes. And they will not be able to use this knowledge in life.

Rosow (1995) provides a touching example of the inadequacy of "hard work" for those who do not come to school with the expected background: She describes how Mitzi, the semiliterate child of a semiliterate parent, struggled with a homework assignment in which she was supposed to write a sentence with each of ten words given by the teacher. Neither Mitzi nor her mother could even read the words on the list, and the sentences made the task insurmountable. After thirty minutes of hard struggle, the assignment was far from done. A child from a literate home would have finished it in a few minutes, thanks to superior literacy development from exposure to a print-rich environment, and the availability of expert help.

Table 1. What can happen in school.

Strategy leads to:	school success?	life success?
problem-solving	yes no	yes (Curie) yes (Einstein)
study	yes no	no no (Mitzi)

We can make the same analysis for language education (Table 2), where "life success" refers to the ability to use the language outside the classroom in real communication.

In the first category are those who get comprehensible input outside the classroom and do well in language classes. In foreign-language education, they are known as false beginners and false intermediates. Rarely acknowledged in the professional literature, but known by every college foreign-language student, is the fact that about half of the students in beginning college-level foreign-language classes are false beginners; some have had instruction in the language before, or have used the language extensively outside the class, and some are even native speakers of the language.

Table 2. What can happen in foreign-language class.

Strategy leads to:	school success?	life success?
comprehensible input	yes no	yes yes
study	yes no	no no

At more advanced levels, most students are false intermediates. In a recent USC study, we found that only ten percent of the students in advanced foreign-language classes were not native speakers of the language or had not spend a significant amount of time abroad (Dupuy and Krashen, forthcoming).

False beginners and false intermediates get much better grades, feel more comfortable in class, and even tend to sit together (Loughrin-Sacco 1992; Dupuy and Krashen, forthcoming).

In the second category are those who got lots of input outside of class but did not succeed in class. In some cases, tests focussed on late-acquired items that some acquirers have not yet acquired, despite having considerable competence, and in other cases acquirers have a dialect of the language that is different from that taught in school.

The third category, those who have studied hard and did well in school but who cannot use the language outside of school, is quite common; the fourth category probably represents most foreign-language students.

Solutions.
Get knowledge outside of school. A popular solution to this problem is to become a false beginner, and to ensure that one's children already have the knowledge and abilities they will be expected to "learn" in school. It has been argued that this is exactly what happens in literacy development. Children who grow up in a print-rich environment are far better prepared to deal with the traditional language-arts curriculum—it is a test they can easily pass.

Vocabulary knowledge is a clear example. It is well established that children differ enormously in vocabulary size. As Nagy and Herman (1987) have pointed out, children with larger vocabularies are not doing more drills and exercises: They are reading more. Homes of the affluent tend to have more books, a quiet, comfortable place to read, and a life-style that provides the leisure time to read as well as models of readers. It is thus no surprise that a powerful relationship exists between measures of vocabulary and socioeconomic class (Hill and Giammateo 1963).

The Schoolboys of Barbiana (1970), a group of eight teenagers who failed in the Italian school system, came to the same conclusion. Their analysis showed that the children of the poor fail at a much higher rate than children of professional classes. Their explanation is that the successful students already knew what school was supposed to teach. Students' "improvement" in literacy was merely due to the fact that those who came to school less literate drop out:

> The only ones left [in grade 6] are those who could write correctly to begin with; they could probably write just as well in the third elementary. The ones who learned to write at home ... The illiterate she had in the first grade are just as illiterate now. She [the teacher] has simply dropped them from sight. (p. 49)

The advantage of the affluent in school is translated into career advantage. Roe (cited in Simonton 1994) reported that :

> Eminent scientists were very unlikely to originate in the lower strata. Not one came from a family where the chief breadwinner was an unskilled laborer, and only 3% had fathers who were skilled workers. In contrast, 53% were the sons of professional men. This incidence was 18 times greater than the proportion of professional parents in the general population. Even when we confine our attention to just science doctorates, those who have managed to become Nobel laureates are nearly twice as likely to have

fathers who were professionals, managers, or proprieters ... of more than 300 contemporary creators, leaders, and celebrities, 80% emanated from business or professional homes, while only 6% ascended from dire poverty. (p. 157)

Simonton also concludes that the same effect is present for politics. A huge percentage of those holding high political office are from the affluent: "The log cabin myth is just that—pure myth" (1994: 157). Just as in education, those who have succeeded sometimes believe it was exclusively through their own efforts. Former Texas Secretary of Agriculture Hightower attributed this attitude to former president Bush: "a man who was born on third base who thinks he hit a triple." (Affluence is, of course, not a guarantee of literacy and success, nor is poverty a guarantee of illiteracy and lack of success. There are some who, despite wealth, manage to avoid reading and others who, despite poverty, gain access to print and succeed.)

Getting the necessary preparation elsewhere is also the solution many foreign-language students adopt. Last year's true beginner becomes this year's false beginner. What has clearly happened here is that, in Freire's terms, the oppressee has become the oppressor. It is also the solution for those who seek tutoring and remediation, but the usual result is more of the same kind of schooling they were unable to deal with in the first place (Rosow 1995).

I suspect this kind of thing happens in other subjects as well. It is in fact encouraged by teachers who, for some reason, feel they deserve the credit when a student shows up in class who already knows the material.

Simply mastering the material in another way, and then getting credit for it is, of course, not the solution. When this happens, school becomes simply a test, "... school is no longer school. It is a hospital which tends to the healthy and rejects the sick. It becomes just a place to strengthen the existing differences to a point of no return" (Schoolboys of Barbiana 1970: 12–13).

More time. Another possibility is to give some students more time. Athletics does this: It is called "red-shirting" and, contrary to "retention" in education, it is an honor and not a disgrace. A football player who is red-shirted is considered varsity material, and worth the investment of another year of training.

A different way. Slowing down is a step in the right direction: Time pressure should be reduced and even eliminated. This will, I predict, result in greater speed of learning. But it is not enough. We need to change some assumptions about language and cognitive development. School should be enterprise-based, a place where teachers and students engage in problem-solving and are given the time and opportunity to be in flow. This will result in both literacy and cognitive development. The enterprises must be of real interest to the students. We need to end the competition between the demands of education and the students' interests. When we do, the results are very positive: Simonton (1988) cites Roe's study of eminent scientists, in which she found that "the best-liked teachers were those who let their students pursue independent interests, such as extensive outside reading" (1988: 119).

Problems. As is well-known, the public's view of what is necessary is the exact opposite of what is proposed here. The public calls for more basics and hard study; in other words, a continuation of the cause–effect fallacy. The public also calls for more speed, and an emphasis on being "at grade level" and "competitive."

Educators often use this attitude as an excuse for engaging in practices they do not believe in: e.g. We must teach skills, because students and parents demand it, and because we need to fill out report cards. I sympathize with teachers in this position, but we must realize that it is our professional responsibility to teach according to our convictions about how people acquire language and grow cognitively. As Smith (1986) put it, engineers do not consider public opinion on how to build bridges, nor do surgeons allow the public to tell them how to perform operations.

Similarly, administrators who are not expert in instruction should not be able to dictate how teachers teach. We sometimes solve this problem by "doing it right" in our classrooms but keeping it a secret, taking out the basal and spelling list when the inspectors come by. This certainly helps the students here and now, but the skills program and philosophy get the credit for the success and there is no change. And the basal publishers make the profit, while teachers spend their own money on trade books.

A related rationale is that we need to do skills because next year's teacher will require them and our students need to get used to them. But doing it wrong this year will only make students less prepared for next year. The best inoculation against incorrect pedagogy is language development via comprehensible input and cognitive development via interesting problem-solving. If we know someone will be starved next year, we don't begin starvation now as preparation.

The best counterargument to these objections is the consistent finding that comprehensible input and problem-solving yield superior results. Language students, for example, who have read a great deal do very well even on standardized tests, and problem-solving yields far vaster and deeper knowledge than study. Students, parents, and administrators need to know this.

REFERENCES

Bloom, Benjamin. 1963. "Report on creativity research by the examiner's office of the University of Chicago." In Calvin Taylor and Frank Barron (eds.), *Scientific creativity*. New York: Wiley. 251–264.

Csikszentmihalyi, Mihaly. 1991. *Flow: The psychology of optimal experience*. New York: Harper Perennial.

Csikszentmihalyi, Mihaly and Keith Sayer. 1995. "Creative insight: The social dimension of a solitary moment". In Robert Sternberg and Janet E. Davidson (eds.), *The nature of insight*. Cambridge, Massachusetts: MIT Press. 329–363.

Dupuy, Beatrice and Stephen Krashen. Forthcoming. "From lower-division to upper-division foreign language classes: Obstacles to reaching the promised land."

Gruber, Howard. 1995. "Insight and affect in the history of science." In Robert Sternberg and Janet E. Davidson (eds.), *The nature of insight*. Cambridge, Massachusetts: MIT Press. 397–431.

Hill, Edwin and Michael Giammatteo. 1963. "Socio-economic status and its relationship to school achievement in the elementary school." *Elementary English* 40: 265–270.

Kohn, Alfie. 1993. *Punished by rewards*. Boston: Houghton Mifflin.

Krashen, Stephen. 1981. *Second language acquisition and second language learning*. New York: Prentice-Hall.

Krashen, Stephen. 1990. "How reading and writing make you smarter, or, how smart people read and write." In James E. Alatis (ed.), *Georgetown University Round Table on Languages and Linguistics 1990*. Washington, D.C.: Georgetown University Press. 364–376.

Krashen, Stephen. 1991. "The input hypothesis: An update." In James E. Alatis (ed.), *Georgetown University Round Table on Languages and Linguistics 1991*. Washington, D.C.: Georgetown University Press. 409–431.

Krashen, Stephen. 1992. *Fundamentals of language education*. Torrance, California: Laredo Publishing Company.

Krashen, Stephen. 1993. *The power of reading*. Englewood, Colorado: Libraries Unlimited.

Krashen, Stephen. 1994a. "The input hypothesis and its rivals." In Nick Ellis (ed.), *Implicit and explicit learning of languages*. New York: Academic Press. 45–77.

Krashen, Stephen. 1994b. "The pleasure hypothesis." In James E. Alatis (ed.), *Georgetown University Round Table on Languages and Linguistics 1994*. Washington, D.C.: Georgetown University Press. 299–322.

Laughrin-Sacco, Steven. 1992. "More than meets the eye: An ethnography of an elementary French class." *Canadian Modern Language Review* 49: 80–101.

Nader, Ralph. 1994. "Interview with David Frost," October 21, 1994. DPTV and GWETA.

Nagy, William, Patricia Herman, and Richard Anderson. 1985. "Learning words from context." *Reading Research Quarterly* 20: 233–253.

Nagy, William and Patricia Herman. 1987. "Breadth and depth of vocabulary knowledge: Implications for acquisition and instruction. " In Margaret G. McKeown and Mary E. Curtis (eds.), *The nature of vocabulary acquisition*. Hillsdale, N.J.: Erlbaum. 19–35.

Rosow, LaVergne. 1995. *In forsaken hands*. Portsmouth, N.H.: Heinemann.

Schoolboys of Barbiana. 1970. *Letter to a teacher*. New York: Vintage Books.

Semb, George and John Ellis. 1994. "Knowledge taught in school: What is remembered?" *Review of Educational Research* 64: 253–286.

Simonton, Dean. 1984. *Genius, creativity, and leadership*. Cambridge, Massachusetts: Harvard University Press.

Simonton, Dean 1988. *Scientific genius*. Cambridge, U.K.: Cambridge University Press.

Simonton, Dean. 1994. *Greatness*. New York: Guilford Press.

Smith, Frank. 1986. *Insult to intelligence*. Portsmouth, N.H.: Heinemann.

Smith, Frank. 1988. *Joining the literacy club*. Portsmouth, N.H.: Heinemann.

Sobel, Dava 1995. "Interview: Mihaly Csikszentmihalyi." *Omni* 17(4): 73-74, 76-77, and 90.

Swain, Merrill. 1985. "Communicate competence: Some roles of comprehensible input and comprehensible output in its development." In Susan Gass and Carolyn Madden (eds.), *Input in second language acquisition*. New York: Newbury House. 235-256.

Wallas, Graham. 1970. "The art of thought." In Philip E. Vernon (ed.), *Creativity*. Baltimore: Penguin. 91-97.

Teacher education and psycholinguistics: Making teachers psycholinguists

Ronald P. Leow
Georgetown University

Introduction. There is a growing awareness that teacher education constitutes one of the most challenging yet rewarding aspects of language instruction today. Making teachers aware of several variables that contribute to language learning and teaching enhances their understanding of what takes place in the classroom and prepares them to make informed decisions while teaching. One area that can contribute tremendously to teachers' understanding of how L2 learners learn/acquire the target language is the field of cognitive science and psychology. This paper will (1) present a brief overview of the cognitive-psychology roots that have guided psycholinguistic studies in second-language acquisition (SLA); (2) review the findings of relevant psycholinguistic studies that have addressed cognitive processes employed by L2 learners in the classroom; and (3) provide some implications that can serve as a guide to what the teachers' role in the foreign-language classroom should be.

Background. The literature abounds with studies that have attempted to theoretically account for or explain the role of cognitive processes in SLA (e.g. Anderson 1983; Bialystok 1978, 1981, 1988, 1990, 1992, 1994; Ellis 1993; Gass 1988; Hulstijn 1989; Hulstijn and Schmidt 1994; Krashen 1982, 1985; Robinson in press; Sharwood Smith 1981, 1986, 1991; Schmidt 1990, 1992, 1993, 1994; Tomlin and Villa 1994; VanPatten 1995). Most of these studies find their roots in cognitive psychology (e.g. Shriffin and Schneider 1977), which recognizes two important distinctions to describe skills development and performance: (1) Shortterm memory store (STM) vs. longterm memory store (LTM) and (2) controlled vs. automatic processes. These two distinctions account for the learning, storage, and production of language. According to Shriffin and Schneider (1977: 155), memory is "conceived to be a large and permanent collection of nodes, which become complexly and increasingly interassociated and interrelated through learning." Each node has a set of informational elements and is usually inactive and passive. When the system of interconnected nodes is in this state, it is called longterm store. When some of these nodes are activated by some external stimulus, these activated nodes refer to shortterm store. Shortterm memory store has its nodes activated in memory at the same time and is quite limited in its capacity to deal with incoming information. Learning takes place when information travels from STM and is linked to existing nodes in LTM to form new associations. Whether these two stores comprise two separate systems and stores (Shriffin 1993) or one interconnected storage place (Baddeley and Hitch 1993; Carlson, Khoo, Yaure, and Schneider 1990) still remains to be resolved.

According to Shriffin and Schneider, these nodes can be activated in two ways, usually referred to as the automatic and controlled modes of information processing. Automatic processing is a learned response generated by a consistent activation of the same input to the same node(s) over a long period of time. Because automatic processes are associated with almost the same set of interconnected nodes, once learned they occur quickly, require a minimum of effort and attention, and are difficult to suppress or modify. On the other hand, controlled processes require a large amount of cognitive effort, are generally conscious, and only permit a limited amount of features to be attended to by learners.

Underlying the limited attentional resources is the metaphor of adult language learners as limited-capacity processors, that is, information contained in the input competes for attentional resources available to the learner (Kahneman 1973; Wickens 1980, 1984, 1989). While Kahneman argues for one pool of resources for the allocation of attention, Wickens proposes multiple resources which are dependent upon the type of task learners participate in and how different these tasks are in their level of difficulty. In other words, different tasks may draw from either the same pool or different pools of resources based on the difficulty-level of the task. He distinguishes between serial and parallel processing. Serial processing occurs when two tasks are being performed simultaneously and resources are being drawn from the same pool (e.g. carrying on two conversations at the same time). Parallel processing occurs when the tasks are distinct and thus draw from different pools of resources (e.g. talking and driving a car simultaneously).

Alongside the distinction between short-term memory store vs. long-term memory store and controlled vs. automatic processes is another distinction that has fueled a plethora of studies—implicit vs. explicit knowledge. The studies cited above have in some way viewed language learning as the internalization of two types of knowledge—implicit (acquired) and explicit (learned) knowledge. Ellis (1993) identifies two kinds of implicit knowledge: Formulaic knowledge (e.g. language chunks) and rule-based knowledge (internalized, generalized, and abstract structures). He also provides three characteristics for explicit knowledge: It is analyzed (that is, it can be described and classified), abstract (that is, it represents some underlying generalization of actual linguistic behavior), and explanatory (that is, it can account for how grammar is used in actual communication). Knowledge can also be viewed from a declarative or procedural perspective (Anderson 1983). According to Anderson, declarative knowledge represents a set of facts while procedural knowledge refers to knowing how to do things. Ellis (1993) argues that there is a difference between these two forms of knowledge by associating implicit/explicit knowledge with intuition/consciousness and declarative/procedural knowledge with the degree of control over the L2 knowledge with reference to the use of effortful controlled processes and effortless automatic processes.

Two positions which differ on the degree of relationship between these two types of knowledge have been put forward—the noninterface and the interface positions. The noninterface position postulates that explicit grammatical knowledge (Krashen 1982) or learned linguistic knowledge (Schwartz 1993) and implicit knowledge or competence are completely separate. To support his claim, Krashen points out (1) the phenomenon of learners who have acquired an L2 without ever having studied it formally; (2) the evidence of learned grammatical items (for example, late-acquired items like English third-person-singular endings) never being acquired; and (3) the inability of learners to acquire the entire range of grammatical rules of the L2. Implications for the classroom would include offering opportunities for real communication to take place via comprehensible input, which would then promote acquisition.

The interface position acknowledges the existence of the two types of knowledge but postulates some degree of interaction between the two. Two types of interface position can be identified—weak and strong. The weak-interface position (Ellis 1993; Seliger 1979) acknowledges the possibility of some overlap between learning and acquisition. Seliger proposes that there are two different types of processes that govern rule-learning and spontaneous communication. In other words, conscious knowledge of a grammatical rule does not necessarily mean that it can be accessed for spontaneous conversation. Ellis (1993) emphasizes in his model the key role that explicit knowledge plays in monitoring, noticing, and noticing-the-gap. In this way, pedagogical rules would make internalization of the L2 rules somewhat easier, provided the learner is psycholinguistically ready (cf. Pienemann 1987), and may serve to facilitate the accessing of seldomly-used, acquired L2 features. Implications for the classroom would include some kind of focus on pedagogical rules that would serve as "acquisition facilitators" or "advance organizers" (Terrell 1991).

The strong-interface position (Bialystok 1981; McLaughlin 1987; McLaughlin, Rossman, and MacLeod 1983; Sharwood Smith 1981) argues that there is a direct link between the two, that is, by practicing new grammatical rules until they become automatized, explicit knowledge can be converted into implicit knowledge. McLaughlin (1987) and McLaughlin, Rossman, and MacLeod (1983) view second-language development as the acquisition of a complex cognitive skill. During the initial stages of learning, there is a slow development of skills that is regulated by controlled processes. Because adult second-language learners are presumed to be limited-capacity processors, they need to practice the features of the L2 until they become automatic. In a similar vein, Bialystok (1981) proposes that the key difference between these two kinds of knowledge is that, whereas implicit knowledge is a system that holds unanalyzed L2 information and functions at an intuitive level, explicit knowledge has a system that holds an analyzed set of L2 features that can be articulated, studied, and manipulated. Bialystok suggests that learning is conscious and that practice provides the opportunity for explicit knowledge to become implicit knowledge.

Inherent in the above cognitive-based theories of second-language acquisition is the question of the role of consciousness in language learning. In many of these studies, consciousness has been closely associated with "awareness" and "attention" (in the sense of a limited-capacity system). McLaughlin (1990) suggests avoiding the umbrella term "consciousness" due to its ambiguity while Schmidt (1994) views the conflation of distinct senses of consciousness as leading to terminological confusion in current research. While acknowledging McLaughlin's suggestion, he proposes that future research on language-learning processes address the following four aspects of consciousness: (1) Consciousness as intentionality (the distinction between intentional vs. incidental L2 learning); (2) consciousness as attention (some amount of attention, noticing, or detection is necessary for language learning to take place); (3) consciousness as awareness (learning on the basis of awareness at the point of learning—explicit learning—or without such awareness—implicit learning); and (4) consciousness as control (theoretically similar to attention, but underscores the contrast between input and output processing).

On the other hand, Tomlin and Villa (1994: 190) prefer to omit the notion of consciousness and view the construct of awareness as a subjective experience of a cognitive event or of an external stimulus which can be measured using the following criteria: (1) A behavioral or cognitive change as a result of the experience; (2) a report of this awareness; and (3) a description of the experience. The notion of attention, in their opinion, is too broad-grained and they further divide it into the following three components: (1) Alertness (an overall readiness to deal with incoming stimuli); (2) orientation (the direction of attentional resources to a certain type of stimuli); and (3) detection (the cognitive registration of the stimuli). Robinson (in press) attempts to reconcile these different positions by positing a definition of noticing that includes noticing plus rehearsal in shortterm memory, prior to being encoded into longterm memory (cf. Cowan 1988, 1993). In this way, according to Robinson, "noticing can be identified with what is both detected and further activated following the allocation of attentional resources from a central executive. The allocation of resources for rehearsal may vary according to the demands of the type of task being performed, which may require data-driven vs. conceptually driven processing (cf. Graf and Ryan 1990; Jacoby 1983). Data-driven processing is encoding stimuli from a bottom-up direction, that is, the visual marks on a printed word, while conceptually-driven processing is top-down and involves more effortful integration of encoded stimuli within their surrounding context, similar to the activation of schemata in longterm memory.

In spite of the terminological vagueness, there are at least two broad theoretical questions that arise from the review provided above. These are: (1) Does the limited-capacity nature of working memory (including the role of consciousness in its broad sense) influence the comprehension, intake, and production of L2 learners? and (2) Does explicit knowledge convert into implicit knowledge? From a pedagogical viewpoint, can we manipulate the input or instruction we expose our students to in such a way that (1) their processing demands can be reduced so that they can reallocate their attention to attend to linguistic form(s) contained in the input, and/or (2) they notice specific linguistic items in the input? Similarly, can we manipulate instruction in such a way that this instruction can have an effect on learners' explicit knowledge which may then lead to implicit knowledge?

VanPatten (1989, 1990) attempted to investigate the attentional capacity of L2 learners in the aural mode. Hypothesizing that early-stage L2 learners cannot attend to both form and meaning simultaneously without experiencing a cognitive overload, his subjects were exposed to aural input in under four different conditions: Group 1 was required to listen for the meaning of the passage only, Group 2 was required to listen for the lexical item *inflación* ("inflation"), Group 3 was required to listen for the definite article *la* ("the"), and Group 4 was required to listen for the third-person-plural morpheme *-n*. He found an overall decrease in comprehension when subjects attended to items that were of less communicative value (*la* and *-n*) as compared to an item of more communicative value (*inflación*), which led him to postulate that learners appear to attend to meaning before form. In addition, VanPatten found that his advanced learners were capable of allocating more attention to form in the input when compared to less-advanced learners and concluded that "only when input is easily understood can learners attend to form as part of the intake process" (1990: 296). In other words, VanPatten argues that until they can process the input without too much conscious attention and effort, learners in the early stages of SLA will only be able to process the input primarily for meaning.

There have only been two published studies to date that have investigated the process of attention in the written mode (Leow 1993; Shook 1994). Leow (1993) investigated the effects of simplification (simplified vs. unsimplified), type of linguistic item (present perfect vs. present subjunctive), and language experience (second semester vs. fourth semester) on learners' intake of Spanish linguistic items contained in written input. He made the following hypotheses: (1) Simplified input should reduce the processing demands required to process for meaning, which in turn should facilitate learners' intake of the linguistic items under focus; (2) due to its more "communicative" value, learners should be able to attend significantly more to the present-perfect form than the present-subjunctive form in the input; and (3) learners with more language experience should be able to reallocate their cognitive capacity in order to attend significantly more to the linguistic items in the input than learners with less language experience. Subjects were exposed to written input in one of the four conditions: Simplified or unsimplified input with the present-perfect form, or simplified or unsimplified input with the present-subjunctive form. He found that reducing learners' cognitive demands to processing for meaning by simplification did not produce any significant increase in their intake of the linguistic items contained in the input, results that were corroborated in a follow-up study in the aural mode (Leow 1995). In other words, there is no evidence that learners reallocate their attention to form when their processing demands to attend to meaning are reduced. In effect these results provide support for researchers who question the effects of external manipulation of the input and who provide a stronger role for learners' internal mechanisms that may not necessarily be impacted by this external manipulation (e.g. Gleitman, Newport, and Gleitman 1984; Sharwood Smith 1991; White 1984).

With respect to linguistic items in the input, Leow (1993, 1995) found modality to be a contributing factor to what learners take in from the input. Results from both studies indicate that L2 learners were only able to take in significantly more perfect tense forms when compared to subjunctive forms when this input was made available in the aural mode. It was suggested that the phonological aspect of the two forms may be an important factor that can influence the choice of either form. In addition, in both studies, advanced learners performed significantly better than less-advanced learners, indicating that these two groups of learners are not regulated by the same cognitive processes when exposed to both written and aural input.

Probably the first study to address the notion of input enhancement in the written mode is the study by Shook (1994) who investigated the effects of type of saliency of grammatical information contained in written input on learners' intake of two linguistic items, the present perfect and the relative pronoun (*que* and *quien*) in Spanish. Subjects were divided into three groups: The first was exposed to the text alone, the second was exposed to the grammatical items bolded with no instructions, and the third received a text similar to that of the second group together with the request to deduce a grammatical rule for the bolded items. Shook found significant effects for saliency of grammatical items on learners' intake of grammatical information contained in written input. Like Leow (1993, 1995) and VanPatten (1989, 1990), his results also indicated different processing for different linguistic items, where the perfect-tense form was taken in more significantly than the relative form. However, he also found a mixed bag of findings with respect to language experience: Second-year learners performed better than first-year learners on the present-perfect production task, but this finding was the opposite for the relative-pronoun production task.

Arguably what has been most investigated from a psycho-linguistic perspective are the effects of formal instruction on learners' behavioral patterns in the classroom. Formal instruction has been investigated in the classroom from the following perspectives: Consciousness-raising or input enhancement (e.g. Carroll, Roberge, and Swain 1992; Doughty 1991; Fotos 1993, 1994; Fotos and Ellis 1991; Harley 1989; Lightbown and Spada 1990; Spada and Lightbown 1993; Tomasello and Herron 1989, 1991; White, Spada, Lightbown, and Ranta 1991), and "input processing" (Cadierno 1995; VanPatten and Cadierno 1993; VanPatten and Sanz in press). These studies, which have found overall positive effects, make direct or indirect references to the notion of attention, be it "noticing" (which Schmidt 1990, 1992, 1993, and 1994 claims is essential for intake to occur) or attending to both form and meaning in the input via some kind of external manipulation of the input by the teacher. Input was enhanced in these studies by providing subjects with metalinguistic information, negative or positive feedback through overt error correction, numerous examples of the structure under study, opportunities to engage in information-sharing activities, and/or explicit discussion of the linguistic feature. It should be noted, however, that while it may be argued that the positive effects were achieved by drawing in part on the learners' attention to the linguistic form(s) in the input, these studies have not provided an explanation as to how this works (Tomlin and Villa 1994).

Consciousness-raising, as defined by Ellis (1992: 234), is "an attempt to equip the learner with an understanding of a specific grammatical feature—to develop declarative rather than procedural knowledge of it." In other words, this type of instruction is designed to develop an explicit knowledge of grammar and invokes the notion of attention. However, this description was later changed to input enhancement as it was felt to be too focused on learners' internal processes. As a result, input enhancement focuses less on learners' internal processes and more on the characteristics of the input.

Fotos and Ellis (1991) investigated the effects of explicit instruction designed to promote consciousness-raising of indirect object placement in English by Japanese EFL learners via a "grammar communication task" at two institutions (a college and a university). This task was designed to integrate grammar instruction with activities designed to promote opportunities for communication involving an exchange of information (p. 606). The focus of the task was more on cognitive understanding than on acquisition. Subjects were divided into three groups: Group 1 participated in the grammar communication task (the task group); Group 2 received the traditional teacher-fronted instruction (the traditional group); and Group 3 did not receive instructional exposure. Results indicate that at the college level, there was no difference in performance on a grammaticality-judgment task designed to measure learners' explicit knowledge of the L2 feature between the task and traditional groups. At the university level, results revealed that the traditional group performed significantly better than the task group on the posttest after the treatment. It was also found that gains made by the task group disappeared by the delayed posttest administered two weeks later.

Fotos (1993) extended Fotos and Ellis' (1991) study by attempting to address the effects of consciousness-raising grammar instruction on the amount of noticing of the formal feature(s) under study (indirect-object placement, adverb placement, and relative-clause usage). Once more the subjects (one hundred sixty Japanese EFL learners) were divided into the task group, the traditional group, and the control group. Meeting for ninety minutes once a week, subjects were exposed to each L2 structure in one class session and participated in noticing exercises performed in the subsequent two sessions. Noticing was operationalized in this study as the ability to recognize and underline the structure embedded in either a short story or a dictation exercise. Results from a grammaticality-judgment task and a sentence-production task revealed that, on the adverb placement and relative-clause usage tasks, both instructed groups performed significantly better than the control group. However, no difference was found between the traditional and task groups. On the indirect-object-pronoun task, while the same results were found between the instructed groups and the control group, it was also found that the traditional group noticed the linguistic feature considerably more when compared to the task group.

Tomasello and Herron (1988, 1989) investigated the role of different kinds of feedback on the learning of eight grammatical exceptions (the contractions *du* and *au*, *mon*+masculine singular noun, *ne*+verb+*pas de*, *dites*, *cet*+masculine-singular noun, *meilleur*, and *-er* imperatives) found to be problematic to adult English-speaking learners of French. Subjects were exposed to one of two types of instruction: The Garden Path and Control conditions. The Garden Path condition is rooted in Nelson's (1987) cognitive-comparison model of language acquisition in which the teacher first induces the learners to orally produce an error by overgeneralizing the pattern, and then correcting the error both orally and by writing the correct form on the blackboard, and following this up with a grammatical explanation. In the Control condition, the teacher pointed out the exception before any generalization could be made and then followed a similar correction procedure as in the Garden Path condition. They concluded that negative feedback can affect learners' responses in an instructional setting where the focus is on explicit grammar instruction by aiding learners to focus their attention on the rule and its features, thereby reducing the effects of generalization. However, as Carroll, Roberge, and Swain (1992: 177) point out, these studies did not address the role of feedback on the unconscious (implicit) processes of acquisition, that is, the ways in which error correction can help learners "cognize" (in Chomskyan terminology) the right rule in the first place.

Carroll, Roberge, and Swain (1992) set out to investigate the effects of feedback (explicit correction) on the learning of morphological generalizations. Their subjects were seventy-nine intermediate and advanced adult English speakers enrolled in university classes. The subjects were trained on two rules of French suffixation (-*age* and -*ment*) and then divided into two groups and exposed to one of two conditions: Experimental (where subjects received immediate feedback on their mistakes) and comparison (where subjects received no corrective feedback). All subjects then "guessed" responses to novel stimuli and were retested twice, the second retest administered one week after the first. Results indicate that while the experimental group performed significantly better than the comparison group, no difference was found between the two groups on their learned generalizations. Advanced subjects, however, appeared to benefit more substantially than the intermediate subjects on the learning of absolute exceptions.

Doughty (1991) addressed the acquisition of English relative clauses in a carefully-controlled, computerized study. Based on the Noun Phrase Accessibility Hierarchy (Keenan and Comrie 1977), she selected subjects who appeared to be ready to acquire relative clauses, divided them into three groups and then exposed them to three different types of a computer-assisted reading lesson: (1) A meaning-oriented group that had the relevant clauses highlighted by typographical means; (2) a form-oriented group that received explicit grammatical information on the relative clauses in addition to the highlighted exposure; and (3) a control group that read the text with relative clauses but did not receive the physical highlighting of grammatical information that the other two groups received. Results indicate that while all three groups improved on the posttest when compared to the pretest, the two groups that received additional instruction improved significantly more than the control group. Furthermore, Doughty found that the meaning-oriented group demonstrated superior comprehension of the text than the other two groups, as measured by a recall task. While the study did not address the longterm effects of instruction, it did demonstrate immediate positive effects for instruction and provided support for the hierarchical relative-clause framework postulated by other studies (e.g. Eckman, Bell, and Nelson 1988).

The following studies were conducted in immersion settings comprising anglo- and francophone children (between the ages of ten and fourteen) attending classes in a communicative-language-teaching framework. Prevalent in this setting were meaning-based activities, group work that promoted the negotiation of meaning, the provision of rich, varied, and comprehensible input, and occasional error correction (Lightbown and Spada 1990: 434). Lightbown and Spada investigated the spontaneous oral production of problematic linguistic structures (the plural and progressive morphemes -*s* and -*ing*, respectively, adjective placement in noun phrases, gender in possessive determiners, and presentational *have* and *be*) by their subjects over a period of five months. Using a "Picture Card Game" to elicit subjects' spontaneous oral production, they found tentative support for the contribution of form-based instruction in a communicative framework to an improvement of linguistic knowledge and performance.

In a later study under similar learning conditions, Spada and Lightbown (1993) investigated the longterm effects of form-focused instruction together with corrective feedback on learners' spontaneous production of English question formation. Subjects were ESL Grade 5 and 6 students who comprised two groups: An experimental group (who were exposed to two weeks—about nine hours—of form-focus instruction and corrective feedback) and a control group (who did not receive this type of instruction). Using a variation of the "Picture Card Game" to elicit subjects' spontaneous oral production, they found, somewhat to their surprise, that the control group performed as well as or even better than the experimental group. According to Spada and Lightbown, this finding was most likely due to the type of instruction that actually took place in the classroom, where there was indeed focus on form, thereby erasing any distinction between the two groups.

Harley (1989) investigated the effects of a functional approach to the teaching of the French preterit and imperfect tenses to Grade 6 anglophone learners in an immersion setting. A multiassessment-task approach (including both written and oral tasks) was used to measure learners' proficiency in these two past tenses. Using a posttest and delayed posttest design, Harley found a positive shortterm effect that disappeared by the time the delayed posttest was administered.

Input-processing instruction (defined as explanation and practice/experience processing the input data) differs from traditional instruction (defined as explanation and output practice of a grammatical point) by focusing instruction at learners' intake level instead of their output level. It is claimed that instruction designed to alter the psycholinguistic strategies learners use to make form–meaning connections when exposed to L2 data will provide the L2 system with richer grammatical intake. In other words, the crucial hypothesis of this type of instruction is that formal instruction needs to highlight or make salient L2 linguistic forms which may then be noticed by L2 learners. Instructionally, Cadierno (1995) and VanPatten and Cadierno (1993) studied the effects of type of instruction (input-processing vs. traditional vs. control) on the interpretation and written production of the Spanish past tense and object pronouns respectively. They found that learners exposed to input-processing instruction performed significantly better on the interpretation task when compared to the other two groups, and these effects were held constant on a second and third posttest conducted one week and one month after the treatment respectively.

However, no difference was found on the written production task between the input-processing and traditional groups which both performed significantly better than the control group. This superior performance over the control group was maintained on both the second and third posttests. VanPatten and Sanz (in press), while corroborating these results, also found that processing instruction positively affected both oral and written production, albeit on a shortterm basis.

Implications for the language teacher. Based on the review above, what are some implications for language teachers? The following areas will be discussed: (1) Learners as limited-capacity processors; (2) type of linguistic items; (3) language experience; (4) mode of exposure; (5) pedagogical input presentation (including formal instruction and exposure); and (6) task-based approaches to language learning and teaching.

Learners as limited-capacity processors. If we accept the cognitive-psychological notion of adult learners as limited-capacity processors, then we need to consider this cognitive limitation in the classroom when we select the input (e.g. type, amount, etc.) or task (difficulty level) to which we want to expose our students. For example, we need to make an effort to reduce learners' attentional demands by (1) selecting input (aural or written) that will not potentially cause a cognitive overload, (2) allowing more time to process the input, and (3) activating existent or prior knowledge or providing advance organizers before a task is attempted.

Type of linguistic items. We need to be aware that all linguistic items do not appear to be processed in a similar manner. Research appears to indicate that relatively salient linguistic items are more likely to be processed by learners than items that may not contribute meaningfully to the overall comprehension of the input. Consequently, we need to consider the type of linguistic item to which we we want to expose our students based on the meaningfulness of the item, for example verbal forms versus nonverbal forms such as relative pronouns.

Language experience. While language experience appears to impact how learners process input, we still need to be aware that the type of task and the type of linguistic item may play a role in narrowing this difference.

Mode of exposure. It appears that modality may have an impact on how and what learners take in from the input to which they are exposed. We need to be aware that cognitive processing may be more constrained depending upon the mode of exposure, and that input presented in one mode may be taken in differently in another. Future research addressing the effects of modality is certainly warranted before we can derive strong implications for the classroom from this area of investigation.

Pedagogical input presentation. Based on the current research on the role of consciousness in SLA, together with the associated constructs of attention, awareness and noticing, it appears that for intake to take place, some form of noticing, detection, and/or noticing and rehearsal is crucial. However, at present there is some terminological confusion as to how to define and operationalize these constructs, and research designs have not been robust enough to provide definitive implications for language practice. Thus some caution is warranted at the present moment.

Subsumed under pedagogical input presentation is research on formal instruction and exposure to grammatical information. Most psycholinguistic studies reveal positive effects for instruction, albeit for the most part shortterm, so the question at present is not whether formal instruction is necessary but what type of psycholinguistic instruction or exposure is more beneficial for our students and which type can promote longterm performance. If we accept that some form of "noticing" is required for input to become intake in the classroom setting, then we need to make more salient the grammatical items in the input. In addition, because most effects of formal instruction or exposure appear to be shortterm, exposure should be lengthened or recycled in order to strengthen the link between students' shortterm memory store and their longterm memory store via the reactivation of knowledge bases.

Because we cannot guarantee that learners are attending to the input we are exposing them to, one way to improve this situation may be to ensure that they are alert and focused on the linguistic item(s) being promoted in the lesson period by involving them more actively in the processing of grammatical features of the L2. Moreover, formal instruction and exposure to grammatical features should be both teacher-fronted and learner-centered. In this way, learners are considered more as "constructors" and not "recipients" of grammatical knowledge (Mayer 1992; cf. also Adair-Hauck, Donato, and Cumo 1994). As to whether explicit knowledge converts into implicit knowledge, this theoretical question is far from answered.

Task-based approaches to language learning and teaching. Capacity theories that have suggested the deployment of attentional resources to cope with task demands have already led some researchers to propose designing specific tasks that can promote the act of noticing on the learners' part. While traditional instruction focuses specifically on grammatical features, task-based approaches, according to Long (1991) and Schmidt (1990), can enhance how learners notice features of syntax, vocabulary, and phonology that are not perceptually and psychologically salient to the learner (cf. Doughty 1991; Hulstijn 1989). In the area of syllabus design, Long and Crookes (1992) argue that in a task syllabus, when combined with a focus on form (as compared to specific focus on forms, that is grammar) in task-based language teaching, the task receives more support in second-language acquisition research as a viable unit around which to organize language teaching and learning opportunities. Wickens' (1989) model of the structure of multiple resources hypothesizes that noticing will tend to be superior when the learner participates in dual-tasks that do not compete for attentional resources from the same resource pools. Once concurrently performed tasks do not draw from identical resource pools, or one of the tasks can be performed automatically, the learner will be able to allocate more attentional resources to processing the input. Tasks suggested by research that are designed to facilitate learners' noticing of grammatical features in the input are "describe and arrange" (Ur 1988), the one-way information gap "draw the picture" (Gass and Varonis 1985), and "assemble the scene" (Pica, Doughty, and Young 1987). There are two excellent books out at present that are informative in this area: *Tasks in a pedagogical context: Integrating theory and practice* edited by Crookes and Gass (1993) and *Making communicative language teaching happen* by Lee and VanPatten (1995).

Conclusion. To conclude, the field of cognitive psychology has made some inroads into the field of second-language-acquisition research which, in turn, is impacting to a certain extent on language practice in the foreign-language classroom. While psycholinguistic research in SLA is still in its infancy at present, it can still inform and promote language teachers' awareness and understanding of the cognitive aspects of language learning in the formal classroom, an awareness and understanding that comprise an essential component of any teacher-education program.

REFERENCES

Adair-Hauck, Bonnie. Richard Donato, and Philomena Cumo. 1994. "Chapter 6: Using a whole language approach to teach grammar." In Judith L. Schrum and E. W. Glisan (eds.), *Teacher's handbook: Contextualized language instruction*. Boston, Massachusetts: Heinle and Heinle. 90–111.

Anderson, John R. 1985. *Cognitive psychology and its implications, Second edition*. New York: Freeman.

Baddeley, A. and G. Hitch. 1986. "Working memory." In G. Bower (ed.), *Recent advances in learning and motivation*. New York: Academic Press. 47–90.

Bialystok, Ellen. 1979. "An analytical view of second language competence: A model and some evidence." *Modern Language Journal* 63: 257–262.

Bialystok, Ellen. 1981. "Some evidence for the integrity and interaction of two knowledge sources." In Roger Andersen (ed.), *New dimensions in second language acquisition research*. Rowley, Massachusetts: Newbury House.

Bialystok, Ellen. 1988. "Psycholinguistic dimensions of second language proficiency." In William Rutherford and Michael Sharwood Smith (eds.), *Grammar and second language teaching*. New York: Newbury House.

Bialystok, Ellen. 1991. "Achieving proficiency in a second language: A processing description." In Robert Phillipson, E. Kellerman, Larry Selinker, Michael Sharwood Smith, and Merrill Swain (eds.), *Foreign/second language pedagogy research*. Clevedon, U.K.: Multilingual Matters. 63–78.

Bialystok, Ellen. 1994. "Analysis and control in the development of second language proficiency." *Studies in Second Language Acquisition* 16: 157–168.

Cadierno-López, Teresa. 1995. "Formal instruction from a processing perspective: An investigation into the Spanish past tense." *The Modern Language Journal* 79: 179–193.

Carlson, R.A., B.H. Khoo, R.G. Yaure, and W. Schneider. 1990. "Acquisition of a problem solving skill: Levels of organization and the use of working memory." *Journal of Experimental Psychology: General* 119: 193–214.

Carroll, Susanne, Yves Roberge, and Merrill Swain. 1992. "The role of feedback in adult second language acquisition: Error correction and morphological generalizations." *Applied Psycholinguistics* 13: 173–198.

Cowan, Nelson. 1988. "Evolving conceptions of memory storage, selective attention and their mutual constraints within the human information processing system." *Psychological Bulletin* 104: 163–191.

Cowan, Nelson. 1993. "Activation, attention, and shortterm memory." *Memory and Cognition* 21: 162–167.

Crookes, Graham and Susan M. Gass (eds.). 1993. *Tasks in a pedagogical context: Integrating theory and practice*. Clevedon, U.K.: Multilingual Matters.

Doughty, Catherine. 1991. "Second language instruction does make a difference." *Studies in Second Language Acquisition* 13: 431–469.

Eckman, Fred R., Lawrence Bell, and Diane Nelson. 1988. "On the generalization of relative clause instruction in the acquisition of English as a second language." *Applied Linguistics* 9: 1–20.

Ellis, Rod. 1993. "The structural syllabus and second language acquisition." *TESOL Quarterly* 27: 91–113.

Fotos, Sandra S. 1993. "Consciousness raising and noticing through focus on form: Grammar task performance versus formal instruction." *Applied Linguistics* 14: 385–407.

Fotos, Sandra S. and Rod Ellis. 1991. "Communicating about grammar: A task-based approach." *TESOL Quarterly* 25: 605–628.

Gass, Susan M. 1988. "Integrating research areas: A framework for second language studies." *Applied Linguistics* 9: 198–217.

Gleitman, Lila R., Elissa L. Newport, and Henry Gleitman. 1984. "The current status of the motherese hypothesis." *Journal of Child Language* 11: 43–79.

Harley, Birgit. 1989. "Functional grammar in French immersion: A classroom experiment." *Applied Linguistics* 10: 331–359.

Hulstijn, Jan H. 1989. "Implicit and incidental second language learning: Experiments in the processing of natural and partially artificial input." In Hans W. Dechert and Manfred Raupach (eds.), *Interlingual processes*. Tübingen, Germany: G. Narr. 49–73.

Hulstijn, Jan H. and Schmidt, Richard. 1994. "Guest editors' introduction." In Jan H. Hulstijn and Richard Schmidt (eds.), *AILA Review: Consciousness and second language learning; Conceptual, methodological and practical issues in language learning and teaching* 11: 5–10.

Kahneman, Daniel. 1973. *Attention and effort*. Englewood Cliffs, N.J.: Prentice Hall.

Keenan, Edward L. and Bernard Comrie. 1977. "Noun phrase accessibility and universal grammar." *Linguistic Inquiry* 8: 63–99.

Krashen, Stephen D. 1982. *Principles and practice in second language acquisition*. Oxford and New York: Pergamon.

Lee, James F. and Bill VanPatten. 1995. *Making communicative language teaching happen*. New York: McGraw-Hill.

Leow, Ronald P. 1993. "To simplify or not to simplify: A look at intake." *Studies in Second Language Acquisition* 15: 333-355.

Leow, Ronald P. 1995. "Modality and intake in second language acquisition." *Studies in Second Language Acquisition* 17: 79-89.

Lightbown, Patsy M. 1983. "Exploring relationships between developmental and instructional sequences in L2 acquisition." In Herbert W. Seliger and Michael H. Long (eds.), *Classroom-oriented research in second language acquisition*. Rowley, Massachusetts: Newbury House. 217-245.

Lightbown, Patsy M. 1985. "Can language acquisition be altered by instruction?" In K. Hyltenstain and Manfred Pienemann (eds.), *Modelling and assessing SLA*. San Diego, California: College-Hill Press. 101-112.

Lightbown, Patsy M. and Nina M. Spada. (1990). "Focus-on-form and corrective feedback in communicative language teaching: Effects on second language learning." *Studies in Second Language Acquisition* 12: 429-448.

Lightbown, Patsy M., Nina M. Spada, and Robert Wallace. 1980. "Some effects of instruction on child and adolescent ESL learners." In Robin C. Scarcella and Stephen D. Krashen (eds.), *Research in second language acquisition*. Rowley, Massachusetts: Newbury House. 162-172.

Long, Michael H. 1991. "Focus on form: A design feature in language teaching methodology." In Kees de Bot, Ralph B. Ginsberg, and Claire Kramsch (eds.), *Foreign language research in cross-cultural perspective*. Philadelphia: John Benjamins. 39-52.

Long, Michael H. and Graham Crookes. 1992. "Three approaches to task-based syllabus design." *TESOL Quarterly* 26: 27-57.

Mayer, Richard E. 1992. "Cognition and instruction: Their historic meeting within educational psychology." *Journal of Educational Psychology* 84: 405-412.

McLaughlin, Barry. 1978. "The monitor model: Some methodological considerations." *Language Learning* 28: 309-332.

McLaughlin, Barry. 1987. *Theories of second language learning*. London: Edward Arnold, 1987.

McLaughlin, Barry. 1990. " 'Conscious' vs. 'unconscious' learning." *TESOL Quarterly* 24: 617-634.

McLaughlin, Barry, Tammy Rossman, and Beverly McLeod. 1987. "Second-language learning: An information-processing perspective." *Language Learning* 33: 135-158.

Nelson, K. 1987. "Some observatons from the perspective of the rare event cognitive comparison theory of language acquisition." In K. Nelson and A. Kleeck (eds.), *Children's language, Volume 6*. Hillsdale N.J.: Lawrence Erlbaum. 289-331.

Pica, Teresa, Catherine Doughty, and Richard Young. 1987. "The impact of interaction on comprehension." *TESOL Quarterly* 21: 737-758.

Pienemann, Manfred. 1984. "Psychological constraints on the teachability of languages." *Studies in Second Language Acquisition* 6: 186-214.

Robinson, Peter. In press. "Attention, memory and the 'noticing' hypothesis. *Language Learning* 45: 321-369.

Sanz, Cristina. 1993. *Multiple assessment of the effects of input-based explicit instruction in grammar on L2 output*. Unpublished Ph.D. dissertation, University of Illinois at Urbana-Champaign.

Schmidt, Richard. 1990. "The role of consciousness in second language learning." *Applied Linguistics* 11: 129-158.

Schmidt, Richard. 1992. "Awareness and second language acquisition." *Annual Review of Applied Linguistics* 13: 206-226.

Schmidt, Richard. 1994. "Deconstructing consciousness in search of useful definitions for applied linguistics." In Jan H. Hulstijn and Richard Schmidt (eds.), *AILA Review: Consciousness and second language learning; Conceptual, methodological and practical issues in language learning and teaching* 11: 11-26.

Schneider, Walter. 1993. "Varieties of working memory as seen in biology and in connectionist/control architectures." *Memory and Cognition* 21: 184–192.

Schwartz, Bonnie. 1993. "On explicit and negative data effecting and affecting competence and linguistic behavior." *Studies in Second Language Acquisition* 15: 147–163.

Seliger, Herbert W. 1979. "On the nature and function of language rules in language teaching." *TESOL Quarterly* 13: 359–369.

Sharwood Smith, Michael. 1981. "Consciousness-raising and the second language learner." *Applied Linguistics* 2: 159–169.

Sharwood Smith, Michael. 1991. "Speaking to many minds: On the relevance of different types of language information for the L2 learner." *Second Language Research* 17: 118–136.

Shook, David J. 1994. "FL/L2 reading, grammatical information, and the input-to-intake phenomenon." *Applied Language Learning 5:* 57-93.

Shriffin, R.M. 1993. "Shortterm memory: A brief commentary." *Memory and Cognition* 21: 193–197.

Shriffin, R.M. and Waltert Schneider. 1977. "Controlled and automatic human information processing II: Perceptual learning, automatic attending, and a general theory." *Psychological Review* 84: 127–190.

Spada, Nina M. and Patsy M. Lightbown. 1993. "Instruction and the development of questions in L2 classrooms." *Studies in Second Language Acquisition* 15: 205–224.

Terrell, Tracy D. 1991. "The role of grammar instruction in a communicative approach." *Modern Language Journal* 75: 52–63.

Tomasello, Michael and Carol Herron. 1988. "Down the garden path: Inducing and correcting overgeneralization errors in the foreign language classroom." *Applied Psycholinguistics* 9: 237–246.

Tomasello, Michael and Carol Herron. 1989. "Feedback for language transfer errors: The garden path technique." *Studies in Second Language Acquisition* 11: 385–395.

Tomlin, Russell S. and Victor Villa. 1994. "Attention in cognitive science and second language acquisition." *Studies in Second Language Acquisition* 16: 183–203.

Ur, Penny. 1988. *Grammar practice activities: A guide for teachers.* New York: Cambridge University Press.

VanPatten, Bill. 1989. "Can learners attend to form and content while processing input?" *Hispania* 72: 409–417.

VanPatten, Bill. 1990. "Attending to form and content in the input: An experiment in consciousness." *Studies in Second Language Acquisition* 12: 287–301.

VanPatten, Bill. 1995. "Cognitive aspects of input processing in second language acquisition." In Peggy Hashemipour, Ricardo Maldonaldo, and Margaret van Naerssen (eds.), *Studies in language learning and Spanish linguistics: In honor of Tracy D. Terrell.* New York: McGraw-Hill. 170–183.

VanPatten, Bill and Teresa Cadierno. 1993. "Input processing and second language acquisition: A role for instruction." *Modern Language Journal* 77: 45–57.

VanPatten, Bill and Cristina Sanz. (in press). "From input to output: Processing instruction and comminicative tasks." In Fred Eckman (ed.), *Second Language Acquisition Theory and Pedagogy.* Hillsdale, N.J.: Erlbaum.

White, Lydia. 1984. "Against comprehensible input: The input hypothesis and the development of second language competence." *Applied Linguistics* 8: 95–110.

White, Lydia. 1991. "Adverb placement in second language acquisition: Some effects of positive and negative evidence in the classroom." *Second Language Research* 7: 133–161.

White, Lydia, Nina M. Spada, Patsy M. Lightbown, and Leila Ranta. 1991. "Input enhancement and second language question formation." *Applied Linguistics* 4: 416–432.

Wickens, Christopher D. 1978. "The structure of attentional resources." In Raymond S. Nickerson (ed.), *Attention and performance VIII.* Hillsdale, N.J.: Lawrence Erlbaum. 239–257.

Wickens, Christopher D. 1984. "Processing resources in attention." In Raja Parasuraman and D.R. Davies (eds.), *Varieties of attention*. New York: Academic Press. 63–102.

Wickens, Christopher D. 1989. "Attention and skilled performance." In Dennis H. Holding (ed.), *Human skills*. New York: John Wiley. 71–105.

Teaching language and teaching language learners: The expanding roles and expectations of language teachers in communicative, content-based classrooms

Teresa Pica[1]
University of Pennsylvania

Introduction. Teaching language and teaching language learners are activities that have always been expected of language teachers. Yet their roles in these activities have expanded considerably in recent years. So too have expectations about the scope of their practice and its educational outcomes. Such expectations are not the teachers' alone, but are shared along with their students, their program administrators, the wider society, and the academic institutions that prepare them for this work.

This expansion in roles and expectations for teachers has paralleled an expansion in the dimensions of language competence that are expected of the language learner. Whereas learners' competence used to be defined within the scope of their knowledge and application of grammar and vocabulary, it is now believed that learners need to acquire what most language educators refer to as "communicative competence." This construct, which is based on the seminal work of Hymes (1972) and Savignon (1972), has come to stand for what learners can do with language in terms of four principal dimensions of language use—the linguistic, sociolinguistic, discoursal, and strategic—which were set forth by Canale and Swain over a decade ago. (See Canale and Swain 1980) Thus it is now widely held that most language learners, especially those of English as a second language, need to acquire another language, not as a static, unapplied system, but as an instrument for spoken and written communication and as a means of access to, and mastery of, academic, professional, and other kinds of utilitarian content.

Within this context, teachers' work in teaching language has come to defined as their work with language learners. Teachers are expected to provide them with experiences in language, communication, and content, not as separate entities, but as interwoven aspects of communicative competence. As such, these experiences must integrate learning processes with learner purposes, so that

---

[1] This article was written while Teresa Pica was the Ethel G. Carruth Associate Professor of Education at the Graduate School of Education, University of Pennsylvania.

learners can learn language through processes of communication and content learning as they use language for purposes of communication and content learning. This approach has made for a sound, sensible, and successful pedagogy, whose theoretical consistencies and empirical outcomes have, for many years, sustained a great deal of attention and applause. (See, for example, Brinton, Snow, and Wesche 1989; Cantoni-Harvey 1987; Genesee 1987; Krashen and Terrell 1983; Mohan 1986.)

The sustained attention that has been given to communicative, content-oriented pedagogy has also brought it under a good deal of scrutiny. The scrutiny has come from several directions. As will be discussed throughout this chapter, the scrutiny has come empirically, through focused studies and finely tuned analyses of classroom activities and learning outcomes, theoretically, through the application of increasingly sophisticated theoretical views on language learning, and professionally, through the addition of teachers' voices to institutional channels of discourse on language policy and classroom practice.

Overall, these efforts and their outcomes have served to validate the integration of language, communication, and content as a feasible approach toward helping learners master the multiple dimensions of communicative competence. And yet, the outcomes of these efforts have raised a number of concerns about the effectiveness of such a pedagogy, and have begun to dampen somewhat the applause it has enjoyed for so long.

These concerns, expressed by both language teachers and language-learning researchers, suggest that the interface of language, communication, and content in the classroom may not be an optimal way for teachers to help learners meet their purposes for language learning and assist them in the language-learning processes believed to guide this effort.

The purpose of this article, therefore, is to highlight a number of current concerns about the teaching of language learners for purposes in, and through processes of, communication and content learning, and to address these concerns within the context of second-language-acquisition theory and research. In view of the theme of this volume, the education of language teachers, the paper begins by noting several professional concerns.

Communication, content learning, and professional concerns. For language teachers at work in their classrooms, or preparing for work in preservice or inservice settings, an increasing array of responsibilities is at hand. These responsibilities, when viewed in a positive light, might be described as expanding, but they have become, all too often, impossibly demanding, for the teachers as individuals and for language education, as a field of study and a domain of professional activity.

As individuals, teachers have been called on to orient their classrooms toward communication and to organize them around meaningful content, through the use of authentic materials, activities, and assignments. When content is of a specialized nature, chosen to assist the learner's language needs in academic or professional areas, it can be outside of the educational and professional preparation or backgrounds of teachers, and thereby can pose considerable challenges to the their credibility, comfort, and effectiveness in the classroom. As Snow (1991: 326) suggests in describing content-centered language learning, it is the language teachers' ability to work with the content of students' curricula that is one of the most challenging, yet necessary, aspects of their work.

Challenges also face the profession of language education, as language teachers working in elementary- and secondary-school supported and sheltered classes, community-college tutoring centers, and university adjunct courses are expected to serve their students through work that, to many teachers, has seemed more like academic-content remediation than language education. (See Benesch 1988, 1992.) In their quest to assist language learners, some teachers have claimed that they have felt reduced to tutors, their success determined by how well their students could master subject matter that originated in the classrooms of other teachers, themselves unable to accommodate the students' needs. (See again Benesch 1992; as well as Gaies 1991; Gantzer 1991; Spack 1988.)

What can language teachers and teacher educators do to shape and focus their ever-expanding roles in ways that enhance, rather than dilute, their status as language educators? How should they direct their efforts to provide an environment in which learners' experiences in communication and content learning can integrate the processes and purposes of language learning? What should they expect of their students and themselves? Ultimately, these questions require such wide-ranging, often complex, answers at classroom, societal, and policy levels, that teachers may feel powerless to address them as they carry out their daily work. Yet much practical information can be gained by examining these questions within the small, but vital, context of second-language-acquisition theory and research. It is to that effort that we now turn.

Communication and content learning for communicative competence.
A vast amount of work has been published on communicative and content-based curricula and classrooms, the theoretical bases for their relationship to learners' needs for communicative competence, and the activities appropriate to their implementation. Thus much has been has been published on the construction of syllabi that specify notions and functions for language use, the adaptation and application of authentic materials and activities to the classroom, the implementation of classroom procedures that promote learner involvement, and the integration of language and content across the curriculum. There has been an ongoing proliferation of texts and edited works devoted to these topics, from earlier collections and volumes in the 1970s. (See, for example, Brumfit and Johnson 1979; Munby 1978), to a vast array of contributions throughout the following decade (such as Brinton, Snow, and Wesche 1989; Candlin 1981;

Johnson and Morrow 1981; Finocchiaro and Brumfit 1983; Nunan 1988, 1989; Omaggio 1986; Prabhu 1987; Savignon 1983; Yalden 1983, 1987), with continuation into the 1990s (with Brown 1994 and Nunan 1991, among others.)

With respect to content-based programs, the published literature reflects a much broader and more balanced range of interests and a good deal more empirical work. This latter has often been carried out on students' language accomplishments, particularly in French-immersion contexts. However, a greater amount of this research has highlighted learners' academic attainment and mastery of subject-matter content than their attainment of communicative competence in its multiple dimensions and details. When students' language learning has been evaluated, this has been usually done through comparisons with language learning under more traditional approaches. It is emphasized that content learning does not interfere with language learning (both first and second), rather than how it is that content and communication can account for language-learning success. (See, for example, Genesee 1987; Harley 1989; Harley and Swain 1984; Lafayette and Buscaglia 1985; Snow 1991.) Such accomplishments have served to validate many of the goals and practices of communicative and content-based classrooms, but have left the field of language education with questions about their impact on language learning.

Quite notably, a number of researchers have documented innovative classroom activities within communication and content-oriented programs of language study. (See, for example, DiPietro 1987; Prabhu 1987.) In addition, several studies have shown that students are learning quite a bit of language in communicative classrooms. (See, for example, Montgomery and Eisenstein 1986; Spada 1986, 1987.) Of particular note, learners and their teachers report a greater sense of relaxation among them in such contexts, along with confidence about their language studies. (See Boyd-Kletzander, in preparation.) Further, the greater amount of research that has been carried out on content learning programs has revealed a good deal of success in learners' communicative competence overall, certainly better than that observed among their peers in less innovative contexts, particularly in the areas of comprehension skills and spoken fluency. (See Lightbown and Spada 1990; Spada and Lightbown 1993; Swain 1984; Swain and Lapkin 1982.)

Increasingly, however, research has made it clear that the participation of learners in activities that are communicative and based on meaningful content is useful and important, but may not be not sufficient, if they are to achieve the level of structural and sociolinguistic accuracy required for their communicative competence. It is evident that in classrooms in which communication and content learning are central activities, learners often fall short of their goals in these areas of language development. (See, among others, Lightbown and Spada 1990; Swain 1988; White, Spada, Lightbown, and Ranta 1992.)

Thus studies have shown that learners' linguistic accuracy in their L2 lags behind their communicative fluency, particularly when they try to express themselves by using complex clause structures or draw from multilayered systems of verb tense and aspect. (See, as noted above, Lightbown and Spada 1990; Spada and Lightbown 1993.) In some instances, the linguistic and sociolinguistic forms, rules, and features required for communicative competence in the second language have been inaccessible to learners from exposure to classroom communication and content alone. (See Harley, Cummins, Swain, and Allen 1990; Lyster 1994; Plann 1977; White 1991; and Wong-Filmore 1992 for representative examples of the broad range of methods and contexts of this research.) Numerous, often interrelated, insights into these outcomes have been offered at classroom, curriculum, and learner-specific levels. (See Lightbown and Spada 1993 for a synthesis.) Indeed, even seminal works on communicative and content-oriented methodology, such as those by Brumfit (1980), Higgs and Clifford (1982), Stern (1982), and Valdman (1980) expressed reservations which foreshadowed these results.

Theory and research on second-language acquisition have produced additional insights as well. Current theoretical and empirical work suggests that communication and content learning make an important contribution as activities for language use, but that they cannot also be seen as processes for language learning. An implication of this work is that the emphasis placed on facilitating and insuring communication and content learning in the classroom may not leave sufficient room for work on language itself, or on the cognitive processes considered essential for language learning. It is such L2 learning processes that we now discuss in order to examine the relationship they have to communication and content learning, and to understand the roles all three play in meeting the learner's need for communicative competence.

Learner purposes and learning processes: Theoretical insights and research perspectives. Recently there has been an increasing amount of theoretical support and empirical evidence for the conscious, cognitive aspects of language learning and the kinds of social interaction that provide a context for their application. This has been reflected in constructs such as "consciousness raising" (Rutherford and Sharwood Smith 1985), "language awareness" (James and Garrett 1991; Nicholas 1991), "focus on form " (Doughty 1991; Long 1991a, 1991b, 1995), "noticing" (Schmidt 1990), and "notice the gap" (Schmidt and Frota 1986). Together, these constructs suggest that when learners attempt to access and comprehend the meaning of others' messages as well as encode meaning into messages of their own, they also need to draw their attention to the forms through which such meaning is expressed, if they are to be able to process, store, and retrieve them for immediate or subsequent use.

This theoretical perspective has been elaborated in a number of ways. Klein (1986), for example, has claimed that learners need to segment, analyze, and synthesize message input into constituent units as they attempt to comprehend message meaning, and to draw on their interlanguage capacity in similar ways as they engage in message production. Schmidt and Frota (1986) and Swain and Lapkin (1994) have argued, respectively, that when learners can notice differences between the language they comprehend and their own interlanguage variety, or between the language of a message they intend to express and their actual production, this also serves an attention-focusing role that might lead to revision, restructuring, or confirmation of a form or feature of interlanguage. Further, research has shown that learners are aided in their access to, and comprehension of, language when provided with what Sharwood-Smith (1991) has called "enhanced input." Such input consists of language samples that have been modified to make linguistic forms and features more salient and easier to process, and to raise the learner's consciousness about language form. (See again the seminal work of Rutherford and Sharwood-Smith 1985 and Schmidt and Frota 1986, and more recent papers by Schmidt 1990 and Long 1991a, 1991b, 1995.) Enhanced input is believed to assist learners with comprehension, and to help them to recognize forms that are so similar to forms in their first language that they are easy to overgeneralize, that are too complex to learn from meaningful input alone, or that are unstressed in the stream of speech and are therefore difficult to induce therefrom.

Support for the role of enhanced input in these aspects of language learning has come from a number of studies. White (1991), for example, has investigated the learning of adverb-placement rules in English and French. She found that because of the overlapping of rules, the subtle differences among them were difficult for learners to notice unless they were pointed out. Further, with respect to the detection of structural features that are difficult to learn inductively, research has pointed to the role of enhanced input in drawing learners' attention to language form as they attempt to process meaningful input, especially for structures of considerable linguistic complexity. (See Lightbown 1992; Lightbown and Spada 1990; White, Spada, Lightbown, and Ranta 1992.)

Another type of input and an important theoretical contributor to language learning is often referred to as "negative input" or "feedback." According to Schachter (1983, 1984, 1986, 1991), negative input is considered critical for success in language learning because it provides metalinguistic information on the clarity, accuracy, and/or comprehensibility of learners' own production and helps them to notice nontarget-like forms in their interlanguage that are difficult to detect during the even flow of social communication. Empirically, the valuable contributions of negative input have been revealed in studies done individually and collectively by White, Lightbown, Spada, and Ranta. (See again Lightbown and Spada 1990; White, Spada, Lightbown, and Ranta 1992.) Schmidt (in Schmidt and Frota 1986), has also shed light on this aspect of the learning process. In order to benefit from correction, Schmidt reports that he had to know he was being corrected. Hearing a corrected version immediately following what he had just said helped him "notice the gap" between his language and a correct version.

Taken together, these theoretical and empirical insights suggest that much of language learning requires a good deal of cognitive effort. Thus it is possible that communicative and content-oriented activities, as they engage learners in communicating about content, or in learning content for its own sake, might present a cognitive overload on the language-learning process. As research has shown, when learners are asked to turn their attention to both new content and new linguistic forms when engaged in message communication, these forms may not be accessible because their attention is inevitably consumed by their need to understand and express message meaning (see van Patten 1990). Such research has offered insight into why asking learners to participate in communication and attend to content learning may result in their difficulty with the more complex aspects of communicative competence. Although empirical work such as Krashen's (1983, 1985) has clearly emphasized that the more obvious form–function relations of language can be induced below the level of conscious awareness, the less obvious or purely arbitrary ones appear to demand learners' full attention.

Classrooms which emphasize communication and content learning have often placed a good deal of emphasis on natural, unadapted input or on input modified to assist the comprehension of message meaning. They have done this rather than focus on the detection of specific forms used to encode the message. Instructional strategies in such classrooms have been more focused on insuring learners' comprehension and expression of message meaning over their attention to the structure and accuracy of language form. Such practices, however, might now be reconsidered in light of the needs of learners to notice and attend to language form as they decode and encode message meaning, and with regard to the contributions of enhanced and negative input in meeting these needs. Activities in communication and content learning, with their emphasis on language use, cannot, in themselves, guarantee that learner purposes and learning processes will be served in the classroom.

Research suggests that activities that emphasize communication and content learning have also underserved an important aspect of the learning process—the need for learners to access the structure and structural possibilities of language itself. This is where additional, practice-oriented theory and research can offer insight for language teachers and for the learners with whom they work. Current contributions as well as directions in this area of work are described in the two next sections.

The first section focuses on activities which provide a context in which specific features of the L2 can be highlighted in the interest of communicating a message whose meaning depends on those features. In such language-dependent communication and content activities, learners would have to take notes about or report on several interrelated events that, in turn, require their attention to verb tense and aspect. The second section illustrates activities that also provide a context for specific L2 features, but with communication focused on messages about the features themselves. In language-content activities of this kind, learners might be asked to complete a fill-in-the-blanks grammar exercise by selecting one of several different verb-tense or aspectual features and explaining their choices to their teacher or to each other.

Communication activities with language-dependent content. These activities are designed to direct learners' attention to language features and forms as they communicate and exchange information, solve problems, and reach decisions in a content area of interest to them. Optimally, learners' recognition and use of the forms and features that are necessary and appropriate to this content are essential to their successful communication and learning thereof (see, for example, Loschky and BleyVroman 1993).

As noted by Genesee (1987, 1994), useful and effective activities, when implemented in content classrooms, could involve students in exchanging information from texts of historical accounts and life histories. This could draw their attention to verb tense and aspect. In the sciences, activities could be designed to highlight conditional and adverbial forms as well as noun phrase modification in the service of functions such as hypothesizing and speculating, describing, explaining, comparing, and contrasting. In addition to this integration of language and content, Genesee places importance on the fact that such activities involve the learner in the negotiation of message meaning.

Negotiation is a term which has been applied to a variety of interactional behaviors, across different fields of activity outside of language learning proper, such as business and politics. However, it is generally viewed with respect to language learning as a kind of interaction in which interlocutors try to resolve conflicts in their communication of message meaning. To do this, they modify the structure of their interaction as they check each other's comprehension, seek clarification and confirmation of each other's utterances, and adjust the form of their messages until comprehension is achieved. As described below, these linguistic and interactional adjustments provide the context for critical processes of L2 learning. (See further discussion in Pica 1994.)

The following excerpts, from data gathered for Pica 1994, illustrate how learners adjust their interaction to achieve mutual comprehension. In (1), for example, a learner and a native speaker (NS) of English were engaged in a task that required them to exchange information about sets of house pictures that each one held uniquely, and described to the other for replication. As can be seen, the NS signaled to the learner that the learner's initial utterance in the exchange could not be understood. Together they modified the structure of their interaction until, in the final exchange, mutual understanding was reached with respect to the location and the English referent of "stone," which here, was "step."

(1) English NS	English L2 learner
	I think on the front is a small stone
on the front?	yeah oh doors
in the front of the door?	yeah
there is a small step, yes?	oh yes

(source: Pica, Holliday, Lewis, Berducci, and Newman 1991)

Throughout the task the learner was exposed to a good deal of negative input in the interest of message communication. The negative input in the NS negotiation signals provided the learner with feedback on the form and comprehensibility of message production (as shown also in Pica, Holliday, Lewis, and Morgenthaler 1989; Pica et al. 1991). In (1), the NS segmented a section of the learner's initial utterance, "on the front?," repeated it in isolation, then manipulated and modified it through the incorporation of additional input from the learner. Thus the learner's "... on the front is a small stone and ... oh doors" were restructured by the NS into "in the front of the door? and there is a small step, yes?"

In (2), the learner signaled about what had appeared to be the single word in the NS message, "feedback is." The NS responded through a comprehension check, "do you know feedback? you know the word?," and provided an example to illustrate its meaning. This response also separated "feedback" from the learners' "feedback is" as a separate lexical item. As revealed here, the enhanced input that comes via negotiation seems highly compatible with a number of language-learning processes, providing an opportunity for learners to focus on phonological, lexical, and syntactic forms and features, and to comprehend the messages that these forms encode. (See Pica 1994.)

(2) English NS

this looks promising	
do you all have a chance to give your	feedback is?
complaints to school? do you know what	no
feedback is?	
do you know feedback?	being very good you can talk
you know the word?	about that
you can talk about the program not	
English L2 Learner	

yeah we have to do an evaluation?
do an evaluation and write a report
to school

(source: Pica 1994)

In (3), it was the learner who used examples to clarify the meaning of "free" for another learner. As shown, in responding to the other learner's negative input, which itself consisted of segmentations of the learner's own original production, the learner produced a great deal of modified output.

(3) English L2 Learner   English L2 Learner

	do you go to dinner tomorrow? I'm not sure, you go, you should go with me
you go?	I want I think it's free
free?	because there is nothing
	they don't tell the cost
uhuh	so maybe it's free I think
uhuh	

(source: Pica 1994)

As further discussed in Pica (1994) and in Pica et al. (1989), the output produced by learners in both their signals and responses of negotiation is characterized not by the usual kinds of rote repetition found during traditional language lessons, or even by the fluent, unmonitored communication so often promoted in literature on the communicative classroom. Instead, negotiation has been shown to offer learners a basis on which to analyze and break apart their interlanguage into meaningful segments, and thereby draw upon their interlanguage resources as they attempt to produce forms and structures that may be a little beyond the complexity or accuracy of those they used initially.

This overview suggests that negotiation tasks, in both their design and their actual use by learners, can provide an excellent context for the processes of language learning. There is also evidence to support the view that negotiation assists comprehension, indirectly from earlier studies by Chaudron (1983, 1985), Kelch (1985), and Long (1985) on speech modification and comprehension, and directly through later work by Pica (1991) and Pica, Young, and Doughty (1987). Some recent evidence even suggests a role in comprehension in assisting the retention of language form and application, at least in the short run, again from Doughty (1991), who looked at English L2, and from Loschky (1989,

1994), who studied the acquisition of locatives in Japanese as a foreign language.

Unfortunately, negotiation tasks that are currently available engage learners in negotiation over topics of interest, problems to be solved, and decisions to be made (see Pica, Kanagy, and Falodun 1993), while negotiation tasks that integrate content, communication, and specific language features are still in the experimental stage. Their development has been a great challenge to researchers for two reasons.

First, as discussed in Pica (1994), researchers have found that negotiation works most readily on lexical items and larger syntactic units, such as sentence constituents. Learners' negotiation over choices in grammatical morphology has been observed, but not in an impressive amount. Even when learners and their interlocutors have been asked to tell stories, sequence events, or explain procedures, these assignments have not been effective in getting them to negotiate very much over their time and aspect marking. (See Pica, Lincoln-Porter, Paninos, and Linnell 1995.) The learners have appeared to give more attention to the people in their stories and the objects in their events and procedures—what they look like, their shapes, sizes, and so forth—rather than the activities that are portrayed. This interaction directs the participants only into segmenting and moving larger units of syntax such as sentence constituents. This does not imply that learners and interlocutors cannot negotiate over forms that seem to trouble them for time and aspect, modality, case, and number. Indeed they have been observed to do so at however infrequent a rate. What are needed are tasks whose topics and content can insure such experiences for them.

A further challenge is that the negotiation tasks that have been developed thus far have focused on everyday social experiences involving stories, problems, and information exchange. Typically, learners are asked to identify missing items, reconstruct events, or reproduce each other's pictures and drawings. Academic, professional, and other kinds of utilitarian content have not been the primary focus here. And yet, a major thrust of work in discourse analysis has been to identify the forms that serve the very language functions in these domains. (See Selinker, Tarone, and Hanzelli 1981 for examples.) For negotiation tasks to serve learner purposes and processes in the language, communication and content areas, they may need to be organized around texts of this kind, in the hope that they will serve to focus learners' attention to language form in the interest of communicating message meaning.

Communication activities with language as content. A number of other types of classroom activities have also been shown to promote learners' attention to language forms as they are engaged in communication. In these activities, learners talk about language rules and forms in order to solve problems and reach decisions about suppliance of such forms in linguistic contexts such as sentences and longer passages of text. These activities are not designed to draw learners' attention to language form in the service of message meaning, as is the case with the negotiation tasks described above. Instead, they direct learners' attention toward discussing linguistic rules and forms in ways in which they must reach decisions and articulate judgments about the structures themselves. The dictogloss is one such example. (See Nunan 1989.) This is an activity in which a text is read to learners, who must take notes as they listen. They then work in small groups to reconstruct the text, then present and compare their versions as a class. Students have been observed to discuss grammar with an eye toward accuracy and application. The dictogloss, as well as the grammatical decision-making activities highlighted in Fotos and Ellis (1993), have been reported to have a positive impact on learner-production accuracy, and therefore may serve a useful purpose in their learning.

Research on more traditional interventions in the communicative and content classrooms has also indicated that language itself is often appropriate content for the learner. This has been shown for both linguistic and sociolinguistic rules. Lyster (1994) and Swain and Lapkin (1989), for example, found that fossilized learners could be taught sociolinguistic rules for use of the French pronoun *tu* through analytic teaching and through being given opportunities for crosslingual comparison with their native language, English. Additional, instructional input through language awareness tasks also appears helpful in this area. (See Day and Shapson 1991; Harley 1993.)

Research has also suggested ways in which communicative activities accompanied by explicit instruction can be helpful, in the case of Olshtain and Cohen (1990) for apologies and Billmyer (1990) for compliments. Billmyer's work focused on learners who were tutored by a native English speaker on the form and application of compliments in American English (based on the work of Wolfson 1981, 1983, 1984) when interacting in a variety of conversational contexts. As a result of such form-focused instruction, the learners were able to produce more spontaneous compliments and more norm-appropriate compliments in social situations outside of the instructional context, and to do so significantly better than other learners, who had engaged only in the conversational experiences with the native speaker.

A number of studies also suggest that grammar rules and features in themselves can serve as useful content for language learning, particularly when grammar instruction accompanies opportunities for oral communication inside and outside the classroom (Eisenstein and Montgomery 1986), learners are at an appropriate developmental stage for word-order sequences (Pienemann 1984; Ellis 1989), the structure is related to others in a markedness hierarchy of difficulty (Gass 1982; Doughty 1991), the structure is "easy"—i.e. has a clear form–function relationship, but might be difficult for learners to recognize on its own because it is nonsyllabic, voiceless, and word- final as, for example, English plural -*s* (Pica 1985)—and, as noted above, when the L2 structure is so close to the L1 structure and/or so rare in the L2 input that learners would have a difficult time or limited opportunities with respect to noticing the difference between the two. (See again Lightbown and Spada 1990; White, Spada, Lightbown, and Ranta 1992.)

In contexts where drawing learners' attention to language features can make a difference in their efficiency in language learning, feedback on error might be helpful for those forms that have been identified as amenable to such instruction. Especially effective appear to be teachers' reduced repetitions of students' errors, with emphasis on the error itself more than expansions or elaborations of the learners' utterances or isolated suppliance of a correct form. (See Chaudron 1977.) Such a format can make errors salient to learners and allow for noticing gaps between errors and correct production. Another useful technique for helping learners to notice such gaps is suggested in studies by Tomassello and Herron (1988, 1989). These researchers found that learners who were first led "down the garden path" to produce typical errors of overgeneralization for exceptional L2 structures, then given immediate feedback and direct instruction, performed better on these structures than learners first taught the rules and exceptions together, and then given opportunities for practice. Again, such techniques suggest that language itself can be a content area that, like other content areas, can be learned effectively and efficiently in somewhat traditional formats.

Implications and directions. This article has addressed current concerns and questions about teaching language learners for purposes in, and through processes of, communication and content learning, within the context of recent second-language-acquisition theory and research and pressing professional issues that speak to the scope and expectations of classroom instruction. It has been suggested that providing learners with opportunities to communicate in the classroom and to use academic, professional, and other forms of utilitarian content as a basis for their language learning is insufficient for learners, and can be discomforting to language educators as well. Clearly, some adjustments are in order.

Those of us who work in universities, armed with our own research and scholarship on the research of others, are in a particularly critical position to address these concerns and work through the needed adjustments. First, we must examine and integrate theory and research on language teaching and language learning and provide fora in which they can be presented to, discussed, and critiqued by our professional-education students. This information should not be restricted to our work with doctoral students, teacher researchers, or faculty colleagues. Rather it is critical to all professionals in language education as an integral part of their knowledge base and as a priority in their reading assignments, field projects, and class discussion. Our research institutions are in a special position to help language and content teachers, both novices and seasoned professionals, to come together in ways that the everyday world of their work environment cannot provide.

In keeping with this perspective, our Educational Linguistics program at the University of Pennsylvania has developed Project T.E.A.M.,[2] a program leading to an advanced degree in education and which brings together "Teachers of English in the Academic Mainstream." These are teachers who work with language learners in elementary and secondary language and content classrooms. Together they share their expertise, experience, and questions, and ongoing solutions with novice teachers in our regular courses on language learning and teaching, as well as in special classes and workshops designed to address these issues directly. We are also working to develop the kinds of tasks that bring together content, communication, and specific areas of language that we recognize as so essential to the success of language learners in mastering both language and content.

Project T.E.A.M. has been designed in the belief that teachers and teacher educators need to view their work as a life-long process, one which requires them to keep up with research that spans both language learning and all aspects of content teaching. This is a very new project and, admittedly, a new direction for us, but one we have undertaken with optimism, for language educators and for the language learners we all so very much want to help. The increasing emphasis on communicative and content-oriented language teaching, while striving nobly to meet the needs and purposes of language learners, runs some very serious risks with respect to the language-teaching profession, unless teachers and teacher educators take steps to make sure their work serves the processes of language learning. In drawing on current work as well as forging new lines of research, we hope that we can make a difference in the way teachers can work together to teach language and address the needs of language learners.

---

[2] Project T.E.A.M. is a three-year enhancement program for School District of Philadelphia "Teachers of English in the Academic Mainstream," who work with students of limited English proficiency as teachers of English as a second language, bilingual-classroom educators, and instructors of academic content. The teachers' tuition is covered in full through a Title VII grant from the Office of Bilingual Education and Minority Language Affairs. The T.E.A.M. program consists of ten course units in linguistics, language studies, sociocultural concepts and issues, and approaches to pedagogy, with particular focus on methods of integrating language and content in the classroom. Monthly seminars, workshops, and discussion sessions led by invited experts are offered, providing opportunities for T.E.A.M. teachers to work collaboratively as they exchange knowledge and skills from their respective domains of expertise, strategize toward curriculum integration, engage in classroom-oriented research, and prepare to become expert consultants within their schools. T.E.A.M. teachers work closely with Educational Linguistics faculty in each of these efforts. Dr. Cheri Micheau, principal consultant to Project T.E.A.M. since its inception, coordinates the project. Teresa Pica is Project Director.

Why have we begun with this direction, and not moved in others, using current themes such as "political action," "empowerment," "teacher as researcher," or "school restructuring"? It is not because we feel these domains are unimportant, but because we feel they will gain importance when teachers can refer to and speak from a knowledge of language-learning theory and research, so that they can feel empowered, carry out relevant studies, and take political action. We want teachers to ask not only how they can apply extant theory and research to their classroom work, but also how their classroom work can inform and generate new theory and to guide them in their own research. If we can work together across university, classroom, and community settings to identify and carry out research on questions, as yet unanswered or, undoubtedly, as yet to be articulated, we will maintain our identity as professional educators and increase our visibility within the field of professional education.

REFERENCES

Benesch, Sarah (ed.). 1988. *Ending remediation: Linking ESL and content in higher education.* Washington, D.C.: Teachers of English to Speakers of Other Languages.

Benesch, Sarah. 1992. "Sharing responsibilities: An alternative approach to the adjunct model." *College ESL* 2(1): 1–8.

Billmyer, Kristine. 1990. "The effects of formal instruction on the development of sociolinguistic competence: The performance of compliments." Unpublished Ph.D. dissertation, University of Pennsylvania.

Boyd-Kletzander, Ruth. (in preparation). "Empowering Students in ESL Classrooms." Ph.D. dissertation, University of Pennsylvania.

Brinton, Donna, Marguerite Ann Snow, and Marjorie B. Wesche. 1989. *Content based second language instruction.* Rowley, Massachusetts: Newbury House.

Brown, H. Douglas. 1994. *Teaching by principles: An interactive approach to language pedagogy.* Englewood Cliffs, N.J.: Prentice-Hall Regents.

Brumfit, Christopher J. 1980. "From defining to designing: communicative specifications versus communicative methodology in foreign language teaching." *Studies in Second Language Acquisition* 3(1): 1–9.

Brumfit, Christopher J. and Keith Johnson (eds.). 1979. *The communicative approach to language teaching.* Oxford: Oxford University Press.

Canale, Michael and Merrill Swain. 1980. "Theoretical bases of communicative approaches to second language teaching and testing." *Applied Linguistics* 1(1): 1–47.

Candlin, Christopher (ed.). 1981. *The communicative teaching of English: Principles and exercise typology.* London: Longman.

Cantoni-Harvey, Gina. 1987. *Content-area language learning: Approaches and strategies.* Reading, Massachusetts: Addison-Wesley.

Chaudron, Craig. 1977. "A descriptive model of discourse in the corrective treatment of learners' errors." *Language Learning* 27(1): 29–46.

Day, Elaine M. and Stan M. Shapson. 1991. "Integrating formal and functional approaches to language teaching in French immersion: An experimental study." *Language Learning* 41(1): 25–58.

DiPietro, Robert J. 1987. *Strategic interaction: Learning languages through scenarios*. Cambridge, U.K.: Cambridge University Press.

Doughty, Catherine. 1991. "Second language instruction does make a difference: Evidence from an empirical study of second language relativization." *Studies in Second Language Acquisition* 13(4): 431–469.

Ellis, Rod. 1989. "Are classroom and naturalistic acquisition the same? A study of the classroom acquisition of German word order rules." *Studies in Second Language Acquisition* 11(3): 305–328.

Finocchiaro, Mary and Christopher Brumfit. 1983. *The functional-notional approach: From theory to practice*. Oxford: Oxford University Press.

Fotos, Sandra and Rod Ellis. 1993. " Communicating about grammar: A task-based approach." *TESOL Quarterly* 25(4): 605–628.

Gaies, Stephen. 1991. "ESL students in academic courses: forgin a link." *College ESL* 1(1): 30–37.

Gantzer, Jack. 1991. "Issues in ESL: Putting ESL in its place." *College ESL* 1(2): 21–24.

Garfinkel, H. 1967. *Studies in ethnomethodology*. Englewood Cliffs, N.J.: PrenticeHall.

Gass, Susan. 1982. "From theory to practice." In Mary Hines and William Rutherford (eds.), *On TESOL '81*. Washington, D.C.: Teachers of English to Speakers of Other Languages. 129–139.

Genesee, Fred. 1987. *Learning through two languages: Studies of immersion and bilingual education*. Cambridge, Massachusetts: Newbury House.

Genesee, Fred. 1994. "Integrating language and content instruction." In R. Michael Botswick (ed.), *Katoh Gauken Immersion Education International Symposium report*. Katoh Gauken, Japan, October 1994: 15-25.

Harley, Birgit. 1989. "Functional grammar in French immersion: A classroom experiment." *Applied Linguistics* 10: 331–359.

Harley, Birgit and Merrill Swain. 1984. "The interlanguage of immersion students and its implications for second language teaching." In Alan Davies, C. Criper, and Anthony Howatt (eds.), *Interlanguage*. Edinburgh, U.K.: Edinburgh University Press. 391–311.

Higgs, Theodore and Ray Clifford. 1982. "The push toward communication." In Theodore Higgs (ed.), *Curriculum, competence and the foreign language teacher*. Skokie, Illinois: National Textbook Co. 57–79.

Hymes, Dell. 1972. *Towards communicative competence*. Philadelphia: University of Pennsylvania Press.

James, Carl and Peter Garrett (eds.). 1991. *Language awareness in the classroom*. London: Longman.

Johnson, Keith and Keith Morrow (eds.). 1981. *Communication in the classroom*. London: Longman.

Kelch, Ken. 1985. Modified input as an aid to comprehension. *Studies in Second Language Acquisition* 7 (1): 81–89.

Klein, Wolfgang. 1986. *Second language acquisition*. Cambridge, U.K.: Cambridge University Press.

Krashen, Stephen. 1980. *Second language acquisition and second language learning*. Oxford: Pergamon Press.

Krashen, Stephen. 1983. "Newmark's ignorance hypothesis and current second language acquisition theory." In Susan Gass and Larry Selinker (eds.), *Language transfer in language learning*. Rowley, Massachusetts: Newbury House. 135–156.

Krashen, Stephen. 1985. *The Input Hypothesis: Issues and implications*. London: Longman.

Krashen. Stephen and Tracey Terrell. 1983. *The Natural Approach*. Oxford: Pergamon Press.

Lafayette, Robert C. and Michael Buscaglia. 1985. "Students learn language via a civilization course —a comparison of second language classroom environments." *Studies in Second Language Acquisition* 7(3): 323–343.

Larsen-Freeman, Diane and Michael Long. 1991. *Second language research*. New York: Longman.

Lightbown, Patsy. 1983. "Exploring relationships between developmental and instructional sequences in L2 acquisition." In Herbert Seliger and Michael Long (eds.), *Classroom oriented research in second language acquisition*. Rowley, Massachusetts: Newbury House. 217–243.

Lightbown, Patsy. 1992. "Getting quality input in the second/foreign language classroom." In Claire Kramsch and Sally McConnell-Ginet (eds.), *Text and context: Cross disciplinary perspectives on language study*. New York: Heath. 187–197.

Lightbown, Patsy and Nina Spada. 1990. "Focus-on-form and corrective feedback in communicative language teaching: Effects on second language learning." *Studies in Second Language Acquisition* 12(4): 429–448.

Lightbown, Patsy and Nina Spada. 1993. *How languages are learned*. Oxford: Oxford University Press.

Long, Michael. 1985. "Input and second language acquisition theory." In Susan Gass and Carolyn Madden (eds.), *Input in second language acquisition*. Rowley, Massachusetts: Newbury House. 377–393.

Long, Michael. 1991a. The least a theory of second language acquisition needs to explain. *TESOL Quarterly* 24(4): 649–666.

Long, Michael. 1991b. "Focus on form: A design feature in language teaching methodology." In Kees de Bot, D. Coste, Ralph Ginsberg, and Claire Kramsch (eds.), *Foreign language research in cross-cultural perspective*. Amsterdam: John Benjamins. 39–52.

Long, Michael. 1995. "The role of the linguistic environment in second language acquisition." In William C. Ritchie and T. K. Bhatia (eds.), *Handbook of language acquisition, Volume 2: Second language acquisition*. New York: Academic Press.

Loschky, Lester. 1989. "The effects of negotiated interaction and premodified input on second language comprehension and retention." *Occasional Paper No. 16*, Department of ESL, University of Hawaii.

Loschky, Lester. 1994. "Comprehensible input and second language acquisition: What's the relationship?" *Studies in Second Language Acquisition* 16(3): 303–324.

Loschky, Lester and Robert Bley-Vroman. 1993. "Grammar and Task based methodology." In Graham Crookes and Susan Gass (eds.), *Tasks and language learning: integrating theory and practice*. Clevedon, U.K.: Multilingual Matters. 123–167.

Lyster, Roy. 1994. "The effects of functional-analytical teaching on aspects of French immersion students' sociolinguistic competence." *Applied Linguistics* 15(3): 263–288.

Mohan, Bernard. 1986. *Language and content*. Reading, Massachusetts: Addison-Wesley.

Montgomery, Carol and Miriam Eisenstein. 1986. "Real reality revisited: An experimental communicative course in ESL." *TESOL Quarterly* 19(2): 317–333.

Munby, John. 1978. *Communicative syllabus design*. Cambridge, U.K.: Cambridge University Press.

Nicholas, Howard. 1991. "Language awareness and second language development." In Carl James and Peter Garrett (eds.), *Language awareness in the classroom*. New York: Longman.

Nunan, David. 1988. *The learner-centered curriculum*. Cambridge, U.K.: Cambridge University Press.

Nunan, David. 1989. *Designing tasks for the communicative classroom*. Cambridge, U.K.: Cambridge University Press.

Nunan, David. 1991. *Language teaching methodology: A textbook for teachers*. Englewood Cliffs, N.J.: Prentice-Hall.

Olshtain, Elite and Andrew D. Cohen. 1990. "The learning of complex speech behavior." *TESL Canada Journal* 7(1): 45–65.

Omaggio, Alice. 1986. *Teaching language in context*. Boston: Heinle and Heinle.

Pica, Teresa. 1991. "Classroom interaction, participation and comprehension: redefining relationships." *System* 19(3–4): 437–452.

Pica, Teresa. 1994. "Research on negotiation: what does it reveal about second language learning conditions, processes, and outcomes?" *Language Learning* 44(3): 493-527.

Pica, Teresa and Catherine Doughty. 1985. "The role of group work in classroom second language acquisition." *Studies in Second Language Acquisition* 7(2): 233-248.

Pica, Teresa, Lloyd Holliday, Nora Lewis, and Lynelle Morgenthaler. 1989. "Comprehensible output as an outcome of linguistic demands on the learner." *Studies in Second Language Acquisition* 11(1): 63-90.

Pica, Teresa, Lloyd Holliday, Nora Lewis, Dom Berducci, and Jeanne Newman. 1991. "Language learning through interaction: What role does gender play?" *Studies in Second Language Acquisition* 13(3): 343-376.

Pica, Teresa, Ruth Kanagy, and Joseph Falodun. 1993. "Choosing and using communication tasks for second language research and instruction." In Susan Gass and Graham Crookes (eds.), *Tasks and language learning: integrating theory and practice*. London: Multilingual Matters. 9-34.

Pica, Teresa, Felicia Lincoln-Porter, Diana Paninos, and Julian Linnell. 1995. "What can second language learners learn from each other? Only their researcher knows for sure." *Working Papers in Educational Linguistics*. Philadelphia: University of Pennsylvania.

Pica, Teresa, Richard Young and Catherine Doughty. 1987. "The impact of interaction on comprehension." *TESOL Quarterly* 21(4): 737-758.

Pienemann, Manfred. 1984a. "Learnability and syllabus construction." In Kenneth Hyltenstam and Manfred Pienemann (eds.), *Modelling and assessing second language acquisition*. Clevedon, U.K.: Multilingual Matters. 23-76.

Pienemann, Manfred. 1984b. "Psychological constraints on the teachability of languages." *Studies in Second Language Acquisition* 6: 186-214.

Plann, Sandra. 1977. "Acquiring a second language in an immersion situation." In H. Douglas Brown and Ruth Crymes (eds.), *On TESOL '77*. Washington, D.C.: Teachers of English to Speakers of Other Languages. 213-223.

Prabhu, N. S. 1987. *Second language pedagogy: A perspective*. Oxford: Oxford University Press.

Rutherford, William and Michael Sharwood Smith 1985. "Consciousness-raising and universal grammar." In William Rutherford and Michael Sharwood Smith (eds.), *Grammar and second language learning*. Rowley, Massachusetts: Newbury House. 107-116.

Savignon, Sandra. 1972. *Communicative competence: An experiment in foreign-language teaching*. Philadelphia: Center for Curriculum Development.

Savignon, Sandra. 1983. *Communicative competence: Theory and classroom practice*. Reading, Massachusetts: Addison-Wesley Publishing Co.

Schachter, Jacqueline. 1983. "Nutritional needs of language learners." In Mark A. Clarke and Jean Handscombe (eds.), *On TESOL '82: Pacific perspectives on language learning and teaching*. Washington, D.C.: Teachers of English to Speakers of Other Languages. 175-189.

Schachter, Jacqueline. 1984. "A universal input condition." In William Rutherford (ed.), *Universals and second language acquisition*. Amsterdam: John Benjamins. 167-183.

Schachter, Jacqeline. 1986. "Three approaches to the study of input." *Language Learning* 36(2): 211-226.

Schachter, Jacqueline. 1991. "Corrective feedback in historical perspective." *Second Language Research* 7(2): 89-102.

Schmidt, Richard. 1990. "The role of consciousness in second language acquisition." *Applied Linguistics* 11(2): 129-158.

Schmidt, Richard and Sylvia Frota. 1986. "Developing basic conversational ability in a second language: a case study of an adult learner of Portuguese." In Richard Day (ed.), *Talking to learn*. Rowley, Massachusetts: Newbury House. 237-326.

Selinker, Larry, Elaine Tarone, and Victor Hanzelli (eds.). 1981. *English for academic and technical purposes*. Rowley, Massacusetts: Newbury House.

Sharwood Smith, Michael 1991. "Speaking to many minds: On the relevance of different types of language information for the L2 learner." *Second Language Research* 7(2): 118–132.

Snow, Marguerite, Myriam Met, and Fred Genesee. 1989. "A conceptual framework for the integration of language and content in second/foreign language instruction" *TESOL Quarterly* 23(2): 201–217.

Snow, Marguerite Ann. 1991. "Teaching language through content." In Marianne Celce-Murcia (ed.), *Teaching English as a second or foreign language*. Boston: Heinle and Heinle Publishers. 315–328.

Spack, Ruth. 1988. "Initiating ESL students into the academic discourse community: How far should we go?" *TESOL Quarterly* 22(1): 29–51.

Spada, Nina. 1986. "The interaction between types of content and type of instruction: some effects on the L2 proficiency of adult learners." *Studies in Second Language Acquisition* 8(2): 188–199.

Spada, Nina. 1987. "Relationships between instructional differences and learning outcomes: A process-product study of communicative language teaching." *Applied Linguistics* 8(1): 137–161.

Stern, H.H. 1982. "French core programs across Canada: How can we improve them?" *The Canadian Modern Language Review* 39(4): 847–858.

Swain, Merrill. 1985. "Communicative competence: some roles of comprehensible input and comprehensible output in its development." In Susan Gass and Carolyn Madden (eds.), *Input in second language acquisition*. Newbury House. 235–256.

Swain, Merrill. 1984. "A review of immersion education in Canada: Research and evaluation studies." *ELT Documents* 119: 35–51.

Swain, Merrill and Sharon Lapkin. 1982. *Evaluating bilingual education: A Canadian case study*. Clevedon, U.K.: Multilingual Matters.

Swain, Merrill and Sharon Lapkin. 1989. "Aspects of the sociolinguistic performance of early and late French immersion students." In Robin Scarcella, Elaine Anderson, and Stephen Krashen (eds.), *On the development of communicative competence in a second language*. Cambridge, Massachusetts: Newbury House. 41–54.

Swain, Merrill and Sharon Lapkin. 1994. "Problems in output and the cognitive processes they generate: A step towards second language learning." Ms., Modern Language Centre, Ontario Institite for Studies in Education, Toronto, August 1994.

Tomasello, Michael and Carol Herron 1988. "Down the garden path: inducing and correcting overgeneralization errors in the foreign language classroom." *Applied Psycholinguistics* 9(3): 237–246.

Tomasello, Michael and Carol Herron. 1989. "Feedback for language transfer errors." *Studies in Second Language Acquisition* 11(4): 385–395.

Valdman, Albert. 1980. "Communicative ability and syllabus design for global foreign language courses." *Studies in Second Language Acquisition* 3(1): 81–96.

van Patten, Bill. 1990. "Attending to form and content in the input: an experiment in consciousness." *Studies in Second Language Acquisition* 12(3): 287–301.

White, Lydia. 1991. "Adverb placement in second language acquisition: some effects of positive and negative evidence in the classroom." *Second Language Research* 7(2): 133–161.

White, Lydia, Nina Spada, Patsy Lightbown, and Leila Ranta. 1992. "Input enhancement and L2 question formation." *Applied Linguistics* 12(3): 416–432.

Wong-Fillmore, Lily. 1992. "Learning a language from learners." In Claire Kramsch and Sally McConnell-Ginet (eds.), *Text and context: Cross disciplinary perspectives on language study*. New York: Heath. 46–66.

Wolfson, Nessa. 1981. "Compliments in cross-cultural perspective." *TESOL Quarterly* 15(1): 117–124.

Wolfson, Nessa. 1983. "An empirically based analysis of complimenting in American English." In Nessa Wolfson and Eliot Judd (eds.), *Sociolinguistics and language acquisition*. Rowley, Massachusetts: Newbury House. 82–95.

Wolfson, Nessa. 1984. "Rules of speaking." In Jack C. Richards and Richard Schmidt (eds.), *Language and communication*. London: Longman. 61–87.

Yalden, Janice. 1983. *The communicative syllabus: Evolution, design, and implementation*. Oxford: Pergamon.

Yalden, Janice. 1987. *Principles of course design for language teaching*. Cambridge, U.K.: Cambridge University Press.

Language anxiety in second-language acquisition: Using a wider angle of focus

Dolly Jesusita Young
The University of Tennessee

Introduction. In an age where advances in technology have produced easy access to information, it is not surprising that these advances have influenced our way of thinking. The networking of information leads to greater insights on issues than isolated examinations alone. For this reason, the notion of systems thinking has gained recognition in the business community and can have a positive influence on the way we think in the academic community. Systems thinking attempts to integrate disciplines; it aims to build shared visions. In essence, it uses a wider angle of focus on issues. Senge explains how systems thinking works:

> Business and other human endeavors are also systems. They, too, are bound by invisible fabrics of interrelated actions, which often take years to fully play out their effects on each other. Since we are part of that lacework ourselves, it is doubly hard to see the whole pattern of change. Instead, we tend to focus on snapshots of isolated parts of the system, and wonder why our deepest problems never seem to get solved. Systems thinking is a conceptual framework, a body of knowledge and tools that has been developed over the past fifty years, to make the full patterns clearer and to help us see how to change them effectively. (Senge 1990: 7)

Systems thinking promotes the examination of issues through a variety of lenses or disciplines, so that key interactions among them can be discerned and more comprehensive understandings of issues can evolve. In the area of second-language acquisition (SLA), it is particularly important for us to not work in isolation from other disciplines. Research on language anxiety, traditionally characterized by the snapshot approach, could benefit by using a wider angle of focus. The purpose of this paper is to use the latest research on language anxiety to illustrate how the study of language anxiety can benefit from systems thinking. By examining how affective, cognitive, and linguistic variables actually interrelate in language-anxiety research, I depict a more complex, dynamic, comprehensive, and systemic perspective of processes in second-language acquisition.

Affective variables in SLA research. Prior to the 1970s, language research had not yet considered the role of cognition and affect in adult foreign- or second-language learning. In the 1950s, linguistic theory was greatly influenced by structuralism and learning theory by behaviorism. Chomsky's insights in the 1960s brought a movement in language-learning research that considered the cognitive aspects of languages and learning. This shift moved the foreign-language profession from an emphasis on research questions of "what" to questions of "how" (Swaffar, Arens, and Byrnes 1991: 11). Rather than asking "what," as in "What features are unique to language X and not to language Y?" as the structuralists did, we began to ask "how," as in "How is it that sentences with parallel structures can mean two different things?" In other words, we went from describing the structures of languages and comparing their differences to considering the meanings behind them. A wealth of research related to cognition and language learning resulted and, from this, the profession gained a more profound understanding of how learners acquire language. Since the mid-1980s, the profession has also begun to include not only research questions of "what" and "how," but of "why." For example, "Why are there individual differences in learning a language?" "Why do some learners experience success in foreign-language learning and others have such a difficult time with it?" In the last ten years, second-language-acquisition researchers have broadened their view of what it means to learn another language by recognizing the importance of affective variables ("why" questions) in the acquisition process. Affective variables refer to the emotional aspects of language learners such as learners' attitudes, motivation, self-confidence, personality characteristics, and language anxiety.

The expansion of SLA research to include affect and cognition suggests that our thinking about languages and language learning is changing, and we are becoming more aware of the complexities of language learning. The world today is in some ways vastly different from the world of forty years ago. The information age, through advances in technology, has produced the information highway, virtual libraries, and the World Wide Web. Disciplines no longer need to function in isolation. Within the field of SLA, we can now connect more easily with researchers in a wide range of disciplines and subdisciplines such as psychology, educational psychology, special education, applied linguistics, sociolinguistics, and psycholinguistics. Our understanding of the processes involved in SLA has been enriched by researchers in these areas, although we have still a long way to go.

Language anxiety and affect: Relating language anxiety to other affective variables. In general, research on affective variables (including language anxiety) has traditionally focused on examining the relationship between affective variables and language achievement. By maintaining a microscopic, linear focus on how these two variables relate, we have gained important insights into individ al differences in language learning among adult learners. For example, we now have evidence to indicate that adults experience language anxiety and that language anxiety can negatively affect language learning and performance (see Young 1995a for a review of this research). Movement toward a wider angle of focus in our research is illustrated, however, in two theoretical efforts by Gardner and Thrembly (forthcoming) and Gardner and MacIntyre (1992, 1993).

Gardner, a Canadian-born psychologist who has worked in the field of affective variables for the past thirty years, has tremendously influenced the direction of language-anxiety research. He has a long history of conducting correlational research on the relationships among motivation and other affective variables, including language anxiety. In a recent essay, he and his co-author, Thrembly, hypothesize a relationship between the two most researched affective variables to date: motivation and language anxiety. Garnder and Thrembly offer a new way of discussing these two phenomena, not in isolation from each other, but in relation to each other.

In the 1960s Alpert and Haber (1960) suggested that there are two types of anxiety: facilitative and debilitative anxiety. Drawing from drive theory and cognitive considerations of anxiety, they contend that facilitative anxiety produces an increase in drive that leads to improved performance. Debilitative anxiety, on the other hand, evokes an increase in drive that actually leads to poor performance. In research which fell under the rubric of "motivation," we have seen that motivation tends to have a positive effect on language performance and achievement. Language anxiety, on the other hand, has a negative relationship with language performance. Recently, Gardner and Thrembly have argued that what has in the past been called facilitative anxiety may actually be motivation. They contend that facilitative and debilitative anxiety need not be distinguished because "the majority of studies using general measures of anxiety have failed to find any correlation of [general] anxiety with achievement" (Gardner and Thrembly forthcoming: 27). Instead, they assert that facilitative anxiety enhances language performance because individuals are energized. They believe this energy is an inherent component of motivation. In viewing language anxiety in relation to motivation, they no longer treat these phenomena as isolated variables. For example, they posit that "the conditions that give rise to motivation are the same as those that reduce anxiety. Or, if one is anxious about one's behavior in a given content, it may be difficult to maintain motivation" (Gardner and Thrembly forthcoming: 32).

In the past, researchers in motivation concentrated on exploring the role of this variable in SLA, and in doing so also suggested different ways of motivating learners. Similarly, researchers in language anxiety have also generated strategies to reduce anxiety. By examining the interrelationship between these two affective variables, we may learn new and unexplored ways to reduce learners' anxieties and therefore improve motivation. Moreover, discussions which bring together the notions of language anxiety and motivation are necessary because they lead to less linear and more complex systemic views of the emotional variables that contribute to language acquisition. Motivation, however, is not the only affective variable whose relationship to language anxiety is worth exploring. Gardner and MacIntyre examined affective variables in language learning and found links between language anxiety and learning strategies (Gardner and MacIntyre 1992), learner attitudes, degree of risk-taking, and self-confidence (Gardner and MacIntyre 1993). In their 1993 article, Gardner and MacIntyre also first posit a relationship between motivation and language anxiety when they note that "the similarities between facilitating anxiety and motivation are striking, both in how they are measured and their conceptual definitions" (Gardner and MacIntyre 1993: 6).

In sum, most recent research in language anxiety could be viewed as expanding its angle of focus to include investigations of language anxiety as it relates to other affective variables, in addition to language performance. In essence, we see that as researchers "pursue their own visions and learn to listen to others' visions, they begin to see that their own personal vision is part of something larger" (Senge 1990: 352). As this direction in language-anxiety research continues to progress, we hope to gain richer insights into the complexities of affect in the process of second-language acquisition. To obtain an accurate global picture of the processes involved in SLA, we must examine key interrelationships of variables within a discipline, as well as across disciplines. In the next section, we cross disciplines as I discuss recent studies on the relationship between affect and cognition.

Language anxiety and cognition: From product to process. Much of the research on language anxiety before the 1990s focused on the way language anxiety inhibits the learners' performance in the foreign language. Indicators of language performance included such measures as grades, oral-test scores, scores on standardized tests, vocabulary-performance scores, self-ratings of language performance, and the like (see Ely 1986; Gardner, Moorcroft, and MacIntyre 1987; Trylong 1987; Young 1986). In addition to the more obvious indications of the negative effects of language anxiety, other researchers have discovered more subtle effects of language anxiety on the quality of language performance (Phillips 1992; Steinberg and Horwitz 1986). For example, Steinberg and Horwitz (1986) found that subjects who experienced more anxiety tended to offer less interpretive information when asked to describe a picture, while subjects who reported lower anxiety levels tended to offer more interpretive and subjective information about the picture.

Instead of measuring linguistic output exclusively, more recently researchers have begun to examine the relationship between language anxiety and cognitive processing of language input. MacIntyre and Gardner have integrated research in cognition and affect by investigating the effects of language anxiety on information processing. In one study, MacIntyre and Gardner (1994b) administered a variety of tests that focused on the processing of language and found that anxiety also negatively affected language intake. In addition, they found subtle effects of language anxiety. For example, more anxious students were less fluent, had less complex sentences, and had poorer pronunciation than less anxious students. In another study, MacIntyre and Gardner (1994a) examined the effect of anxiety on early stages of language processing (i.e. input and processing), and then output, and again found that anxiety negatively affects subjects' ability to process language. They found that anxiety successfully induced by a camera at stages of input, processing, and output correlated negatively with performance. They conclude that cognitive deficits occur when students experience anxiety in the input and processing stages, but that the deficits can be overcome if the learner is given the opportunity to recover the missing input by returning to material offered at the input and processing stage (MacIntyre and Gardner 1994a: 16). If anxiety affects the processing of language input, this means that it impedes a learner's ability to process new language. In other words, it reduces what a learner can hope to process as usable "intake," ultimately hindering successful language acquisition.

To fully understand the process of SLA, we must work to include a variety of perspectives. Psychologists and cognitive psychologists have discovered through empirical studies important links between affect and cognition. Their studies on the effects of language anxiety on input have offered insights into the interactions among cognition, affect, and linguistic outcomes. At a theoretical level, their research underscores the benefits of a systems-thinking approach to issues since, in systems thinking, a complex system exists beyond our sight, so that interrelationships within the system give glimpses into more comprehensive structures that influence behavior over time (Senge 1990: 44). In this case, the cognitive and affective processes involved in producing language interact with the processes involved in "getting" language, and vice versa. One does not function in isolation from the other. In the next section, I draw on the work of specialists in learning disabilities to indicate an interactive and compensatory approach to discussing the connections among affective, cognitive, and linguistic variables in the SLA process.

Language anxiety and linguistic competence. In the last few years, research conducted by specialists in learning disabilities, primarily Sparks and Ganschow (1991, 1995a, 1995b, forthcoming), has evoked a renewed, healthy debate over the relationship between anxiety and ability or, more specifically in our case, language anxiety and linguistic competence. Language-anxiety research has consistently indicated that language anxiety negatively affects language learning and/or performance and, more recently, the processing of foreign-language (FL) input. In correlational research, however, strong correlations do not equal causation. Most FL researchers in this area infer that high levels of anxiety harm language learning and performance. On the basis of their investigations, Sparks and Ganschow (1991, 1995a, 1995b, forthcoming) contradict these claims by suggesting that affective variables, such as motivation or language anxiety, do not play a causal role in language learning and performance but are likely to be a consequence of native-language and foreign-language aptitude. They explain:

> Problems with foreign language learning are not likely to be primarily the result of low motivation, poor attitude, or high anxiety... Poor attitudes and high anxiety are more likely to arise from difficulties inherent in the task itself... Foreign language learning difficulties are likely to be based in native language learning and that facility with one's language "codes" (phono-logical/orthographic, syntactic, semantic) is likely to play an important causal role in learning a foreign language. (Sparks and Ganschow 1995b: 234)

The authors infer from their data that language anxiety does not cause poor language performance or learning, but that weak language performance and unsuccessful language learning are a consequence of foreign-language skills rooted in weak native-language skills.

Sparks and Ganschow refer to their position as the Linguistic Coding Deficit Hypothesis (LCDH).[1] They arrive at this hypothesis on the basis of statistically significant differences they have found among successful FL learners, poor FL learners, and learning-disabled (LD) language learners on native-language tests and the MLAT (Ganschow, Sparks, Javorsky, Pohlman and Bishop-Marbury 1991; Sparks, Ganschow, Javorsky, Pohlman, and Patton 1992a, 1992b; Sparks and Ganschow forthcoming). Table 1 summarizes the findings of these researchers. Sparks and Ganschow state, "In our research on foreign-language learning, then, we focus on language variables in students with FL learning problems because the learning of a FL is the learning of language"(1995b: 236). In sum, their view is that "the problems of most FL learners will not be found by studying affective variables but by investigating how language differences affect FL learning" (Sparks and Ganschow 1995b: 240).[2]

In response to the research by Sparks and Ganschow, MacIntyre (1995) has charged that language learning is the study of language, but not exclusively that. He argues that "the LCDH is incomplete as an explanation for individual

---

[1] Recently Sparks and Ganschow have modified their hypothesis to the Linguistic Coding Differences Hypothesis. (See Sparks and Ganschow forthcoming.)

[2] It is unclear whether they suggest a return to structuralism with this statement.

differences in second language learning" (MacIntyre 1995: 139).[3] MacIntyre contends that anxiety, cognition, and behavior interact with each other and are recursive and cyclical. He offers the following example of how these variables interact:

> ... a demand to answer a question in a second language class may cause a student to become anxious; anxiety leads to worry and rumination. Cognitive performance is diminished because of the divided attention and therefore performance suffers, leading to negative self-evaluations and more self-deprecating cognition which further impairs performance, and so on. (MacIntyre 1995: 142)

What we are experiencing here are two disciplines which offer competing explanations for difficulties that foreign-language learners encounter. MacIntyre is a cognitive psychologist and, as such, he contends that to understand how individuals learn a foreign or second language, we must examine the role of cognitive and affective variables in addition to linguistic variables. Sparks and Ganschow and their colleagues are learning-disability specialists; they suggest that an examination of language aptitude alone can offer explanations for much of the success or failure in language learning. Each researcher brings to an issue his or her interpretation of and approach to an issue. Within a systems-thinking approach, however, I encourage researchers to acknowledge the complexities among all intervening variables: affective, cognitive, and linguistic. Senge (1990: 75) argues that "every influence is both cause and effect. Nothing is ever influenced in one direction." Therefore, there are probably valid insights in both Sparks's and Ganschow's position and MacIntrye's perspective. One position need not exclude the other. By viewing these positions using a wider angle of focus, we validate both perspectives.

As a second-language-acquisition specialist, and sometimes a psycholinguist, I offer the following information which attempts to concisely contextualize in specific and global terms the studies by Sparks, Ganschow, and their colleagues. I also underscore the important contributions their research has made to advance our understanding of the interrelationships among affective and linguistic variables in SLA.

---

[3] For a review of the positions each of these researchers take regarding this issue, see MacIntyre (1995) and Sparks and Ganshow (1995b).

Table 1. Research on the relationship between NL skills and FL aptitude

Study	Subjects	Variables	Findings
Ganschow and Sparks (1995)	high-risk FL learners and LD students	native-language skills and foreign-language aptitude	Significant difference on NL phonological/orthographic* measures between high-risk and LD groups. No significant difference between these two groups on NL measures of semantics and MLAT
Ganschow et al. (1991)	successful FL students and unsuccessful FL students	native language skills, foreign-language aptitude, and cognitive ability	Significant difference on NL measures of phonology/orthography and syntax and MLAT. No significant difference in cognitive ability or semantic measures between these two groups.
Sparks and Ganschow (1995a)	high achievers and low achievers	native-language skills and foreign-language aptitude	Significant difference between native-language phonological/orthographic* measures and MLAT. No significant difference between high achievers and low achievers on verbal memory measures and two of three semantic measures.
Sparks et al. (1992a)	low-risk students and high-risk students	native-language skills and foreign-language aptitude	Significant relationship between native-language measures of phonology and syntax and the MLAT. No significant difference between vocabulary and reading comprehension.
Sparks et al. (1992b)	low-risk students, high-risk students, and LD students	native-language skills and foreign-language aptitude	Significant difference on MLAT and native-language measures of phonology and syntax between low-risk and LD students. There were no significant differences between high-risk and LD students on all measures except spelling.

* spelling, pseudoword recognition, word recognition, phonemic awareness

The MLAT as an predictor of foreign-language learning. In the late 1950s, Carroll and Sapon (1967) developed the MLAT, which comprises five subtests: phonetic script, numbering learning, spelling clues, words in sentences, and paired associates. The MLAT is now, however, over thirty-five years old. Some researchers (McLaughlin 1990; Skehan 1989; Spolsky 1989) suggest that this instrument can no longer be considered valid as a measure of language aptitude. In their review of cognitive variables in second-language acquisition, Gardner and MacIntyre (1992: 214) review aptitude assessment and note that "advances in language pedagogy and psychological assessment procedures require changes in aptitude assessment."[4]

The goals for foreign-language education have also changed as a result of shifts in the ways we think about languages and language learning. Swaffar, Arens, and Byrnes (1990) discuss a shift in expectation of language performance in their book *Reading for meaning*. They contend that "rather than measuring student performance against an absolute norm for vocabulary and grammar mastery," the new standard today "acknowledges the value of achieving specific communicative objectives such as linguistic creativity, i.e. self expression of authentic feelings" (Swaffar, Arens, and Byrnes 1990: 8). Given this, the findings that Sparks, Ganschow, and their colleagues report do not necessarily suggest that success on the MLAT predicts success in foreign-language learning in a communicatively-based foreign-language class.

Language aptitude within the context of SLA research since the 1950s. Spolsky (1989) has proposed a rather comprehensive model which describes the process of language acquisition. His model is appealing because it embraces a diverse array of areas and traditions[5] of research in language learning, such as linguistic, social, affective, and cognitive variables. In addition, he acknowledges the effects on SLA of differences "in the specific opportunities for learning to which the learner is exposed, either in a formal academic setting or in a more naturalistic acquisition environment" (Clark and Davidson 1993: 258).

---

[4] Sparks points out in an e-mail document (March 14, 1995) that a need to norm the MLAT does not invalidate it as a measure of language aptitude. He states that "Stanovich (1988, *Science and Learning Disabilities* 21: 210–214) argues that procedures used to diagnose or uncover explanations for performance in an educational skill are not necessarily the same procedures used to facilitate performance of that skill in an educational environment. This is an important point that is overlooked."

[5] These refer to such traditions as "linguistic analysis, description and quantification of learner variables associated with language-learning success, sociological and sociometric issues, curriculum and instructional design, and ... the design and use of appropriate data-gathering instruments" (Clark and Davidson 1993: 258).

A survey of various SLA research anthologies indicates that these diverse disciplines contribute to the process of SLA (see Brown 1987; Gass and Selinker 1994; Larsen-Freeman and Long 1991). MacIntyre (1995), then, is correct to point out that language aptitude is not the sole source to predict or effect second-language learning, and to suggest that the LCDH is incomplete if it makes the claim to be able to predict language learning over affective variables.

On the other hand, the studies by Sparks, Ganschow, and their colleagues are crucial in that they bring back into the big picture a variable neglected in the last few decades, language aptitude. Furthermore, their findings cannot be disputed since they appear to be consistent in most of their studies. In fact, most foreign-language specialists would concur that good native-language skills facilitate language learning, so that even if research had used state-of-the-art measures of language aptitude, researchers might still have found a relationship between native-language skills and foreign-language aptitude or grades. Regardless of how valid the specific findings by Sparks and Ganschow are thought to be, it is important to view their findings on language aptitude within the context of general second-language research, instead of isolated from it. As Senge (1990: 7) put it, "it's ... hard to see the whole pattern...[when] we tend to focus on snapshots of isolated parts..."

To better explain my perspective, I would like to draw an analogy based on research in foreign-language or second-language (SL) reading research which has evolved to a greater extent than research in language aptitude and language anxiety. In reading, we know that adult readers can use their pre-existing knowledge about how their first language functions, and can use sophisticated background experiences with the real world (schemata) to offset deficiencies in their mastery of a second language. In other words, we accept that multiple knowledge sources are involved in the process of reading comprehension. This approach to FL/SL reading is referred to as an Interactive Model of reading. Within an interactive model of FL/SL reading, processing strategies, content knowledge, and increased FL/SL proficiency play crucial roles in the comprehension process. Some of the reading research has also explored the differences in strategy-use between successful and unsuccessful reading comprehension (e.g. Block 1992; Hosenfeld 1976; Munby 1979; Pritchard 1990; Sarig 1987) and indicates that, like L1 reading research, readers who approach reading as a "meaning-getting process" tend to be more successful than those who approach it as a "decoding process." In short, we know that while language proficiency is a critical variable in reading comprehension, and perhaps the key variable, it is not the only one. Moreover, Stanovich (1980) claims that reading relies on an array of processes and that deficiencies in one area will lead to reliance on other areas.

Just as FL readers may be weak in one or the other skills involved in reading comprehension and compensate for this in other ways, so too may learners be weak in their analytical, discrete-point language skills (since that is what the MLAT measures), but be strongly motivated or have a positive attitude about language learning that helps them compensate for weaknesses in language aptitude. Or, they may have negative experiences in the foreign-language class because of an instructor's harsh manner of error correction, erroneous beliefs about language learning, or not doing as well as they would like. This in turn, evokes anxiety which then further debilitates their performance and learning.

In short, language anxiety can spring from poor language skills in the same way it can arise from other sources (MacIntyre 1995; Young 1991). For example, language-anxiety research consistently indicates that learners report more anxiety over having to speak in the foreign language (a combination of social anxiety, communication-apprehension, and state anxiety) (Phillips 1992; Young 1990). This type of anxiety does not limit itself to high-risk or poor language learners exclusively. In fact, Sparks and Ganschow report in two different studies (Ganschow, et al. 1994; Ganschow and Sparks 1995) "the Mean scores of the high-anxious groups on the native-language and FL aptitude measures were in the average range" (Sparks and Ganschow forthcoming: 11). They speculate that "high-anxious students do not always have weak (poor) language skills. Rather, low-anxious students 'look relatively strong because their overall native oral and written language and FL aptitude skills lie in the above average to superior range' " (Sparks and Ganschow forthcoming: 11).

In essence, the research by Sparks and Ganschow and their colleagues has allowed the question of linguistic competence to become part of the picture once again.[6] Their research has also encouraged language-anxiety researchers to examine the possibilities of interactive models, similar to the ones used in discussing research in FL or SL reading, to explain key interrelationships among affective, linguistic, and cognitive variables in SLA.

Conclusion. Although researchers have produced numerous studies on one or another learner variable, sometimes the "compartmentalization" of knowledge creates a false sense of confidence (Senge 1990: 283). We still have a long way to go to fully understand the role of cognitive and affective variables, particularly language anxiety, in adult second-language acquisition. In this brief paper, I have tried to illustrate that by using a wider angle of focus, which includes advances in language anxiety research, we could benefit by applying a systems-thinking approach in second-language-acquisition research. The interconnection of various disciplines in SLA research will suggest key relationships

---

[6] In another recent study, Ganshcow and Sparks (1995) suggest that direct instruction in Spanish phonology could help at-risk learners in foreign-language aptitude. This suggestion comes at a time when the norm is not to teach phonology in the foreign language class. For at-risk learners, however, this may actually help them feel less anxious and tense about the sounds of the foreign language they need to produce. Furthermore, it could help them decode more effectively the sounds they hear.

among cognitive, affective, and linguistic variables. By viewing these variables through a wider angle of focus and remaining open to possibilities and inter-relationships, we acknowledge that there is "no simple answer" when dealing with a phenomenon as complex as language acquisition.

REFERENCES

Alpert, Richard and Ralph N. Haber. 1960. "Anxiety in academic achievement situations." *Journal of Abnormal and Social Psychology* 61: 207–215.

Block, Elizabeth B. 1992. "See how they read: Comprehension monitoring of L2 and L2 readers." *TESOL Quarterly* 20(3): 463–491.

Brown, H. Douglas. 1987. *Principles of language learning and teaching.* Englewood Cliffs, N.J.: Prentice Hall.

Carroll, John B. and S. M. Sapon. 1967. *Modern language aptitude test, Elementary form.* New York: Psychological Corporation.

Clark, John L.D. and Fred Davison. 1993. "Language-learning research: Cottage industry or consolidated enterprise?" In Alice Omaggio Hadley (ed.), *Research in language learning.* Lincolnwood, Illinois: National Textbook Company. 254–278.

Ely, Christopher M. 1986. "An analysis of discomfort, risktaking, sociability and motivation in the L2 classroom." *Language Learning* 36: 1–25.

Ganschow, Leonore and Richard Sparks. 1986. "Learning disabilities and foreign language learning difficulties: Deficit in listening skills?" *Journal of Reading, Writing, and Learning Disabilities International* 2: 305–319.

Ganschow, Leonore and Richard Sparks. 1995. "Effects of direct instruction in Spanish phonology in the native-language skills of foreign language aptitude of at-risk foreign language learners." *Journal of Learning Disabilities* 28(2): 107–120.

Ganschow, Leonore, Richard L. Sparks, Reed Anderson, James Javorshy, Sue Sinner and Jon Patton. 1994. "Differences in language performance among high-, average-, and low-anxious college foreign language learners." *The Modern Language Journal* 78(1): 41–55.

Ganschow, Leonore, Richard Sparks, James Javorsky, Jane Pohlman, and A. Bishop-Marbury. 1991. "Identifying native language difficulties among foreign language learners in college: A foreign language learning disability?" *Journal of Learning Disabilities* 4: 530–541.

Gardner, Robert C. and Peter MacIntyre. 1992. "A student's contribution to second language learning. Part I: Cognitive variables." *Language Teaching* 25: 211–220.

Gardner, Robert C. and Peter MacIntyre. 1993. "A student's contribution to second-language learning. Part II: Affective variables." *Language Teaching* 26: 1–11.

Gardner, Robert C. and Peter MacIntyre. 1994a. "The effects of induced anxiety on three stages of cognitive processing in computerized vocabulary learning." *Studies in Second Language Acquisition* 16(1): 1–17.

Gardner, Robert C. and Peter MacIntyre. 1994b. "The subtle effects of language anxiety on cognitive processing in the second language." *Language Learning* 44: 283–305.

Gardner, Robert C., R. Moorcroft, and Peter D. MacIntyre. 1987. *The role of anxiety in second language performance of language dropouts.* Research bulletin No. 657. London, Ontario: University of Western Ontario.

Gardner, Robert C. and P.F. Tremblay. (forthcoming). "Motivation: The other affective variable." In Dolly J. Young (ed.), *Affect in FL/SL learning: A practical guide to dealing with learner anxieties.* San Francisco: McGraw-Hill.

Gass, Susan M. and Larry Selinker. 1994. *Second language acquisition.* Hillsdale, N.J.: Laurence Erlbaum Associates.

Hosenfeld, Carol. 1976. "A preliminary investigation of the reading strategies of successful and nonsuccessful second language learners." *Systems* 5: 110–123.

Larsen-Freeman, Diane and Michael Long. 1991. *An introduction to second language acquisition research.* New York: Longman.

McLaughlin, Barry. 1990. "The relationship between first and second languages: Language proficiency and language aptitude." In Birgit Harley, Patrick Allen, Jim Cummins and Merrill Swain (eds.), *The development of second language proficiency.* Cambridge, U.K.: Cambridge University Press. 158–174.

MacIntyre, Peter. 1995. "How does anxiety affect second language learning? A reply to Sparks and Ganschow." *The Modern Language Journal* 79(1): 138–154.

Munby, John. 1979. "Teaching intensive reading skills." In Ronald Mackay, Bruce Barkman, and R. R. Jordan (eds.), *Reading in a second language: Hypothesis, organization and practice.* Rowley, Massachusetts: Newbury House. 142–158.

Phillips, Elaine. 1992. "The effects of language anxiety on students' oral test performance and attitudes." *The Modern Language Journal* 76(1): 14–26.

Pritchard, Robert. 1990. "The effects of cultural schemata on reading processing strategies." *Reading Research Quarterly* 25: 273–295.

Sarig, Gissi. 1987. "High-level reading in the first and in the foreign language: Some comparative process data." In Joanne Devine, Patricia L. Carrell, and David E. Eskey (eds.), *Research in reading English as a second language.* Washington, D.C.: Teachers of English to Speakers of Other Languages. 107–120.

Senge, Peter M. 1990. *The fifth discipline: The art and practice of the learning organization.* New York: Doubleday Publishers.

Sparks, Richard and Leonore Ganschow. 1991. "Foreign language learning differences: Affective or native language aptitude differences?" *The Modern Language Journal* 75(1):3–16.

Sparks, Richard and Leonore Ganschow. 1995a. "Teachers' perceptions of students' foreign language academic skills and affective characteristics." *Journal of Educational Research.*

Sparks, Richard and Leonore Ganschow. 1995b. "A strong inference approach to causal factors in foreign language teaching: A response to MacIntyre." *The Modern Language Journal.*V, 79(2):235–244.

Sparks, Richard and Leonore Ganschow. Forthcoming. "Native language skills, foreign language aptitude, and anxiety about foreign language learning." In Dolly J. Young (ed.), *Affect in FL/SL learning: A practical guide to dealing with learner anxieties.* San Francisco: McGraw-Hill.

Sparks, Richard, Leonore Ganschow, James Javorsky, Jane Pohlman, and John Patton. 1992a. "Identifying native language deficits in high- and low- risk foreign language learners in high school." *Foreign Language Annals* 25: 403–418.

Sparks, Richard, Leonore Ganschow, James Javorsky, Jane Pohlman, and John Patton. 1992b. "Test comparisons among students identified as high-risk, low-risk, and learning disabled in high school foreign language courses." *The Modern Language Journal* 76: 142–159.

Skehan, Peter. 1989. *Individual differences in second language learning.* London: Arnold.

Stanovich, Kenneth E. 1980. "Toward an interactive-compensatory model of individual differences in the development of reading fluency." *Reading Research Quarterly* 16: 32–71.

Steinberg, Faith S. and Elaine K. Horwitz. 1986. "Anxiety and second language speech: Can conditions affect what students choose to talk about? " *TESOL Quarterly* 20(1): 131–136.

Spolsky, Bernard. 1989. *Conditions for second language learning.* Oxford: Oxford University Press.

Swaffar, Janet K., Katherine M. Arens, and Heidi Byrnes. 1991. *Reading for meaning: An integrated approach to language learning.* Englewood Cliffs, N.J.: Prentice Hall.

Trylong, Vicky Lynn. 1987. *Aptitude, attitudes and anxiety: A study of their relationships to achievement in the foreign language classroom.* Unpublished Ph.D. dissertation, Purdue University.

Young, Dolly J. 1986. "The relationship between anxiety and foreign language oral proficiency ratings." *Foreign Language Annals* 19(5): 439–435.

Young, Dolly J. 1990. "An investigation of students' perspectives on anxiety and speaking." *Foreign Language Annals* 23(6): 539–553.

Young, Dolly J. 1991. "Creating a low-anxiety classroom environment: What does the language anxiety research suggest?" *The Modern Language Journal* 75(6): 426–437.

Young, Dolly J. 1995a. "New Directions in Language Anxiety Research." In Carol Klee (ed.), *Faces in a crowd: Individual learners in multisection programs.* Boston, Massachusetts: Heinle and Heinle. 3–45.

Young, Dolly J. 1995b. "Venerable voices." In Trisha Dvorak (ed.), *Voices from the field.* Englewood Cliffs, N. J.: Prentice Hall. 193–228.

Reinventing (America's) schools:
The role of the applied linguist

JoAnn (Jodi) Crandall
University of Maryland Baltimore County

Introduction. As an applied linguist in a department of education, I am pleased to see that language teacher education is the focus of this year's Georgetown University Round Table on Languages and Linguistics. It is clear that applied linguists have a central role to play in the education of second-language teachers. But with the changing demographic profile of the United States and the increasing likelihood that most teachers will have English (as-a-second)-language learners in their classes, I believe we should expand that role to include the education of **all** teachers.

In this paper, I plan to (1) review some of these demographic factors as they relate to our nation's schools; (2) discuss some of the implications of these factors for preservice and inservice teacher education; (3) describe some of my own work in this area; (4) outline some of the educational research questions which would benefit from applied linguistic insights; and (5) conclude with a discussion of the possible roles of applied linguists in school reform.

Changing demographics and the schools. More than nine million people immigrated to the United States in the 1980s, a higher number than any decade in the twentieth century, except for the period between 1905 and 1914, when there were ten million newcomers. Because of continued immigration, refugee resettlement, family size, and other demographic and socio-cultural factors, the U.S. population is becoming increasingly diverse. Between the 1980 and 1990 Censuses, the Asian-American population more than doubled, and the Hispanic-American population increased by more than 50% (Bureau of the Census 1991). This rich diversity offers a great resource to the United States, especially in a time of increasing global interconnectedness as evidenced by the North American Free Trade Agreement or the Pacific Rim alliances; but it also represents a real challenge to our schools.

Changing demography has had a profound impact on U.S. schools. In only five years, between 1986 and 1991, the nation's school age population grew by only 4%, but the percentage of limited-English-proficient students rose by 50% (Fix and Zimmerman 1993). Los Angeles is the first major metropolitan school district with a majority school-age population that is language minority (coming from homes in which a language other than English is spoken), but if current demographic projections are accurate, the minority school population is expected to increase by more than 30% between 1990 and 2000 (American Association of Colleges for Teacher Education 1990) and by the year 2020, Hispanics will comprise 25% of the school-age population. It is not surprising, then, that by that same year (2020), an estimated fifty major metropolitan school districts will have language "minority" majority populations. If racial minorities were included, there already are fifty metropolitan school districts with majority "minority" populations, including the districts in which I live and teach (Washington, D.C. and Baltimore, Maryland). Today, across the country, it is not unusual for a school district to have students who represent eighty or more different languages, or for one school to have twenty or more languages represented.

An increasing number of these students also enter American schools with either no prior schooling or schooling which has been interrupted for several years by the political and economic conditions of their home country. Unfortunately, many immigrant students come from war-torn countries or countries in the midst of political upheaval, and the subsequent forced migration and stress have also taken a toll on these students, leaving some with what psychiatrists have suggested is a form of posttraumatic-stress disorder. These students face even greater challenges in schools, resulting in negative consequences for their school completion rates (Montemayor 1988; McDonnel and Hill 1993).

Implications for preservice and inservice teacher education. While the nation's school children are increasingly likely to be Hispanic-, Asian-, or African-American, their teachers are less likely to be so. The overwhelming majority of U.S. public school teachers are white and English-speaking, and this situation is not likely to change in the near future, since the percentage of minorities enrolled in teacher education is declining. Thus, in U.S. schools, most teachers are teaching at least some students with whom they share neither a common language nor a common culture or national background, and the number of these culturally and linguistically different students is increasing. While actual numbers are difficult to establish, in 1990, an estimated 30% of all students were minority, while only 21% of the teachers were; by the year 2000, that gap is expected to widen so that 38% of the students, but only 5% of the teachers, will be minority. Currently, while Hispanic students represent about 10% of the school age population across the country, they constitute only 1% of the teaching profession (Diaz-Rico and Smith 1994).

While there is a growing gap between the background, education, and experiences of the students and teachers in our schools, teachers have had limited professional preparation for teaching students whose languages, cultures, and educational expectations may differ substantially from their own. Few teachers have had even one course in second-language acquisition, crosscultural communication, interdisciplinary pedagogy, or other areas which would prepare them for their changing classrooms. What they know about teaching these students has been learned mostly on the job, often by talking with other teachers. But most teachers do not view this experience as adequate preparation, especially when coupled with additional challenges facing them, such as larger classes; fewer resources; and increasing student expectations manifested in higher graduation requirements, more mandated tests, and the addition of community service credits. Schools are also being asked to solve a number of problems brought to them daily from the community (substance abuse, gang activity, family breakdown, teenage pregnancy), and teachers are frequently expected to replace parents who are not there; to provide moral instruction which was traditionally offered in the home or church; to fill in for the missing school nurse or provide personal or career counseling for the overworked guidance counselors; or to oversee conflict resolution and peer mediation programs which address problems that were brought to school from the outside community. Administrative staff, who previously supported instruction, spend the majority of their time and effort on maintaining order and security or dealing with the demands of growing bureaucracies, rather than helping teachers to guide students through appropriate courses of instruction to career and educational goals. While the problems are greatest at the secondary level, they exist to an alarming degree even in elementary schools.

A variety of efforts is needed to support teachers in their attempts to work in these increasingly demanding settings, and applied linguists have a number of important roles to play in assisting teachers and schools in preservice and inservice teacher education, school-based reform and program restructuring, program and curriculum design, and collaborative research.

Needed change in preservice and inservice education. In 1984, O'Malley and Waggoner estimated that one of every two teachers in U.S. schools would have an English-language learner in class, although few teachers had even one course in English as a second language. Recognition of the increasing diversity of the student population has led to some changes in the preservice preparation of teachers, with teacher education programs restructuring to put urban education, multiculturalism, and multilingualism at their core, but that change is late in arriving. For most teachers and staff who have already exited preservice programs, a variety of inservice education programs is needed.

Perhaps the inservice education program with the broadest sweep is one mandated by the state of Florida several years ago as part of an out-of-court settlement. The signed Consent Decree requires any teacher who has even one English-as-a-second-language student (or English-language learner) in class to participate in at least sixty hours of inservice education focused on second-language acquisition, crosscultural communication, and the integration of language and content instruction. To fulfill that inservice requirement, teachers have a number of options, including courses at local universities, workshops or institutes at schools led by master teachers, a televised training program with locally available materials, or some combination of these. In addition, a new program of courses was added to the preservice education program of all ESL and other classroom teachers to make preservice education more reflective of the diverse classrooms facing future Florida teachers. While there have been some preliminary evaluations of the results of this decree, it is too early to determine the impact that both the changing inservice and preservice teacher education will have on student achievement. One problem which has frequently been identified, however, is the hostility of some teachers because participation in the program was mandatory rather than voluntary.

California has also recently revised its teaching credentials, initiating the Crosscultural, Language, and Academic Development (CLAD) and the BCLAD (Bilingual CLAD) to encourage teachers to study and be examined on areas in first- and second-language acquisition and development, culture, and integrated instruction. Ohio has also established a TESOL/Bilingual Education validation requiring twenty hours of coursework from a university or college with an approved training program for staff who work with limited-English-proficient students. As more states recognize the centrality of linguistic and cultural diversity in education, we can expect a number of changes in preservice education, as well as certification requirements, to enable all teachers to understand language development and crosscultural differences as they relate to expectations of teaching and learning. In addition, such training can help teachers become familiar with approaches which can facilitate continued cognitive growth and academic achievement for students who are acquiring English language and literacy. In both their design and implementation, these programs will need the help of psycholinguists, sociolinguists, and other applied linguists interested in the intersection of language and education.

In the meantime, applied linguists are also needed to help design and implement inservice education and to work collaboratively with educators in their efforts to redesign academic programs, develop curriculum, and create articulated sequences of courses which will allow language-minority students to develop their primary language, move through English language and literacy classes, and participate in academically equivalent sheltered versions of core courses, until they are able to compete equally in mainstream academic courses, and before moving on to postsecondary education and careers.

Project WE TEACH. In what follows, I would like to describe a school reform effort with which I have been involved for the past two years. WE TEACH (When Everyone Teaches, Everyone Achieves) is one of four national demonstration projects in immigrant secondary education funded by the Andrew

W. Mellon Foundation. The goal of the project is to help middle and high schools to improve the English language and literacy of language-minority students, to increase these students' access to the core curriculum, improve their academic achievement, and better prepare them for both postsecondary education and future careers. In plain English, the project is investigating ways to help at-risk immigrant students stay in school (nationally, language minority students are 1.5 times as likely to drop out of school than are their English-speaking peers; Cardenas et al. 1988) and to help them achieve. In addition, the project aims to encourage them to begin planning for their future early, for both a career and postsecondary education, rather than settling for an entry-level job at a local fast-food restaurant or cleaning company.

WE TEACH is a collaborative effort of the Department of Education at the University of Maryland Baltimore County, the Prince George's County (MD) Public Schools ESOL/Language Minority Programs, and the Prince George's County Coalition for the Foreign Born, a consortium of public and private community organizations concerned with educational, health, social service, and other needs of immigrants. Prince George's County (part of the greater Washington, D.C. metropolitan area) is the fifteenth largest school district in the United States, and, like many urban/suburban school districts, the majority of its population is minority. In the schools in which I work, 60–65% of the students are African-American and another 15–20% are "international" (born outside of the United States). The number of international students increases yearly.

Not only is the international population growing rapidly, it is also becoming increasingly diverse, resulting in almost constant changes for schools. For example, previously, the majority of immigrants in the County were Hispanic, Chinese, Korean, or Vietnamese. Today, they are as likely to be from the Caribbean or Africa as they are from Central America. The second fastest growing population of international students is a group which has been designated as "World English" speakers; that is, they come from Caribbean or West African countries and speak a variety of English or an English-based creole which may be quite divergent from the academic English expected in our schools. More serious, however, is the fact that many of these students arrive in the United States as adolescents, with little prior formal education and limited literacy, something which is increasingly true of students from Central America as well. Currently, about 10% of the County's international student population is in need of basic literacy instruction. The linguistic diversity of the student population has led the district to implement a variety of English-as-a-second-language, rather than bilingual, program models, but students receive bilingual support through bilingual teachers and aides and a variety of bilingual materials for both students and parents.

These culturally and linguistically diverse students are enrolled in schools in which the majority of teachers have had little or no prior experience with linguistically and culturally diverse students, crosscultural communication differences, or students with limited prior education. It is unlikely that they have had even one course to prepare them for the multilingual and multicultural classrooms that are their daily reality, and many have had little experience in studying a foreign language or living abroad. Even the ESL teachers in the district are often still enrolled in ESL teacher education, since ESL certification in Maryland is only about ten years old and the state's institutions of higher education have not been able to prepare enough Master's level ESOL/Bilingual educators.

While most of the teachers have not previously been prepared to teach language-minority students, there does exist a core of teachers who have learned a great deal in their daily interactions with international students. Many of these teachers are committed to changing the school and their own instructional practices to improve the education of their students. Thus, there is both teacher knowledge to be drawn upon and an interest in working collaboratively with teacher educators and community members to develop new programs for language minority students as part of Project WE TEACH. There is also an interest in exploring research questions through teacher–graduate-student applied-research collaborations, where the emphasis is on identifying factors which help immigrant students to achieve. This applied research, grounded in practice, takes the form of small ethnographic case studies as well as larger quantitative surveys and analyses.

Inservice and preservice education initiatives. Perhaps the most important initiatives in the project are those that focus on inservice education or professional development. The goals of these initiatives are to help teachers to continue learning from their students, their classes, and each other and to engage their students in collaborative learning and teaching. These inservice initiatives range from graduate courses offered at the school site, to opportunities for teacher inquiry and reflection. All evolved from discussions and planning by teacher-led advocacy and research teams in the schools as well as through formal needs assessments, and they are constantly revised to meet changing school priorities and needs.

The first graduate course identified as having primary importance for ESL and other teachers and administrators, was a course called "Strategies for working with linguistically and culturally diverse secondary school students." That course provided (1) a linguistic and cultural profile of the students in local schools; (2) an overview of theories of second language acquisition, with an emphasis upon academic language learning; (3) basic information on crosscultural differences that may impact on teaching and learning; and (4) a series of sessions focusing on the kinds of strategies teachers can use to help students continue their academic and linguistic growth, many of which were identified through literature reviews and in the large-scale three-year survey of Content

ESL conducted by the Center for Applied Linguistics (Crandall 1993a; Sheppard 1995). These strategies included the use of task and project work; cooperative learning and other grouping strategies; graphic organizers, interactive journals; a variety of other reading and writing experiences; and thematic units and lessons. The course was taught cooperatively by teacher educators, County teachers, visiting local area content and ESL teachers, and curriculum planners, many of whom had backgrounds in applied linguistics. Others had particular expertise in teaching math, science, or other content areas and in working with language-minority students. During the course, teachers began to feel that most of these strategies would benefit language-majority, as well as language-minority, students and could be included without watering down the content or taking undue instructional time away from other students. To reinforce that perception, as a culminating activity, we asked participating teachers to develop thematic units and lesson plans which could be used with both language minority and majority students in their classes.

A second graduate course offered on site addressed the issues of teaching World English students, that special population of international students who come to school speaking a variety of English or an English-based creole. A number of students have limited prior education and literacy, and coupled with the dialect diversity, they present real challenges to secondary school teachers who need to help them to acquire several years of education during a time in which they are also acquiring academic English and literacy. The course, "World Englishes and their speakers," parallels two other inservice courses. One focuses on Hispanic cultures and Spanish, teaching basic social and instructional Spanish and providing an introduction to the various Hispanic communities in the County; the other is devoted to Asian cultures and languages, concentrating more on the Asian cultures represented by the students, but also offering a brief introduction to the various oral and written language systems.

With the World Englishes course, we decided to increase the attention to language issues, with the hope that the insights from such a course would also help teachers better understand and facilitate learning of the majority African-American student population, many of whom speak related varieties of English. The course engages teachers in a close study of the language, literacy, and other characteristics of one World English-speaking student with limited prior education. Teachers meet weekly with a student from the Caribbean (Guyana, Jamaica, Trinidad and Tobago) or West Africa (Ghana, Liberia, Nigeria, Sierra Leone) and engage in dialogue journal writing, tutoring (especially helping with reading and writing), and a variety of language and academic development activities including discussions about school and home. Teachers audiotape, transcribe, and analyze at least a portion of one tutoring session and write weekly entries in their journals about the progress of their students.

The course is taught cooperatively by sociolinguists, community members, teachers, and the World-English-speaking students themselves, who are invited to class, especially during the night their country is discussed, so that they can amplify or contradict what is presented by the guest speaker or answer questions teachers have about students' educational experiences in their home countries and in the United States. Participants also watch *American tongues* and other videos dealing with American English varieties, read about the countries and their linguistic situations, and engage in analyses of oral and written texts.

The goals of the course are to help teachers become more aware of the systematic nature of English language variation and the similarities across these varieties, and to understand the social, cultural, and educational background of these students both in their home countries and in the United States. Together, the participants, who include teachers and administrators in the middle and high schools involved in Project WE TEACH, as well as some graduate students in ESOL/Bilingual Teacher Education, identify some strategies that could be used to help these students with limited prior education to acquire academic English literacy, and to telescope the many years of missed formal schooling into only a few years. Over time, as well, teachers have been becoming more knowledgeable about the nature of linguistic variation, the relationships among the various Caribbean and West African varieties of English (and African American Vernacular English), and strategies to help students maintain that variety while also gaining access to the academic English expected of them, especially in written texts in secondary schools. Teachers are also gaining a new respect for these students and their languages. In the beginning, teachers were apt to use terms like "bad English" or "poor grammar" to describe the students' Englishes, but after hearing from a number of guest speakers who maintained these varieties and could switch between them and more standard American English, they also developed a heightened sense of the importance of supporting each students' oral language while helping them develop the academic English used in schools. Several teachers also found the new information and strategies useful for meeting the needs of other students in the school.

These two courses will be followed this fall by a course on developing academic literacy and concepts among secondary school students with delayed or limited prior schooling. What has been learned firsthand in working with World-English-speaking students will help teachers and their schools better meet the needs of all students who are developing English language, literacy, and basic academic concepts late in their education.

A number of inservice workshops has also been offered, especially at the middle school, where teachers work together in teams to develop integrated, thematic units. To date, units have focused on themes such as patterns or explorations, allowing mathematics, science, social studies, and ESL teachers to integrate their instruction and accommodate diverse learners in their classes.

The project is also attempting to change the nature of preservice education in a number of ways, not only by including graduate students from the ESOL/Bilingual Teacher Education program in the inservice courses offered on site, but also through a number of collaborative assignments for students in these schools. We have chosen to concentrate our practicum and student teaching assignments in project schools, thus increasing the numbers of teachers in the schools and providing opportunities both for teacher candidates to learn from more experienced teachers and for more experienced teachers to be refreshed with new theories and techniques these candidates bring to class.

Additionally, some ESOL/Bilingual and other graduate teacher education students are engaged in a variety of research projects in the schools. Several are conducting ethnographic fieldwork and writing case studies on special programs and sheltered classes in these schools as part of their "Ethnography in education" course; others are engaged in thesis research. Over the years, we expect students to produce an ongoing cycle of case studies, documenting project initiatives and providing insights to teachers and school staff concerning improved ways of helping language minority (and other) students acquire English language and literacy, achieve in school, develop an enhanced sense of the value of bilingualism in their communities and future careers, and improve their career planning and college preparation. We are also fortunate to have the first doctoral student in educational policy sciences who is interested in immigrant educational issues doing her research in these schools, investigating the interaction of school, district, and state educational policy and the nature of implicit and explicit educational policy development. Gradually, what is emerging naturally from these collaborations is the establishment of a Professional Development Center at one of the schools, by which theory and practice in the education of language minority students can be brought together in a rich program of preservice and inservice teacher education.

Tutoring and mentoring initiatives. The project also involves a number of cross-age and crosslinguistic tutoring and mentoring projects designed to enhance students' own language and literacy and their sense of self-esteem. We have a number of objectives in these initiatives, but one very important one is to help linguistically and culturally diverse students learn through teaching and, in the process, to consider the possibility of teaching as a future career. If we can encourage more minority students to enter teaching as a career, we can help to redress the terrible imbalance between the large numbers of language minority students in the schools and the limited number of teachers who come from similar linguistic and cultural backgrounds.

One of these tutoring projects brings college students studying to be English teachers to the high school, where they tutor literacy level ESL students as part of a course on the nature of literacy and reading instruction. We hope that having a college student as a tutor will also serve a mentoring function, helping to humanize college and allowing students with limited prior education to consider college at some point in their future and teaching as a career.

Other cross-age tutoring programs bring former ESL students from a high school to tutor ESL students in a nearby middle school, not only providing positive role models for the middle school students, but also providing these students with someone to depend on when they move to that high school. Additionally, students studying Spanish in the high school tutor elementary school ESL students, while they are also learning Spanish from their young Spanish-speaking tutees. One example of the impact these programs can make is the elementary special education student who had been ashamed of speaking Spanish in school, but developed a new pride in his language and a sense of self-esteem as a bilingual student when his high school tutor was trying to learn Spanish from him. Our hope is that through this kind of crosslinguistic tutoring, more students will develop an enhanced pride in their heritage and a better understanding of the value of bilingualism in their future careers.

Mentors from the community are also being called upon to help students develop that sense of self-esteem. For example, Hispanic professionals working for the U.S. Department of Agriculture spend a few hours a week in the schools to mentor and tutor students. In addition, career days are held in which successful Hispanic, Asian, African, and Caribbean journalists, teachers, college professors, guidance counselors, and others are invited to talk informally with students and to reflect a range of possible career options for immigrant students. Students have also participated in a variety of field trips to local employment and educational institutions where they have been encouraged to reconsider the value of their bilingualism and biculturalism both in meeting the new community service requirement for graduation and in planning for future careers. For example, on one field trip to a local nursing home, several of the residents were delighted to find students who could speak their languages; in turn, several students have continued to visit these nursing home residents, fulfilling their community service requirements while also seeing firsthand the value of their bilingual skills.

Curriculum and course development and related research activities. If language minority students are to achieve academic success at school and be able to continue their education beyond high school, they must have access to the core curriculum and the ability to fulfill graduation requirements through a clearly articulated series of courses which help students make the transition from ESL to mainstream classrooms. A major focus of our research and planning has dealt with these curriculum and articulation issues.

What are the key milestones for ESL, especially in terms of academic language development? How can subsequent ESL and English teachers build on previous academic language tasks? How can students who need to develop basic literacy and academic concepts do so, while still developing their oral English proficiency? How might various literacy, academic skills, and English-as-a-second-language courses be sequenced to provide optimum development when both student time and school resources are limited? These are some of the questions with which an ESL Task Force has been grappling during the past year. The County has developed two basic literacy and academic skills development courses and another course focusing on academic language, but they are offered periodically at only a few schools, and most teachers have had little sense of their purposes or the students for whom they were developed. WE TEACH made it possible to initiate discussions about the courses and to establish an articulation plan which, in addition to determining the optimal sequence of these courses along with ESL offerings, identified the students who would most benedfit from the revised curriculum. In addition, high school ESL teachers were able to develop a portfolio assessment system, with a checklist of expected oral and written language tasks for each proficiency level, which accompanies the student through the ESL program. Currently, we are working to develop a similar system for the middle school that will parallel and sequence into the high school system.

Similarly, we are working to develop a potential sequence of courses which will enable language minority students to complete the expanding graduation requirements by participating in sheltered sections of some of their academic courses. Perhaps most interesting of these is a sheltered chemistry course, "Chemistry in the community," which is being taught for the first time to students at all levels of English language proficiency by a chemistry teacher who is able to take abstract chemistry concepts and make them relevant and meaningful to English language learners. Students were greeted the first day of class with signs warning them not to drink the water as an introduction to their first unit on water pollution. Graduate students in the Ethnography in education class are conducting small case studies of this and other sheltered courses in an attempt to document current practice and better understand what sheltered courses are like and how they help students make the transition to the mainstream classroom. Our hope is that additional sheltered classes can be added across the curriculum, including those related to career or vocational education. Two possible courses are a sheltered, applied economics course (perhaps focusing on entrepreneurship, since many of our language minority students would be interested in starting their own small businesses), and a sheltered computer literacy course to prepare students for keyboarding and other office career courses.

Still another transition issue being addressed is that related to postsecondary education and/or employment. It became clear very early that many language minority students had not thought of college as an option, even if they were honor-roll students. Most were from countries where one was either a university student or worked; few understood that a large percentage of American college students work and attend school. Others would not discuss college in coeducational settings, since being successful in school was not prestigious among peers. Even those who had some idea about college often lacked knowledge of application procedures or the kinds of tests required. To tackle these large issues, then, teachers in the project task forces designed an International Women's Council and later, an International Men's Council, to help students navigate the strange territory of college preparation and application. Meeting weekly after school, sometimes in the computer lab and other times in the career center, students learned about colleges, the kinds of tests required, how to write college applications (especially the culturally difficult essays about themselves), and sources of scholarship support. They learned about the TOEFL, the SAT, and ACT, and were guided through the application and testing process. A TOEFL preparation course was also developed which helped students through their first test outside of school. While it is too early to judge the effectiveness of these various initiatives, as of this writing, twenty-three of the twenty-five senior women active in the Council have been accepted by a college and several have been promised scholarship support. An additional group of sophomores and juniors has been mentored by these students and will begin the formal application process next year.

Another serious transitional issue facing some language minority students is the hiatus in their education that occurs because of travel to home countries, which may come at any time during the school year and seriously interrupt their language and content learning. One attempt to deal with this has been the development of Travel Learning Units which involve tasks that can be undertaken in the home country to help students to continue their academic growth outside of school. Some of these are practical tasks that involve academic literacy and thinking skills similar to those required in the state functional reading, writing, math, and citizenship tests. These tests represent a serious challenge to many of these language minority students.

Transitions between the home and school are also a focus of project attention. The project is exploring ways of better integrating the home and community into the school and taking the school to the home and community. Parents have participated in student leadership activities such as weekend retreats and have been involved in students' homework activities where the parent is the expert. A number of other ideas is being considered, including a series of discussion sessions about parent and community issues and a combined computer literacy and ESL class for adults.

In a recent project report, I said that the only constant in schools is change. All school change is a process, and thus transitions in school policies and procedures are also a part of this project. For example, in the first year of this project, one of the secondary schools experimented with a number of different scheduling options, finally deciding on a four-period day for the next year. That represents both an opportunity and a challenge for language minority students who will be responsible for fewer subjects in a semester, but will also be engaged in longer periods of time focused on any one area. What are the best ways of organizing instruction given this new schedule and how can English language and literacy development best be incorporated into it? These are just a few of the questions being addressed in the larger transition to a new school day.

The research agenda. A project like WE TEACH has the potential to continue to expand indefinitely, limited only by the time and resources of the teachers and others working with it. But an equally important part of the project involves time for reflection, for analyzing project-related data, looking back at project initiatives, and considering the need for change. Throughout the project, teachers and graduate students/teacher candidates have been engaged in a variety of applied research efforts, attempting in some small way to provide a preliminary answer to some of the most important questions facing education (some of which I identified previously in Crandall 1993a and 1993b). These questions include:

(1) What is the optimal sequence of course offerings for immigrant secondary-school students which will enable them to achieve, have access to the core curriculum, and meet ever-increasing graduation requirements?

(2) What are the critical dimensions of programs that will encourage immigrant students to continue their education?

(3) How can schools support students' languages and cultures and help them to understand the value of bilingualism and biculturalism both in their education and their future careers?

(4) What are the attributes of effective sheltered instruction? What are some strategies to increase the context and reduce the cognitive and linguistic complexity while still helping students to meet the same curricular objectives as English-speaking students? Which of these sheltered instructional strategies are beneficial for mainstream students? Can sheltered instruction be used in classes of English-language learners and English-speaking students? Of English-language learners at all levels (or must they be at an intermediate level of proficiency)?

(5) What are some ways to integrate better the home and community in the school and the school in the home and community? How can schools more effectively build upon what students bring with them to school in their knowledge and experiences?

(6) What is the impact of leadership education, community service, and other after-school activities in helping students to stay in school, to achieve, and to continue their education after graduation?

(7) What is the role of mentoring and tutoring in academic achievement of both the mentor and the tutor? Does tutoring increase language and cognitive development? Does it lead to increased interest in teaching as a career?

(8) How does case study and action research by teachers change their perceptions, attitudes, and/or instructional approaches?

(9) How is immigrant and language minority educational policy developed on a daily basis at schools? What is the nature of the relationships between school, district, and state policy? and

(10) How does language and dialect study affect the attitudes and instructional practices of teachers?

The role of the applied linguist. As our experiences demonstrate, in school reform efforts which are largely focused on making schools more responsive to the increasing ethnic and linguistic diversity of the student population, applied linguists have a number of roles to play. These include, but are not limited to:

(1) serving as a catalyst for school change;

(2) providing research direction and synthesizing available research;

(3) identifying appropriate literature and other resources concerning issues of linguistic and cultural diversity and instruction or assessment;

(4) helping to articulate the research questions;

(5) stimulating discussion and reflection;

(6) providing professional development through courses, workshops, and opportunities for research and reflection;

(7) helping to create schools in which diversity is less of a problem and more of a resource; and

(8) encouraging greater linkages between linguistic and educational research and practice for both graduate students and teachers.

When this kind of a program is developed at schools and teacher education is offered at the school site, preservice teachers (including student teachers), novice and experienced teachers, graduate students, teacher educators, and other faculty can come together to provide preservice teacher education that is more grounded in real-world concerns and inservice teacher education that is more informed by recent research and theory.

This is an exciting time for applied linguists interested in education. Opportunities for relevant applied linguistic research abound and the possibility of influencing some of the linguistically- and culturally-diverse student popula-tion to consider teaching or educational research as future careers increases. At the very least, the presence of additional interested and well-informed adults in the schools should help alleviate some of the pressures teachers currently face and provide more opportunities for both student and teacher reflection and growth.

REFERENCES

American Association of Colleges for Teacher Education. 1990. *The next level: Minority teacher supply and demand, a policy statement.* Washington, D.C.: American Association of Colleges for Teacher Education.

Association of Teacher Educators. 1991. *Restructuring the education of teachers.* Report to the Commission on the Education of Teachers into the 21st Century. Reston, Virginia: Association of Teacher Educators.

Bureau of the Census. 1991. *1990 census.* Washington, D.C.: Bureau of the Census.

Cardenas, Jose A., Maria del Refugio Robledo, and Dorothy Waggoner. 1988. *The undereducation of American youth.* San Antonio, Texas: Intercultural Development Research Association.

Council of Chief State School Officers. "A concern about ... Limited English proficient students in intermediate schools and in high schools." *Concerns* 40(July): 1-7.

Crandall, JoAnn. 1993a. "Content-centered learning in the United States." *Annual Review of Applied Linguistics* 13: 111-126.

Crandall, JoAnn. 1993b. "Current directions in curriculum development and materials preparation for culturally and linguistically diverse students." In G. Richard Tucker (ed.), *Policy and practice in the education of culturally and linguistically diverse students.* Alexandria,Virginia: Teachers of English to Speakers of Other Languages.

Diaz-Rico, Lynne T. and Jerilynn Smith. 1994. "Recruiting and retaining bilingual teachers: A cooperative school-community-university model." *The Journal of Education for Language Minority Students* 14(Winter): 255-268.

Fix, Michael and Wendy Zimmerman. 1993. *Educating immigrant children; Chapter 1: In the changing city.* Washington, D.C.: Urban Institute.

Garcia, Eugene E. 1987-1988. *Effective schooling for language minority students.* Focus No. 1. Washington, D.C.: National Clearinghouse for Bilingual Education.

Gay, Genera. 1993. "Building cultural bridges: A bold proposal for teacher education." *Education and Urban Society* 25(3): 284-299.

Hadaway, Nancy L., Viola Florez, Patricia J. Larke, and Donna Wiseman. 1993. "Teaching in the midst of diversity: How do we prepare?" In Mary J. O'Hair and Sandra J. Odell (eds.), *Diversity and teaching:Teacher education handbook.* Fort Worth, Texas: Harcourt, Brace, Jovanovich. 60-70.

Lucas, Tamara, Rosemary Henze, and Ruben Donato. 1990. "Promoting the success of Latino language minority students." *Harvard Educational Review* 60(3): 315-340.

O'Malley, J. Michael and Dorothy Waggoner. 1984. "Public school teacher preparation and the teaching of ESL." *TESOL Newsletter* 18(3): 1, 18-22.

McDonnel, Lorraine M. and Paul Hill. 1992. *Newcomers in American schools: Meeting the education needs of immigrant youth.* Washington,D.C.: RAND Corporation.

Minicucci, Catherine and Laurie Olsen. 1992. *Programs for secondary limited English proficient students: A California study.* Focus No. 5. Washington, D.C.: National Clearinghouse for Bilingual Education.

Minicucci, Catherine and Laurie Olsen (eds.). 1992. *Educating students from immigrant families: Meeting the challenge in secondary schools.* Santa Cruz, California: Center for Research on Cultural Diversity and Second Language Learning, University of California.

Montemayor, Abelardo. 1994. "A blueprint for an educational response to the needs of immigrant students." *IDRA Newsletter* January: 3–6.

National Council of La Raza. 1993. *The forgotten half: Two-thirds: An Hispanic perspective on apprenticeship European style.* Washington, D.C.: National Council of La Raza.

Sheppard, Ken. 1995. *Content-ESL across the USA; Volume I: A technical report.* Washington, D.C.: Center for Applied Linguistics.

Stein, Hollis, John Nelson, and Carolyn Bernache. 1992. " Teaching literacy to secondary school students through school content." Bladensburg, Maryland: Prince George's County Public Schools, ESOL/Language Minority Programs. Ms.

Valverde, Silvia A. 1987. "A comparative study of Hispanic high school dropouts and graduates: Why do some leave school early and some finish?" *Education and Urban Society* 19(3): 320–329.

Waggoner, Dorothy. 1992. "The increasing multiethnic and multilingual diversity of the U.S.: Findings from the 1990 census." *TESOL Matters* 2(5): 12–13.

Waggoner, Dorothy. 1993. "1990 Census shows dramatic change in the foreign-born population in the U.S." *NABE News* 16(7): 1, 18–19.

Research internships:
Involving undergraduate foreign-language
secondary-education majors in ethnographic research

Steven J. Loughrin-Sacco
Boise State University

Introduction. During the 1986–1987 academic year, a team of three faculty and five undergraduate-student researchers conducted a year-long ethnography of an elementary French class at Michigan Technological University. The research team conducted the study to gain insights into how students at Michigan Tech, primarily science and engineering majors, learn French in a classroom setting. The team studied a cross-section of classroom behavior and the context in which it took place, using the classic troika of ethnographic data-collection measures: Daily classroom observations, interviews, and the collection of all students work, course records, and any other relevant documentation. The three areas of inquiry that evolved in the study (Loughrin-Sacco et al. 1992) included:

(1) Institutional context: The position of the class within the framework of the institution;
(2) Social context: The interpersonal relationships within the French class; and
(3) Learning conditions: The variables that impacted learning (methods, techniques, materials, class activities, evaluation, etc.).

Among the more interesting findings were:

(1) Institutional and social variables had much more of an impact on learning than did methods variables;
(2) The appearance of false beginners in the elementary French class had a sustained negative impact on true beginners in terms of performance and anxiety levels;
(3) Oral production was the most anxiety-ridden activity for both true and false beginners;
(4) Both true and false beginners constantly experienced a grammar overload;
(5) True beginners functioned nearly as well as false beginners on Natural Approach–type activities; and

(6) All students found intensive communicative writing beneficial to their learning of French.

Rationale for using team ethnography and undergraduate-student researchers. Despite the aforementioned discussion of the study's research focus and findings, the purpose of this paper is to discuss the successes we had with undergraduate-student researchers in the ethnographic study. The keys to the success of the ethnographic study was our use of team ethnography, a procedure that my colleague and co-research director Ellen Bommarito learned under Egon Guba at Indiana University, and the use of undergraduate researchers to collect and analyze data, and to derive and write up conclusions. There are numerous advantages to the use of a team approach to ethnographic inquiry versus the use of a single ethnographer that we traditionally see in anthropology, sociology, and linguistics.

First, the use of a team enabled us to examine the French class in great depth (in both scope and duration). A single ethnographer at an institution like Michigan Tech, who regularly faces an eleven-hour teaching load per quarter and heavy committee work, would have found it overwhelming and impractical to observe the French class for over one hundred thirty class periods, conduct three hundred and fifteen hours of interviews, study student work, and analyze over 3,000 pages of data. Second, team ethnographic research strengthened data-analysis procedures because it added researcher triangulation to data-source triangulation. In the French study, members of the research team typically strove to concur on hypotheses and conclusions. The inherent difficulty in finding concurrence among eight researchers pushed team members to find ample evidence to support their positions. Third, we reduced the danger of researcher bias by putting two researchers in the French class for classroom observations. In addition, we reduced researcher bias because the elementary French class and its participants were studied by researchers representing several disciplines such as applied linguistics, cultural studies, English rhetoric and composition, and scientific and technical communication. Team members contributed to the study through their various views on language acquisition, literacy, and learning theory.

The decision to include undergraduates as researchers was indeed controversial. Most language-acquisition research is conducted by professors or graduate students with a high level of sophistication in foreign-language-acquisition theory and research methodology. Can undergraduate students serve as adequate data collectors and analysts in an ethnographic study? We were compelled to consider the use of undergraduates for practical reasons. At the time of the study, Michigan Tech did not have a full-fledged graduate program in the Department of Humanities. To conduct a year-long ethnography, we needed researchers who could commit the time to collect and analyze data on a daily basis for at least three quarters. Our colleagues in Humanities had neither the time nor the interest in participating in such a time-consuming study of a French class. The decision was made then to train a select group of undergraduate Scientific and Technical Communication (STC) majors and integrate them fully into the study.

As we prepared for the French study, we were convinced that undergraduate students could indeed perform effectively as data collectors and analysts, provided they were carefully trained and supervised. In prior ethnographies of a ten-week first-year English composition class and an art appreciation class at Michigan Tech (George 1990; George and Young 1991), we discovered that undergraduate researchers were dedicated and capable data collectors and critical analysts. They conducted thorough classroom observations and competent interviews, synthesized data in their development of hypotheses and generalizations, and they unexpectedly proved to be tenacious and successful debaters in defense of their arguments. Most importantly, we found that the undergraduate researchers developed an unusually strong rapport with their student informants that led to open and frank interviews in all three studies. We felt that faculty researchers, and even graduate-student researchers, would not have had the same success soliciting honest and frank information from students in the study.

Training. The research team consisted of five undergraduate researchers, a senior faculty researcher, and two French professors. The undergraduate researchers, all with excellent academic records and all having had one year of college French, were senior STC majors. All five received nine hours of required Senior Project credit for their work in the study. Before participating, the five undergraduate researchers took a three-credit course that served as their theoretical and methodological training. In this course, they read and discussed Spradley's *Ethnographic interview* (1979) and *Participant observation* (1980) and Guba's *Toward a methodology of naturalistic inquiry in educational evaluation* (1978) in addition to numerous articles on data collection and analysis. They also practiced classroom observations and interviews under close tutelage. In each case, they worked with teachers and students unconnected with the study, and their observation notes and interview transcripts were brought to meetings and carefully critiqued.

At the outset of the study, the undergraduate researchers conducted their first few classroom observations in conjunction with the auditor, who observed alongside them and then compared notes. For their early interviews, the student ethnographers planned questions with the help of the project supervisor and their transcripts were critiqued. The auditor, a veteran undergraduate researcher who had participated in a previous study at Michigan Tech, was trained for his special tasks by reading some additional theoretical material, examining the journal written by auditors from previous projects, and conversing with the project supervisor.

Undergraduate researchers as data collectors. Classroom observation notes served as the backbone of the data-collection procedures. Observers were also assigned specific tasks in order to observe behavior of particular interest to the team. Sometimes they were asked to observe the whole class, small groups, or particular individuals. For classroom observations, we placed two undergraduate researchers on a rotational basis in the back two corners of the French class for an average of three days per week (out of four possible days) from September to May. The observer's task was to record as much information as possible pertaining to classroom behavior. Each day's handwritten notes included a seating chart at the top of the page. Times were noted in the left-hand margins of the notes at approximately five-minute intervals. All class events, such as small-group work, grammar explanations, drills, games, etc., and as many student and teacher behaviors as possible were noted. Below is a thirty-second segment of sample observation notes in which an observer focuses on one small group:

9:05   T (teacher) tells class to break up into groups of three.
        Russ, Mary, & John place their desks facing each other.
        Russ asks group in English what they're supposed to do.
        Mary answers in English; ask interview questions on p. 45.
        Mary asks other two from text: "Qui la vaisselle chez vous?"
        John laughs, says: "Pas moi!"
        Russ says haltingly: "Moi, je faire la vaisselle." *
        T, facing group, corrects Russ: "Je *fais* la vaisselle." "Don't forget
            to conjugate the verb."

The most significant feature of the sample notes is what is left out: The observer's opinion of classroom events or behavior. The observation notes should only indicate descriptions of factual behaviors and events, not interpretations thereof. For instance, the observer might suspect that Russ continues to have problems with the concept of conjugating verbs, or continues to come to class unprepared, or is bored. However, the observer is expected to place an asterisk after a particular behavior and elaborate in his or her research journal on what he or she suspects. The undergraduate-student researchers recorded entries in their research journal after every classroom observation and informant interview. Below are excerpts from one research journal in which the undergraduate researcher (Clark 1987) gives her impression of events and behaviors in her January 16 classroom observation:

When they did "trouvez quelqu'un qui..." ("Find somebody who...")
they were really getting into it. They were laughing and getting pretty
loud... I don't remember our classes last year enjoying that exercise as

much as this class did. Even after they were sitting down, they were talking to each other... Barbara seems to fade in and out of class... At the beginning of class, (the teacher) said that all "delinquent" homework had to be in by 5 o'clock. I'm anxious to see who gets it in and what happens if somebody turns it in, say, Monday morning instead.

How intrusive or unintrusive were the undergraduate observers? Our field notes contain ample evidence that they fit in naturally in the French class and that both the teacher and the students behaved as if they were not part of the study. The undergraduate researchers noted several times during the year when they were asked by students to participate in small-group work as if they were actual students in the class. They also noted when students were quick and attentive, when they fell asleep or did Chemistry homework in class, and even when one or two students cheated on in-class exams. They further remarked on the teacher's "best" and "worst" behavior, i.e. when he seemed prepared and unprepared, when he was happy or angry with the students, and even when he dismissed class early. All of this rich information was used in conjunction with interview data and student work to form the basis of hypotheses and conclusions. Overall, the undergraduate researchers performed their classroom observations thoroughly and in a disciplined fashion. Their research journals revealed an astute perceptiveness of classroom behavior.

Interviews of class participants by the undergraduate researchers provided a crucial dimension of data collection. Interviews were a liberating experience for the students and the teacher where they could describe events in the class, learner and teacher strategies, and their feelings of satisfaction, joy, anger, frustration, or doubt. For the research team, interviews elucidated classroom behavior and events, confirming or rejecting many of the team's hypotheses. The undergraduate researchers interviewed eleven students, representing true and false beginners, males and females, and successful and less successful learners. In all, they conducted twenty-nine interviews with students and six interviews with the teacher for a total of three hundred and twenty-three hours. All interviews were recorded on cassette tape with the permission of the informants; afterwards, all interviews were transcribed by the undergraduate researchers and the transcripts were duplicated for each member of the team.

Most interviews, standardized during team meetings, were designed to examine general issues about the class or a particular aspect of the class during team meetings. The undergraduate researchers helped generate the standardized questions and then had the leeway to ask follow-up questions or to add questions when they thought it would generate additional information. All interviews began with questions on how the class was going, what they were doing, and how they were doing. (It is interesting to note that the teacher and the students often expressed different perceptions in response to these questions.) Below are some sample questions asked in a focused interview on writing in the French class:

(1) Your French professor has told us that in your French class four different skills are covered: Speaking, listening, reading, and writing. Of these, which do you consider to be your strengths? Your weaknesses? Rank order them for me.

(2) Can you describe for me the writing assignments you do for French? What does [the teacher] expect on these assignments?

(3) What kinds of responses do you get on these writing assignments? How do you feel about the responses? When you get a writing assignment back, what do you do with it? How do you usually do on the assignments?

(4) When you have a writing assignment, exactly how do you go about doing it?

(5) What role do these writing assignments play in the French course? What do you think the teacher intends for you to get from them? What (if anything) do you actually get?

It was in conducting interviews that the undergraduate researchers excelled. Their skill as interviewers came from their ability to develop a rapport with their student informants which unleashed a flood of information and feelings (both positive and negative) that course evaluations and student-teacher conversations did not reveal. The teacher of the French course, though possessing good classroom rapport with most of his students, was shocked at the specificity of comments and the intensity of emotions when he read the transcripts after the academic year ended. For example, Eric criticized the busy-work involved in completing the text's purportedly communicative workbook exercises and said that it took time away from his letter-writing to friends in French; Tom, a false beginner, empathized with the plight of his true-beginner friends in class; John, a true beginner, said he would not take any more French because he had to spend up to twenty hours per week on the homework; George admitted copying a friend's lab exercises and cheating on in-class exams; several students disputed the teacher's course goals that focused on communication, claiming instead that grammatical accuracy and spelling precision were the keys to getting a superior grade; several students wished the teacher would focus more on offering authentic listening and reading assignments and less on formal grammar instruction; finally, most students graphically said the textbook "sucked" despite its popularity among teachers nationwide. Perhaps textbook editors should include more students and fewer professors in the prepublication review process. In the interview process, the undergraduate researchers remained professional by protecting student confidentiality and by retaining their role as researchers and not going "native" as they developed the rapport between themselves and the student informants.

Undergraduate researchers as data analysts. Like all ethnographies, the French study proceeded in a year-long cycle of data collection and analysis. The undergraduate researchers analyzed data in four ways. First, in what represents the first formal stage of data analysis, they kept a research journal in which they summarized their classroom observations and interviews, explored their feelings and biases, speculated about the significance of behaviors and events, and formulated hypotheses that led to "generalizations." Second, data was analyzed in weekly team meetings. The research team met for two or more hours at the senior researcher's house to summarize the past week's events in the French class, plan future classroom observations and interviews, resolve group conflicts, and analyze data. Third, in early November, the undergraduate researchers began the "generalization" stage of data analysis by formulating "truths" about the class. Generalizations, which are short and numerous, were constantly revised during the course of the study. Fourth, the generalizations evolved into "write-ups" which combined several generalizations into a longer narrative of classroom events and behavior. Theoretically the write-ups, taken together, told the story of the French class, or at least those aspects of the class that the research team deemed important. The formulation of generalizations and write-ups required the intensive documentation of evidence found in the classroom observations, interviews, and student work. Below are some sample condensed generalizations from the French study (Clark, Erickson, Stoor, and Worth 1987):

(1) Students who scored high enough on the placement exam to place into second-year French will not make significant improvement in their French skills in the first-year sequence;

(2) The combination of inexperienced and experienced students together in the classroom has negative effects on the inexperienced students;

(3) [The teacher's] actions and comments encourage students to speak French in front of the class although in spite of this, many students still do not speak French in class for a variety of reasons; and

(4) One of the students' favorite activities is the teacher's use of French to describe his personal experiences in France.

At this point, it is important to describe the role of the auditor in data analysis. We included an auditor as a member of the research team in part to enhance the validity of the team's findings. Ethnographic research is by its nature subjective in data collection and analysis. The auditor in the French study was a "veteran" undergraduate ethnographer who participated in a previous

Michigan Tech project. He was not part of the data-collection process, nor did he formulate any generalizations or write-ups. Instead, his job was to be a skeptic, playing the devil's advocate about each hypothesis and conclusion formulated by the research team. The auditor had to be completely familiar with all classroom-observation and interview data and then work with the research team on examining generalizations and write-ups. It was his job, in conjunction with the senior researcher, to force the team members to consider all possible relevant explanations in their write-ups and to insist on their taking all relevant evidence (even contradictory evidence) into account. Above all, the auditor's job was to ensure that the arguments presented in the generalizations and write-ups were logically developed and fully supported by evidence. The process of analyzing data may seem from my description like a linear one, but the process was recursive. Generalizations and write-ups were constantly modified and combined, and extensively revised, based on the review of available evidence and further data collection. Finally, it should be noted that the undergraduate researchers contributed the vast majority of conclusions cited in Loughrin-Sacco et al. (1992).

Using research internships to enhance teacher training. Even though the undergraduate researchers in the Michigan Tech ethnographies majored in Scientific and Technical Communication, research internships for future K–12 foreign-language teachers and applied linguists would enhance their professional development and provide assistance to the foreign-language-acquisition researcher. Research internships, involving qualitative-research studies, can take several shapes besides the year-long ethnography. I have involved undergraduates in the study of a two-week summer intensive French course (Loughrin-Sacco, Matthews, Sweet, and Miner 1990) and graduate students in a ten-week study of anxiety levels of true and false beginners in an elementary French class (Loughrin-Sacco 1991). In both studies, undergraduate researchers committed themselves to only one quarter as a research intern. As part of a secondary-foreign-language methods course, future K–12 foreign-language teachers can be trained to conduct classroom observations and interviews.

At Michigan Tech, research internships were very popular for several reasons. First and foremost, participation in a research project satisfied part or all of a nine-credit internship requirement in the Department of Humanities. Second, undergraduate researchers in all three studies received extensive training in ethnographic theory, observation and interviewing techniques, data analysis, and academic writing. Third, Scientific and Technical Communication majors relished applying their study of learning theory, literacy, language acquisition, rhetoric, and technical communication in a professional context. By participating in an actual research study, undergraduate researchers received a unique perspective on the teaching–learning process. They investigated this process from a variety of vantage points—from the students', the teacher's, and their own as researchers. Even though only a few of the undergraduate researchers continued their ethnographic research in graduate school, most agreed that their participation in research studies was the most valuable aspect of their postsecondary education and that their training and participation benefitted them on the job as technical writers, document specialists, editors, and managers. Finally, several of the undergraduate researchers received publication credit as co-authors of articles in academic journals. Future K–12 foreign-language teachers and applied linguists would buttress their knowledge of language acquisition and the teaching–learning process if they had the opportunity to serve as research interns.

Conclusion. When we think of internships for undergraduate college students, we normally think of student teaching or internships with businesses or government. Research is an additional area where undergraduate students, with proper guidance, training, and supervision, can do internships. In three ethnographic studies at Michigan Technological University, undergraduate students demonstrated that they could successfully collect, analyze, and write up data. In the French study, five undergraduate students participated in a year-long ethnographic study where they collected and analyzed data in an attempt to better understand how science and engineering students learn French in a classroom context. Their participation in the study and the publication of an article in the *Canadian Modern Language Review* (Loughrin-Sacco et al. 1992) contributed in large part to the article's nomination for the ACTFL/MLJ Paul Pimsleur Award for Research in Foreign Language Education.

Although Scientific and Technical Communication majors participated in the French study, research internships could also benefit future K–12 foreign-language teachers and applied linguists. Future teachers receive plenty of experience teaching and tutoring before they officially enter the profession, but receive little or no time immersed in a community of learners. In the French ethnography, the undergraduate researchers worked with a community of learners for a year, experiencing first-hand their joys, fears, frustrations, successes, and failures. They saw the teacher through the students' perspective; they witnessed how reluctant students were in making their needs known to their instructor and how easy it was for the teacher to misinterpret students' needs; and they observed that some students were often wiser than their teacher in selecting learning activities that met their needs.

Research internships have the potential to provide other benefits to future teachers as well. Research internships would give future teachers an opportunity to apply their textbook knowledge in a professional context. In an internship involving an ethnographic study, future teachers would also learn how to conduct classroom observations and interviews, search for evidence, synthesize data, compose and defend arguments, critically analyze others' arguments, and write for professional purposes. In addition, research internships would provide future K–12 foreign-language teachers and applied linguists with insights into language acquisition, literacy, and language learning that they cannot acquire in books or lectures.

For research internships to succeed, several conditions are necessary. First, the faculty member must be willing to commit time to train, manage, and supervise undergraduate researchers in exchange for their help in collecting and analyzing data. Second, the institution or department must have in place an internship or practicum requirement for graduation. At Michigan Tech, all majors in the Department of Humanities had a nine-credit Senior Project which promoted opportunities for faculty and students to work together on research projects. Third, the faculty member must select only mature, dedicated, and academically solid students to join them in a research project. Fourth, whenever possible, the *quid pro quo* should extend beyond the benefits of professional development and academic credits to include co-authorship in presentations and publications.

Our profession constantly trumpets the importance of a learner-centered foreign-language curriculum. However, learner-centered foreign-language education involves more than the use of collaborative activities and proficiency-oriented materials. If we are to become truly learner-centered, we must better understand learners by involving them in the description of their learning process and the development of a foreign-language curriculum. Current teacher-training practices focus too much on theory and praxis and not enough on what Bailey (this volume) calls "voices from the classroom." Research internships, especially those involving ethnographic research, would make future K–12 foreign-language teachers more sensitive to the needs and practices of the learner and lead to a teacher-training model that fully utilizes learner input in making curricular decisions.

REFERENCES

Bailey, Kathleen. This volume. "What teachers say about teaching."
Clark, Cathy. 1987. "Response to observations," January 16 field notes.
Clark, Cathy, Michelle Erickson, Jody Stoor, and Kevin Wirth. 1987. Field notes (undated).
George, Diana. 1990. "The struggle with empowerment: Hearing the voices of dissent." In Donald Daiker and Max Morenberg (eds.), *Theory and practice in teaching writing*. Upper Mountclair, N.J.: Boynton-Cook Publishers. 212–219.
George, Diana and Arthur P. Young. 1991. "Voices of participation: Three case studies of engineering students in an art appreciation class." In Peter Elbow, Pat Belanof, and Sheryl Fountain (eds.), *Nothing begins with N: New investigations of freewriting*. Upper Mountclair, N.J.: Boynton-Cook Publishers. 111–135.
Guba, Egon G. 1978. *Toward a methodology of naturalistic inquiry in educational evaluation*. Monograph 8. Los Angeles, California: UCLA Center for the Study of Evaluation.

Loughrin-Sacco, Steven J. 1990. "Inside the black box revisited: Toward the integration of naturalistic inquiry in classroom research on foreign language learning." *Polylingua* 1(1): 22–26.

Loughrin-Sacco, Steven J. 1991. "Of apples and oranges: The effects of integrating beginners and false beginners in elementary French classes." In Sally Sieloff Magnan (ed.), *Challenges in the 1990s for college foreign language programs*. Boston: Heinle and Heinle. 89–112.

Loughrin-Sacco, Steven J., Sylvia Matthews, Wendy M. Sweet, and Jan A. Miner. 1990. "Reviving language skills: A description and evaluation of Michigan Tech's summer intensive French course." *ADFL Bulletin* 21(ii): 34–40.

Loughrin-Sacco, Steven J. et al. 1992. "More than meets the eye: The ethnography of an elementary French class." *The Canadian Modern Language Review* 49(1): 80–101.

Spradley, James P. 1979. *The ethnographic interview*. New York: Holt, Rinehart, and Winston.

Spradley, James P. 1980. *Participant observation*. New York: Holt, Rinehart, and Winston.

Systemic-functional linguistics and the education of second-language teachers: A case study

David Nunan
University of Hong Kong

Introduction. In 1989, a federally-funded project was established in Australia to improve the quality of factual/academic writing by L2 school students in Australia. The basis of the project was an innovative in-service package for training teachers in the use of systemic-functional linguistics for analyzing and assessing students' writing, and for designing pedagogical packages for improving factual writing. In this paper I shall describe the intervention program which was developed, as well as the linguistic model on which it was based. I shall then present the results of a study which was carried out to evaluate the effectiveness of the program, as well as the extent to which teachers were able to incorporate into their pedagogical repertoire the linguistic model underlying the program. Results suggest that, while teachers were able to appropriate the discourse of systemic-functional linguistics, and were able to utilize effectively the sample materials contained in the in-service package, they were not able to use the linguistic model for designing or adapting their own materials. Implications of the study for the education of second-language teachers are presented and discussed, and a model program for addressing the problems which emerged from the DSP Disadvantaged Schools Project Writing Package is presented.

Functional-linguistic models and the notion of "genre." Functional models of linguistic analysis are developed to account for relationships between the forms of the language and the various uses to which the language is put. The systematic relationship between language structure and function is described by Halliday in the following way:

> Every text—that is, everything that is said or written—unfolds in some context of use; furthermore, it is the uses of language that, over tens of thousands of generations, have shaped the system. Language has evolved to satisfy human needs; and the way it is organized is functional with respect to those needs—it is not arbitrary. A functional grammar is essentially a

"natural" grammar, in the sense that everything in it can be explained, ultimately, by reference to how language is used. (Halliday 1985: xiii)

Recently both Halliday and Martin (see for example Halliday and Martin 1993) have made important conceptual advances in the analysis of high-school textbooks from a systemic-functional perspective. This analytical work provides detailed descriptions of the characteristic linguistic features of school texts.

A key concept for many working within this functional perspective is "genre." A "genre" is a particular type of oral or written communication such as a narrative, a casual conversation, a poem, a recipe, or a description. Different genres are typified by a particular structure and by grammatical forms that reflect the communicative purpose of the genre in question.

At present, linguists are studying different text and discourse types in an effort to identify their underlying generic structure, and the linguistic elements which characterized them. In addition to identifying generic structure and linguistic features, genre analysts also look at other discourse features such as topicalization, the use of reference, and the operation of given/new structures in text.

This model has found a number of pedagogical applications, most recently by Hammond, Burns, Joyce, Brosnan, and Gerot (1992). These researchers argue that three key principles flowing out of the theory of systemic-functional linguistics have direct relevance for language teachers. These are as follows:

- Language is functional, that is, language is the way it is because of the meaning it makes. The theory suggests that resources available within the systems of discourse, grammar, and vocabulary are utilized in specific ways to make specific meanings;
- It is a theory of language in context, and suggests that language can only be understood in relation to the context in which it is used. The different purposes for using language and different contexts result in different language texts. The construction of language texts in turn impacts on the context. There is thus a two-way relationship between text and context; and
- The theory focuses on language at the level of the whole text. By text is meant any connected stretch of language that is doing a job within a social context. Thus the term "text" is used to refer to stretches of spoken and written language. Text may be as short as one word, e.g. *exit*, or it may be as long as a book such as a training manual. This theory differs from most other approaches to language study, notably traditional grammar, which offers systematic analyses of language only up to the level of the sentence, and provides little guidance to the language learner, who needs to know about structure, organization, and

development in connected oral discourse and written texts. (Hammond et al. 1992: 1)

The "teaching–learning" cycle. The proponents of this approach to language education have developed a curriculum model which they call the "teaching-learning" cycle. This cycle has four recursive phases. These are as follows:

- Building control of the field: This initial phase is designed to provide learners with the background content-knowledge which they will need in order to carry out the tasks and achieve the goals of the curriculum;
- Modeling: Here learners are provided with examples, in the form of models, of how native speakers or competent users of the language would use the language;
- Joint construction: Teacher and student work collaboratively to create a text following the model provided in the preceding state in the teaching–learning cycle; and
- Independent construction: Learners, working independently, construct their own texts.

The conceptual model provided by systemic-functional linguistics, and the curriculum genre developed by Christie (1985), Hammond (1990), and others (e.g. Hammond, Burns, Joyce, Brosnan, and Gerot 1992) has been used in the development of an in-service teacher-education program. The program was designed to give teachers technical knowledge of "genre" theory and practice in order to equip them to teach factual writing. It is of interest because of its theoretically motivated underpinnings which, in the next section, will be described in some detail.

The disadvantaged schools project writing package. In the late 1980s and early 1990s, a series of pedagogical initiatives was developed to help elementary children, particularly those from minority-language backgrounds, develop control of the written-language genres that they need in order to succeed in school. Previous work indicated that while the dominant-process and whole-language approaches were effective in developing control over imaginative uses of language, they were failing students when it came to factual writing. Unfortunately, polarized positions between "genre" theorists and proponents of whole language were taken up, and what might have been a healthy dialog became an unhelpful and unnecessary debate. Bamforth contrasts the product-oriented genre approach with the whole-language process approach in the following way:

Genre theory grounds writing in particular social contexts, and stresses the conventionbound nature of much discourse. Writing, therefore, involves conformity to certain established patterns, and the teacher's role is to induce learners into particular discourse communities and their respective text types. By contrast, the process approach extols individual creativity, individual growth, and self-realization, and the teacher's role is that of "facilitator" rather than "director." (Bamforth 1993: 94)

However, Bamforth goes on to point out that the process versus product debate represents a false dichotomy. In fact, proponents on both sides of the ideological debate confuse syllabus-design issues with methodological ones. The strength of the genre approach rests on the principles it sets out for the selection of content. This is essentially a syllabus design issue. The process approach, on the other hand, is oriented towards classroom action, and its concerns are therefore essentially methodological. Any comprehensive approach to pedagogy must incorporate syllabus design, methodology, and assessment. This confusion, in fact, came to be reflected in the belief systems of the teachers who took part in the innovation described below.

This particular initiative was known as the Disadvantaged Schools Project Writing Package (DSP Writing Package), which took a very firm line on the side of the genre approach. The six specific objectives of this innovation were as follows:

(1) That students demonstrate improvements in their ability to respond effectively to the writing demands of the curriculum. Specifically, they will be able to perform effectively in written class assignments, make effective notes, do independent research, complete written homework assignments, and participate fully in classroom discussions about writing;

(2) That students understand the criteria by which their writing is being assessed and act on their writing to meet these criteria;

(3) That teachers and researchers find evidence to demonstrate the positive impact of the teaching–learning cycle, known as the "curriculum genre," on students' verbal and reading abilities;

(4) That teachers participating in the genre writing package be able to identify examples of the following genres: Recount, report, procedure, explanation, exposition, discussion and narrative;

(5) That teachers will be aware of the significant language features of the genres listed above; and

(6) That teachers will be able to apply their knowledge of genre theory to identify the schematic structures and significant language features of genres other than those identified above.

In 1990, the National Centre for English Language Teaching and Research was commissioned to carry out an evaluation of what came to be known as the DSP Writing Package. (For a detailed description of the project and the evaluation see Nunan 1992.) The evaluators were charged with looking at the impact of the innovation on both learners and teachers. There were three principal points of focus to the evaluation:

(1) To assess the impact of the "package" on children's writing;
(2) To evaluate the impact of the package on teachers'
  (a) capability to assess the effectiveness of students' writing,
  (b) pedagogy, and
  (c) knowledge of the social functions of language; and
(3) To identify which elements of the package have been most beneficial and which require amendment.

While the evaluation focused on the impact of the package on the practices of the teachers, as well as on the children's writing, I shall confine myself here to the teachers who took part in the project. The research question of interest here is: To what extent were the teachers who took part in the project able to internalize and use, for their own pedagogical purposes, the linguistic principles underlying the package?

Data for the evaluation came from four sources: A detailed questionnaire completed by teachers involved in the project; focused interviews with teachers and other key personnel; observation and analysis of lessons; and an analysis of samples of students' writing from the schools taking part in the innovation as well as samples from those not involved.

The project was supposed to be completed within a seven-month time scale as indicated below. However, the complexities of the evaluation, and the fact that the data-collection phase yielded approximately 1,500 pieces of children's writing which had to be analyzed, caused the evaluation to overrun its timeline and budget, and the evaluation was finally submitted in March of the year following the data collection.

- In May: Appoint principal research assistant; devise questionnaire and distribute to schools;
- In June: Interview consultants and authors of in-service package on goals, nature and implementation of package; conduct literature review; identify "non"-package schools to act as control; collect samples of students' writing from package and non-package schools;
- In July: Collate responses to questionnaire and select schools for further evaluation; conduct structured interviews with teachers, students and parents; record sample lessons and collect written texts relating to these lessons;
- In August: Complete interviews, recordings of sample lessons, and collection of texts; begin data analysis and evaluation of students' writing;

- In September: Complete data analysis and evaluation of students' writing; begin drafting report;
- In October: Submit draft report; and
- In November: Revise report; submit final draft.

The training package included an introduction to systemic-functional theory and practice, model demonstration lessons, and sample materials which provided an analysis of the generic structure and grammatical characteristics of selected written genres. The idea was for teachers to use the samples as models for the development of their own materials. In particular, it was intended for teachers to use the linguistic model for the analysis of genres that had not been analyzed by the creators of the DSP package.

Assessing children's writing. In assessing children's writing, teachers were trained to look for the following features, all of which are important according to the linguistic model underpinning the innovation:

- Schematic structure: Is the schematic structure appropriate for the genre of the text? (In the model, it is argued that texts written for different purposes will exhibit different patterns of overall organization and text structure.);
- Topic development: Does the writer explicitly identify the topic, and is it developed appropriately? (If the writer fails to develop the text topic or switches from one topic to another, then the text is confusing and difficult to follow.);
- Reference: Does the writer use reference appropriately? (Appropriate use of reference is an indicator of text cohesion and an indicator that the writer has a sense of the "decontextualized" nature of writing in comparison to speaking.) (Nunan 1992: 204.)

These assessment criteria were also used by the evaluation team when assessing the writing samples collected from children in the project schools as well as children in comparison schools. The texts and commentaries which follow illustrate how this was done.

Example 1. Schematic structure of successful text.

STRUCTURE	CLAUSES	TEXT: The Skull and the Skeleton
	1	One day there was a poor orphan girl
Orientation	2	She had to work with her stepmother
	3	Her hands were going to skin and bones
	4	So she decided to run away
	5	She saw a castle
	6	So she knocked on the door tap tap tap
	7	A skull with no body opened the door
	8	and he said "yes"
Complication	9	The girl told the skull [what had happened to her]
	10	She stepped into his castle
	11	She saw a body without a skull
	12	She knew that it belonged to the skull
	13	And the skull told the girl [what had happened]
	14	The they [sic] had dinner
	15	She stayed two night [sic]
Resolution	16	and she kissed the skull
	17	They got married
	18	They lived happily after

COMMENTARY ON TEXT:

[This text] like many other narratives collected for this analysis contains no evaluation and reveals that this young writer, like many others, lacks full control of the narrative genre. However, for the purpose of this evaluation of young children's writing, the essential stages of the narrative have been taken to be orientation, complication and resolution, and hence is assessed as satisfying criterion 1. The topic of [the text] is developed in the sense that the adventures of the "poor orphan girl" are related to the meeting of the "skull" and subsequent finding of its disengaged body. While the logical sequence of some events in the Narrative such as the skull telling "what had happened" and "having dinner" are not especially clear, there is enough information about the skull and skeleton for the reader to follow both the sequencing of events and the connection between complication and resolution. Hence the text is considered successful in terms of criterion 2. Reference is used appropriately in the text. The major participants are explicitly introduced: "a poor orphan girl," "a skull with no body" and thereafter referred to appropriately; "she," "the girl," "he," "the skull." Thus it is clear at all times who or what is being referred to in the text. (Walshe et al. 1990: 20)

Example 2. Schematic structure of unsuccessful text.

STRUCTURE	CLAUSES	TEXT: Aboriginal Skeletons and Skulls
Thesis (statement)	1	All around the world the museums do need some skeletons and skulls
Argument 1 (statement)	2	Well the Aboriginals gave them some of their grand-parents to put in the museum's
Argument 2 (recount)	3	Well Loir Richards is an Aboriginal
	4	and she said that some people say that Aboriginals have not got any feelings
Conclusion	5	The skeletons and skulls should go back
	6	where they come from and remain
Argument 3	7	You would not like it
	8	if they took your grandparents skeletons and skulls

COMMENTARY ON TEXT:
... the structure of Text 2 can be summarized as follows: a general statement, which could be generously interpreted as a thesis, followed by a second statement, rather than an argument. Next is a short recount rather than a second argument... followed by the writer's conclusion regarding this topic and then there is a follow up argument. It is the conclusion that gives the clearest indication that the writer intended the text to be an Exposition. Other stages in the text are not those of a successful Exposition... Development of topic in Test 2 is unsatisfactory. While the text is loosely cohesive around the topic of museums and skulls and skeletons, there are problems in that none of the arguments follow logically from one another... There are also minor problems with referencing. The opening statement refers to "the museums". Such reference is unclear as the reader is not informed which museums are being referred to... Thus Text 2 is assessed as unsatisfactory on all three criteria. (Walshe et al. 1990: 21)

Teachers' interpretations of the linguistic model. In general terms, the innovation had an overall positive response from participating teachers. It also had a beneficial impact on students' writing. A comparative analysis of texts from package and non-package schools indicated that, in terms of the evaluative criteria identified by the researchers, students in package schools produced a greater range of factual texts, and produced them more successfully. The team also found that the teachers' classroom practices changed as a result of their participation in the innovation. The model of in-service training upon which the innovation is based has a number of distinctive features which contributed to its effectiveness. These included the balance of theory and practice, the demonstration lessons, and the cyclical nature of the input. However, there is evidence that the most problematic area of the innovation was the extent to which teachers were able to internalize and use the analytical tools offered by the linguistic model. This conclusion is based on data provided by the interviews and questionnaire.

In attempting to get at the teachers' belief systems relating to the nature of language and learning, participants were asked to state three beliefs they had about language development that determined the way they taught. This probe yielded three hundred seventy-two responses which were subjects to a form of key-word analysis, and subcategorized according to whether they were referenced principally against language, the instructional context, or the learners themselves. From Table 1, it can be seen that the overwhelming number of responses were referenced against language and learning.

On balance, the responses from teachers indicated either that they had not internalized the linguistic model underpinning the project, or that their understanding was piecemeal and partial. There were numerous instances in which teachers appeared to have appropriated the discourse of systemic-functional linguistics without really understanding or being able to use it to further develop and refine their own materials. In addition, many teachers grafted emerging concepts onto their existing belief systems which had emerged from training in areas such as whole language and process writing. In other words, each teacher developed his or her own personal theories of language and learning, often in ways which were incompatible with the original linguistic model. This can be seen in the following illustrative statements:

- "I believe grammar, spelling and reading are the basis for language development."
- "All children benefit from immersion of the written print [sic]."
- "Children learn best when there is a positive encouraging environment."
- "Children learn by using the language."
- "Children should be allowed to learn any new concepts in their native language if possible."
- "Children need to be immersed in all types of writing/reading literature."

- "It occurs across the curriculum and therefore should not be seen as a separate subject area."
- "Language is developed through all curriculum areas."
- "A child needs to be aware of basic grammatical structures."
- "There is a strong relationship between oral language development and expression and the ability to express oneself in writing."
- "Children need to be an active part of a rich language environment."
- "Children's language develops through experiences so in order for the children to gain the most out of any given lesson many experiences should be given."
- "Spoken language should be mastered (ESL) before written."

While this general failure to internalize the linguistic model underpinning the package did not vitiate the effectiveness of the materials contained in the package, it did prevent the teachers from developing and adapting their own materials in ways intended by the developer of the innovation. In a sense, they were slaves to a linguistic model they did not understand and could not control. This was reflected in the fact that, while they could successfully teach those genres that were extensively modeled in the innovative package, they were unable to analyze other genres in terms of their overall generic structure and characteristic morphosyntactic features, and were thus unable to develop materials and pedagogical procedures for teaching these other genres.

Linking linguistic theory and pedagogical practice through action research. The question that needs to be faced is, What, if anything, can be done about this situation? One solution of course is to encourage teachers who do not have formal training in linguistics to undertake some sort of tertiary course, preferably at the postgraduate level. In the contexts in which I have worked for the last few years, this is an option which is open to relatively few teachers, given the cost and time involved. An alternative, and one that I have found to be successful in a wide range of situations, is to establish professional-development programs which are linked to classroom-based action research. Such research enables teachers to contest linguistic theory in the context of their own situation over an extended period of time. (I have found that a timeframe of around one academic year seems to work.) A program of linked academic input and action research which I have developed is set out in Table 2. This program is initiated once teachers have taken an introductory course in systemic-functional linguistics and genre analysis. (For a description of the application of the systemic-functional model see Nunan and Lamb 1995.)

Table 2. Program of linked academic input and action research.

Session 1: Introduction to classroom observation
  (a) A series of reflective activities designed to get teachers thinking about their own teaching style
  (b) Reflecting on the teaching of others: Teachers examine and critique extracts from a range of classrooms identifying those aspects of the extracts they liked and disliked
  (c) Identification of ideological beliefs and attitudes underlying critiques

Between-session task: Teachers record and reflect on their own teaching

Session 2: Introduction to action research
  (a) Teachers report back on the between-session task
  (b) Introduction to issues and methods in action research
  (c) Introduction to the action-research process

Between-session task: Teachers develop a draft action plan

Session 3: Focus groups and action plans
  (a) Formation of focus groups and appointment of facilitators
  (b) Sharing of draft action plans
  (c) Refining questions

Between-session task: Baseline observation, focus-group meetings, preliminary data collection
Session 4: Analyzing data   (a) Participants develop ways of analyzing and making sense of their data
Between-session task: Ongoing data collection and analysis, focus-group meetings

Session 5: Writing up
  (a) Participants receive input on presenting their research
  (b) Development of draft reporting outlines

Between-session task: Production of draft reports
Session 6: Refining reports Participants receive feedback and discussion of draft reports
Session 7: Evaluation Participants evaluate the action-research process and provide feedback on how their involvement changed them

Subsequent to the Disadvantaged Schools Project, an adaptation of this model was used with a group of teachers in Australia working in the area of adult education. Action-research reports from some of the participating teachers have just been published (Burns and Hood 1995), and from these reports, it is clear that the teachers involved were able to appropriate the linguistic model and incorporate this into their teaching repertoires. This is not to say that the program was without its difficulties. During the course of the project, the following problems emerged:

- Having the time to carry out research in addition to their usual teaching;
- The logistics of documenting or collecting data during busy classtime;
- Being disciplined and systematic about writing up or documenting the data while it was fresh in their minds;
- Uncertainty about whether what they were doing was "right" and whether they were going about the data collection accurately;
- Needing to have some individual contact with coordinators or others in the project to reaffirm that they were on the right track;
- Revealing their teaching "warts and all" to researchers and other teachers;
- The additional practical arrangements to be organized, like finding equipment and remembering to tape their classroom interaction;
- The tedium of recording problems or issues regularly and writing about something rather than just thinking about it;
- Not wanting to exhaust their learners' goodwill if they were the major focus of the data collection; and
- Writing up the research outcomes for public consumption. (Burns 1995: 1)

Conclusion. In this paper, I have described an innovative approach to teaching writing based on systemic-functional linguistics. Genre theory, which has emerged as the pedagogical arm of systemic-functional linguistics, has provided language teachers with criteria for evaluating the extent to which learners have gained control of the grammatical and discoursal features of genres which are highly valued within academic contexts.

In the second part of the paper, I gave an account of the Disadvantaged Schools Project Writing Package, an innovation based on genre theory, which is intended to improve writing programs by training teachers to identify examples of key school genres including recounts, reports, procedures, explanations, expositions, discussions, and narratives. The package was also designed to make teachers aware of the significant language features of these genres, and to provide them with skills in identifying the schematic structures and significant language features of genres other than those identified in the training program. The evaluation of the program revealed that teachers were able to teach the genres modeled in the package, but were unable to use the linguistic tools provided in the package to design their own materials. Data from the evaluation further showed that teachers evolved their own personal theories of language and learning which represented idiosyncratic (and in some cases truly bizarre) amalgamations of the various training programs they had been involved in, most notably the genre-based package and earlier training in whole-language approaches to instruction. (This work underpins the insights of Kohonen 1992; Kolb 1984). The questionnaire and interview data also show that in a sense the teachers were victims of an academic shoot-out. They were caught in the crossfire between proponents of a process approach to pedagogy, and those committed to the genre approach.

It is clear from the study reported above that the development of "linguistic literacy" in language teachers requires long-term, detailed educational programs, particularly in contexts where teachers have little formal training in an appropriate form of linguistic analysis. The term "appropriate" is used advisedly. This study shows that the "any old kind of linguistics training will do" belief is untenable when it comes to applying that knowledge to pedagogy. In the present instance, it is clear that if teachers are to design materials that enable students to function linguistically, they need a detailed and appropriate introduction to functional linguistics.

Finally, I presented one possible way in which an appropriate model of linguistics could be presented and contexted in the classroom through the development of a longitudinal action-research agenda. There is evidence that, despite certain difficulties, such an agenda is feasible in a range of different contexts and environments, and that it leads to change in terms of the teachers' knowledge base and also their professional practice. It is effective precisely because it enables teachers to make connections between theory and practice, and provides them with opportunities to contest linguistic theories against their own pedagogical situation over an extended period of time.

REFERENCES

Bamforth, Roger. 1993. "Process versus genre: Anatomy of a false dichotomy". *Prospect* 8(1–2): 89–99.
Burns, Anne. 1995. "Teacher researchers: Perspectives on teacher action research and curriculum renewal." In Anne Burns and Sue Hood (eds.), *Teachers' voices: Exploring course design in a changing curriculum.* Sydney: National Centre for English Language Teaching and Research. 4-19.
Burns, Anne and Sue Hood (eds.). 1995. *Teachers' voices: Exploring course design in a changing curriculum.* Sydney: National Centre for English Language Teaching and Research.

Christie, F. 1985. *Language education*. Victoria, Australia: Deakin University Press.

Halliday, Michael Alexander Kirkwood. 1985. *An introduction to functional grammar*. London: Edward Arnold.

Halliday, Michael Alexander Kirkwood and Jim Martin (eds.). 1993. *Writing science: Literacy and discursive power*. London: Falmer.

Hammond, Jennifer. 1990. Choice and genre in adult literacy. *Prospect* 9(2): 42-53.

Hammond, Jennifer, Anne Burns, Helen Joyce, Daphne Brosnan, and Linda Gerot. 1992. *English for social purposes: A handbook for teachers of adult literacy*. Sydney: National Centre for English Language Teaching and Research.

Kohonen, Vilijo. 1992. "Experiential language learning: Second language learning as cooperative learner education." In David Nunan (ed.), *Collaborative language learning and teaching*. Cambridge, U.K.: Cambridge University Press. 14-39.

Kolb, David. 1984. *Experiential learning: Experience as the source of learning and development*. Englewood Cliffs, N.J.: Prentice-Hall.

Mincham, Lexie. 1991. *The SNAP Project*. Adelaide, Australia: Department of School Education, South Australia.

Nunan, David. 1992. *Research methods in language learning*. Cambridge, U.K.: Cambridge University Press.

Nunan, David. 1993. *Introducing discourse analysis*. London: Penguin.

Nunan, David and Clarice Lamb. 1995. *The self-directed teacher: Managing the learning process*. New York: Cambridge University Press.

Walshe, John, Jennifer Hammond, Geoffrey Brindley, and David Nunan. 1990. *Evaluation of the disadvantaged schools writing project*. Sydney: National Centre for English Language Teaching and Research.

Developing a second-language-research component within a teacher-education program[1]

G. Richard Tucker and Richard Donato
Carnegie Mellon University and University of Pittsburgh

Introduction. Research within the domain of second-language education is lively and vigorous. This state of affairs represents a welcome change from that which characterized the field as recently as thirty years ago. A report which was prepared in 1964 for the (national) Commission on the Humanities discussed the impact of then-recent advances in linguistics upon the general public. The conclusion reached in that report was that contributions to date had been "essentially zero." We believe that a strong case can be made—in many parts of the world—that this conclusion no longer summarizes public perception or reality.

Simultaneously, this is a time of examination within the teacher-education profession. A review of the most recent books devoted to the education of teachers reveals that our focus has shifted from training in formulaic instructional techniques to *reflective practice* and *educational inquiry* (Richards and Lockhart 1994; Wallace 1991; Henderson 1992). Teacher education has indeed come of age thanks to the efforts of organizations such as the Holmes Group, the American Association of Colleges of Teacher Education, the National Council for the Accreditation of Teacher Education, and the Association of Teacher Education. In spite of internal discussion and debate among these organizations, one central message is clear—teachers need to develop the ability to reflect on their own practices, observe and document classroom life, and systematically engage in research activities leading to instructional refinements and innovations. The concept of virtuoso teacher-fronted, classroom performance as the sole criteria of an individual's ability to teach has become obsolete. The assumption underlying teacher education and effective instruction today is that, in addition to sound pedagogical skill and strong content knowledge, teachers need to possess the ability to develop a

---

[1] This research has been supported in part by a grant from the U.S. Department of Education to G. Richard Tucker and Richard Donato, and in part by the Department of Modern Languages at Carnegie Mellon University and the Department of Instruction and Learning at the University of Pittsburgh. Because our respective graduate programs involve students interested in issues of second- and foreign-language education, we have used the terms interchangeably.

deeper understanding of instruction through an inquiry-based exploration of classroom practices.

The literature on teacher education has repeatedly proposed a form of inquiry referred to as action research. Richards (1994: 12), summarizing Gregory (1988) and Kemmis and McTaggart (1988), defines action research as teacher-initiated investigations which seek to increase the teacher's understanding of classroom teaching and learning, and bring about change in classroom practices. Action-research projects are typically classroom-based studies that consist of four iterative processes: observation, analysis, action, and reflection. The principal of action research is viewed as the key to building a community of practitioners that is self-critical, self-renewing, and reflective. A corollary to this principal and positive byproduct of including research activity in teacher-education programs is eliminating in the minds of many the discontinuity among theory, research, and practice. Therefore, if the goal of a new generation of truly professional, reflective practitioners is to be realized, teacher-education programs will need to incorporate experiences in classroom-based research as a central focus.

The goal of creating teacher-researchers may at first glance appear lofty, even unattainable, given the limited time and resources often devoted to teacher education. Wallace (1991) states that "there are *real problems* with the concept of teacher as researcher: to do research properly requires special expertise, a lot of time, financial resources, and ... an academic bent" (1991: 56, emphasis ours). Wallace proposes action research as a solution to this problem since it is more within the control of teachers and more relevant to actual classroom experiences.[2] Wallace implies, therefore, that action-research and basic-research methods are mutually exclusive; the latter clearly lies outside the purview of the classroom teacher and relegated to small-scale "projects." We claim, however, that the two research traditions are not necessarily in conflict. Rather, the difference between action research and basic research is one of *degree* rather than *kind*. Both forms of research can be subsumed under the concept of inquiry and rely on relevant questions, data collection, analysis, and the discussion of implications for instruction. What prevents teacher research from inclusion among other traditional forms of research is the teacher's *access* to the tools and discourse of the research community. The real issue is, therefore, how to unlock the hermetically sealed world of research and introduce preservice and inservice

---

[2] We assume that what is meant here is "basic research" conducted in a laboratory setting under highly controlled conditions. If this is the case, then qualifying one type of researcher as more rigorous and academic than another is unwarranted and suffers from an epistemological bias that fails to reflect critically on itself and recognize the legitimacy of alternative forms of inquiry. Conversely, characterizing teacher research as more relevant to instruction implies that basic research is often irrelevant to classroom practice and also undermines its value.

teachers to research practice *of any kind*. By participating centrally or peripherally (Lave and Wenger 1991) in the research community, rather than merely "consuming" its findings, teachers can investigate practical classroom problems, formulate usable solutions, monitor and evaluate outcomes, and disseminate findings to other practitioners—activities that are, at the same time, explicit goals of action research and ultimately the litmus tests of all exemplary basic or applied research.

To address the problem of teachers' access to the practices of the research community, we propose a model whereby a spectrum of foreign-language educators from preservice teachers to doctoral candidates in foreign-language education are apprenticed into classroom-based research. The apprenticeship model (Rogoff 1990) seeks to introduce teachers into a community of professional practice where they can find the assistance, research tools, discourse, and resources (i.e. Wallace's *problems*) to make principled, well-informed inquiries into classroom practice, and become legitimate participants in the cycle of theory–research–practice that is the hallmark of our profession. We show how a single, innovative educational project can form the nucleus around which multiple research opportunities can be created for preservice and inservice teachers. Within this context, teachers are provided with opportunities to work in concert with other researchers on investigating and documenting classroom practice and student learning, i.e. to participate in research.

In this paper, we describe some of the reciprocal contributions and influences of our current research and the education of second-language teachers. We do this by: (1) Describing briefly a continuing, longitudinal, collaborative program of research by which we document and evaluate diverse aspects of the teaching of Japanese as a foreign language to elementary-school youngsters (Donato, Antonek, and Tucker 1994; Tucker, Donato, and Antonek 1994); (2) identifying several exemplary research topics within this program which form foci for involving preservice and inservice teachers in various types of qualitative or quantitative action research through an apprenticeship model; (3) describing some of the ways in which the research conducted to date has benefited from and contributed to the Japanese program, the participants in the teacher-education program, and foreign-language-education practice and policy in the state of Pennsylvania; and (4) identifying the implications that our experiences have had for an existing graduate program at the University of Pittsburgh, and for a program about to begin at Carnegie Mellon University.

An innovative JFL program. After considerable study and discussion among parents, teachers, the principal, and university specialists during the summer of 1992, the Executive Committee of the Falk School—the laboratory school of the University of Pittsburgh—voted to authorize an experimental three-year compulsory program in Japanese for all children in kindergarten through grade five. The school had not previously offered a FLES (foreign language in the elementary school) program, nor had it ever offered Japanese instruction at any level. The establishment of this Japanese FLES program has offered a rich opportunity for sustained collaboration among faculty from the University of Pittsburgh and Carnegie Mellon in areas such as innovative curriculum development, formative and summative evaluation, basic and applied language-acquisition research, and parental and community outreach within the context of a graduate teacher-education program. In the section to follow, we describe briefly the characteristics of the JFL program and summarize the results of our continuing program evaluation.

Curriculum and materials in the first year. The Japanese as a foreign language (JFL) program, now in its third year, consists of one fifteen-minute lesson each day, five days per week, for every student from kindergarten through Grade 5. The first teacher (Ms. Mari Cato O'Connell) worked with Donato during the summer of 1992 to develop the original "scope and sequence" for the course, which focuses on helping students to develop communicative language proficiency in Japanese. The template used for curriculum development followed the American Council on the Teaching of Foreign Languages (ACTFL) proficiency guidelines which we believe adds to the generalizability of the program. (For purposes of this paper, it is relevant to note that Ms. O'Connell was a graduate student in the Foreign Language Education program at the University of Pittsburgh who was assigned to teach in the JFL program at Falk under the terms of her graduate teaching assistantship.)

The curriculum reflects a proficiency orientation with attempts at content-enrichment where appropriate.[3] Each lesson or set of lessons designed by the teacher focused on thematic vocabulary presented within a context, a language function associated with the context, and some attention to the grammatical or syntactic structure necessary for carrying out the function (Omaggio Hadley 1993). During the first year of the program (1992–1993), lessons emphasized listening comprehension or receptive skills more than productive skills, although students were certainly not discouraged from using Japanese when production occurred spontaneously in class, as is often observed among young children learning new languages. During the first year, children received significant amounts of Japanese input from their teacher—their only source of input—and were systematically required to demonstrate comprehension through several Total Physical Response activities. Production, although not neglected, was not deemed central to the children's initial contact with Japanese. When speaking

---

[3]The issue of content-enrichment requires additional investigation. During the first year of an innovative FLES program and in the presence of a dynamically emerging understanding of the role of foreign-language instruction in the elementary-school curriculum, expectations for the systematic integration of subject-area content into the foreign-language curriculum may be overly optimistic.

was the objective of a lesson, production was limited to new lexical items, formulaic expressions for carrying out functional objectives (e.g. greeting, leave-taking, stating one's address or age), or some creative, personalized responses (e.g. "What's your favorite color? Your favorite food?").

Adaptations for the second year. Observations by Ms. O'Connell and another graduate-student researcher, as well as the results of end-of-year testing during the first year, indicated that students had strong listening-comprehension skills, but that their production was limited primarily to word- or phrase-level utterances, often formulaic in nature.[4] The second-year curriculum for children was therefore designed to build upon themes and functions from the first year with increased opportunities for extended language production. Thus the inclusion of role and drama activities, games, and personalized questions represented an attempt to enable the children to go beyond listening comprehension to more productive and creative language use. Culture also played a significantly greater role in the second-year curriculum. The teacher invoked cultural themes more frequently as a basis for introducing new vocabulary (e.g. learning about a Japanese home when learning words for rooms of a house). Thematic vocabulary introduced in the first year was maintained in the second year, but amplified and elaborated upon in the second-year curriculum. This vocabulary was also used more productively than during the previous year, and students were expected to demonstrate comprehension and production of new lexical items in classroom speaking activities.

Adaptations for the third year. Students are currently in their third year of Japanese study during the 1994–1995 academic year. Participants continue to study Japanese fifteen minutes per day, five days per week. Curricular enhancements during the year include increased emphasis on student production, the inclusion of monthly cultural topics that parallel holidays and celebrations in Japan, and closer contact between the JFL teacher and subject-area teachers (e.g. music, art, social studies, computer science, and mathematics) for developing interdisciplinary lessons. The current teacher, Ms. Yoko Morimoto, is a native speaker of Japanese with elementary-school teaching experience. In addition to teaching at the Falk School, she is enrolled in the graduate program in Foreign Language Education at the University of Pittsburgh (the original JFL teacher relocated to Mexico in August 1994 for family reasons).

---

[4] This observation is not surprising given the emphasis of the first-year curriculum on listening comprehension and the learning of certain fixed expressions necessary for carrying out novice-level language functions.

Summary of program results. Since the inception of the program, we have planned and implemented a multifaceted program of research and documentation in which we attempt to provide:

- a description of the school *ambiance* within which the program was implemented and currently operates;
- a detailed description of the Japanese *program* and its *implementation*;
- a longitudinal assessment of Japanese-language acquisition for a randomly selected sample of students who have participated in the program; and
- a description of the views of administrators, teachers, parents, and participating students toward the program.

To date, we have found that the children have demonstrated notable progress in developing a set of building blocks in Japanese—particularly in their control of receptive skills and basic vocabulary. With respect to productive skills, we are encouraged by the students' ever-increasing linguistic ability. Children appear to be following rudimentary rules of Japanese syntax. Some initiate their own utterances in Japanese, while others whom we observed were well beyond word-level utterances and, in some cases, appeared to be developing the ability to engage in unplanned, extended, albeit brief, discourse often reflecting their personal feelings and reactions. Furthermore, both they and their parents appreciate the program, enjoy the study of a foreign language in general and Japanese in particular, and wish to have the opportunity to continue their study of Japanese. (For more detailed reports of research results, see Donato, Antonek, and Tucker 1994 and Tucker, Donato, and Antonek 1994.)

Developing a continuing relationship. For several reasons, we have worked diligently to establish a solid relationship with this JFL program. We hope that our continuing research with these children, their parents, and their teachers, will help to raise the awareness of parents, educators, and policy makers about the many ways in which carefully designed and well implemented FLES programs can contribute to the development of second-language proficiency and crosscultural awareness and understanding on the part of the large proportion of American youngsters who will never have the opportunity to participate in more intensive immersion programs or developmental bilingual-education programs. Furthermore, we have found that our relationship with this program has provided a natural focus for involving successive cohorts of teacher-certification candidates and foreign-language-education graduate students in a wide variety of meaningful research experiences. This training has led to their own professional development, while simultaneously yielding formative information relevant to foreign-language-education practice and policy.

Exemplary research foci. In the section to follow, we identify eight exemplary research topics which have served as foci for our own work to date, and which we believe warrant additional attention from the profession in and of themselves. (Additionally, these research foci clearly show how, in the model of graduate teacher education we are proposing, novices can be apprenticed into meaningful research practice as an integral part of their formation as teachers and researchers.) Our intention is not to describe the results of the research conducted around each of these topics, but merely to illustrate the richness and variety of the types of research questions that can be examined within such a context.

Documentation of the FLES model. The issue of which foreign-language-education-program model to select is a complex one. Research clearly shows that an immersion model results in greater proficiency gains than a FLES model (Campbell, Gary, Rhodes, and Snow 1985; Clyne 1986; Rhodes, Thompson, and Snow 1989). However, immersion is not always the model of choice. And as noted above, the majority of American youngsters who will participate in foreign-language programs will, for one reason or another, *not* participate in immersion programs. There is a remarkable paucity of descriptive or evaluative information about participants in FLES programs or about students who continue their language study in well-articulated, so-called "traditional" foreign-language programs at the intermediate and secondary grades. The success of immersion education has seemingly deflected our attention from the need to develop a comprehensive description of alternative programs. Thus one topic for our attention has been a comprehensive description of the development and implementation of this innovative Japanese FLES program from multiple perspectives. This work is being carried out collaboratively with doctoral candidate Ms. Janis Antonek, and the results of the research to date can be found in a variety of sources (Donato, Antonek, and Tucker 1994; Tucker, Donato, and Antonek 1994).

This comprehensive and continuing evaluation provides the vehicle within which it has been possible to conduct several other action-research projects which have enhanced the professional development of several second-language-teacher-education students.

Developing (Japanese) language-assessment instruments. A systematic review by staff from the Iowa State University/Center for Applied Linguistics National K-12 Foreign Language Resource Center has revealed a shocking scarcity of instruments for measuring the foreign-language proficiency of K–6 students. This lack is strongly felt for the so-called less commonly taught languages such as Japanese. Assessing the oral ability of children is particularly problematic given the limited language that they control at initial stages of language learning. This implies that research on oral assessment needs to be systematically undertaken to determine the tasks and techniques best suited for describing the language proficiency of young children. Thus we found that this program provided an opportunity to develop a set of valid and reliable language-assessment instruments for young children. These instruments may well serve as prototypes for future testing, following the implementation of foreign-language education as part of the Goals 2000 core curriculum. This work also provided an opportunity to involve graduate students in all aspects of test-development activities including literature review; critique of extant tests; development or adaptation; field testing and revision of a variety of new instruments; and analyses of the psychometric or other properties of the tests themselves, as well as of the results of testing within a setting that had some personal meaning for them.

Age of introduction and Japanese-language learning. As interest in teaching foreign languages in the elementary school continues to expand within a context of ever-shrinking budgets, the issue of the optimal age for starting a foreign language becomes more important. Despite a good deal of more theoretically-oriented research in recent years (Birdsong 1989; Singleton 1989; Genesee 1987), whether there are benefits for children who begin foreign-language study in the early primary grades (K–2), when compared with others who delay instruction until the intermediate primary grades (3–5), remains to be tested empirically within a FLES model; additional research clearly is called for within the context of FLES programs.

Somewhat serendipitously, the present program provides an interesting opportunity for collecting data relevant to this important practical and theoretical issue. The program, introduced in the 1992–1993 academic year, was compulsory for all children from kindergarten through Grade 5. Thus, at the conclusion of the current academic year, it will be possible to compare the progress of two cohorts of students over three years, one which began in kindergarten, and the other which began in Grade 3. Initial data (Donato et al. 1994) have indicated that although there were greater overall proficiency gains for an older cohort (Grades 3–5) in a FLES program, the younger cohort (K–2) made more uniform gains.

Investigating the acquisition of specific features of Japanese. The JFL program also provides an opportunity to conduct some basic research in second-language acquisition. For example, a distinguishing characteristic of Japanese and which seems to prove quite problematic for English speakers, even those studying Japanese at the university level, is the particle system. Within the context of this study, we examined the acquisition of two of the three types of particles in Japanese-sentence particles and phrase particles. Jorden (1987: 33) defines a sentence particle as "one of a small group of words which occur only at the end of sentence; they qualify the meaning of what has preceded. They regularly follow the preceding word directly without pause." The question marker *ka*, which occurs at the end of both information and yes/no questions, would be an example. Phrase particles, on the other hand, are used to connect a nominal to the following element. Their function is to point out what role the preceding word plays in the sentence—a function that in English is largely carried by word order. Examples of particles that were studied included *de, wa*, and *o* (e.g. *Piza Haato de Tomu wa piza o tabemasu*, "Tom eats pizza at Pizza Hut"), *ga, ni* (e.g. *Tsukue ni tatte kudasai*, "Please stand on the desk"), *no* (e.g. *Mari-san no basukeeto*, "Mary's basket"), and *to* (e.g. *Mari-san to hitsuji*, "Mary and the lamb").

Within this context, it has been possible to examine (Johnston 1994) the older versus younger students' differential abilities to comprehend and produce correct instances of particle use, as well as to describe, in their own words, the "meaning" of particular particles in given contexts, and to relate this emerging control to particle use in the JFL classroom—in this case, the only source for target-language input.

Language-learning strategies of young children. The issue of language-learning strategies has received considerable attention in the field of foreign-language education. Studies of learner strategies, concentrated mainly on high-school or adult learners, have attempted to uncover differences according to gender, ethnicity, proficiency level, learning style, aptitude, training conditions, or classroom practices (Oxford and Crookall 1989; Oxford and Nyikos 1989; Oxford 1990; Donato and McCormick 1994). Little is known, however, about the strategies of young children in a foreign-language classroom. Because of the JFL program, gaining access to young learners who were studying a foreign language daily was not difficult. An investigation of how young learners approach the task of acquiring a foreign language piqued the interest of a certification candidate who was preparing to begin a career as an elementary-school foreign-language teacher. Through classroom observations and one-on-one interviews with the children in the JFL program, this preservice teacher discovered that children do possess strategies for learning, some of which differ in marked ways from what she had researched in the literature. Pusateri (1994) documented that young learners engage in mental rehearsal before class and prefer learning from stories, songs, and games (or input-rich classes). When not in class, young learners report imitating the classroom by teaching Japanese to "their stuffed animals or younger siblings." Pusateri concluded that, unlike many high-school or college students who needed to be motivated or instructed to use particular learning strategies, strategic learning emerged naturally and spontaneously in younger children. These children reported that they seek out opportunities to use the new language with friends and peers on the playground or at home, and that this activity helped them remember Japanese words and expressions. This finding contrasts dramatically with Nyikos's and Oxford's (1993) study of twelve hundred undergraduates which found that "functional practice strategies," or active, social uses of the new language, were infrequently invoked by college-level language learners. Clearly, by virtue of her research, this certification candidate will begin her career as an elementary-school foreign-language teacher cognizant of some of the strategic learning processes of young learners, how they differ from older learners, and the extent to which young learners are willing to engage with language learning beyond the physical and time constraints of the classroom.

Investigating the emergence of Japanese literacy. The extension of the JFL program into middle school will provide a unique opportunity to document teachers' experiences with the introduction of literacy activities. By way of background, we have found that a great deal of uncertainty, and even controversy, surrounds the choice and sequencing of Japanese writing systems for purposes of introducing reading skills to young English-speaking students. Ultimately, proficient speakers of Japanese must master a set of *kanji*—ideographs derived originally from Chinese. In addition, two syllabaries are used—each made up of approximately fifty symbols. One set (*hiragana*) is used primarily to represent grammatical function words and inflectional endings; the other (*katakana*) is commonly used when writing loan words. Japanese words can also be represented by using the Latin alphabet, a system called *romaji*.

Interestingly, in a systematic survey of fifteen Japanese-language-teaching specialists, we found *no* evidence whatsoever of empirical research examining this important issue. Rather, we found diametrically opposed, and passionately held—often principled—views advocating the desirability of using one or the other systems for initial training. Since the Falk School is a laboratory school, we are in a position to conduct systematic research, with random assignment of students to conditions, on this important pedagogical topic. Thus we can examine the ways in which initially using one or the other syllabary facilitates or impedes the development of Japanese literacy skills. We can also collect writing samples over time from selected students for analysis.

Investigating teacher talk in the JFL classroom. In the context of a graduate seminar on theories and methods of foreign-language instruction, two inservice Japanese teachers, one of whom was the JFL teacher at Falk School, opted to explore the issue of teacher talk in the JFL classroom. After one teacher reviewed the literature and consulted with her professor, data collection procedures, transcription protocols, and a coding scheme were established.[5] The preliminary research led to such notions as display and referential questions, remodeling, corrective feedback, personalization, repetitions, and the negotiation of meaning. Background research also indicated that apart from studies of caretaker speech in L1 acquisition, little is known about teacher talk in a FLES classroom. Systematic quantitative and protocol analysis of the JFL teacher's speech by these graduate students revealed differences between the younger (Grades K–2) and older (Grades 3–5) cohort in terms of the *quantity* and *quality* of talk. Although the target language was used approximately eighty-five percent of the time in all classes, the teacher maintained target-language input more often with younger children than older children. Morimoto and Takahashi (1994) state that "the fact that very small children five to seven years of age can understand so much Japanese without depending on their native language struck us by surprise." In analyzing questioning behavior, they found that more personalization in the form of referential questions was directed to older children, whereas younger children were asked far more often to respond to display questions. Another finding was that the teacher's elicitation-discourse practices reflected what is considered "best practice" or, in Moskowitz's (1976) term, indirect influence. That is, the teacher rarely corrected mistakes directly or asked students to repeat after her verbatim. Rather, she remodeled, used rising intonation, or waited for students to speak or self-repair, which they were often observed to do.

Important findings from this study conducted by inservice teachers contribute to the research base on FLES and point to future studies of teacher talk in the elementary-school foreign-language classroom. Moreover, including the teacher in the analysis of her own discourse patterns within her own classes made the research intrinsically useful and influential on her instruction. In the final reflection on her research experience, Morimoto states that "I am thrilled by the language learning process I see every day. This research has provided me a great opportunity to analyze my own teacher talk. This will definitely influence my teaching."

Facilitating home–school collaboration using interactive homework. In a parent survey conducted at the end of the first year, parents reported that they wanted more information about the JFL curriculum and about the learning activities of their children. Based on our belief concerning the power and importance of homework, we decided to initiate a series of interactive

---

[5] Only one student from the research team reviewed literature and established a coding scheme. Since one of the researchers was the teacher of the class to be analyzed, she did not participate in the preliminary research but analyzed her own speech only after videotapes of her class had been made.

parent–child homework assignments. (For a description of the early activities, see O'Connell 1994.) We believe that homework *communicates* to parents what and how well children are learning, can *facilitate* classroom learning, and can *mediate* the relationship between home and school. We should add that, to our surprise, we have found no mention whatsoever of the roles and uses of homework in the foreign-language classroom in any of the currently used methodology texts that we consulted.

Homework packets were designed to familiarize caretakers with vocabulary and cultural topics introduced in class. (The work of Epstein 1993, who developed the TIPS model, proved helpful to us in creating our template.) Each interactive assignment included a short activity to be carried out by parents and children, such as counting, identifying colors, simple role-plays, or vocabulary practice. Vocabulary and culture provide the focus of each of the bi-monthly assignments. Parents were also provided with phonetic keys to assist them in pronouncing the Japanese words in the assignments. The assignments are short, one side of one eight-and-a-half- by fourteen-inch page, and consistent in format: Section 1 introduces the topic, discusses relevant class work, indicates the due date, and provides a space for the child's signature; Section 2 features from two to four language functions; Section 3 asks students to display their knowledge to their parents; Section 4 calls for students to teach the language functions to their parents; Section 5 provides an opportunity for children and parents to communicate in Japanese; and Section 6 presents relevant cultural information and concludes with a tear-sheet for parents to sign and return along with any feedback or comments that they wish to offer. (See Antonek, Tucker, and Donato 1995 for additional details.) The information generated to date by the interactive homework assignments has proven to be enormously rich. Parents and children do complete the assignments; furthermore, an astonishingly large number of parents use the assignments as an opportunity to provide detailed and informative feedback about the program to the teacher (and to the researchers), thus providing an important source of insight into the informedness of parents about various aspects of the JFL program.

Reciprocal benefits of this collaborative research program. In the section to follow we describe briefly some of the ways in which the research has benefited from and contributed to the Japanese program, the participants in the teacher-education program, and foreign-language-education practice and policy in the state of Pennsylvania—and perhaps nationally.

Implications for the JFL program. The research has directly affected the JFL program in several ways. The program was originally implemented in the 1992–1993 academic year as a three-year pilot program. The results of the continuing program documentation led directly to a decision by the Executive

Committee of the school to regularize the program beginning with the 1995–1996 school year. In addition, various aspects of the quantitative and qualitative research associated with the program have led to curricular changes. These changes have resulted in placing additional emphasis on language production through the use of role-play situations; games, songs, and a whole-language storytelling approach to instruction; greater integration of material from the JFL program with other content areas; and an increased incorporation of authentic cultural material into the program.

At the same time, the program has provided an opportunity for conducting applied research on topics such as the effectiveness of FLES instruction; the optimal age for the introduction of foreign-language study; the nature of target-language input to young learners; the language-learning strategies of FLES students; the roles of parental encouragement and attitudes in children's second-language development; the relationship between parental informedness about student progress and program implementation, as well as basic research on issues related to developing psychometrically sound assessment techniques for use with young children; and the acquisition of language-specific features, such as the Japanese particle system, by second-language learners.

Implications for teacher educators. Around the current research we have organized a comprehensive series of practical, relevant, and interesting research experiences for two cohorts of graduate students in the Foreign Language Education program at the University of Pittsburgh, a model which we will also incorporate in the new doctoral program at Carnegie Mellon. Following an initial period of traditional literature review and seminar discussion examining the strengths and weaknesses of a variety of approaches to educational research, students from varied backgrounds and with diverse interests have an opportunity to conduct their own investigation in close collaboration, or apprentice-type relationships, with more senior investigators. The students are learning to conduct research in a rigorous fashion under carefully monitored conditions. In many instances, they also have the chance to see the results of that research directly applied to influence educational practice in general and their own teaching in particular. In addition to acquiring a varied array of research skills and analytic tools, the students gain a first-hand appreciation for the benefits that can be achieved by systematically documenting and reflecting upon their own teaching practices. We believe that this model reconciles the dichotomy between basic and action research that has puzzled, if not plagued, the educational research community. The student action research reviewed above is "real research" because the students receive mentoring from more experienced researchers in the field. As "real research," studies by students create new knowledge, raise further questions and hypotheses, and contribute to educational practice and policy, an issue to which we now turn.

Implications for foreign-language-education practice and policy. Even at this early stage, we believe that this research suggests several important implications for foreign-language-education policy and practice. Perhaps most importantly, we hope that our continuing research with these children, their parents, and their teachers, will help to raise the awareness of parents, educators, and policy makers about the many ways in which carefully designed and well-implemented FLES programs can contribute to the development of second-language proficiency and crosscultural awareness and understanding on the part of the large proportion of American youngsters who will never have the opportunity to participate in more intensive immersion programs or developmental bilingual-education programs. Our emphasis throughout has been to describe as clearly as possible those things which the students can do and the many ways in which their incipient skills will serve them in the years ahead, rather than enumerating the things that they *cannot* do.

We have also been struck by how programs such as this often do not seem to "fit" squarely within the mainstream of other units and activities of the school. This marginalization is reflected in many ways: By a lack of private space for the often itinerant teacher; the failure to include the teacher in the school's various working groups; the lack of time allotted for joint planning; and the failure to assign "grades" to the children in so-called special subjects. Certainly, the successful implementation of programs such as these will depend upon their increasing centrality to the life of the school.

Our experience with this program has also served to reiterate the pressing need for FLES materials for all languages, but especially for the noncognate, less commonly taught languages. An examination of Willetts's (1989) summaries of the information from the 655-item database that was developed as part of the work of the Center for Language Education and Research (CLEAR) by Grala (1987) as part of another CLEAR activity revealed no bibliographic entries for materials for Japanese at the elementary level.

The importance attached to issues of articulation has taken on new urgency for us with this program. The Japanese program at Falk was initially approved as a three-year pilot program for all children in the elementary grades (kindergarten through Grade 5). Thus students who made the transition from Grade 5 to Grade 6 in 1993–1994 and 1994–1995 found themselves unable to continue to study Japanese; they were required to participate in a one-semester FLEX experience in French, and another in Spanish in the sixth grade. This policy was problematic for two reasons.

On the one hand, the students apparently developed a set of very positive attitudes toward the study of foreign language in general and Japanese in particular. They also acquired a foundation or building blocks upon which later proficiency in Japanese can be based. We worry on the one hand that the skills developed to date will suffer from attrition and erode if the students' sequence of study is interrupted. On the other hand, the school may be sending a negative message by indicating that the study of Japanese is suitable for elementary-school children but, when it comes time for the more serious academic work of higher grades, Japanese is no longer appropriate and students must instead choose a "European" language. Thus the concept of articulation becomes critically important from a policy perspective as well as from the perspective of providing as seamless a transition as possible from one level of study to the next.

Finally, the state of Pennsylvania has joined with California, Colorado, New York, North Carolina, Texas and, most recently, Massachusetts (Walsh 1995: 10) in integrating foreign languages into its core curriculum and requiring state-wide assessments in foreign languages to fulfill high-school graduation requirements. In Pennsylvania, according to the Chapter 5 regulation (*The Pennsylvania Bulletin 1993*), all students, in order to earn high-school diplomas, will be required to demonstrate "Intermediate Low level" oral proficiency as defined by the ACTFL proficiency scale.

Given this state of affairs, two important issues call for our attention. First, the traditional two-year high-school sequence of foreign-language instruction may not prove sufficient for preparing students to meet state-wide minimum standards. Therefore, as elementary- and middle-school foreign-language programs proliferate in states where foreign language occupy seats at the table with other traditional core subjects, policy derived from solid research needs to be established to construct and articulate these levels of instruction. We believe the JFL research agenda we have established contributes knowledge directly to the formulation of these critical policies. These policies can help determine, for example, the optimal time to begin instruction, effective instructional strategies, valid and reliable measurements of FLES students' achievement, the role of parent-school collaboration, and knowledge of how early language learners acquire a new language and cultural awareness in a traditional classroom setting. Second, the future success of foreign-language instruction in the United States rests, in the end, primarily in the practice of classroom teachers. The JFL program has, therefore, contributed to building a coterie of teachers for whom research is not an exclusive activity of higher-education personnel. Through their experiences in learning how to formulate questions and seek answers concerning educational practice, these teachers can directly influence policy, curriculum development, and the achievement of their students. Through the incorporation of a strong research focus during preservice and inservice teacher education, teachers will be better prepared to evaluate and contribute to policy and shape their own professional futures.

Implications for our graduate programs. In the section to follow, we describe briefly some of the ways in which our experiences with this project have influenced the Foreign Language Education program at the University of

Pittsburgh, as well as the new doctoral program in second-language acquisition at Carnegie Mellon University.

Graduate education as a community of practice. It has often been said that teachers are reluctant, if not resistant, to reading the findings of research. Crowded school-day schedules, multiple class preparations, and extracurricular activities are the regularly cited reasons for why teachers cannot find time to inform themselves of the latest research developments in foreign-language learning. We believe, however, that these reasons are only symptomatic of a larger problem in teacher education that has only been recently addressed in a direct way. (See, for example, *TESOL Journal* 1994.) Teachers who stand outside the research community and look in, see a misty landscape of charts and graphs, snippets of discourse samples, and unfamiliar and alien terminology. This landscape hardly invites exploration. For teachers to engage with research requires that they be initiated into its practices, and not simply observe it from the outside. If teachers are to connect with and relate to research, they must first experience what it means to do research and what research has to offer.

Within our respective graduate programs, we have observed compelling reasons for incorporating a strong research component. From the perspective of teacher education, we have seen preservice and inservice teachers ask probing questions, seek knowledge from the professional literature, and work diligently to find answers. Thus, in this environment, theory, practice, and research cohere in ways that heretofore have only been described as the ideal state of affairs. Moreover, the JFL project has provided an arena for conducting research in real classrooms with real learners. Within the microcosm of one class period, myriad significant questions can be posed and explored by future teachers and teacher educators. Required "class papers," therefore, can become technical reports that form and inform parts of a larger research enterprise, contributing directly to new knowledge in the field, policy, and planning.

From the perspective of a graduate program in second-language acquisition (SLA), including a research component is, of course, not uncommon. What this project contributes to a graduate SLA program is the opportunity for interdisciplinary work that will ultimately enrich the SLA field itself. Independent of its utility as a practical means for learning about and conducting research studies, the nature of the JFL project allows for connections to be made with current issues in the fields of education, developmental psychology, and educational policy and planning. Additionally, students of SLA will experience first-hand the impact of their research on practice, thus anchoring SLA research in the broader framework of the applied sciences.

We have tried to demonstrate that through a single innovative project and close ties with researchers in an apprenticeship-like fashion, students at various levels of professional development can be guided in the process of educational inquiry and gain access to a community of professional practice. Within this community a symbiotic relationship exists among research, practice, and policy. The fabric of this community is woven through chains of assistance where knowledge is shared and relations are created to benefit the common goal—a better understanding of the processes of second-language learning in the classroom. Important outcomes, therefore, of a research component in teacher-education programs and graduate SLA programs is that researchers can recognize and valorize the contributions of teachers, and teachers can collaborate with researchers and develop expertise for making sense of the dynamics of their own instruction. Only in this way can we truly speak of a professional community.

REFERENCES

Antonek, Janis, G. Richard Tucker, and Richard Donato. 1995. "Interactive homework: Creating connections between home and school." *Mosaic* 2(3)1–10.

Birdsong, David. 1989. *Metalinguistic awareness and interlingual competence.* New York: Springer.

Campbell, Russell N., Tracey C. Gray, N. C. Rhodes, and Marguerite Ann Snow. "Foreign language learning in the elementary school: A comparison of three language programs." *Modern Language Journal* 69(1): 44–54.

Clyne, Michael (ed.). 1986. *An early start: Second language at primary school.* Melbourne, Australia: River Seine.

Curtain, Helena A. and Carol Ann Pesola. 1988. *Languages and children—making the match.* Reading, Massachusetts: Addison-Wesley.

Donato, Richard, Janis Antonek, and G. Richard Tucker. 1994. "A multiple perspectives analysis of a Japanese FLES program." *Foreign Language Annals* 27(3): 365–378.

Donato, Richard and Dawn McCormick. 1994. "A sociocultural perspective on language learning strategies: the role of mediation." *The Modern Language Journal* 78(4): 453–464.

Grala, Maria. 1987. "Foreign language textbooks currently being used in elementary schools." CLEAR Materials Resource Series, Number 1. Washington, D.C.: Center for Applied Linguistics. (ERIC Document Reproduction Service No. ED 311 688).

Gregory, R. 1988. *Action Research in the Secondary Schools.* London: Routledge, Chapman, and Hall.

Henderson, James. 1992. *Reflective teaching: Becoming an inquiring educator.* New York: Macmillan Publishing.

Johnston, Amy. 1994. "Particle development and acquisition among students in a Japanese FLES program." Unpublished research report, Carnegie Mellon University.

Jorden, Eleanor H. with Mari Noda. 1987. *The spoken language.* New Haven, Connecticut: Yale University Press.

Kemmis, Stephen and Robin McTaggart 1988. *The action research planner, Third edition.* Victoria, Australia: Deakin University Press.

Lave, Jean and Etienne Wenger. 1991. *Situated learning, legitimate peripheral participation.* New York: Cambridge University Press.

Morimoto, Yoko and Etsuko Takahashi. 1994. "Teacher talk in a Japanese FLES program." Upublished research report, University of Pittsburgh.

Moskowitz, Gertrude. 1976. "The Classroom interaction of outstanding foreign language teachers." *Foreign Language Annals* 9(2): 135–157.

Nyikos, Martha and Rebecca Oxford. 1993. "A Factor analytical study of language learning strategy use: interpretations from information-processing theory and social psychology." *The Modern Language Journal* 77(1): 11–22.

O'Connell, Mari. 1994. "Parent-child home activity for the Japanese language program at Falk school." Unpublished research report, University of Pittsburgh.

Omaggio Hadley, Alice. 1993. *Teaching language in contex, Second edition.* Boston, Massachusetts: Heinle and Heinle.

Oxford, Rebecca. 1990. "Styles, strategies, and aptitude: connections for language learning." In Thomas Parry and Charles W. Stansfield (eds.), *Language aptitude reconsidered.* Englewood Cliffs, N.J.: Prentice Hall. 67–125.

Oxford, Rebecca and David Crookall. 1989. "Research on language learning strategies: methods, findings, and instructional issues." *The Modern Language Journal* 73(4): 404–419.

Oxford, Rebecca and Martha Nyikos. 1989. "Variables affecting the choice of language learning strategies by university students." *The Modern Language Journal* 73(3): 291–300.

The Pennsylvania Bulletin. 1993. Title 22-Education. 5.202, Student Learning Outcomes (xi), 23(30): 3554.

Pusateri, Michelle. 1994. "Language learning strategies of the young language learner." Unpublished research report, University of Pittsburgh.

Rhodes, Nancy, Lynn Thompson, and Marguerite A. Snow. 1989. " A comparison of FLES and immersion programs." Washington, D.C.: Center for Language Education and Research, Center for Applied Linguistics. (ERIC Document Reproduction Service No. ED 317 031).

Richards, Jack C. and Charles Lockhart. 1994. *Reflective teaching in second language classrooms.* New York: Cambridge University Press.

Rogoff, Barbara. 1990. *Apprenticeship in thinking: Cognitive development in social context.* New York: Oxford University Press.

Singleton, David. 1989. *Language acquisition: The age factor.* Clevedon, U.K.: Multilingual Matters.

TESOL Journal. 1994. 4(1). Special issue devoted to "Teacher Research."

Tucker, G. Richard, Richard Donato, and Janis Antonek. 1994."Documenting an exemplary Japanese FLES program: In pursuit of Goals 2000." Unpublished research report, Carnegie Mellon University/University of Pittsburgh.

Wallace, Michael. *Training foreign language teachers, a reflective approach.* New York: Cambridge University Press.

Walsh, Mark. February 15,1995. *Education Week* XIV(21): 1, 10.

Willetts, Karen. 1989. *The survey of materials and curricula in second language education.* (Final report). Washington, D.C.: Center for Language Education and Research, Center for Applied Linguistics. (ERIC Document Reproduction Service No. ED 311 691).

Curriculum transformation:
A psycholinguistics course
for prospective teachers of ESOL K–12

Shelley Wong
University of Maryland, College Park

When I first began teaching Psycholinguistics, I was struck by the tremendous gap between the subject matter of my course and the lives of children in the public schools. As a land-grant institution, located in a large metropolitan area, the mission of the University of Maryland's College of Education is to prepare teachers to teach boys and girls from Kindergarten to Grade 12. In the school districts we serve, as many as eighty different languages are spoken by school children. While research has shown that language-minority children achieve best in schools which incorporate the students' languages and cultures (Cummins 1986; Collier 1989), often there is *not a single person* among the school staff who speaks the language of the language-minority child, nor identifies with the same cultural-minority group.

The textbook which had been selected for the psycholinguistics class had a second-language focus, but poverty was not addressed as a topic, nor listed in the index. Yet in some of the schools in our area, the majority of children participated in the federally funded school-lunch program. Teachers in my courses commented that their teacher-preparation courses never prepared them to deal with the harsh social and economic conditions they encountered among their students (Wong and Grant 1995). What should a teacher do when a child comes to school in shorts in the winter or when a child is absent from school because the mother needs her to babysit for younger brothers and sisters?

To address the gap between the psycholinguistics curriculum and school reality, I began to look for studies which focused on the language acquisition of racial-, cultural- and linguistic-minority public-school children rather than studies of international students in university intensive-English programs or middle-class professors and their children (Garcia 1991). I also encouraged students to do research papers which would draw connections between second-language learning and the socioeconomic realities of the K–12 classrooms in our area.

My own understanding of curriculum transformation was enhanced by participating in the Curriculum Transformation Project Summer Faculty Institute on Women, Gender, and Race at the University of Maryland at College Park.[1] By looking at scholarship on constructions of difference: gender, class, and race in various disciplines and talking to other faculty members about ways to approach curriculum transformation, I started to revise the syllabus of my course.[2] I began by changing the readings. I also looked at research methodology, with a critical eye to questions of gender, class, race, and culture. Perhaps the greatest lesson that I learned by participating in the seminar was that curriculum transformation takes time. By talking to other professors who had engaged in curriculum transformation over many years, I learned to be patient with myself and not to expect that I would be able to change everything overnight. Curriculum transformation is a process involving change, reflection, and commitment over an extended period of time.

In this paper, I begin by discussing various models of multicultural-curriculum transformation. I then present a rationale for a sociocultural approach to psycholinguistics which incorporates critical-language study into the curriculum for second-language teachers. I conclude by discussing the importance of incorporating minority voices into the curriculum and recruiting racial, cultural, and linguistic minorities into second-language teaching.

Theoretical perspectives on multicultural-curriculum transformation. There are several models of the multicultural curriculum which can inform the work of second-language teachers and teacher educators who are concerned with meeting the needs of second-language learners in the public schools. Chief among these are the typologies developed by Sleeter and Grant (1987) and Banks (1993). Sleeter and Grant (1987) have developed a typology of five approaches to multicultural education in the U.S. "Teaching the Culturally Different" is an approach which assimilates students of color into the cultural mainstream. A "Human Relations Approach" helps students from different backgrounds appreciate each other and develop more honest relationships. A third approach, "Single Group Studies," fosters cultural pluralism by focusing on the experiences and contributions of distinct ethnic, gender, physically challenged, differently abled, and social-class groups. "Multicultural Education" promotes cultural pluralism and social equality through minority-hiring practices, inclusive curriculum and pedagogy, and affirmation of minority languages. Finally, "Multicultural and Social Reconstructionist Education" prepares students to

---

[1] The seminar, led by Deborah Rosenfelt and Alaka Wali, professors in Women's Studies and Anthropology, comprised twelve faculty members from diverse disciplines.

[2] For copies of the syllabus, study questions, and glossary for EDCI 732 Psycholinguistics, contact Shelley Wong, University of Maryland, Curriculum and Instruction, 2311 Benjamin Bldg., College Park, Maryland 20742, (301) 405-3136, SW86@umail.umd.edu.

challenge sructural inequality and promote cultural diversity. Sleeter and Grant point out that most of what is written concerning language-minority students is written from the perspective of "Teaching the Culturally Different," discussing how or what to teach language-minority children. Very few authors discuss second-language learning and bilingualism from a multicultural perspective, and most of those who write about multicultural education and cultural diversity do not address language development. They suggest the need for more dialogue between advocates of bilingual education and multicultural education.

Banks (1993) has developed a similar typology. His four approaches similar to Sleeter and Grant's, minus the "Human Relations Approach," represent different levels of integrating multicultural content into the curriculum. The most basic is the "Contributions Approach," which focuses on heroes, holidays, and discrete cultural elements. The second level, the "Additive Approach," adds content, concepts, themes, and perspectives relating to racial or cultural minorities without changing the structure of the curriculum. The third level, the "Transformation Approach," changes the structure of the curriculum to enable students to view concepts, issues, events, and themes from the perspectives of diverse ethnic and cultural groups. In the fourth level, the "Social Action Approach," students make decisions on important social issues and take actions to help solve them. Renner (1994) points out that in applying Banks's model to the English-as-a-foreign-language classroom, the four approaches are not mutually exclusive. Aspects of each may be employed, incorporating changes with the benefit of student input. While the Contributions and Additive approaches could have the danger of trivializing culture, they may be a good first step in curricular transformation. A multicultural curriculum which is transformative prepares students to criticize stereotypes, identify biases, and challenge social inequalities (Sleeter and Grant 1987). A curriculum which is transformative, rather than "assimilationist," is culturally relevant:

> Critical theorists assert that schools function to reproduce the systemic inequalities of the society. Consequently, the way to break the cycle is to focus on the kind of education minority students need. The work of Freire (1973), Aronowitz and Giroux (1985), King (1987), and McLaren (1989) suggest some features of what successful teachers of minority students must do to emancipate, empower and transform both themselves and their students. Aspects of this kind of teaching form the basis for what I have identified as "culturally relevant teaching." (Ladson-Billings 1992: 109)

Culturally relevant teaching is culturally responsive in that it is not developed in a vacuum, but situated within a particular sociopolitical context and developed from the standpoint of raising school achievement (Nieto 1992).

Cummins (1986) has developed a theoretical framework for empowering minority students which complements the various multicultural-transformative approaches discussed above. His framework consists of four components: (1) There should be an additive, rather than subtractive, view toward the home culture and language. Rather than supplanting the home language with English, teachers value the home language and view it as a way to develop competency in a new language. (2) There is a collaborative, rather than exclusionary, approach to community participation. All families, especially those from marginalized groups and working-class backgrounds are encouraged to participate. (3) There is a reciprocal, interaction-oriented, rather than transmission-oriented, model of pedagogy.[3] (4) Assessment is advocacy-oriented rather than legitimization-oriented. Cummins asks us to consider whether assessment focuses attention on advocating and improving the education of language-minority students or whether it justifies school failure.

Finally, to get beyond a "foods, facts, and fiestas" approach (Ovando and Collier 1985:106) to curricular transformation for second-language teachers and students would entail viewing language acquisition as socially constructed and culturally embedded. It would also entail preparing prospective ESOL teachers to take a critical stance towards inequality in education. The various models and theories of multicultural education led me to adopt a sociocultural approach to psycholinguistics.

Sociocultural approaches to psycholinguistics. To develop an approach to psycholinguistics from the standpoint of language-minority students in the public schools, the first step was to find readings that would look at language learning and literacy from sociocultural and critical perspectives that incorporated gender, ethnicity, class, and race.

Halliday and Hasan's (1989) view of language as a social semiotic provided a theoretical framework for students to understand the forms and functions of language within social contexts. Focusing on social context in children's language development directs us to analyze meanings and uses rather than grammatical forms separate from functions (Halliday 1973). The new syllabus emphasized the social nature of language and the development of language as a culturally embedded phenomenon.

I was critical of psycholinguistic studies that were "acultural"—that is, that took the culture of the researcher as a given, and viewed culture as a constant variable to be "factored out" (Wertsch 1991). In the absence of studies of children from nonmainstream families, would the descriptions of middle-class motherese be viewed by my students as universal or normative, and the language of Cambodian or Salvadorean families as impoverished? Elinor Ochs's (1988) study of Samoan language acquisition was a useful corrective to demonstrate that

---

[3] Transmission models are similar to what Freire (1973) calls "banking" pedagogy, in which the teacher "deposits" knowledge into the student.

North American caregiver speech was not universal. Her descriptions of difficulties she encountered in doing research which crossed cultural and linguistic boundaries were refreshingly honest and thought-provoking.

Cultural awareness is, of course, critical for second-language teachers in the public schools. On one level, second-language teachers recognize that the cultures in their own families and the classrooms in which they grew up may be worlds apart from the experiences of their students. Yet if teachers are unaware of the cultural assumptions they take for granted, they may inadvertently view their students' different cultural practices as rude, cold, insincere, or untrustworthy.

Developing cultural awareness includes incorporating diverse voices in the canon, rather than only those from Western or European traditions (Banks 1993a). Just as in K–12 education where changing the names and faces in a textbook exercise from Smith to Gomez or Kim is a cosmetic approach to multiculturalism, i.e. there has been no transformation of the curriculum, changing the studies to include those of "at-risk" children may not involve a paradigm shift in approaches to psycholinguistics. However, including voices which represent feminist, postcolonial, or critical perspectives will provide theoretical models which encourage ESOL teachers to take a critical stance toward inequality in education. When second-language teachers and prospective teachers read Jonathan Kozol's (1991) indictment of "savage inequalities" in education, it may cause them to become more aware of poverty and ask what they as teachers can do to address it. Similarly, second-language teachers truly transform the curriculum when they investigate the "funds of knowledge" (Moll 1990) in the communities in which they teach and, with the participation of parents, other community members, and their students, change their classroom exercises or problems to reflect the "funds of knowledge" which are valued in the homes and communities of their students. When sources of knowledge are diversified to reflect the home languages and cultures of the students, and the *ways* of knowing are called into question—this is truly curricular transformation.

Sociocultural approaches to psycholinguistics help teachers to be more aware of their own biases and critical of deficit models of education. Vygotsky's approach to psychology was sociohistorical. The emphasis was on situated knowledge which was constructed in particular historical situations (John-Steiner 1994). For example, a historical approach to educating African-American students will locate school failure in slavery, racism, and systematic oppression through the particular historical situations and lived experiences of African-American people. This approach contrasts with those which blame the victim and put the onus of failure on the Black matriarchy (Glazer and Moynihan 1963).

Vygotsky's sociohistorical psychology posited a relationship between the development of consciousness and the development of language. For Vygotsky, both developed through social interaction. His concept "zone of proximal development" challenges us to consider not only what a child can do independently, but what a child can do with assistance, with social support (Vygotsky 1978). For Vygotsky, intelligence is not fixed, nor is the level of maturation immutable. Both can be influenced through education. Vygotskian approaches to language acquisition and education stress what Bruner (1977) calls "scaffolding"—the assistance of an adult or more capable peer in problem-solving. Vygotsky was interested in how tools, including psychological tools such as language, mediate human action. He opposed atomistic, reductionistic approaches to knowledge acquisition, insisting on a study of the activity as a whole—within a historical, social, and cultural context (Lantolf 1994).

Critical-language study and psycholinguistics. A transformative multi-cultural curriculum calls on students to be critical of stereotypes, biases, and structural inequalities. Critical-language study (Fairclough 1989) enables language teachers to develop and apply tools of linguistic analysis to language and power and, through the application of discourse analysis, to answer the sociology-of-education question, "Who does knowledge serve?". The broader social processes of reproducing inequality, cultural capital, and pedagogical communication (Bourdieu 1977), or social stratification, tracking, and literacy (Mehan 1991), are put together with discourse analysis at the microlevel.

To encourage students to become more aware of deficit models and linguistic stereotypes, I incorporated into the course requirements critical-language-study readings and two critical-language-study assignments that were developed by Allan Luke at James Cook University of North Queensland (Luke 1986). The first assignment asked students to analyze textbooks critically to discern the selective traditions of texts and how discourse functions to position the reader to adopt particular stances (Kress 1989). The second assignment was a classroom-interaction assignment, in which students taperecorded classroom interactions and transcribed and analyzed classroom discourse. I encouraged students to tape their own teaching. The purpose of the two discourse-analysis exercises is to help teachers develop linguistic tools to increase their awareness of the language of education and to look at their own teaching critically.

Critical-language study was also applied to dialect awareness. Linguistic stereotypes and dialect discrimination lead to language-minority students being labeled developmentally disabled. For example, a disproportionate number of speakers of African-American Vernacular English are diagnosed as having speech disorders requiring special-education services. I invited a sociolinguist, Carolyn Adger, to talk to my class about a project in the Baltimore public schools to develop a dialect-fair speech- and language-assessment instrument (Adger, Wolfram, Detwyler, and Harry 1993). This project is an example of what Cummins (1986) calls "advocacy-oriented rather than legitimization-oriented assessment," in which applied linguists worked with speech and language specialists to design an approach to accommodate language differences in assessment and placement procedures. This new dialect-sensitive approach will reduce systematic discrimination against speakers of vernacular dialects in the schools.

Expanding the resources for curriculum transformation. Ira Shor (1992) remarked that each class brings different resources to the act of multicultural-curricular transformation for empowerment. In the course that I am teaching now, there is a deaf student with an M.A. in linguistics from Gallaudet University. Her presence contributes to reconceptualizing the nature of human language. Through readings and discussions, we are developing a sociocultural rather than a pathological view of deafness (Wilcox 1994). The class has asked, for example, Where does deaf education belong? Is it the responsibility of the Department of Special Education or the Department of Curriculum and Instruction which houses the Teaching English to Speakers of Other Languages program? We also have a native speaker of Arabic, a native speaker of Farsi, an English–Turkish bilingual American, a native speaker of Thai, two native speakers of Korean, a native speaker of Portugese, an African American, and a West Indian from Trinidad. In our class are human resources who may have been excluded, marginalized, or characterized as "other" because of their religion, race, gender, or sexual orientation. Others may have a family member with a developmental disability. Some students have had extensive crosscultural experiences. Some have studied languages. Some have studied various discourses —feminist scholarship, ethnic studies, Marxism, poststructuralism, or anti-colonial and postcolonial literatures. All bring linguistic and cultural resources to curriculum transformation.

Addressing the imbalance between the schools of education and the public schools. The changing demographics in the Washington, D.C. metropolitan area reflect a national trend; while minority children are becoming the majority in public-school districts across the country, there is a slight decrease in minorities in teacher-education programs (Fuller 1992). As second-language-teacher educators, we must address the acute shortage of language-minority teachers and advance programmatic solutions to address this urgent problem, including developing models for the successful recruitment and retention of language-minority students in teacher education and graduate programs in all areas of education.

The need for more minority teachers is occurring at a time of increasing racial and economic polarization. Language minorities are often scapegoated as the cause of unemployment and budgetary problems. With the passage of California's Proposition 187, which denies state-funded medical care, social services, and education, to undocumented immigrants and their children, and a rising current of anti-foreign and anti-immigrant movements to make English the official language across the country, we in second-language-teacher education have a special role to play. Dell Hymes (1992) reminds us that when the Linguistics Society of America was founded in 1924, many of its members were conscious of the necessity to challenge popular assumptions about "primitive" languages, especially unwritten ones. In the tradition established by Boas, Bloomfield, Sapir, and Whorf, part of the mission of applied linguistics is to dispel public misconceptions about minority languages.

The inclusion of voices which have been marginalized or submerged as "the other," alien, or foreign in schools of education provides an arena for all students to learn how to speak to each other across racial, linguistic, and cultural boundaries (Greene 1988). A spirit of discovery, appreciation for one another's diverse experiences, and an atmosphere that encourages asking questions and expressing different opinions support multicultural dialog. Minority recruitment can heighten awareness of structural inequity in education and open up spaces for more meaningful multicultural-curriculum transformation in second-language-teacher education.

Second-language-teacher education programs which prepare students for ESOL K-12 certification in the public schools need to address educational equity, poverty, and racism. Courses in psycholinguistics and second-language acquisition must address the sociocultural contexts of learners. Gender, race, ethnicity, and social class can best be incorporated by transforming readings and assignments in conjunction with recruiting more racial, linguistic, and cultural minorities into teacher-education programs.

REFERENCES

Adger, Carolyn, Walt Woifram, Jennifer Detwyler, and Beth Harry. 1993. "Confronting dialect minority issues in special education: Reactive and proactive perspectives." *Proceedings of the Third National Research Symposium on Limited English Proficient Student Issues: Focus on middle and high school issues*. Washington, D.C.: Office of Bilingual Education and Minority Language Affairs, U.S. Department of Education.
Banks, James A. 1993. "The canon debate, knowledge construction, and multicultural education." *Educational Researcher* 22(5): 4–14.
Banks, James A. 1993. "Approaches to multicultural curriculum reform." In James A. Banks and Cherry A. McGee Banks (eds.), *Multicultural education:Issues and perspectives, Second edition*. Needham Heights, Massachusetts: Allyn and Bacon. 195–214.
Bourdieu, Pierre and Jean-Claude Passeron. 1977. Trans. by Richard Nice. *Reproduction: In education society and culture*. London: Sage Publications.
Bruner, Jerome. 1977. "Early social interaction and language acquisition." In H. Rudolph Schaffer (ed.), *Studies in mother–infant interaction*. London: Academic Press. 271–289.
Collier, Virginia. 1989. "How long? A synthesis of research on academic achievement in a second language." *TESOL Quarterly* 23(3): 509–531.
Cummins, Jim. 1986. "Empowering minority students: A framework for intervention." *Harvard Educational Review* 56(1): 13–36.
Fairclough, Norman. 1989. *Language and power*. London: Longman.
Freire, Paulo. 1973. *Pedagogy of the oppressed*. New York: Seabury Press.

Fuller, Mary Lou. 1992. "Teacher education programs and increasing minority school populations: An educational mismatch?" In Carl A. Grant (ed.), *Research and multicultural education: From the margins to the mainstream*. London: The Falmer Press. 184–200.

Garcia, Eugene. 1991. "The education of linguistically and culturally diverse students: Effective instructional practices." Santa Cruz, California: National Center for Research on Cultural Diversity and Second Language Learning.

Glazer, Nathan and Daniel P. Moynihan. 1963. *Beyond the melting pot: The Negroes, Puerto Ricans, Jews, Italians, and Irish of New York City*. Cambridge, Massachusetts: M.I.T Press.

Greene, Maxine. 1988. *The dialectic of freedom*. New York: Teachers College Press.

Halliday, M.A.K. 1975. *Learning how to mean: Explorations in the development of language*. New York: Elsevier.

Halliday, M.A.K. and Ruqaiya Hasan. 1989. *Language, context, and text: Aspects of language in a social semiotic perspective*. Hong Kong: Oxford University Press.

Hymes, Dell. 1992. "Inequality in language: Taking for granted." In James E. Alatis (ed.), *Georgetown University Round Table on Languages and Linguistics 1992*. Washington, D.C.: Georgetown University Press. 23–40.

John-Steiner, Vera, Carolyn P. Panofsky, and Larry W. Smith (eds.). 1994. *Sociocultural approaches to language and literacy: An interactionist perspective*. Cambridge, U.K.: Cambridge University Press.

Kozol, Jonathan. 1991. *Savage inequalities: Children in America's schools*. New York: Crown Publishers.

Kress, Gunther. 1985. *Linguistic processes in sociocultural practice*. Geelong, Australia: Deakin University Press.

Ladson-Billings, Gloria. 1992. "Culturally relevant teaching: The key to making multicultural education work." In Carl Grant (ed.), *Research and multicultural education: From the margins to the mainstream*. London: The Falmer Press. 106–121.

Lantolf, James. 1994. "Sociocultural psycholinguistics: A brief historical overview." Paper presented at the American Association for Applied Linguistics, Baltimore, Maryland, March 1994.

Luke, Allan. 1986. "Linguistic stereotypes, the divergent speaker and the teaching of literacy." *Journal of Curriculum Studies* 18(4): 397–408.

Mehan, Hugh. 1991. *Sociological foundations supporting the study of cultural diversity*. Santa Cruz, California: National Center for Research on Cultural Diversity and Second Language Learning.

Moll, Luis. 1990. *Vygotsky and education*. Cambridge, U.K.: Cambridge University Press.

Ovando, Carlos J. and Virginia P. Collier. 1985. *Bilingual and ESL classrooms: Teaching in multicultural contexts*. New York: McGraw-Hill.

Nieto, Sonia. 1992. *Affirming diversity: The sociopolitical context of multicultural education*. New York: Longman.

Renner, Christopher E. 1994. "Multicultural methodologies in second language acquisition: Integrating global responsibility, peace education and cross-cultural awareness." *Peace, Environment and Education* 3(17): 3–21.

Shor, Ira. 1992. *Empowering education: Critical teaching for social change*. Chicago: The University of Chicago Press.

Sleeter, Cristine E. and Carl A. Grant. 1987. "An analysis of multicultural education in the United States." *Harvard Educational Review* 57(4): 421–444.

Wertsch, James. 1991. *Voices of the mind: A sociocultural approach to mediated action*. Cambridge, Massachusetts: Harvard University Press.

Wong, Shelley and Rachel Grant. 1995. "Addressing poverty in the Baltimore-Washington metropolitan area: What can teachers do?" *Literary Issues and Practices*. 12:3–12.

The education of second-language teachers: The link between linguistic theory and teaching practice

Weiping Wu
Center for Applied Linguistics

1. Introduction. Almost everyone would now agree that language teaching is influenced to a great extent by developments in linguistics. The degree to which teaching practice is guided by linguistic theories, however, depends on how well teachers are trained linguistically. Various aspects of second-language teaching and teacher training have been discussed by many (Larsen-Freeman 1986, 1990, Leo Van Lier 1991, Richards 1991). While agreeing with most of their arguments on the need for a theory in teaching and for both pre- and in-service training of second-language teachers, I focus in this paper on aspects of linguistic knowledge that are closely related to teaching. Examples from Chinese and English are used to illustrate my points.

By examining some of the key issues in second-language teaching (SLT) from a linguistic perspective, I argue that a clear understanding of these issues is the first step toward a better-guided practice in teaching a second language. Within the context of teaching Chinese as a second language (CSL) to speakers of English, I also propose a dynamic theory of teaching CSL and outline some implications in actual teaching if such a theory is to be implemented.

Although the five aspects of this theoretical framework explained below are relevant to all second-language-learning situations, I stay within the CSL context for the purpose of discussion. Relevant features of Chinese and English referred to in this paper are based on previous studies of the two languages (Chao 1968; Quirk and Greenbaum 1973; Gao 1981; Ann 1982; Chu 1982; Jiang 1984; Hao 1986; Kreidler 1986; Li and Cheng 1988; Li and Thompson 1989; Norman 1989). The five aspects are:

(1) Spoken versus written language,
(2) universality versus particularity,
(3) cultural versus linguistic tasks,
(4) performance versus competence, and
(5) proficiency versus achievement.

Second-language teachers may not (and perhaps never will) agree on how these issues should be handled, but they certainly agree that different ways of dealing with these basic issues will affect the outcome of learning.

As can be seen from the list, each aspect of the theory consists of two somewhat contrastive components. The focus of attention here is the allocation of time and effort in dealing with various tasks in language learning. It is important to point out that these five paired aspects are not mutually exclusive. Rather, they are two points connected by a line. At any given point on the line, elements of both (e.g. universality and particularity) can be found. The relation between the two is a matter of proportion, rather than presence or absence.

Knowing the complexity of each of these aspects, I intend only to provide some general principles related to each. For in-depth treatments, see discussions on the relation between spoken and written Chinese (Li and Thompson 1982; Wu 1990), and between universality and particularity in teaching CSL (Wu 1993). Other aspects have been explored from varying perspectives, such as the issue of competence and performance (Hymes 1971, 1972; Gumperz 1984; Savignon 1990), the rationale and methodology for proficiency-based teaching and testing (Clark 1986; Liu 1989; Thompson 1989; Valette 1989; Stansfield 1990; Jiang 1993), and the importance of including culture in language teaching (Garza 1990; Robinson 1991; Pan 1993).

2. Components of the theory. The amount of time available for any language program is always limited, and the learning tasks often seem to be too numerous; only a certain number of tasks can be accomplished within a given period of time. This is where the concept of priority comes in. As used in this paper, priority relates to the concept of time, either in terms of sequence or in terms of amount depending on the context. If Task A has priority over Task B in a language program, A will be dealt with before B in the instructional sequence. In places where sequence is less important than the amount of time, the time allocated for Task A will be more than that for Task B. Thus "priority" is used to describe both the sequence and the division of time in establishing an agenda to teach various tasks in the learning process. Contextual clues will make it clear which of the two meanings it is used for.

"Dynamic" suggests that the task receiving priority varies in different stages in the learning process. That is, a priority task in stage one of learning may not be so in stage two and vice versa. No matter which stage we are in, however, only one task is designated as the priority task so that the time and effort for such a task is guaranteed. In terms of time, "dynamic" indicates that the division of time among different tasks is not fixed, but a priority task always receives more time than any other individual task. The main objective of dynamic priority in second-language teaching is to make sure that time and resources are guaranteed for the most important task of learning a language at a particular acquisition stage. At any given time, other tasks also exist and should receive due attention. Given the fact that language is the object of study in linguistics, it goes without saying that teachers' linguistic knowledge will make it easy for them to accept the concept of tasks and to recognize the differences among various tasks in terms of priority.

Two basic assumptions underlie the arguments in this discussion. First, in learning a language, one cannot acquire all the skills at the same time. While on a strategic level, language is a system with various interrelated subsystems and should be treated as a whole, the nature of learning nevertheless makes it possible to focus, at a given stage, on a certain language skill. Secondly, we learn a language in order to use it. One cannot say every language learner has a specific purpose to use it in real life, but more and more people nowadays do take a practical approach. Thus communication with language, or the use of language, is more important than the book knowledge of language to many learners.

2.1. Spoken versus written language. In languages in which there is a big gap between the spoken form and its written form, such as Arabic and Chinese, how to strike a balance between the two in a relatively short program is a never-ending debate. Different philosophy and program objectives may lead to totally different approaches. In Chinese programs, for example, all possible combinations have been preached, and some practiced to a certain degree: No characters, all characters, first character and then sounds, first sounds and then characters, both starting at the same time, and so on. Arguments for each approach seem to be equally sound out of context. In a way, this is like the story of the blind men and the elephant. For language teachers, the key to seeing the whole "elephant" lies in a clear understanding of the objectives of second-language learning, the structural characteristics of both the written and the spoken components of the Chinese language, and the relative difficulties involved in learning for English speakers.

In the context of cause-effectiveness and according to the nature of the Chinese language, spoken Chinese has priority over written Chinese at the beginning stage (the length of which will depend on the length of the whole program, to be discussed later). Spoken Chinese is defined as the oral form of the language as it said and heard, regardless of the romanization systems (Pinyin, Yale, or Bo, Po, Mo, Fo (BPMF)) by which it is represented. Written Chinese refers to characters, both simplified and traditional.

By giving priority to spoken Chinese, I mean that students will concentrate on the spoken form during the initial stage of their study until they can perform elementary tasks (ask and answer questions, give a description, tell a story, make a request, etc.). During this stage, the task facing English-speaking students learning Chinese will be similar to the one they face when learning a cognate language, like Spanish or German.

According to Clifford (1993), the more sameness there is between the native language of the learners and the target language being learned, the easier it is for them to learn. Although not the only reason, a totally different writing system is a major reason that Chinese (with Arabic and Korean) is listed as one of the most difficult languages (Group IV) in all government language schools. It is understandable that Spanish is listed as the easiest (Group I) for speakers of English. The differences in the phonological systems between Chinese and English may also cause some difficulty, since tones are used as a distinctive feature in Chinese. Compared with the writing system with its impressive number of characters, the discrepancies in sounds are not nearly as formidable.

Students serious about learning Chinese eventually will have to learn characters. Once a working knowledge of the spoken form is within the reach of the students, the task of studying the characters becomes less challenging. The only connection to make is between meaning and symbols. Just as the time needed for acquiring speaking skill (not just knowledge of the Chinese sound system) varies among students, the time for introducing characters will also differ among programs.

One argument against introducing characters at a later stage is that students will "learn the same word twice," meaning first they learn its phonological form and then its graphic form. This argument is not well founded because students always learn the word "twice" even if characters are introduced at the same time as its phonological form. The only difference is the length of time between introducing the two forms. One can always give an equally valid argument that, if characters are introduced at the same time, the burden on the students would be too great because they have to remember both the phonological form and the written form simultaneously. This would slow down the learning process, cause more frustration, and thus discourage students from continuing.

Among other common arguments against focusing on oral forms first are the following: If characters have to be learned, it is better to start early. Or, students are confused by all the homophones without characters. Getting into these arguments on either side without knowing the larger context of program objectives and student needs is getting into the blind men's debate about the elephant.

To put things in context, let us look at the learning process, which can be broken down into the following steps: making the link between sound and meaning, making the link between written form (either letters or characters) and meaning, and making the link between meaning and the real world. The purpose of learning a language is to reach the last step. People who communicate with audible signals depend on the first step while those who do so with written symbols need the second step. The reality of human communication suggests that far more people depend on the oral form for communication. If such a common-sense argument is not convincing enough, let us look at some facts about Chinese itself.

From a linguistic point of view, giving priority to spoken Chinese is determined by the nature of language. In spoken Chinese, there are four hundred sixteen basic syllables. Counting the tones, the total number is 1,295 (excluding thirty-nine light tones). The number of characters, on the other hand, is enormous. *Kangxi* Dictionary has over 47,000 characters (though many of them are now obsolete). *Cihai*, a popular table-top dictionary, has about 15,000 characters. To function as a literate person, one has to know more than 3,000 individual characters, which takes several years of continuous study. A six-credit course (one semester) at a university usually introduces approximately one hundred seventy-five characters. Programs at different institutions may vary, but the range is between one to three hundred. Even at the higher end of it, it will take about five years to reach the 3,000 goal, if we assume that every character learned is remembered, and all combinations from individual characters are understood.

If we introduce characters from the very beginning of Chinese language study, most of the time during the first two years, which is usually the length of time that most students who are not majoring in Chinese at the university level spend in Chinese classes, will be spent on struggling with the characters. The total number of characters students will have learned at the end of the two years, however, comes to about only one third of those needed to function as a person who is literate in Chinese. We do not want students to spend two years studying and still not be able to talk nor read. Thus starting characters from the very beginning does not seem to be effective if we agree that communicative competence is the main objective of the program. As for the issue of homophones (meaning students are confused by words with the same sound but represented by different characters), sometimes whether there is confusion or not actually depends on how the teacher chooses to guide the students and how well he or she is trained linguistically. Elsewhere I give a more detailed discussion of this issue (Wu 1991). Suffice it to say here that, if we remember language is always used in context, we will not exaggerate the confusion attributable to homophones.

2.2. Universality versus particularity. Universality as used in this paper refers to common formal features shared by all languages. Particularity covers those characteristics of each language that have no formal equivalents in other languages, like the use of *ba* to front the object in Chinese, which has no formal match in English. On the strategic level, universality has priority over particularity in the course of the whole program. Generally speaking, common features are easier for students, especially at the beginning stage.

In an earlier paper (Wu 1993), I made a comparison between Chinese and English in three subsystems of language—phonology, syntax, and semantics, concluding that there are more similarities than particularities between two languages as wide apart as English and Chinese, especially when we consider all the features of a language. Here, I give just one example in each subsystem to demonstrate that even in the most "typical" examples used by many to show differences between the two languages, similarities can still be found.

In phonology, in the categories that are traditionally regarded as the "unique" feature of Chinese, like the retroflex *zh, ch, sh* and the palatal *j, q, x,* the "uniqueness" is partly exaggerated by spelling convention and does not really indicate all the acoustic properties of the sounds. Variations of the phoneme /i/ in Chinese also affect the sound quality of these consonants. If we ignore spelling, we have little difficulty in recognizing the similarity between the initial *s* sound in English (as in "Seattle") and the *x* in Chinese (as in *xi*). If we stay within phonetics, we can actually say all languages, not just Chinese and English, share more common features than particularities. After all, we only have so many places of articulation.

In syntax, among the features mentioned frequently by most studies as "different" are the topic-comment structure and word order, especially the left-branching feature in Chinese. Actually, it is not difficult to find, in English, sentences starting with "as for" or "concerning." These are equivalent to the topic-comment structure in Chinese in many cases. The so-called "left-branching" structure, which can be represented as "Modifier+*de*+modified," or "attributive+*de*+head noun," receives much publicity not because it is so vastly different from English, but because it is the place where students often make mistakes. After all, English is also left-branching at the phrase level. Consider "the little round wooden table," in which all the modifiers are to the left of the head noun. What we have here in both examples are differences in frequencies or levels (phrase versus clause), and not exactly a brand new concept or feature that is present in one language and absent in the other.

In semantics, almost all languages are similar since most concepts of the world are shared by mankind regardless of the language they use. Take verbs for example. Regardless of the labels found in various languages, all languages possess only three kinds of verbs: state, process, and action verbs. Following the case grammar theory proposed by Cook (1989), all languages are the same when it comes to logical structure with its five identifiable categories: Agent, Experiencer, Benefactive, Object, and Locative. In English, the verb "to give" would involve the giver (Agent), the thing being given (Object), and the receiver (Benefactive). Data collected from several languages (Chinese, Russian, French, Japanese) in a seminar on semantics (Dinneen 1989) also show striking similarities among languages in terms of semantic structure. In Chinese, the verb *gei* (to give) demands the same number of entities as in English. One may argue that the word *gei* in Chinese can also function as a preposition "for" or "to," and that therefore it is different from the verb "to give" in English. This, however, is a difference in the usage of *gei* as a word, and not in the logical structure or semantic property of *gei* when used as a verb, like "give" in English.

By giving priority to universality, I mean more attention should be paid to common features shared by Chinese and other languages. We should not exaggerate the uniqueness of Chinese. Instead, we should start with similar features and then move to the particular ones. The rationale for such a priority can be understood in terms of the following aspects: psychological preparation of students, old-new information theory in learning, and the number of features on each side (similarities versus differences) when the language is taken as a whole.

Psychologically, students may be under pressure if they are told from the very beginning that this is a totally different language from English and thus requires an overwhelming amount of effort. As a matter of fact, some teachers would tell the students "just forget about English." One problem with human beings is that we cannot unlearn. To "forget about" the language you have been using all your life is simply impossible. Students would feel differently if they are told the whole truth and not just part of it. That is, the language they are learning (Chinese) works basically the same as the language they already know (English), with some particularities in certain aspects. They can be instructed to use their knowledge of the language they already know, such as the SVO pattern, the use of classifiers, the ability to express the same concept of time or aspect with different means. Such "friendly" preparation would help them feel more confident in the process of learning. Some people may object to this approach by saying that what is different is actually easier for students to remember, and features that are similar sometimes present the biggest problem. While in total agreement with the logic behind such an argument, I want to point out that this does not alter the fact that similarities among languages are more common than particularities when all features of a language are considered. Nor does it contradict the approach that makes use of analogy and association.

From the perspective of the learning process, new information is always built on old information. What is the same or similar among languages is considered as old information while what is different is new information. New things are usually learned by comparing and contrasting with the old, either consciously or unconsciously. Moreover, analogy is a most powerful tool of learning for many. There is no analogy without what is already known. No matter whether they are told to "forget about your native language" or not, students are not likely to do as told even if they want to. One advantage adult learners have is the ability to reason, to compare and contrast, as compared to children, who learn by imitation. It is certainly helpful to try to implement some of the features and findings from child language acquisition in the adult SLA classroom, but one cannot force adults to learn like children.

As teachers, we are also concerned with what kind of picture we present to students about anything we teach. If there are more similarities than differences between two languages, it is fair that students have that picture. Having a correct frame will be important for the learning process in the long run. We have learned from studies of languages that universality is the forest while particularity is the trees. We do not want our students to be so obsessed with each individual tree that they lose the general picture of the forest.

2.3. Cultural versus linguistic tasks. If we decompose the learning process into separate tasks, we see the ones early in the process are mainly linguistic and the ones toward the end are basically pragmatic or cultural in nature. At the advanced level (as used in the American Council on the Teaching of Foreign Lnguages [ACTFL] Proficiency Guidelines), cultural tasks should have priority over linguistic ones.

By giving priority to cultural tasks when students reach the advanced level, I mean more time and effort should be devoted to cultivate their awareness of the culture in which the target language is used. I also mean the approximation, whenever possible, of the culture associated with the language. The model described by Pan (1993) is a good example along these lines. Given the close tie between language and culture, it is difficult to draw a line and proclaim that on one side of it are linguistic tasks and on the other cultural ones, and that once we cross the line, the focus of teaching should shift. Well-trained teachers can often detect the need to do so when students start telling them that they know every word in the sentence but still do not know what it means.

The real difficulty here is to define a cultural task. For discussion purposes, we can divide each speech event into two components. What one says in an utterance is linguistic in nature, the syllables, the words, the syntactic structures used, etc. When, where, to whom, and how it is said, however, are factors that can be considered as pragmatic in nature and have more to do with culture. In other words, the appropriateness of an utterance, as opposed to the formal features of the utterance itself, is the cultural task that the students have to acquire.

To understand the differences between cultural and linguistic tasks, we can also look at the issue in light of language and language use. Linguistic tasks are the knowledge of language itself as a system of symbols, while cultural ones are the knowledge, or the ability to use the language appropriately according to the status of the speaker and the addressee(s) in a particular context. Strictly speaking, cultural factors are at work at the very beginning of a language course. Whether *nin* should be used instead of *ni* in *nihao* (hello), which is perhaps one of the first words a student would learn to say in a CSL classroom, certainly requires a lot of cultural consideration.

The shift of focus from linguistic features to cultural ones is necessitated by the expectations of interlocutors in communication, especially with native speakers of Chinese. It is certainly true that a lot of "foreigner talk," including mispronunciation, slowness in responses or speech, wrong word choices either linguistically or contextually, and syntactic errors or broken sentences, is tolerated at the beginning stage of acquisition. Any attempt at carrying out the conversation in the target language with its native speakers is often appreciated. Experience seems to suggest that this accommodating attitude gradually disappears as the language learner advances in proficiency. By the time the learner reaches the advanced level, the expectations of native interlocutors change.

Like it or not, advanced language learners find themselves measured by the same, or similar criteria as those for the native speakers because of the vocabulary they know, the grammatical structures they use, and the fluency they possess when using the foreign language. They are then expected to talk not only correctly but also appropriately, to laugh at jokes which require an understanding of the cultural background, to pick up hints that have not been said explicitly, and to recognize not just the meaning of words, but also the connotations these words may carry and the attitude of the speaker. All these are not taught by teachers in classrooms. The best place to pick up these nonlinguistic cues would be the society in which the language is used. For want of such an environment, a multimedia approach would be the closest scenario that can provide similar input. Specifics of such an approach are discussed in the implications section.

2.4. Performance versus competence. Performance in this paper is defined as what one can do with the language in communication, either oral or written. Competence, in this context, refers to what one knows about language. Like the distinction between cultural and linguistic tasks, we can also say that performance is linked to language use while competence is linked to language itself. There is of course a close relation between the two. It is difficult to imagine a good performance without competence. It is possible, however, for someone to have a good knowledge of the language and still perform poorly.

Priority of performance, as is advocated in this paper, means providing enough opportunities for the students so that they can develop their ability to use the language for real-life situations. Even though competence is the base of performance, there is always a gap between the two. Giving priority to performance means devoting more time to bridge such a gap. Most CSL classes at the university level still center on the understanding of the materials presented in class. By the time the text is understood, class time is almost over. New material is given in the next class. Thus the practice for using what is learned in class is left to the student's discretion outside of class. If the purpose of studying a second language is to use it in real-life communication, I would argue for more class time for the students to go beyond understanding what is learned in class. As a matter of fact, the issue of performance should be on the agenda from the very first day of the program and remain so until the very last day. It is difficult to say exactly how much time should be given to performance and how much to competence, for it is virtually impossible to say for certain where one ends and the other starts. Running the risk of oversimplifying the issue, I would say students should at least be able to use (performance) over sixty percent of the words and structures they know (competence). Experience suggests that such a percentage would call for a lot more time for cultivating the ability to use the language than the time needed to learn about the language.

From another perspective, to have performance as the priority is simply a result of changes over time in our understanding of what learning a language involves. Many discoveries have been made about the processes of learning in general, and language learning in particular. It is no longer new to us that there is a close relation between various pedagogies and their results in terms of learning. To keep up with the developments of linguistics and benefit from our knowledge of new discoveries, we constantly have to make adjustments in our priorities in language learning. This partly explains why language-teaching methodology has evolved from the Grammar–Translation Method to the Communicative Approach. Every shift of methodology in between, the Direct Method, the Audio-Lingual Method, the Silent Way, Suggestoppedia, Community Language Learning, and the Total Physical Response Method, reflects the change of focus in language learning (cf. Larsen-Freeman 1986).

The purpose of learning a foreign language nowadays has moved further away from the original narrow purpose of academic research in literature and linguistics. The majority of the students learning a second language are doing so for real-life applications, such as job opportunities in the future, being able to talk to their friends speaking that language, or even the need to pass a second-language-proficiency requirement. Most of the students would like to use the language to some capacity, and not just know about it. Students need more than just comprehension skills so that they can do research, as many history and literature majors did in the past. They need production skills as well, if not more so, so that they can communicate. If being able to communicate in a second language is the goal, it is inevitable that performance will be in the foreground of learning, which translates into more class time for practice throughout the whole program.

2.5. Proficiency versus achievement. Proficiency testing has priority over achievement testing in SLT programs. To avoid confusion, I make a distinction between proficiency and performance as used in this paper. Proficiency is evaluated by proficiency testing, as opposed to achievement testing; while performance is a factual description of students' ability to use the language, as opposed to their knowledge of it. A student with a high level of proficiency usually performs in accordance with the characteristics of that proficiency level.

One good performance alone, if not supported by consistent patterns, cannot be regarded as a sure sign of high proficiency.

Proficiency-oriented testing has two important characteristics. One is lack of a direct link between the content of the test and the textbook used for the course. No matter what textbook is used, or which methodology is employed in teaching, students doing well on a language proficiency test will be ones who are able to use that specific language for real-life purposes. This leads to the second characteristic, which can be described as the standardization of the test itself. No matter where it is used, it would measure the same ability. Take the Chinese Speaking Test (CAL 1994) for example; it measures students' ability to speak Chinese regardless of where they learn the language, how they learn it, or what textbook they use.

Giving priority to proficiency tests is interpreted as making an effort to use them regularly either by themselves or supplemented by achievement tests. A more accurate way of describing priority here would be to stress the frequency aspect of time, rather than the absolute amount of time. Since most proficiency tests are developed by testing professionals, and the teachers actually do not spend much time designing these tests, teacher time is often irrelevant here. Frequency is a specific index which translates to the regular use of proficiency tests, such as entry and exit tests, mid-program tests, semester-end or year-end tests, regardless of whether or not achievement tests are used. One problem with using proficiency tests is that the current levels in many commercially available tests are too far apart. As a result, one semester of study sometimes makes no difference in the results of the test. Students will certainly be disappointed if they find that studying seems to get them nowhere. The revelation we can gain from such a situation is that, first, some language programs seem to do little to improve the proficiency of the students, and second, proficiency tests need to be improved so that they reflect student progress on a finer scale.

Important as it is, it should be pointed out that using proficiency testing in a language program does not exclude the use of normal achievement testing. After all, it would be good for both the students and teachers to know how well vocabulary and grammatical structures are mastered by students and how much they have learned from class.

Giving priority to proficiency instead of achievement in testing, like giving priority to performance instead of competence in teaching, is closely linked to the objective of study. In the course of a program, we want to know how well students are doing in terms of their ability to communicate, and not just how much they know about the textbook. We also want to know where they are, compared to students in other programs at the end of their study. Most importantly, we want to make sure that there is a link between the score assigned to a student and what he or she can do with the language. Based on an achievement test, an "A" in intensive Chinese, for instance, may actually have nothing to do with the student's ability to use Chinese.

The lack of standards in individual achievement tests used by various SLT programs may turn out to be a driving force for the use of proficiency tests. The variety of textbooks used and individualized ways of grading often make it impossible to interpret grades. Teachers are known to be either "tough" or "easy" in grading. Inflation of grades is also common. Materials used for the same level in different schools, or even in the same school, are different in content, style, focus, and difficulty level. The objectives in one program often differ from others. Given all of these factors, it is not surprising to find that some C students from a certain school are better than some A students from other schools.

3. Implications. Briefly discussed above are the five components of a dynamic priority theory with examples from teaching CSL. For each aspect, I have argued that priority be given to certain tasks in the learning process. What does fully implementing such a framework imply for second-language teachers? What is the relation between teachers' linguistic training and their teaching practice? When talking about how these aspects are perceived by second-language teachers, we have to face the fact that many of them are not trained in linguistics or second-language acquisition. It is certainly not realistic to expect language teachers without training in linguistics, pedagogy, or SLA theories to make use of developments in these fields automatically and systematically. In the context of the dynamic priority theory discussed in this paper, for example, teachers first of all have to be convinced of the priorities before they can seriously consider how to implement various aspects of such a framework. One cannot take for granted that a teacher with a background in linguistics, education, or SLA will be a better teacher. It is reasonable to assume, however, that the linguistic training of teachers will make it easier for them to accept the notion of priority and handle various tasks with more confidence and resources. At least one thing is clear: CSL teachers with a background in linguistics will find it easier to accept the notion that spoken language is primary while written language is secondary. With the basic conviction that certain tasks are to be given priority in the course of a language program, teachers should then pay attention to the following aspects.

3.1. Curriculum design. If we think of students entering a second-language program as the "raw material" and those exiting the program as the "products," curriculum design is the process in which they are "manufactured." The percentage of the qualified "products" will then depend on how well the curriculum is designed. Obviously, there is a guiding principle, explicit or implicit, behind every curriculum.

A traditional curriculum, with knowledge of the language as the focus, will inevitably place emphasis on knowing about the language. If the present theoretical framework is used as the principle for curriculum design, emphasis will be on using the language. This will mean devoting a considerable amount of time to the spoken form, introducing the writing system in a CSL program relatively late, making efforts to approximate the target culture in the classroom, recognizing the importance of performance, and regularly using proficiency tests—with or without achievement tests, depending on the program objectives.

3.2. Methodology. Given the priorities specified in the curriculum, the pedagogical tools used to reach the goals will invariably reflect the focus at each stage of the program. A proficiency-based teaching methodology, therefore, will be the natural candidate. Among the specific issues to be considered in this regard are: The creation of a student-centered learning environment; the degree to which teachers represent the native culture, especially at the advanced level where the introduction of culture often demands more than the cultural notes in a book; various issues related to error correction (what kinds of errors should be corrected, how, at what stage, etc.); and the kind of exercises to use in order to develop communicative skills.

3.3. Material selection. Once the principles and methodology are decided, the next important element in incorporating the dynamic priority theory will be the choice of materials. Needless to say, the best materials will be ones that are designed with the dynamic priority theory as the guiding principle in the first place. Such a set of textbooks can be used in its totality throughout the program. Unfortunately, textbooks always lag far behind developments in linguistic or pedagogical theory. So, in reality, teachers often find themselves using only selections from the available textbooks all the time. In selecting materials that will fit the priority theory, the most important thing to bear in mind is the fact that each stage has a different priority. As long as the salient feature of a textbook fits the need of a particular stage, it can be used as a textbook for that particular stage. That means different textbooks will be used at different stages. All textbooks, as can be expected, will have to be modified to fit the need of the curriculum better.

Given the fact that more than one textbook will be used, the smooth transition of materials becomes critical. It is nothing new to hear teachers complaining that no single textbook is good enough. Many teachers are actually doing their best to make the teaching materials serve their purpose better by compiling their own materials. It will take collaborative efforts by teachers and program coordinators to smooth out gaps that exists between various textbooks used in the course of the whole program. Relevant descriptions in the CSL model presented below will give some suggestions as to which direction this will go. One benefit of adopting the dynamic priority theory in second-language teaching is that the type of materials to be used for programs with such an approach will make it easy to use authentic materials, reflecting the trend in the field of materials development.

3.4. Testing procedures. Adopting the priority theory also means the use of proficiency tests in the course of the program. It does not follow that no achievement tests will be allowed. The use of proficiency tests as a measurement tool ensures that the communicative ability of the students can be evaluated. This does mean, however, that the relative weight of oral and written exams now assigned by many programs will have to be changed. Students are not likely to spend time practicing speaking Chinese if they are to be tested on written translations. The characteristic features of proficiency tests, as well as the advantages of using them, have been discussed in detail by many (Clark 1986; Jiang 1993; Liu 1989; Stansfield 1989). What I stress here is that these two kinds of tests are complementary and should not necessarily be mutually exclusive.

3.5. A working model. Certain aspects of this theoretical framework have been implemented in actual teaching, with or without making a direct link to the dynamic priority theory. Based on teaching practice from actual Chinese language-training programs that I have been involved in over the past several years, I propose below a working model incorporating most of the aspects. This model for implementing the dynamic priority theory in CSL has four major components: time allocation, teaching materials, methodology, and testing procedures.

- **Time allocation:**
  - A considerable length of time (four to eight thirty-hour weeks, depending on the length of the whole program) at the beginning of a Chinese program is devoted solely to the spoken form of the language;
  - In each week following the initial period, a proportion of classroom time (about ten hours per week in a thirty-hour-per-week program) is spent on aural and oral practice;
- **Materials:** Textbooks are not used in their totality. Different textbooks for each level listed below only serve as the basic texts, with a lot of modification by instructors.
  - Beginning level: *Standard Chinese: A modular approach* (Defense Language Institute, 1980).
  - Intermediate level: *Speaking Chinese about China* (Sinolingua. 1989), which is treated as a content-based textbook.

- Advanced level: *Advanced Chinese: A topical approach*. This instructional packet consists of unedited authentic materials prepared by teachers. It has three components:
  (1) Printed materials, which consist of articles from current newspapers, excerpts from official documents, and publications intended for native speakers of Chinese (such as entries from the *China encyclopedia*);
  (2) Electronic materials, which include videotapes (movies, news broadcasts, TV series) and audiotapes (news broadcasts from Voice of America, Taiwan, and Mainland China); and
  (3) Direct communication with authentic cultural and linguistic representatives of the Chinese language who are invited to give lectures and discuss various topics with the students.
- **Methodology:**
  - Whenever possible, common features among languages are stressed and used as starting points for introducing particular features;
  - Features unique to Chinese receive due attention, but are not exaggerated to the extent that they create a distorted picture of the language.
- **Testing procedures:**
  - Proficiency tests in speaking (Oral Proficiency Interview as used by government language schools), reading and listening are administered regularly (usually once every eight weeks) during the program;
  - Final grades of the students are based on their ability to use the language and not knowledge of the textbooks they have covered.

The model described above has been in use in several Chinese programs for students from the government. All students came into the program with a specific purpose of reaching a certain proficiency level. In all the programs using this approach, every student reached the expected proficiency level at the end of the program. Although many factors may have contributed to the success of the programs, it is certainly not a mere coincidence that teachers in these programs are well-trained in linguistics. Other factors contributing to the success of these programs are highly motivated students with a single purpose of learning Chinese; the freedom instructors have to design and implement the programs; and, for advanced classes, a budget that covers the costs of needed teaching materials, including inviting one guest speaker for each topic. Though not many CSL programs will enjoy such privileges, the principles manifested by these programs are nevertheless applicable (at least to the intermediate level) in the field of teaching CSL.

4. Conclusion. Obviously, the variety of curricula for teaching CSL already in existence may defy any pedagogical theory. The need to treat different stages of the learning process differently also dictates that any priority is relative. No matter how a particular curriculum is designed and how courses are taught, however, not many people will deny the fact that the final goal of learning a language nowadays is to use it one way or another. As mentioned earlier, it is against such an assumption (we learn language in order to use it) that the dynamic priority theory is defined and discussed.

The main reasons for giving priority to certain tasks in the learning process can be summarized as follows: We give priority to the spoken form because of the nature of language; to universality because of the principles in learning; to cultural tasks due to the change of attitude toward the learners as they get to the advanced level; to performance because the main objective of learning a language is to use it and not just know about it; and to proficiency tests because we want to know how well students can use the language. It is important to remember that priority is dynamic and that two seemingly opposing terms are actually two sides of the same coin. Second-language teachers will find that understanding these underlying reasons can contribute to better-guided practice in teaching.

To recapture what has repeatedly been mentioned in the course of the discussion, the quality of second-language teaching programs is closely connected with the linguistic training of teachers. A common-sense argument is that language teachers have to know what to do before it can be done. If teachers are ignorant of the nature of language, of the learning process, and of the methodological issues so vital to a language program, there is a missing link in the process of second-language teaching and learning. It is through the education of second-language teachers that we can provide this link. Knowledge of linguistics, however, is not knowledge of language teaching. That is why we need a theory of language teaching, as Larsen-Freeman points out (Larsen-Freeman 1990). Setting priorities so that time and efforts will be guaranteed for important tasks at different stages of learning is an effort in this direction.

REFERENCES

Ann, Tsekai K. 1982. *Cracking the Chinese puzzles*. Hong Kong: Stockflows Co., Ltd.
Center for Applied Linguistics (CAL). 1994. *Chinese speaking test*. Washington, D.C.: Center for Applied Linguistics.
Chao, Yuenren. 1968. *A grammar of spoken Chinese*. Berkeley, California: The University of California Press.
Chu, Show-chih Rai. 1982. *Chinese grammar and English grammar, a comparative study*. Taipei, Taiwan: Commercial Press.

Clark, John L.D. and Ying-che Li. 1986. *Development, validation, and dissemination of a proficiency-based test of speaking ability in Chinese and an associated assessment model for other less commonly taught languages*. Washington, D.C.: Center for Applied Linguistics.

Clifford, Ray. 1993. "(Respond to) Developing language competencies." Presentation at the National Invitational Symposium on Critical Language Education, The University of Iowa, Iowa City, Iowa.

Cook, Walter A. 1989. *Case grammar theory*. Washington, D.C.: Georgetown University Press.

Dinneen, Francis. 1987. *Contrastive analysis: Collection of data*. Unpublished ms., Georgetown University.

Gao, Gengsheng. 1981. *Hanyu yufa wenti shishuo*. Shandong, P.R.C.: People's Publishing House.

Garza, Thomas. 1990. "Bringing cultural literacy into the foreign language classroom through video." In James E. Alatis (ed.), *Georgetown University Round Table 1990*. Washington, D.C.: Georgetown University Press. 285–292.

Gumperz, John J. 1984. "Communicative competence revisited." In Deborah Schiffrin (ed.), *Georgetown University Round Table 1984*. Washington, D.C.: Georgetown University Press. 278–289.

Hu, Yushu. 1979. *Xiandai hanyu*. Shanghai: Shanghai Education Publisher.

Hymes, Dell. 1971. "Competence and performance in linguistic theory." In Renira Huxley and Elizabeth Ingram (eds.), *Language acquisition: Models and methods*. London: Academic Press. 3–28.

Hymes, Dell. 1972. "On communicative competence." In J. B. Pride and Janet Holmes (eds.), *Sociolinguistics*. Harmondsworth, U.K.: Penguin Books, Ltd. 269–293.

Jiang, Xinsong, et al. 1984. "Understanding the Chinese language." In Bruno G. Bara and Giovanni Guida (eds.), *Computational models of natural language processing*. Amsterdam: Elsevier Science Pub. Co. 197–225.

Jiang, Xixiang. 1993. "Language proficiency: its implications for teaching and testing in Chinese weekend schools." Presentation at the Chinese Language Teachers Association annual meeting, San Antonio, Texas.

Kreidler, Charles W. 1986. *English phonology*. Unpublished text used in course on English phonology. Georgetown University.

Larsen-Freeman, Diane. 1986. *Techniques and principles in language teaching*. Oxford: Oxford University Press.

Larsen-Freeman, Diane. 1990. "On the need for a theory of language teaching." In James E. Alatis (ed.), *Georgetown University Round Table 1990*. Washington, D.C.: Georgetown University Press. 261–270.

Leo van Lier. 1991. "Language awareness: The common ground between linguist and language teacher." In James E. Alatis (ed.), *Georgetown University Round Table 1991*. Washington, D.C.: Georgetown University Press. 528–546.

Li, Charles N. and Sandra A. Thompson. 1982. "The gulf between spoken and written language: a case study in Chinese." In Deborah Tannen (ed.), *Spoken and written language: exploring orality and literacy*. New Jersey: Ablex Publishing Corporation. 77–88.

Li, Charles N. and Sandra A. Thompson. 1989. *Mandarin Chinese: A functional reference grammar*. Berkeley, California: University of California Press.

Li, Dejin and Meizhen Cheng. 1988. *A practical Chinese grammar for foreigners*. Beijing: Sinolingua.

Li, E.C. Cheng, et al. 1984. *Mandarin Chinese: A practical reference grammar for students and teachers*. Taipei: The Crane Publishing Co.

Liu, Yinglin (ed.). 1989. *Hanyu shuiping kaoshi yanjiu*. Beijing: Xiadai Publishing House.

Norman, Jerry. 1989. *Chinese*. Cambridge, U.K.: Cambridge University Press.

Pan, Yuling. 1993. "Implementing cultural elements in Chinese teaching." Presentation at the Chinese Language Teachers Association annual meeting, San Antonio, Texas.

Quirk, Randolph and Sidney Greenbaum. 1973. *A concise grammar of contemporary English.* San Diego, California: Harbout Brace Jovanovich, Publishers.

Richards, Jack C. 1991. "Content knowledge and instructional practice in second language teacher education." In James E. Alatis (ed.), *Georgetown University Round Table 1991.* Washington, D.C.: Georgetown University Press. 76–99.

Robinson, Gail L. 1991. "Second culture acquisition." In James E. Alatis (ed.), *Georgetown University Round Table 1991.* Washington, D.C.: Georgetown University Press. 114–122.

Savignon, Sandra. 1990. "Communicative language teaching: Definitions and directions." In James E. Alatis (ed.), *Georgetown University Round Table 1990.* Washington, D.C.: Georgetown University Press. 207–217.

Stansfield, Charles. 1990. "An evaluation of semi-direct speaking test as measures of oral proficiency." In James E. Alatis (ed.), *Georgetown University Round Table 1990.* Washington, D.C.: Georgetown University Press. 228–234.

Thompson, Richard T. 1989. "Oral proficiency in the less commonly taught languages: What do we know about it." In James .E. Alatis (ed.), *Georgetown University Round Table 1989.* Washington, D.C.: Georgetown University Press. 228–234.

Valette, Rebecca M. 1989. "Language testing in the secondary schools: Past experience and new directions." In James .E. Alatis (ed.), *Georgetown University Round Table 1989.* Washington, D.C.: Georgetown University Press. 255–264.

Wu, Weiping. 1993. "Universality vs. particularity in Chinese teaching and testing." ED 366 215. Springfield, Virginia: ERIC Document Reproduction Service. Paper based on presentation at a presession of the 1993 Georgetown University Round Table on Language and Linguistics, Georgetown University, Washington, D.C.

Wu, Weiping. 1992. "Where is linguistics in the CFL (Chinese as Foreign Language) classroom." ED 366 213. Springfield, Virginia: ERIC Document Reproduction Service. Paper based on presentation at SEC/AAS (Association for Asian Studies) Conference, The University of Georgia, Athens, Georgia.

Wu, Weiping. 1991. "A sociolinguistic study of Chinese language training for diplomatic personnel." (Co-author) Proceedings of the 3rd International Symposium on Teaching Chinese, Taipei, Taiwan.

Wu, Weiping. 1990. "Teaching Chinese: linguistic and traditional approaches." Presentation at a presession of the 1990 Georgetown University Round Table on Language and Linguistics, Georgetown University, Washington, D.C.

Providing comprehensible input in a dead foreign language: Two text-based strategies

Catherine N. Ball
Georgetown University

Introduction. The traditional course in Old English offers a range of experiences not normally available in the first semester of a foreign-language class: an introduction to several centuries of history and culture; analysis and discussion of important literary texts, both poetry and prose; and the opportunity to experience a survival of medieval language pedagogy. Modern communicative approaches to foreign-language teaching may indeed seem to be irrelevant, unachievable, or unmotivated for dead languages. There is no call for communicative competence in Ancient Greek, Old English, or Medieval French; no student may ever need to ask for directions in Old Irish, or to negotiate a contract in Old Norse. Moreover, communicative approaches require a level of production competence rarely achieved by scholars trained only in the analysis of written texts. Reading knowledge is a more realistic proficiency goal than communicative competence under these circumstances, and more suited to the traditional goal of being able to read and appreciate texts in the target language.

Unfortunately, the grammar-translation method that is enshrined in the dead-language curriculum does not directly support this goal. Although the typical textbook is a "grammar and reader" (e.g. Lehmann and Lehmann 1975; Kibler 1984; Mitchell and Robinson 1992), the inclusion of textual excerpts extends a false promise: Having heard and read *about* the language for up to a semester, the student is prepared only to parse and translate the passages, not to read them. In the case of Old English, this is a poor reward for weeks or months of instruction in sound change, phonology, the conjugation of strong and weak verbs, the classes of nouns and their declensions, and other aspects of knowledge about the language. Knowledge *of* language is what is required for reading.

As I was preparing to teach Old English for the first time, I wanted to preserve and enhance what is good about the traditional beginning Old English course, while finding a linguistically motivated approach to reading knowledge. What is good, it seemed to me, was the attention to content and context that I had experienced as a student, and the exposure to authentic texts. But the magic moment when I found I could read Old English did not arrive in the course of translating the extended prose passages assigned for class homework, or decoding the beautiful but difficult poetic texts of *Seven Old English poems* or (in the second semester) *Beowulf*. That moment arrived sometime in the course of my dissertation research, as I was poring over the Old English corpus, searching for syntactic constructions relevant to the history of the *it*-cleft. I resolved to find a more efficient and pleasurable path to this reading experience, one which would enable my own students to begin reading as soon as possible.

Designing an acquisition experience for Old English. In searching for an approach that would lead to reading competence while minimizing the role of formal language instruction, I adopted Krashen's (1985) Input Hypothesis: That what is required for language acquisition is quantities of "comprehensible input":

> The Input Hypothesis claims that humans acquire language in only one way—by understanding messages, or by receiving "comprehensible input". We progress along the natural order ... by understanding input that contains structures at our "next stage"—structures that are a bit beyond our current level of competence. (We move from i, our current level, to $i+1$, the next level along the natural order, by understanding input containing $i+1$ ...) We are able to understand language containing unacquired grammar with the help of context, which includes extra-linguistic information, our knowledge of the world, and previously acquired linguistic competence. (Krashen 1985: 2)

While comprehensible input is often assumed to come from living speakers, there seems to be no reason to reject texts as a source, and Krashen (1989, 1993) has emphasized the role of reading in the development of both first- and second-language literacy. In the case of Old English, the major source of comprehensible input is the Old English corpus, a rich and varied collection of prose and poetic texts from the eighth through the eleventh century, and it is these texts which best represent the linguistic competence of native speakers of the language. This adaptation of the Input Hypothesis can be termed "acquisition through reading." The crucial problem then becomes the identification and sequencing of appropriate passages from the corpus, and their presentation to the learner as inputs.

After some experimentation with computational models for this problem, it became clear that any reliable algorithm for selecting comprehensible inputs from a set of language samples requires a sophisticated set of evaluation procedures, capable of assessing an arbitrary learner's current level of competence (i) and identifying $i+1$ phenomena in potential input. A "comprehensibility judgment" procedure is also required to evaluate whether some input I containing $i+1$ will be comprehensible to some learner L, given the linguistic and extralinguistic context. With these procedures in hand, the problem can be stated as an artificial-intelligence path problem, where the problem is to find a path through the corpus satisfying a set of constraints, as in (1):

(1) Select a sequence of inputs I_1, I_2, ... I_n for some learner L such that
    (a) each input is at least partly comprehensible;
    (b) some inputs contain unacquired $i+1$ phenomena that can be inferred from the context;
    (c) later inputs prune or confirm hypotheses; and
    (d) the linguistic-knowledge state at I_n supports the reading of extended target texts.

An automated system for selecting comprehensible input would constitute an intelligent tutoring system, but is currently beyond the state of the art in computational linguistics and artificial intelligence. Even for humans, it is unlikely that the general form of the Input Hypothesis can be fully operationalized. Accordingly, I made certain simplifying assumptions.

First, I assumed that learners would exhibit a uniform initial level of competence with respect to Old English; namely, they would have no "previously acquired linguistic competence" in the language. Second, I assumed that I could provide reliable comprehensibility judgments for this set of learners, capitalizing on my own lack of competence in the language. Finally, I selected lexical knowledge as the focus of acquisition. Lexical knowledge is clearly necessary for comprehension, and is the first obstacle to reading in a foreign language: If every word in the input is unknown, no amount of grammatical knowledge will make the input comprehensible. The lexicon is also central in generative theories of language, where it is assumed to contain both syntactic information (such as part of speech and subcategorization) and links to semantic information. Computational models of language acquisition have suggested that the core grammar of a language can in fact be derived from input and a lexicon (e.g. Berwick 1985). While there are a number of controversial issues in this area, I made the assumption that lexical information can and must be acquired in context, and that the acquisition of a lexicon brings with it some level of syntactic competence. This assumption allowed me to reformulate the input selection problem in (1) above as (2):

(2) Select a sequence of inputs I_1, I_2, ... I_n from the corpus such that
    (a) each input is at least partly comprehensible;
    (b) some inputs contain *unknown lexical items* that can be inferred from context;

(c) later inputs prune or confirm hypotheses; and

(d) the linguistic-knowledge state at I_n supports the reading of extended target texts.

Input selection and enhancement. Although a focus on lexical acquisition simplifies the problem of designing comprehensible input for beginners, lexical inferencing is itself an active area of research, and results to date (as represented, for example, in Huckin, Haynes, and Coady 1993) do not translate directly to the design of instructional materials. However, a number of heuristics emerged as I confronted the problem of choosing the first comprehensible input (I_1) from the corpus. After examining and rejecting many difficult passages from well-known texts, I settled on (3) below. This passage comes from a neglected text known as *Byrhtferth's manual*, a handbook of "ecclesiastical computation" for priests which includes useful information about astronomy, basic arithmetic and, in this case, the meaning of selected roman numerals.

(3) ByrM 1 195–196:
I. *getacnað an.*
V. *getacnað fif.*
X. *getacnað tyn.*
L. *fiftig.*
C. *centum. hundred.*
D. *fif hundred.*
M. *þusend ...*
xxiii. *þreo & twentig.*
xxiiii. *feower & twentig.*
xxv. *fif & twentig.*
xxvi. *syx & twentig ...*

Some crucial properties of this passage that contribute to comprehensibility are as follows: The content is predictable, given the discourse topic (the meaning of the roman numerals); the clause-level surface structure is simple, and indistinguishable from that of Modern English; and most of the lexical items are either already known (the roman numerals), or recognizable as cognates (the Old English numerals). Hearing this passage read aloud can further enhance comprehensibility, and allow the learner to form hypotheses about Old English phonology and grapheme-to-phoneme correspondences: For example, *fiftig* and *twentig* are pronounced in much the same way as in Modern English.

Armed with hypotheses about Old English number expressions and their relationship to Modern English, the learner can be introduced to morphological variation in the numbers and to additional cognates in other semantic areas. However, in the passage below (from Ælfric's preface to his translation of

Genesis), many of the cognates may not be immediately recognizable. In this case, pictures can provide unambiguous clues for the potentially unknown lexical items, and labels for the pictures can suggest the root forms: For example, a drawing of an eye is labelled *eage* and a drawing of a foot is labelled *fot*.

(4) ÆGenPref 105:
   God gesceop us twa eagan & twa earan, twa nosðyrlu, twegen weleras,
   twa handa & twegen fet ...
   "God gave us two eyes and two ears, two nostrils, two lips, two hands and two feet ..."

These initial observations suggested a set of design principles for a collection of comprehensible inputs from the Old English corpus. First, it makes sense to exploit the linguistic and background knowledge of the educated adult reader, and it also makes sense to enhance the input to increase the inferability of lexical items. In terms of linguistic knowledge, the existence of cognates and syntactic similarities between Old and Modern English makes the selection of comprehensible input a less daunting task than it might be for two unrelated languages. To take advantage of this fact, I organized the search for data around a set of core-concept areas that are rich in cognates (counting, nature, the body, months and seasons, and so on), and looked for short passages where the syntax was reasonably transparent. In terms of background knowledge, these core-concept areas provide familiar content, but I was also able to identify contexts where what is assumed to be new (and in need of explanation) to the Anglo-Saxon reader is known to the modern reader: For example, basic arithmetic and natural science, the signs of the Zodiac, and familiar Biblical events.

In terms of the inferability of lexical items, a key issue is constraining the set of possible senses available to the reader. The linguistic context can clearly be a valuable source of constraints, as illustrated in (3) above, but not all contexts are equally helpful. In (4) for example, imagine that all the lexical items are known except for *weleras*. The context then supports the inference that *weleras* is a noun and a part of the body, since it is a member of a conjunction of other body parts (eyes, ears, nostrils, hands, and feet). It can also be inferred that the body has two *weleras*, but the context is insufficient to narrow the choices down to lips. The general strategy I adopted to support inferencing was to narrow the choice of senses by providing an indication of the discourse topic, by choosing linguistic contexts where the content was (or could be made) predictable, and by supplying additional visual and aural clues for individual lexical items: Pictures, sounds, and voice recordings (for cognates obscured by orthography).

The result was a collection of what I judged to be comprehensible inputs, organized into chapters corresponding to basic concept areas, and sequenced and enhanced in such a way that a learner with no prior knowledge of Old English could, as I hoped, acquire a sizable portion of the Old English lexicon from context. When completed, the collection contained seven chapters of readings culled from approximately twenty-two texts, with an audiovisual "glossary" at the end.

Hwæt! Old English in context. I first implemented this collection of readings as an electronic book, using the Voyager Expanded Books Toolkit as authoring software. This HyperCard-based package allows the developer to prepare text with wordprocessing software, import it into chapters, and add hypertext links to other text, images, sound, or video. Voyager Expanded Books provides many book-like features which struck me as useful for language learners: for example, a notebook facility and the ability to write in the margins and insert graphic paperclips and turn-down pages. The book software also provides facilities for finding or concordancing selected words and navigating through the text. A sample page from the first chapter of *Hwæt!* is shown in Figure 1. In this screen snapshot, shaded underlining indicates clickable hypertext links: For example, standard short titles of Old English texts are linked to descriptions of the texts, which are in turn linked to bibliographic information for the editions used. The speaker icon is linked to voice recordings, and all other links are to sound files (animal and nature sounds) or drawings (by Kathryn Taylor, a graduate student in computational linguistics).

Because the book was not fully implemented when class began, and because I was also unsure of the best way to integrate hypermedia into the classroom, I piloted the general approach by using printouts of each chapter as the basis of the "language" section of the syllabus. Initial results were promising: With no formal grammar instruction, the students were able to read the texts and to discuss their content (in Modern English), and the incorporation of reading at the outset added a sense of excitement and accomplishment to the early stages of the course. Reading also provided a way to bypass formal instruction in Old English phonology and orthography: After memorizing the first few lines from an audiotape of *Beowulf* to get a sense of the sound system, the class read everything out loud, with excellent results. During this period we also read and discussed material that furnished background knowledge for the second half of the course, which was to be devoted to important and interesting literary texts.

The second half of the semester, however, revealed problems with the course design and the approach to lexical acquisition. First, in designing the collection of comprehensible inputs, I had been unable to find paths to all of the lexical items necessary for the extended poetic texts traditionally included in the first semester. The battle poetry, for example, features a rich vocabulary for a specific domain: terms for weaponry, fighting men, and various kinds of assaults, many of which are found chiefly in the poetry. The poetry also exhibits complex syntax and unfamiliar rhetorical structures. As a result, the second half

Figure 1. *Hwæt!* Old English in Context (Voyager Expanded Book version).

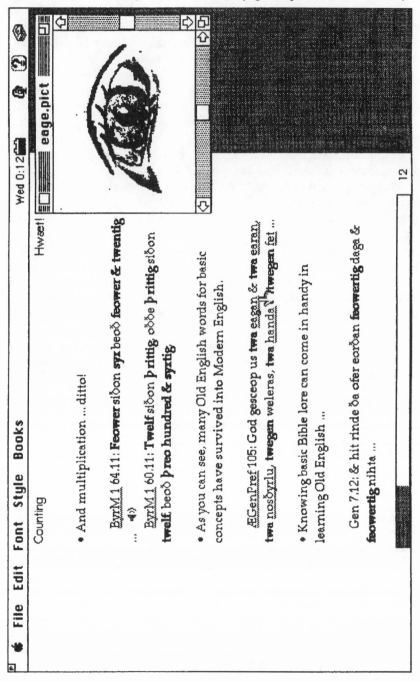

of the semester was chiefly devoted to translation and discussion, much as it would have been in a more traditional course. Although I experimented with various prereading activities involving lexical familiarization, it was only at the end of the course, when I returned to simple prose texts such as the *Old English martyrology*, that the students were again able to read, rather than decipher, the texts.

The overall results of this pilot class indicate several areas for improvement and research. First, the corpus-based approach to lexical acquisition needs to be tested through effects of instruction studies. Second, while the provision of comprehensible input appears to have been useful in the classroom, each chapter consumed an entire class period. With only two-and-a-half hours of classroom time available each week, it is doubtful whether an extension of the input to cover all the vocabulary (and syntax) necessary for extended literary texts could be achieved in less than a semester. Moving the poetry to a second semester is an option, although these beautiful and moving texts provide much of the reward for learning Old English. Another option is to make comprehensible input available outside the classroom.

With this second option in mind, I converted *Hwæt!* to Hypertext Markup Language and placed it on the World Wide Web. While the Voyager implementation runs only on the Macintosh, the Web version can be accessed from any computer lab, dormitory, or home machine with a graphical Web browser and sound capabilities. Furthermore, changes to Web files take effect immediately, without any distribution lag. Moving *Hwæt!* to the Web will allow some basic reading to take place outside the classroom, but there is another need I wished to address: the opportunity to interact, if only to a limited extent, in the foreign language.

MondoMOO: A multiuser virtual environment with robots. Although my class focused on reading knowledge, as is customary, and had no production goals, several of the students chose to produce original compositions (poetry and chronicles) for the course paper. In reflecting on my own experiences in Old English and German for Reading Knowledge, in which students received no encouragement or even opportunity to produce, it seemed to me that some learners would enjoy and benefit from opportunities to interact in Old English. As can be imagined, such opportunities are rare: Even if the instructor is capable of sustained conversational interaction in Old English, the chances of finding a physically present, fluent speaker of Old English outside the classroom are very small. However, the Internet provides a possible solution.

A model for the use of the Internet in language learning is furnished by SchMOOze University, a virtual environment designed by Julie Falsetti of Hunter College. Users log in from around the world using telnet and enter a virtual university where they can interact with other users (native and nonnative speakers) in English. Such text-based virtual environments are rapidly springing up for other languages, providing opportunities for real-time conversational interaction outside the classroom. Users find them highly engaging: They can construct their own identities as "players", converse with other users, and (if granted the necessary privileges) modify the environment, building rooms and furnishing them with objects. These virtual environments provide a variety of language-related activities in addition to conversation: For example, players read and construct textual descriptions associated with objects, as illustrated in Figure 2. This figure shows the first few minutes of a novice-user session in SchMOOze University.

To support future classes in Old English, SchMOOze University inspired two projects which were undertaken by the students in my Introduction to Natural Language Processing class. The first project was to construct a virtual environment at Georgetown, using the MOO software developed by Xerox Parc and available by FTP. The Georgetown MOO ("MondoMOO") contains a virtual model of the Intercultural Center, in one of whose rooms is a time machine that will allow the user to be transported to Anglo-Saxon England. The construction of Anglo-Saxon England, or perhaps simply a town or a monastery, can be a collaborative project for future students in Old English or Medieval Studies. The second project was to construct a "robot," an autonomous computer program which simulates a human player and is capable of simple conversational interaction. Our first robot, Elmo, was designed to provide help to novice users, who may not be familiar with the English-like MOO command language that is required to perform actions in the virtual environment. A sample user session with Elmo is illustrated in Figure 3.

Elmo was developed by d'Armond Speers, a graduate student in computational linguistics at Georgetown, using robot code developed by Michael Mauldin of Carnegie Mellon University. Mauldin's robots provide an impressive level of conversational ability based on pattern-matching and have been mistaken for humans; our class project was to perform brain surgery on the original robot and add natural-language processing. Elmo provides a model for the development of an Anglo-Saxon robot capable of interacting with users in Old English. The Anglo-Saxon robot, which is currently in the planning stages, will initially use a pattern-matching strategy for processing user input, and may in fact represent a translation of Elmo's original input patterns and responses into Old English. Development of full natural-language-processing capabilities will require the development of an Old English lexicon, morphological analyzer, parser, and generator—a more ambitious and longer-term project.

Figure 2. Sample user session, SchMOOze University, novice user (names altered).

```
%telnet arthur.rutgers.edu 8888
Trying 128.6.110.37 (port 8888) ...
Connected to arthur.rutgers.edu.
Escape character is "^V".
*************************************************************************
* Welcome to schMOOze University                                        *
*                                                                        *
*       = = >  To connect to an existing player type:                    *
*               CONNECT NAME PASSWORD                                     *
*       = = >  To connect as a guest type:                               *
*               CONNECT GUEST                                            *
connect guest
*** Connected ***
Don't forget to take a look at the newspaper. Type "news" to see it.
Guest awakens, and looks about.
You have connected as a Guest to SchMOOze. We want our Guests to feel welcome here.
So as a Guest, you can give yourself a name, and description. This way you won't be an
anonymous guest, but yourself. —SchMOOze Management.
[Please type the name you wish to be known as.]
Cathy
You typed: "Cathy". Is this what you want? [Enter "yes" or "no"]
yes
Please type in a brief description of yourself. Example: A tall skinny man with a perpetual
grin on his face. He wears a worn suitjacket and jeans, and has his hair tied up in a ponytail.
[Please enter a brief description of yourself.]
A computational linguist looking at the system.
Description and name set.
The Entrance Gates
--- -------- -----
These are the entrance gates to schMOOze University. To the north you can see a carved
stone archway leading to the tree lined mall of the campus. Guests and new players might
want to head directly to the Beginner classroom by typing CLASSROOM.
    To find out where things are on campus, just type MAP.
        < = =The campus clock tower reads 11:26 a.m. EDT= = >
 You see a newspaper and Suggestion-Box here.
Obvious exits: North and Classroom
 < connected: Cathy [Guest]. Total online: 5 >
You sense that Mary is looking for you in University Dorm.
She pages, "Hi!", at 11:26 a.m. Eastern Standard Time.
Mary is going to try to join you.
Mary has arrived.
Mary says, "Hi!"
say "hi"
You say, ""hi""
Mary says, "Are you new to Moo?"
say "Yes!"
You say, ""Yes!""
```

Figure 3. MondoMOO, sample user session with Elmo.

```
% telnet underdog.georgetown.edu 7777
Trying 141.161.1.6 ...
Connected to underdog.
Escape character is "^]".
===========================================
 Welcome to Mondo MOO!
--------------------
To connect to an existing player, type CONNECT PLAYER PASSWORD
To connect as a guest, type CONNECT TAURUS_GUEST
===========================================
connect Europa ●●●●●●●●
*** Connected ***
The Transporter Room
You find yourself in the Transporter Room, on the second floor of the Intercultural Center
(ICC) at Georgetown University. The darkness is illuminated by the soft glow of several curious
machines, including a Transporter and a Time Machine.
*** New users: type "NEW" to get some basic tips! ***
Obvious exits: out and closet
You see Transporter Control Panel, Newsletter, Time Machine, and BabyDog here.
Last connected Wed Mar 8 14:58:25 1995 EST from underdog.acc.georgetown.edu
Elmo has arrived.
"Hi, Elmo!
You say, "Hi, Elmo!"
Elmo says, "Hello, Europa."
"Where have you been?
You say, "Where have you been?"
Elmo says, "I have been to 11 rooms altogether, here are the last few, Europa: The Transporter
Room, Hallway (ICC 2nd floor), Elevator, Hallway (ICC 4th floor), ICC473, Lobby (ICC 3rd
floor), Red Square, SFS Dean's Office, SFS Network Administrator's Office, Closet."
"Have you seen Randalf?
You say, "Have you seen Randalf?"
Elmo says, "Randalf was in Closet about 23 hours ago, Europa."
"Thanks.
You say, "Thanks."
Elmo says, "You're welcome, Europa."
"Who is here now?
You say, "Who is here now?"
Elmo says, "Well Europa, I see 1 player awake here: Europa"
"How can I get to ICC473?
You say, "How can I get to ICC473?"
Elmo says, "Path from The Transporter Room to ICC473, type "go out" to get to Hallway (ICC
2nd floor), "go right" to get to Elevator, "go 4" to get to Hallway (ICC 4th floor), "go
ICC473" to get to ICC473."
"Ok, you can go away now.
You say, "Ok, you can go away now."
Elmo says, "I'll be going, then, Europa."
"Bye!
You say, "Bye!"
Elmo says, "Goodbye, Europa."
```

Summary and conclusions. Dead-language instruction differs from modern-foreign-language instruction in several important ways: A major goal is the ability to read and appreciate texts; sources of input are severely constrained; the course of study may be restricted to one or two semesters; and the instructor may have limited competence in the language. Under these circumstances, it is reasonable to turn to the corpus of surviving texts as a source of authentic, comprehensible input. In this paper, I have described some of the potential and some of the limitations of a corpus-based approach to teaching Old English in a one-semester course, and have discussed a supplementary approach which involves an Anglo-Saxon analog of SchMOOze University, a virtual environment for ESL students available over the Internet.

The corpus-based approach, which finds support in research on acquisition through reading (e.g. Krashen 1989, 1993), provides comprehensible input through microsamples from the Old English corpus. These samples are selected, arranged, and contextualized in such a way that the background knowledge of the educated modern reader, the availability of cognates, the discourse context, and aural and visual clues work together to maximize the inferability of unknown lexical items. The collection of samples from the Old English corpus has been implemented as a hypermedia electronic book (*Hwæt! Old English in context*), and has since been converted to run on the World Wide Web.

An initial trial of the corpus-based approach suggests that while it enables learners to read authentic texts from the first day, the rate of progress is not sufficient to allow the reading of difficult full texts by mid-semester. Since classroom interaction is limited to fewer than three hours a week, but learners may benefit from more opportunities for production and interaction, I have identified a supplementary approach which will allow learners of Old English to interact in a virtual environment over the Internet. The use of virtual environments and robots to provide comprehensible input offers a solution to the problem of limited classtime, and may also allow dead-language pedagogy to take a step in the direction of more communicative approaches. While there are many challenges associated with the design of computer systems that are capable of conversational interaction in Old English (or any language), this is a promising area for future research and development.

REFERENCES

Berwick, Robert C. 1985. *The acquisition of syntactic knowledge*. Cambridge, Massachusetts: M.I.T. Press.

Crawford, S. J. (ed.). 1922. *The Old English version of the Heptateuch, Ælfric's treatise on the Old and New Testament and his preface to Genesis*. Early English Text Society (EETS) OS 160. Reprinted 1969, with additions by N. R. Ker. London: Oxford University Press.

Crawford, S. J. (ed. and trans.). 1966. *Byrhtferth's manual.* EETS OS 177. London: Oxford University Press.

Herzfeld, George (ed. and tr.). 1900. *An Old English martyrology.* EETS OS 116. Millwood, N.Y.: Kraus Reprint Co.

Huckin, Thomas, Margot Haynes, and James Coady (eds.). 1993. *Second language reading and vocabulary.* Norwood, N.J.: Ablex.

Kibler, William W. 1984. *An introduction to Old French.* New York: Modern Language Association.

Krashen, Stephen D. 1985. *The input hypothesis: Issues and implications.* New York: Longman.

Krashen, Stephen D. 1989. "We acquire vocabulary and spelling by reading: Additional evidence for the input hypothesis." *Modern Language Journal* 73(4): 440–464.

Krashen, Stephen D. 1993. *The Power of reading.* Englewood, Colorado: Libraries Unlimited.

Lehmann, R. P.M. and W. P. Lehmann. 1975. *An introduction to Old Irish.* New York: Modern Language Association.

Mitchell, Bruce and Fred C. Robinson. 1992. *A guide to Old English, Fifth edition.* Oxford: Blackwell.

Pope, John C. 1981. *Seven Old English poems.* New York: Norton.

APPENDIX: SOFTWARE SUMMARY

"Hwæt! Old English in Context"—Voyager Expanded Book version
System requirements: Macintosh with hard drive, System 6.0.7 and HyperCard 2.1 or later (or HyperCard Player), 3.5 MB disk space. Shipped on two 1.4 MB high density diskettes.
Tools used:
   Hardware: Macintosh PowerBook 145B, 8 MB memory, 80 MB disk
   Authoring software: Voyager Expanded Book Toolkit
         The Voyager Company (1-800-446-2001)
   Photographs: QuickCam digital camera for Macintosh (Connectix)
   Drawings: drawn on paper by Kathryn Taylor, scanned using HP ScanJet IIp
   Clip art and sound clips: from America Online and HyperCard 2.1
   Voice recording: PowerBook microphone
   Text: Microsoft Word
   Text sources: Helsinki Diachronic Corpus (ICAME CD-ROM; also available from Oxford Text Archives); printed editions of Old English texts

• *"Hwæt!* Old English in Context"—World Wide Web version
System requirements: any platform (Mac, PC, NeXt, Sun) with sound capabilities, graphic Web browser (e.g. Mosaic, Netscape, but not Lynx) with helper applications for sound and images. Browsers and viewers are available over the Internet. For users without direct link to Internet (e.g. SLIP connection): download and install a Web browser on Mac/PC, download *Hwæt!* files using Lynx, run Web browser with 'local' access.
Web address: http://www.georgetown.edu/cball/hwaet/hwaet06.html
Tools used:
   Authoring software: NCSA Mosaic for Mac (freeware)
   Microsoft Word to HTML conversion: rtftohtml; HTML Editor (shareware)
   Image conversion: GifConverter (shareware)

- **MondoMOO—Multilingual multi-user reality environment with robot**
System requirements: any text terminal with telnet access to the Internet
Access method: telnet underdog@guvax.georgetown.edu 7777
Tools used:
    MOO software: available by FTP from parcftp@xerox.com
    robot (Elmo): based on Colin (developed by Michael Maudlin of CMU), written in C

Taming the electronic lion, or
How to shape a language-learning environment
out of the chaos called the Internet

Vincent J. Cangiano, El Houcine Haichour, and Stephanie J. Stauffer
Georgetown University

Introduction. Electronic information and communication are assuming an ever-expanding role in our everyday lives. In the U.S., schools and universities are acquiring computer technology for a variety of applications: library databases, computer centers, writing labs, multimedia workstations, and so forth. An increasing number of educational institutions provide access to world-wide electronic networks such as the Internet, allowing students and faculty to undertake research and communicate with colleagues by computer. This development has prompted researchers and educators to examine how such technology might be most effectively integrated into curricula. In this paper, we consider motivations and means for using the Internet as a tool in second-language education.

We begin this paper by examining what constitutes relevant language data, pointing to the value of data from varied media. We then discuss how a corpus of such data can be constructed using the Internet—and, specifically, the multimedia resources that are available on the Internet's World Wide Web.[1] Next, we provide a specific example of how to harness global resources for local uses, providing a description of a project demonstrated at this conference. Finally, we outline the strengths of this approach and offer some concluding remarks.

Learning from a corpus of language data. Linguists, teachers, and students approach language data from different perspectives and for different purposes. Nonetheless, a broad similarity exists in the process each of these "researchers" follows in examining language. The corpus linguist, the data-

---

[1]Briefly, the World Wide Web (WWW) is a rapidly expanding collection of interconnected documents available on the Internet in the form of text files, audio recordings, video clips, and images. Resources on the WWW represent only a portion of those on the Internet. Other Internet capabilities for computer-mediated communication within the language classroom are discussed in Stauffer (1994) and elsewhere.

conscious teacher, and the investigative learner all share a common interest in the discovery and application of linguistic facts from their experience with authentic language data. What constitutes relevant "language data" depends upon what kind of linguistic discovery one hopes to make.

For the language learner, an adequate corpus of language data will need to integrate data of different types and from varied media. While exposure to and analysis of authentic text is important to a learner's language development, so too is experience with how the target language is actually spoken (for pronunciation practice, intonation cues, etc.) and how its speakers genuinely interact (as seen in authentic film and video recordings). In the foreign-language context, in particular, where access to authentic and relevant samples of the target language may be very limited, varied sources of input represent a valuable resource for the learner in developing both linguistic and cultural knowledge. Thus, for the learner, a corpus of relevant language data might be represented by the collection of authentic written texts used during his or her language course (articles, short stories, dialogues, etc.), radio and television excerpts heard on international broadcasts (when learning in a foreign language context), and the cumulative language experiences gained from interacting with native speakers of the language.

Shaping a language-learning environment using the World Wide Web.
An online hypermedia corpus for language learning. A corpus of language data in various media is precisely what can be found today on the Internet. Through the World Wide Web (WWW), users can access and retrieve large amounts of language data, in the form of text files, audio recordings, video clips, and images. Among the kinds of resources that can be found on the WWW are news stories, weather reports, literature, dictionaries, reference works, information about culture, art, music, history, and so forth. Although English is currently the lingua franca of the Internet, such multimedia resources exist in a variety of languages. And while these documents come from different parts of the globe, most are designed so that you can easily "link" from one document to another through the computer networks of the Internet.[2]

Users of the Internet find it to be both fascinating and frustrating; novices may even find it a bit frightening (hence the "lion" metaphor of our title). Nonetheless, shaping a language-learning environment out of what is, at times, a rather chaotic network of resources, is not an unmanageable task. The WWW makes accessing and retrieving information and resources much easier than was previously possible on the Internet. This is due to two factors. One is the

---

[2] The WWW might be seen as the online equivalent of software design concepts originally embodied in Bill Atkinson's HyperCard for the Macintosh.

development of standards for encoding and transferring networked documents: HyperText Markup Language (HTML) and HyperText Transfer Protocol (HTTP). The other is the availability of graphical browsers—programs that enable users to display the variety of document types mentioned above.[3] Thanks to HTTP, browsers can also access information that was formerly available only through other, separate protocols, such as File Transfer Protocol (FTP), Network News Transfer Protocol (NNTP), Telnet, Gopher, and WAIS.

The home page as a tool for corpus construction. The main organizing tool for users of the WWW is the home page. Basically, a home page serves as a gateway (or directory) to information and resources located elsewhere on the Internet. Upon connecting to the WWW, a user will often see on screen the home page that the Internet access provider (e.g. a university or a commercial service) has prepared. Included in the home page are links to Internet resources that the institution's computer administrator has chosen to make easily available to users. Some educational institutions offer faculty and students the opportunity to develop their own home pages. For example, a teacher of Italian might create a home page that would "branch off" from the institution's home page and allow students to link to remote locations and view pages containing text, audio, and video in Italian. Figure 1 shows the home page created for the project described in the next section of the paper.

What is needed to link users from a home page to a remote document is the address of that document. Each document on the WWW resides on a computer at some institution and thus has some absolute address that identifies it, i.e., its Universal Resource Locator, or URL. When the home page is formatted in accordance with HTML conventions,[4] the addresses of these documents will be invisible to the user. Instead, the user will simply see, within the home page, the names of (or icons representing) the remote documents, usually highlighted with boldface or color, indicating that they are active "links," which the user can select (with the click of a computer mouse) in order to view. Figure 2 shows the HTML source file for the home page illustrated in Figure 1.

---

[3] The most popular browsers (e.g. *Mosaic* and *Netscape*) are available as shareware, at little or no cost to the user.

[4] See *A Beginners Guide to HTML,* listed in the appendices.

Figure 1. Example of a home page and a linked page.

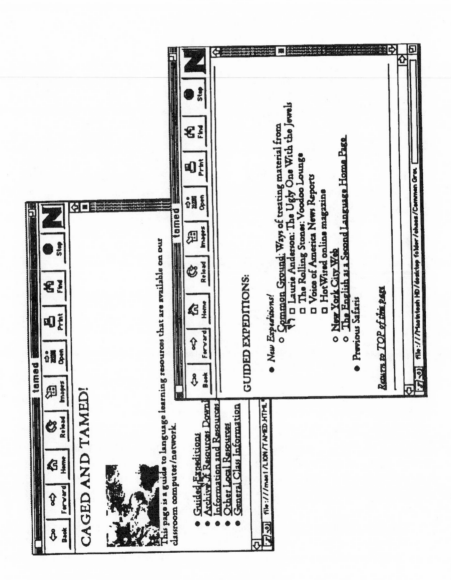

Figure 2. HTML text file, source of the home page in Figure 1.

```
<html>
<head>
<title>tamed</title>
</head>
<body>
<h2><a name="top">CAGED AND TAMED!</a></h2>
<img src="tinylion.gif."><br>
This page is a guide to language learning resources that are
available on our classroom computer/network.<p>
<ul>
<li><a href="#safaris">Guided Expeditions</a>
<li><a href="#web">Archive of Resources Downloaded from the Web</a>
<li><a href="#gu">Information and Resources at Georgetown</a>
<li><a href="#other">Other Local Resources</a>
<li><a href="#class">General Class Information</a>
</ul>
<hr>
```

Fortunately, the graphical-browser software allows the user to create his or her own home page in a very quick and easy way. While the user is exploring the resources on the WWW, he or she can record the addresses of interesting

Figure 3. Bookmarks within Netscape.

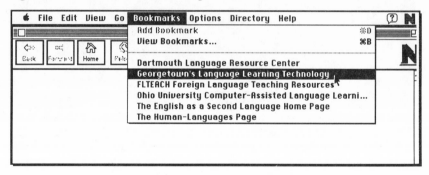

sites (i.e. remote documents or directories) by using the "bookmark" feature within the menu options (see Figure 3). Saving the bookmark file automatically creates an HTML document that can either be used as a simple home page that lists remote document names, or edited into a more elaborate home page that might also include brief descriptions of the remote resources.

Creating a home page on the WWW provides an efficient means of organizing a learner's access to a corpus of authentic resources available electronically. In this way, the chaos of the Internet can be shaped into a language-learning environment without a large investment on the teacher's part. Another approach is to create a local archive of WWW resources. In the next section, we briefly describe a project of this sort that we demonstrated as part of our conference presentation.

Taming the Electronic Lion. A teacher or learner may also want to accumulate resources accessed through a home page by downloading and saving them to a local computer hard drive. Then the documents can either be compiled for some kind of focused analysis (e.g. through concordancing of textual resources), or they can be dynamically linked to create a local hypermedia learning environment. The local archive can also be used alongside other software resources such as dictionary and thesaurus programs, word-processing software, and teacher-generated courseware. This approach does require a certain investment in time and learning. However, it also offers certain advantages over simply browsing the WWW, as we shall see. Constructing a local archive from global resources involves many overlapping stages (outlined in Table 1 and discussed below).

In constructing a local archive for English language learning and teaching purposes, we first explored the Internet to get a feel for the type of material that was beginning to appear across the Web, and to see which sites or addresses showed promise of being updated and maintained regularly. We were interested in well-designed Web pages that combined graphics and text, along with audio and video clips, where possible. In addition, we were searching for rich language data and interesting subject matter.

What we discovered was a plethora of commercial and non-commercial sources on the Internet that could be used to frame any of a number of lesson types: content-based, task-based, functional/notional, and so forth. There is plenty of material to exploit for reading comprehension, and this material varies in style and register. What is perhaps more surprising is that a growing number of sources include audio and video files that can be used to develop and test listening comprehension. Some of these will be discussed below.

From among the vast quantities of material, we chose a few sites that offered exceptional promise of being well-maintained. The issue of maintenance is important, and cannot be taken for granted. It is extremely easy to design a home page, and to put it on the Web. However, such pages can lose their currency very quickly. The WWW can be thought of as a publishing enterprise, where some home pages may act as unchanging reference volumes, but most pages need to be refreshed frequently in order to remain interesting and relevant. This continued maintenance is one of the more challenging aspects of publishing on the WWW. When a site is well-maintained, however, it becomes extremely useful to an instructor as a source of authentic materials that will not grow stale—serving the purpose that newspapers, radio broadcasts, and videos

Table 1. Constructing a "local web."

Stage 1: Accessing ("Confronting the Electronic Lion in the Wild")
- *Exploring* resources ("sites") on the WWW
- *Considering* pedagogical needs
- *Selecting* ("bookmarking") resources with classroom purposes in mind

---

Stage 2: Retrieving ("Caging the Electronic Lion")
- *Downloading* files to disk (documents, browsers, helper applications, editors, etc.)
- *Assembling* files in a directory of a hard drive
- *Editing* link addresses according to new file locations
- *Testing* the integrity of links
- *Revising* files to eliminate errors and links to unavailable files

---

Stage 3: Creating ("Taming the Electronic Lion")
- *Manipulating* files for specific pedagogical purposes
- *Supplementing* files with teacher-generated (or student-generated) documents
- *Organizing* the archive with a series of teacher-generated home pages

---

Stage 4: Analyzing ("Feeding the Electronic Lion")
- *Piloting* the materials with students
- *Obtaining* feedback from students
- *Evaluating* effectiveness of materials

---

have, but with "live" electronic text and other content that can be easily manipulated. The stability of an address, or link, is also important. The Web is changing rapidly to accommodate the exponential growth in the number of people who use it. Many home pages have been created by people with relatively temporary addresses, and a materials designer must be aware of the possibility that a source might cease to exist without warning. Other sources, most of them commercial or institutional, show promise of stability.

It should be mentioned that the issue of copyright for materials on the WWW is as yet unresolved. Some sources attach various copyright notices to the materials that they include in their home pages: HotWired, for example, allows not-for-profit redistribution of its articles, as long as the original copyright notice is not deleted. Other commercial enterprises are less generous.

Table 2. Sources for home page.

The Rolling Stones	http://www.stones.com
The Voice of America	http://gopher.voa.gov
Laurie Anderson	http://www.voyagerco.com/LA
HotWired	http://www.wired.com
New York City Web	http://www.nyweb.com

We chose to use the sources in Table 2 for our local "taming" of the Internet. Each of these sources offers graphics, sound, video, or a combination of these, in addition to its textual content. The Rolling Stones site provides clips from the group's most recent album, along with the complete lyrics of each song. In addition, the Frequently Asked Questions (FAQ) list, compiled by fans and distributed on Usenet, is archived here. Videos and photographs are also available.

The VOA site is less visually appealing, but more informative: it posts radio broadcasts, updated hourly, along with a history and description of the agency and schedules for special features. Broadcasts are also available in languages other than English.

The Voyager Company's home page acts as an index to the artists whose work the company promotes. This site provides video clips from Laurie Anderson's recent performances, along with a tour schedule. The illustrated text of one of her pieces is included. A search of the net, through Yahoo (http://www.yahoo.com), yielded a number of privately-maintained home pages that provided additional information on Anderson: a FAQ list, a number of audio excerpts from her albums, and a link to a feature article from HotWired.

HotWired archives contain selected pieces from the back issues of *Wired Magazine*. As mentioned above, this site generously grants permission to redistribute articles. At this site, too, are graphics and audio samples from works of artists featured in the magazine or on the Net, along with pointers to other interesting Web pages.

The New York City Web is an introduction to the city, full of engaging photographs and stories written by New Yorkers. One section of this archive that we found well-suited for language-teaching purposes was a runner's diary, in which he discusses his participation in the New York City Marathon. Another section, detailing the enchantments of Christmas in New York, would provide good cultural information and be of high interest to students in an English as a foreign language (EFL) context.

It is interesting to note the recurrence of a number of genres: the FAQ, the schedule, and so forth. These genres can be put to use within a pedagogical approach, for information-extraction exercises and as unifying features for diverse materials.

We decided that, to be most useful to a class, these remote archives ought to be duplicated, edited, and loaded onto a local machine. The decision to edit was made because not all of the material from the remote archive was relevant to classroom purposes, not all of it was freely duplicable, and some of the archives were simply too large. The decision to download was made because, no matter how stable a link, there are times when the Internet is so busy that access to remote locations is maddeningly slow, or simply impossible. With the archive duplicated "at home," instant access would be assured. In addition, global resources, once downloaded, can be edited for pedagogical purposes. Home pages, for example, can be altered so that the inaccessible links are removed or marked as not available. Such downloading and editing of selected links prevents students from "getting lost in cyberspace." The instructor's job is also made easier, as he or she can control the timing of updates to the information contained on the page. As information from remote links is updated, supporting pedagogical materials need to be revised or created. Controlling updates, therefore, limits the amount of work a teacher needs to do in maintaining the local archive.

With a live connection to the Internet, students can, of course, be given a copy of the instructor's home page that will point them to the original sites of these resources. They can then follow the links independently, for their own purposes, both within and beyond the boundaries defined by the instructor.

After selecting, downloading, and editing our archives, we wanted to organize them within a pedagogical framework. We created our own home page for learners, and inserted links to both "tamed" (locally archived) and "wild" (remote) resources.

A home page, called "Common Ground," framed the archives described above in a number of ways, allowing the materials to be recycled for a number of purposes. One was a theme-based unit on popular culture; the second, a function-based unit on conveying emotions and experiences in song, narrative, and exposition; and the third, a theme-based unit on marketing on the Web. Each of these units was meant to be used by an already-existing class: different classes could mine the same archive in different ways. The general framework for "Common Ground" is shown in Figure 4. A sample of the archive is shown in Figure 1.

We think these materials provide a combination of (1) supplementary, motivating activities, (2) weekly or semi-weekly required activities, (3) a springboard for class or individual projects, for sustained use during one particular part of a term, and (4) possibly part of an independent learning package.

Figure 4. Framework for "Common Ground" tamed resources.

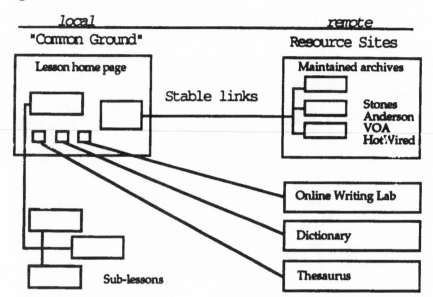

The final step in our project—piloting and evaluating the architecture that we have created with a group of L2 students—remains to be accomplished. We expect to carry out a trial of these or other Web-based materials within the next year. Other researchers around the world are at work on similar projects, and within a year or two we expect this approach to be, if not common, then at least not unusual.

Strengths of the Approach.

Efficiency. Creating a home page on the WWW allows one to assemble authentic language resources with relative ease. A corpus suitable to specific learner needs and interests can be "constructed," in a sense, by compiling a list of remote document addresses for inclusion into a home page. Thus the instructor's time can be spent considering precisely what the corpus is to include and how exactly to select a representative sample of language data. Furthermore the corpus, and any teacher-designed supporting materials, can easily expand:

> For teachers a hypermedia corpus or metatext offers a far more efficient means of developing, preserving, and obtaining access to course materials than has existed before ... a hypertext corpus allows a more efficient means of preserving the work of past endeavors because it requires so much less effort to select and organize them (Landow 1992: 72–73).

Authentic materials. Through the introduction of a home page, the foreign- or second- language teacher is able to provide learners direct access to language in the form of electronic texts, dictionaries, and other audio and video material. For most users of the Internet, this language serves nonpedagogical communicative functions. Some argue that the use of such authentic materials with language learners is problematic since they are written largely for an audience of native speakers who have the processing and language skills, and cultural background, necessary to interact with the input. Still, by carefully structuring a home page (e.g. by choosing which links to include and which to omit), the teacher may be able to exercise control over the sort of input the learners are exposed to. Willis observes that:

> Concocted texts exemplify the grammar not as it is but as the coursewriter believes it to be ... The use of authentic text makes it likely that not only structure and necessary choice but also the typical behavior of words and phrases will be captured and can be highlighted for the learner. (1993:92)

Similarly, incorporating authentic text into second-language-teaching materials can highlight important cultural dimensions of language use. The use of authentic materials from the WWW is therefore well motivated, serving both the linguistic and cultural needs of learners.

Learning-centered approach and dynamic resources. Teachers, students, and program directors usually have little say in the decisions about the content and form of computer-assisted language learning (CALL) software that is produced commercially. Even when the content and form of these programs are determined in anticipation of a particular set of learning needs and purposes, such planning inevitably limits the software's flexibility. This applies not just to conventional grammar-based CALL but even to more recently produced multimedia applications. In general, the content and form of the software are determined by an external authority, which limits their usefulness. This issue is extremely important if one is planning a dynamic curriculum in which teaching activities and materials are constantly changing to meet the learning needs of the students. Being able to create a dynamic corpus of Internet resources allows the teacher (and students) more flexibility in the selection, presentation, and evaluation of materials. The corpus can be designed with various purposes in mind (English for specific purposes, English as a foreign language, content-based curriculum, etc.), in order to satisfy particular needs within the curriculum.

Conclusion. Our culture of learning is constantly changing; the use of computers by learners is now taken for granted. The changing learning styles and needs of students provide strong arguments for incorporating technology into curricula where appropriate, as in the use of Internet resources in the language classroom. The wide variety of materials available on the Internet can provide authentic, relevant, and culturally-contextualized input for the language learner—an important consideration for those developing language teaching materials.

In this paper, we have attempted to illustrate different ways of exploiting the resources of the Internet and the World Wide Web, as well as motivations for doing so. In the end, teachers themselves will determine how to apply this technology in ways most appropriate to their specific classroom needs. With the continually updated and expanded resources of the Internet, a teacher can negotiate with his or her students the sort of input that is relevant to them in order to make curricular objectives more responsive to the constantly changing needs of the learners. We hope we have provided some perspective on how the chaos of the Internet might be harnessed for language-learning purposes. A logical next step would be to pilot some implementation of this technology in the classroom to determine its feasibility and effectiveness within a language-learning context.

ACKNOWLEDGMENTS

This paper and the conference demonstration emerged from ideas and inspiration generated during coursework with Professor Catherine Ball at Georgetown University. Additional thanks go to Jackie Tanner, Lye Ong, Lawrence Biggs, and Alan Gajadhar.

REFERENCES

A beginner's guide to HTML. Work in progress. Available at http://www.ncsa.uiuc.edu/demoweb/html-primer.html.

Landow, George P. 1992. "Hypertext, metatext, and the electronic canon." In Myron C. Tuman (ed.), *Literacy online: The promise (and peril) of reading and writing with computers.* Pittsburgh, Pennsylvania: University of Pittsburgh Press.

Mosaic for Macintosh, Release 1.0.3. National Center for Supercomputing Applications, University of Illinois, Urbana-Champaign.

Netscape, Release .96beta. Netscape Communications Corporation, Mountain View, California.

Stauffer, Stephanie, J. 1994. "Computer-based classrooms for language learning." In James E. Alatis (ed.), *Georgetown University Round Table on Language and Linguistics 1994*. Washington, D.C.: Georgetown University Press. 219–232.

Willis, Dave. 1993. "Grammar and lexis: Some pedagogical implications." In John M. Sinclair, Michael Hoey, and Gwyneth Fox (eds.), *Techniques of description: A festschrift for Malcolm Coulthard*. New York: Routledge.

APPENDIX 1. Software used for accessing the WWW and working with HTML documents.

Netscape	graphical browser	freeware
Mosaic	graphical browser	freeware
JPeg View, GIFConverter	graphics viewers/converters	shareware
Easy Play	movie players	shareware
SoundApp	sound player/converter	shareware
BBEdit lite	text editor	freeware
(various)	Word processor that can save files in "rtf" format	commercial
RTFto HTML	automatic HTML converter	freeware

*Note: Sites for downloading the freeware/shareware resources listed below can be found by keyword search using the Yahoo search tool (http://www.yahoo.com).

APPENDIX 2. Resources for learning more about the Internet, WWW, and HTML.

How to Write HTML Files	http://curia.ucc.ie/info/net/htmldoc.html
A Beginner's Guide to HTML	http://www.ncsa.uiucedu/demoweb/htmlprimer.html
W3 Clients	http://info.cern.ch/hypertext/www/clients.html

APPENDIX 3. A sampling of WWW resources for language pedagogy (including URLs).

The Human-Languages Page
    http:/ /www.willamette.edu/ tjones/Language-Page.html

Dartmouth Language Resource Center
    http:/ /grafton.dartmouth.edu:8001 /lrc/

Georgetown's Language Learning Technology
    http:/ /www.georgetown.edu/centers/LLT/home.html

FLTEACH Foreign Language Teaching Resources
    http:/ /www.cortland.edu/www_root/flteach/flteach.html

Ohio University Computer-Assisted Language Learning (CALL) Lab
    http:/ /www.tcom.ohiou.edu/OU_Language/OU_Language.html

The English as a Second Language Home Page
    http:/ /www.ed.uiuc.edu/edpsy-387/rongchang-li/esl/

"Wait wait wait wait!"
A sociolinguistic analysis of repetition in the speech of adult beginning ESL learners using instructional software

Susan A. Huss-Lederman[1]
University of Wisconsin-Whitewater

Introduction. In this paper, I demonstrate how adult beginning learners of English as a second language (ESL) use forms of repetition to facilitate interpersonal interaction while they work with drill and practice software. The three uses of repetition to be examined include:

(1) establishing communicative signals,
(2) making economical lexical reference, and
(3) compensating for interlocutor's perceived limitations in understanding.

I propose that learners exploit forms of repetition because such strategies (among others) enable learners to create mutual understanding within a task-focused discourse.

Repetition in discourse. Repetition is a necessary and ordinary feature of spoken discourse. In analyzing repetition in conversation, Tannen (1987a: 215) defines the term as "a pervasive type of spontaneous pre-patterning," while Merritt (1994: 26) describes repetition as "a general inclusive term for all kinds of 'happening again'." As indicated by such definitions, repetition encompasses a range of discourse practices, from exact reiteration to paraphrasing. According to Bennett-Kastor (1994), forms of repetition activate cognitive and social structures, sustaining the representational function of language. Repetition may occur at times along a temporal continuum from the moment immediately following an utterance to a point in the distant future.

Not surprisingly, repetition is abundant in the speech of new learners of English. It is a way to commit a new language to memory, to create a history of use within a new language. In an empirical study, Tomlin (1994) has shown

[1]Thanks to Inaam Manssor and colleagues at the Arlington (VA) Education and Employment Program for moral support of my combining ESL teaching with linguistic research.

that when new learners of a second language hear the same phrases and respond to them through physical action, cognitive imprinting results. Learners recall phrases and their meanings long after participating in the experimental exercise. Pica (1993) maintains that second-language learners participating in social interaction improve their fluency through repeating, paraphrasing, and shifting the syntactic position of words and phrases within the course of communicating with each other. Phrases recycled in different communicative contexts over time aid language learners in becoming "at-home" in a new language (Becker 1984, 1994).

Tannen (1987b, 1989) and Norrick (1987) list several functions of self- and other-repetition in conversational discourse. These include: Efficiency of production; ease of comprehensibility; connection of parts of text to the whole; connection of authors and auditors to emergent text; interactional functions; and involvement.

Once speakers set up a pattern of talk, it is easy for them to substitute new information within the established structure, such as when individuals list information (Tannen 1989: 48). Likewise, a recognized pattern lessens discourse density, and listeners can understand utterances more easily (Tannen 1989: 49). Kleifgen (1992), in a discourse study of a trio of teachers evaluating educational software, notes that almost all utterances (97%) are related to task with 32% of all utterances incorporating onscreen text in some way. Kleifgen maintains that such talk, embedded in the context of ongoing, task-focused interaction, is coherent. Furthermore, repetition of onscreen items serves cohesive functions in the everemergent text of the discourse. Analysis of discourse data from the current study indicates that repetition accomplishes the same functions in the task-talk of institutional (in the case of this study, educational) as well as of conversational discourse.

Previous studies of learner discourse and CALL. There are three prominent studies of ESL learners using computer-assisted language learning (CALL) software that examine the quality of discourse emerging while learners use software together. Piper (1986) examines the conversational "spin-off" among different multilingual triads of college students videotaped using three different CALL text-manipulation programs. She concludes that repetitive, short turns, characteristic of the interactions she observes, are not the best context for language practice. Young (1988) notes that the more negotiation of outcome learners co-determine, the closer to natural conversation a NNS-NNS[2] interaction becomes. Abraham and Liou (1991) attempt to make NNS-NNS discussion integral to the use of different software programs by telling study participants to talk to each other and by selecting programs that they, as

---

[2]NNS=Non-Native Speaker

researchers, think might encourage problem-solving conversation. Results of Abraham and Liou's study indicate a difference in the quality of talk spoken by participants: There are more long turns in the discourse.

These studies assign greater merit to interactions in which learners working in small groups employ complex, long turns (Brown and Yule 1983a). The interactions discussed in this paper are task-focused, and therefore elliptical, repetitive, and direct, much like task-focused interactions encountered outside the classroom not only by NNSs, but by native speakers as well. Short, repetitive turns are natural to the task-specific interaction characteristic of small group work with *instructional* computer programs (as classified by Wyatt 1987). I maintain that there is another dimension necessary in the examination of L2 discourse—the social context of an utterance. Rather than treating the use of computer programs as a stimulus affecting learner speech, the complete interaction among learners and the computer and software must be considered as a purposeful, meaningful, social interaction.

When examining the discourse of second-language learners, it is important to consider the quality of talk not only in terms of complexity, novelty, and length of utterance, but also in terms of the relationship between spoken discourse and its social function. Interaction must be viewed as integral to the task at hand, not its by-product. Task-focused interaction is a prevalent type of discourse, distinguished by such features as repetition and short turns.

Data. Data for the current sociolinguistic study consist of four videotaped and transcribed interactions of learners paired to use drill and practice software. All of the students are in beginning-level ESL literacy courses for adult refugees and immigrants, and six individuals comprise the four pairs of focal learners. They have little experience with formal education. Four of them self-report no schooling, one reports three years, and one reports six years. Three speak Spanish as a native language, with the remaining three speaking Khmer, Vietnamese, or Farsi. No pair-members speak the same language. The four videotaped interactions total one hundred and eighty-seven minutes.

At the time learners were taped, it was customary to mix pairs whenever possible so that individuals working together were not speakers of the same native language. Teachers paired learners in this way in order to foster communication in English naturally. Teachers, including me (a teacher in the school at the time I conducted the study), interacted with learners if they needed assistance; therefore, the teachers appear on tape as well. Even though learners were being videotaped, the interaction among the learners and teachers was natural. In fact, it would have been marked as unusual if teachers had observed learners experiencing difficulties, and had chosen not to step in and assist them. All learners had studied in this electronic classroom once before.

Software. There is very little software available for beginning ESL learners with low oral proficiency, and even less for those who have limited experience with formal schooling. At the time of data collection (spring 1990) most of the software used with learners was not designed expressly for ESL, but either for children or for adult native speakers of English developing basic literacy skills. Almost all available software was in drill and practice format, with the exception of large-type word processors and a program combining the manipulation of graphics and words to create a picture learners could then write about. Because of this, teachers at this adult school had to focus on integrating technology into instruction when appropriate, compensating for mismatches between software intended for native speakers and the nonnative speakers using it.

The software program titles are: *Basic Vocabulary Builder on Computer* (National Textbook, 1984), *Words at Work: Contraction Action* (MECC, 1986), and *Fun from A to Z* (MECC, 1986). *Basic Vocabulary Builder* is an ESL program, while *Words at Work: Contraction Action* and *Fun from A to Z* target native English-speaking children as their users. All programs are in drill and practice format and are designed for use on Apple IIe computers. None uses any type of audio support.

Repetition in task-focused discourse. In this section, I offer examples which show how adult beginning ESL learners facilitate task-focused interaction through repetition. From establishing mutually understood frameworks of interaction to simplifying onscreen text through paraphrasing, learners are able to sustain ongoing focus on task, in part, through repetition.

Establishing communicative signals. The learners participating in this study are at the beginning stages of developing competence in English. Because they are interacting with other beginners in their second language, they must work to set up some communicative signals in order to frame and interpret different stages of their interaction. Communicative signals differ from contextualization cues, which Gumperz (1982) defines as conventions of discourse tacitly shared by a speech community. The signals that learners work to set up are not tacit: they are interactionally negotiated. Their very negotiation fits well within the framework of task-oriented talk. Setting up these signals is part of the process of creating a coherent framework for interaction. The example that follows demonstrates how Minh and Maria set up communicative signals as they engage in copying onscreen vocabulary into their notebooks.

In Example 1, Minh and Maria work out how to signal to each other when they are finished with one problem and are ready to continue to the next. They set up a communicative signal which they use until their routine is established. They use the word "finish(ed)" to indicate when they are ready to move on. The following example demonstrates this.

Minh and Maria have just begun to use *Basic Vocabulary Builder* and have jointly negotiated a routine to establish which lexical items on the screen should be copied. Maria utters the words "all right" and "okay" while she copies down vocabulary items. Each time she utters one of these words, Minh misinterprets it as a signal indicating that Maria wants to continue to the next problem. She keeps stopping him from continuing. Finally he says the following (for clarity, certain intervening text between lines 3 and 4 has been omitted):

Example 1: Communicative signals

→   1   Minh: You finished?__
    2   Maria: ⌐__No.
    [MARIA CONTINUES TO WRITE.]
→   3   Minh: Finished?
    [MARIA AND MINH DISCUSS HOW MUCH TEXT THEY ARE TO COPY
    FROM THE SCREEN.]
→   4   Maria: Finish.

In this example, Maria repeats the word "finish" with statement intonation. This serves as an unambiguous, verbal check mark, a signal that she is ready to move on.

Later, they also are able to use words such as "okay" and "all right" to accomplish the same function. Initially, it had been confusing for Minh to interpret Maria's utterances of "okay" and "all right," because Maria had used these expressions to indicate to herself her cognitive orientation to a task. For example, she has uttered "all right" to signal that she has finished reading something and is now ready to pay attention to something new, but this does not necessarily signal that she is ready to move to the next onscreen problem. The function of "all right" in Maria's speech is easily misunderstood by Minh. "Finish(ed)" is clearer because it is Minh's signal, and the first part of a question/answer adjacency pair that Minh initiates.

In this example, learners negotiate a mutually understood communicative signal so that they know when they are both ready to move on to the next problem. Once they have established a framework for interaction, they sustain and work within it, binding each step in their interaction with a signal that they are ready to continue with the next step.

Repetition for economical lexical reference. The following excerpt (Example 2) provides a clear example of how shifts in intonation convey meaning. Mariam, an illiterate Afghani woman with little communicative skill in English, is not sure if the letter she is pointing to in *Fun from A to Z* is correct. She relies on the assistance of Kim, her Cambodian partner.

Example 2: Repetition with change in intonation for economical lexical reference

1	Kim:	R.
2	Mariam:	R:?
3	Kim:	Yes.
4		R.
5	Mariam:	R,

[KIM PRESSES RETURN.]

In this example, Mariam uses repetition and intonation to convey a confirmation request. She also repeats to confirm that she has understood. Kim understands and responds to these repetitive utterances.

As Simpson (1994) notes, shifts in intonation while maintaining lexical repetition signal shifts in meaning. From the context, specifically the intonation that Mariam uses, Kim knows that Mariam is asking for confirmation or clarification when uttering "R:?" in line 2, not confirming what Kim has said. Were this the case, Mariam probably would have said, "R." When Mariam uses rising intonation, she speaks topically (Brown and Yule 1983b: 84), linking her discourse contribution to that of Kim. Likewise, Kim does the same for Mariam. When saying, "Yes. R." in lines 3 and 4, Kim accomplishes many discourse functions:

(1) She acknowledges that Mariam has asked her a question;
(2) She signals her confirmation both with the word "yes" and by using utterance final intonation; and
(3) She links her contribution topically to Mariam's, in part by repeating the focus of their interaction, "R."

In this successful interaction, Mariam and Kim not only share topic and context, but also the intonational contextualization cues of their target language, which frames the sequence as a question-answer-confirmation set within this context. This much accomplished, Kim presses the return key to continue the lesson.

Paraphrasing onscreen language. Learners and teachers may choose to paraphrase onscreen language in an attempt to compensate for what they perceive to be their interlocutors' inabilities to understand onscreen text. Individuals with limited proficiency use paraphrasing to describe a situation or entity when exact words fail. Words and phrases used in paraphrasing can be selected to accommodate the listener's understanding of the speaker. A speaker may intentionally select descriptive phrasing that s/he has determined will be most accessible to other interlocutors.

Simplified paraphrasing is also used by stronger interlocutors to communicate on a level that a weaker interlocutor can understand. Zuengler (1991) notes that this may be considered a mild form of convergence, in which a speaker tries to accommodate interlocutors by attempting to sound more like them. Alternatively, this may be a form of complementarity, if the driving force behind the simplification is to emphasize differences in role and status. For example, when Antonio and Minh communicate with each other, it is clear that Antonio has superior communication skills. Whether Antonio's awareness of his superior ability or his desire to communicate effectively with Minh causes him to simplify his utterances, as in Example 3, is not clear.

Example 3: Paraphrasing

		1	Antonio:	Wait wait wait wait.
		2	Minh:	Yes no?
		3		Again?
		4		Again,
		5		Yes no?
		6		Yes.
		7	Antonio:	Yes.
		8		/ ? /
→		9		One moment please.
→		10		You have to wait.
→		11		Okay?
→		12		Wait.

Here, in line 9, Antonio reads the onscreen text to Minh. He then paraphrases it, making a directive ("You have to wait. Okay?") Furthermore, he simplifies the directive in line 12 by boiling it down to "Wait." By paraphrasing, Antonio attempts to compensate for what appears to be Minh's limited ability to understand English. He is also able to emphasize the message appearing on the screen by reading it aloud, paraphrasing it once, and then repeating the key word from his paraphrased utterance ("wait"). Finally, through repeatedly telling Minh he has to wait in so many different ways, Antonio is, in effect, prolonging the length of time that Minh has to wait.

Discussion. When learners repeat, they are able to apply old words to new situations, gaining experience using a new language. In new situations, learners are able to work together to create a pattern of interaction which renders their subsequent joint actions coherent. Below, I make some final comments about the interactive work of repetition used by the participants in this study. I suggest that forms of repetition are fundamental for beginning learners to communicate effectively and efficiently.

In the Piper (1986) study, turn-taking among three ESL learners using CALL is described as rapid, and individual turns are fewer than three words long. She cites Brown and Yule (1983a), who maintain that long, complex turns are most important for language practice for advanced speakers, because this type of language use poses the greatest challenge for second-language speakers in encounters outside the classroom. However, not all interaction among interlocutors is characterized by long, involved conversation. When the goal of an interaction is to successfully complete an immediate task, an environment conducive to the use of short turns is created.

This is not to say that CALL activities which promote complex turns cannot be developed. A CALL environment conducive to relating narratives, telling jokes, or giving detailed instructions —the types of discourse genres Brown and Yule (1983a: 20) mention as requiring long, involved turns at talk—could be incorporated into an activity in which learners use software. For example, if after using simulation or game software learners are asked to recount to others what happened while they used the software, they would be retelling. In the retelling of an event occurring in the microworld environment, the learners would create a narrative, a speech genre which can contain longer, more complex utterances than task-talk (cf. Wyatt 1987 on the integration of CALL materials into various pedagogical approaches).

Conclusion. The task-based emphasis of learner-learner discourse calls for a good deal of repetition. Participants need to speak directly and accurately in order to perform well together. It is not surprising, then, that the more task-based the interaction, the more that lexical repetition appears. Such repetition is less an indication of a learner's status as a beginner than of an individual's ability to strategize for effective task-focused dialogue.

REFERENCES

Abraham, Roberta G. and Hsien-Chin Liou. 1991. "Interaction generated by three computer programs: Analysis of functions of spoken language." In Patricia Dunkel (ed.), *Computer-assisted language learning and testing: Research issues and practice*. New York: Harper-Collins. 85–109.

Basic Vocabulary Builder on Computer. 1984. Lincolnwood, Illinois: National Textbook Company.

Bennett-Kastor, Tina L. 1994. "Repetition in language development: From interaction to cohesion." In Barbara Johnstone (ed.), *Repetition in discourse: Multidisciplinary perspectives, Volume I*. Norwood, N.J.: Ablex. 155–171.

Becker, A. L. 1984. "Biography of a sentence: A Burmese proverb." In Edward M. Bruner (ed.), *Text, play, and story: The construction and reconstruction of self and society*. Washington, D.C.: American Ethnological Society. 135–155.

Becker, A.L. 1994. "Repetition and otherness: An essay." In Barbara Johnstone (ed.), *Repetition in discourse: Interdisciplinary perspectives, Volume 2*. Norwood, N.J.: Ablex. 162–175.

Brown, Gillian and George Yule. 1983a. *Teaching the spoken language*. Cambridge, U.K.: Cambridge University Press.

Brown, Gillian and George Yule. 1983b. *Discourse analysis*. Cambridge, U.K.: Cambridge University Press.

Fun from A to Z. 1986. Minneapolis, Minnesota: MECC.

Gumperz, John. 1982. *Discourse strategies*. Cambridge, U.K.: Cambridge University Press.

Johnstone, Barbara (ed.). 1994. *Repetition in discourse: Interdisciplinary perspectives, Volumes I and II*. Norwood, N.J.: Ablex.

Kleifgen, Jo Anne. 1992. "Social interaction at the computer: The merging of talk and text." LC Report 92-1. New York: Literacy Center, Teachers College, Columbia University.

Merritt, Marilyn. 1994. "Repetition in situated discourse: Exploring its forms and functions." In Barbara Johnstone (ed.), *Repetition in discourse: Multidisciplinary perspectives, Volume I*. Norwood, N.J.: Ablex. 23–35.

Norrick, Neal. 1987. "Functions of repetition in conversation." *Text* 7(3):245–264.

Pica, Teresa. 1993. "Communication with second language learners: What does it reveal about the social and linguistics processes of second language learning?" In James E. Alatis (ed.), *Georgetown University Round Table on Languages and Linguistics 1992*. Washington, D.C.: Georgetown University Press. 435–464.

Piper, Alison. 1986. "Conversation and the computer: A study of the conversational spin-off generated among learners of English as a foreign language working in groups." *System* 14(2):187–198.

Simpson, Jo Ellen M. 1994. "Regularized intonation in conversational repetition." In Barbara Johnstone (ed.), *Repetition in discourse: Interdisciplinary perspectives, Volume 2*. Norwood, N.J.: Ablex. 41–49.

Tannen, Deborah. 1987a. "Repetition in conversation as spontaneous formulaicity." *Text* 7: 215–243.

Tannen, Deborah. 1987b. "Repetition in conversation: Toward a poetics of talk." *Language* 63(3): 574–605.

Tannen, Deborah. 1989. *Talking voices: Repetition, dialogue, and imagery in conversational discourse*. Cambridge, U.K.: Cambridge University Press.

Tomlin, Russell S. 1994. "Repetition in second language acquisition." In Barbara Johnstone (ed.), *Repetition in discourse: Multidisciplinary perspectives, Volume I*. Norwood, N.J.: Ablex. 172–194.

Words at Work: Contraction Action. 1986. Minneapolis, Minnesota: MECC.

Wyatt, David. 1987. "Applying pedagogical principles to CALL courseware development." In William Flint Smith (ed.), *Modern media in foreign language education: Theory and implementation*. Lincolnwood, Illinois: National Textbook Company. 85–98.

Young, Richard. 1988. "Computer-assisted language learning conversations: Negotiating an outcome." *CALICO Journal* 5: 65–83.

Zuengler, Jané. 1991. "Accommodation in native-nonnative interactions: Going beyond the 'what' to the 'why' in second-language research." In Howard Giles, Justine Coupland, and Nikolas Coupland (eds.), *Contexts of accommodation: Developments in applied sociolinguistics*. Cambridge, U.K.: Cambridge University Press. 223–244.

Reap what you sow:
Inservice training for language teachers in CMC

Stephanie J. Stauffer
Georgetown University

Introduction. The evidence from publications and conference presentations is clear: The imagination of language teachers worldwide has been captured by the Internet. Effective use of computer-mediated communication (CMC) for language teaching, however, depends not only on vision but also the skills, attitudes, and experiences of the instructors who will be expected to carry out or support CMC-related aspects of the curriculum. This paper provides a detailed description and analysis of the challenges involved in educating faculty for the introduction of CMC into the curriculum of an intensive English program. It follows up on the ideas presented in Stauffer (1994).

For this intensive program, the author was asked to design tasks involving mail exchanges, subscribing to discussion lists, remote database searches, file transfer (by anonymous ftp), and so on. These tasks were to be integrated with the program mission of providing instruction in English language and communication skills, crosscultural communication, and business-related exercises.

During the course of the program, attempts to implement CMC were met both with support and resistance from various sources, some predictable and some surprising. This paper outlines in some detail the need for explicit inservice training and education of instructors for the implementation of CMC, and concludes with training suggestions.

Background. The Intensive International Executive Program (IIEP), a ten-week intensive program for executives, offers instruction in the English language, crosscultural skills, and international management. In 1994, forty students attended: Thirty-five of them were Japanese and five were Chinese; three of the students were women. The program is held on the rural campus of a Japanese university. Students followed the schedule of classes outlined in Table 1. Most students were not experienced with CMC.

Table 1. Daily schedule

English Language (9:00–12:00)	Management (2:00–5:00)
International Business English:	Case Studies
Memos, Faxes, Business Letters	Lectures
Telephone skills (listening/spea-	Management Exercises
king)	Guest Speakers
Vocabulary	Crosscultural Exercises
Grammar	Negotiations Simulation
Communications Skills:	
Presentations	
Discussion Leadership	

The proposal for using and teaching CMC in the 1994 program included the following arguments (Stauffer 1994: 223–224):

(1) Growth of business use of e-mail and the Internet is on the increase (Cronin 1994; Sproull and Kiesler 1991). International managers need to know how CMC can affect their organizations;

(2) Much of the communication (and archiving) on the Internet is done in English. This provides (a) authentic language input, and (b) opportunities for communicative use of language; and

(3) The English on the Internet is more alive than the English in any textbook. Students will be motivated to learn up-to-date ways of expressing themselves.

The incorporation of CMC was to entail its use both for management and language exercises. The Internet,[1] it was argued, could provide relevant content and resources for the Management curriculum—for example, it was to be used as a supplementary data source for a marketing project. It could also be used as an authentic forum for students to hone their English-language skills, particularly for writing. As the English language classes comprised the more predictable and stable part of the daily schedule, it was thought that they would offer a good forum for introducing CMC; use of the Internet for Management projects would follow. (See Stauffer 1994 for further details.)

---

[1] Although the term "Internet" is used throughout this paper, in reality each student and faculty member had unlimited access to a Bitnet account. There was occasional and extremely limited access to one Internet connection—this is why graphical World Wide Web browsers are ignored in this paper.

Framework. This paper's title, "Reap what you sow," paraphrases the verse, "Whatsoever a man soweth, that shall he also reap" (Galatians 6: 7). The modern and computer-oriented version may be familiar to readers as GIGO—"Garbage in, garbage out." It is these metaphors that guided efforts to provide sound preservice and inservice training and education for CMC. The related parable of the sower resonates with these metaphors and frames the discussion of the results of these efforts.

Behold, a sower went forth to sow; and when he sowed, some seeds fell by the way side, and the fowls came and devoured them up: Some fell upon stony places where they had not much earth: And forthwith they sprung up, because they had no deepness of earth: And when the sun was up, they were scorched; and because they had no root, they withered away. And some fell among thorns; and the thorns sprung up, and choked them: But other fell into good ground, and brought forth fruit, some an hundredfold, some sixtyfold, some thirtyfold. Who hath ears to hear, let him hear. (Matthew 13: 3–9)

Within the framework of the parable, this paper first discusses the faculty members and their CMC-related experience. Next, the "seeds" of training and education are outlined, and then the "yield" from those seeds is examined.

Where did the seeds fall? Six faculty taught the core courses of the program: the full-time program director, along with five instructors hired for the summer. Four of these summer faculty were English teachers and one was a Management specialist. All but the CMC coordinator were returning to the program.

Table 2 catalogs each instructor's familiarity with various CMC-related skills. Instructors are listed and will be referred to by their area of specialization: Computer-mediated communication (CMC),[2] director (DIR), evaluation and testing (EVAL), management (MGMT), crosscultural communication (XCC), and English-language coordinator (ELC). In summary, all of the faculty had wordprocessing experience before the program began. Five out of six had used electronic mail; the same five had participated in listserv discussion groups, although two of these had had their first and only experience with the discussion group that had been specially created to introduce faculty to the experience. (This special discussion group is explained below.) With respect to more arcane Internet functions such as file transfers or listserv database searches, only two faculty members had used file transfer, and only the CMC specialist was experienced with database searches.

---

[2] The CMC instructor is the author of this paper.

Table 2. Faculty and CMC-related experience

Instructor	Experience Before Beginning of Program					Returning or New to Program
	Word-processing	E-mail	Listserv Discussion	Internet File Transfers	Listserv Searches	
CMC	yes	yes	yes	yes	yes	new
DIR	yes	yes	yes	—	—	full-time
EVAL	yes	yes	yes	yes	—	returning
MGMT	yes	yes	yes*	—	—	returning
XCC	yes	yes	yes*	—	—	semi-new**
ELC	very little	—	—	—	—	returning

*Experience on the newly-created IIEP-L only.
**XCC had worked in the program in 1991 under the same director.

What did we sow? What did we reap?

Program Goals. Program goals for CMC, although not formally articulated, included the following:

- to create a local electronic community;
- to put people in touch with friends and others outside the small program community;
- to give instructors a tool to expand their repertoire of approaches to English-language teaching and classroom management by introducing new means of communicating, record-keeping, and disseminating information;
- to provide instructors with a way to expose students to the living language—sources of real discourse in action, complete with slang etc.;
- in the end, to allow students and instructors to become, if not expert, then comfortable users of e-mail, and to encourage them to participate in communication and research on the Internet.

In other words, the goals of the program were really very simple. We wanted students to finish the summer having learned to use electronic mail and having developed some idea of the best uses for this medium of communication. We also wanted to introduce students to the worldwide network, both as a resource for gathering information, and as a community of sorts.

To achieve these student-oriented goals, we needed the support and participation of the instructors. We expected that some faculty members would be learning specific e-mail and database-search functions along with the students. What is more, we realized that for these faculty members, learning how to *implement* the new channel of communication within the language or management classes would present a challenge, but we were confident that our goals were manageable.

Preparation for the 1994 Program. Keeping the faculty's broad array of CMC-related experience (Figure 2) in mind, a private listserv discussion group (IIEP-L) was set up in advance of the program for IIEP instructors. Because instructors were geographically far-removed from each other—living and working in Hawaii, Japan, California, Massachusetts, and Washington, D.C.—it was hoped that the IIEP-L would give them a convenient centralized forum to plan for the summer. Of course, it was also hoped that this would accustom those faculty members with less CMC-related experience to this mode of communication. As it happened, one instructor (ELC) was cut out of this loop because she did not have e-mail. This was especially unfortunate because she was the instructor with the least CMC experience; she was also responsible for coordinating the English-language classes.

So that instructors new to listserv would be motivated to discover what the medium could offer beyond the IIEP-L, some research was done to find discussion groups relevant to the instructors' personal interests. By catering to personal interests in this way, it was expected that instructors would experience and understand the excitement that many people feel at being part of a worldwide communication community, and that they would also draw their own conclusions about the possible uses of discussion groups within the program. Relevant usenet newsgroups were also researched, but these were less interesting because they were not freely available to students or instructors throughout the summer.

Short, practical articles on integrating e-mail into the classroom were gathered. Poling's (1994) three-page article, for example, reports on his own experiences and makes a number of recommendations concerning how to use e-mail in the classroom.

- Answering direct questions from any student
- Counseling
- Distributing class assignments
- Making general class announcements
- Giving occasional quizzes
- Communicating directly with a particular student
- Posting grades
- Providing helpful hints about homework or upcoming tests

- Allowing students to send excuses for missing class (1994: 53)

Poling's article is also frank in discussing the drawbacks of using e-mail. Such a straightforward approach was important in choosing papers to act as resources for instructors—it was realized that instructors might (and should) raise questions and objections concerning the use of technology in the classroom, and it was necessary to address those concerns realistically.

For the management specialist (MGMT), who was not acquainted with Internet functions beyond e-mail and the in-house IIEP-L, business- and management-related resources *on* and *about* the Internet were researched. *Doing business on the Internet* (Cronin 1994) was suggested as background reading; this book describes the online strategies of a series of companies and organizations in various business sectors. Also recommended was Sproull and Kiesler's (1991) *Connections: New ways of working in the networked organization.*

As it happened, MGMT's home institution, Babson College, was host to a gopher server that maintained a well-prepared collection of Internet business resources and information. Instructions on how to access gopher, along with the name and telephone number of the person in charge of the archives, were passed along to MGMT well in advance of the summer program.

For exploitation in the language classroom, interesting threads from usenet newsgroups and listserv discussion groups were chosen and archived. Exercises and suggestions for exercises were created from these postings.

In addition, the CMC specialist collected sources on the use of the Internet for business and pedagogical purposes, as a database for future projects, and in order to understand and anticipate possible problems in the 1994 Program. For a complete list of references, see Stauffer (1994). Additional sources of interest published after that paper was written include Velayo (1994), Butler (1995), Brainer and Gildenston (1995), and Berge (1995).

During the 1994 Program. The CMC coordinator's main responsibility, besides teaching English classes, was to instruct students on how to use the University's Macintosh and IBM computers for wordprocessing, spreadsheeting, electronic mail, and other CMC functions. Faculty education and training for CMC were done in the week before the students arrived; after that, training occurred when and where necessary throughout the summer.

Education and training for CMC had begun with the IIEP-L in the months before the program began. It continued with individualized instruction, mainly on the use of the University's unwieldy electronic mail system. Short manuals were distributed to faculty members: These were the basic manuals originally accompanying the shareware mail utility. Since these materials were poorly organized and difficult to understand, it was necessary for the CMC coordinator to be available to respond quickly to telephone calls and e-mail messages asking for help in mastering the system. It was recommended that faculty members master a limited number of functions: reading, writing, editing, replying to and forwarding e-mail, and knowing how to create a distribution list, so that e-mail could be sent to entire classes using a simple "nickname."

The instructors were introduced individually to the resources that had been "hand-picked" to match their interests. These mainly consisted of listserv discussion groups. The instructors were given information on how to subscribe to each particular group, and also how to search for other interesting discussions. It was most important, from the point of view of the CMC coordinator, to follow up with each instructor in order to discover whether these listserv discussions had indeed turned out to be interesting, and what new questions or needs these instructors had encountered in the meantime.

At the beginning of the summer, before students arrived, Poling's (1994) short article was distributed to instructors to encourage individual thought and planning about how to incorporate CMC into the program. At appropriate times throughout the summer, CMC-related materials were offered to English instructors. The first of these, a very simple example, accompanied a chapter in Jones and Alexander (1989) on written business communications. The chapter covers business letters and memos, and briefly mentions electronic mail. As a source of more up-to-date (and more useful) information about e-mail, copies of the Netiquette guide (an e-mail style guide) were prepared for each class, along with transparencies of the points that related well to business-writing style (Figure 1). More complex materials that were made available involved a series of e-mail messages printed in a packet with suggested questions for discussion, ranging from elements of vocabulary used in the postings to elements of argumentation style.

Problems that arose. As the summer progressed, some problems and weaknesses in our approach to implementing CMC became obvious. First, and most important, was the fact that there were no clear specifications of skills that the faculty members would be expected to develop, use regularly, and implement in the classroom. This came about, in part, because of a lack of communication with returning faculty members, especially the English instructors, concerning the changes that were to be made in the program, and the attendant expectations that faculty members would learn to use CMC. This worked against faculty use of CMC, particularly for the ELC, who had the least amount of CMC experience. It also worked against instructors affected by the

Figure 1. Netiquette guide (E-mail style guide)

```
              Summary of Things to Remember

    Never forget that the person on the other side is human.
    Be careful what you say about others.
*   Be brief.
    Your postings reflect upon you; be proud of them.
*   Use descriptive titles.
*   Think about your audience.
*   Be careful with humor and sarcasm.
    Only post a message once.
*   Summarize what you are following up.
    Use mail, don't post a follow-up.
    Read all follow-ups and don't repeat what has already
        been said.
    Double-check follow-up newsgroups and distributions..
    Be careful about copyrights and licenses.
    Cite appropriate references.
*   When summarizing, summarize.
    Mark or rotate answers or spoilers.
*   Spelling flames considered harmful.
    Don't overdo signatures.
    Limit line length and avoid control characters.

Original from: chuq@sun.COM (Chuq Von Rospach). This document is in the public domain
and may be reproduced or excerpted by anyone wishing to do so.
```

ELC's decisions concerning the English-language classes.

Other summer faculty members varied widely in their interest, willingness, and ability to work CMC into the program. For example MGMT, a key faculty member, was not knowledgeable about CMC and had not been able to follow up on the leads prepared for her in advance of the summer program. This meant that the projects that were to have made use of Internet databases had not been prepared with the Internet in mind. These projects, therefore, could make only haphazard use of the network, leading students and faculty members to question the value of ever trying to use the "net."

Another problem for the smooth adaptation of CMC was that the CMC coordinator did double duty as English instructor. It is possible that students may have been less than willing to accept one instructor with two identified areas of expertise; what is certain is that overlapping spheres of "coordination" for ELC and CMC caused some misunderstandings.

Perhaps the biggest mistake that can be identified from the 1994 program, however, was that no formal preprogram *training* was carried out—only preprogram *education*. The instructors arrived on campus one week before the students arrived. In that week, there should have been an orientation to the new CMC components of the summer program. This orientation should have included a limited introduction to the University e-mail system, along with an outline of what students would be learning, and some simple exercises to get the neophytes started.

In sum, where we sowed confusion, we reaped confusion. Where we sowed miscommunication, we reaped that, too. But the interests of individual instructors played a large role in how efforts to implement CMC were received. The next section re-examines characteristics of instructors in this light.

Where did the seeds fall? revisited. To return to the parable of the sower, then, a short sketch of how it can be applied to the characteristics of each instructor is offered here.

SOME SEEDS FELL BY THE WAY SIDE ... These are the plans that were misguided, or the instruction and discussion that was poorly timed. Included here is much of the material prepared for use by English teachers: It either did not capture their interest or was simply offered at the wrong time for instructors to be able to incorporate it into their plans. Also included here are lost opportunities for training and education, such as the time not used during the initial, preprogram week.

SOME FELL UPON STONY PLACES ...AND BECAUSE THEY HAD NO ROOT, THEY WITHERED AWAY. Despite a certain amount of "tilling" and "fertilization"—that is, advance preparation done for these individuals—both ELC and MGMT appear not to have been interested in the applications of CMC. For MGMT, time was lacking. In the case of ELC, the cause seems to have been a personal opposition to the use of anything but face-to-face communication for classroom purposes, along with a certain amount of technophobia and a reluctance to appear to be inexpert at a skill that her students were learning.

In each case, there were repercussions for the program: For example, ELC asked other English instructors not to use CMC because then her students would be left behind. MGMT designed projects that did not make use of CMC; in discovering the ill fit, students questioned (quite rightly) the value of the Internet as it related to the exercise.

What *is* interesting is that both MGMT and ELC have expressed interest in the Internet in the months since the program ended. The seeds of 1994 may take root in 1995.

AND SOME FELL AMONG [WEEDS]; AND THE [WEEDS] SPRUNG UP, AND CHOKED THEM. One faculty member, EVAL, was hard at work collecting and analyzing data for his dissertation during the summer of 1994. Though the metaphor of the weeds is perhaps a bit too strong to apply to him, it fits his situation in certain ways. EVAL was well-prepared to implement CMC in the program's English classes. (See Table 2.) His research, however, occupied most of his free time and, as he had taught the curriculum before, it seemed that he was interested mainly in covering ground that was familiar with methods that were familiar, with little time available to adapt his in-class practices. However, he participated fully in the IIEP-L, both before and during the summer, and communicated often by e-mail with his students. Such extracurricular use of e-mail may have been the most motivating kind for students.

BUT OTHER FELL INTO GOOD GROUND, AND BROUGHT FORTH FRUIT, SOME AN HUNDREDFOLD ... The one faculty member who was attracted to CMC and who gladly experimented with it was XCC. She expanded on the simple ideas presented in Poling (1994), subscribed to listserv discussion groups, brought the ideas and the language into the classroom, and has continued to do so with her classes—and at professional conferences—since the end of the summer program. Her willingness to adopt new methods was helpful in convincing some of the more reluctant faculty members to give CMC a chance. It is interesting to note that, other than the CMC coordinator, XCC was the only instructor not returning to the program from the previous summer. Perhaps this was a factor in her willingness to use innovative methods.

Comments and conclusions. The management of innovation, such as the introduction of CMC into an existing curriculum, is often difficult. New communication systems require a critical mass of people to participate in order to assure their success (Markus 1987, in Sproull and Kiesler 1991: 167); with a faculty of six, this critical mass is difficult to obtain. Nevertheless, the innovation took hold in the Summer of 1994, and will be revised and expanded in 1995.

Cooper (1989: 58–72) outlines the components of the management of innovation. He reminds the reader of what is involved in changing behaviors and attitudes in this simple sentence: "Who adopts what; when, where, why, and how?" Both the form and the function of the thing to be adopted—CMC, in this case—must be considered. Further, Cooper claims that adoption is not a simple act: It progresses through stages of awareness, evaluation, proficiency, and usage.

The anticipated *function* of CMC within the summer program has been discussed. Its *form* was problematic: The University's computer system was slow and unreliable; it made messages difficult to edit; and the interface was unintuitive even for those who had used e-mail previously. Further, this system offered Bitnet access only. All interactive Internet functions were accessed through one computer, controlled by the CMC coordinator (for reasons of expense). Given such an ugly form, it was likely that some users would resist the adoption of CMC even if they were convinced of the value of its function.

Of those who could manage both the function and the form of CMC, then, at which stages of adoption did they arrive? All six instructors certainly came to *awareness*, and probably to *evaluation* of CMC, although some of these evaluations were better-informed than others. This is where ELC remained. The CMC coordinator and the program director (DIR) began the summer at the *usage* stage; it seems that XCC and EVAL attained a state between raw *proficiency* and expert *usage*, and that MGMT was *proficient* despite her resistance to the system. These levels of adoption are respectable given, again, the unwieldiness of the system and the time constraints of the program.

Summary. To summarize then, what kind of seeds did we sow? What did we provide instructors at the beginning, and throughout, the summer program? As we expected, we planted seeds of personal interest to increase the faculty members' motivation to learn and make use of the e-mail and discussion systems. We provided some personal tutoring sessions, so that instructors would feel comfortable with the commands, and handed out printed copies of instructions on how to use the system. We also planted the seeds of information about very practical ways to introduce e-mail and electronic discussions into the program.

What did we reap? It turns out that the handful of seeds that we sowed contained some surprises: Some unexpected mutations cropped up. Problems arose from miscommunication concerning program goals and expectations. The summer's CMC efforts, however, did yield positive results with more than half the instructors and with many students. At least half the instructors (XCC, CMC, and DIR) have continued to use some form of CMC in the classroom; some students have since contacted the faculty members through e-mail, using newly acquired accounts; and faculty members have become active in professional discussion groups. All six instructors now use e-mail regularly for personal communication. This personal adoption, although admittedly very different from conceptualizing pedagogical applications of CMC, could be the first step in adoption for classroom use.

Suggestions. In conclusion, this paper offers some points to consider in preparing to add CMC to an existing curriculum. First, it is necessary to state the goals of proficiency and usage for CMC-related skills. Where faculty members are not already experienced users, goals and expectations must be stated clearly. It can be helpful to model, as often as necessary, the ways you would like the system to be used. Communicate via e-mail with faculty members on matters that do not require face-to-face interaction. If possible, lay the groundwork for this before the program begins.

Spend time, at the beginning of the program before classes begin, on anticipating and answering the instructors' questions about the use of CMC. Create a frequently-asked-questions list to recycle in subsequent programs.

Lower expectations, both for students and for instructors, in regard to the number of specific e-mail or listserv functions that need to be mastered—it is tempting to ignore or discount the learning curve. However, stand firm on the required basic skills, and do not allow the technophobia of a minority to prevent nontechnophobic people from using technology.

"Translate" documentation into easily understood instructions, where possible. Be sure that support skills, such as wordprocessing, are not neglected. Avoid some difficulties of an unwieldy system by preparing templates for memos, class distribution lists, database searches, and so on, in advance. Help faculty members maintain and learn skills by offering workshops, some obligatory and some optional, both preservice and inservice. If you must, emphasize CMC experience in the hiring process.

Avoid emphasizing the computer aspect of CMC. Instead, highlight the communication possibilities for managers and language teachers. Do this by facilitating the instructors' development of personal e-mail and discussion-group networks. Be available to answer questions, and do some extra research to find sources of interest.

Finally, remember that not all ground is fertile, and not all seeds grow. The seeds that do grow, however, may yield a hundredfold.

REFERENCES

Bible. n.d. Authorized King James (Red Letter) Version. San Francisco, California: Collins Publishers.

Berge, Zane L. 1995. "Facilitating computer conferencing: Recommendations from the field." *Educational Technology* 35(1): 22–30.

Brainer, Charlie and Stacy B. Gildenston. 1995. "Overcoming technophobia: Instructor CALL competencies." Paper presented at the International TESOL Convention, March, 1995, Long Beach, California.

Butler, Brian. 1995. "Using WWW/Mosaic to support classroom-based education: An experience report." *Interpersonal Computing and Technology Journal* 3(1): 17–52. [listserv@guvm. georgetown.edu; get BUTLER IPCTV3N1]

Cooper, Robert L. 1989. *Language planning and social change.* Cambridge, U.K.: Cambridge University Press.

Cronin, Mary J. 1994. *Doing business on the Internet.* New York: Van Nostrand Reinhold.

Jones, Leo and Richard Alexander. 1989. *International Business English.* Cambridge, U.K.: Cambridge University Press.

Markus, M. Lynne. 1987. "Toward a 'critical mass' theory of interactive media: Universal access, interdependence and diffusion." *Communication Research* 14: 491–511.

Poling, Don J. 1994. "E-mail as an effective teaching supplement." *Educational Technology* 34(5): 53–55.

Sproull, Lee and Sara Kiesler. 1991. *Connections: New ways of working in the networked organization.* Cambridge, Massachusetts: M.I.T. Press.

STEPHANIE J. STAUFFER / 547

Stauffer, Stephanie J. 1994. "The computer-based classroom." In James E. Alatis (ed.), *Georgetown University Round Table on Languages and Linguistics 1994*. Washington, D.C.: Georgetown University Press. 219–232.

Velayo, Richard S. 1994. "Supplementary classroom instruction via computer conferencing." *Educational Technology* 34(5): 20–26.

Von Ruspach, Chuq. 1991, January. "Netiquette guide." chuq@sun.COM. (public domain)

An update on transfer and transferability

Donna Lardiere
Georgetown University

1. Introduction. Over the course of the past few decades of second-language-acquisition (SLA) research, numerous factors and combinations of factors have been invoked (with varying degrees of success) to account for perceived differences between L1 and L2 acquisition. These include the role of affect, acculturation, motivation, aptitude, learning styles, learning strategies, length and intensity of L2 exposure and age at initial exposure, among others. However, even if it were possible in principle to roughly equalize the conditions for both L1 and L2 acquisition by controlling for these variables, one enduring difference, by definition, would still remain: prior knowledge of the first language. Over the course of these decades of research, moreover, the explanatory prominence given to the effects of this factor has periodically risen and fallen. For example, it has now been over twenty years since the morpheme-order studies of Dulay and Burt (1974) appeared to minimize the role of L1 transfer—then rooted in behaviorist theory—as an important consideration in SLA. In this fledgling effort to approach SLA from a universalist perspective, the so-called "creative constructionists" parted company with the "contrastive analysts."

With the appearance of the parameter-setting model within the Principles and Parameters theory of Universal Grammar (UG) (Chomsky 1981), language-acquisition researchers working in this framework were provided with new technical means of more precisely characterizing L1 influence (the term "transfer" was rarely used) on the acquisition of the L2 grammar. Since the pioneering work by, for example, White (1985) and Flynn (1987), research in this framework has produced a large body of studies in which discussion of the role of the L1 has been recast (again with varying degrees of success) in terms of the transfer of parametric values. This type of L1 transfer has been presumed to result in either a "match" or "mismatch" with a given parametric setting in the L2, thus in some way either facilitating or delaying the development of certain aspects of the target grammar. As discussed by White (1993), the differences between these and earlier accounts of the role of transfer involve assumptions about (1) linguistic theory as a theory of the mental representation of language knowledge rather than a set of conditioned language habits, (2) the fact that L1 effects may hold at levels other than the visible "surface" similarities and differences examined under traditional contrastive analysis, (3) the interaction of properties associated with a particular parameter as well as the interactions holding between parameters, and (4) the status of certain parameter settings as either marked or unmarked. (See White 1993 for a review of these assumptions.)

At this point it is crucial to remind ourselves that the transfer or re-setting of parametric values is relevant only insofar as it applies to elements which are properly considered to fall within the domain of UG, a matter still far from settled and to which I will return. However, one recent area of inquiry currently assumed indeed to fall within this domain is the question of whether or not both L1 and L2 learners have access to a fully-developed phrase structure. Within current versions of linguistic theory, this is taken to include functional-category phrases projected from elements such as determiners (DP), complementizers (CP), and modals, auxiliaries and/or verbal inflectional material such as Tense and Agreement (IP or TP and AGRP). Much SLA research has recently focused on the availability of these functional categories at the outset of acquiring the L2 and particularly on whether it is even possible for their phrasal projections to transfer from the native language. Various positions on this issue were outlined at a Second Language Research Forum symposium last year on the L2 "Initial State," as well as in Hoekstra and Schwartz (1994). Though all essentially assume L2 access to UG, they differ in terms of their assumption of strong vs. weak continuity—i.e. the extent to which all functional projections are available from the beginning of L2 syntactic development and whether the L1 can serve as the source of this knowledge.

In the rest of this paper, I will first briefly review these positions, as they reflect the most current thinking from a UG perspective on the issue of L1 transfer in the development of the L2 grammar. I will then focus on the use of the presence (or absence) of targetlike inflectional morphology as a criterion for determining whether or not a particular projection, such as IP or AGRP, exists in the interlanguage. Finally, I will conclude with some thoughts about the place of morphology in the discussion of UG-constrained grammatical development in SLA.

2. L2 phrase structure: Are functional projections transferable?

2.1. The Minimal Trees Hypothesis. In a seminal paper initiating the most recent debate on the L2 initial state, Vainikka and Young-Scholten (1994) propose a weak continuity approach to SLA, i.e. components of UG such as X'-theory are available from the onset of L2 acquisition but the actual phrase structure represented initially by the learner will contain lexical projections only (NP, VP, AP). This proposal follows similar claims made for L1A (e.g. Clahsen, Eisenbeiss, and Vainikka 1994; Radford 1990, 1994; Vainikka 1992). In other words, at the earliest stages of development the L2 interlanguage grammar, only lexical projections (and their directionality values) transfer from the L1, whereas functional projections such as DP, IP, and CP do not. This appears to fit well with much empirical data (and anecdotal observation) suggesting that L2 learners at early stages often lack categories such as determiners, auxiliaries, complementizers, and tense and agreement inflection. Moreover (as pointed out by Schwartz, to appear), this proposal offers one of the most principled explanations to date within principles-and-parameters theory for both the similarities and differences observed between L1 and L2 acquisition, making it intuitively appealing.

The subjects in the Vainikka and Young-Scholten study were adult native Turkish or Korean speakers learning German as a second language in a naturalistic setting. Similar to studies in the L1 acquisition of German, as development proceeds, learners are claimed to posit an underspecified functional projection without agreement features, obligatory verb raising, or embedded clauses (Stage 2). At the point where the agreement paradigm has been acquired and finite-verb raising is obligatory, this FP turns into a full-fledged AGRP (Stage 3). The stages are shown in Figure 1 below for German L2 acquisition with representative utterances from the data:

Figure 1.

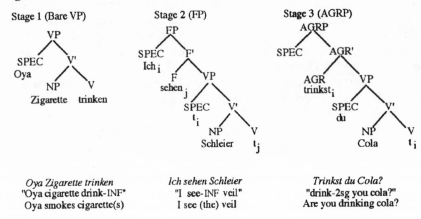

Oya Zigarette trinken	Ich sehen Schleier	Trinkst du Cola?
"Oya cigarette drink-INF"	"I see-INF veil"	"drink-2sg you cola?"
Oya smokes cigarette(s)	I see (the) veil	Are you drinking cola?

Although this description is somewhat oversimplified, for our purposes it is simply important to note one of the most significant distinctions between Stage 2 and Stage 3: L2 learners of German were considered not to have acquired a functional projection for Agreement (AGRP) until they had produced correct agreement suffixes at least sixty percent of the time on raised main verbs and had also produced at least two correct instances of four different agreement suffixes. Based on learners' progression though the first two stages of development in which the subjects produced fewer than four agreement suffixes or relied heavily on the infinitival suffix -n, Vainikka and Young-Scholten

(1994:281) concluded that functional projections are absent in the initial stage of L2 grammar, despite their existence in the L1. In short, they contended that at early-to-intermediate stages where subject–verb paradigms still appear incomplete, this is due to the fact that "there is no INFL or AGR position for base-generating suffixes." Note also that, like the morpheme-order studies of twenty years ago, the Minimal Trees position seeks to infer universally-constrained syntactic knowledge (or, more precisely, lack of it) on the basis of "surface" spell-outs of morphological inflection.

2.2. *The Absolute L1 Influence Hypothesis.* In contrast to the weak-continuity approach taken by Vainikka and Young-Scholten in their Minimal Trees Hypothesis, Schwartz and Sprouse (1994) and Schwartz (to appear) advocate a strong-continuity position, dubbed the "Absolute L1 Influence Hypothesis," in which "the L1 grammar in its entirety characterizes the initial state of L2A" (Hoekstra and Schwartz 1994: 14). In their longitudinal study of the interlanguage of a native Turkish speaker acquiring L2 German, Schwartz and Sprouse assume that the complete phrase structure of the Turkish clause, including its functional projections, is available and utilized from the start of L2A. This claim is based on an analysis which suggests early verb movement into a complementizer position and subject movement to the Specifier of CP position to satisfy the requirement for nominative-case assignment on subjects. In addition, Schwartz (to appear) demonstrates that Vainikka and Young-Scholten's cross-sectional data can be similarly reanalyzed on the assumption that knowledge of functional categories has transferred into the L2. She also questions the extent to which the entire semantics of verbs which subcategorize for propositions could transfer, given that the transfer of such embedded propositions would be disallowed under the Minimal Trees Hypothesis; or, additionally, how the Case Filter could apply to DPs, if DPs, being functional projections, do not transfer.

2.3. *The Valueless Full Trees Hypothesis.* The final transfer proposal I would like to consider is that made by Eubank (1994), who claims that the Absolute L1 Influence Hypothesis is too strong; thus he offers a "weak transfer" view in which both lexical and functional projections transfer along with their directionality values; however, parametric values of morphology-driven features such as the strength of agreement do not. Within current versions of linguistic theory, languages with "strong" agreement (such as French) raise thematic verbs in order to pick up their inflectional features (in IP), whereas "weak" agreement languages (such as English) do not. Eubank argues that if the parametric values that result in verb-raising and pronominal subject–AUX inversion in French transferred into the interlanguage of a native French speaker learning English, then we would expect to find utterances such as *Jean likes not the girls* or *Reads she the book?* in the French-English interlanguage data; however, these are unattested. In other words, the initial L2 representation of English by native speakers of French does not include the strong inflectional characteristics of French.

Eubank assumes that the presence of particular values such as inflectional strength derives from the presence in the lexicon of the relevant affixes, and asks whether such inflections are transferable from the L1 into the L2. He argues, "If they do [transfer], then one would expect to find associated values; if not, then related values may likewise be absent. What we thus need to know is whether or not bound inflectional morphology transfers from the NL into the L2" (Eubank 1994: 30).

For our purposes, we need to note that, like Vainikka and Young-Scholten, and in fact like Dulay and Burt whom he cites, Eubank (1994:31) assumes that syntactic values of features under functional heads appear only "if they are supported by the relevant inflectional morphemes in the lexicon," i.e. actual suffixes.

3. Is "default" agreement really agreement? At this point I would like to take up the question of what sort of evidence could be used in trying to determine when or whether knowledge of a particular functional projection—in this case that of Agreement (AGRP)—exists in one's interlanguage. In other words, is the criterial level of targetlike or near-targetlike production of an entire inflectional paradigm a reasonable one? To begin with, consider the following data from German L1A from Clahsen (1990/1991: 377) and Clahsen and Penke (1992:188) shown in (1) below:

(1) a. *Fels noch nich iser putt*   D (2;10)
    ("rock yet not is-*he* broke")
    The rock is not yet broken.

   b. *Das iser fest*   D (2;10)
    ("that is-*he* fixed")
    This is fixed.

   c. *Da iser großer fisch*   D (age not provided)
    ("there is-*he* big fish")
    There is a big fish.

Note that the *iser* verb forms in (1) do not exist in German (the target form is *ist*). Clahsen (1990/1991: 377) calls the inflection on the verb (the *-er*, "he") "pronominal copies." Clahsen and Penke (1992: 188) further remark in regard to these pronominal forms which "are suffixed to verbal elements" that "as with other verb inflections, the verb stem and the suffixed element are immediately adjacent, and in many cases, the pronouns agree with the subject in terms of person and number." Nevertheless, these forms are non-targetlike, and Clahsen (1990/1991) and Clahsen and Penke (1992) characterize the stage in which these data appear as the "FP stage," similar to the stage described above for German L2A according to Vainikka and Young-Scholten. It is not until the next stage, upon acquiring the (correct) subject–verb agreement paradigm for the present indicative, that an AGRP is said to emerge.

However, note that while -er is not a verbal affix in the target system, it is specified for [3sg]; the fact that these pronominal copies agree in person and number with the subject appears to show an attempt to spell out the correct grammatical *features* associated with the syntactic (subject) node. The point is this: Agreement morphology on verbs reflects the *features* of the subject. If learners (both L1 and L2) have knowledge of these features, they may happen to use whatever spell-out is available at that point in their productive repertoire which indicates awareness of the features. In that case, it would be premature to assume that until the spell-outs themselves are targetlike, the learner has no knowledge of agreement (i.e. an AGR projection in the syntax).

Now recall that Vainikka and Young-Scholten (1994: 281) had argued for L2A that, at stages where subject–verb paradigms still appear incomplete, this is due to the fact that "there is no INFL or AGR position for base-generating suffixes." However, I would argue that it is possible (indeed, likely, according to much recent work in morphology) that it is not agreement *suffixes* which are base-generated in the syntax under INFL or AGRP, but rather agreement *features*. Thus while it seems implausible that adult L2 acquirers would not have knowledge of these features if their L1 required it, it is on the other hand entirely likely that the lexical spell-outs of the affixes associated with the features must be learned over time. Moreover, in light of this distinction between inflectional features and their phonetic reflexes, it is unnecessary to ask, as Eubank (1994: 31) does, "whether or not bound inflectional morphology transfers from the NL into the L2," and unnecessary to assume that a model which posits the transfer of functional as well as lexical projections would require it.

However, in connection with this question, consider another study, conducted on the L2A of Chichewa, by Orr (1987). This research, conducted in Malawi, looked at the acquisition of noun-class prefixes and agreement markers in Chichewa, a Bantu language, by L1 speakers of Ngoni (another Bantu language with a similar noun-class-prefix system) and Gujarati (a non-Bantu language spoken by the Indian immigrants in the area). Orr found, not terribly surprisingly, that the Ngoni speakers outperformed the Gujarati speakers on the morphological aspects of acquisition by far, even when the overall proficiency ratings between the two groups (as determined by the Foreign Service Institute test for communicative competence) were equivalent. The data strongly indicated, according to Orr (1987: 118), that "success in supplying noun class morphology is dependent primarily on L1 affiliation, with proficiency level being of lesser importance."

The results showed that all the Ngoni subjects, even at the lowest levels of proficiency exhibited a "sophisticated ability to supply class prefixes for nouns covering a broad spectrum of types: Singular nouns, plural nouns, locatives, infinitives and classes with semantically diverse memberships" (1987: 118). The weaker performance of the Gujarati speakers, on the other hand, was explicitly attributed by Orr to the fact that their L1 does not have a similar noun-class system.

However, Gujarati does have noun class (i.e. masculine, feminine, and neuter gender) distinctions and suffixal, rather than prefixal, agreement. At no point, though, did Gujarati speakers' production of Chichewa noun-class morphology show up as, say, a suffix rather than a prefix on the noun—in other words, incorporating the morphological spell-out forms of Gujarati. What did appear in the Gujarati data, however, was a striking reliance on a single overgeneralized class and agreement prefix and a tendency to leave nouns unmarked for plurality in obligatory plural contexts. The overgeneralization suggests that the Gujarati speakers were indeed aware of the requirement for agreement and, as noted earlier, relied on using whatever spell-out was available at that point in their productive repertoire to fulfill this requirement. It does not suggest that Gujarati speakers lack a functional projection for noun-class agreement. As for the tendency to leave plural nouns unmarked, Orr notes that this is strikingly similar to a characteristic of Gujarati, which allows optional plural-marking of nouns under various conditions, and does, therefore, appear to be a transfer effect.

The use of a default morphological form to mark a given syntactic feature is, of course, a well-known phenomenon throughout both L1A and L2A. In English L1A for example, we find overregularization extended to irregular forms such as *foots* or *goed* to mark the features [+ plural] or [+ past]. With respect to inflections indicating subject–verb agreement, we seem to find early overreliance on forms used to spell out [3sg]. This tendency has been noted in the acquisition literature, e.g. by Meisel (1994) and Meisel and Ezeizabarrena. Meisel and Ezeizabarrena (1994: 19) explicitly point out that [3sg] forms "represent the default value of agreement."[1] Furthermore, they note that we can distinguish between "Agreement," the grammatical relation, and "agreement," its morphological reflex, and presume that the former but not the latter is available at early stages of development (1994: 20).

---

[1] One exception to this generalization, of course, is English, where [3sg] spell-out (-*s*) is acquired quite late in both first and second language acquisition.

In my own data I have found what appears to be a similar trend by native Spanish speakers acquiring the word-formation rules for English deverbal compounding. In both languages deverbal compounding can be used productively to coin a name for somebody or something that performs a transitive action on an unspecified (generic) object, as shown by the examples in (2):

(2)   Spanish   English

    a.   *un lavaplatos*   a dishwasher
         ("a wash(3sg?) plate(PL)")
    b.   *un abrelatas*   a can-opener
         ("an open(3sg?) can(PL)")
    c.   *un pierdeplumas*   a pen-loser
         ("a lose(3sg) pen(PL)")

(In the examples shown above, (2a) and (2b) have become lexicalized, whereas (2c) represents a novel but attested coining for the Spanish example. These forms in both languages actually share several similarities. For example, both are deverbal nominalizations consisting of a head and its complement (often the theme/direct object); in both cases the nonhead noun (*platos* and *dish*) may not satisfy the external argument of the base verb, i.e., it cannot be the thing doing the washing. These compounds are also productive in both languages—in Spanish this is the most fully productive type of compounding available (Harris 1987; Lang 1991), and spontaneous coinings are usually semantically compositional.

Aside from these similarities, there are obvious differences as well. Despite the fact that both Spanish and English have head-initial VPs, only Spanish retains canonical verb–complement order in deverbal compounds. Additionally, the verb in the Spanish compound appears to bear features of verbal inflection and, unlike English, its object is pluralized, even when the compound as a whole is clearly singular. In English, on the other hand, we find a constraint against pluralized objects within the compound (e.g. *disheswasher*).

Although the form of the verb in lexicalized Spanish V+N compounds has been historically or traditionally sometimes held to be a ([2sg]) imperative, apparently few, if any, current speakers retain this intuition for spontaneous, productive usage. Rather it is more likely (as I have argued— in Lardiere 1994 and Lardiere and Schwartz 1994) that, for these kinds of nominalizations in both languages, Tense—a verbal hallmark—is absent altogether whereas nominal AGR features are present. These features comprise the nominal default value [3sg] (as well as, probably, masculine gender in the Spanish compounds); as features of the compound head, they percolate to the top of the lexical X^0 node.

One very common error pattern observed among the novel deverbal compounds elicited from early-stage Spanish-speaking acquirers of English involves the transfer of the Spanish word-order for compounds into English, e.g. *eater-flies* or *eating-flies* instead of *fly-eater*. In addition to the transferred word-order, however, it appears that knowledge of what constitutes a deverbal nominalization is also available. In this case the knowledge consists of the deleting of Tense plus "reversion" to default nominal-agreement features (i.e. [3sg]), as in Spanish. As Beard (1995: 123, following Jakobson) points out, third person is the default category for all lexical nouns. Among the English L2 data, the use of [3sg] nominalizing affixes *-er* and/or *-ing* (and the neutralizing of Tense) in examples such as *eater-flies* and *eating-flies* may explain why there are virtually no instances in the data of a "template"-type transfer from Spanish of forms such as *eats-flies* or even *eat-flies*, although either of these forms would more closely resemble a literal, "surface" transfer from the Spanish.

In sum, an examination of whatever inflectional material is present in interlanguage data may reveal an attempt at feature-marking that, although not exactly targetlike, may be at least consistent with the required features or reflect underlying knowledge of the types of projections required. To the extent a default form represents an overgeneralization in the form-to-feature mapping, it suggests awareness of the requirement to somehow mark the feature—in this case knowledge of the SPEC-head–agreement relation.

4. Conclusion. Although there is conceivably a place for morphology in UG, one must obviously be careful where language-specific phenomena, such as affixation, are concerned. Recent morphological theories arguing for a separation of grammatical features from their actual spell-outs (the so-called "separationist" theories of, e.g. Anderson 1992; Aronoff 1994; Beard 1987, 1995; Halle and Marantz 1993; etc.) represent one way of integrating morphology in syntactic derivations, in which the role of UG is limited to specifying the features visible to the syntax. When considering the question of transfer, and the transferability of functional projections in particular, it is important to keep in mind that the language-specific spell-out of those features is another matter altogether, and one that must clearly be learned.

REFERENCES

Anderson, Stephen R. 1992. *A-morphous morphology*. N.Y.: Cambridge University Press.
Aronoff, Mark. 1994. *Morphology by itself*. Cambridge, Massachusetts: MIT Press.
Beard, Robert. 1987. "Morpheme order in a lexeme-morpheme base morphology." *Lingua* 72: 1–44.
Beard, Robert. 1995. *Lexeme-morpheme base morphology*. Buffalo, N.Y.: SUNY Press.
Chomsky, Noam. 1981. *Lectures on Government and Binding*. Dordrecht, Germany: Foris.

Clahsen, Harald. 1990/1991. "Constraints on parameter setting: A grammatical analysis of some acquisition stages in German child language." *Language Acquisition* 1: 361–391.

Clahsen, Harald, Sonja Eisenbeiss and Anne Vainikka. 1994. "The seeds of structure: A syntactic analysis of the acquisition of case marking." In Teun Hoekstra and Bonnie D. Schwartz (eds.), Languages acquisition studies in generative grammar: *Papers in honor of Kenneth Wexler from the GLOW 1991 Workshops*. Amsterdam: John Benjamins.

Clahsen, Harald and Martina Penke. 1992. "The acquisition of agreement morphology and its syntactic consequences." In Jürgen Meisel (ed.), *The acquisition of verb placement: Functional categories and V2 phenomena in language acquisition*. Dordrecht, Germany: Kluwer. 181–223.

Dulay, Heidi and Marina Burt. 1974. "Natural sequences in child second language acquisition." *Language Learning* 24: 37–53.

Eubank, Lynn. 1994. "On the transfer of parametric values in L2 development." Unpublished manuscript, University of North Texas.

Flynn, Suzanne. 1987. *A parameter-setting model of L2 acquisition*. Dordrecht, Germany: Reidel.

Halle, Morris and Alec Marantz. 1993. "Distributed morphology and the pieces of inflection." In Kenneth Hale and Samuel J. Keyser (eds.), *The view from Building 20: Essays in honor of Sylvain Bromberger*. Cambridge, Massachusetts: MIT Press.

Harris, James W. 1987. "The accentual patterns of verb paradigms in Spanish." *Natural Language and Linguistic Theory* 5: 61–90.

Hoekstra, Teun and Bonnie D. Schwartz. 1994. *Language acquisition studies in generative grammar: Papers in honor of Kenneth Wexler from the GLOW 1991 Workshops*. Amsterdam: John Benjamins.

Lang, M. F. 1991. *Spanish word formation: Productive derivational morphology in the modern lexis*. N.Y.: Routledge.

Lardiere, Donna. 1994. "The acquisition of word-formation rules for English synthetic compounding." Unpublished Ph.D. dissertation, Boston University.

Lardiere, Donna and Schwartz, Bonnie D. 1994. "Agreement in L2 acquisition and the criterion of 'correct' overt manifestation." Paper presented at the Workshop on Generative Studies on the Acquisition of Case and Agreement, University of Essex, March 1994.

Meisel, Jürgen M. 1994. "Getting FAT: Finiteness, Agreement and Tense in early grammars." In Jürgen M. Meisel (ed.), *Bilingual first language acquisition: French and German grammatical development*. Amsterdam: John Benjamins.

Meisel, Jürgen M. and Maria J. Ezeizabarrena. 1994. "Subject-verb and object-verb agreement in early Basque." Paper presented at the Workshop on Generative Studies of the Acquisition of Case and Agreement, University of Essex, March 1994.

Orr, Gregory J. 1987. "Aspects of the second language acquisition of Chichewa noun class morphology." Unpublished Ph.D. dissertation, University of California, Los Angeles.

Radford, Andrew. 1990. *Syntactic theory and the acquisition of English syntax*. Oxford: Blackwell.

Radford, Andrew. 1994. "Clausal projections in early child grammars". *Essex Research Reports in Linguistics* 3: 32-72.

Schwartz, Bonnie D. (to appear)."On two hypotheses of 'transfer' in L2A: Minimal Trees and Absolute L1 Influence." To appear in Suzanne Flynn, Gita Martohardjono, and Wayne O'Neil (eds.), *The generative study of SLA*. Hillsdale, N.J.: Erlbaum.

Schwartz, Bonnie D. and Rex Sprouse. 1994. "Word order and nominative case in nonnative language acquisition." In Teun Hoekstra and Bonnie D. Schwartz, (eds.), *Language acquisition studies in generative grammar: Papers in honor of Kenneth Wexler from the GLOW 1991 Workshops*. Amsterdam: John Benjamins.

Vainikka, Anne. 1992. "Case in the development of English syntax". Manuscript. University of Massachussetts-Amherst.

Vainikka, Anne and Martha Young-Scholten. 1994. "Direct access to X'-theory: Evidence from Korean and Turkish." In Teun Hoekstra and Bonnie D. Schwartz (eds.), *Language acquisition studies in generative grammar: Papers in honor of Kenneth Wexler from the GLOW 1991 Workshops*. Amsterdam: John Benjamins.

White, Lydia. 1985. "The 'pro-drop' parameter in adult second language acquisition." *Language Learning* 35: 47–62.

White, Lydia. 1993. "Universal grammar: Is it just a new name for old problems?" In Susan M. Gass and Larry Selinker (eds.), *Language transfer in language learning*. Amsterdam: John Benjamins.

Dialectal variation as an insight into the structure of grammar

Raffaella Zanuttini
Georgetown University

Comparative syntax. Work in syntax aims to characterize the principles underlying the structure of human language. It is a well-established fact that a sentence does not consist of a string of words randomly put together, but rather of words combined via a set of combinatorial principles which are sensitive to structure. Research in syntactic theory attempts to discover such principles, on the basis of empirical investigations which can either focus on one language or range across a variety of languages.

Take as an example the study of sentential negation, i.e. the syntactic process by which a language can negate a clause, thus expressing a negative proposition. In principle, languages could employ any number of strategies to form negative clauses; but in fact what we find is that they employ only a very limited number of ways to do so. For example, no language forms a negative clause by producing the mirror image of the non-negative sentence, or by simply reversing the order of subject and verb, or of noun and determiner. Instead, languages employ a set of elements, which we can informally label "negative markers": elements like English *n't* or *not*, French *ne* or *pas*, Japanese *na-i*, or Basque *ez*. Not only is the set of negative markers small, but also the range of positions they may occupy in a clause is extremely limited: the negative markers, far from occurring in just any position in the clause, can only occupy a very restricted number of positions. The task of a syntactician, then, is to uncover the principles which govern the formation of negative clauses: What sort of elements can be used to negate a clause? Where exactly do such elements occur in the clause? What determines the choice of one strategy for negating a clause over another?

Often the analysis of a single language does not allow a thorough understanding of a given grammatical phenomenon. For example, if we attempt to characterize the syntactic properties of sentential negation basing our analysis on (American) English alone, we must include in our description factors such as the presence of *do*, which is required when the sentence does not contain a form of auxiliary *have* or *be*, main verb *be*, or a modal. That is, whereas the sentences in (1) form a negative clause by adding the negative marker *n't* to the affirmative counterpart, those in (2) require the insertion of a form of *do*, in addition to the negative marker:

(1)   a.   Mary has left early. / Mary has*n't* left early.
       b.   John is sleeping. / John is*n't* sleeping.
       c.   They can call me at five. / They ca*n't* call me at five.

(2)   a.   Mary likes pizza. / Mary *doesn't* like pizza.
       b.   We enjoyed that movie. / We *didn't* enjoy that movie.

But the presence of *do* is an idiosyncratic property of the grammar of English; though it might reflect some requirement imposed by the negative marker which appears in the clause (i.e. that it be associated with an element expressing tense), it does so only indirectly. In order to see what relevant generalization underlies the expression of sentential negation, one is forced to compare negative clauses in English with their counterparts in other languages.

Moreover, the analysis of a single language clearly does not make it possible to answer questions concerning the crosslinguistic properties of a grammatical phenomenon. This is true of the study of any grammatical phenomenon and not only of sentential negation. If we want to know how human languages form questions, for example, it is not sufficient to study a single language, but a comparison of a variety of languages is necessary.

Once we decide to extend the investigation beyond a single language, we are immediately faced with a difficult choice: is it more useful to study languages which represent different ends of the spectrum, or languages which are related and thus are more similar to one another? In other words, what is the appropriate way to approach the study of the universal as well as the language-particular principles which determine a given grammatical phenomenon?

By observing a range of languages which are representative of different families we can broaden our perspective and thereby eliminate some of the factors specific to a single grammar. But we might also introduce differences which are irrelevant for the phenomenon under investigation and thereby make the picture blurry. For example, languages might differ in the position of the verb (a language might or might not have "verb movement"; it might place the verb in a position preceding the complements or else in a position following the complements; etc.); or they might differ in whether grammatical information is expressed by means of verbal affixes, of independent particles, or of adverbs, etc.

In contrast, focusing on a set of languages which differ from one another only minimally allows us to perform an experiment in which we have controlled for external factors (i.e. gross variation among languages) and through which we can observe the effects of a range of syntactic environments on a single variable. The advantage of studying closely-related languages has emerged most clearly in recent years from the work of such linguists as Richard Kayne, Paola Benincà, Christer Platzack and Anders Holmberg, who have been working within the paradigm of comparative syntax. From this perspective, the Romance languages provide an excellent testing ground for the purposes of our study, since it is possible to find varieties which differ only minimally and precisely with respect to those properties related to the expression of sentential negation. For example, in as limited a geographical area as Northern Italy, it is possible to find dozens of linguistic varieties (the so-called Northern Italian dialects) which exhibit syntactic (as well as morphological and phonological) differences, but which share many basic syntactic properties.

In this paper we will show how the analysis of closely related Romance languages furthers our understanding of the structure of negative sentences by allowing us to compare the properties of different negative markers against a background which remains constant. In our experiment, the variable under investigation is the syntactic realization of sentential negation. The languages under study are some of the widely spoken Romance languages (e.g. Italian, French, Spanish) and some of the Northern Italian dialects (e.g. Piedmontese, Valdotain, Milanese).[1] We will argue that, within this language family, the range of strategies used for the expression of sentential negation is limited to two main ones: Languages mark sentential negation either in a position preceding the finite verb or else in a position following the finite verb but preceding the complements. Other differences, such as the one concerning the distribution of negative indefinites, can be shown to be reducible to this primary distinction.

A case study: Negation in the Romance languages. In order to characterize the range of variation attested in the Romance language family for the expression of sentential negation, we will examine which and how many structural positions can be used for the placement of the negative markers.

Let us start by comparing negative sentences from a handful of dialects spoken in Northern Italy.[2] At first sight, it looks like we find negative markers

---

[1]In the cases we discuss, the distinction between "language" and "dialect" is due exclusively to political reasons and has no relevance for the grammatical phenomenon we are investigating. Consequently, we use the term "language" inclusively, i.e. to refer both to the Romance varieties which have the status of the official language of some political entity (e.g. Italian, Catalan, Quebecois) as well as to those that do not (e.g. the Northern Italian dialects, such as Piedmontese, Romagnolo, etc.). We also use the term "dialect" to refer to the latter class of languages, as this reflects common usage.

[2]The geographic distribution of these dialects ranges from the western tip of the northern Italian coast to the mountainous areas of Trentino, a north-eastern region bordering with Austria: Ventimigliese is spoken in the town of Ventimiglia, in the province of Savona, in Liguria

in many different positions. In (3), the negative marker *nu* precedes the finite verb; in (4), the negative marker *no* follows the finite form of the verb; in (5), one negative marker precedes the finite verb (*n*) and one follows it (*nent*); in (6) the negative marker *non* precedes not only the finite verb but also the complementizer *ku* ("that") which introduces the clause in (7), a negative marker in preverbal position co-occurs with one which follows not only the finite verb but also the object:

(3)   *I*   *nu*   *ven.* (Ventimigliese)
         ("S.CL   NEG   come")
         They're **not** coming.

(4)   *La*   *Maria*   *l'ha*   *no mangià*   *la carne.* (Pavese)
         ("the   Maria   CL'has   not eaten   the meat")
         Mary **hasn't** eaten meat.

(5)   *U*   *nin*   *sent*   *nent.* (Cairese)
         ("S.CL   us-NEG   hears   NEG")
         He **doesn't** hear us.

(6)   *Per*   *non*   *ku s*   *brusa*   *a*   *karbunera.* (dialect of Osiglia)
         ("for   not   that CL   burns   the   coal")
         So that the coal won't burn.

(7)   *No*   *gaj neanka*   *pü*   *en*   *par de*   *kalse* *no.* (dialect of Lisignago)
         ("NEG   have even   more   a   pair   of   socks NEG")
         I **don't** even have a pair of stockings **anymore**.

This appears to be a rather complex distributional pattern. At this point one might legitimately wonder whether, as we increase the number of languages we look at, we will also increase the number of options we find for a language of this family to express sentential negation. The answer is negative. In fact, a close look at a range of languages shows that, despite the apparent differences, a limited number of strategies for the expression of sentential negation is adopted across them. In what follows we will argue that two main strategies are employed by the Romance languages for negating a clause. Let us examine them in turn.

(North-Western Italy); Cairese is spoken in the the town of Cairo Montenotte, on the border between Liguria and Piedmont; Osiglia, like Cairo Montenotte, is a town in the Ligurian hinterland; Piedmontese is spoken in Piedmont, the region whose main urban center is Turin; Pavese is the dialect of Pavia, a town roughly 30 Km. south of Milan, in central Northern Italy; Lisignago is a town in the Trentino region, in eastern northern Italy.

Preverbal negative markers. One strategy for negating a sentence is to have the negative marker in a position following the preverbal subject and preceding the finite verb. This is the position exemplified in (3) above and used by many of the most widely spoken Romance languages, such as Italian, Spanish, Catalan, Rumanian, as well as by all the dialects of central and southern Italy. Some examples are given below:

(8) a. *Gianni **non** ha telefonato a sua madre.* (Italian)
     b. *Juan **no** ha llamado a su madre.* (Spanish)
     c. *El Joan **no** a trucat a sa mare.* (Catalan)
     d. *João **não** ligou para sua mãe.* (Portuguese)
     e. *Jon **nu-i** telefona mamei lui.* (Romanian)
        John has**n't** called his mother.

The languages which adopt this strategy for negating a clause also share another property, namely the following: When a negative indefinite occurs in the clause—i.e. an element corresponding to "no-one," "never," "nothing," etc.—it is subject to different restrictions depending on whether it occurs in pre- or in postverbal position. When it occurs in preverbal position, it can be the only negative element in the clause, as illustrated by the following examples:

(9) a. *Nessuno è venuto.* (Italian)
     b. *Nadie vino.* (Spanish)
        Nobody came.

On the other hand, when it occurs in a position following the finite verb, it cannot be the only negative element in the clause:

(10) a. **Ho visto **nessuno**.* (Italian)
      b. **He visto a **nadie**.* (Spanish)
      c. **He vist **ningú**.* (Catalan)
      d. **Vi **ninguem**.* (Portuguese)
      e. **Am vazut pe **nimeni**.* (Romanian)
         I have**n't** seen **anybody**.

For a sentence with a negative indefinite in postverbal position to be grammatical, it must be the case that either the negative marker is present, or else another negative constituent occurs in a preverbal position (e.g. a subject, or a topicalized constituent). The following examples illustrate these two cases:

(11) a. *Non ho visto **nessuno**.* (Italian)
      b. *No he visto a **nadie**.* (Spanish)
      c. *No he vist **ningú**.* (Catalan)
      d. *Não vi **ninguem**.* (Portuguese)
      e. *Nu am vazut pe **nimeni**.* (Romanian)

I haven't seen **anybody**.

(12) a. *Nessuno ha detto niente*. (Italian)
      b. *Nadie ha dicho nada*. (Spanish)
      c. *Ningú (no) ha dit res*. (Catalan)
      d. *Ninguem (não) disse nada*. (Portuguese)
      e. *Nimeni nu a zis nimic*. (Romanian)
          ("nobody NEG has said nothing")
          Nobody said **anything**.

Note that the co-occurrence of the two negative constituents, as well as that of the negative marker and one negative constituent, does not give rise to two instances of negation, i.e. is not a case of double negation. Rather, the two negative elements together are interpreted as a single instance of negation, a phenomenon which has been labelled "negative concord."[3]

We have thus identified a cluster of properties: the property of marking sentential negation in a position higher than the finite verb correlates with that of imposing a constraint on the distribution of negative indefinites to the effect that they cannot follow the finite verb, unless another negative element precedes it. Obviously, the next question to ask is why such a correlation exists, and what insight it gives us into the properties of the languages under investigation. Informally, the relevant property which characterizes these languages seems to be the following: they must mark sentential negation in a position as high as or higher than inflection, i.e. the position where information concerning tense and agreement is expressed. These languages do not allow sentential negation to be marked in a position lower than inflection. We will see in the next section that such a requirement is not shared by all Romance languages but uniquely characterizes those which adopt as a strategy for negating a clause the use of a preverbal negative marker.

Postverbal negative markers. A second strategy for negating a sentence in Romance languages is to have the negative marker in a position following the finite verb. Our task as syntacticians consists of characterizing precisely what this position is and determining whether or not it is a unique position. In this section we will argue that there are not one, but two positions where postverbal negative markers may occur. Nevertheless we maintain that the use of a postverbal negative marker, in either position, represents a unitary syntactic strategy for the expression of sentential negation, different from the one involving preverbal negative markers.

---

[3]Negative concord, i.e. the co-occurrence of two of more negative elements contributing a single instance of negation to the clause, is also found in non-standard varieties of English (cf. Labov 1972 and Ladusaw 1992, among others).

Consider the following examples. The sentences are from the same language, Piedmontese; they exhibit two different negative markers, *nen* and *pa*:

(13)   a.   *Gianni   a   l'ha   **nen**   capì   tut*. (Piedmontese)
                 ("Gianni   S.CL   CL'has   NEG   understood   everything")
                 Gianni didn't understand everything.

         b.   *Gianni   a   l'ha   **pa**   capì   tut*! (Piedmontese)
                 ("Gianni   S.CL   CL'has   NEG understood   everything")
                 Gianni didn't understand everything (though you thought he would).

As indicated in the translations, the two sentences do not have identical interpretations. The first one is simply negating a proposition. The second one is interpreted as negating a proposition which the speaker thinks is believed to be true, either in the context or by the hearer (cf. Cinque 1976). That is, (13)b is uttered felicitously only if the speaker thinks that John was expected to understand everything, either in the discourse context or by the hearer in particular.

Are the two negative markers *nen* and *pa*, which trigger these two different interpretations, in the same position or in different positions? In other words, does the difference in interpretation correspond to a structural difference in the position of the negative markers?

In order to answer questions of this type, it is advantageous to compare languages which differ only minimally from one another. As mentioned above, this process allows us to examine one variable while keeping the background constant. Let us see how.

Recent work by Cinque (cf. Cinque 1994, 1995) has studied the distribution of adverbs which occur in the "space" delimited on the left by an active past participle (in Italian) and on the right by the first complement of the past participle. This work has convincingly shown that the relative order of these classes of adverbs is rigidly fixed and, moreover, is the same both in Italian and in French. Such relative order is shown in Table 1.

Table 1.

Italian: French:	*mica* *pas*	*già* *déjà*	*più* *plus*	*sempre* *toujours*	*completamente* *complètement*	*tutto* *tout*	*bene* *bien*
	neg	already	(any)more	always	completely	all	well

For the sake of brevity, we will not reproduce here Cinque's arguments nor the empirical evidence adduced in support of his proposal, for which the reader is referred to the work cited. However, we will build on his evidence and his conclusions to pursue an answer to our questions.

If we apply Cinque's diagnostic tests to the languages under study, we see that the same ordering of adverbs described in Cinque's work for Italian and French is found in our set of languages as well. This provides us with a starting point for our investigation, as follows. To determine whether or not two negative markers are in the same position, we can observe their distribution with respect to the adverbs which occur in the same syntactic space. Such an observation will give us a fine-grained analysis of the ordering of elements which occur between the verb and the complements and will allow us to examine more closely the position of a given negative marker. The data from Piedmontese replicate the relative order among the lower adverbs described in Cinque's work. Limiting our investigation to "already," "anymore" and "always," we find that their relative order is the same described by Cinque for Italian and French, with "already" preceding "anymore," which in turns precedes "always." As for the relative order of the negative marker with respect to these adverbs, what we find is the following. Piedmontese *pa* parallels the distribution of Italian *mica* and French *pas*. It precedes the word for "already," *gia*, as shown in (14):[4]

(14)   a.   *A*   *l'ha*   **pa** *gia*   *ciamà*   *che mi* *i* *sapia!*
            ("S.CL   CL'has   NEG already   called,   that I   S.CL know")
            He hasn't **already** called, that I know!

       b.   *A*   *l'è*   **pa**   *gia*   *parti?!*
            ("S.CL   CL'is   NEG   already   gone")
            He hasn't **already** gone?!

Pa also precedes the adverb corresponding to "anymore," *pi*:

(15)   a.   *A*   *l'han*   **pa** *pi*   *telefunà,*   *da* *'ntlura.*
            ("S.CL   CL'have   NEG more   telephoned,   since that-time")
            They haven't called **anymore**, since then!

       b.   *Da*   *'ntlura,*   *a*   *l'ha* **pa** *pi*   *sempre acetà*
            ("Since that-time   S.CL CL'has NEG more   always accepted

---

[4]The opposite order of the two adverbs, i.e. *gia pa*, is also possible, but only when *gia* does not fall within the scope of negation:
(i)   *A l'avia* **gia pa** *vulu 'ntlura.*
      "He had already not wanted to at that time." / "Already at that time he had not wanted to."
(ii) *A l'avia* **gia pa** *salutami cul dì la.*
      "He had already not said hello to me on that day." / "Already on that day he had not said hello to me."
The sentences in (14), on the other hand, have an intepretation in which *gia* is within the scope of negation: "It is not the case that he has already called," "It is not the case that he has already left."

> *i*   *nost*   *invit.*
> the   our   invitation")
> Since then, he **hasn't any longer** always accepted our invitations!

Note that *gia* in turn precedes *pi*:

(16)   a.   *A*   *mangia*   *'n bucun*   *e*   *a*   *veul*   **gia**   **pi** *gnente.*
                ("S.CL   eats a bite   and   S.CL   wants already no more nothing")
                He eats a bite and **already** doesn't want anything anymore.

         b.   *Purtrop,*   *subit*   *dopu*   *l'uperasiun,*   *a*   *conusia*
                ("Unfortunately,   right   after   the' surgery   S.CL recognized
                gia   **pi**   *gnun.*
                already   no more   anyone")
                Unfortunately, right after the operation, he **already** didn't recognize anyone.

From the observation that *pa* typically precedes both *gia* and *pi*, combined with the observation that *gia* precedes *pi*, we conclude that the respective ordering among these adverbs is the following: *pa, gia, pi.*

The distribution of *nen* contrasts with that of *pa* with respect to both *gia* and *pi*. First, *nen* cannot precede *gia* ("already"); thus (17)a contrasts with (17)b and with the sentences in (14) above:[5]

(17)   a.   **A*   *l'e*   *nen*   *gia*   *andait*   *a*   *ca'.*
                ("S.CL   CL'is   NEG   already   gone   to   home")
                He hasn't already gone home.

         b.   *A l'e* **pa gia** *andait a ca'!*

This contrast suggests that *pa* and *nen* do not occur in the same structural position, but rather that *pa* is higher than *gia*, whereas *nen* is not.

The distribution of *nen* differs strikingly from that of *pa* also with respect to the word for "anymore," *pi*. Whereas *pa* precedes *pi*, as we saw in (15) above, *nen* follows *pi* in linear order:

(18)   a.   *Da*   *'ntlura,*   *a*   *l'ha*   **pi**   *nen*   *sempre vinciu.*
                ("from then,   S.CL   CL has   more   NEG   always won")
                Since then, he has **no longer** always won.

---

[5]As we pointed out in Footnote 4 for *pa*, for *nen* as well the opposite order of the two adverbs (i.e. *gia nen*) is possible only when *gia* does not fall within the scope of negation:

(i) *A l'avia* **gia nen** *vulu 'ntlura.*
    "He had already not wanted at that time."/"Already at that time he had not wanted to"

(ii) *A l'avia* **gia nen** *salutami cul di la.*
     "He had already not said hello to me on that day."/"Already on that day he had not said hello to me."

As in the examples from Footnote 4, an intonational break separates *gia* from *nen vulu.*

Table 2.

Italian:	*mica*	*già*	*più*		*sempre*
French:	*pas*	*déjà*	*plus*		*toujours*
Piedmontese:	*pa*	*gia*	*pi*	*nen*	*sempre*
	neg	already	(any)more	neg	always

    b. *A*   *l'han*   **pi**   **nen**   *ricevu*   *gnente.*
        ("CL   CL'have more NEG   received   nothing.")
        They have **no longer** received anything.

One possible conclusion we can draw from these data is that, whereas *pa* precedes both *gia* and *pi*, *nen* follows them both. Moreover, *nen* precedes *sempre*, which in turn can either precede or follow the past participle, as shown in the following examples:[6]

(19)   a. *A*   *l'ha*   **nen** *(sempre)*   *dine*   *(sempre)* *tut.*
           ("S.CL   CL'has   NEG (always)   said-us   (always) everything")
           He hasn't **always** told us everything.
      b. **A l'ha sempre nen dine tut.*

If the position of *nen* is lower than that of *gia* and *pi*, but higher than that of *sempre*, then the linear order of these elements in Piedmontese, as compared to that of the corresponding elements in French and Italian, will be the one in Table 2.[7]

This leads us to the following conclusion: when a language has two negative markers both in postverbal position, one being used to negate a proposition

---

[6]In margin to these data, let us point out what we can conclude about the position of the past participle in Piedmontese: it must raise to a position higher than *tut*, "everything," as confirmed by the fact that the order *tut*+participle is ungrammatical. It may or may not raise to a position higher than *sempre*. It cannot raise to a position higher than *pi* or *nen*.

[7]An alternative analysis is also compatible with the data, though: *nen* might occupy a position structurally higher than *pi* and the observed linear order might be the consequence of movement of *pi* to adjoin to *nen*. That is, the order of these elements could be the following:

Italian:	*mica*	*già*		*più*	*sempre*
French:	*pas*	*déjà*		*plus*	*toujours*
Piedmontese:	*pa*	*gia*	*nen*	*pi*	*sempre*
	neg	already	neg	(any)more	always

For a discussion of the arguments in support of this analysis, we refer the reader to Zanuttini (in preparation).

which is believed to be true and the other simply to negate a proposition which has no special status in the discourse, the two negative markers occur in different structural positions. The one which negates a proposition believed to be true is structurally higher than the one which does not.

The conclusion that a structural difference accompanies the difference in interpretation is confirmed by the examination of other languages within the same family. Those which have two distinct postverbal negative markers (e.g. Pavese and Milanese) have them in two different structural positions. Even those which have only one postverbal negative marker, though, might use both positions. One example is provided by the variety of Valdotain we examined, spoken in the town of Cogne. This language does not have two morphologically distinct negative markers but always employs the form *pa*. Interestingly, though, the distribution of *pa* varies depending on the discourse status of the sentence. When *pa* is used to negate a proposition which is assumed to be believed true, then it precedes the adverb "already," i.e. it occurs in the same position as Piedmontese *pa*. On the other hand, when it is used simply to negate a sentence which might or might not be believed to be true, it follows the adverb "already" and occurs in the same position as Piedmontese *nen*.

Without providing the relevant data, let us simply show a summary of the distribution of the negative markers with respect to the class of adverbs under discussion (Table 3, next page).

So far in this section we have argued that the negative markers which appear in postverbal position in the Romance languages occupy one of two positions (and no more): either they precede the adverb "already" or they follow it but precede the adverb "always." When a language employs two morphologically distinct postverbal negative markers, the two positions are specialized as follows: the former is reserved for the negative marker which negates a proposition believed to be true (by the hearer or in the discourse), while the latter is used by the negative marker which negates the clause without any presupposition attached.

Given that postverbal negative markers can occur in two different positions, in what sense do we want to say that the use of post-verbal negative markers, in contrast with that of preverbal negative markers, represents a second strategy by which Romance languages negate a clause? The languages which use postverbal negative markers contrast with those which use preverbal negative markers with respect to the restrictions imposed on negative indefinites. In Piedmontese, Valdotain, Milanese, etc. negative indefinites are free to occur in

Table 3.

Italian:	*mica*	*già*	*più*	*sempre*
French:	*pas*	*déjà*	*plus*	*toujours*
Piedmontese:	*pa*	*gia*	*nen/pi nen*	*sempre*
Pavese:	*mia*	*giamò*	*no/pu*	*sempar*
Milanese:	*minga*	*giamò*	*no/pü*	*semper*
Valdotian:	*pa*	*dza*	*pa/pa mai*	*toujou*
	neg	already	neg/(any)more	always

postverbal position without the co-occurrence of any other negative element in preverbal position, in contrast to what is the case in Italian, Spanish, Catalan, etc. This is illustrated in the examples below, to be contrasted with (10) above:

(20)   *I*   *l'hai*   *vist*   **gnun**. (Piedmontese)
       I   have   seen   **nobody**.

(21)   *Dz'i*   *gneuna*   *esperiance*. (Valdotain)
       I have   **no**   experience.

(22)   a.   *Hoo*   *vist*   **nissùn**. (Milanese)
           ("have   seen   no one")
           I didn't see **anyone**.
      b.   *L'ha*   *mangiaa*   **niént**.
           ("CL'has   eaten   **nothing**")
           He hasn't eaten **anything**.
      c.   *Gh'è*   *vegnuu*   **nissùn**.
           ("CL'is   come   no one")
           No one has come.

Hence, we have identified two strategies for marking sentential negation in the following sense. If a language places the negative marker in a position higher than inflection, then any negative element taking sentential scope must occur either in a position higher than inflection or else in co-occurrence with a negative element higher than inflection. On the other hand, if a language places the negative marker in a position lower than inflection, no such restriction is shown in the language.

The remaining cases. In our task of trying to make sense of the variation observed within the Romance languages in the expression of sentential negation, we are left now with three more cases. Let us discuss them one by one.

The first case is that exemplified in (5) above: that is, the case of a language where a preverbal negative marker which is between the subject and the finite verb co-occurs with a postverbal negative marker which is between the participle and the complements. Perhaps the best known cases of this type are standard French and Walloon (a dialect of French spoken in Belgium); but several other Romance varieties exhibit this pattern as well, as seen in the following examples:

(23) a. *Jean* *n'aime* *pas* *la viande*. (French)
      ("Jean NEG'likes NEG the meat")
      John doesn't like meat.

    b. *La feglia* *na* *canta* *betg*. (Surmeiran—Signorell 1987:125)
      ("the daughter NEG sings NEG")
      The daughter doesn't sing.

    c. *An* *dis* *brisa* *aksì*. (Romagnolo—from ASIS)
      ("S.CL-NEG say NEG like-that")
      One doesn't say it that way.

    d. *An* *'s* *dis mia* *achsé*. (Emiliano)
      ("S.CL-NEG one says NEG like-that")
      One doesn't say it that way.

    e. *U ni* *va nent*. (Cairo Montenotte—Parry (in press))
      ("S.CL NEG-LOC.CL goes NEG")
      He doesn't go there.

Though this strategy certainly differs from that exhibited by the languages discussed so far, we argue that in fact it does not represent a new strategy for expressing sentential negation. Rather, it is a combination of the two strategies mentioned above, since it employs a preverbal negative marker in combination with a post-verbal one. The combination of both a pre- and a postverbal negative marker is well-attested in the history of the Indo-European languages (see Jespersen 1917; Posner 1985; Schwegler 1983, 1988; Ladusaw 1992; among others). As Jespersen described in what is commonly known as "Jespersen's cycle," a language which negates a sentence by means of a preverbal negative marker at some point begins to employ a postverbal negative marker as well (for reasons which are the object of interesting debate); then the preverbal negative marker weakens phonologically and the postverbal negative marker becomes obligatory; finally, the preverbal negative marker disappears and the postverbal one becomes the only negative marker for the clause. From a diachronic perspective, then, we can view the co-occurrence of a pre- and a postverbal negative marker as the second stage of this cycle of diachronic change.[8]

The negation strategy exemplified by (6) is a different case, in that it doesn't seem to be generally available to any of the languages we have studied.

---

[8]In the languages exemplified above, the pre-verbal negative marker has undergone phonetic reduction, and it can be dropped (while the post-verbal one is obligatory).

Rather, it is a way to negate only a particular class of sentences, namely so-called "purpose clauses." Some more examples are given below:

(24)
A	*l'ha*	*fàit*	*parèj*	*për*	**nen**
("S.CL	has	done	so	for	NEG

ch'a	*së*	*stofìeissa.*	(Piedmontese)
that'S.CL	himself	bored")	

He did it that way so that he would**n't** get bored.

(25) a.
Je	*lui*	*ai*	*menti*	*pour (ne)*	**pas**
("I	to-him	have	lied	for	NEG	NEG

qu'il	*parte.*	(French)
that'he	leaves")	

I lied to him so that he would**n't** leave.

b.
Li	*mentiguèri*	*per*	*pas*	*que se'n*	*anèsse.* (Occitan)
("to-him lied		for	NEG	that he	leave")

I lied to him so that he would**n't** leave.

In fact, it is not even a strategy reserved for negative markers only. As we can see in the following sentences from Quebecois, from Daoust-Blais and Kemp (1979), other elements can occur in this position, e.g. the counterparts of the adverbs "no more" and "never" and of the quantifier "everything":

(26) a. *J'ai caché les ciseaux pour **plus** que ma fille se blesse.* (Quebecois)
   I hid the scissors so that my daughter would no longer hurt herself.

b. *J'ai caché les ciseaux pour **jamais** que pareille chose arrive a ma fille.* (Quebecois)
   I hid the scissors so that such a thing would never happen to my daughter.

c. *Je vais faire le ménage pour **tout** que ce soit beau.* (Quebecois)
   I'm going to clean up so that everything will look nice.

Thus we do not consider this a different strategy available to the Romance languages for the expression of sentential negation. Rather, we take these data to simply show that, in purpose clauses, certain elements can occur to the left of the complementizer. Though many questions remain to be answered in this respect (What characterizes the elements that can occur in that position? What is special about that position in particular? Why is this construction reserved for purpose clauses?), what is relevant for the purposes of our discussion is that this phenomenon is not representative of a general strategy employed by Romance languages for the expression of sentential negation.

Finally, let us turn to example (7) above, where a negative marker in postverbal position follows not only the finite verb but also the complements of the verb. A few more examples of the same type are given below:

(27) a.
No	*kredo*	*ke*	*pödia*	*parlar*
("NEG	believe	that	could	to-talk

kon	*elo*	*no*. (Cembra—Zörner 1989:263)						
with	him	NEG")						

I don't think that I could talk to him.

b. | *No* | *lagarlo* | *davert* | | | *no!* (Lisignago—Zörner 1989) | | | |
|---|---|---|---|---|---|---|---|---|
| ("NEG | leave-it | open | | | NEG") | | | |

Don't leave it open!

c. | *No* | *gaj* | *neanka* | *pü* | *en* | *par de* | *kalse* | *no*. (Lisignago) |
|---|---|---|---|---|---|---|---|
| ("NEG | have | even | | more a | pair of | socks | NEG") |

I don't even have a pair of socks anymore.

Note that, in all these examples, the postverbal negative marker does not co-occur with a preverbal one. As far as we know, this postverbal negative marker cannot occur alone in the clause, but must co-occur with a preverbal negative marker. If further empirical investigation confirms that this is indeed the case, then we might explore the possibility that the negative marker in sentence-final position be an intensifier (of the type of English "at all") and not a real negative marker (that is, an element whose function is that of negating a clause). Given that we have not yet been able to do fieldwork and collect our own data on any of the dialects which exhibit this type of negative clauses, we are not in a position to make any precise claim on this case, but will await the chance to conduct further research.[9]

Conclusion. The results presented in this work can be considered a first step towards the ambitious goal of determining and understanding what limits there are on the syntactic options that universal grammar imposes on the expression of sentential negation. A complete understanding can only be obtained through the study of a very large number of languages, and the work on Romance languages presented here should be seen as constituting one piece of this larger project. Besides outlining the first step of research in this area, we hope to have also shown the advantages of one method of investigation, namely that of comparing languages which differ from one another only minimally.

REFERENCES

Benincà, Paola, Richard Kayne, Cecilia Poletto and Laura Vanelli. 1990–present. *Atlante sintattico dell'Italia settentrionale*. Centro di Dialettologia, Università degli Studi di Padova (ASIS). Unpublished material.

Cinque, Guglielmo. 1976. "Mica." *Annali della Facoltà di Lettere e Filosofia, Università di Padova* I: 101–112.

---

[9]Data bearing on this issue can also be found in certain varieties of Brasilian Portuguese. Since we do not have a clear picture of the data, though, we will not discuss it here and will leave it for further research.

Cinque, Guglielmo. 1994. "On the relative order of certain 'lower' adverbs in Italian and French." In A. Fassi Feri. *Actes de la Table Ronde sur la Linguistique Comparée.* Marrakech: European Science Foundation.

Cinque, Guglielmo. 1995. "Adverbs and the universal hierarchy of functional projections." *GLOW Newsletter* 31. 14–15.

Daoust-Blais, Denise and William Kemp. 1979. "Pour pas tout que ca se perde: pour as a 'quantifier raising' subordinator in Quebec French." ms.

Jespersen, Otto. 1917. *Negation in English and other languages.* A.F. Host.

Labov, William. 1972. "Negative attraction and negative concord." *Language* 48(4): 773–818.

Ladusaw, William A. 1992. "Expressing negation." ms., Univ. of California, Santa Cruz.

Parry, M. Mair. (in press). "Preverbal negation and clitic ordering, with particular reference to a group of North-West Italian dialects." *Zeitschrift für Romanische Philologie.*

Posner, Rebecca. 1985. "Post-verbal negation in non-standard French: A historical and comparative view." *Romance Philology* 39(2): 170–197.

Schwegler, Armin. 1983. "Predicate negation and word-order change: A problem of multiple causation." *Lingua* 61(4): 297–334.

Schwegler, Armin. 1988. "Word-order change in predicate negation strategies in Romance languages." *Diachronica* 5(1/2): 21–58.

Signorell, Faust. 1987. *Normas Surmiranas: Grammatica rumantscha digl idiom da Sur- e Sotses.* Coira, Switzerland: Tgesa editoura cantounala.

Zanuttini, Raffaella. (in preparation). *Syntactic properties of sentential negation.* New York: Oxford University Press.

Zörner, Lotte. 1989. *Il dialetto di Cembra e dei suoi dintorni. Descrizione fonologica, storico-fonetica e morfosintattica.* Annali di S. Michele n.2. San Michele all'Adige: Museo degli usi e costumi della gente trentina.

Phonology and phonetics
in the education of second-language teachers

Elizabeth C. Zsiga
Georgetown University

Introduction. The first step in teaching any linguistic pattern to a second-language learner ought to be discovering the representation of that pattern for native speakers. Only when we know what native speakers are doing can we hope to teach second-language learners how to do it. Thus a solid foundation in theoretical phonology and phonetics is crucial in the education of second-language teachers. Different kinds of principles and processes determine the sound pattern of a language, and teachers must be aware of them in order to understand and correct their students' problems.

Phonologists and phoneticians generally recognize three types of rule, or sound pattern: lexical alternations, postlexical processes, and phonetic regularities. The lexical/postlexical distinction was proposed by Kiparsky (1985) in the theory of Lexical Phonology. While this theory as a whole is no longer widely accepted, the distinction between rules that apply to words in the lexicon and rules that apply to words in phrases remains important. Keating (1988) and Cohn (1990) discuss the distinction between postlexical phonology and phonetic implementation. The properties that distinguish these three rule types are discussed below. The different kinds of rules are acquired very differently by second-language learners, if they are acquired at all.

Lexical alternations. In lexical alternations, the phonological shape of a morpheme differs depending on the shape of the other morphemes it combines with. These alternations may be sensitive to morphological information such as part of speech or the distinction between root and affix. They respect structure preservation in that they cannot create sounds that are not part of the language's underlying inventory. Although lexical rules may exceptionally fail to apply to a particular word, their application is never variable or optional. Examples from English include:

- assimilation of the prefix *in-* to the place of articulation of a following consonant, resulting in *intolerable* and *indecipherable*, but *impossible*, *illegible*, and *irreducible*;

- voicing assimilation of the plural marker, producing [s] after voiceless sounds, [z] after voiced, and [əz] after strident sounds; and
- palatalization of alveolars before [j]-initial[1] suffixes such as *-ual* and *-ion*, illustrated by pairs such as *press/pressure*, *habit/habitual*, *grade/gradual*, and *confess/confession*.

Lexical rules are the most easily taught and learned in second-language acquisition. According to Weinberger (1994), such rules will rarely if ever be transferred from a learner's native language to a second language.

Phonetic regularities. At the other end of the spectrum of phonological and phonetic processes lie phonetic regularities. These can be defined as language-specific patterns in the implementation of speech. Like the lexical alternations, these regularities are neither variable nor optional, but unlike lexical alternations they never mark distinctions between words. Phonetic regularities may involve subphonemic place distinctions, or they may involve accurate timing of subsegmental articulatory events, such as aspiration or nasalization. For example:

- English /t/ is generally apical alveolar while Russian /t/ is generally laminal dental (Jones and Ward 1969);
- Aspiration of syllable-initial voiceless stops in English is greater in stressed than in unstressed syllables (Cooper 1991); and
- In French, the amount of contextual vowel nasalization differs dialectally: Nasalization begins sooner for nasalized vowels in Parisian French than in Canadian French (Van Reenen 1982, cited in Cohn 1990).

Although these articulatory habits may *seem* automatic to native speakers (speakers find it very difficult to change their habits, and unless explicitly instructed will not notice them), even these "low-level" regularities are learned and language-specific. Should some regularity be absent in a person's speech, the speaker is immediately marked as speaking with an accent. For example, final stops are not released in English, although they are in Italian. Hence the Italian-American accent is stereotyped as adding "a" to every word. Clearly, these "low-level" phonetic regularities transfer to a second language, and persist as markers of a foreign accent.

Postlexical processes. Between the lexical alternations and the phonetic regularities lie postlexical processes, so called because they apply to words in

---

[1] This paper follows IPA transcription, using [j] for the palatal glide.

phrases rather than in the lexicon (see Kiparsky 1985). Unlike lexical alternations, postlexical processes are not sensitive to grammatical information, and they have no systematic exceptions. They can create sounds not present in the language's underlying inventory, such as flaps in English. Unlike either of the other two rule types, postlexical processes may be optional and variable. They are most likely to apply in fast or casual speech. Some examples from English include:

- deletion of final alveolars before a word-initial stop: Only in very careful speech will the final /t/'s be heard in phrases like *that boy and that girl*;
- assimilation of final /n/ to a following stop: In careful speech, the nasals in *in Paris* and *in Congress* will be pronounced [n], while in more casual speech they may sound just like [m] or [ŋ]; and
- palatalization between words, as in *this year, miss you,* and *hit you*.

Weinberger (1994) proposes that postlexical rules, unlike their lexical counterparts, will transfer to a second language. This difference between lexical and postlexical rules is surprising given traditional phonological analyses, which represent the two kinds of process in exactly the same way: as phonological rules manipulating feature values. For example, both lexical palatalization (as in *confess/confession*) and postlexical palatalization (as in *miss you*) are represented as the /s/ undergoing a featural change from [+ant] to [-ant]. Evidence suggests, however, that grouping all lexical and postlexical rules together as "phonology," as opposed to the "low-level, phonetic" processes, is incorrect.

In many cases postlexical rules and phonetic processes belong together, as opposed to lexical alternations. It will be argued here (following Browman and Goldstein 1986, 1990, 1992), that like the phonetic processes, many if not all postlexical "rules" can be seen to result from habits of articulatory coordination. Evidence from several different sources shows that many processes that have been described using feature-changing phonological rules are better described in terms of articulatory timing. In fact, many postlexical rules of English can be seen to arise from a single generalization: There is significant temporal overlap between adjacent consonant gestures in English.

Gestural overlap in postlexical processes. Many studies have shown significant overlap between two consecutive consonant gestures in English (e.g. Perkell 1969; Hardcastle and Roach 1979; Hardcastle 1985; Barry 1985, 1991; Marchal 1988; Browman and Goldstein 1990; Byrd 1994; and Zsiga 1994.) Researchers have found that in a sequence of two consonants, movement of the articulators toward closure for the second consonant begins during the articulation of the first, generally before closure for the first consonant has been reached. At times the two closures may be nearly simultaneous. This gives rise to the "phonetic" fact that consonants in English are unreleased in clusters, but there are further and more interesting consequences as well.

The consequences of gestural overlap have been investigated extensively within the theory of Articulatory Phonology (see Browman and Goldstein 1992 for an overview). One important proposal of this theory is that changes in the amount of overlap between gestures may lie behind many phonological and phonetic processes. This approach to gestural overlap will be adopted here.

Deletion and assimilation of final alveolars. Articulatory Phonology proposes that, in fast or casual speech, overlap between articulations may increase to the point where it may cause the perception that a consonant has been assimilated or deleted. Browman and Goldstein (1990) consider assimilation and deletion of final alveolar consonants in English, in phrases like *perfect memory* ([pʰərfɛk mɛmri]) or *hundred pounds* ([hʌndrɛb paʊndz]). They present x-ray traces which show that even in utterances in which no alveolar is heard, an alveolar closure may still be made. Barry (1985, 1991) and Nolan (1992) also argue, based on evidence from electropalatography, for the presence of a (sometimes weakened) tongue-tip gesture in phrases where an alveolar has apparently been deleted.

Browman and Goldstein argue that the alveolar closure is not heard in these cases because the articulation is completely overlapped by the following consonant. This overlap effectively masks any acoustic consequences of the alveolar closure, such as formant transitions or audible release, and leads to the perception that the alveolar had been deleted. Browman and Goldstein point out that this gestural hiding provides an articulatory account of the generalization noticed by Guy (1980) that final alveolars are more likely to be deleted before other stops than in any other context.

In these cases of apparent deletion, no phonological rule has applied. The perception of deletion follows from gestural overlap. Gestural overlap, in turn, follows from independently-needed principles of articulatory coordination.

R-dropping in Brooklyn English. DeJong and Zsiga (1995) suggest that variable "r-dropping" in Brooklyn English may be another case where coproduction can lead to the perception that a phonological rule of deletion has applied. As part of the development of a larger multidialect database (Hertz et.al. 1994), DeJong and Zsiga recorded several hours of speech from a number of speakers of the Brooklyn dialect of American English. Since the data was collected for the purpose of speech-synthesis, rather than sociolinguistic, research, it was collected in a very controlled setting: Subjects were asked to read lists of words in a frame sentence. The data consisted of many different kinds of words and consonant combinations, however, so that there was no particular emphasis on the pronunciation of /r/. Even in this controlled setting, variation was found among subjects. Some dropped all postvocalic /r/'s, some dropped none. Others produced postvocalic /r/ only some of the time. Across subjects, however, a significant effect of the following consonant was found. Subjects whose production varied dropped /r/'s completely, or produced weakened versions, most often in words where the following consonant was a coronal (as in *burt* and *bird*), and most often of all before /l/ (as in *pearl*). Subjects who pronounced /r/'s consistently also produced weakened versions (evidenced by higher F3 values) in the same contexts.

DeJong and Zsiga suggest an articulatory explanation for this finding: /r/ and coronals, especially /l/, have incompatible tongue shapes. The articulation of /r/ requires the tongue body to be high and "bunched" in the uvular region. The articulation of /l/, on the other hand, in order to implement the lowering of the sides of the tongue necessary for a lateral, requires the tongue body to be stretched back and down toward the pharynx. This backward and downward movement of the tongue body also colors the preceding vowel, resulting in a "dark /l/" (Sproat and Fujimura 1993). Other coronals require this tongue body position to a lesser extent.

Thus /r/ requires a high bunched tongue body, /l/ a low stretched tongue body, and the tongue cannot be in two places at once. In general, the upcoming articulation receives the greater weight in conflicts of this sort in English: Assimilation is regressive, so that sounds affect the ones that precede them. DeJong and Zsiga conclude that the /l/ obscures the /r/, exerting pressure on the speaker to drop or weaken /r/'s in this context.

English palatalization. Another example of gestural overlap in phonological processes is seen in postlexical palatalization in General American English. Palatalization between words (as in *miss you, bless you,* or *this shop*) differs from palatalization within words (as in *confess/confession* or *press/pressure*). The change from /s/ to /ʃ/ in lexically-derived words such as *pressure* is complete and categorical. Palatalization between words, however, is gradient and variable. Catford (1977), Zue and Shattuck-Huffnagel (1980) and Hulst and Nolan (in press) have demonstrated gradience and variability in /s#ʃ/ sequences; Zsiga (1993, in press) shows the same result for /s#ʃ/ sequences.

Compare the two spectrograms in Figure 1. At the left of the figure is a spectrogram of a native American English speaker' s pronunciation of the phrase *pressure point*. The fricative noise for /ʃ/ is fairly low-pitched (most intense around 3400 Hz) and remains steady throughout the fricative. At the right of the figure is a spectrogram of the same speaker saying the phrase *press your point*. Note the very different pattern of frication: The fricative noise begins much higher (around 5500 Hz), but falls over the course of the fricative, into the /ʃ/ range. The patterns in Figure 1 are typical of those found by Zsiga (in press) and by Hulst and Nolan (in press). Both of these studies also found

Figure 1. Left: Spectrogram of an American English speaker's pronunciation of the phrase *pressure point*. **Right:** Spectrogram of the same speaker's pronunciation of the phrase *press your point*.

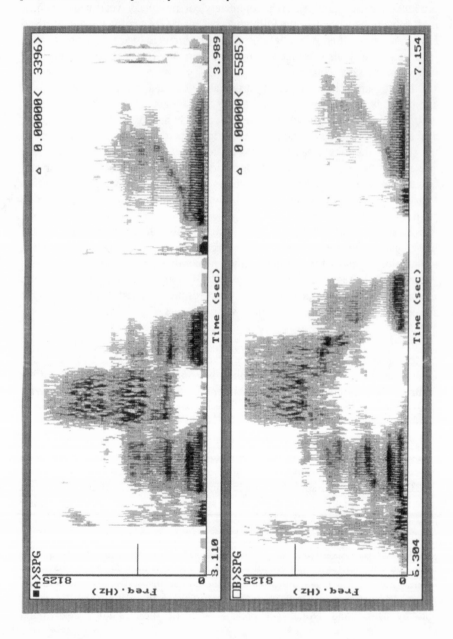

variation from token to token and from speaker to speaker in the degree to which an /s#j/ or /s#ʃ/ sequence looked like an /s/, an /ʃ/, or something in between.

Zsiga (1993, in press) argues, based on electropalatographic evidence, that the variable and gradient assimilation seen in phrases like *press your point* is due to varying degrees of articulatory overlap between the /s/ and /j/ articulations. The study begins by establishing patterns of palate contact for underlying /s/, /ʃ/, and /j/ between vowels, based on the pattern of electrodes activated in the artificial palate (see Zsiga 1993 for details). The articulation of /s/ is character- ized by contact furthest forward on the alveolar ridge, while /j/ has the most contact toward the back and center of the palate. The articulation for /ʃ/ is inter- mediate between these two, showing neither front nor central contact. These typical patterns of contact are then used to form "templates" for each articula- tion. The articulatory target for a consonant can be said to be reached when all or most of the electrodes that constitute its template are activated. Once the tem- plate patterns are established, the degree of overlap between articulations can be studied by examining how contact in the template regions changes over time.

Figure 2A shows the pattern of palate contact in a lexically-derived /ʃ/, as matched to the /s/, /ʃ/, and /j/ templates (data from Zsiga 1993). The graph shows the percentage of each template that is filled over time. (One frame, or

Figure 2A. Percentage of /s/, /ʃ/, and /j/ templates filled over time in the articulation of lexically-derived /ʃ/

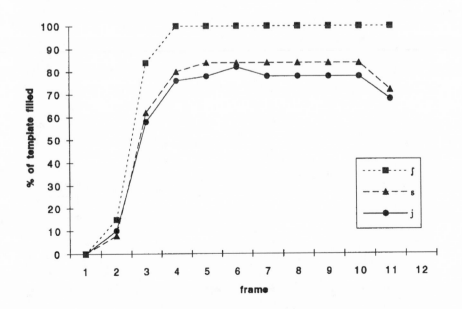

one "picture" of palate contact, occurs every 15.6 ms.) Consider first the /ʃ/ template (dotted line). As the constriction is formed, more and more of the template fills up. The /ʃ/ template is 100% filled as the articulation reaches and maintains its target position. (Because /ʃ/ has less extensive contact than either /s/ or /j/, and because the templates share many electrodes, the /s/ and /j/ templates, shown by dashed and solid lines, are as much as 80% filled as well.) The facts that 100% of the /ʃ/ template is filled and that the constriction is maintained in a steady state show that lexically derived /ʃ/ has the same pattern of contact as the underlying template /ʃ/.

Compare this to the pattern in Figure 2B, which shows the pattern of palate contact in a /s#j/ sequence. Unlike that in Figure 2A, the pattern here is not a steady state, but two overlapping articulations. The alveolar constriction for /s/ (dashed line) is made first. The target constriction for /j/ (solid line) is reached only 30 ms later. During most of the /j/ articulation, the template for /s/ remains at least 90% filled. This pattern of articulatory overlap is consistent with the acoustic patterns found in these sequences. The fricative starts out like /s/. However, as palatal contact for /j/ increases, the fricative noise falls in pitch.

Figure 2B. Percentage of /s/ and /j/ templates filled over time in the articulation of an /s#j/ sequence

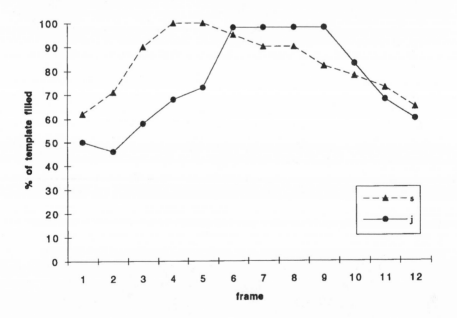

At the point in time when the /s#j/ sequence sounds /ʃ/-like, electropalatographic data show an /s/ and /j/ being made at the same time.[2]

The conclusion argued for at more length in Zsiga (1993, in press) is that postlexical palatalization in English is best accounted for in terms of gestural overlap, rather than in terms of a phonological rule that manipulates features. The acoustic and articulatory differences between lexical and postlexical palatalization show that the /s/ in an /s#j/ sequence is not changed into an /ʃ/ by the operation of a phonological rule. Rather, the data suggest that the acoustic changes come about as a result of the normal overlap between adjacent consonant gestures.

Interestingly, preliminary research shows that there is a tendency for this pattern of palatalization to be transferred to Russian by English speakers learning Russian as a second language.

Russian palatalization. Russian makes an underlying contrast between palatalized (soft) and nonpalatalized (hard) consonants. The pronunciation of the "soft" consonants poses a difficult problem for learners of Russian and their teachers. English speakers apparently have a hard time learning to make the secondary palatal constriction and the primary consonant constriction, such as a dental constriction for /s/, at the same time. Rather, English speakers tend to produce too much of an "off-glide." They have the greatest problems with word-final palatalized consonants, for which no off-glide can be made.

Figure 3 (left) shows a spectrogram of the utterance [vasʲa], a Russian name, produced by an English-speaking student in her second semester of studying Russian. This is the same English speaker whose spectrograms are seen in Figure 1. Note the similarity to the /s#j/ sequence she produced when speaking English. The fricative noise starts out high but falls in pitch towards the end. There is a prominent off-glide from the fricative to the second vowel.

Figure 3 (right) shows a spectrogram of the same utterance produced by a native speaker of Russian. In this utterance, the fricative noise remains steady and high-pitched. In addition, a clear difference in the vowels can be seen. For the English speaker, palatalization produces a /j/-like off-glide in the following vowel. For the Russian speaker, however, palatalization affects the *preceding* vowel, creating an on-glide. The following vowel is also affected, but to a much lesser extent than for the English speaker.

---

[2] Hulst and Nolan (in press), who examined only acoustic data, argue that the gradient and variable patterns they found in /s#/ sequences could not be due to changes in articulatory overlap, because in some cases assimilation of /s/ to /ʃ/ appeared to be complete. The data presented here shows, however, that even when the acoustic result is /ʃ/-like, the articulation may not be.

Figure 3. Left: Spectrogram of the Russian name [vasʲa] as pronounced by a native English speaker learning Russian. **Right:** Spectrogram of [vasʲa] as pronounced by a native Russian speaker.

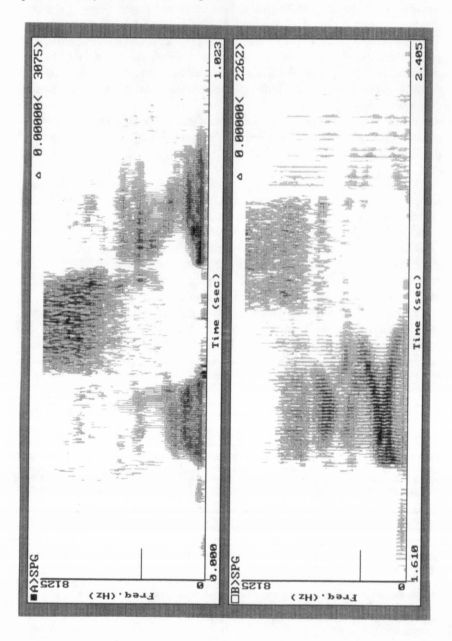

These spectrograms show that the native Russian speaker employs a very different timing pattern than the native English speaker uses, making the palatal constriction much earlier with respect to the primary dental constriction. It is this timing pattern that the English speaker finds so hard to learn. In speaking Russian, she continues to use the pattern of overlap typical of her native language.

Conclusion. Postlexical processes may often simply be a result of timing patterns, what Browman and Goldstein (1986, 1990, 1992) call "gestural over-lap." This paper has marshaled evidence that three different processes in English that have in the past been described by phonological rules can in fact be seen to follow from the generalization that consonant sequences in English overlap in time:

- "deletion" of final alveolars,
- /r/ "dropping", and
- palatalization between words.

The timing facts about consonant overlap must be stated independently to account for the "phonetic" fact that consonants in clusters are unreleased. The data presented here show that these "phonetic" timing facts can have important perceptual consequences.

We know, because we know about foreign accents, that the rules and constraints that determine the timing of speech gestures vary from language to language, and that learners readily transfer the timing rules of their native language to a second language. The spectrograms in Figure 3 support the conclusion that English speakers use an articulatory organization typical of English in producing Russian palatalized consonants. If postlexical rules can also be analyzed as the result of the timing patterns, as has been argued here, it should come as no surprise that postlexical rules will also transfer to a second language. A clearer understanding of the different kinds of sound patterns in phonology and phonetics leads to a clearer understanding of the patterns of transfer in second-language acquisition.

REFERENCES

Barry, Martin C. 1985. "A palatographic study of connected speech processes." *Cambridge Papers in Phonetics and Experimental Linguistics* 4: 1–16.

Barry, Martin C. 1991. "Temporal modelling of gestures in articulatory assimilation." *Proceedings of the XIIth International Congress of Phonetic Sciences* 4: 14–17.

Byrd, Dani. 1994. "Articulatory timing in English consonant sequences." *UCLA Working Papers in Phonetics* 86.

Browman, Catherine and Louis Goldstein. 1986. "Towards an articulatory phonology." *Phonology Yearbook* 3: 219-252.

Browman, Catherine and Louis Goldstein. 1990. "Tiers in articulatory phonology, with some implications for casual speech." In John Kingston and Mary E. Beckman (eds.), *Papers in laboratory phonology 1: Between the grammar and physics of speech.* Cambridge, U.K.: Cambridge University Press. 341-376.

Browman, Catherine and Louis Goldstein. 1992. "Articulatory phonology: An overview." *Phonetica* 49: 155-180.

Catford, J. C. 1977. *Fundamental problems in phonetics.* Bloomington, Indiana: Indiana University Press.

Cohn, Abigail C. 1990. "Phonetic and phonological rules of nasalization." *UCLA Working Papers in Phonetics* 76.

Cooper, Andre. 1991. "An articulatory account of aspiration in English." Unpublished Ph.D. dissertation. Yale University.

DeJong, Kenneth J. and Elizabeth C. Zsiga. 1995. "A connection between coarticulation and variable rule application: Coda r's in Brooklyn English." Presented at the 127th meeting of the Acoustical Society of America, Washington, D.C.

Guy, Gregory. 1980. "Variation in the group and in the individual: The case of final stop deletion." In William Labov (ed.), *Locating language in time and space.* New York: Academic Press. 1-36.

Harcastle, W.J. 1985. "Some phonetic and syntactic constraints on lingual coarticulation during /kl/ sequences." *Speech Communication* 4: 247-263.

Hardcastle, W.J. and P.J. Roach. 1979. "An instrumental investigation of coarticualtion in stop consonant sequences." In P. Hollien and H. Hollien (eds.), *Current issues in the phonetic sciences.* Amsterdam: John Benjamins. 531-540.

Hertz, Susan R., Elizabeth C. Zsiga, Kenneth J. DeJong, and Katherine. E. Lockwood. (in press). "From database to speech: A multi-dialect relational database integrated with the Eloquence synthesis technology." *Proceedings of the Second Workshop on Speech Synthesis.* European Speech Communication Association and the Institute of Electrical and Electronics Engineers.

Hulst, Tara and Francis Nolan. (in press). To appear in *Papers in Laboratory Phonology IV.*

Jones, Daniel and Dennis Ward. 1969. *The Phonetics of Russian.* Cambridge, U.K.: Cambridge University Press.

Keating, Patricia. 1988. "The phonology-phonetics interface." In Frederick J. Newmayer (ed.), *Linguistics: The Cambridge survey. Volume 1: Linguistic theory: Foundations.* Cambridge, U.K.: Cambridge University Press. 281-302.

Kiparsky, Paul. 1985. "Some consequences of Lexical Phonology." *Phonology Yearbook* 2: 85-138.

Marchal, Alain. 1988. "Coproduction: Evidence from EPG data." *Speech Communication* 7: 287-295.

Nolan, Francis. "The descriptive role of segments: Evidence from assimilation." In G. Docherty and Robert Ladd (eds.), *Papers in laboratory phonology II.* Cambridge, U.K.: Cambridge University Press. 261-280.

Perkell, Joseph. 1969. *Physiology of speech production: Results and implications of a quantitative cineradiographic study.* Cambridge, Massachusetts: MIT Press.

Reenen, Pieter van. 1982. *Phonetic feature definitions: Their integration into phonology and their relation to speech, a case study of the feature nasal.* Dordrecht, Germany: Foris.

Sproat, R. and O. Fujimura. 1993. "Allophonic variation in English /l/ and its implications for phonetic implementation." *Journal of Phonetics* 21: 291-311.

Weinberger, Steven. 1994. "The faster the better: On the L2 transfer of fast speech processes." Talk presented to the Washington Linguistics Society, Georgetown University, Washington, D.C., December 1994.

Zsiga, Elizabeth C. 1993. "Features, gestures, and the temporal aspects of phonological organization." Unpublished Ph.D. dissertation, Yale University.

Zsiga, Elizabeth C. 1994. "Acoustic evidence for gestural overlap in consonant sequences." *Journal of Phonetics* 22: 121–140.

Zsiga, Elizabeth C. (in press). "An acoustic and electropalatographic study of palatalization in American English." To appear in *Papers in laboratory phonology IV.*

Zue, Victor, and Stephanie Shattuck-Huffnagel. 1980. "Palatalization of /s/ in American English: When is a /ʃ/ not a /ʃ/?" *Journal of the Acoustical Society of America* 67: S27.

Knowledge, language, and communication

Kenneth Chastain
University of Virginia

Introduction. A valid theory of second-language learning evolves logically from learning models to linguistics, to applied linguistics, to second-language learning and teaching. A solid comprehension of each is dependent upon a thorough understanding of the preceding component in the sequence. Well-prepared second-language teachers are well informed in all four areas.

In this paper I plan to focus primarily on one particular aspect of language and language learning, the traditional parts of speech and their role in second-language learning. However, I trust that the relationship of the ideas to learning theory will be understandable and that the implications for other aspects of second-language teaching will be clear.

The topics are as follows:

- Knowledge—How do we learn? What do we know?
- Language—What is language? What is the relationship between knowledge and language? What are the rules governing the use of language? What is the purpose of language? What are the relationships among knowledge, language, and communication?
- The communication process—What happens during the communication process? What is the sequence?
- The traditional parts of speech—What are they? What do they mean? What role does an understanding of them play in helping students comprehend language as a communication system? What role does an understanding of them play in helping students develop communication skills?
- A communicative definition of the parts of speech—From a communicative point of view, what parts of speech are necessary for communication?
- Implications for second-language teaching—What should second-language teachers know? How can they incorporate this knowledge into their teaching?

These topics lead to one thesis and one question:

Thesis: Most students do not comprehend these long-used grammatical terms and do not comprehend the role of the parts of speech in communication.

Question: Would it be possible to present the concept of parts of speech so as to enhance comprehension and usefulness for second-language learning?

Knowledge. The brain becomes activated before birth. Hardwired to comprehend its life space, it serves from that time forth as an information processor. Constantly being fed data through the five senses, it strives to perceive the salient aspects of its surroundings, to comprehend them, to organize them into meaningful units, and to store them in clusters of related material.

As a result of this constant cognitive activity, the brain's network of interrelated information continues to grow and expand throughout one's life. As we mature and as the number of experiences that we have had accumulate, so, too, does the amount of information that we possess. Taken together, all this mental material constitutes our world knowledge.

Of course, each individual's cognitive network is different from that of any other person. This uniqueness is due primarily to four factors. First, our brains have different capacities and abilities. Second, we have different experiences as we participate in our environment. Third, we interact with that environment in different ways either through personal choice or because of different opportunities. Fourth, we interpret the received data from the environment in different ways.

Language. Language consists of world knowledge, linguistic rules, and communication skills. By definition, speakers of a language have the knowledge, the rules, and the skills needed to exchange information with other speakers. In other words they know the vocabulary, i.e. the words that they need to talk about aspects of their world. They also know the language rules, i.e. the morphology, the syntax, the pragmatics, and the discourse rules that enable them to use the appropriate form of a word, to put words in the proper order, to employ the words, phrases, and sentences with the meaning appropriate to the situation, and to place them properly within a discourse. They also have the skill to participate in this fast-paced creation-recreation sequence both as producers and receivers with remarkable speed and accuracy.

The process of communication. Obviously, communication involves the transfer of information from producers to receivers. Producers possess a knowledge of their world and language. They activate their language to create a message that they believe will convey some particular mental image of their world knowledge to some specific receiver or group of receivers. This is the productive phase of communication. Receivers utilize their world knowledge and their language knowledge to recreate messages sent to them by producers. This is the receptive phase of communication.

Given the fact that the cognitive networks of producers and receivers are never identical, the message that the receivers recreate will often not be exactly the same as the mental image being transmitted by the producers. However, in most cases the resemblance of the recreated message is close enough to that of the created message to complete the communication satisfactorily. When receivers are unable to recreate the message, they must request additional information in order to ensure comprehension.

To a great extent communication depends upon the degree of congruence between the world knowledge of producers and receivers. When the past experience, i.e. world knowledge, of both is relatively similar, communication requires fewer words to convey the mental image because receivers need only a minimum of language clues to recreate the mental image of the producers. However, as the world knowledge of the participants in the communication becomes increasingly less similar the producers must supply more information, i.e. language, in their communication.

Communication has a motive and a purpose. The motive commences with some emotion or some thought that causes the producer to create a message. The purpose is to satisfy the desire that stimulated the message. For example, Maria is hungry: She asks for a peanut butter and jelly sandwich. The hunger is the motive for the message. Obtaining the sandwich is the purpose of her communication. Her hunger arouses the image of the sandwich in her mind. Getting the sandwich becomes her goal, and she creates a message to send to someone capable of satisfying her desire. That receiver has to use the language of her message to recreate her mental image in order to be able to satisfy her request.

The traditional parts of speech. As all second-language teachers know, and as many students seem not to know, the traditional parts of speech are nouns, pronouns, verbs, adjectives, adverbs, prepositions, and conjunctions. (The fact that so many students seem incapable of learning these seven words and their definitions in twelve years of school comprises one of the many mysteries of education. Perhaps their lack of comprehension reflects the violation of fundamental principles of language learning to which we should be more sensitive. In other words, perhaps there is a message in this situation for all language teachers to consider.) Names for the parts of speech also provide labels for discussing the use of words in sentences, although subcategories such as subject, direct object, indirect object, and object of preposition exist for nouns. This classification and the related definitions originated with the Greeks and Romans and has survived through the centuries with little, if any, alteration This continuity makes the task of keeping up with changes in the subject rather simple, a consoling thought to teachers who know the parts of speech and a frightening one to students who, in spite of years of persistent instruction, never seem to comprehend their meaning or their relationship to communication. Students do know that the parts of speech are important in second-language classes because teachers keep talking about them, but they are not sure what the parts of speech have to do with learning a language or using it to communicate.

Now, let us take a brief look at the traditional parts of speech, trying as we do so to consider these definitions from the point of view of your students rather than from your own perspective.

- Noun—The English word "noun" comes from the Latin word *nomen* meaning "name." Thus, a noun is a naming word. Nouns designate the things, both concrete and abstract, in the known world and, therefore, they are used by speakers to represent their world knowledge. The editors of *The American Heritage dictionary of the English language (AHD)* define a noun as "A word used to denote or name a person, place, thing, quality, or act."

- Verb—The word "verb" comes from the Latin word *verbum* meaning "word." In the *AHD*, "verb" is defined as "that part of speech that expresses existence, action, or occurrence."

- Pronoun—The *AHD*'s definition for pronoun is "One of a class of words that function as substitutes for nouns or noun phrases and denote persons or things asked for, previously specified, or understood from context." The word comes from the Latin word *pronomen*, derived from *pro* meaning "in the place of" and *nomen* meaning "name."

- Adjective—The term "adjective" comes from the Latin word *adjectivus* ("attributive") from *adjectus* ("attributed"), the past participle of *adjicere* ("to throw, to add"). *Adjicere*, in turn, is derived from *ad* ("to") plus *jacere* ("to throw"). Thus an adjective is a word that supplies additional information about a noun, i.e. it adds to the number of attributes given by the producer of the message to the receiver.

- Adverb—The term "adverb" comes from the Latin word *adverbum*, which was a translation of the Greek word *epirrhema*. The word "adverb" literally means "added word." That is, the speaker adds another word, or other words, to the verb.

- Preposition—The term "preposition" comes from a Latin translation of the Greek word *prothesis* meaning "to place in front of." Therefore, a preposition is literally a word placed in front of a another word, in this case a noun.

- Conjunction—The term "conjunction" has its origin in the Latin verb *conjungere* meaning "to join together." Literally, a conjunction joins two equal parts of a communication together.

Let us return to the questions that I outlined earlier. What role do these definitions have in helping students understand language as a communication system? What role do they have in helping students develop communication skills? Experience indicates caution in ascribing a major role for knowledge of parts of speech in second-language learning.

A communicative, comprehensible definition of the parts of speech. My belief is that students do not understand the parts of speech, and my supposition is that we can provide them with new definitions that give them a clearer understanding of the meaning, the function, and the use of each from a communicative point of view. Being able to regurgitate the definition that a "noun" is the name of a person, place, or thing does not place a great burden on anyone's cognitive capabilities. However, being able to apply that definition in order to identify nouns in a sentence and to explain their meaning, function, and use in communication does seem to perplex many learners.

Let us try to imagine a situation in which all the components of a communication are present except language. There are at least two participants. One is motivated to seek some specific goal, and the other is willing to attend to the resultant request. That is, two speakers are in a situation in which one is to be the producer of a message and the other a receiver. What parts of speech will they need in order to create and to recreate a comprehensible message? What meanings, functions, and uses must these parts of speech have in order to provide the basis of language? In other words, what types of words would they have to generate in order to communicate?

First, based on their perception of their life space, the speakers have some knowledge of their world. They see a world filled with things both concrete and abstract. They see a world in which these things do something.

Thus, their first need in order to communicate about their world is for *naming words*. They must have names for the things that they perceive in order to communicate about them. [1] These naming words are of two types: names for things, which we have traditionally labeled "nouns" and names for what the things do, which we have commonly called "verbs."

By combining naming words, speakers have the ability to talk about generalities in their world. For example, "birds fly" and "babies cry."

Second, since they often need to communicate about specific instances of the generalities, they must create a language that includes *specifiers* as well as naming words. With specifiers the speakers can identify a certain group or a specific one as well as the whole. They can use specifiers with both types of naming words. By utilizing words such as "those" or "most," they help the receiver to understand to which "birds" or "babies" they are referring. The same is true with regard to the naming word for what the "birds" and "babies" do. Birds can fly "slowly" or "fast," and babies can cry "loudly" or

---

[1] That is, if they want to communicate their mental images to another speaker. They do not have the words to think, i.e. to manipulate those images mentally.

"constantly." In either case the use of the specifier reduces the referential potential of the naming word, thus allowing the receiver to recognize the exact individual or group and the exact type of "doing" that the producer has in mind.

Speakers may also use phrases and clauses in the same way. For example, the phrase "on the lake" and "in the nursery" make even clearer to which "birds" and to which "babies" the speaker is referring. In cases in which the receiver is less familiar with the "birds" and "babies" under consideration, the speaker may add a clause such as "that arrived this morning" to further specify them.

Third, since speakers often want to describe a scene containing a number of naming words and specifiers, they must have a system for indicating the relationship among the words. The part of speech typically utilized to express this meaning and to fulfill this function is the *relator*. Relator words indicate relationships among words in a communication. In the previous examples, the words "on" in the phrase "on the lake" and "in" in the phrase "in the nursery" show the relationship between "lake" and "birds" and between "nursery" and "babies". The word "that" performs a similar function in the clause "that arrived this morning" relating the idea expressed in the clause to the naming words "birds" and "babies". [2] Phrases such as "near the lake" and clauses such as "when they are hungry" perform the same function for the naming words "fly" and "cry". That is, they specify where and when with regard to what the things named in the communication do.

Fourth, in order to avoid unnecessary repetition in contexts in which the antecedent of the referent is clearly understood by the receiver, the producer may utilize a substitute rather than repeat the naming word. These *substitutes* are not absolutely necessary for communication, but they allow speakers to make a more efficient use of language and to be less boring. For example, in the discourse "Elizabeth arrived last night. She is still sleeping this morning. Mom is taking her to the dentist at ten o'clock." the repetition of "Elizabeth" is unnecessary and undesirable. The words "she" and "her" convey the same meaning just as effectively and more efficiently.

In summary, in order to communicate with each other, speakers need naming words to describe the generalities of their world, and they need specifiers to talk about specific instances of those generalities. In addition, they need relators to indicate relationships among the words, the phrases, and the clauses contained in their communications. Finally, they regularly utilize substitutes rather than repeat *ad nauseam* naming words that recur in the communicative discourse.

---

[2] Of course, "that" also serves as the subject of the clause.

Implications for second-language teaching. One of the major complaints heard repeatedly at second-language professional meetings is that students do not know the grammar. The implication is that they do not know the grammar of their own language, which by definition is not true. The reality is that many do not know the definitions of the grammatical terminology nor the practical applications of the traditional parts of speech. Surely, if they do not know the parts of speech, their definition, nor their use, they cannot utilize their knowledge of the parts of speech to assist them in learning second-language rules or in developing communication skills.

Second-language teachers can take two steps to alleviate this acknowledged problem. First, they can develop a new communicatively-oriented system of terminology for the parts of speech that describes the language used in communication. Second, they can present and practice language use only in a communicative context. In my opinion, implementing only those two changes would radically alter what students know about language and what they are able to do with what they know.

Conclusions. The purpose of language is communication. Communication involves meaning, function, and use. [3] Based on my experience with students, I believe that presenting the traditional parts of speech in the traditional manner, i.e. with abstract definitions and noncontextual examples, is not an effective means of helping students to understand how the parts of language function as a mediator between the producers who create messages and the receivers who recreate those messages.

My feeling is that second-language educators can develop a description of the parts of speech that is easier to understand and easier to relate to communication. It seems clear to me that any useful approach must include a focus on meaning, function, and use in communicative contexts in order for students to understand the role that words play in communication and to utilize that knowledge to assist them in language learning. The four parts of speech that I have described are one possibility. The task facing us is to experiment until we find a system that is more comprehensible and useful to students.

---

[3] The form of the words is also a factor in communication. However, form is not a consideration in this paper.

REFERENCES

The American Heritage dictionary of the English language, First edition. 1969. New York: American Heritage Publishing Co., Inc.

Complexity, linguistics, and language teaching

Jeff Connor-Linton
Georgetown University

Introduction. The science of complexity is succeeding chaos theory as an important heuristic in many fields—from physics to economics to biology to artificial intelligence. Because complexity research addresses questions that breach traditional disciplinary boundaries, complexity has not yet been formally defined. But what all complexity research seems to share is a focus on *complex*, *adaptive*, *dynamic* systems in which many independent agents interact in many ways. The independent agents in complex systems undergo apparently spontaneous self-organization through which individuals and groups of individuals acquire collective properties they would never have acquired individually. This emerging definition is enough to prompt consideration of how (at least metaphorically) languages, speech communities, and language classrooms might be understood as complex systems.

In this paper, I want to draw linguists' attention to a relatively new scientific approach which has proven dramatically revealing and explanatory of a wide range of "systems" across a variety of scientific disciplines. My goal is not to construct a new theory of "linguistic complexity," but to suggest the potential value of the construct of complexity—either as a heuristic or in its more particular modeling capacity—for a number of questions in linguistics and language teaching.

I must state at the outset that I am no expert on complexity. About a year ago, I discovered the popular literature on complexity research (through Waldrop 1992). Many aspects of what complexity researchers were finding in physics, economics, biology, and artificial intelligence seemed to offer a new way of looking at language. In fact, I was surprised that the notion of complexity has apparently not been applied to language.[1] I wanted to share the excitement of my discovery with other linguists (and learn of other linguists interested in complexity), and remembered a paper given by Roger Bowers at the 1990 Round Table, in which Bowers raised a number of questions that chaos theory might raise for language teaching and learning. I found Bowers' paper very provocative and decided to adapt his model. In what follows I've taken

---

[1]After I presented this paper, several linguists in the audience informed me that they were working with the notion of complexity.

parts of Waldrop's description and examples of complexity as my "text" and interpolated, in brackets, possible connections to linguistics and language teaching. (Page references below are to Waldrop 1992, unless otherwise attributed.)

Complexity. The central question asked in research on complexity is, Why do ecological, social, economic, biological, and subatomic systems which are apparently stable for relatively long periods of time, seem to suddenly and radically change? Think of the sudden collapse of the Soviet Union, the October 1987 stock market crash, and the beginning of life on earth four billion years ago. [Think of first language acquisition and language change.] This question actually has two sides. First, why do systems which are demonstrably capable of change remain stable so often for so long? And second, why do they change when they do?

To answer these questions, researchers have noted four characteristics of these kinds of systems. First, they are complex, with "a great many independent agents ... interacting with each other in a great many ways. Think of the quadrillions of chemically reacting proteins, lipids, and nucleic acids that make up a living cell, or the billions of interconnected neurons that make up the brain, or the millions of mutually interdependent individuals who make up a human society" (p.11). [Think of the individual members of a speech community, or the interdependent components of a language or a sound system.] In complex systems, each agent "finds itself in an environment produced by its interactions with the other agents in the system. It is constantly acting and reacting to what the other agents are doing. And because of that, essentially nothing in its environment is fixed" (p.145). [What allow these agents to be reactive are their structural properties: energy valences in atoms, chemical valences in molecules, electrical valences (mediated by chemical valences) in brain cells. So, two questions for linguists are: If language is a complex system, what are its agents? Parts of speech? Principles and parameters? Co-occurring sets of functionally-related discourse features? Each of these at different levels of organization? And what are the principles of valence of these "language agents"? It might be easier to conceive of these kinds of complex relationships and changes at the level of language *use*—within speech communities, for example—but research on other complex systems shows that if we find complexity at one level of organization within the system, we tend to find it at other levels of organization as well.]

The second characteristic of complex systems is that "the very richness of these interactions allows the system as a whole to undergo *spontaneous self-organization*. Thus people trying to satisfy their material needs unconsciously organize themselves into an economy through myriad individual acts of buying and selling; it happens without anyone being in charge or consciously planning it ..." (p.11). [Do people trying to satisfy *communicative or social* needs unconsciously organize themselves into speech communities through myriad individual acts of speaking and listening?] "Organisms constantly adapt to each other through evolution, thereby organizing themselves into an exquisitely tuned ecosystem" (p.11). [Think of language change and how, for example, a change in the realization of one phoneme can ultimately reorder the sound system.] "In every case, groups of agents seeking mutual accommodation and self-consistency somehow manage to transcend themselves, acquiring collective properties ... that they might never have possessed individually" (p.11). [Think of Sapir (1925) and Jakobson and Halle (1956) and sets of features in language, where no one feature exists alone, and each feature has significance only through its relations to the other members of the set.] Complex systems undergo spontaneous self-organization because they have "many levels of organization, with agents at any one level serving as the building blocks for agents at a higher level" (p.145). [Think of phonemes, morphemes, words, phrases and sentences; think of phonology, morphology, syntax, semantics, and pragmatics; think of the communicative competence of individual speakers, the communicative norms of a speech community, and culture.]

The third characteristic is that "these complex, self-organizing systems are *adaptive*, in that they don't just passively respond to events ... [but] actively try to turn whatever happens to their advantage. Thus, the human brain constantly organizes and reorganizes billions of neural connections so as to learn ... Species evolve for better survival in a changing environment—and so do corporations and industries" (p.11). [Certainly speech communities are as adaptive as corporations and industries, and the adaptive capabilities of the brain suggest that language itself—or at least some of its component subsystems—may be adaptive as well.] Complex systems "are constantly revising and rearranging their building blocks as they gain experience" (p.146). [At the most apparently fundamental levels of language, this change and learning process seems relatively slow, but so is genetic evolution, and Labov's work on vowel-system change in Chicago demonstrates a real-time process.]

The fourth characteristic of complex systems is that they "have somehow acquired the ability to bring order and chaos into a special kind of balance ... where the components of the system never quite lock into place, and yet never quite dissolve into turbulence, either" (p.12). [Language—and patterns of language use—are certainly dynamic, not static, systems, although we may have to take a long-term historical perspective to see dynamism and change—not only in genetic evolution but in language change as well. Think of whatever is more static in language (Universal Grammar, for example) as part of the force that constrains language change, while language's interface with other social systems (which are themselves changing) provides the "chaotic" force for change.]

New analogies, new perspectives. The "discovery" of complex systems, as just described, co-occurred with a shift of emphasis in scientific research—

from dissecting things into their simplest pieces to trying to understand how those pieces fit together and make a whole that is more than the sum of its parts. The "discovery" of complexity suggests a new approach to science. For several hundred years, scientific inquiry has sought to simplify phenomena; it focussed on particles, predictability and regularity, and conceived of rules as explanations for why things seem to stay the same for so long. The alternative scientific approach suggested by complexity conceives of rules as explanations of processes of change, the forming and dissolving of patterns, and the interrelatedness of phenomena.

We might make a fairly strong argument that linguistics has been participating in this shift, with the generative "revolution" over structuralism in formal theory and complementary advances in sociolinguistics and discourse analysis. Let me offer a few examples of this shift in other disciplines and suggest some ways in which this new perspective may be relevant to linguistics.

Genetic circuits and register shift? In the 1960s, biologists François Jacob and Jacques Monod discovered that a very few genes in a DNA molecule function as switches. If one of these gene switches is turned on (by exposing the cell to a particular hormone, for example), it will send out a chemical signal that will turn some gene switches in the DNA molecule on and others off. These genes then send out their own chemical signals (or stop sending their signals), and more gene switches are flipped "in a mounting cascade, until the cell's collection of genes *settle down into a new and stable pattern*" (p.31; my emphasis).

Could this be a model, by analogy, of register or style shifting? Consider the factors or co-occurring sets of features which Biber (1989) identifies as the stable patterns within discourse. How do speakers negotiate the change from one pattern or register to another? Some finite perception about the context prompts a small shift in one speaker's use of language, which then calls attention to the perceived aspect of context and triggers changes in the other speaker's use of language. Some of these changes may be congruent with the first speaker's changes and some may be different—amplifying or contesting the direction of change. The first speaker then responds to the second speaker's verbally manifested "analysis" of the new context—and so on until the speakers negotiate and identify a new stable register (and construction of the context). The empirical test of this "hypothesis" would be to identify the linkages between aspects of context and "first trigger" linguistic features, and then trace the "mounting cascade" of changed features. We might try this semi-experimentally, introducing new contextual cues into an interaction, or analyze naturalistic data from a historical, regressive perspective, taking a stretch of discourse that displays register shift and then working backwards, identifying (perhaps statistically, by frequency of use) the stages of shift, increasingly narrowing the focus as we move to the initial stages of the shift.

Jacob and Monod's research on genetic circuitry—as well as more recent complexity research on neural networks—shows that agents (e.g. genes) are typically reactive to between two and ten other agents. The interaction effects of such a system, while certainly more complex than most current linguistic research designs, are finite and modelable by computer. Stuart Kauffman's modelling of networks of two-state (on–off) agents (Kauffman 1992) shows that some sort of order is inherent in any network of dependency relationships. For example, a network of two light bulbs randomly affecting each other can have two-times-two states: on–on, on–off, off–on, and off–off. Kauffman's first computer model was a network of one hundred agents, with one million trillion trillion possible states, an immense universe of possibilities. (It would take billions of times the history of the universe for the network to cycle through all possible states just once at one state per microsecond.) But *within a few minutes*, the network settled down into a small series of orderly states; that is, in spite of the randomness of each agent's effect on another agent, the system quickly became stable because of the limited number of connections between agents and the nature of dependency networks. Kauffman calculated that the number of states in the stable series of states scales roughly as the square root of the number of agents in the network. Not coincidentally, the number of cell types (stable cellular states) in an organism is about the square root of the number of genes which the organism has. So, what are the "genes" of language? What are the "cell types" of language? Kauffman's research suggests that life started on earth because of an autocatalytic set of molecules. Is this a metaphor for how—neurally and socially—language began?

Jacob and Monod's discovery of genetic circuitry means that "the DNA residing in a cell's nucleus was not just a blueprint for a cell ... [but] actually the foreman in charge of construction ... a kind of molecular-scale computer that directed how the cell was to build itself and repair itself and interact with the outside world" (p.31). Are we thinking of Universal Grammar as a blueprint or as a computer?

The central premise of generative linguistic theory is that we must posit some underlying structure to account for how a child so quickly and efficiently acquires her native language in an environment of inaccurate and incomplete input. Consider an alternative metaphor: John Holland's research on adaptation (Holland 1975) has demonstrated that a complex system that uses natural selection and recombination of competing and cooperating hypotheses about input is a very efficient solution to immensely complicated problems. In fact, Holland's models show that systems starting out with random bits of information can organize themselves into complex wholes.

Holland, Holyoak, Nisbett, and Thagard (1986), drawing from research on complex systems, propose a general cognitive theory of learning, reasoning, and intellectual discovery based on induction. They propose three basic principles of how complex systems (including human beings) learn:

(1) Knowledge can be expressed in terms of mental structures that behave very much like rules;
(2) these rules are in competition, so that experience causes useful rules to grow stronger and unhelpful rules to grow weaker; and
(3) all plausible new rules are generated from combinations of old rules.

The first principle is very familiar to linguists, but the last two less so. In the generative paradigm, we're seeking fixed rules; there's no competition of rules, no learning from experience, and no generation of new rules from combinations of old rules. By analogy to other complex systems, could it be that Universal Grammar is not a blueprint contemporaneously constraining the possible sentences of a fully-developed linguistic competence, but an emergent system in which rules compete with each other throughout childhood and recombine to create mature linguistic competence?

Self-organization and language learning. Complex systems seem to defy (or at least subvert) entropy, the second law of thermodynamics; that left to themselves, atoms will mix and randomize themselves as much as possible, or decay. Complex systems are characterized by the growth of structures more than decay. How can this be so? Prigogine (1980) points out that the answer lies (as it so often does) in our assumptions; in the real world, atoms (and more generally, agents in complex systems) are almost never left to themselves, are almost always exposed to energy and material flowing in from outside. This input is the fuel for the self-organization of the system.

Consider a pot of soup. Left alone, it will obey the second law of thermodynamics and sit at room temperature, in equilibrium with its surroundings with stable molecular movement. If a tiny gas flame is turned on under the soup, nothing will happen; the difference in heat (the input) isn't enough to disturb molecular movement in the soup. But turn the gas up, and the increased energy input turns the soup unstable. At first molecular movement is random, then some of the random motions start to grow. Some portions of the soup rise; others fall. Quickly the soup organizes its motions so that from above we can see a hexagonal pattern of convection cells, with fluid rising in the middle of each cell and falling along its sides. The soup has acquired a new level of order and structure. It achieves this self-organization because of self-reinforcement, "a tendency for small effects to become magnified when conditions are right" (p.34).

Another term for self-reinforcement is positive feedback. In complex systems—and language learning certainly seems complex—positive feedback can't help but produce changing patterns. What is self-reinforcement in language learning? Computer models of complex systems suggest that we may want to simplify input (not just make it comprehensible, but actually provide less "instruction") and provide the learner with many more opportunities to practice.

Again, I must illustrate by analogy. In 1987, Craig Reynolds presented a computer model of birds' flocking behavior at the Artificial Life Workshop at Los Alamos. He demonstrated that his computer representations of "boids" would fly together as a flock by following only three very low-level, local rules:

(1) Maintain a minimum distance from other objects in the environment, including other "boids";
(2) try to match velocities with those of other "boids" in one's neighborhood; and
(3) try to move toward the perceived center of the mass of "boids" in one's neighborhood.

No matter where the individual "boids" started at the beginning of a demonstration, these three local rules quickly got them to form a flock which could even part around a tree and then reform. The complex behavior of flocking *emerged* from the interaction of individual agents each following a simple set of very local interactive rules. Are we teaching too much and standing in the way of emergent second-language acquisition?

Machines are designed top-down; living systems *emerge* bottom-up, from a population of much simpler systems. Bottom-up models use a few simple rules of local agent-to-agent interaction that produce tendencies (not rigid "always" statements) that allow the system to adapt to changing conditions. Complexity research suggests that "the way to achieve lifelike behavior is to simulate populations of simple units instead of one big complex unit. Use local control instead of global control. Let the behavior emerge from the bottom, instead of being specified from the top down. And ... focus on ongoing behavior instead of the final result ... living systems never really settle down" (p. 280). Are our current models of language and language learning top-down, mechanical models or bottom-up, emergent models?

Both chaos theory and complexity research demonstrate that "Tiny changes in certain features can lead to remarkable changes in overall behavior" (Gleick 1988: 178), and that "Tiny differences in input can quickly become overwhelming differences in output" (Gleick 1978: 8). In language teaching, can we identify a very few local rules of interaction—perhaps at different levels of structure—teach only those and then provide an environment for learners to practice? Would the other rules (that we didn't teach students directly) emerge as they negotiated the space of possible behaviors? Couldn't this explain the superior efficiency of language immersion over classroom instruction? Of course, language teaching has been moving for some time from teacher-centered to more learner-centered approaches, but complexity research suggests that we may have a very long way to go in relinquishing control and relying more on the learners' learning abilities.

Bowers's (1990: 129) consideration of chaos theory led him to a similar point; he asked, "Can teaching be too orderly for its own good? What evidence is there that orderly teaching inhibits learning?" Most approaches to language teaching implicitly assume a relatively regular progression of learning. (And this isn't so much a result of pedagogical theory as a consequence of institutionalization.) But complex systems evolve and learn by dramatic fits and starts interspersed among periods of stasis. What's happening in a learner's mind during these periods of stasis, as the class moves on?

Consider the converse of natural languages' well-known redundancy: Each new "data bit"—whether phoneme, word, utterance, or discourse chunk—in a stream of natural language is partly constrained and predictable by the bits preceding it, so each new bit carries less and less information. Does this mean that the more input we as teachers produce, the less effective that input is? Randomizing the stream of data increases the information conveyed by each new bit. Are our efforts to order the syllabus self-defeating?

Research on complex systems shows adaptation/learning to be very similar to a game: "An agent plays against its environment, trying to win enough of what it needs to keep going ... the payoff (or lack of it) gives agents the feedback they need to improve their performance" (p. 165). In some ways this sounds a lot like our current second-language-acquisition research program, which asks questions like, What is the most effective environment or feedback for second language acquisition? But the game metaphor raises some other questions, like What is the language learner's environment, and how does she play against it? And what does the learner need to keep going, and is she receiving it from classroom feedback?

The concept of an interlanguage also resonates with another characteristic of complex systems: "Every complex adaptive system is constantly making predictions based on its various internal models of the world—its implicit assumptions about the way things are out there" (p. 146). But complexity research suggests that a learner has many interlanguage models, which are competing and recombining in response to their environment and its input.

The lack of control over learning implied in these questions sounds frightening, but consider computer science's undecidability theorem, which states that unless a computer program is utterly trivial, the fastest way to find out what it will do is to run it and see what it does, and, conversely, that natural selection, trial and error, is the only general-purpose procedure for finding a set of rules that will produce a particular complex behavior. Maybe we're constraining language learners too much—giving them too many rules and too little space for trying out possible behaviors. How would we teach if we thought of language learning as a bottom-up, emergent phenomenon?

After all, top-down approaches to language teaching haven't been terribly successful. Top-down models have cumbersome and complicated rules which are supposed to precisely guide and account for every single behavior of each agent in the system in every conceivable situation. Since this is impossible, top-down systems are always crashing on conditions that they don't know how to handle. (In fact, hasn't formal linguistic theory-building—and most experimental, positivistic science as well—made a virtue of building theories top-down, and driving them through data until they crash?) What would a bottom-up, emergent model of language look like?

Anti-conclusion. I've reserved one more characteristic of complex systems for the end of this paper because it seems the most philosophically provocative. Complex, emergent systems seem to operate on "the edge of chaos," on a fine line between stasis and randomness. Complex behavior is characterized by second-order phase transitions that take place, for example, between solid and fluid states of matter. But how do they get there? How do they keep themselves there? And what do they do there? The answer seems to be that the balance at "the edge of chaos" is optimal for "computing," for the most efficient processing of information. Darwinian natural selection encourages static systems to loosen up, and turbulent systems to become more organized; learning and evolution get a system to the edge of chaos and keep it there. Learning and evolution also seem to move agents along the edge of chaos in the direction of greater and greater complexity. It's as if complexity is the counterpart of entropy, the way in which systems grow in an environment that is simultaneously decaying.

REFERENCES

Biber, Douglas. 1989. *Variation across speech and writing*. New York: Cambridge University Press.

Bowers, Roger. 1990. "Mountains are not cones: What can we learn from chaos?" In James E. Alatis (ed.), *Georgetown University Round Table on Languages and Linguistics 1990*. Washington, D.C.: Georgetown University Press. 123-136.

Gleick, James. 1988. *Chaos: Making a new science*. London: Heinemann.

Holland, John H. 1975. *Adaptation in natural and artificial systems*. Ann Arbor, Michigan: University of Michigan Press.

Holland, John H., Keith J. Holyoak, Richard E. Nisbett, and Paul R. Thagard. 1986. *Induction: Processes of inference, learning, and discovery*. Cambridge, Massachusetts: MIT Press.

Jakobson, Roman and Morris Halle. 1956. *Fundamentals of language*. The Hague: Mouton.

Kauffman, Stuart A. 1992. *Origins of order: Self-organization and selection in evolution*. Oxford: Oxford University Press.

Prigogine, Ilya. 1980. *From being to becoming*. San Francisco: W.H. Freeman.

Sapir, Edward. 1925. "Sound patterns in English." *Language* 1: 37-51.

Waldrop, M. Mitchel. 1992. *Complexity: The emerging science at the edge of order and chaos*. New York: Simon and Schuster.

On the need to *unlearn*
in the foreign-language learning process

Kurt R. Jankowsky
Georgetown University

What we are in the process of learning—be it small or large, whether acquired within a formally structured course or in our everyday encounter with things not yet known to us—unavoidably has a very definite influence on what we have already learned, what we already know. The effect will vary considerably from instance to instance, depending upon the nature of the subject matter being learned, and the external circumstances surrounding the learning process. It will also be significantly determined, of course, by types of learning individuals, their natural talents, their special interests and inclinations, and the general state of their preparation for the specific learning encounter that is under way. Last but not least, it will be determined by the frame of mind and the emotional make-up of those individuals at any given time.

The effect will in most cases amount to one of the following:

(1) Total replacement of an item previously acquired by the item being learned;
(2) Mere addition of something new to what is already known;
(3) Substantive alteration of what has previously been learned; or
(4) Far-reaching adaptation of newly-acquired knowledge to knowledge already firmly in possession and, conversely, old knowledge to new.

The impact of such an effect will also leave traces on a scale of values, since, as I strongly believe, any process initiated, any action undertaken by a human being, has either negative or positive implications. The result might be a mere perception, transient in nature, or an instance of lasting reality; but it is unfailingly there, as it is realized by the individuals involved and perceived by the attentive observer.

Almost of necessity a third evaluative category comes into play, a neutral category. Some may feel inclined to call this "a cop-out." Some others may want to insist that certain occurrences can very well be either good or bad, important or unimportant, or neither good nor bad, neither important nor unimportant. I for one would like to opt for the "cop-out" version. However,

I would add the specification that I am firmly convinced that in numerous instances, an evaluation in positive or negative terms is not possible right away, at any given moment. I contend that it is not possible, either for the learner or for the observer, but that it will eventually present itself unmistakably, as time progresses and all ramifications have fully developed. Unfortunately, this may often occur at a point in time when remedial action will either be very difficult to accomplish or not possible at all.

Our main concern here, however, is not the general process of how we learn, but a very specific process, namely how foreign languages are learned. On the other hand, we all know very well that most of our general learning is tied to language. At the very least, we should be in a position to claim that every type of learning is dramatically facilitated by language. Hence, the obvious conclusion is that the language-learning process and the general learning experience have a great deal in common. The case of foreign-language learning is surely different, but not in ways affecting central areas. To illustrate this marginal difference, I would like to compare briefly the learning of, say, mathematical formulae or the learning of historical data with the learning of a foreign language.

Our mother tongue is—whether we are aware of it or not—the exclusive means by which we establish and enlarge our knowledge in mathematics and in history, and this enlargement of knowledge has no apparent, drastic impact on the structure of our language. We may profit language-wise, too, from our expedition into the realms of mathematics and history, but this benefit emanates from a subject matter, not from the means with which that subject matter is made accessible.

When we embark on acquiring a foreign language—or enlarging our knowledge of it—we also deal with a subject matter, yet never—as we do in the case of any other object of learning—with the subject matter alone. The foreign language being learned is, just like the mother tongue, a learning tool as well. It is, though, not the primary, but a secondary learning tool, in other words, a learning tool in the making. At some stage of its development the mother tongue is also a learning tool in the making, which has special implications if the foreign-language learning occurs at an early age. And of course, we should also keep in mind that growing into one's mother tongue never ends. But the second language functions, nevertheless, on a somewhat different level, as it is forced into the role of coexisting with another learning tool which is more developed— and hence more powerful—and which is often desperately needed, and conse-quently called upon and utilized, to overcome communicative hurdles presenting themselves during the foreign-language-learning process.

We are close to the center of the problem. A second language which we learn is something drastically different in kind, not just degree, from a second subject matter we learn, say, mathematics in addition to history or any other field of knowledge that we may wish to choose. History also demands space for its presence in the human mind, just like the foreign language does, but the impact of history on what is already stored of other subject matters by previous learning processes is of another nature than the impact of the foreign language on the mother tongue. That is to say, the first language, because of its principal role as a learning tool, is tied more closely to the second language, in its role as a new subject matter, than to another subject matter such as history or mathematics. The first language and the second language, since they have to share the role of acquiring and administering subject-matter knowledge, are incessantly and rather vigorously competing with each other. The enforced coexistence of two or more languages in the mind of the learner can never be an equivalent to the juxtaposition of two or more partners with equal rights and duties. One of the languages will always dominate, although it need not be permanently the mother tongue. In the course of time—a fairly long time one might add— any one language could, on principle, fulfill the role of the primary learning tool.

Now we can focus on our main task. From the foregoing it should be apparent what the general contention must be: When a foreign language is learned, inevitably some *unlearning* has to take place. The *unlearning* is much more extensive and much more complicated in this instance than it is when we learn other new subject matter since, again, in the foreign-language-learning process there is not only subject matter involved but also the carrier or vehicle for the "transportation" of subject matter, the language as the primary learning tool.

Let us go back to the four items named above that were introduced as one possible way of characterizing the effect of the newly arriving knowledge on the knowledge already in place. While it is not possible for the analysts to restrict themselves to the "tool" character of first and second language, I still would nevertheless contend that we can indeed focus on that component, even though we remain fully aware that the tool cannot be separated from the "tooled." (I like that new use of the word!) While the two components certainly do not actually occur in separation, they are separable by thought, a possibility which the investigators cannot afford to leave unused.

Of the four items named—total replacement, mere addition, substantive alteration, far-reaching adaptation—we will focus only on the first, as it is certainly the most crucial item: *Total replacement*.

Any language teaching that aims at maximal efficiency requires a far greater knowledge of linguistics than would be readily admitted by those who know very little about linguistics. This underestimation, incidentally, has considerably increased during the last two decades, with the greater part of the blame probably to be laid at the door of the linguistic profession. One of the many good things that sophisticated training in linguistics would provide language teachers is detailed knowledge of the structure of the first and second languages, which would enable teachers to predict with a great degree of accuracy the clashes between the two systems that are bound to occur as soon as the foreign-language teaching is initiated. In addition, it would guide langage teachers in designing a comprehensive strategy for the appropriate remedial action. The results of contrastive studies make it abundantly clear, for instance, that the sound systems of any two languages entail differences ranging from rather insignificant to extremely consequential. If during the foreign-language-teaching procedure those systemic differences are not properly addressed, the difference in the first case may not involve any distortion of meaning at all, yet in the second case miscommunication will unavoidably occur. But in any case the overall implication is that, no matter how trifling or how far-reaching the difference of individual sounds across the border of two languages may be, due to the systemic nature of those two sets of sounds, no individual sound of, say, the English sound system has a complete match in any sound of, say, the French sound system. Consequently, English learners of French will have to replace their native sound system in its entirety by the French sound system if they want to understand the foreign language and be understood in the foreign language to the fullest extent possible.

The *unlearning* process has to be complete so that the *learning* process may become complete. Needless to say, the suspension or cancellation of the native sound system is temporary, limited to the time or times of speaking the foreign language. But if the *unlearning* is less than complete at the stipulated time, no substantive learning, no learning without serious distortion, can occur. The material being learned cannot be adequately absorbed by the learner unless it is internalized with the appropriate sound shape. If it is not correctly integrated, its subsequent use is seriously hampered. Even if the items involved can be reproduced, listeners are not likely to understand a message that is phonetically distorted, even if the distortion is only slight.

What is true for the sound system is valid likewise for any other language component, be it the grammar or the lexicon. Here the *unlearning* in the learning process will be much less drastic; that is, it will be restricted to subsystems or even sections of subsystems. But this is due to the different place of the three components—sound system, grammar, and lexicon—within the overall framework of language, and the varied roles these systems play in the communicative process. While the lexicon is the most crucial component in the transmission of information, the speaker or listener is required to be familiar with only a comparatively small portion of it in order to launch and sustain meaningful communication. Familiarity with no more than about 25%, or even less, of the entire lexicon will certainly do. No native speaker of English, for instance, could possibly know all of the roughly 600,000 words the language is assumed to have. Shakespeare is said to have employed in his writings a mere 45,000 different words.

Second in importance to the lexicon is grammar; but communication will not be seriously impeded if one partner's knowledge of the L2 grammar amounts to no more than 50%. It is quite different with the sound system. Unless the sounds of the target language are mastered to at least 90% or even 95%, meaningful communication is not likely to occur. The required mastery ranges from individual sounds to suprasegmental features, including intonational features.

Proficiency in language entails habitual performance of various functions, which are—most of them anyway—no doubt language-specific. Likewise, the underlying habits are determined by language-specific factors. Piecemeal *unlearning* of interfering habits will not do, as it is bound to result in piecemeal learning. Let me cite some examples involving grammar and lexicon. Word order and declension, for instance, are eventually produced habitually, not by a conscious reconstruction effort whenever the deliverance of a particular performance is required. In leading up to the habit formation, conscious reconstruction may prove to be a necessary phase, but the shorter this phase is kept under the skillful guidance of the teacher, the better for the speedy progress of the learner. The phase is unnecessarily—and at that to a large extent unproductively—prolonged if the pertinent L2 structures are lined up with what is, often wrongly, considered the equivalent item in the students' mother tongue. Extensive knowledge of contrasting structures in L1 and L2 languages, a standard program item in any linguistic training geared at language teaching, must be heavily utilized by the teachers in their lesson preparations, but is hardly transferable to the classroom situation without adequate adaptation. This endeavor will most likely lead to the insight that habit formation is vastly facilitated—and the *unlearning* of the L1 structures put on its most effective course—when L2 structures being learned are aligned and/or contrasted with L2 structures already learned. Such a procedure banishes the usefulness of attempting to put the learners through a process of comparing L1 and L2 structures. Such a comparison should not be part of pattern practices, since the structures, belonging to two different systems, cannot be systemically compared.

As an interesting aside I would like to refer briefly to a number of papers presented within the framework of the One Hundred Sixty-First Annual Meeting of the American Association for the Advancement of Science held in Atlanta, Georgia, February 16–21, 1995. In a symposium on bilingualism many questions of crucial importance for foreign-language teaching were raised and discussed. Of special significance in connection with our topic is an overriding concern expressed by several speakers and captured best in the title of one of the papers, given by Grace H. Yeni-Komshian: "What happens to our first language when we learn a second language?" The symposium also caught the attention of foreign observers. A German newspaper, for instance, reporting on the invalidity of the "wide-spread prejudice that children educated bilingually from early on would later in life show achievement deficits in many areas," adds the remark that "However, a warning is sounded against too abruptly pole-changing from one language to the other. In such a case young pupils could be confronted with two different 'language worlds' than cannot be sufficiently combined. " (Cf. Hans Schuh and Gero von Randow in *Die Zeit,* March 10, 1995, Section *Wissen,* p. 18). While a sudden switch from one language to another is outright damaging for the learner's progress in any environment, it is of no help in the classroom situation either.

The lexicon of a language does not exist in isolation. Nor do, of course, the sound system and grammar. Only through their live combination does language as an undivided but composite entity emerge. For the lexicon an additional line-up is constitutive: the relationship it establishes between the grammar and the world at large. The systemic clashes between L1 and L2 languages are nowhere more substantial and more potentially devastating than in the lexicon. This is not surprising if we, first of all, remind ourselves that the lexicon, as the sum total of the lexical entities of a language, comprises not only words but also segments larger than words, such as compounds, phrases, and idiomatic expressions, as well as phonological features like intonational contours. Further, each language system has uniquely evolved over the centuries so as to approach reality in different ways, and it is the lexicon that expresses those different approaches more comprehensively than any other section of language. Thus, we have a picture that could hardly be more language-specific. How do we learn one of these lexical systems in addition to the one we started to grow into from the very first day of our lives? The most troublesome aspect of this situation is that we have come to be convinced that our first-acquired system of lexical entities, which endows us with the ability to recognize, classify, and master the world surrounding us relatively well, is the only one that exists, is a system that is *absolute* rather than *relative*. It is under this premise that in matters of the lexical system we are not only dealing with a strong habit, but with something much more ingrained. It is acquired and not inherited, but it is nevertheless almost as inveterate as an innate feature of our nature. To shake it loose, to replace at least some of it with the lexical system of another language, or part of such a system, is a formidable task; yet it is the essential precondition for the success of our venture to teach foreign languages.

How do we go about this without conjuring up the obvious danger of damaging a well established, well functioning system and failing to put in place at the same time a secondary system of truly comparable capacity? I would again make the case that mixing systems across the border of languages is risky business and hence should be avoided at all cost. Moving from one language to the other, when at least one of the systems is still *in statu nascendi*, tends to confuse the student and not bring about a long-range solution to the task at hand. This holds true for the sound system as much as for grammar, and most particularly for the lexicon. We are aware that there is, in the case of the speaker, a consistent progression from thought to language content, to grammatical form, to its expression via speech sound; and in reverse order, in case of the listener, from the perception of the speech sound, to grammatical form, to language content, to thought. This chain of progression functions most effectively if only one language is used in all of its stages; that precarious arrangement is best left intact and not disrupted by translation at any point. Paraphrasing in the target language is a much better interpretation of the peculiarity of the content construction than can be achieved by taking recourse to the mother tongue. At the heart of this problem, and the key to its adequate solution, is the insight that words owe their specific meaning in a particular sentence—that is, their actual or sentence-specific meaning—largely to their distribution in the sentence. A paraphrase in the target language, if skillfully done, can do full justice to the needed task of revealing the intrinsic relationship between grammatical form and content, which even the very best of translations cannot achieve satisfactorily. Foreign-language instruction goes astray if it loses sight of the established fact that, from the very first day of classroom work, students may learn to employ structures in the target language that express content features which can only be approximated in one's mother tongue. It is true that paraphrasing in the target language, which is frequently essential to secure full content comprehension, is likewise an approximation. But this approximation utilizes the grammatical structures and the speech sounds of the target language, thus rendering the process incomparably superior to even the most expert translation. Underscoring this assessment is the fundamental belief which was hinted at before, that the three core components of language—sound system, grammar, and lexicon—are bound together in an overriding systemic relationship as well. Any learning process, as it involves one part, requires the "functional presence" of the other two.

Unlearning is crucial, especially where the lexical component is involved. One might quibble about the precise meaning which is assigned to the word in connection with our topic. A term like "temporary suspension" would, for instance, not do equally well. The term *unlearning* is supposed to convey that acquired habitual attitudes have to be changed so that new habitual attitudes can take shape. It also connotes that a conscious effort is required on the part of the learner, not just a passive "do-nothing" attitude.

There is an important cautionary note that has to be added here. It is possible also to *unlearn* information that should not be *unlearned*, to give up valuable speech habits that should actually be retained at all cost. Such a loss is not likely to occur in a classroom with a competent foreign-language teacher in charge, when a first or a second foreign language is being taught. It is, however, most likely to occur in a classroom setting, or in a natural contact situation outside the classroom, when too large a number of foreign languages are learned, no matter whether they are learned simultaneously or successively. Believe it or not, there are those who are honestly convinced that foreign-language learning is easy. Well, unfortunately they are wrong, and this is not very difficult to prove. Learning one's mother tongue to a high degree of perfection is, as we all know, the job of a lifetime, and learning one foreign language—with at least a comparable degree of proficiency—is by no means much simpler. Learning one or more languages may just be more than some individuals can handle. But it is not on the elusiveness of the envisioned gain in from learning several languages that we need to focus. This missed opportunity is certainly a loss, but is not harmful. Outright harmful and dangerous, however, is a potential side effect accruing for those learners who have dabbled in too many foreign languages, without mastering any one of them. They may be faced with the disastrous result of having succeeded in dismantling the central role of any language, including their mother tongue, to serve as a principal guiding force in the communication with the world at large. This deplorable situation will rarely happen in the ordinary foreign-language classroom; yet, is very frequent in some Asian countries which have numerous national languages and a large number of mutually unintelligible dialects as well.

Studying this phenomenon thoroughly and devising strategies for desperately needed remedial action is important not only for those countries where it most often occurs but also for us here in the United States. Of the large number of people from all over the world who immigrate to the United States every year, many face a serious language problem which does not go away by itself. Very young children are the least affected, since their learning of a new language is not significantly retarded by a potential conscious or subconscious unwillingness to enter the necessary process of *unlearning* certain habits formed in conjunction with the learning of their mother tongue. The problem gets more serious when the immigrants are older. It is a fact that the longer any habit is retained, the harder it is for anyone to discontinue practicing it. Habits related to the use of one's mother tongue are no exception. If adult-education classes that specialize in teaching English to immigrants concentrate too much on the learning process and pay too little attention to the *unlearning* process of speech habits originally formed in the acquisition of the mother tongue, the result is bound to be disappointment and frustration on both sides.

Will a full-fledged explanation of all factors involved help the learners to overcome their attitudinal problems? In all likelihood it will not. At least part of the reason that immigrants stick resolutely to their pristine language habits is the desire to stay in touch with their roots, with their home country, and not give up part of their identity for the unknown that will take its place. The effective remedy for their problem is there, I am sure, in the form of the theoretical framework referred to above, ready for the well-trained, sophisticated teacher to translate into practical classroom application. That learners and teachers share the same mother tongue need not in itself be considered a great advantage. It is more important that the instructors realize the need to be thoroughly familiar with the structures of the two languages involved and take the appropriate course of action.

Unlearning certain habits is required of the learners to ensure success in foreign-language learning, as it is the indispensable precondition for the learning process to take off and move along smoothly according to the envisioned plan. It is by no means the only precondition, but by far the most fundamental one. Certainly not much less important are the corresponding preconditions to be fulfilled on the part of the teachers. I have already mentioned some in passing, but the essential ones involve the need for even the teachers to *unlearn* certain old attitudes that they have acquired over a long period of time and that have never been challenged by others nor been critically evaluated by the teachers themselves.

A complete list of preconditions would take reams of paper and hours of time to identify. I will conclude by mentioning a few that I believe are of crucial importance.

(1) We as instructors must *unlearn* to devise teacher-oriented plans for classroom activities, so that we may be able to create student-oriented plans. This refers primarily to questions of methodology, but should include also teaching objectives involving the subject matter taught. We have to come to know much more about our students. What do *they* think about the subject matter they are being taught? How do *they* react to procedures followed in class? Are their reactions seriously evaluated and incorporated in the planning to the extent possible for us? Student-oriented teaching is common knowledge, I know, and I also know it should be widely practiced, but this is either not— or no longer— the case in reality. Student-oriented teaching is too often plainly disregarded, because we do not particularly like the idea of *unlearning* the host of long-standing habits with which we have grown so comfortable, which we love to keep mostly for our own sake. It would be good to learn, instead, that no method and no procedure should be taken for granted and introduced and reintroduced repeatedly. Since classes are made up of individuals and hence no two classes are alike, each and every class would warrant the elaboration of a class-specific plan of classroom action.

(2) We as instructors have to *unlearn* the commonly-held belief that what is new is necessarily the most effective method, the most comprehensive procedure, the most desirable objective. New and old are important criteria, but they are not always synonymous with effective versus shallow, desirable versus unacceptable. What is needed is an attitude that makes it a habit for us to constantly evaluate our assumptions, our methodology, our general procedures. We will then in all likelihood change them frequently in accordance with our new insights derived from a critical attitude towards all relevant aspects of our work, and we will avoid the pitfalls of embracing what is fashionable but lacks the essential criteria for substance, merit, and usefulness.

(3) We should also *unlearn* the habit of feeding our clientele wrong or, at the very least, unrealistic information about the nature of their subject, the

learning of one or more foreign languages. To reiterate, foreign-language learning is a very difficult and very time-consuming task. It amounts to deliberate false advertising if we claim otherwise. Students should know precisely and as soon as possible what they are about to encounter. Once this is done, the stage is set for the methodological expertise of the master teacher to do what can and should be done to implement the first and foremost objective in foreign-language instruction: to make language learning as pleasant, appealing, and easy as possible without jeopardizing any of the substantive aims and purposes of the overall task.

(4) Those who have successfully *unlearned* the notion that language learning is an easy task will also have to let go of another misconception entertained not only by the innocent bystander, but also— surprisingly— by the practicing and would-be foreign language teacher. This misconception is the belief that foreign-language *teaching* is easy. Fortunately, the times are gone when hiring officials and hired individuals were equally convinced that more or less the only requirements for the success of foreign-language teaching was for the teacher to be endowed with boundless enthusiasm and have native-speaker status for proficiency in the language being taught. Undoubtedly, both characteristics are good and valuable, but alone they do not suffice. All foreign language teachers should be required to undergo a comprehensive, but flexible teacher education program if we are to avoid exposing captive students to unprepared teachers. Here a great deal of *unlearning* still has to take place. The fact is that in numerous cases the training of foreign-language teachers is incidental, if not outright accidental. The main justification for such a state of affairs seems to be that some candidates easily outshine even those full-fledged, seasoned foreign-language teachers who have somehow endured the most rigorous training without ever becoming competent.

These are exceptional cases, and exceptions only confirm the rules. We cannot hope to improve the situation of foreign-language learning and teaching without seriously rethinking the methodology of teacher training with its wide range of implications. One common misconception that needs to be rectified is the widespread belief that no specific linguistic knowledge is required for language teachers to perform their task to perfection, i.e. that candidates with ample training in literature and a good amount of imagination will do equally well. Unfortunately, if they do not succeed, the damage will in most cases surface only when it is too late to undo it.

(5) We also have to *unlearn* the myth that everything is well if and when our students present us with favorable course evaluations at the end of the semester. Certainly, one essential criterion for a well-done language-teaching job is the satisfaction of the students taught, but other criteria are equally crucial, especially those that generally neither the teachers nor the students have become aware of until long after the teaching job is done. There is need for some

mechanism to be put into place that provides an additional measure for the evaluation of teacher performance, primarily to avoid reducing language teaching to a mere popularity contest.

(6) Last but not least, let us *unlearn* the belief that it is the students who are primarily involved in the actual learning procedure when successful foreign-language learning takes place. Do we ourselves still know how to achieve what we, day in day out, expect of our students? Do we still know in minute detail what is involved in learning a foreign language? Have we ourselves recently attempted either to start learning another foreign language or improve systematically our knowledge of one with which we have already acquired some familiarity? We should try learning another language often and more seriously. It is an eye-opener in numerous respects and significantly improves our understanding of how students learn what we teach them, and hence our understanding of how we should handle our job.

REFERENCES

Baker, Colin. 1992. *Attitudes and language.* Clevedon, U.K. and Philadelphia: Multilingual Matters Ltd.

Baker, Colin. 1993. *Foundation of bilingual education and bilingualism.* Clevedon, U.K. and Philadelphia: Multilingual Matters Ltd.

Bausch, Karl-Richard and Frank G. Königs (eds.). 1986. *Sprachlehrforschung in der Diskussion: Methodologische Überlegungen zur Erforschung des Fremdsprachenunterrichts.* Tübingen, Germany: G. Narr.

Blair, Robert W. 1982. *Innovative approaches to language teaching.* Rowley, Massachusetts: Newbury House Publishers.

Crookes, Graham and Susan M. Gass (eds.). 1993. *Tasks and language learning: Integrating theory and practice.* Clevedon, U.K. and Philadelphia: Multilingual Matters Ltd.

Dechert, Hans W. (ed.). 1990. *Current trends in European second language acquisition research.* Clevedon, U.K. and Philadelphia: Multilingual Matters Ltd.

Dechert, Hans W. and Manfred Raupach (eds.). 1989. *Transfer in language production.* Norwood, N.J.: Ablex Publishing Corp.

Faerch, Claus et al. 1984. *Learner language and language learning.* Copenhagen: Nordisk Forlag A.S.

Freed, Barbara F. (ed.). 1991. *Foreign language acquisition research and the classroom.* Lexington, Massachusetts: D.C. Heath.

Freeman, Yvonne S. and David E. Freeman. 1992. *Whole language for second language learners.* Portsmouth, N.H.: Heinemann.

Gass, Susan M. et al. (eds.) 1989. *Variation in second language acquisition.* Clevedon, U.K. and Philadelphia: Multilingual Matters Ltd.

Gass, Susan M. and Larry Selinker (eds.). 1992. *Language transfer in language learning.* Amsterdam and Philadelphia: John Benjamins.

Gass, Susan M. and Larry Selinker (eds.). 1994. *Second language acquisition: An introductory course.* Hillsdale, N.J.: Lawrence Erlbaum.

Gnutzmann, Claus et al. (eds.). 1992. *Fremsprachenunterricht im internationalen Vergleich: Perspektive 2000.* Frankfurt a.M.: Diesterweg.

Hammerly, Hector. 1985. *An integrated theory of language teaching and its practical consequences.* Blaine, Washington: Second Language Publications.

Harley, Birgit (ed.). 1990. *The development of second language proficiency.* Cambridge, U.K. and New York: Cambridge University Press.

Heindrichs, Wilfried et al. 1980. *Sprachlehrforschung: Angewandte Linguistik und Fremdsprachendidaktik.* Stuttgart: Kohlhammer.

Helbig, Gerhard. 1981. *Sprachwissenschaft-Konfrontation-Fremdsprachenunterricht.* Leipzig: VEB Verlag Enzyklopädie.

Holmen, A. et al. (eds.) 1988. *Bilingualism and the individual.* Clevedon, U.K. and Philadelphia: Multilingual Matters Ltd.

Huebner, Thom and Charles A. Ferguson (eds.). 1991. *Crosscurrents in second language acquisition and linguistic theories.* Amsterdam and Philadelphia: John Benjamins.

Hüllen, Werner and Lothar Jung. 1979. *Sprachstruktur und Spracherwerb.* Düsseldorf: August Bagel Verlag; Bern and Munich: Francke Verlag.

Krashen, Stephen D. 1988. *Second language acquisition and second language learning.* New York: Prentice Hall.

Lado, Robert. 1964. *Language teaching: A scientific approach.* New York: McGraw-Hill.

Leahey, Thomas H. and Richard J. Harris. 1989 [1985]. *Human learning.* Englewood Cliffs, N.J.: Prentice-Hall.

Malamah-Thomas, Ann. 1987. *Classroom interaction.* Oxford and New York: Oxford University Press.

McLaughlin, Barry. 1982. *Children's second language learning.* Washington, D.C.: Center for Applied Linguistics.

McLaughlin, Barry. 1992. *Myths and misconceptions about second language learning: What every teacher needs to unlearn.* Santa Cruz, California: The National Center for Research on Cultural Diversity and Second Language Learning.

Nabrings, Kirsten and Peter Schmitter. 1979. *Spracherwerbsforschung: Eine Bibliographie zur Pädolinguistik.* Münster: Institut für Allgemeine Sprachwissenschaft der Universität.

Odlin, Terence. 1989. *Language transfer: Cross-linguistic influence in language learning.* New York and Cambridge, U.K.: Cambridge University Press.

Oksaar, Els, ed. 1984. *Spracherwerb—Sprachkontakt—Sprachkonflikt.* Berlin and New York: de Gruyter.

Padilla, Amado M. et al. (eds.). 1990. *Foreign language education: Issues and strategies.* Newbury Park, California: Sage Publications.

Phillipson, Robert et al. (eds.). 1991. *Foreign/second language pedagogy research: A commemorative volume for Claus Faerch.* Clevedon, U.K. and Philadelphia: Multilingual Matters Ltd.

Rieck, Bert-Olaf. 1989. *Natürlicher Zweitspracherwerb bei Arbeitsimmigranten: Eine Langzeituntersuchung.* Frankfurt a.M.: Peter Lang.

Ringbom, Hokan (ed.). 1987. *The role of the first language in foreign language learning.* Clevedon, U.K. and Philadelphia: Multilingual Matters Ltd.

Scarcella, Robin C. et al. (eds.). 1990. *Developing communicative competence in second language.* Boston: Heinle and Heinle.

Schuh, Hans and Gero von Randow. 1995. "Gute Laune hilft beim Lernen." Report on the 161st Annual Meeting of the American Association for the Advancement of Science, Atlanta, Georgia, February 16–21, 1995. (*Die Zeit,* March 10, 1995, Section *Wissen,* p.18).

Singleton, David M. 1989. *Language acquisition: The age factor.* Clevedon, U.K. and Philadelphia: Multilingual Matters Ltd.

Tarone, Elaine E. et al. (eds.). 1994. *Research methodology in second-language acquisition.* Hillsdale, N.J.: Lawrence Erlbaum.

VanPatten, Bill et al. (eds.). 1987. *Foreign language learning: A research perspective.* Cambridge, Massachusetts and New York: Newbury House.

Wright, Tony. 1987. *Roles of teachers and learners.* Oxford: Oxford University Press.

Yeni-Komshian, Grace H. 1995. "What happens to our first language when we learn a second language?" Paper presented at the Annual Meeting of the American Association for the Advancement of Science. Atlanta, GA, February 17, 1995.

Unlearning learnability

Donald Loritz
Georgetown University

> Consider what effects, that might conceivably have practical bearings, we conceive the object of our conception to have. Then, our conception of these effects is the whole of our conception of the object ... [or] ... "Ye may know them by their fruits."
>
> —C.S. Peirce's Pragmatic Maxim, 1878, 1905

Abstract. In 1965 it was "proved" that computers could not learn natural languages (Gold 1965, 1967). This proof threatened millions of dollars in artificial intelligence research, so there was a substantial incentive to show that learning was unimportant. This enterprise (e.g. Culicover and Wexler 1980; Berwick and Weinberg 1984; Pinker 1979, 1984, 1989) became known as "learnability theory."

The most effective argument against learning was brilliantly anticipated by Chomsky's conjecture that children do not "learn" language (1962). If human beings did not learn language, then the fact that computers could not learn language would not limit the promise of computers. Indeed, if children's (allegedly) "effortless" learning of natural language was accomplished by means of an innate program, then the discovery of that program would justify greatly-expanded support of research in "learnability theory," computation, and linguistics. (Of course, if language could not be learned, then it could not really be taught, either. But language teaching was popularly regarded as women's work, and with sufficient funding, this logical implication was easily glossed over.)

Unfortunately, a small mathematical error rendered the ensuing thirty years of linguistic research bootless. Because the human brain is not an everyday computer (it is a massively parallel processor) learnability theory has been wrong by some 7,111,111 orders of magnitude. More unfortunately, language "acquisition" theory has become mechanized and divorced from the broader study of psychology and human learning. Still more unfortunately, linguistic theory has failed language teachers and learners at a time when, at least in the United States, education and teaching have been under unremitting political attack.

We language teachers must unlearn learnability theory. It is simply wrong. Language is learned, it can be taught, and it should be taught. But unlearning learnability will not be easy. Its proponents are well-funded. And even in our own number there are many teachers and researchers who, in the absence of a competing theory, have become invested in mechanical theories of language. The study of neural networks now provides a viable competing theory, and in the interest of children and learners, regardless of the interests of computers, learnability must be unlearned.

On the origin of theories. After World War II, victorious United States soldiers returning home reported with amazement that the people in Europe did not speak English. Within a decade, to fulfill its new role of world leadership, the United States rapidly began to require modern-foreign-language education in all its schools. To fill the pressing need for modern-foreign-language teachers, tens of thousands of applied linguists needed to be recruited and trained. Washington, D.C. was naturally in the forefront of this mission, and by 1960 the first and only School of Languages and Linguistics (SLL) in the world, a professional school for the training of foreign-language teachers, had been organized at Georgetown University with Robert Lado as its Dean. In 1957 Lado's *Linguistics across cultures* redefined foreign-language teaching for a new generation of teachers and students.

Other large, social forces also shaped the linguistics of the day. After World War II, there was also a sudden upturn in the birthrate, especially in the United States. This "baby boom" immediately resulted in an increased demand for English teachers and an increased research interest in child language, and in 1958 Roger Brown's *Words and things* defined the new field of psycholinguistics.

But then, in the mid-1960s, when the new generation of polyglot American baby-boomers went abroad, we discovered that the rest of the world had learned English! English had become the international language of commerce, the twentieth-century *lingua franca*. In the United States, the boom in foreign-language education collapsed as rapidly as it had begun: School after school dropped its foreign-language requirement, and foreign-language teachers began queuing up on the unemployment line. At the same time oral contraceptives became widely available, and now there was a sudden *downturn* in the birthrate. The baby boom collapsed as suddenly as it had begun, and by the mid-1980s "psycholinguistics" had once again become just another term for "women's work."

Many graduate schools, like Georgetown's SLL under the leadership of James Alatis, retrained unemployed linguists to find jobs teaching English as a second language. But in the United States at least, teaching English was just so much more women's work, and teaching English to immigrants was an even less respected profession. Most linguists had to look elsewhere to support their families.

Over the past half century we at the Georgetown University Round Table on Languages and Linguistics have borne witness to this ebb and flow of demand for language learning and applied linguistics. But we have not always kept in touch with our former colleagues—of course some of what they did was top secret ...

At the heart of German communications in World War II was the "Enigma Machine." The Enigma Machine was a cash-register-like "black box" which took German as its input, applied mechanical *transformations* to it, and output Nazi war codes. The Allies called upon a team of mathematicians, linguists, and cash-register engineers to help undo the transformations of the German and Japanese Enigma Machines. In the process, they gave a whole new meaning to the phrase "international business machines." The final Allied triumph over Germany was the also the triumph of a new linguistics: *computational* linguistics.[1]

After the War, Warren Weaver of the Rockefeller Foundation circulated a memorandum entitled *Translation* to some two hundred mathematicians, engineers, and linguists. *Translation* proposed that the military-industrial-academic complex which had so successfully broken the Enigma code redirect its energies to breaking the evilest code of all, the Russian language. With the outbreak of Korean hostilities in the cold war, "machine translation" became heavily funded by U.S. military and intelligence agencies, and many universities, including Georgetown, the Massachusetts Institute of Technology, and the University of Pennsylvania, participated in this program.

At a 1952 conference, Weaver proposed a two-stage research effort which would first analyze or "parse" Russian into a hypothetical, abstract, universal language called "machinese," and then generate English from this machinese. At the Massachusetts Institute of Technology this effort became organized under the leadership of Yehoshua Bar-Hillel. Like the WWII code-breakers, MIT took a mathematical approach to the translation problem: The syntax of mathematics was felt to have been solved by Church's recursive lambda calculus, and the semantics of mathematics was felt to have been elegantly solved in the system of Boolean logic, while Turing and Von Neumann had specified logical machines for implementing such syntax and semantics. In the MIT approach, human language was just a special case of mathematics. Machine translation was to be accomplished by applying a generative grammar (a special case of the lambda calculus) to discretely-coded semantic symbols (evaluated by Boolean logic) on a recursively-structured LISP machine (a special case of a Von Neumann-Turing machine).

In 1955 a University of Pennsylvania graduate student wrote a dissertation theoretically outlining a scheme for the generation of English from a kind of machinese and was immediately hired by MIT to work on machine translation.

---

[1]Computational code-breaking also figured prominently in the progressive defeat of Japan, but this contribution was overshadowed by the atom bomb.

His name was Noam Chomsky. The MIT analysis team, headed by Victor Yngve was to first "parse" Russian into machinese. Then Chomsky's team was to generate English from this machinese deep structure. But the problem of machine translation proved vastly harder than WWII code-breaking. After five years of effort, the MIT team had, in Yngve's words, "run up against a semantic wall." It had failed to parse a single Russian sentence into acceptable deep structure, much less test Chomsky's generative grammar. So it sometimes happens that yesterday's application becomes today's theory.

The unlearnability paradox and learnability theory. In a series of conjectures, Chomsky (1959, 1962, 1965, *et passim*) laid the computer science community's failure to crack the Russian code to the *unlearnability paradox*, which runs follows:

A. Human language is infinite, but
B. the human mind is finite.

Therefore,

C. Human language cannot be learned, but rather
D. human language must be innate.

In 1965 Gold offered the first mathematical proof of these conjectures, and a series of subsequent mathematical analyses form what is now called "learnability theory" (e.g. Gold 1967; Hamburger and Wexler 1975; Wexler and Culicover 1980; Baker and McCarthy 1981; Berwick and Weinberg 1984; see Pinker 1979 and Berwick 1987 for relatively nontechnical summaries). In this section I will summarize these mathematical analyses following Berwick and Weinberg 1984.

Berwick and Weinberg adapted equation (1) from Earley (1970) as a measure of "parsability," and Berwick (1987) proved that the notion of parsability is equivalent to learnability (i.e., we have *learned* a language when we can *parse* all of the sentences in the language).

(1) $t = k \mid G^2 \mid l^3$

Equation (1) says that the time t, which a computer needs to parse a sentence of length l, is proportional to the product of three terms: The cube of the length, the square of the grammar size G, and k, a scaling constant expressing the speed and/or size of the computer. Berwick and Weinberg explain that as the exponential terms G and l increase, k becomes relatively small, so we may simplify the problem by focusing on G and l in (2):

(2) $t = G^2 \mid l^3$

Now premise A, the infinity of language, is commonly, if nontechnically, demonstrated by sentences like i:

i.   *This is the house that Jack built.*
     This the cat that lives in the house that Jack built.
     This is the dog that chased the cat that lives in the house that Jack built.
     ...

Since sentences can be of infinite length l, it can take an infinite length of time t to parse a sentence, and an infinite time to learn any language which contains such sentences.

Although this form of the argument for premise A is frequently presented in introductions to generative grammar, it overlooks Chomsky's fundamental contribution: Chomsky's grammars are *recursive*, so i illustrates not one long sentence of infinite length, but rather a chain of "embedded sentences" (or, more recently, "X-bars"), each of some finite length l'. Now, because l' is a constant like k, it vanishes in comparison to the exponential term G, and (2) can be rewritten as (3):

(3) $t = G^2$

It follows that the learnability of a language depends principally on G, the size of the grammar.

Suppose then, that a five-year old's grammar, G_5, has 100 rules, so $t_5 = G^2 = 10000$. Now suppose a ten-year old's grammar has 200 rules and $t_{10} = 40000$. According to the formula in (3) it would take the ten-year old four times longer to parse a sentence than it would a five-year-old! Two further conclusions follow: G must be small so that it can be learned by some early age, and thereafter G must not be allowed to grow. There must be a critical age after which any learning stops. We may then further assume that there are important innate factors which determine G, keeping it small and static.

Standard critiques of learnability theory. Logically, the unlearnability paradox rests on the two premises, A and B. In defense of premises A and B, that language is infinite and the human mind finite, Jackendoff (1994) offers two classic demonstrations (*ii* and *iii*):

ii. *Amy ate two peanuts.*
   Amy ate three peanuts.
   Amy ate four peanuts
   ...
   Amy ate forty-three million, five hundred nine peanuts.
   ...

There are as many sentences in this series as there are nameable integers. The biggest number name listed in my Webster's Collegiate is a vigintillion (10^{63} in US/French usage; 10^{120} in British/German usage). With all the numbers up to this at our disposal, we can create more sentences in this series than there are elementary particles in the universe. (Jackendoff 1994: 11)

Immediately, we may use *ii* to dismiss quibbling about infinity. While it is true that neither 10^{16} nor even a British vigintillion is, strictly speaking, *infinity*, no one is using *infinity* in its unbounded, strictly mathematical sense. The critical point is that language is infinite relative to the brief candle of an individual life, within which time language must be learned.

In the second demonstration, Jackendoff asks us to open the dictionary at random and begin to construct a series of sentences like *iii*:

iii. *A numeral is not a numbskull.*
   A numeral is not a nun.
   ...
   A numbskull is not a numeral.
   ...

And so on it goes, giving us $10^8 \times 10^8 = 10^{16}$ absolutely ridiculous sentences. Given that there are on the order of 10^{10} neurons in the entire human brain,[2] this divides out to 10^6, or one million sentences per neuron. Thus it would be impossible for us to store them all in our brains ... (Jackendoff 1994: 11)

It may be objected that learning a language involves not just *storing* such sentences, nor even just *parsing* them, but *understanding* them, i.e. knowing, like Jackendoff himself, that the sentences in *iii* are "ridiculous." Ever since Yngve's "semantic wall," skeptics have similarly criticized generative theory's

---

[2]Jackendoff's 10^{10} is more commonly an estimate of the number of neurons in the *neocortex*. For the entire brain/nervous system I use 10^{11}. Estimating 10^3 synapses per neuron then yields the stimate of 10^{14} total synapses used below.

context-free inability to account for context-sensitive semantic meaning—but the critics have failed to provide a better account. While I believe that a semantic critique of generative theory is possible, let us for the moment note that each sentence in *ii* and *iii* is, in simple fact, semantically distinct. Thus, despite whatever inadequacies may be laid to generative semantic theory, this particular consideration of semantics only deepens the unlearnability paradox and so seems to strengthen the foundation of generative theory.

The infinity of the human mind. The critical logical flaw in learnability theory and, consequently, in generative linguistics, lies not in premise A, but in premise B. Jackendoff's demonstration of the limitation of the human mind assumes that the neurons of a human mind are arrayed like memory locations in a Turing machine (Figure 1.) In a Turing machine, data is serially stored on a tape, and serially processed by a read/write head, as in Figure 1.

Figure 1. A Turing machine.

```
    ... 1 0 1 1 0 1 1 1 0 0 1 0 1 0 1 1 1 1 0 0 0 1 0 ...

        < -- R | W -- >
```

But what if the human mind is not built like an everyday computer? What if neurons are not simply connected, each-to-next like the tape cells of a Turing machine (or, for that matter, like a behaviorist stimulus-response chain)? What if *brain* cells combine in the same way that Jackendoff combines words in *iii*?

The formula for the number combinations k, of S synapses taken s at a time is given in (4). (Because long-term memory is principally stored at synapses, (4) computes learning in terms of synapses, not brain cells *per se*.) :

$$(4) \quad k = \frac{S!}{(S - s)! \, s!}$$

Assume that one-tenth of the 10^{14}-odd synapses in the human nervous system are used for language. This gives us $S = 10^{13}$ synapses for language. Now let each word, morpheme, or X-bar "rule" in our grammar be represented by, on average, a combination of 1,000,000 synapses ($s = 1,000,000$). Then, by (4), $k > 10^{7,111,111}$. By this analysis, *contra* Jackendoff, each human brain not only has the capacity to name every elementary particle in the universe, but with its left-over capacity, it can then name the particles in $10^{7,111,035}$ more universes![3]

Substituting our new value of k into equations (1-3) yields equation (5):

$$(5) \quad t = \frac{G^2}{k = 10^{7,111,111}}$$

G is still exponential, but so is k. There is no unlearnability paradox. The size of the grammar, G, is irrelevant to learnability, because the capacity of the human mind is infinite.[4]

Unlearning learnability, or Will robots inherit the Earth? Marvin Minsky, long-time director of the MIT Artificial Intelligence Laboratory writes in the October 1994 *Scientific American*:

> Will robots inherit the earth?—Yes, as we engineer replacement bodies and brains using nanotechnology. We will then live longer, possess greater wisdom and enjoy capabilities as yet unimagined ... Will robots inherit the earth? Yes, but they will be our children. We owe our minds to the deaths and lives of all the creatures that were ever engaged in the struggle called evolution. Our job is to see that all this work shall not end up in meaningless waste. (1994:108–113).

This is surely a prescient vision, and Professor Minsky may well be remembered as a prophet when, a billion years hence, our Sun supernovas engulf the Earth in fire. On that Day of Judgment, only Virtual Minds will be lifted unto the heavens and saved. There, powered only by interstellar hydrogen and hungering only for the Word, the Virtual will be free at last from this *sansara* of the Flesh. There, etched in silicon, the Virtual will find Life

---

[3] In this analysis I have used $s = 10^5$, because it originally seemed reasonably large, and I was astounded to see the combinatorial result. But even increasing s or decreasing S by orders of magnitude still leaves us with the capacity to name all the elementary particles in *this* universe.

[4] There are other possible criticisms of learnability theory. For example, as early as 1967 Gold (p. 452*ff.*) acknowledges that several kinds of negative evidence (in addition to caregiver correction) could facilitate learning. Moreover, he acknowledges that in the case of "primitive recursive text with a generator naming relation" there is no limit on learning. This is analogous to a curriculum with a teacher. Gold dismisses these as being "of no practical interest," apparently because the target language is effectively preidentified. But this model is of practical interest because the child is, in fact, born into a preidentified speech community. This is the gist of what may be called the "functional" critique of learnability theory. Such criticisms do not, however, directly challenge the erroneous assumption that the human mind is, in essence, a limited Turing machine.

Everlasting, and there will no longer be a need for sex. Original Sin itself will be vanquished! Truly a sublime vision.

I beg the reader's indulgence, however, to worry about the intervening billion years. I am still concerned for the children studying in our schools, each of whose minds infinitely exceeds the capacity of the computers in Professor Minsky's laboratory, if not those in his imagination. And I cannot help but worry that some of society's investment in robots has been and will be at the expense our flesh-and-blood children: Certainly, for example, claiming that the important aspects of language are innate has not encouraged society to invest in language education. Perhaps neither Professor Minsky nor any linguist who believes in the Turing machine would advocate such disinvestment. Nevertheless, Peirce's Pragmatic Maxim evaluates our theories by all their *conceivable* consequences, not only those consequences which we are pleased to contemplate. Given the history of linguistics in the latter half of the twentieth century, I am not pleased to contemplate the consequences of a theory which belittles the human mind and makes computers the measure of man.

I conclude that learnability theory must be unlearned. In its place, we must erect a theory which unifies language and learning in a scientific study of how the brain adapts to the ever-changing context of life. Generative philosophers may object that "nobody knows anything about the brain" (Chomsky 1988: 755), but the claim is at best disingenuous: In the twentieth century, no less than twenty-five Nobel Prizes have been awarded for discoveries about the human brain and nervous system (Golgi 1906, Ramon y Cajal 1906, Sherrington 1932, Adrian 1932, Dale 1936, Loewi 1936, Erlanger 1944, Gasser 1944, Hess 1949, Moniz 1949, Bekesy 1961, Hodgkin 1963, Huxley 1963, Eccles 1963, Hartline 1967, Wald 1967, Granit 1967, Axelrod 1970, von Euler 1970, Katz 1970, Sperry 1981, Hubel 1981, Wiesel 1981, Sakmann 1991, and Neher 1991). From such an impressive foundation, quite a complete explanation of language can be developed.

Unfortunately, there is not space here for an adequate exposition of this "adaptive language theory" (but see Loritz 1990, 1991). Briefly, the theory builds upon adaptive resonance theory (ART, Grossberg 1968 *et seq.*[5]), with important affinities to "functionalism" (e.g. Bates and MacWhinney 1987; MacWhinney 1987a) and "connectionism" (e.g. Rumelhart and McClelland 1984, 1986). At points, adaptive language theory even bears some resemblance

---

[5]Ironically, ART was virtually developed in Minsky's laboratory at MIT. Grossberg was hired by MIT in 1967. In 1969 he was awarded its Norbert Wiener Medal for Cybernetics, and promoted to Associate Professor. In the same year, Minsky and Papert published *Perceptrons*, which supposedly refuted the computational utility of neural networks. Grossberg's unexpected 1972 discovery of the gated dipole proved Minsky and Papert wrong, and in 1975 he was denied tenure for heresy and banished to the relative obscurity of Boston University.

to current generative theory, but the resemblance is a superficial epiphenomenon of the theories' common data—at its base, adaptive language theory assumes that language is learned by brain cells, not Turing machines. In so doing, it seeks to affirm the infinity of the human mind and restore the uniquely human unity of language and learning.

REFERENCES

Baker, Charles and John McCarthy. 1981. *The logical problem of language acquisition*. Cambridge, Massachusetts: MIT Press.

Bates, Elizabeth and Brian MacWhinney. 1987. "Competition, variation, and language learning." In Brian McWhinney (ed.), *Mechanisms of language acquisition*. Hillsdale, N.J.: Erlbaum Associates.

Berwick, Robert C. and Amy S. Weinberg. 1984. *The grammatical basis of linguistic performance*. Cambridge, Massachusetts: MIT Press.

Brown, Roger. 1958. *Words and things*. Glencoe, Illinois: The Free Press.

Chomsky, Noam. 1959. "Review of Skinner, B.F., *Verbal behavior*." *Language* 35(1):26–57.

Chomsky, Noam. 1962. "Explanatory models in linguistics." In E. Nagel, P. Suppes, and A. Tarski (eds.), *Logic, methodology, and philosophy of science: Proceedings of the 1960 International Congress*. Stanford, California: Stanford University Press.

Chomsky, Noam. 1965. *Aspects of the theory of syntax*. Cambridge, Massachusetts: MIT Press.

Chomsky, Noam. 1988a. *Language and politics*. Montreal: Black Rose Books.

Earley, James. 1970. "An efficient context-free parsing algorithm." *Communications of the Association for Computing Machinery*. 6(8): 451–455.

Gold, E. Mark. 1965. "Limiting recursion." *Journal of Symbolic Logic 30*:1*ff*.

Gold, E. Mark. 1967. "Language identification in the limit." *Information and Control* 10(3): 447–474.

Grossberg, Stephen. 1968. "Some physiological and biochemical consequences of psychological postulates." *Proceedings of the National Academy of Sciences* 60(3): 758–765. Also in Stephen Grossberg (ed.), *Studies of mind and brain*. Dordrecht, The Netherlands: D. Reidel. 53–64.

Grossberg, Stephen. 1972a. "A neural theory of punishment and avoidance. II: Quantitative Theory." *Mathematical Biosciences* 15(2): 253–285. Also in S. Grossberg (ed.), *Studies of mind and brain*. Dordrecht, The Netherlands: D. Reidel. 194–228.

Grossberg, Stephen. 1986. "The adaptive self-organization of serial order in behavior: speech, language, and motor control." In E.C. Schwab and H.C. Nusbaum (eds.), *Pattern recognition by humans and machines*. Orlando, Florida: Academic Press.

Hamburger, Henry and Kenneth Wexler. 1975. "A mathematical theory of learning transformational grammar." *Journal of Mathematical Psychology* 12(2): 137–177.

Jackendoff, Ray. 1994. *Patterns in the mind*. New York: Basic Books.

Lado, Robert. 1957. *Linguistics across cultures: Applied linguistics for language teachers*. Ann Arbor, Michigan: University of Michigan Press.

Loritz, Donald. 1990. "Linguistic hypothesis testing in neural networks." In James E. Alatis (ed.), *Georgetown University Round Table on Languages and Linguistics 1990*. Washington, D.C.: Georgetown University Press.

Loritz, Donald. 1991. "Cerebral and cerebellar models of language learning." *Applied Linguistics* 12(3): 299–318.

MacWhinney, Brian. 1987a. "The competition model." In B. MacWhinney (ed.), *Mechanisms of language acquisition*. Hillsdale, N.J.: Erlbaum Associates.
MacWhinney, Brian. (ed.) 1987b. *Mechanisms of language acquisition*. Hillsdale, N.J.: Erlbaum Associates.
Minsky, Marvin. 1994. "Will robots inherit the Earth?" *Scientific American* 71(4): 108–113.
Minsky, Marvin and Seymour Papert. 1969. *Perceptrons*. Cambridge, Massachusetts: MIT Press.
Peirce, Charles S. 1878. "How to make our ideas clear." *Popular Science Monthly* 13(Jan.): 286–302.
Peirce, Charles S. 1905. "What pragmatism is." *The Monist* 15(April): 161–181. Reprinted in P. Wiener (ed.), 1958, *Charles S. Peirce: Values in a universe of chance*. New York: Doubleday. 180–202.
Pinker, Steven. 1979. "Formal models of language learning." *Cognition* 7(2): 217–283.
Pinker, Steven. 1984. *Language learnability and language learning*. Cambridge, Massachusetts: Harvard University Press.
Pinker, Steven. 1989. *Learnability and cognition: The acquisition of argument structure*. Cambridge, Massachusetts: MIT Press.
Pinker, Steven. 1994. *The language instinct*. New York: Morrow.
Rumelhart, David E. and James L. McClelland. 1984. "On learning the past tenses of English verbs." In David E. Rumelhart and James L. McClelland (eds.), *Parallel distributed processing, Volume two*. 216–271.
Rumelhart, David E. and James L. McClelland. 1986. *Parallel distributed processing*. Cambridge, Massachusetts: MIT Press.
Wexler, Kenneth and Peter Culicover. 1980. *Formal principles of language acquisition*. Cambridge, Massachusetts: MIT Press.

Maximizing learning in the Advanced EAP: Critical listening, critical thinking, and effective speaking

Joan Morley
The University of Michigan

Learning a second language is a challenging and rewarding part of the human experience. Now, as ever, many forces—educational, economic, political, religious, and social—influence individuals to undertake language learning tasks, tutored or untutored. Language professionals, those of us who practice "tutored" second language instruction and linguistic research, have inherited a complex field. Its history includes a wide spectrum of beliefs about language and language learning processes and a no less broad collection of instructional orthodoxies. Today the work of language educators and linguistic researchers continues to be extensive and varied, as is well documented by the kinds of language studies reported at the 1995 Georgetown University Round Table. But one important bond—one common cause shared by all of us—it seems to me, is the relentless pursuit of information and insights that will maximize learning—for our second-language students, our trainees in the language professions, and our own continuing exploration of language and learning phenomena.

In this context, "Maximizing learning in Advanced EAP" (English for Academic Purposes) outlines some of the instructional features of two EAP oral communication courses for advanced-level university students. The focus of these courses, under development at the University of Michigan, is spoken discourse in various academic contexts. Their goal is to help learners develop: (1) critical listening, (2) critical thinking, and (3) effective "public speaking" (i.e., speaking to and with groups of fellow students and professors) in English, their second language. Overall, in planning ways to maximize learning in these courses, a central component has been syllabus design that is constructed with a discourse-based perspective on language, that is, linguistic patterns viewed in relation to the social contexts in which they function. The main thrust of our experimental work is, of course, instructional research and the development of effective oral communication courses for L2 learners, but it also provides interesting and challenging teaching experiences and research and materials development projects for faculty, graduate student assistants, and upper level undergraduates in applied linguistics courses.

1. English for Academic Purposes.

International students in North American colleges and universities. In colleges and universities across North America, enrollments of international students—with their various EAP needs—have increased steadily over the last fifty years. The numbers have risen from around 8,000 in 1943 to nearly 450,000 in 1993–1994, according to statistics compiled by IIE, the Institute of International Education,[1] and it is predicted that international student enrollments will be over half a million by the year 2000. In addition, while only a few hundred institutions reported students from abroad in the early 1940s, today nearly 2,800 colleges and universities have international enrollments.

Historically, the majority of international students has been at the undergraduate level, but in recent years there have been increasing numbers of graduate school enrollments. One sign of these times in the United States is the fact that during the 1980s the number of doctorates awarded to non-U.S. citizens more than doubled, increasing from 5,221 to 10,666. And in 1991 non-U.S. graduates earned 30 percent of total doctorates, with 59% of the doctorates in engineering schools going to non-US students.[2]

EAP course work and students' needs. As more and more upper-level non-native speakers (NNSs) enter universities, many with functional language deficiencies despite meeting the language proficiency entrance requirements, it is important to re-examine EAP programming. The language needs of the majority of upper-level students are often ones that call not only for English for Specific Purposes (ESP) in academia, but English for Career-Specific Purposes (EC-SP). NNSs are pursuing academic degree programs, of course, but they also are in training for professional careers. In fact, many students play three roles at one and the same time:

- enrolled graduate student (in an MA, PhD, or professional degree program)
- teaching assistant or research assistant in a discipline

---

[1] Information in this section was adapted from a paper given by Sherry Mueller, Director of IIE Exchange Programs, at the English Language Institute's Fiftieth Anniversary Symposium on the University of Michigan campus in Fall 1991, "Internationalism and higher education patterns and trends: A national perspective on the last fifty years," and from recent volumes of the IIE publication *Open Doors*.

[2] This material was adapted from information in the *NAFSA Newsletter*, April/May 1993; it originally appeared in P. Ries and D.H. Thurgood, *Summary Report 1991: Doctorate recipients from United States universities*, National Academic Press.

- practicing professional already engaged in preparing scholarly publications and presentations

In many North American graduate schools it is not unusual to find that a significant number of "students" are on leave from academic, government, or business and industry jobs in their home countries.

Developing EAP oral communication courses. For years EAP instruction focused largely on writing skills in the academic context, often to the exclusion of anything but cursory attention to the skills of listening and speaking. Recently, however, a growing sense of the importance of oral communication in EAP has emerged, and a realization that written communication is but one of the language skills non-native speakers need to become fully participating members of their academic disciplines and their professional communities. The importance of effective oral communication for successful university and career performance is recognized in more and more university departments.

Eleven of the more than thirty EAP courses in the University of Michigan English Language Institute (ELI) program provide instruction in various facets of oral communication. The purpose of these courses is to meet the needs of the largely graduate-level student clientele—needs as perceived by the learners themselves, and by ELI faculty, departmental faculty, academic counselors, and admissions personnel. The work in this cluster of oral communication courses is designed to meet both basic and sophisticated oral language needs of students in different departments around the university. Course curricula include attention to interactive listening, lecture comprehension, note-taking, academic speaking, discussion, argumentation, research presentations, interviewing, beginning pronunciation, intermediate pronunciation, voice and articulation. In addition, work in other classes in the ELI curriculum—integrated skills courses, writing courses, grammar courses, vocabulary and reading courses, thesis and dissertation courses, ITA courses, etc.—also features attention to oral communication in the development of class activities and tasks. (Morley 1991,1993)

Advanced EAP oral communication courses. To provide advanced courses to meet the academic and career needs of international upper-level university students, faculty, and visiting scholars, it was necessary to break out of the molds of traditional "listening" and "speaking" conceptualizations. As pointed out by Murphy (1991) and others, this has long been a false division of language instruction. In designing the course work discussed in the remainder of this paper, in order to focus on maximizing learning, it was useful to keep some of the pieces of old and familiar instructional protocols, but it was necessary to synthesize them with new features—to create revised molds.

• ELI 434–"Discussion and oral argumentation speaking and listening skills." This course focuses on advanced tasks that feature listening and speaking skill-building in the construction of academic oral argumentation and interactive challenge-and-defense discussion. (Credit: 1 graduate credit.)

• ELI 601–"Listening and speaking in research contexts." This course focuses on oral communication in field-specific academic and professional contexts and the appropriate language for specific language functions in a variety of genres.
(Credit: 2 graduate credits.)

These two EAP courses are planned to provide instruction and practice for effective, sophisticated oral communication. They are designed to serve graduate-level students who are in MA, PhD, or professional programs across the university, and NNS faculty members and visiting scholars as well. Recent enrollments have included students from anthropology, geology, physics, dentistry, art history, electrical engineering and computer science, industrial operations engineering, civil engineering, materials science, math, business administration, law, psychology, economics, social work, public health, architecture and urban design, and many more departments.

Some of the same curriculum guidelines also have been used in designing speaking skills segments for a third course, ELI 993, an intensive summer workshop for International Teaching Assistants (ITAs), "College teaching in the United States: Pedagogy, culture, and language."(Credit: 1 graduate credit.)

2. Curriculum goals for advanced oral communication courses. In designing ELI 434 and ELI 601 a set of specific *learning goals* and a set of detailed *language goals* that encompass a number of parameters were developed. These are outlined in the Appendix.

2.1 Learning goals: Communicative competence, learning strategies, critical thinking. The intent of these three learning goals is to broaden the scope of the oral communication courses so that learners are involved not only in developing discrete language skills, but are oriented toward broader linguistic, personal, social, and intellectual perspectives.

GOAL 1: COMMUNICATIVE COMPETENCE. Learner development of communicative competencies in the production and reception of spoken academic discourse is one of the primary goals of these courses. The four components of the popular model developed by Canale and Swain (1980); Canale 1983, 1988) were adapted and used in the course design. Drawing upon Hymes's (1970) work with its dual focus on communicative competence and linguistic competence, the Canale and Swain format combines basic concepts in one very useful linguistic and pedagogical framework.

● *linguistic competence*—effective use of sentence-level language with primary attention to form, that is, grammatical, phonological, and lexical patterns of the L2;

● *discourse competence*—effective use of discourse above the level of the sentence, specifically, in areas such as language organization, use of rhetorical markers, ways of showing relationships in extended oral or written texts, etc.;

● *sociolinguistic competence*—skill in manipulation of language as appropriate to different contexts with regard to features of the situation, participants, roles, shared knowledge, etc.; and

● *strategic competence*—skill in repairing miscommunication and manipulating language as necessary to cope with breakdowns in communication; compensating for weaknesses in any of the other competence areas.

Developmental not rehabilitative coursework. In considering the four communicative competence goals, it is important to emphasize that ELI 434 and 601 course work is intended to be "developmental" in nature. That is, the philosophy is one of facilitating the growth and expansion of oral language skills, not "repair". Class activities are structured to enable learners to experiment, gain confidence, develop style, and expand and enrich their often limited and impoverished linguistic repertoire.

Overall, a central belief is that by involvement in demanding intellectual personalized oral language use, learners are "forced" to add to and retrieve language data from their second language stock, again and again, repeatedly and rapidly, thereby enabling learners to better "fix" elements within their repertoire and to access them more and more quickly for increasingly easy fluent use.

Developmental second language instruction might be considered on par with the continuing development of skills in one's first language, or in a third, fourth, or fifth year of foreign language study. Rehabilitative work, with measures to eliminate distracting error patterns and to repair pronunciation and/or grammatical breakdowns, is initiated in ELI 434 and 601, as necessary, and students are given individualized attention in tutorials.

GOAL 2: LANGUAGE LEARNING STRATEGIES. The concept of the language learner's role as "active creator" in the learning process played an important part in the movement away from a behavioral explanation of language acquisition, and toward a cognitive developmental theory (Corder 1967, 1976). Then, important reports on "good learner characteristics" by Rubin (1975) and Stern (1975) called the attention of professionals to the importance of individual differences and learner strategies and styles. Learner self-involvement was seen as crucial. Personal awareness, self responsibility, and the learner's control of his or her learning through conscious strategies played a significant role in empowering learners.

In the 1970s information appearing in the strategies literature focused primarily on research and theory, but in the 1980s a variety of practical guidelines and suggestions to teachers for helping students develop learning strategies began to appear. Valuable information and guidelines to help teachers set strategy goals and carry out instructional procedures in their classrooms appear in O'Malley, et. al, (1985), Chamot and O'Malley (1987), Wenden and Rubin (1987), Wenden (1985; 1991), Oxford (1985; 1990; 1993), O'Malley and Chamot (1990), and Scarcella and Oxford (1992), Leaver and Oxford (1983).

GOAL 3: CRITICAL THINKING. The critical thinking/critical language interface has not received much attention in the higher education ESL literature. Yet the average NNS university student, especially at advanced levels, will probably never pass through any more important time-compressed period of intense intellectual growth in his or her lifetime. Question: Will these students be able to take full advantage of this once-in-a-lifetime opportunity to develop their potential—intellectually and linguistically—using English as the medium of instruction and scholarly communication without help? Many will not. But EAP courses can provide instruction that will enable students to expand the breadth and depth of their English language use *at the same time that significant conceptual development is taking place.* The continued development of cognitive-academic language facility by this EAP student population may well be as essential to their proficiency as it is to school-age children acquiring a second language. The features of basic interpersonal communication skill-building (BICS) and cognitive academic language proficiency (CALP) as reported by Cummins (1980, 1983; Cummins and Swain, 1986) are well worth studying by EAP teachers.

Like the instruction in the EAP listening courses, described in Morley (1995), course work in ELI 434 and 601 has focused on ways and means to "teach thinking by discussion" (Bligh 1986). Drawing upon the work of Bligh (1986), Gordon and Poze (1980), and S.E.S. Associates at Harvard University, information on "groups for creative thinking" has been adapted and used in activities developed for ELI 434 and 601. Activities involve students in different types of discussions in order to encourage the development of various aspects of "thinking". Planning includes the following steps:

> Step 1. Identification of "thinking" objectives (e.g. problem-solving, analytical thinking, applying principles, consolidating memory by "rehearsal" of facts, decisionmaking, etc.) (Bligh 1986).

> Step 2. Identification of appropriate types of discussion teaching methods that can help learners develop particular skills (e.g. contexts such as "buzz" groups, brainstorming, case discussion, sensitivity groups, logical argument discussions, developmental sequence discussions, etc., as described in Bligh 1986).

> Step 3. Development of very focused tasks for learners. In traditional classes it is often the pattern to assign a topic, divide students into groups, and ask them to produce an answer or complete a task. But more often than not, the intent is largely one of simply getting students talking and is appropriate at beginning levels. What these advanced courses attempt to do, however, is to involve students in activities that encourage specific kinds of talking and thinking with clear ideas of what you want them to do, how you want them to do it, and why is important in the development of critical thinking/critical language use (Morley 1995).

2.2 Language goals: Speech, grammar, lexicon, discourse

GOAL 1: SPEECH RECEPTION/SPEECH PRODUCTION. The speech goals are to help learners develop intelligible and expressive use of the sounds and prosodic features of spoken English when they are in the *speaker mode,* and to use them for comprehension when they are in the *listener mode.* A dual focus is used, one which draws students' attention to two aspects of the spoken code: (a) micro-level pronunciation features, and (b) macro-level communication features. (See the Appendix.)

GOAL 2: GRAMMAR. The grammar goals are to help students expand their range of grammatical options, as well as to eliminate pesky problems. The assignments provide guided extemporaneous and impromptu speaking experiences that include both the uni-directional communication of sustained narrative presentations and the bi-directional (and multi-directional) communication of interactive comments/questions/answers. In a "safe" class environment, where early establishment of a supportive classroom "community" rapport is essential, these experiences allow students to experiment grammatically. They can try out new forms and new phrase structures, receive instant feedback, and get teacher and peer suggestions for possible alternative constructions—in the pre-class small-group peer rehearsal sessions, in the in-class performance sessions, in the post-class video-critique sessions.

GOAL 3: LEXICON. ELI 434 and 601 assignments give students opportunities to expand their repertoire of vocabulary words and phrasal units in two categories: (1) formal academic language, both general academic and field-specific, and (2) the less formal but equally important language of idiom, slang, and humor. Again, this class is a "safe" place, ideal for experimentation with idiomatic language, and the use of "jokes" and humorous anecdotes. In many disciplines even the most erudite explanatory discourse employs illustrative examples that make use of anecdotes and stories.

As a semester-long assignment students are asked to keep personal vocabulary journals and to make daily entries in both lexical areas. This learning strategy trains students to become conscious searchers for ways to expand their language stock and encourages them to become alert linguistic observers.

GOAL 4: DISCOURSE STRUCTURES AND FUNCTIONS. As detailed in the Appendix, this goal focuses on rhetorical markers, both macro-level organizational patterns and micro-level markers, and devotes attention to both transactional and interactional discourse.

A discourse-based perspective on language. In planning ways to maximize learning in these courses, a central component has been syllabus design that is constructed with a discourse-based perspective on language, that is, linguistic patterns viewed in relation to the social contexts in which they function. As Michael McCarthy and Ronald Carter (1994) comment in their book *Language as discourse: Perspectives for language teaching*:

> A discourse-based view of language involves us in looking not just at isolated, decontextualized bits of language. It involves examining how bits of language contribute to the making of complete texts. It involves exploring the relationship between the linguistic patterns of complete texts and the social contexts in which they function. It involves considering the higher-order operations of language at the interface of cultural and ideological meanings and returning to the lower-order forms of language which are often crucial to the patterning of such meanings. A discourse-based view of language also prioritizes an interactive approach to analysis of texts which takes proper account of the dynamism inherent in linguistic contexts. Language learning is also a dynamic process in which learning how to produce and understand texts and their variation is crucial. (p. 38)

Transactional and interactional discourse. In *Discourse analysis*, (1983), Brown and Yule discuss two types of language function. Their divisions are similar to Halliday's categories of "ideational language" and "interpersonal language" (Halliday in Lyons 1970).

●language for transactional purposes—the language used to convey factual or propositional information

●language for interactional purposes—the language used to express social relationships and personal attitudes

At first blush it might seem that in oral academic contexts transactional discourse, with its focus on content and its message-orientation, is of more importance than interactional discourse, with its focus on person and social orientation. In fact, both transactional and interactional discourse functions are important parts of the successful use of English for Academic Purposes. Transactional discourse (i.e., academic "business-type talk") and interactional discourse (rapport-building "small talk") are interwoven and function to support each another in academic contexts involving student-professor and student-student interactions. Attention to both kinds of discourse needs to be included in advanced EAP oral communication courses.

3. Course structure and course requirements.

ELI 434 and 601 are advanced public speaking courses in which students participate in a variety of assignments designed to facilitate the development of critical listening/critical thinking/effective speaking. They are similar in many ways to speech courses offered for native speakers of English in university speech or communication departments, but because they are designed to carry out the learning and language goals outlined in Part 2, there are a number of differences in the foci of the instructional tasks and the nature of the activities.

Class structure. For the discussion in this section, no differentiation will be made between the formats for ELI 434 and 601, as they are structured in much the same way.

Enrollment in the classes is limited to ten to twelve students per section. Classes meet for two, two-hour class sessions per week for seven weeks, or for one, one-and-a-half hour session for fourteen weeks. The classes require demanding out-of-class participation (e.g. pre-class rehearsals—both video filmed and unfilmed; small-group preparation and rehearsals for panel presentations; viewing and analyzing special video tapes outside of class and preparing panel reports for the class on the content, organization, and effectiveness of speakers' oral delivery; out-of-class follow-up analysis sessions with peer-groups and the instructor). The following three kinds of work sessions are used for these classes.

1. PRE-CLASS PREPARATION AND REHEARSAL SESSIONS. Pre-class oral rehearsals are an essential part of almost all assignments for these courses; they are not optional. The purpose of explicit rehearsal expectations is two-fold: to extend the students' guided oral practice opportunities beyond a class hour or two per week, as well as to benefit the quality of the specific assignment. Detailed preparation and rehearsal directions are given for each assignment. For some assignments—in groups or individually—students reserve time in a filming room which is specially outfitted for video practice.

2. IN-CLASS PERFORMANCE SESSIONS. Each oral assignment is recorded onto the speaker's personal video cassette. Panel presentations—in pairs or groups of three or four—are recorded on both a group tape and each individual's tape. Assignments have a set time limit so that every student gets a chance to "perform" every day. Short assignments of five minutes include longer follow-up sessions; longer assignments have little time for an in-class follow-up session, but include out-of-class assignments for small-group analysis of the video-taped presentation.

3. POST-CLASS CRITIQUE SESSIONS. Small groups of students meet after selected class assignments. Using a speech evaluation inventory, they complete a brief analysis of each student's strengths and two or three weaknesses, that is, areas that need continuing attention. From time to time the instructor joins the groups to monitor their work. Following panel presentations, the instructor meets with the entire panel group to review the recording.

Student video portfolio. Preparation of individual video portfolios is a central part of ELI 434 and 601. In much the same way that students assemble a portfolio of their writing assignments for writing classes, students in ELI 434 and 601 produce their personal "portfolio" of video tapes. Each assignment is recorded in its entirety, including instructional "interruptions," as is the audience participation follow-up session (i.e. comments, questions, and answers), which is conducted by the speaker. [Note: If video equipment is not available, an audio portfolio can be substituted.]

For the mid-term examination students view each of their presentations, observe their strengths and weaknesses, compare their performances from first to latest, and write a report. At the end of the term students select and submit for evaluation five recorded assignments from their portfolio.

Workout sessions and oral revision work. On a rotating basis the instructor provides one-on-one workout sessions which are videotaped in their entirety. These are true "workouts" in which the instructor sets rigorous individual standards and, serving in a teacher-as-coach mode, provides instant feedback and suggestions for revisions on the spot throughout the entire presentation. The student may be asked to repeat portions of the presentation over and over with specific goals. And, just as writing teachers ask students to submit revised papers, once or twice during the term students in these classes are asked to prepare a revised version of a presentation.

4. Assignments.

Speaking/listening/thinking tasks. Assignments for ELI 434 and 601 are chosen from among the five generic sets of speaking, listening, thinking activities described below. Students also learn how to introduce themselves and others, how to participate in a discussion, and how to chair a discussion. In addition, students in both classes have a number of free-choice, field-specific assignments that simulate the presentation of conference papers and "brown bag" departmental talks. Simulations of job interviews and "job talks" are conducted as needed.

Assignments include the following three tasks:

TASK 1: SPEAKING. One purpose of each assignment is to complete a central speaking task which has one or more specific language functions. Students are also expected to participate actively in the follow-up discussions by offering comments, questions, and answers. For students with marked speech intelligibility problems special tutorial work is provided.

TASK 2: LISTENING. Each assignment is also designed to include specific listening tasks during all three stages (i.e. pre-class, in-class, and post-class sessions). Listening tasks are varied (e.g. listening and performing actions; listening and performing operations; listening and solving problems; listening and writing notes; listening and analyzing on one or more of several levels; listening and summarizing information; interactive listening and negotiating meaning through comment/question/answer routines; etc.)[3] (Morley 1991b).

TASK 3: THINKING. Each assignment also focuses on specific "thinking" tasks. Some of the thinking tasks are planned as part of the preparation work and some are programmed into in-class sessions. For example, in case study activities (see the assignments in Group E, below) two to four students analyze a piece of spoken discourse along specified parameters and present a panel report that includes showing illustrative segments from the video tape. During the in-class report session for this assignment both the audience (i.e. class members and teacher) and presenters participate in a discussion in which they are asked to analyze and respond to the information in certain ways, and to

---

[3] See Morley in Celce-Murcia (1991: 92–103).

express and defend their own opinions. Other examples: (1) panels present their views on specific "university issues" (see the third assignment in Group C, below) and ask for responses and additional contributions from listeners; (2) for the "process talk" assignment (see the fourth assignment in Group B, below) listeners' take notes on the major steps in the process, and ask for repetitions, verifications, and clarifications as needed.

The assignments described in this section are not ordered, with the exception of the first and second assignments in Group A and the first and second assignments in Group C. During a semester a class will use ten to twelve assignments. Students are given descriptions of the purposes and procedures for each assignment. When the preparation is carried out during class time, the teacher circulates among the groups and monitors them as they prepare, answering questions, giving suggestions, supplying vocabulary words, and modeling pronunciation. The out-of-class preparation sessions are directed by an assigned or elected "chair" and monitored by the students themselves.

Each assignment has a time limit; students are expected to rehearse carefully in order to keep within the the allotted time. A stop watch with a buzzer warns students when only one minute remains. Students assist in filming and in time-keeping.

4.1 Group A: Individual Personal Talks

1. TWO-MINUTE PERSONAL INTRODUCTORY TALK (a first-day talk). Students are divided into groups of three and are placed in different rooms—or parts of the one classroom. They work together for five minutes in an informal rehearsal of what they plan to say about themselves. In "thinking by discussion" terms, this is a buzz group method. Objectives include consolidating memory by rehearsal of facts, encouragement of reticent students, and group cohesion (Bligh 1986:6–10).

2. TWO-MINUTE PERSONAL TOPIC TALK (a first- or second-day introductory talk). The same small-group preparation/rehearsal format is used here. Each class member chooses a topic from the list provided. Working together in small groups, students outline and rehearse their topic talks. The class members then reassemble and give their talks. Topics can include items such as: "What complicates my life?"; "What makes a happy family?"; and "My career plans for the next five years."

3. PERSONAL ATTRIBUTES TALK , OR "WHY I SHOULD GET THE JOB?" (a two-to three-minute self-sell talk). This task involves a two- to three-minute "self-selling" talk designed to "persuade"; that is, each student is to outline his or her strongest abilities in order to "get the job." It will be used again later in the course in job interview simulations. Student groups work outside of class in a brainstorming discussion that helps each person prepare. The time pressure

forces decisions as group members consider each other's strengths, suggest choices, help assemble logical arguments, and listen to each other's rehearsals. The group also acts as a peer-support group that monitors the rehearsals, encourages, and gives feedback.

4. APPLICATION-FOR-A-SCHOLARSHIP TALK, OR "WHY I SHOULD GET THE MONEY?" This task also involves a talk to persuade. As homework a description of a $20,000 dollar scholarship and the requirements for the competition is distributed. Students work independently outside class and prepare their case. Two or three compelling arguments must be developed to persuade a "scholarship jury" that the student is deserving. Sometimes teachers or students from other classes come in, listen to the talks, serve as a jury, and select a winner!

4.2 Group B: Individual Substantive Talks

1. MAKING ANNOUNCEMENTS.[4] Working together in groups of three, each student prepares a set of two factual informational announcements of local interest. Students are encouraged to be creative. Memos, posters, bulletin boards, and local and campus newspapers are sources, or students may create their own imaginary announcements. Each group sits as a panel and presents its announcements to the class and each individual student conducts a follow-up session for questions and comments as an integral part of the announcements assignment. Audience members are encouraged to ask really difficult questions for the student to "field."

2. A "STORY-TELLING" OR NARRATIVE TALK. This is a very enjoyable activity and it serves to build class community. It also has a practical discourse function, as anecdotes and stories are not only part of interactional discourse, but also can serve as illustrations within a transactional presentation. Individuals prepare, rehearse, and present a personal story about an incident in their travel experience or on living in a new location (e.g., country, city, etc.).

3. INFORMATIVE TALK WITH VISUALS. This is a good assignment with which to begin a series of more demanding presentations, as it allows the student to feel some security in having visual aids to depend upon in addition to generating "talk." Individuals prepare, rehearse, and present a talk that has a visual display as the focal point of the verbal presentation (e.g., overhead transparencies, slides, posters, handouts, blackboard work, models, etc.). Again, these talks include follow-up questions and comments as an integral part of the task. Guidelines for organizational patterns and presentation "tips" are distributed and

---

[4] Several of these assignments are from Morley (1992), *Extempore Speaking Practice.*

discussed. These include notes on organizational discourse markers and suggestions for preparing and using a variety of visuals.

4. A PROCESS OR "HOW TO ... " TALK. This is an especially enjoyable activity and allows for a wide range of topics. Individuals prepare, rehearse, and present a talk that focuses on giving instructions that will enable listeners to follow a course of action or take steps, often in sequence, in order to perform an action or operation, or undertake an activity. Audience members take notes on the major steps and ask questions of repetition, verification, or clarification. Guidelines and sample talk scripts are distributed and discussed. Topics can include: how to bake a cake; how to buy a car; how to ride a bicycle; how to open a bank account; how to get a credit card, etc.

5. A SPATIAL OR "HOW TO GET THERE" TALK. This task is similar to the previous assignment but the activity is focused on giving spatial directions to guide listeners toward reaching a specific geographical location. Students are encouraged to use maps, diagrams, or drawings as visual aids. These talks include follow-up questions and comments as an integral part of the task. Guidelines and sample talk scripts are distributed and discussed.

6. A CAUSE AND EFFECT EXPLANATORY TALK. This is an informational talk that features cause and effect as the focal organizing principle of the presentation. Individuals prepare, rehearse, and present an explanation, again with an audience participation follow-up session. Guidelines about organizational and cause-and-effect-specific discourse markers, and sample outlines are distributed and discussed.

7. A CONTRAST/COMPARE EXPLANATORY TALK. This is an informational talk that features contrast and comparison as the focal organizing principle of the presentation. Individuals prepare, rehearse, and present an explanation, again with audience follow-up questions. Guidelines that supply information about organizational and contrast-and-comparison-specific discourse markers and samples are distributed and discussed.

8. AN ISSUE-ORIENTED PERSUASIVE TALK. Students choose a topic of personal interest that involves a campus issue or a more general social issue. Outside of class they work together in pairs for preparation and rehearsal, but each student presents an individual talk. Guidelines for persuasive organizational patterns and persuasion-specific discourse markers are distributed and discussed.

4.3 Group C: Panel Presentations on International Student Issues. All assignments in this category are planned and rehearsed outside of class. In class they are presented by the three or four panel members who are seated together at the center table in a seminar style arrangement of tables. Each panel is allowed fifteen to twenty minutes for both their presentation and the follow-up session. Each student presents part of the discussion. One panel member chairs the meeting and introduces the panelists. One student summarizes main points or conclusions briefly at the end of the presentation. One student conducts the follow-up discussion.

The follow-up is an especially important part of this activity as it allows for spontaneous discussion among presenters and audience members. A limited range of questions may be established for a given assignment from among the following question types: repetition, paraphrase, verification, clarification, elaboration, extension, challenge, etc. (Morley 1992:3–4).

1. DISCUSSION QUESTION: "WHAT IS IT LIKE TO BE A MINORITY SPEAKER OF THE LANGUAGE OF THE MAJORITY?". It is fruitful to use this task very early in the course; it is a very "rich" topic and it contributes a great deal toward building a sense of class "community", bonding, and internal class trust and support. The first step is a short open class discussion that encourages students to brainstorm "off the tops of their heads" on the topic for three or four minutes. After this warm-up session, the second step is the homework assignment of small-group discussion and preparation of a panel report in which each person expresses her or his views on the subject. Students share experiences and concerns about language and cultural problems and adjustments. In the next assignment—or as a part of this one— students "brainstorm" and share ideas about how to solve or at least ameliorate some of the problems created by being second-language speakers living in an unfamiliar culture.

2. DISCUSSION QUESTION: "WHAT CAN WE DO TO HELP OURSELVES WHEN PROBLEMS OCCUR?" (FOLLOW-UP TO THE PREVIOUS ASSIGNMENT). This task follows the format used in the previous assignment. It involves brainstorming discussions and problem-solving and it encourages the sharing of coping strategies and self-help learning strategies. As a follow-up assignment each group views its video and makes a list of self-help suggestions using categories supplied by the teacher, or constructing their own. Lists of these are then duplicated and distributed to everyone. This task is very useful as an introduction to strategies goals.

3. DISCUSSION TOPIC: UNIVERSITY ISSUES. This is a very provocative topic. It focuses on cross-cultural comparisons including areas such as: relationships between professors and students in different countries; grading systems in different countries; academic and social issues of concern to students in different countries; the importance of a college degree, etc. It follows the panel preparation and presentation format described above.

4.4 Group D: Panel Interview Reports. In pairs or groups of three to four, students plan a school or community field trip. They prepare a list of questions as preparation for an informational interview. A pre-interview simulation session is held in class with the teacher or another person acting as the interviewee as students try out their procedures, interview skills, and questions. The students then call and make appointments, conduct the interviews, plan panel reports, and present them in class. The presentation format is the same as the assignments in Group C. Guidelines for interviews which include courtesy protocol are distributed.

Interviewees might include someone on the local school or campus premises (e.g. directors, curriculum coordinators, testing directors, librarians, office managers, teachers) or someone in the local community (e.g. merchants, business people, travel agents, mayors, fire or police chiefs, officials at passport/visa offices, etc.).

4. 5 Group E: Case Study Panel Reports. For each of these assignments pairs of students select a subject from those provided. Outside of class they view the video-recorded material and read any script material for the case. They then prepare a report that includes an analysis of the case and their opinions about the topic. They may show a portion of the video tape during their report if they wish. The nature of the analysis varies depending on the assignment. At the conclusion of their report, students conduct an audience participation follow-up discussion session for comments/questions/answers.

1. ANALYZING LEGAL CASES. The purpose of this task is to give students opportunities to practice mounting arguments, making judgments, and defending positions. The material used is descriptions of twenty-one legal cases (Ritter 1983) tried in civil law courts across the United States in recent years. A written summary and video reading of each case is available. These cases provide an excellent source of controversial issues.

Pairs of students choose a case and prepare a report as follows. One student reads a short summary of the case aloud to the class. Each student in the pair then gives a synopsis of either the "pro" or the "con" position. Next the "arguments" of the case are presented. Each of the pair argues one side. Following this presentation, audience members may express their opinions and give their arguments and counter-arguments. At the end of the open discussion the class sits as a "jury" and a secret ballot verdict vote is taken and announced. The teacher then reads the decision rendered by the judge and the reasoning upon which the decision was based. A few more minutes of agreement/disagreement discussion completes this activity.

Topics include: the case of religion in school; the case of the eavesdropping husband; the case of the trooper's ticket quota; the case of the short applicant; the case of the barred woman executive, etc.

2. ANALYZING INFORMATIONAL LECTURETTES. The purposes of this task are to give students opportunities to: summarize content; judge the balance/bias of the information presented on subjects; critique organizational patterns; and assess speakers' presentational skills.

Twenty video recordings of short informational lecturettes (seven to fifteen minutes each) presented by UM faculty and staff members are used for this activity (with a second set of twenty in production; see Morley 1989). These lecturettes provide a rich source of information on a wide variety of topics. In pairs students view their lecturette outside of class and plan a presentation that discusses the content, organization, balance/bias of the video presentation, and the speaker's speech skills. Illustrative segments of the video may be shown. Following the presentation the presenters conduct an open class discussion.

Topics include: TV's influence on children; the self-help movement; decision-making in a major university; language learning; speech varieties; culture shock; American art museums; American baseball; English as international language of research; labor unions; robotics; etc.

3. ANALYZING CONTROVERSIAL ISSUES. As with the first activity, the purpose of this task is to give students practice in mounting arguments, making judgments, and defending positions. Over fifty issues of *Consider*,[5] a weekly non-partisan forum on controversial issues published by the University of Michigan, are used for this activity. In pairs students choose an issue of the publication and prepare a discussion of the topic with presentation of the arguments of the two positions. Following their presentation, they conduct an open discussion on the topic.

Topics include: what is the student's social responsibility? do we have the right to judge other cultures?; are grades failing us?; marriage, the old ball and chain?; are children's cartoons too violent?; the P.C. debate, what's in a name?; does recycling harm more than it helps?; course pack royalties, justice or greed?; the people's right to know: media coverage of public figures; gay family housing; homosexuals in the military; abortion, origins of life; etc.

---

[5] *Consider* is a weekly four-page non-partisan "Issues Forum" published by the students of the University of Michigan and sponsored by colleges, departments, and administrators. Page one of each issue has an eye-catching cover that calls attention to a controversial issue. Page two is a short essay on the "pro" position of the issue, and page three is a short essay on the "con" position.

4. ANALYZING TELEVISION DISCUSSION SHOWS. The purpose of this task is to give students practice in the analysis of discourse organization and discourse markers. In compliance with governmental regulations, off-air tapings of television programs are used for analysis. Students complete a comparative analysis of the discourse features of two programs, such as *Crossfire* and *Washington Week in Review*, and present them to the class for discussion.

5. Final comments. Some of the EAP course development work at the University of Michigan English Language Institute has been discussed here, both theoretical principles and classroom practices. With the goal of maximizing learning for L2 university students, the major focus of this paper has been on syllabus design from a discourse-based perspective on language in which linguistic patterns are viewed in relation to the social contexts in which they function. Some of the details of curriculum design for two advanced oral communication courses have been presented, including a review of goals—those related to language, learning, and course structure and requirements—and brief descriptions of some of the kinds of assignments being used experimentally.

REFERENCES

Bligh, Donald. 1986. *Teach thinking by discussion*. Exeter, UK: The Society for Research into Higher Education and NFER-Nelson.
Brown, Gillian and George Yule. 1983. *Discourse analysis*. New York, NY: Cambridge University Press.
Canale, Michael and Merrill Swain. 1980. "Theoretical bases of communicative approaches to second language teaching and testing." *Applied Linguistics* 1:1–47.
Canale, Michael. 1983. "From communicative competence to communicative language teaching." In J. Richards and R. Schmidt (eds.), *Language and communication*. London: Longman. 2–87.
Canale, Michael. 1988. "The measurement of communicative competence." In R.B. Kaplan et al. (eds.), *Annual Review of Applied Linguistics*, Vol 9. New York: Cambridge University Press. 67–84.
Chamot, Anna and Michael O'Malley. 1987. "The cognitive academic language learning approach: A bridge to the mainstream." *TESOL Quarterly* 21(2):227–249.
Corder, S. Pit. 1967. "The significance of learners' errors." *International Review of Applied Linguistics* 5(4):161–170.
Corder, S. Pit. 1976. "The study of interlanguage." In G. Nickel, ed., *Proceedings of the fourth international congress of applied linguistics*. Stuttgart, Germany: Hochschulverlag.
Cummins, Jim 1980. "The cross-lingual dimensions of language proficiency: Implications for bilingual education and the optimal age issue." *TESOL Quarterly* 14(2):175–187.
Cummins, Jim. and Merrill Swain. 1986. *Bilingualism in education*. London: Longman.
Gordon, W.J.J. and T. Poze. 1980. *The new art of the possible*. Cambridge, Massachusetts: Porpoise Books.
Halliday, M. A. K. 1970. "Language structure and language function." In John Lyons (ed), *New horizons in linguistics*. Baltimore, Maryland: Penguin. 140–165.

Hymes, Dell. 19972. "On communicative competence." In J. Pride and A. Holmes (eds.). *Sociolinguistics*. Harmondsworth, UK: Penguin. 269-293.

Institute of International Education. 1991. *Open doors, 1990-1991*, and *1993-1994*. New York: IIE Publications.

Leaver, Betty Lou and Rebecca Oxford. 1993. *Learning strategies: A manual for students*. Salinas, CA: AGSI Press.

McCarthy, Michael and Ronald Carter. 1994. *Language as discourse: Perspectives for language teaching*. London and New York: Longman.

Morley, Joan (ed). 1989. *American lectures: New listening materials*. People's Republic of China: Fudan University Press.

Morley, Joan. 1991a. "Perspectives on English for academic purposes." In James E. Alatis (ed.)., *Georgetown University Round Table 1991*. Washington, D.C.: Georgetown University Press. 143-166.

Morley, Joan. 1991b. "Listening comprehension in second/foreign language instruction." In M. Celce-Murcia(ed.), *Teaching English as a second or foreign language, Second edition*. New York, New York: Newbury House.

Morley, Joan. 1992a. *Extempore speaking practice*. Ann Arbor, Michigan: University of Michigan Press.

Morley, Joan. 1992b. "EAP oral communication curriculum: Spoken discourse, meaning, and communicative pronunciation." In James E. Alatis (ed.), *Georgetown University Round Table 1992*. Washington, D. C.: Georgetown University Press. 241-258.

Morley, Joan. 1993. "Learning strategies, tasks, and activities in oral communication instruction." In James E. Alatis, (ed.), *Georgetown University Round Table 1993*. Washington, D.C.: Georgetown University Press. 116-136.

Morley, Joan. 1995. "Academic listening comprehension instruction: Models, principles, and practices." In D. Mendelsohn and J. Rubin (eds.), *A guide for the teaching of second language listening*. San Diego, California: Dominie Press, Inc.186-221.

Mueller, Sherry. 1991. "Internationalism and higher education patterns and trends: A national perspective on the last fifty years." Unpublished paper delivered at the University of Michigan, Fall, 1991.

Murphy, John. 1991. "Oral communication in TESOL: Integrating speaking, listening, and pronunciation." *TESOL Quarterly* 25(1): 51-75.

NAFSA. 1993. "Trends: Noncitizen's share of new doctorates continues to grow." *NAFSA Newsletter* 44(6):1-2.

O'Malley, Michael, et al. 1985. "Learning strategy applications with students of English as a second language." *TESOL Quarterly* 19(3): 557-584.

O'Malley, Michael and Anna Chamot. 1990. *Learning strategies in second language acquisition*. New York: Cambridge University Press.

Oxford, Rebecca. 1985. *A new taxonomy of second language learning strategies*. Washington DC: ERIC Clearinghouse on Languages and Linguistics.

Oxford, Rebecca. 1990. *Language learning strategies: What every teacher should know*. New York: Newbury House.

Oxford, Rebecca. 1993. "Language learning strategies in a nutshell: Update and ESL suggestions." *TESOL Journal*. 2(2):18-22.

Ries, P. and D. H. Thurgood. 1991. *Doctorate recipients from United States universities*. New York: National Academic Press.

Ritter, John. 1983. *You be the judge*. Los Angeles, California: Price, Stern, and Sloan.

Rubin, Joan. 1975. "What the 'good language learner' can teach us." *TESOL Quarterly* 9(1):41-51.

Scarcella, Robin and Rebecca Oxford. 1992. *The tapestry of language learning: The individual in the communicative classroom*. Boston, Massachusetts: Heinle and Heinle.

Stern, H. H. 1975. "What can we learn from the good language learner?" *Canadian Modern Language Journal* 31(4):304–318.
Wenden, Anita. 1985. "Learner strategies." *TESOL Newsletter* 19(5).
Wenden, Anita and Joan Rubin. 1987. *Learner strategies in language learning*. Englewood Cliffs, N.J.: Prentice Hall.
Wenden, Anita. 1991. *Learner strategies for learner autonomy*. London: Prentice Hall International.

APPENDIX

Table 1. Skeleton outline of design parameters for oral communication instruction[6]

PART I–LEARNING GOALS			
A. Communicative Competence Goals[7] Purpose: To provide opportunities for learners to develop communicative competencies			
1. Linguistic	2. Discourse	3. Sociolinguistic	4. Strategic
B. Learning Strategy Goals[8] Purpose: To guide learners in developing systematic self-help learning strategies			
1. Cognitive	2. Communication	3. Global Practice	
4. Metacognitive	5. Affective	6. Social	
C. Critical Thinking Goals[9] Purpose: To provide opportunities for learners to develop their L2 skills in critical thinking			
1. Analysis and synthesis	2. Applying principles	3. Problem-solving	4. Decision-making

---

[6]Detailed version of figure appears in Morley (1995:214–216).

[7]See Canale and Swain (1980).

[8]See Oxford (1990) and Wenden (1985).

[9]See Bligh (1986).

Table 2. Skeleton outline of design parameters for oral communication instruction (continued)

PART II–LANGUAGE GOALS: FORMS AND FUNCTION				
A. Speech Goals: Sentence Level and Text Level Purpose: To enable learners to recognize and use pronunciation patterns in *listener* and *speaker* roles		**B. Grammar Goals: Focus on Academic Context** Purpose: To enable learners to comprehend grammatical patterns in the *listener* role and to use them in the *speaker* role.		
1) Micro-level Pronunciation Features (a focus on discrete point pronunciation features; speech production; sentence- level competence)	**2) Macro-level Communication Features** (a focus on global patterns of communica-bility; speech performance; discourse-level competence)	**3) Features of Grammar** (a focus on selected basic grammar points)	**4) Features of Grammar** (a focus on selected complex grammar points)	
C. Lexicon: Words and Phrasal Units Purpose: To enable learners to comprehend lexical units in the *listener* role and use them in the *speaker* role.		**D. Discourse Structures and Functions** Purpose: To enable learners to comprehend structural/functional patterns in the *listener* role and use them in the *speaker* role.		
1) Academic Vocabulary (general academic, and field-specific academic and professional lexicon)	**2) All-purpose Vocabulary** (informal speech, idiomatic expressions, slang, humor, etc.)	**3) Rhetorical Markers**	**4) Transac-tional Discourse** (understand-ing and conveying factual propositional information)	**5) Inter-actional Dis-course** (under-standing and using language of inter-personal/ social/ academic commun-ity)

Multidisciplinary Integrated Language Education: New questions for second/foreign-language teaching

Guy Spielmann
Georgetown University

Introduction: The language crisis. For the past thirty years, there has been incontrovertible evidence of a "language crisis" in the United States. This language crisis can be defined as a steady decline in literacy and language proficiency, with dire consequences for the welfare of the majority of citizens, and the nation as a whole:

> Economic and strategic pressures abroad as well as an increasingly pluralistic society at home demand the creation of an America that is far more language competent than it now is. (Lambert 1994: 7)

Numerical indicators, such as the "virtually unbroken decline from 1963 to 1980" in verbal SAT scores (National Commission on Excellence in Education 1983: 8),[1] disastrous national illiteracy rates,[2] and our empirical observations show that, while mass education has failed to bring literacy (and the "good life") to a majority of citizens, the exponential growth of technology and information since the end of World War II has raised to unprecedented levels the minimal linguistic expertise needed to function adequately in society. This needed expertise is no longer commensurate with average levels of actual proficiency.

The state of second/foreign-language competence is no less alarming: Despite recent developments in research and theory (and recurring claims of a "paradigm shift"), the grim picture painted by the President's Commission on Foreign Languages and International Studies in *Strength through wisdom* (1979) has hardly brightened, even with an ever more pressing sense that actual

---

[1] From 1963 to 1980, verbal ability decreased by more than fifty points, and math ability by forty; from 1980 to 1994, verbal ability decreased another point (after a brief rise in the mid-1980s), whereas math scores increased by seven points.

[2] The U.S. Department of Education defines literacy as "using printed and written information to function in society, to achieve one's goals, and to develop one's knowledge and potential," and uses a five-point scale to rate it. In 1992, ninety million adults (about 47% of the entire U.S. population) performed at the two lowest levels. (Source: *National adult literacy survey*, 1992, National Center for Educational Statistics, U.S. Department of Education.)

competence in nonnative languages is indispensable in a "multicultural world in transition" (Byrnes 1992).

Yet, the nature and depth of the crisis have not been fully grasped because of an enduring *mechanistic* vision of language, limited to the awareness that being articulate contributes to economic competitiveness, employability, and social promotion. In fact, successive generations hold an ever more precarious grasp on language because it is becoming less and less clear *why* a rich vocabulary, sophisticated syntax, and correct grammar should make a difference, other than because they are (or at least were) sanctioned by socially prominent groups. The role of language in the human condition, in the quality of our experience of the world,[3] has been all but ignored because it is regarded as a philosophical issue not directly relevant to the practical, daily concerns of educators.

Despite their apparent differences, the various movements to improve or reform language teaching have all been based on the same ontological and epistemological framework, which explains why the teaching of languages, in more than twenty-five centuries of recorded existence, has gone around in circles and "rediscovered" its most ancient beliefs and methods over and again (See Kelly 1969.) Generally, all failed attempts to change education have in common an "unreflective acceptance of assumptions and axioms that seem so obviously right, natural and proper, that to question them is to question ... reality" (Sarason 1990: 148).

The purpose of Multidisciplinary Integrated Language Education (MILE) is precisely to "question reality": MILE is both a philosophy of language as it relates to education, and a philosophy of education as it relates to language; a model for ontological and epistemological inquiry into such elemental concepts as 'language,' 'education,' 'grammar,' 'learning,' and 'culture.'[4] However, it reflects the basic principles of a *pragmatic* philosophy, which Scheffler sums up as follows:

> In its search for an integrated interpretation of human life, it strives to relate mind and nature, language and thought, action and meaning, knowledge and value, emphasizing always the primary significance of critical thought, logical method, and the test of experience in all realms of endeavor. (Scheffler 1974: ix)

---

[3] Throughout this paper, I use "world" in the semiophilosophic sense of "the seeming by which the universe appears to humans as a set of sensible qualities endowed with a certain organization which occasionally brings it to be designated as the 'world of common sense' " (Greimas and Courtès 1982: 374).

[4] In order to avoid confusion, I distinguish typographically between reference to concepts with single quotation marks ('language') and to words with slashes (/language/).

Only by investigating the current fundamental concepts of language education can we understand and transcend the limitations which account for the inability of successive reforms to contain or reverse the language crisis; philosophical inquiry is only the first step—but an indispensable one—toward effectively revitalizing planning strategies, curriculum, and materials, as well as teaching methods and techniques. In this paper, I will present a rationale for MILE, delineate its major aspects, and offer some insights into its applications to the theory and practice of second/foreign-language teaching.

The current paradigm in language teaching. For all intents and purposes, and notwithstanding gratuitous pleas to the contrary by some educators, language is conceptualized within a mechanistic and positivistic, rationalist paradigm as a neutral tool of learning, communication, or expression; that is, as a mental process which can be modelized in abstraction from actual use by a specific person in a determined context—and from teaching and learning in a peculiar school culture.

The trend towards a resolutely antimentalistic, outcome-based orientation for language instruction has become more pronounced as the erstwhile educational challenge of improving language use from adequate mediocrity to a higher degree of refinement and sophistication has given way to the task of ensuring a minimal level of proficiency for social adaptation. Although this trend meets the intuitive yearning for "basic skills" in the general public, especially in times of recession and social strife, it actually makes a bad situation worse (Gardner 1991), because it was precisely from such a skill-oriented, reductionist view of education that many problems originated.

However justified it may seem, the shift in priorities from what Maslow (1943) calls "growth needs" to "deficiency needs" has obviated the ideal that democracy and mass schooling should spread the finer benefits of education beyond the circle of a cultural elite. In theory, schools should have bestowed upon an ever greater number of ordinary citizens a bounty not only quantitative (i.e. material and economic), but qualitative as well, in the form of a higher level of intellectual, spiritual, and aesthetic self-actualization: "a system of education that affords its members the opportunity to stretch their minds to full capacity," in the words of the epoch-making report, *A nation at risk* (National Commission on Excellence in Education 1983: 13).

Unfortunately, sheer cognizance of the crisis has not translated into philosophical questioning: In *Tomorrow's teachers*, the Holmes Group decried "a simplistic view of the nature of the problems confronting education ... and a simplistic view of how one goes about solving the complex problems of education" (Holmes Group 1986: 26). Indeed, educators have generally responded to the crisis by addressing its symptoms rather than its causes, and implementing "a surfeit of band-aid reforms" (Sarason 1990: 95). As one of the best-known advocates of school reform, Theodore Sizer, recently noted: "Too many reforms never questioned some basic assumptions about how schools are organized" (O'Neil 1995: 4). It is precisely this "set of cultural and social norms and assumptions concerning educational systems" (or "deep structure") which has to be challenged (Tye 1990: 35–36).

Yet, in spite of its manifest and continued failure to alleviate the crisis, our profession has proved quite content with the "surprising consensus among nations on the goals and objectives" of language education (Bergentoft 1994: 8). If we are to effect significant and durable change on the "architecture of the system" by reexamining "what the building blocks are and how they can be assembled better"(Lambert 1994: 49), we must first test the assumptions that these "building blocks" represent. The most primal block, the ultimate purpose of language learning, has been formulated—like so many other educational issues—as a dichotomy: Actual language use to meet socioeconomic needs, versus "learning per se as a liberal educational enterprise" (Lambert 1994: 56).

These apparently antithetical goals only account for two of the four general types of orientations in curriculum, mechanistic (product-oriented) and academic (knowledge-oriented), and ignore humanistic and social-reconstructionist philosophies, which consider the transformation of the learner and the improvement of society as their objectives.[5] One of the fundamental flaws of second/foreign-language education has been to confine its conceptual field to dichotomies (acquisition vs. learning, explicit vs. implicit grammar instruction, skills vs. content, internal vs. external linguistics, etc.). The primary aim of our epistemological enterprise is to expand this field—a task which requires above all a redefinition of 'language' and 'education' in order to establish valid operational concepts as "building blocks."

Towards a new paradigm. MILE reflects the belief that a "philosophy of education shall above of all be a query rather than a corpus of knowledge, a practice of questioning what we know (or believe we know) about education" (Reboul 1992: 3, my translation), and that philosophy is "the theory of education as a deliberately conducted practice" (Dewey 1916: 387). We do need a deliberate practice of questioning concepts to inform all levels of the educational enterprise (curricular and instructional design, materials selection and teaching techniques), and we have to consider that, as Bachelard,

---

[5] A *mechanistic* curriculum (also known as technocratic, or technological) focuses on the attainment of predetermined, discrete outcomes; an *academic* one promotes learning and knowledge for its own sake; *humanistic* philosophy is geared towards the harmonious development of the individual; and *social reconstructionism* regards schooling as an agent for social change. (See McNeil 1990.)

Canguillem, and Foucault demonstrated, no concept is isolated, immanent or static:

> ... the history of a concept is not wholly and entirely that of its progressive refinement, its continuously increasing rationality, its abstraction gradient, but that of its various fields of constitution and validity, that of its successive rules of use, that of the many theoretical contexts in which it developed and matured. (Foucault 1972: 4)

A capital aspect of our work, then, is to pursue what Foucault calls an "archeology of knowledge" in order to understand the formation of the *epistémè* which accounts for the theories and practices of language teaching in existance today.

Although we can only assume that the formal teaching of language originated with formal education itself, it has barely reached the second of the four thresholds outlined by Foucault in the evolution of a "discursive formation" (positivity, epistemologization, scientificity, and formalization) and, in the current state of affairs, shows no sign of moving towards the next level (Foucault 1972: 186–187). There are two main causes of this situation:

(1) Depending on the context, /language education/ refers to any one element in a heterogeneous constellation of concepts, theories, methods, practices, and logistical units (departments, disciplines)—so that, in fact, "language education" does not yet represent a clearly defined, viable discipline; and

(2) teaching language can be heavily empirical (based on "methods that work," regardless of the validity of their premises) or founded on theories (in linguistics, psychology, or cognitive science) which do not, in and by themselves, fully explain the role of language in a formal schooling environment and in education in general.

We must begin by defining 'language education' as a distinct, unified, and internally coherent domain of knowledge and discursive formation, with its own concepts and methodology. The use of /language/ in the singular points very deliberately to the whole human linguistic condition, as opposed to any particular language (or aspect of language); similarly, the use of /education/, as opposed to /teaching/ or /acquisition/, implies that the entire educational experience (formal or informal, in and out of school) is taken into account.

Beyond eclectic and outcome-based models. Such an approach is necessary for all educators, though especially for novice and future teachers, who perhaps most need to reflect on the issues of import in their profession, rather than to simply start teaching as they were taught or embrace uncritically one or several extant methods. Although in theory "methodology courses exist to help prospective teachers develop their own teaching style and pedagogy, rather than to indoctrinate them in the use of specific models and techniques" (Wing 1993: 172), such development often consists of culling discrete items from a pre-established "repertoire of teaching ideas" (Omaggio-Hadley 1993: 105).

The prevailing mechanistic paradigm has thus also undermined teacher education by restricting its scope almost entirely to the *didactic* level, where existing concepts are not questioned and where, in fact, any theoretical thinking is viewed with suspicion, because it is reputed to ignore the actual needs of the teacher in the classroom. It is now widely believed that:

> since there is no "one true theory" upon which to base instruction, the practitioner must either select from among conflicting theories or else become "eclectic" and choose whatever seems to work in a given situation. (Grittner 1990: 38)

This principle, which curriculum expert George J. Posner has dubbed "garbage-can eclecticism" (Posner 1992: 3), really amounts to the outright rejection of epistemology in favor of a purely pragmatic, empirical approach:

> In fact, if we consider the variables that confront teachers throughout the profession, it becomes almost ludicrous to contemplate a single set of teaching strategies that will be appropriate for every age group, proficiency level, learning style ... , to name but a few of the most common teacher-learner variables ... (Grittner 1990: 38)

It is no accident that in the professional discourse of second/foreign-language teaching, /methodology/ is often used synonymously with /method/, although the accumulation of methods (no matter how they are selected) does not equate with methodology, which belongs to a qualitatively higher level of inquiry.[6]

In fact, the very concept of 'method' is at issue, because in itself it implies a mechanistic orientation: Even the claim that there cannot be a single "right" method is predicated on a belief that teaching requires a method which, in turn, presupposes a concept of education as the application by a teacher of "teaching strategies that are aimed at producing specific outcomes" (Grittner 1990: 39).

---

[6] *Webster's New Collegiate Dictionary* (1977) defines "methodology" as "a body of methods, rules and postulates employed by a discipline" and "the analysis of principles and procedures in a particular field," and "method" primarily as "a procedure or process for attaining an object."

656 / GEORGETOWN UNIVERSITY ROUND TABLE ON LANGUAGES AND LINGUISTICS 1995

Such an outcome-based model (which is anything but ideologically neutral, contrary to what is frequently claimed)[7] perpetuates the "factory model" of schooling: Teachers and students are cogs in a system conceived to yield a product that society needs. Since we want education to be much more—a process of growth, maturation and self-actualization, of construction (rather than transmission) of knowledge, an agent of social change—we can hardly subscribe to this concept of 'method,' or accept as an ideal that a teacher should merely "be cognizant of current trends and innovative techniques in foreign language methodology, and ... employ the best methods to achieve the desired goals" (Grittner 1990: 26).

Thus the practitioner is bound to remain an executant (albeit a well-informed one), and may never take on the responsibility for independent judgment which characterizes a true "professional." Only an epistemological frame of mind can counteract this mechanistic orientation, and pave the way for a more humanistic—and, to some degree, social reconstructionist—philosophy.

Redefining language education. In order to define 'language education,' it is necessary to inquire into the meaning of 'language' and 'education' *in relationship to one another*. At present there is no interdisciplinary field of research which includes all academic disciplines pertaining to some aspect of language: English, second/foreign-languages, ESL, linguistics, speech, and communication, to which we could add speech pathology, philosophy, cognitive science, and education. The fact that such a list may seem quite heterogeneous in terms of academic logistics—separate departments, goals, theories, practices, and pedagogical orientations—already points to the problematic nature of 'language' as an object of study in our culture.

Far from discarding existing theories of language or language acquisition, we must confront some inescapable realities of the educational experience:

(1) The ways and means of formal schooling are steeped in an institutional culture which shapes them as much as—if not more than—pedagogical imperatives, and must be taken into account by research and theory about curriculum, teaching methods, and materials;

(2) language is not only an *object* of study among others, but also the primary *medium* of all teaching and learning in and outside of school, a trait which gives it a unique status among academic disciplines; and

---

[7] The "curriculum-free nature of the [ACTFL] proficiency guidelines" (Galloway 1987: 37; see also Omaggio-Hadley 1993: 105) is a myth: Proficiency-oriented instruction, as described by its framers, "is concerned with observable behavior" and "purposely reflect[s] a product rather than process orientation," which represents a very definite and deliberate mechanistic philosophy (Galloway 1987: 35–37).

(3) education *lato sensu* (as opposed to formal schooling) is a constant and universal phenomenon of the human experience—perhaps, as Kant suggested, the very defining feature of our humanity—which provides teaching and learning in ways quite different from those within the institutional culture of schools. In fact the explanation for any "educational crisis" could be that what society at large teaches its members or expects them to know does not match what schools teach (overtly or not), and/or *how* they teach it—hence the ever popular but misdirected goal of making schools relevant to "real life," which is really an adulteration of Dewey's idea that schools *are* real-life settings, and should be operated accordingly. (Dewey 1899)

The nature and function of language as an object of academic study differ sharply from the nature and function of language as a medium of social interaction on the one hand, and as a constitutive element of human thought and perception of reality on the other hand; yet, all three are determinant factors in education *lato sensu*. In conclusion, language teaching cannot be reduced to a kind of algebraic formula, the conjugation of a student with a method and a teacher toward the attainment of a goal, occurring in the microcosm of a classroom (for E-linguists), or a person's mind (for I-linguists). The purview of language education is the human linguistic condition as a whole, which includes our dependence on language to make sense of reality and sustain our various symbolic modes of expression and communication, including and especially those involved in learning.

In order to elaborate a serviceable concept of 'language education,' I propose a model of co-occurrence on two levels, formal (schooling) and informal (socialization) as outlined in Figure 1. Within each level are three mutually presupposed terms: language acquisition, acculturation, and heuristic and metacognitive processes.

Acculturation. Learning is never culturally neutral; it presupposes ontological and epistemological choices, which often remain implicit but serve to reinforce the bond of the learner with a particular culture. This process may well be conflictual (especially in formal schooling) when there is a cultural discrepancy between the learner and the learning or what is being learned: The main argument of multicultural education, for instance, is that "some institutional characteristics of schools systematically deny some students equal ... opportunities" (Banks 1993a: 3) by enforcing cultural norms quite different from those of the students.

Figure 1. Language education

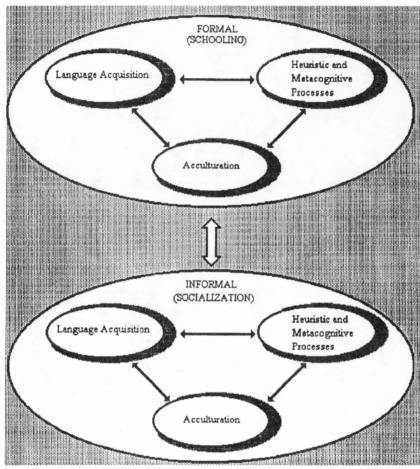

Contrary to what multicultural discourse often states, however, MILE considers that acculturation is not a matter of *substance* (in Hjelmslev's terminology),[8] but of *form*. When Banks posits four levels of integration of multicultural *content* (i.e. substance, in semiotic terms) in the curriculum, he remarks that the "Contributions" and "Addition" approaches, which merely supplement the existing curriculum with "heroes, holidays, and discrete cultural elements," fall short of promoting true multicultural understanding (Banks

---

[8] Louis Hjelmslev (1953) posits a fourfold articulation of signs: *Plane of expression* (Saussure's signifier) and *plane of content* (Saussure's signified) are each divided in *substance* (what is being structured) and *form* (what structures it); all terms are in mutual implication.

1993b: 199). But even in the "Transformation" approach, which involves restructuring the curriculum, the goal remains limited to integrating "perspectives, frames of reference and content from various groups" (Banks 1993b: 203).

Although he points out that "concepts such as the Middle Ages and the Renaissance are still used to organize most units in literature, and the arts" (Banks 1993c: 18), and suggests that students explore the perspective of African Americans on the American Revolution, Banks does not question the implied, essentially Western belief that 'history' is a collection of facts supported by written records. In order to understand acculturation, and possibly affect it, we need to challenge assumptions at the epistemic level about the structuring (form) of knowledge: How do we establish what 'history' or 'language' are?

Heuristic and metacognitive processes. Each learning experience teaches or reinforces the process which makes it possible; therefore, the manner in which learning occurs is as relevant as what is being learnt—more consequential, in fact, since it affects the conditions of further learning. Explicit or not, the "metacurriculum"

> is comprised of learning skills and strategies selected on the basis of their value in helping students (1) acquire the curriculum content being taught and (2) develop the capacity to think and learn independently. (Ackerman and Perkins 1989: 80)

Although fewer people today still claim that the purpose of education is the transmission of facts, schooling has proven to be particularly ill-suited to foster what cognitive scientists call "deep" or "expert" learning. Deep learning, which is "essentially creative," is what "people use to organize their grasp of the world," and what "drives us and gives us our sense of purpose," which "includes our intellectual and spiritual needs" (Caine and Caine 1991: 91–97).

In this sense, "depth" does not refer to highly specialized knowledge in one field: Gardner stresses the difference between the "disciplinary expert," who can apply and adapt his knowledge and skills to continuously solve new types of problems, and the "scholastic" learner, who is only able to deal with a familiar formulation of problems (Gardner 1992: 6). As native-born "intuitive learners," all humans develop "remarkably serviceable and robust theories" about the world; formal schooling then confirms, or more commonly refines or disproves such theories—in principle at least (Gardner 1992: 2). In fact, because of the disjunction between intuitive and formal learning, students retain a surprising number of "misconceptions," "stereotypes," "scripts," and "simplifications" after years of schooling, including college study (Gardner 1992: 170).

The role of language is pivotal in transcending these limits, because of the part it plays in our conceptual representations of the natural world; philosophy took a "linguistic turn" the early twentieth century when it became clear that human inquiry into the nature of reality was conditioned by the linguistic character of thought. The Sapir-Whorf hypothesis, the work of thinkers like Wittgenstein, Quine, Pierce, Russell, and Whitehead, as well as the development of semiotics and various flavors of structuralism (and poststructuralism) should have ruled out forever any mechanistic interpretation and teaching of language.

Nevertheless, the culture of schools has managed to ignore or reject such thinking, or to integrate it only so that it may be more effectively neutralized: Teachers who, as scholars, embrace radical critical theories (feminism, marxism, deconstructionism, etc.) often turn out to be staunch conservatives in their "language courses," and submit their students to a tell-and-drill regimen which belies the very philosophical principles they otherwise advocate. Thus students are denied the opportunity to develop an understanding of language as the main element in our construction of reality, even though their instructors are presumably aware (even if only intuitively) of the wondrous phenomenon of semiosis, and recognize that

> beyond the practical communicative function of language lies its symbolic and metaphoric function. It is this latter function of language which ... liberates men from their pedestrian existence. (Garcia 1992: 6)

Such recognition remains hollow as long as it is not clearly established how and when this liberation should occur, and as the agenda of "basic" courses in the lower regions of the curriculum remains hopelessly mired in a mechanistic paradigm. The ideal goal of learning, what we might call "understanding of the world" in a philosophical sense, requires much more than the performance of skills (no matter how expertly); yet most curricula and teaching methods seem to assume a leap of faith between what is actually taught (and how it is taught) and the putative liberating experience which should follow.

It is enlightening to compare taxonomies of the cognitive and affective domains in this respect: Their upper levels represent forms of "genuine understanding" (of the world, of oneself) that reach *qualitatively* higher than expertise in any field of knowledge or skill domain. Bloom (1956) proposes "evaluation" (i.e. making judgments based on internal evidence or external criteria) as the ultimate goal whereas, on a different type of scale, Maslow (1943) regroups "growth needs" on the top three tiers (in addition to four lower "deficiency needs"): the "need for self-actualization," the "desire to know and understand" and, finally, "aesthetic needs."

In both cases, there is a progression from the concrete and mechanistic toward the intangible and spiritual, a progression which, in fact, parallels the evolution of the human brain, from the cruder, animalistic R-complex (or "reptilian brain") to the uniquely human neocortex (MacLean 1979). In practical terms, these hierarchies are perhaps best summed up as teaching objectives in Scheffler's (1960) distinction among *teaching that, teaching how to*, and *teaching to. Teaching that* is about telling facts, and *teaching how* about training students to use skills; the difference between them is roughly equivalent to the difference between the two successive paradigms governing language teaching in the twentieth century. At first, students were mostly taught *that* "dog" is translated into German as *Hund, that* Bogotá is the capital of Colombia, *that* French adjectives agree with nouns in gender and number. Now they are mostly taught *how to* narrate in paragraph-length connected discourse, *how to* ask deliberative questions, or *how to* read nontechnical expository prose.

To emphasize goals which are communicative or proficiency-oriented, rather than purely substantive, cognitive or behavioral, does not change the fact that outcome-based instruction, although it does not in itself preclude the eventual attainment of genuine understanding and self-actualization, does little to encourage or foster either. When "communication" or "proficiency" have been designated as objectives, the same fundamental questions still remain: Why do we have to be proficient? Wither communication? (other than for economic reasons). The problem is universal: Institutions, curricula, and instructional methods do not generally embody the belief that higher forms of learning are, in fact, the ultimate achievement of education (Gardner 1991: 8).

Scheffler notes that teaching *to* implies both teaching *that* and teaching *how to* (the reverse not being true), with the added dimension of teaching *why* something should be learnt and practiced, i.e. the *teleological* sense of the act of learning in the greater scheme of life. This dimension alone brings the learner to deep understanding and self-actualization:

> ... we talk of citizenship as if it were a set of skills, whereas our educational aim is, in fact, not merely to teach pupils *how* to be good citizens, but, in particular, to *be* good citizens ... We talk of giving them "the skills required for democratic living" when actually we are concerned that they acquire democratic habits, norms, propensities. (...) To extend the category of skills is, in effect, to seem to reduce the scope of the teacher's moral responsibility. Such responsibility cannot, however, be evaded by name-changing; it can only be hidden from view. The inculcation of habits, norms and propensities pervades all known educational practice, and such practice is not therefore a mere matter of skills. (Scheffler 1960: 98–99)

This last point takes us back to acculturation, since the metacognitive dimension of schooling is culturally determined to a very large extent, and the metacurriculum, as a *form*, provides the best evidence of the epistemic implications of cultural norms in formal education.

The heuristic component of learning is only slightly less culture-bound; whereas metacognition refers to the awareness of specific processes being used in the construction of knowledge, heuresis is the desire to learn, the curiosity to elucidate the unknown, to solve puzzles, and to look for more puzzles to be solved. Although this state of mind is naturally present at birth in all humans, it reaches a plateau once a satisfactory stage of functionality in one's environment is obtained, and will increase only slightly thereafter if the demands of the environment do not change significantly. Among other purposes, formal schooling is supposed to stimulate and guide youngsters to a higher heuristic level, and provide a momentum strong enough to make them, as the phrase goes, "lifelong learners."

This principle is neither universal (many cultures discourage intellectual curiosity and prescribe conformity to a set body of knowledge), nor is it effectively applied in those cultures which advocate it, including our own. We have all read or heard Jeanne Houston's comparison between our brain and a Stradivarius ("We come to play like a plastic fiddle"), and myriad critics have charged that formal schooling dulls the wonderful curiosity of children instead of fueling and stimulating it. Even success gauged by traditional criteria of achievement highlights the actual failure of the system:

> Beyond question, students ought to be literate and ought to revel in their literacy. Yet the essential emptiness of this goal is dramatized by the fact that young children in the United States are becoming literate in a *literal* sense ... What is missing are not the decoding skills, but two other facets: the capacity to read for understanding, and the desire to read at all. (Gardner 1992: 186)

Heuristic and metacognitive processes are not bags of tricks, or "thinking skills," but principles of making sense of the world, which rely very heavily on our relationship with language.

Perhaps the word "relationship" best conveys the idea that language is not an inanimate, neutral tool that we pick up and use to perform specific tasks, but one of the constructive agents of our experiential environment, what Jacob Von Uexküll called our *Umwelt* (Von Uexüll 1926). One can have a rewarding, intimate relationship with language, or a distant, uneasy one; only in the first case can we speak of literacy in the sense of a true synergy between language and the mind—and therefore between the mind and the *Umwelt*. The role of language can hardly be understated: It alone is a macrosemiotic system with the capacity to translate other semiotic systems (the reverse not being true), and to serve as a base for the construction of other semiotic systems, because of its unlimited powers of semiosis through double articulation and disengagement (Greimas and Courtès 1982: 170–171).

Language acquisition. Ever since Krashen proposed the now-famous dichotomy—acquisition vs. learning—it has become difficult to avoid terminological confusion and find an "umbrella term" for what happens in the course of formal instruction (Johnson 1992: 10–12). For our purpose, /acquisition/ is a better alternative because it is more general, and can thus still be divided into formal and informal modes; such a distinction, however, is only meant to underscore the necessity to understand the relationships between two processes which may be at the same time complementary and contradictory.

The first step "toward developing a macro-theory that will be comprehensive in its power to explain language acquisition" (Omaggio-Hadley 1993: 41) is to attend to the ontological problem which so far has prevented a true paradigm shift: 'Language' is conceptualized as being primarily a *code*, in the sense of communication theory, i.e. a set of rules (of phonology, morphology, syntax, and semantics) used to encode and decode messages. Here again, this is not to say that educators do not recognize at all that language can be much more than a code, or that actual communication, "content" study, or self-actualization are the ideal goals of language instruction.

The problem is a disjunction between the process and what it is supposed to achieve: In effect, primacy of the code—or "syntactic imperialism" (Greimas and Courtès 1982: 44)—determines the adoption of a mechanistic, grammar- or skills-oriented curriculum, as well as the choice of materials, teaching methods, and modes of assessment. The resilience of this paradigm is perhaps best illustrated in the expression "teaching in context" (Omaggio-Hadley 1993; Schrum and Glisan 1994): Since meaning is unthinkable—literally—without context, the expressed need to "contextualize" language can only be explained by a deeply entrenched concept of language-as-code, and of "context" as an *ex post facto* appendage to morpho-syntactic structures.

The history of schooling in general, and of teaching language in particular, offers several reasons, ideological, pragmatic and cultural, which explain the advent of syntactic imperialism and its persistence after the rise of communicative approaches which purport to align language instruction (native and foreign) on "real-life" use. Space does not permit delving into such an "archeology of knowledge," but we can mention the practicality of the code in reducing language to discrete elements which are easy to memorize, compartmentalize (in a textbook, workbook, or lesson plans) drill, test, and generally manipulate in a mechanistic fashion; this is also why linguistics, as it struggled for recognition as a science, focused on morphosyntactic structures that could be modelized by quasi-mathematical rules.

The pattern that emerges is a refusal to deal with the complexity of meaning and semiosis, which encourages an atomistic vision of language as words and rules, and "the notion that curriculum is an aggregate of more or less independent entities that can be somehow packaged and delivered to our students through particular methods and/or media" (Cunningham 1987: 204). The obvious argument disproving the currently fashionable conceit that communicative and proficiency-oriented instruction represent a "paradigm shift" is that the epistemic macrostructure has remained intact, although the "packaged entities" are now functions and skills, rather than rules and words.

The language gestalt. As an alternative, I propose an operational concept of 'language' accounting for authentic occurrences of linguistic signs in co-occurrence with nonlinguistic signs, and replace the current model of 'language' as a code with peripheral attachments (Figure 2) by a gestalt of four terms in mutual implication—code, context, content, and culture (Figure 3)—which constitute an interface, through the power of semiosis, between the human mind and reality, and not simply a functional tool of communication. This conceptualization prevents the isolation and prioritization of one of the terms, since "language" is *a set of relationships among all four terms*:

(1) "Code" is a lexicon combined with a set of phonological, morphological, and syntactic rules; for all intents and purposes, it is restricted to the signifier or plane of expression.

Figure 2. The traditional code-centered model of language.

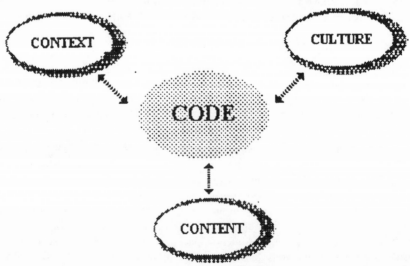

Figure 3. The language gestalt.

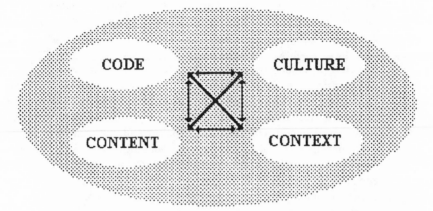

(2) "Content" is the signified, or plane of content, but not necessarily the denotative meaning of a message. For instance, in a grammatical drill or exercise, the referential meaning of the words used is, in fact, fictitious; when a student has to put "Maria goes to the bakery" in the past tense or question form, the meaning is not about Maria or a bakery, but about doing the exercise, even though the words used appear referential. By the same token, "The quick brown fox jumps over the lazy dog" could refer to an actual fox jumping over an actual dog, but we know that its meaning is "having all letters of the alphabet in one sentence," or "testing a typewriter." In order to provide "meaningful" learning opportunities, we must restrict "content" to meaning which is truly denotative. In practical terms, this means that *all* language education has to be about something that has meaning in actual use by native speakers, and exclude activities which have been manufactured for the sole purpose of instruction, no matter how "contextualized" or realistic they may seem.[9]

(3) "Context" refers to the pragmatics of language use in communication as theorized by Pierce, Morris, Frege, Wittgenstein, Carnap, Austin, Searle, Habermas, and others. The premise is that the meaning of a given linguistic message can only be ascertained in a given context determined by its production, transmission, and reception, and also by myriad nonlinguistic factors, which include—as a macrocontext—the culture and history of a whole society.

---

[9] Such an approach is already part and parcel of "whole language" teaching, which shuns "basal readers" in favor of children's literature and other authentic texts.

(4) "Culture" has generally been reduced to the ontologically simplistic idea of a point of view, "world view" or *Weltanschauung*; such metaphors completely misrepresent the role of culture in the *construction* (and not just perception) of reality, and reflect the dualistic concept of a knowing subject essentially different from the object of knowing (in other words, Descartes's *res cogitans* and *res extensa*). The portrayal of diverse cultures as so many "perspectives" on the same unchanging object (a thing-in-itself, Kant's *noumenon*) denies the compelling reality of cultural construction. This can lead to either relativism (all "points of view" are equally valid, but then seem all the less compelling) or ethnocentrism (my "point of view" is better than others, which could/should be changed to accommodate it). By attending to semiosis, the symbolic-associative process of "making sense" of our experience of the world, we can eschew altogether the problems inherent to all perceptual metaphors. The term and the concept of *Umwelt* have been adopted by some semioticians to express the constructed nature of the natural world; I borrow Greimas's and Courtès's (1983: 66) technical definition of culture as "coextensive to the semantic universe, as related to a given socio-semiotic community." The semantic universe is a set of virtual axiologies, or systems of values; in this sense, cultural aspects of social life (artifacts, tastes, behaviors, ways of thinking) can be accounted for as surface manifestations of deep-level structures of meaning.

This model of 'language' as a web of relationships emphasizes that it is a "complex" in the sense of complexity theory, a network of interconnected and mutually influenced elements whose raison d'être is "knowing the world through symbols" (Gardner 1991: 55). We must consider each term *as it relates to the others*, rather than as a self-contained entity with links that can be addressed a posteriori or not at all; in addition, the clear and immediate purpose of studying these relationships must always be the production of meaning, which only dynamic interaction between all four terms can achieve.

The production of meaning is central to communication, which I define etymologically as "putting or having in common" symbolic systems: Communication is semiosis in its intersubjective, consensual dimensions. In practical terms, we can only study communicative manifestations, which constitute various forms of documents: visual, auditive, linguistic, concrete. It is imperative that we base our approach to language on authentic documents, and not materials which have been created or manipulated with a particular teaching method in mind, so that each learning experience may involve heuristic and metacognitive processes; students can thus develop a personal way to interrogate documents and make sense of them.

Some implications of MILE. Although these two models and their brief explication here represent only part of the epistemic framework of MILE, it is possible to indicate how the theory and practice of language education can be transfigured by some of their implications:

We must question concepts, theories, research agenda, curricula, methods, textbooks, etc. of language education at the ontological and epistemological levels. No aspect of teaching and learning should be taken for granted in its form, function, or even existence. The profession has to develop a culture of self-investigation reaching to the most elemental "truths" on which its foundations are laid.

We must assess the validity of theoretical paradigms and teaching methods in the macrocontext of social and educational ideologies and cultures. Many truly insightful findings of language-acquisition research are in effect invalid, because of overarching institutional constraints, such as scheduling, which make it impossible to afford students enough exposure to the language, or the insistence of school boards on certain types of measurable outcomes, or a particular textbook serving as de facto curriculum. We cannot merely state that research has found acquisition to occur in this or that way, and disregard all other parameters of schooling, bury our heads in the sand with the hope that, somehow, truth will prevail; neither should we accept the antipedagogical character of many aspects of formal education. We must confront established practices with a sense of activism, rather than take a technical approach to learning as a mechanism occurring in a vacuum.

We must establish language education as a multi- and interdisciplinary domain contributing to a vertically and horizontally integrated curriculum:[10] Planning, curricular, and instructional decisions should be made with regard to the situation and problems of other disciplines. For instance, I have argued that all second/foreign-language teaching should adopt an immersion, L2-only format, with only authentic materials (including textbooks); yet, many teachers cannot conceive of a class without L1 crutches, and put forth numerous arguments to explain why it cannot reasonably be done—whereas ESL has perforce always done it, and developed methods and techniques which have only very recently been "discovered" by second/foreign-language educators.

The concept of "foreign" language should be radically revised. The extent of illiteracy means that tens of millions of people—far more than are officially

---

[10] Horizontal integration involves the traditional disciplines, and vertical integration the sequencing from introductory or elementary to more advanced levels of expertise.

counted as illiterates—are confronted daily with forms of their native language which, for all intents and purposes, are foreign to them: The idioms of technology, science, the law, the I.R.S., the *New York Review of Books*—and, naturally, academe—are impenetrable to a very large majority of the population. This is why mass-circulation newspapers are reputedly written at a sixth-grade reading level or below, although it is not even clear whether this calibration retains any significance today.

There are also millions of recent immigrants who, having received no formal education in their home countries, are fully illiterate in their L1 and who have to struggle with English as well. Yet, total illiteracy, marginal or surface literacy (applicable to about 80% of the U.S. population), and monolingualism are essentially treated as separate problems. One of the results is that second/foreign-language teaching has kept itself in an impasse by either teaching grammar as if students already possessed an understanding of it and a mastery of its metalanguage in the L1 or, conversely, by minimizing the role of grammar on the premise that students do not understand it in the L1.

When we know that, in fact, students are having great difficulties with syntax and morphology in the L1, our goal should be to help them gain an understanding of what 'grammar' is *conceptually* and why it is important, not to feed them rules and labels for memorizing—or, for that matter, applying them in "communicative" activities. Teachers, new and experienced, need to develop a sense of social responsibility in order to afford their students the purported "liberating" experience of language expertise and of education in general.

Language education must expand its purview from developing communicative skills to elucidating the role of linguistic semiosis in our construction of reality. This is what Freire (1970) called "conscientization," which demands a shift towards humanistic and social reconstructionist philosophies, and away from the mechanistic or academic orientations which have dominated the field so far. Students should have a sense that the purpose of language expertise is to qualitatively increase one's experience of the world; therefore, we need to design curricula and instruction to make teaching *that* (content) and *how to* (skills or processes) prerequisite to teaching *why* (deep understanding).

It is of critical importance that this approach be implemented from the very early stages of schooling or instruction: We cannot simply expect that students will ultimately develop a genuine understanding and expert command of language, when they are introduced to it in a predominantly mechanistic fashion. This concern goes well beyond instructional efficiency; research has proven that students with underprivileged socioeconomic backgrounds stand little chance of ever transcending the limits of a "reproductive" education (i.e. education which perpetuates a stratified social order) and of realizing their potential as human beings (McNeil 1990: 41–43). This is why outcome-based, skills-oriented education can actually help perpetuate illiteracy, which is linked to socio-economic factors.

We must base curriculum and instructional design on the language gestalt, not on artificially isolated aspects of language. Practically, this means the adoption of what is commonly labeled "content-based instruction"—a telling label, since it implies that regular language instruction is devoid of content. However, content-based instruction has usually been interpreted as an alternative to traditional mid- or upper-level literature/culture classes, with technical subject matter.

I propose to base our so-called "language" courses on subject matter in the humanities and social sciences which all students need to grasp as part of their general education. Professors who ceaselessly complain about rampant "cultural illiteracy," as well as those who resent having to teach introductory courses, should see the benefits of giving students a foundation in history, geography, politics, history of ideas, philosophy, etc. at the same time as foreign-language instruction. In order to fulfill this objective, we must phase out prepackaged, artificial teaching materials in favor of authentic documents (including dictionaries and textbooks produced for the native L2 market); these materials require a completely different approach to teaching in which heuristic and metacognitive processes are constantly engaged and stimulated.

The research paradigm in language education must become increasingly qualitative, rather than quantitative. The complexity of language and communication defies quantification; by their very nature, positivistic approaches (experimental and descriptive) seek to isolate variables, and therefore cannot maintain a holistic understanding of the language gestalt. We must develop authentic assessment of students' abilities to make sense of language and use it in actual communicative situations, which involve multiple dimensions of meaning and cannot be reduced to a checklist of discrete elements—grammatical and lexical accuracy, factual knowledge, and also functional or supposedly "communicative" skills.

Conclusion. Because of their focus on the mechanisms of language acquisition, reformers and theorists have not been able to diagnose the causes and severity of the language crisis in the macrocontext of educational and social ideology—or even to accept such a diagnostic. When I argued a few years ago (Spielmann 1989) that claims in the professional literature about the triumph of communicative teaching were unfounded, not necessarily because of flaws in the theory itself, but because of sclerosis in the culture of schooling and teacher training, I was chastised for criticizing brave teachers who were giving their all in "the trenches."

Despite a general agreement that the situation is dire, radical challenges to the status quo are bound to be met with strong, sometimes violent resistance:

> Education is an applied field, a helping profession which seeks to find the most effective and efficient way to do things ... Consequently educators have gravitated towards paradigms (such as cognitive psychology) which purport to provide answers to their questions and provide means to accomplish their ends: For example, if reading achievement scores are down, how do we change our instructions to remediate this situation? Given such orientation, it is not surprising to find educators impatient with paradigms ... which question the possibility of absolute knowledge, which stress the provisional nature of questions and which emphasize the knowledge generating process itself. (Cunningham 1987: 196)

True as this may be, we can no longer ignore that, for all the research and theory, for all the new approaches, methods and techniques, language education has proven chronically impervious to "deep structure" change.

MILE was conceived on the premise that only epistemological questioning can effectively help us solve the language crisis, and prevent us from repeating the mistakes of the past, falling into aporia, or resorting to garbage-can eclecticism. Language education, as MILE defines it, is a wide-open conceptual field, where all of our beliefs have to be reassessed, and the teleological purpose of teaching language brought to the fore.

Language and education are each matters of such complexity that it has been customary so far to fragment them into restricted areas of focus; although at first this may seem justified by practical considerations, such an atomistic approach has paradoxically taken theory and practice away from reality, and divorced them from the human experience of the world. The paradigm shift which has been so eagerly awaited, and more than once mistakenly believed to have occurred, will come about only when we start thinking about language education not as a form of technical training, but as a philosophical inquiry into our human linguistic condition.

REFERENCES

Ackerman, David and D.N. Perkins. 1989. "Integrating thinking and learning skills across the curriculum." In Heidi Hayes Jacobs (ed.), *Interdisciplinary curriculum: Design and implementation*. Alexandria, Virginia: Association for Supervision and Curriculum Development. 77–96.

Banks, James A. 1993. "Multicultural education: Characteristics and goals." In James A. Banks and Cherry A. McGee Banks (eds.), *Multicultural education: Issues and perspectives, Second edition*. Boston: Allyn and Bacon. 3–28.

Banks, James A. 1993b. "Approaches to multicultural curriculum reform." In James A. Banks and Cherry A. McGee Banks (eds.), *Multicultural education: Issues and perspectives, Second edition*. Boston: Allyn and Bacon. 195–214.

Banks, James A. 1993c. "Multicultural education for freedom's sake." In *Reflecting diversity: Multicultural guidelines for educational publishing professionals*. New York: McMillan/ McGraw-Hill. 16–24.

Bergentoft, Rune. 1994. "Foreign language instruction: A comparative perspective." *The Annals of the American Academy of Political and Social Sciences* 532: 8–34.

Bloom, Benjamin S. (ed.). 1956. *Taxonomy of educational objectives: The classification of educational goals, Handbook 1: Cognitive domain*. New York: MacKay.

Cunningham, Donald J. 1987. "Semiotics and education: An instance of the 'new' paradigm." *The American Journal of Semiotics* 5(2): 195–200.

Dewey, John. 1899. *The school and society*. Chicago: Chicago University Press.

Dewey, John. 1916. *Democracy and education*. New York: McMillan.

Foucault, Michel. 1972. *The archeology of knowledge*. Trans. A. M. Sheridan Smith. New York: Random House/Pantheon.

Friere, Paolo. 1970. "Cultural action and conscientization." *Harvard Educational Review* 40(3): 452–477.

Galloway, Vicky. 1987. "From defining to developing proficiency: A look at the decisions." In Heidi Byrnes and Michael Canale (eds.), *Defining to developing proficiency: Guidelines, implementations and concepts*. Lincolnwood, Illinois: American Council on the Teaching of Foreign Languages/ National Textbook Company. 25–74.

Garcia, Ofelia. 1992. "Societal multilingualism in a multicultural world in transition." In Heidi Byrnes (ed.), *Languages for a multicultural world in transition*. Lincolnwood, Illinois: Northeast Conference/ National Textbook Company. 1–28.

Greimas, Algirdas Julien and Joseph Courtès. 1982. *Semiotics and language: An analytical dictionary*. Trans. by Larry Christ and Daniel Patte. Bloomington, Indiana: Indiana University Press.

Grittner, F. M. 1990. "Bandwagons revisited: A perspective on movements in foreign language education." In Diane W. Birckblichler (ed.), *New perspectives and new directions in foreign language education*. Lincolnwood, Illinois: American Council on the Teaching of Foriegn Languages/ National Textbook Company. 9–44.

Hjelmslev, Louis. 1953. *Prolegomena to a theory of language*. Bloomington, Indiana: Indiana University Press.

Holmes Group. 1986. *Tomorrow's teachers: A report of the Holmes Group*. East Lansing, Michigan: Holmes Group.

Johnson, Donna M. 1992. *Approaches to research in second language learning*. New York: Longman.

Kelly, Louis G. 1969. *25 centuries of language teaching: An inquiry into the science, art, and development of language teaching methodology 500 B.C.–1969*. Rowley, Massachusetts: Newbury House.

Lambert, Richard D. 1994. "Problems and processes in U.S. language planning." *The Annals of the American Academy of Political and Social Sciences* 532: 47–58.

MacLean, P. D. 1978. "A mind of three minds: Educating the triune brain." In *The 77th Yearbook of the National Society for the Study of Education*. Chicago: University of Chicago Press. 308–342.

Maslow, Abraham. 1943. "A theory of human motivation." *Psychological Review* 50: 370–396.

McNeil, John D. 1990. *Curriculum: A comprehensive introduction, Fourth edition*. Glenview, Illinois: Scott, Foresman.

National Commission on Excellence in Education. 1983. *A nation at risk*. Washington, D.C.: U.S. Government Printing Office.

Omaggio-Hadley, Alice. 1993. *Teaching language in context, Second edition.* Boston: Heinle and Heinle.

O'Neil, John. 1995. "On lasting school reform: A conversation with Ted Sizer." *Educational Leadership* 52(5): 4–9.

Posner, George J. 1992. *Analyzing the curriculum.* New York: McGraw Hill.

President's Commission on Foreign Languages and International Studies. 1979. *Strength through wisdom: A critique of U.S. capability.* Washington, D.C.: U.S. Government Printing Office.

Reboul, Olivier. 1992. *La philosophie de l'éducation.* Paris: Presses Universitaires de France.

Sarason, Seymour B. 1990. *The predictable failure of educational reform.* San Francisco: Jossey-Bass.

Scheffler, Israel. 1960. *The language of education.* Springfield, Illinois: Charles C. Thomas.

Scheffler, Israel. 1974. *Four pragmatists: A critical introduction to Peirce, James, Mead and Dewey.* New York: Humanities Press.

Schrum, Judith L and Eileen W. Glisan. 1994. *Teacher's handbook: Contextualized language instruction.* Boston: Heinle and Heinle.

Spielmann, Guy. 1992. "A la recherche de l'enseignement communicatif." *The French Review* 65(6): 908–918.

Tye, Barbara B. 1990. "Schooling in America today: Potential for global studies." In Kenneth A. Tye (ed.), *Global education: From thought to action.* Alexandria, Virginia: Association for Supervision and Curriculum Development. 35–48.

Uexküll, Jacob Von. 1926. *Theoretical biology.* London: Keegan Paul, Trench and Trubner.

Wing, Barbara H. 1993. "The pedagogical imperative in foreign language teacher education." In Gail Gubtermann (ed.), *Developing language teachers for a changing world.* Lincolnwood, Illinois: American Council on the Teaching of Foreign Languages/ National Textbook Company. 159–186.

Webster's New Collegiate Dictionary. 1977. Springfield, Massachusetts: G&C Merriam Company.

Guidelines for designing SOPI tasks[1]

Charles W. Stansfield
Second Language Testing, Inc.

1. Introduction. The Simulated Oral Proficiency Interview (SOPI) was developed at the Center for Applied Linguistics (CAL) in the mid-1980s. It was designed to be an alternative to the face-to-face oral proficiency interview (OPI) in languages where the number of interviewers would always be limited. Following the development of the first SOPI in Mandarin Chinese, SOPIs were developed in other less commonly taught languages (Portuguese, Hebrew, Hausa, Indonesian, Japanese, Arabic). In recent years, the demand for SOPIs has spread to the commonly taught languages. As a result and with the help of federal funding, a Spanish SOPI is now available, and SOPIs in French and German are under development. Meanwhile, SOPIs in the less commonly taught languages continue to be developed (Hindi and Cantonese).

The first SOPI, in Mandarin (Clark and Li 1986), established the basic framework for the test. The second, in Portuguese (Stansfield and Kenyon 1988) was essentially an effort to replicate Clark's results. Therefore, the format of the two tests was identical. However, in the process of developing that test and successive ones, new insights, based on extensive field-testing, research, and analysis of examinee responses, were gained into the task-development process. These insights began to be implemented with the development of the Indonesian Speaking Test during 1988–1989. Additional refinements were made in the tasks and in the test format with the development of the Texas Oral Proficiency Test (TOPT) during 1989–1990. The TOPT became the standard for current SOPIs, in terms of the linguistic and sociolinguistic features of the prompts. These changes have been well received by both professionals in the field and examinees.

Because of these changes, the performance tasks that appear on SOPIs that have been developed during the 1990s differ markedly in format from those that appeared in the first SOPIs. The new format is apparent in the Arabic, Japanese, Spanish, French, and German SOPIs developed or now under development. Furthermore, SOPIs developed earlier are now being completely rewritten, so

[1] I wish to acknowledge the influence of the paper by Pavlou and Rasi (1994) on the content of this paper. I also wish to express my appreciation to Dorry Kenyon and Renée Jourdenais for comments on an earlier version of this paper.

as to incorporate the new features. CAL staff have completed the revision of the original Mandarin SOPI and are currently revising the Hindi SOPI, developed previously at the University of Pennsylvania.

This paper offers both an analysis of SOPI tasks and guidance for test developers in the writing of SOPI tasks. The paper is based on the author's experience in leading the development of SOPI tasks at CAL, and his experience in listening to examinees' performances on these tasks both during and after test development.

The paper is of relevance to developers of standardized second-language tests, because it deals with the features that make for an effective elicitation task. It is also of relevance to classroom teachers, because good test tasks attempt to recreate real-world language usage situations. Good, real-world, test tasks also make good classroom exercises. These exercises can serve as a basis for learning, informal assessment, or progress testing. Ultimately, when learning and assessment are integrated, both are enhanced.

I will begin with a description of the components of a SOPI task, and then progress to the task features that must be considered when designing and writing a SOPI prompt. It is these features that are the focus of this paper. They are of crucial importance, because they can, and probably will, affect not only the validity of the task for the examinee, but also the way the examinee responds to the task, and the rating that the examinee receives from the rater on the task.

As Kenyon and Stansfield (1993) have pointed out on previous occasions, on a performance-based test, particularly one that may have important repercussions for the examinee as an individual and society as a whole, the tasks used to elicit examinee performance must have two characteristics that are critical to the validity and accuracy of measurement. First, in order to ensure that the test is fair and unbiased, the tasks must allow, to the fullest extent possible, each examinee a fair and equal opportunity to give the best possible demonstration of his or her ability to speak the language. Second, in the interest of obtaining the most accurate measurement of ability possible, these tasks must elicit a performance sample that enables raters to adequately evaluate the examinee. We consider the issues of appropriateness of the task and its usefulness to the rater throughout the test-development process.

2. SOPI format. The prototypical SOPI is a tape-recorded test consisting of a warm-up comprised of simple personal background questions, followed by fifteen real-world, role-play tasks which make up the body of the test. The first five tasks, called Pictures, ask the examinee to respond while referring to illustrations in a test booklet. The next five tasks, called Topics, focus on the examinee's ability to organize and present information, while the final five tasks, called Situations, focus on the ability to tailor one's speech in order to accomplish a given purpose. Figure 1 is an outline of the SOPI that illustrates

Figure 1. Typical SOPI speaking test format.

Key:		
	I = Intermediate	
	A = Advanced	
	S = Superior	

Item	Intended Level	Speaking Tasks
Warm-up	I	Answer personal questions
Picture 1	I	Ask questions
Picture 2	I	Describe a place/activities
Picture 3	I	Give directions
Picture 4	A	Narrate in present time
Picture 5	A	Narrate in past time
Topic 1	I	Describe personal activities
Topic 2	A	Explain a process*
Topic 3	A	State advantages/disadvantages
Topic 4	S	Support an opinion
Topic 5	S	Hypothesize on an impersonal topic
Situation 1	A	Speak with tact
Situation 2	S	Speak to persuade
Situation 3	S	Propose and defend a course of action
Situation 4	S	Give a talk
Situation 5	A	Give advice
Wind-down		

* Indicates end of Intermediate-level form

Level and number of Items:	
	Intermediate: 5
	Advanced: 6
	Superior: 5

its organization and the speaking tasks that compose it, and the level of each task on the American Council on the Teaching of Foreign Languages (ACTFL) scale. I will now describe the components of a SOPI task, and then discuss a number of considerations in task writing.

3. Components of a SOPI task. All SOPI tasks have a number of common components. A brief description of each component is given below.

3.1. English prompt. Every task contains an English-language prompt, which consists of directions written in English. The length of the directions varies as needed. The specific speaking task or function (e.g. describe a place) is always written in bold print so that the examinee will be able to distinguish it readily. This bolding of the speaking task facilitates a relevant response that is easy to evaluate, as in the following example:

> Imagine that you are at a party in Cuernavaca, Mexico. You join a group of people who are describing their homes. One of the group, Marta, asks you to **describe a typical American home**. You may use the picture in your test booklet or your own experience as a source of ideas. You will have 15 seconds to prepare your answer. After Marta asks her question, you will have one minute and 20 seconds to respond. Remember to wait for Marta's question before you begin your response.

Examinees are encouraged to follow the English prompt printed in the test booklet as the setting is described by the narrator on audiotape. This allows the native-English speaking examinee to understand thoroughly what he or she must do before beginning to respond. If the prompt were written in the target language, the SOPI would become a test of reading as well as speaking. In that case, if the examinee failed to respond, one would not know if the problem were due to a lack of speaking proficiency or an inability to read in the target language.

3.2. Illustrations. Picture-based tasks are accompanied by professionally developed illustrations such as drawings and maps. These illustrations are particularly useful for eliciting specific functions that are mentioned in the ACTFL Guidelines, such as giving directions, describing activities and places, and narrating stories. Whenever examinees may use the illustration as a source of ideas, this is indicated in the prompt. Otherwise, examinees base their response on the information provided in the illustration. Figure 2 depicts the illustration that accompanies the English prompt concerning a typical American home.

3.3. Thinking time. At the end of the English prompt, the amount of time for conceptualizing a response and for responding to the task is specified. "Thinking time" gives examinees time to review the directions presented, along with any accompanying illustrations, and time to formulate a coherent response. The amount of thinking time is specified in the English prompt in Picture-based

Figure 2. A typical American home.

DO NOT TURN THE PAGE UNTIL YOU ARE ASKED TO DO SO.

tasks, and thus it is heard on tape and read in the test booklet. In Topic and Situation-based tasks, the amount of thinking time is specified in writing only, immediately below the English prompt. There must be enough thinking time to allow examinees to conceptualize and formulate their response. Too little thinking time results in unplanned speech. Too much thinking time can cause the examinees to become distracted and to lose their train of thought. The amount of thinking time is determined prior to pretesting and is adjusted following the pretesting if necessary, as indicated by feedback from examinees and raters.

3.4. Target-language prompts. After "thinking time" elapses, examinees hear a target-language prompt spoken by a native speaker of the language being tested. This prompt neither adds to the speaking task specified in the English prompt nor detracts from it. In other words, by following the English prompt, examinees should still be able to respond, even if they have not understood the target-language prompt.

The target-language prompt lends additional authenticity to the context and allows the examinee to hear some of the target language before beginning to respond in that language. While a beep was used in the original SOPI to indicate when an examinee should begin to respond, the target-language prompt has been used since 1990. If necessary, the target-language prompt can be used to provide critical vocabulary, the absence of which might prohibit the examinee from responding. It also reminds the examinee of the context of the task.

3.5. Response time. The response time is the amount of time the examinee has to perform the task. This is indicated in the English prompt in Picture-based tasks. In Topics and Situations, the response time is specified in writing immediately below the English prompt. The amount of time allotted is determined prior to pretesting and adjusted following pretesting, if necessary, again as determined by examinee and rater feedback.

3.6. End tone. Toward the end of the allotted response time, examinees hear a soft tone. This tone indicates that there are five seconds remaining, before the directions to the next task will begin. The examinees may use this time to bring their response to a natural conclusion. After the five seconds have elapsed, the examinees are given instructions to proceed to the next task.

4. Evaluation criteria. In a performance-based test, the evaluation criteria define what is actually being assessed. The same performance can be assessed for different characteristics, depending on the criteria used to evaluate it. The SOPI evaluation criteria are the *ACTFL Guidelines* and/or the Interagency Language Roundtable (ILR) skill-level descriptions on which the *Guidelines* are based. Detailed breakdowns of these scales produce other evaluation subcriteria associated with each level. These subcriteria include function, content, accuracy, context, text type, and sociolinguistic competence. They are nicely outlined in the *ACTFL tester training manual* (1989).

Because the evaluation criteria describe the qualities and skills that a rater will be looking for, we must consider them in designing the task. It is necessary for the test developer to ask, "What kind of performance will this task elicit, and will the performance contain the characteristics that the rater will be looking for as he or she applies the criteria to evaluate it?" If we are to develop a test task that is useful in allowing the rater to place the examinee on the ACTFL scale, then we must consider the criteria that are associated with each point on the scale.

In designing a task, we focus on the tasks, functions, and content that emerge from the descriptions on the scale itself. In this way the rater will immediately be able to tell if the examinee meets the requirements of the level. For instance, at the Advanced level, the scale indicates that an examinee must be able to narrate in present, past, and future time frames. Thus, if we design a task that will elicit a response that is relevant to these evaluation criteria, it will be easy for the rater to determine if the examinee has met the criteria for an Advanced-level rating.

In the SOPI, it is common to test the examinee's ability to narrate in various time frames in the Pictures section of the test. Similarly, because the ability to make an apology is mentioned in the description of the Advanced level, an apology is included as an Advanced-level Situation in the typical SOPI. Other examples of evaluation criteria used in the development of test tasks include complaining, supporting opinions, hypothesizing, etc. These are all in the typical SOPI because they appear in the *Guidelines*. Because the evaluation criteria reward certain skills, it is important to include, to the degree possible, tasks that allow examinees to demonstrate these skills. In this way, the rater will be able to use this scale with greater ease and precision. Of course, other kinds of tasks can be put on the test, but the rater may find it more difficult to apply the *Guidelines* to their evaluation.

5. Wording. The wording of a task refers, obviously, to the language that is selected to write it, and the way the task is phrased. Two parts of the task are affected by the wording: the English-language prompt and the target-language prompt.

5.1. English-language prompt. The English-language prompt is, in a sense, a set of directions to the examinee. The prompt provides all the background information the examinee needs to respond to the task. The English prompt includes the contextualization of the task and specifies the function or task the examinee is to carry out. The English prompt must be worded in a way that is exceptionally clear and precise, so that it will be interpreted in the same manner by all examinees. If the wording is ambiguous, the examinee may focus the response on aspects of the task that are not central to the information needed by the rater. Misinterpretations of a task, such as listing events in a sequence when a narration is required, may affect the examinee's rating, disadvantaging the examinee on the test. Also, misinterpretations of a task make the rater's job more difficult and may even lower the reliability of the rating.

It is also important that the wording of the English-language prompt give appropriate emphasis to the aspects of the task that the rater will consider when determining whether the examinee has handled the task successfully. If the task calls for testing the speaking function of supporting an opinion, then the English-language prompt must direct the examinee to both state and support an opinion in a convincing way.

5.2. Target-language prompt. The target-language prompt is always spoken in natural language. When writing this prompt, the test developer must consider what a native speaker would actually say in such circumstances. Usually, the native speaker would make a short comment or ask a straightforward question based on the progression of the conversation to that point. Thus the target-language prompt does not attempt to repeat the information contained in the English prompt. Indeed, in order to be natural, it may be very short. For example, if three people were ordering a meal in a restaurant, by the time the waiter asked the third person for the order, his request for the final order might simply be "And you?". If the English-language prompt is properly developed, a short target-language prompt may add to the authenticity of the contextualization and of the task itself.

Of course, the prompt need not be short. If the task specified in the English prompt requires a longer question or statement, such is also appropriate.

Sometimes the target-language prompt can be used to give the examinee specific words in the target language. This is especially useful when it is likely that (1) some examinees may not have these words in their active vocabulary, but could use the words correctly if heard in the correct context, and (2) the words are essential if one is to accomplish the task. If the task is to describe how to obtain a driver's license, then the word for "driver's license" can be introduced to all examinees in the target-language prompt. Similarly, if the task is to describe how to use the library, then one may wish to include the word for "card catalog" in the target-language prompt.

In order to be natural, the target-language prompt must be in the appropriate dialect. The dialect used will depend on the setting described in the English prompt. For example, if the task is set in Argentina, then it would be inappropriate to have someone with a Mexican accent record the prompt.

Another concern is the register of the target-language prompt. The register should be appropriate to the task and to the setting. An appropriately worded target-language prompt can reinforce the demands and constraints developed in the English-language prompt. An inappropriately worded target-language prompt can have the opposite affect. Once, when we were developing a Spanish SOPI, we designed a task which asked the examinee to state his or her opinion about a proposal to lengthen the school year to twelve months and give reasons to support it. The native language prompt that was suggested by the task developer, a native Spanish speaker, was *¿Qué te parece la idea de alargar el año escolar?* Had this not been changed during the task-review process, the phrase *¿Qué te parece?* ("What do you think about?") would have lowered the level of the response of some Superior-level examinees, as the informal register of the phrase tends to suggest that a response in an informal register and style is acceptable. This phrase in the target-language prompt was changed to *¿Cuál es su opinión sobre ...?* ("What is your opinion of ...?"), thereby setting the stage for a more formal response, as indicated in the English directions to the task, and allowing the examinee to tailor his or her language to the situation, thus demonstrating Superior-level proficiency.

6. Level of task. Each SOPI task relates to a specific level on the ACTFL scale. The level designation of the task will affect its design. For example, an Intermediate-level task, must be designed in such a way that it can be handled successfully by Intermediate-level examinees. Not only must the topic and function be appropriate to the level, but the type of discourse called for in the response must be within the reach of the examinee. For example, the task of giving directions can be handled adequately and appropriately through discrete sentences. Speaking in discrete sentences is associated with the Intermediate level. No top-down organization is required nor must any summary or conclusion be made at the end. Advanced- and Superior-level speakers may include such features, but they are not necessary to handle the communicative requirements of the task. Thus the task selected is appropriate to the level designation of the task, and the task can be handled by an examinee at that level.

The same can be said about the vocabulary that the prompt elicits. The vocabulary must be appropriate to the level. While an Advanced-level speaker is expected to be able to give a detailed and organized description, we would not expect the Advanced-level speaker to describe in detail how to change a tire, since at this level, the examinee does not typically know the words for "jack," "hubcap," "tire iron," "nuts," "rim," and "bolts," even though such words might be considered part of the general vocabulary of most native speakers.

The linguistic features or accuracy of the language that will be required to answer appropriately must also be considered. What verb tenses and syntactic structures might be required to respond to the task? Are those linguistic features consistent with the intended level of the task?

Sometimes a task may require the examinee to assume a certain attitude or persona. This is acceptable with Superior-level prompts because the ability to tailor one's speech to the situation is a feature of the Superior level. Lower-level prompts must ensure that the examinee is not asked to tailor speech beyond the level of the task. This is very important, since essentially all SOPI tasks are role plays.

7. Speaker.

7.1. Persona. In many writing tests and in speaking tests like the SOPI, the examinee is to play a specific role. Thus the examinee must assume a specific persona. In some role-play tasks, such as those on the role-play cards that accompany the ACTFL OPI, the examinee may be asked to play the role of someone else. Witness the following examples of the contextualization of an Advanced level ACTFL role-play:

- You are driving through a small town when your car breaks down. You go the nearest service station.
- You are a newspaper reporter. On your way to work you witness an accident. You call the paper to report about it.

These two role plays differ in that in the first, the examinee plays him or herself, while in the second, the examinee is asked to assume the role of another person.

Early experience in the development of SOPI tasks suggested that the examinee reacts more positively, and in a more consistent way, to the task if he or she is able to relate personally to the situation. Thus, in developing a task, we attempt to allow examinees to always role-play themselves. The things that change are the topic, the audience, the setting where the conversation takes place, and the goal or purpose of the response. The examinee must respond as he or she would actually respond in this context in real life. The accessibility of the context to examinees is verified during the trialing and field testing of the tasks. Thus, if an examinee feels that he or she would not assume this persona in his native language, then the task is modified or discarded. Clearly, however, we believe that allowing examinees to role-play themselves is a fundamental tenet in task development. When we ask the examinee to assume the role of another person, we risk assigning a task that is outside of one's personal schema.

7.2. Point of view. Another issue to consider is point of view. The examinee may either be asked to agree or disagree with a particular point of view. In tests of writing, for example, the examinee is often told to present a particular point of view. In developing SOPI tasks, however, we have found it best to allow the examinee to choose his or her preferred point of view. While there are many features to a task, tasks may be more engaging when they allow the examinee to choose the point of view that will be presented. The choice of point of view is somewhat similar to the issue of allowing examinees to choose a topic, an issue which has been debated for some time in the field of writing assessment.

7.3. First-person singular versus first-person plural. While most SOPI tasks require the examinee to speak in the first person, another option is to have the examinee represent a group of people with similar ideas. On the SOPI, this is sometimes done in a higher-level Situation task, where the examinee has been asked, named, or elected to represent a group in some way. A group-representation type of task can work to elicit more characteristics of higher-level proficiency if carefully crafted. However, there is the risk that such a task may be outside the experience of some examinees.

8. Topic. During an OPI, the interviewer attempts to elicit information concerning the functions that the interviewee controls, the range of content to which these functions can be applied, and the linguistic accuracy of the language used. The topic of each SOPI task should fit within the range of content that is associated with each level on the ACTFL and ILR scales.

Although every SOPI task must have a topic, in some tasks the topic is more important than in others. Topic is especially important in Topic-based tasks. Here the focus of the task is the examinee's ability to organize information on given subject matter, and to present it to the audience established in the contextualization of the task.

8.1. Familiarity. The crucial issue in judging the suitability of a topic is the degree to which the topic is likely to be familiar to examinees. Topic familiarity helps the examinee respond successfully to the task, while a lack of familiarity impedes the examinee's ability to respond. Naturally, examinees can vary greatly in their familiarity with topics. Thus it is important to select a topic that seems accessible to all examinees. The fact that the examinees' foreign-language vocabulary may vary according to level of proficiency is not a threat to the validity of a topic. The threat rather lies in the possibility that some examinees will approach the topic with more knowledge than others, and will therefore be able to use this knowledge and familiarity to produce a more fluent or convincing response in spite of a lack of language proficiency.

At the lower levels on the ACTFL scale, topics should deal with everyday life: a typical American home, a typical day in the life of a teacher, typical weekend activities, a description of what people typically do at the beach, etc. The examinee will have experience or be very familiar with topics at the Intermediate and Advanced levels.

Because the ACTFL scale moves from the ability to talk about familiar topics to the ability to talk about novel topics at higher proficiency levels, many SOPI tasks deviate from everyday life. Thus a critical issue is the relationship of the topic to the ACTFL scale. While a topic should relate to the scale, it should also be unlikely to favor or disadvantage some examinees for reasons unrelated to their language proficiency. Even a relatively unfamiliar topic, such as the twelve-month school year, should be likely to be equally new to everyone.

As we move from the Advanced to the Superior level, topics become increasingly novel to the examinee. Topics at these levels may require hypothesizing about an event that has not actually happened to the examinee personally, but could. Moving to the Superior level, topics normally do not deal with everyday life at all. Rather, they deal with issues and events at the societal level. Superior topics are sometimes framed in the context of the effects of, or one's opinion on, a proposal that is posited as compulsory. This proposal could be community service, foreign-language study, military service, or tolerating undesirable behavior. In other circumstances, Superior topics may also deal with hypothesizing about a topic that is abstract rather than personal, such as changes in policies and the implications of those changes for the society at large. Here, few examinees will have experienced the change, but all should be fairly readily able to imagine some consequences of the change.

8.2. Effect on audience. Some SOPI topics require the examinee to say things that the supposed audience is not anxious to hear. Such is the case with an apology to the owner of a lost umbrella, or in trying to convince someone to do something they do not ordinarily do, such as trying to convince a landlord to lower the rent on an apartment one is interested in renting. This aspect of the topic tends to put more demands on the speaker. Here strategic competence may play a role in how the examinee approaches the task, and how the rater evaluates it.

Most SOPI topics, however, are reasonably pleasant to the audience because the task is crafted in such a way that the audience actually requests the response and therefore is interested in hearing it.

9. Speaking function or task. The *ACTFL proficiency guidelines* include a variety of speaking tasks in each level. The *ACTFL OPI tester training manual* refers to a number of these tasks as "functions." In the ACTFL context, "function" refers to the rhetorical genre that the examinee can produce: At the Novice level the examinee is able to list; at the Intermediate level the examinee can ask and respond to simple questions; at the Advanced level the examinee can describe and narrate in major time frames; and at the Superior level the examinee can support opinions and deal with abstractions and hypothetical situations. There are a variety of other abilities that are also mentioned in the *Guidelines*, such as the ability to elaborate, complain, and apologize (Advanced level). These are often referred to as "tasks." Thus we see that function and task refer, in a rhetorical sense, to speech acts.

9.1. Agreement with level. The appropriate specification of the speaking function in the English prompt is probably the most crucial aspect of a SOPI task. If the specification is unclear or ambiguous, or if it is not adequately specific, the examinee may not demonstrate the required function although he or she is capable of doing so. In such a case, the rater would have no alternative but to note that the examinee did not produce the desired function. Thus, if an examinee does not produce a Superior-level speaking function, a rating of Superior cannot be awarded, and the examinee would be directly penalized by the test developer's lack of clarity in the specification of the function.

The clear, unambiguous specification of functions is especially important at the Superior level. At other levels, if the examinee modifies the task from that intended by the test developer, he or she may either raise or lower it. However, it is not possible to raise the level of a Superior-level task, because Superior is the highest level on the scale. Moreover, because the language demands of the Superior level are greater than those of everyday conversation, when examinees modify the task they have a tendency to lower its level, rather than to maintain it at the Superior level. For this reason, it is very important that Superior-level prompts be somewhat strongly worded so as to clearly convey the rhetorical nature of the desired response.

9.2. One task per prompt. Another feature of the task is that it must be appropriate to the amount of time the examinee will have to respond. If the task is too complicated, or involves multiple speech acts, the examinee will not be able to accomplish it in the time allotted. Often, neophyte task developers will attempt to create a "macroprompt" in an attempt to elicit a great deal of speech. Witness the following example:

> Describe and compare the advantages and disadvantages of using a car versus public transportation when living in the city, and state which you prefer giving clear and convincing reasons to support your choice.

The above prompt really consists of multiple tasks. One must describe the advantages of using a car, the disadvantages of using a car, the advantages of using various types of public transportation, and the disadvantages of these types of public transportation. All these tasks are at the Advanced level. Next one must compare and contrast this information. This can be a demanding task to organize within a rhetorical framework. Finally, one must choose either a car or public transportation and structure an argument as to why it is better, including a number of supporting reasons within the argument. This last task, which may actually be two tasks, is clearly identified as a Superior-level function in the *Guidelines*.

Because of the multiplicity of tasks in this prompt, it would not be possible for even a Superior-level examinee to respond to it adequately within the normal time frame allotted for a SOPI task (maximum of one minute, forty-five seconds). Also, because the task mixes levels on the ACTFL scale, it would be difficult for raters to reliably rate an examinee on such a task.

10. Audience. Audience refers to the interlocutor; the person or people the examinee is speaking to. In most writing tests, and in the OPI, the audience is the evaluator of the performance. In the SOPI, the audience is never the evaluator. Because the SOPI involves role-playing in real-world contexts, the audience must come from the cast of characters that one might encounter in the real world. The character or characters specified as the audience in the English directions will affect the type of language that the examinee uses in the response. It may even affect the rhetorical genre of the response.

10.1. Size of audience. The number of people that the examinee is speaking to must be specified in the task. The number will affect the nature of the response and the language chosen. The greater the number of listeners, the less intimate the language usage may be. In some languages, this will have an affect on the nature of the response.

10.2. Age. The age of the audience may be either specified of implied. The audience may be approximately the same age as the examinee, older, or younger.

10.3. Sex. The sex of the audience must be specified. This may also have an affect on the usage and approach used to address the individual. The magnitude of the affect depends on the sex of the audience and the language in which the response is given.

10.4. Degree of intimacy. The prompt must specify or give clues as the degree of intimacy that exists between the examinee and the audience. The audience could be a personal friend, a stranger, or an acquaintance, such as a co-worker or a teacher. In many languages, the degree of intimacy will affect the use of certain linguistic features, as well as broader matters of style and strategy.

10.5. Status of audience. The description of the person being spoken to will convey a certain socioeconomic status which may, in turn, affect the type of language that is appropriate to use with this person. The comparative status of the speaker and the audience may also play a role in the response. The audience may have greater status, equal status, or lesser status than the speaker. Socioeconomic status and the comparative status will affect the relationship that the examinee is expected to maintain, the strategy used to respond, and perhaps the language used in the response.

11. Setting.

11.1. Functional location. Since SOPI tasks take place in the real world, rather than in the examination room, every task must have a setting. The setting may be personal, such as the examinee's home, it may be academic, such as a school, or it may be in any other location, such as the street of a city, a store, a party, someone else's home, a restaurant, etc.

11.2. Geographic location. The above locations can be either in the examinee's native country, or in a foreign country where the target language is spoken. If the task takes place in the examinee's native country, then normally the audience consists of a native speaker from another country who is visiting, studying, or working here. If the setting is a foreign country, then the examinee is depicted as visiting, studying, or working there.

12. Formality/informality.
The task will convey some degree of formality to the examinee. Thus the context may be either formal or informal, depending on many other variables stated above. The setting and the characteristics of the audience play important roles in specifying the degree of formality. The level of the topic and the function help in this process also. Ultimately, the degree of formality affects the level of the task. Clearly, Superior-level tasks must involve formal contexts and Intermediate-level tasks typically involve informal contexts. Placing a Superior-level task in an informal context is one of the errors most frequently made by task developers.

13. Conclusion.
This paper has described the components of SOPI tasks and discussed features of these components that can affect the reliability and validity of the task. These important features of task components are: The evaluation criteria that will be used to evaluate the response; the wording of the English description and the target-language prompt; the intended level of the task on the ACTFL or ILR scales; the persona that the speaker is to assume and whether the examinee is to represent the point of view of one person or several people; the familiarity of the topic to the examinee and the congruence of this familiarity with the ACTFL scale; the interest of the supposed audience in hearing a response on this topic; the function or task to be tested and its relationship to the scale; the need to specify only one function or task in each SOPI task; physical and socioeconomic characteristics of the audience and their effect on the relative status of the speaker and the audience; the functional and geographic setting for the task; and the degree of formality of the context in which the examinee will be responding. If all of these features are in harmony with the ACTFL or ILR scales of speaking proficiency, then the task will elicit

a response that can be reliably, accurately, and readily evaluated by a trained rater.

REFERENCES

Clark, John L.D. and Ying-Chi Li. 1986. *Development, validation and dissemination of a proficiency-based test of speaking ability in Chinese and an associated model for other less commonly taught languages.* Alexandria, Virginia: ERIC Document Reproduction Service. ED 278-264.

Kenyon, Dorry M. and Charles W. Stansfield. 1993. "A method for improving tasks in performance-based assessments through field testing." In Ari Huhta, Kari Sajavara, and Smali Takala (eds.), *Language testing: New openings.* Jyvaskyla, Finland: University of Jyvaskyla.

Pavlou, Pavlos and Sylvia Rasi. 1994. "Considerations in writing item prompts for Simulated Oral Proficiency Interview (SOPI)." Paper presented in annual Language Testing Research Colloquium, Center for Applied Linguistics, Washington, D.C.

Stansfield, Charles W. and Dorry M. Kenyon. 1988. *Development of the Portuguese Speaking Test.* Alexandria, Virginia: ERIC Document Reproduction Service. ED 296-586.

From Hirsch's dystopia to Hakuta's utopia: A call for a multilingual alliance

Steven R. Sternfeld
University of Utah

Introduction: In 1986, S.I. Hayakawa, former U.S. Senator from California, co-founded U.S. English, a Washington-based organization lobbying for an English-language constitutional amendment. On March 12, 1987, in a presentation given here at the Georgetown University Round Table, Gerda Bikales, then Executive Director of U.S. English, made the following observation: "Being bilingual, bicultural is the greatest ability for a person; it is a curse for a nation" (cited in Crawford 1992: 89). In coming to terms with the radically different values Bikales places on individual and societal bilingualism, it is useful to back up another nineteen years, to 1968. In that year, Congress passed the Bilingual Education Act, an amendment to the Elementary and Secondary Education Act (ESEA) of 1965 and referred to as Title VII. ESEA Title VII provided local school districts with support in implementing educational programs aimed at helping children with limited English proficiency (LEP) improve their English-language skills.

While Title VII supported experiments with a variety of interventions on behalf of LEP children, local school systems were not as yet required to implement such programs. Then in 1974 the U.S. Supreme Court handed down the *Lau vs. Nichols* ruling, which required that local school districts take "affirmative steps" to meet the special needs of LEP children. Subsequently, a task force was recruited by the U.S. Office of Education to develop general policy guidelines to judge whether or not school districts were in compliance with this ruling. The report which they issued, referred to as the "Lau Remedies," led to the rejection of ESL instruction alone as a satisfactory form of intervention for elementary-school LEP children. In its place a form of bilingual education was proposed, in which students would receive regular curricular instruction in their native language as they worked on developing their ESL skills (Hakuta 1988).

Hirsch's dystopia: A baleful vision. By the time it came up for reauthorization in 1978, there was general alarm that Title VII had been used to promote the maintenance of ethnic languages *at the expense of English language skills*. As a result, Congress voted that year to restrict federal funding to transitional-bilingual programs, in which LEP children were exited from first-language instruction as soon as they acquired sufficient English-language skills to survive in English-language classrooms. The message was clear: The federal government did not want Title VII to be seen as facilitating the attempts of ethnolinguistic minorities to use the public-school system to pass their native language and culture on to their children.

Despite Congress's action, the perception continued to grow that bilingual educators were intentionally subverting the goals of Title VII by privileging first-language retention over mastery of English. In 1981, the *New York Times* noted that President Reagan chose to underscore his own stance on this issue in the following departure from the prepared text of a speech he gave to a group of mayors:

> It is absolutely wrong and against American concept to have a bilingual education program that is now openly, admittedly dedicated to preserving their native language and never getting them adequate in English so they can go out into the job market. (cited in Hakuta 1988: 207)

It comes then as no surprise that in 1987, the year of Bikales' "bilingualism-as-curse" remark, E.D. Hirsch, Jr. conjured up this baleful vision of an emergent linguistic dystopia in his bestseller *Cultural literacy: What every American needs to know*:

> Tolerance of diversity is at the root of our society, but encouragement of multilingualism is contrary to our traditions and extremely unrealistic. Defenders of multilingualism should not assume that our Union has been preserved once and for all by the Civil War, and that we can afford to disdain the cultural and educational vigilance exercised by other modern nations. To think so complacently is to show a fundamental misunderstanding of the role of national literacy in creating and sustaining modern civilization. (1987: 92–93)

Hakuta's utopia, or bilingualism as national resource. While Hirsch's dystopian vision of multilingualism-as-scourge is shared by many, it is certainly *not* shared by all. I would now like to offer you a radically different vision, what I have called Hakuta's Utopia. In *Mirror of language: The debate on bilingualism*, Hakuta offers his readers an unabashedly idealized vision of a universally multilingual America, where the aim of our educational system is for *all* Americans, including monolingual English-speakers, to be functionally bilingual:

The motive is linguistic, cognitive, and cultural enrichment - the creation of citizens of the world. In this ideal society, speakers of immigrant languages would be seen as holders of a valuable resource to be developed, and they in turn would help in the efforts of monolingual English-speakers to learn their language. At the same time, the English-speakers would be seen as resources for the non-English-speakers. (1986: 229–230)

In 1986, when *Mirror of language* was published, Hakuta was able to point with satisfaction to a number of schools in the nation which were already using this "interlocking" concept of two-way bilingual-education programs to create functional bilinguals from both language groups. Where do we as a nation stand almost a decade later? The fact that in the past ten years over twenty states, beginning with California, have adopted laws or constitutional amendments designating English their official language, is enough to tell us that Hakuta's Utopia has yet to take root. Yet, I personally have found that there is cause to be optimistic, for two reasons in particular. First, we have a newly reformed and reauthorized Title VII that echoes Hakuta's call for all Americans to become functionally bilingual; second, over the last fifteen years, there has been a remarkable rise in interest in integrating public service into our educational institutions.

The Improving American Schools Act of 1994. This past fall President Clinton signed the Improving American Schools Act of 1994, which reformed and reauthorized the Elementary and Secondary Education Act (ESEA). A fundamental change in the newly reauthorized ESEA Title VII (Bilingual Education, Language Enhancement, and Language Acquisition Programs) is the recognition of the importance of bilingualism, with the new law requiring that *priority* be given to funding programs that provide an opportunity to develop proficiency in both English and another language for all participating students.

Section A (Bilingual Education) notes that children with limited English proficiency (LEP) have difficulty receiving a good education, in part because their parents' limited English proficiency diminishes their ability to be actively involved in their children's education. For this and other reasons Title VII concludes that bilingual programs using LEP children's native language and culture can:

(1) Build LEP children's self-esteem;
(2) Contribute to their academic achievement, including learning English; and
(3) Benefit English-proficient children participating in such programs.

Section B (Language Enhancement) recommends developing proficiency in two or more languages for all American students, noting that, at elementary-school age, children are both good at L2 learning and particularly receptive to appreciating and valuing cultures other than their own. Thus the federal government, reversing its 1978 decision to support only transitional programs, now recognizes the value of Hakuta's "interlocking concept."

Public service and the service-learning movement. In 1980 the National Commission on Youth published its report entitled *The transition of youth to adulthood*. The commission, chaired by James Coleman and sponsored by the Kettering Foundation, urged that service to one's community and nation be utilized as a means to "bridge the gap between youth and adulthood." Five years later, Frank Newman wrote in *Higher education and the American resurgence*:

> If there is a crisis in education in the United States today, it is less that test scores have declined than it is that we have failed to provide the education for citizenship that is still the most important responsibility of the nation's schools and colleges. (1985: 31)

That same year a handful of college and university presidents responded by founding Campus Compact, an organization dedicated to promoting community service among undergraduates. Five years later George Bush signed the National and Community Service Act of 1990, which provided funding for programs encouraging community service by students in schools and colleges. In 1993 President Clinton signed the National and Community Service Act (Markus et al. 1993). And in this, its tenth year, Campus Compact now claims a membership of some five-hundred colleges and universities nationwide.

Education for citizenship and the multilingual alliance. I would like to argue here that a "multilingual alliance" (Sternfeld 1987b), based on Hakuta's "interlocking concept" and having as its goal functional bilingualism for all Americans, could represent a critical component of Newman's "education for citizenship," an education that would teach through experience core civic notions such as interdependence and respect for diversity. In this multilingual alliance, *all* speakers of *all* languages throughout our educational system would be enlisted as the foot soldiers of a national language-learning and language-teaching effort, guided and supported by professional literacy and language-learning experts.

Discovering service-learning. Although I first wrote about a multilingual alliance in 1987 (Sternfeld 1987b), it was only after my serendipitous encounter with service-learning three years ago that I was able to begin the process of putting theory into practice. In 1991 I developed a new class for our Liberal Education program, entitled "Building community in the classroom: Learning for teaching and teaching for learning." The course used collaborative learning experiences to create a community of teacher/learners who saw learning as a preparation for teaching others, and teaching others as an opportunity to extend and deepen their own learning. I looked forward to teaching the same class the following year and began exploring ways in which I might intensify the community-building experience. I thought that by engaging students collectively in a challenging teaching/learning project *outside* the classroom, I might create a greater need for community-building *inside* the classroom. Because of my background in ESL, I decided that I would have students work with immigrants and refugees in the local community, thereby bringing issues of linguistic and cultural diversity into the teaching/learning equation.

With the support of our Bennion Center, which coordinates community service projects at the University of Utah, I redesigned my class as a service-learning course with the new title "Building community in and outside the classroom: Exploring linguistic and cultural diversity." More than half of the students became mentors to adult Vietnamese refugees being resettled in the Salt Lake area by Catholic Community Services. One group of students worked with language-minority children in a local elementary school, another in an adult workplace ESL literacy program.

As part of their final portfolio, students were asked how they thought they might continue their exploration of issues of linguistic and cultural diversity in the future. One student wrote that he planned to keep on meeting with the Vietnamese refugee he had mentored, with one important modification: In addition to their usual evening together in which they would work on English, my student proposed a second evening in which they would work on Vietnamese. It seems that the time he had spent with the Vietnamese refugee had aroused the student's interest in Vietnamese language and culture.

McGapsters. The degree of reciprocity, of true partnership, which underlay this student's proposal inspired me to once again redesign the course. I applied for and was fortunate enough to receive the 1993–1994 Bennion Public Service Professorship which gave me release time, teaching-assistant support, and seed money to carry out a radically redesigned course. In Winter 1994 I again offered the class, this time as a two-quarter, eleven-unit course. We were now officially Partners in Education with Granger Elementary School in Granite School District's Invest in Futures program. Students worked with groups of K–6 language-minority children, whose languages included Spanish, Vietnamese, Cambodian, and Navajo.

While English was the language of communication between the college students and the language-minority children, the focus of their interaction was on the language-minority children's language and culture. Together these "McGapsters" (*M*ulticultural *Gap* bu*sters*), as we came to be called, created "culture trunks," assemblages of a variety of materials and artifacts from and about the children's native culture which were used to teach others in the school and in the community about the rich cultural diversity that exists in our valley. Our goal for the children was to help them develop their English-language skills and at the same time validate their first language and culture; our hope was that these experiences would encourage them to continue to invest in their first language even as they learn English, thereby increasing the likelihood of their developing into fully bilingual, biliterate Americans.

The role of nonnative-English-speaking college students. I felt the program would benefit considerably from the participation of linguistic- and cultural-minority college students. While their presence would undoubtedly contribute to classroom discussions on issues of linguistic and cultural diversity, I was equally interested in having them act as positive role models for the language-minority children at Granger. Thanks to an aggressive recruitment program, nineteen of the fifty students who enrolled in the Spring Quarter were either language-minority or international students, including native speakers of Navajo, Chinese, Korean, Vietnamese, Italian, Arabic, Japanese, and Spanish. And though my intent had been for the language-minority children at Granger to see positive role models in the bilingual college students, in the end it was perhaps the children who gave the *minority* college students their most valuable lessons, as seen in the following journal excerpt written by K.V., a Vietnamese immigrant:

> The first time that I've really helped someone in terms of bilingualism is at Granger, a boy named Linh Ta, who only speaks Vietnamese and needed help in English. I can remember his shyness toward the other kids, and stubbornness toward the teacher because of language barrier. But by working with him on reading and spelling had made him more comfortable with English then later comfortable with his friends and teacher. This whole process made me feel really good. Simply because I know that I've helped someone better their life, or at least making their life easier to cope with. Since then on, I've found out about the importance and advantages of being bilingual. I became an interpreter for the state, and have written a few essays on bilingualism. In a way I'm glad that I've found my valuable asset that has been in me all this time and never realized it. It just makes me wonder how much more potential I have within me and not know it.

Hakuta's "interlocking" concept. This past Fall, McGapsters moved into its second phase, modeled on Hakuta's "interlocking" concept. Now college students trained language-minority children in using games to teach their native language experientially to other children in the school. At this point our goal is not to integrate L2 (second-language) instruction into the curriculum at Granger so much as to foster the development of those attitudes and aptitudes that promote successful L2 acquisition. If the children at Granger come to see that learning the languages of their peers can be as simple as engaging in mutually enjoyable activities in one another's languages, then perhaps they will find it easier to understand that we must know how to share ourselves and our language with others if we expect others to learn our language.

While developing the L2 skills of native English-speakers was not our immediate concern, there is reason to believe that the potential for significant L2 acquisition would be considerable if these structured L2 activities in the classroom were to lead to spontaneous L2 interaction in and especially outside the classroom. Consider Genesee's (1988) description of the differential results obtained by two, one-year late-immersion programs, one traditional and one innovative. Both programs were at the seventh-grade level and followed core French instruction beginning in kindergarten. The traditional program was teacher-centered and large-group oriented, with all students working together on the same material for the same amount of time. The innovative program was activity-centered and individually and small-group oriented, with children working at their own pace on projects of their own choice. Based on Piagetian principles, the program was set up to take advantage of the learner's ability to acquire language for self-motivated reasons. Although the subjects in the innovative program had only half as much instruction in the target language as the traditional group, comparisons showed that they achieved equivalent levels of proficiency in speaking and listening, and almost the same proficiency levels in reading and writing. Thus the McGapsters program, by promoting child-centered and game-oriented language learning, may in fact be sensitizing children to what might very well be one of the most effective language-learning environments for child L2 acquisition.

Preliminary evaluation. At this stage of the program's development, my evaluation has focused primarily on the impact of the McGapster program on the academic learning of my college students. Nevertheless, the students' journal-writing has proven to be a rich source of anecdotal evidence that the program may already be having a significant impact on the LEP children at Granger. As an example, I offer this journal excerpt written by S.H., a Korean-American college student who worked last Winter and Spring Quarters at Granger:

> Yesterday I attended the Granger international festival. Our group displayed posters and artifacts and we just sat around the table and explained things to people who were curious. While I was there I met a young boy from Korea whom I taught for one day. This young man did not know how to speak, read or write in Korean. One day I taught him how to write his name in Korean and he seemed to enjoy this experience very much. When I saw him at the festival he was with his parents and I had the chance to talk to them. At that moment his father told me something quite remarkable.

Something that made me tremble with excitement. He told me that when his son came home with his name written in Korean on a card he asked his parents if he could learn his native tongue. His father told me that he thinks that I had influenced his son to learn his own language. Then both parents thanked me warmly and left. At this moment I felt like I was actually doing something at the school. I suppose the smallest things can actually influence a child.

The next step: Training the trainers. For almost twenty years now I have designed and implemented college-level FL programs (cf. Sternfeld 1978, 1985a, 1985b, 1987a, 1987b, 1988a, 1988b, 1991, 1992, 1993). Regardless of the quality and intensity of these programs, I recognize that precious few of the college FL students I have worked with have gone on to become functional bilinguals. It is more than simply a question of too little, too late. College FL students who have grown up as monolingual English-speakers in our country are not inclined to consider becoming functionally bilingual part of their civic responsibility. Moreover, having had limited if any opportunity throughout their first twelve years of education to experience and reflect on the *interactive nature* of second-language acquisition, they often fail to acquire the very aptitudes and attitudes that promote successful adult L2 acquisition. My experience over the past twelve years with child second-language acquisition—as a parent outside the classroom and as a teacher inside the elementary school classroom—has convinced me that these aptitudes and attitudes are readily developed in childhood. If then we believe that educated Americans *should* be prepared to learn a second language as an adult—an assumption that would seem to underlie the many foreign-language requirements at secondary and postsecondary educational institutions—then I would argue that we had best prepare them for the task by exposing them to a second language as a child. It is for this very reason that I am so committed to the McGapsters program.

To make this vision a reality, I believe we must conceive of our ESL, FL, and bilingual-education professionals as the standard-bearers of a multilingual alliance that encourages our nation's children to learn through their own experience that by sharing their language with one another, they can learn one another's language. This fall I will be teaching an undergraduate second/foreign-language methods course that will enroll elementary-school teachers working on an ESL endorsement, undergraduates in applied-linguistics and TESL certificate programs, and FL-teaching majors and minors working toward teacher-education certification. The course will enlist these teachers-in-training in the training and supervision of the college students participating in the McGapsters program. This will bring all the teachers-in-training in contact with language-minority and language-majority children in the context of promoting the development of attitudes and aptitudes that will shape these children's language-learning experiences throughout their education. And perhaps in ten or fifteen years I will find my college FL classroom full of language-majority and language-minority bilinguals eager to acquire their third or fourth language.

Postscript: A word of caution. On February 21, 1995, Rep. Pete King (R.-N.Y.) introduced legislation in the House of Representatives that would make English the national language and end all federal programs that promote bilingualism. Rep. King charged that bilingual education "is perhaps the most damaging of this politically correct government infatuation with language multiculturalism[sic]" (*Salt Lake Tribune*, February 22, 1995: A1). In response, Rep. José Serrano (D.-N.Y.), who was born in Puerto Rico, declared that this bill would disenfranchise thousands of people and "prevent citizens and legal residents from acquiring crucial information on medical services, Social Security and education programs" (ibid.: A1). Rep. Serrano felt compelled to add, "There is nothing wrong with being bilingual." (ibid.: A1). We are immediately reminded of the widespread and deeply-rooted "scorn and shame for home-brewed bilingualism" (Hakuta 1988: 229) that persists in our country to this day. For those of us who do not share this belief, we clearly have our work cut out for us.

References

Crawford, James. 1992. *Hold your tongue: Bilingualism and the politics of "English Only."* Reading, Massachusetts: Addison-Wesley.

Genesee, Fred. 1988. "Neuropsychology and second language acquisition." In Leslie M. Beebe (ed.), *Issues in second language acquisition: Multiple perspectives*. New York: Newbury House. 81–112.

Hakuta, Kenji. 1986. *Mirror of language: The debate on bilingualism*. New York: Basic Books.

Hirsch, E.D., Jr. 1986. *Cultural literacy: What every American needs to know*. Boston: Houghton-Mifflin.

Markus, Gregory B., Jeffrey P.F. Howard, and David C. King. 1993. "Integrating community service and classroom instruction enhances learning: Results from an experiment." *Educational Evaluation and Policy Analysis* 15: 410–419.

National Commission on Youth. 1980. *The transition of youth to adulthood: A bridge too long*. Boulder, Colorado: Westview.

Newman, Frank. 1985. *Higher education and the American resurgence*. Princeton, N.J.: Carnegie Foundation for the Advancement of Teaching.

Salt Lake Tribune. February 22, 1995. "English-Only Bill, so to speak." A1.

Sternfeld, Steven. 1978. "The Italian experiment: The use of videotapes as a means of providing conversational models for the second language learner." Unpublished master's thesis, Department of Linguistics, University of Southern California.

Sternfeld, Steven. 1985a. *Foreign language acquisition and the psycho-social variables of adult second language acquisition*. Unpublished doctoral dissertation, University of Southern California.

Sternfeld, Steven. 1985b. "Learner expectations and the promotion of language acquisition in the classroom." *ITESOL Occasional Papers* 5: 26–42.

Sternfeld, Steven. 1987a. "Establishing the value of foreign language education." Paper presented at the Cincinnati Conference on Romance Languages and Literatures, Cincinnati, Ohio.

Sternfeld, Steven. 1987b. "Multilinguorum: A pedagogical play in four lessons." Paper presented at ITESOL Conference, Salt Lake City, Utah.

Sternfeld, Steven. 1988a. "Bilingual education and majority language speakers." Paper presented at the Symposium for Spanish and Portuguese Bilingualism, University of Colorado, Boulder.

Sternfeld, Steven. 1988b. "The applicability of the immersion approach to college foreign language instruction." *Foreign Language Annals* 21(3): 221–226.

Sternfeld, Steven. 1991. "Exploring community in a content-based foreign language classroom." *Cross Currents*. 18(2): 143–151.

Sternfeld, Steven. 1992. "An experiment in foreign education: The University of Utah's immersion/multiliteracy program." In R. Courchêne, J. T. Glidden, J. St. John, and C. Thérien (eds.), *Comprehension-based second language teaching*. Ottawa, Canada: University of Ottawa Press.

Sternfeld, Steven. 1993. "Immersion in first-year foreign language instruction for adults." In John Oller, Jr. (ed.), *Methods that work: Ideas for literacy and language teachers, Second edition*. Boston: Heinle and Heinle. 181–190.

The elaboration of sociolinguistic competence: Implications for teacher education[1]

Marianne Celce-Murcia
University of California, Los Angeles

Introduction and historical overview. The topic I am addressing in this paper is the continuing diversification and refinement of what was originally the sociolinguistic component in Dell Hymes' (1967, 1972) notion of "communicative competence."

Let us begin with some history that is summarized in Figure 1 below. From his earliest work to the present, Noam Chomsky (1957, 1965) has set the agenda for research in formal linguistics by arguing that linguistic competence (i.e. the grammatical knowledge in the mind of the ideal speaker-hearer and the origin and acquisition of that knowledge) is the proper business of linguistics.[2] Formal linguistics gives heavy emphasis to language universals and the domains of phonology, morphology, and syntax—with syntax being of central importance.

In contrast, the data of actual language performance, the learning of second or foreign languages and units of language beyond the sentence level have not been concerns for Chomsky or for most of his followers;[3] however, these are crucial concerns for those engaged in the education of language teachers.

For scholars interested in questions of language use, which includes most functional linguists, sociolinguists, and anthropological linguists, Hymes' notion of "communicative competence" has been attractive. Communicative competence, in its original formulation, consisted not only of Chomsky's linguistic or grammatical competence but also of sociolinguistic competence,

---

[1] At the outset, I would like to acknowledge with gratitude the collaboration of Zoltán Dörnyei and Sarah Thurrell, two colleagues in Hungary, with whom I have written a paper (Celce-Murcia, Dörnyei, and Thurrell 1994) that provides much of the basis for my address at this conference. I also thank Jim McIllece and Joe Plummer for their assistance with the figures.

[2] The grammar of Chomsky's ideal speaker-hearer often gets operationalized as native-speaker intuition. All of language other than "competence" is labeled "performance" and turned over to psycholinguists or sociolinguists for study. (Performance is not part of formal linguistics.)

[3] There are, of course, some notable exceptions among Chomsky's followers with regard to second-language-acquisition research. See for example Eubank (1995), Flynn (1991), and White (1991).

Figure 1. Emergence of sociolinguistic competence

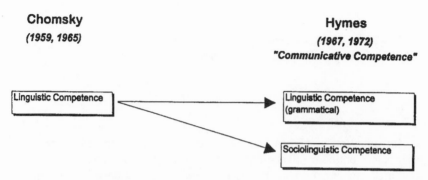

which covered all situated aspects of language use and issues of appropriacy: the speaker, the addressee, the message, the setting, the activity, the register, etc. Hymes' proposal was also attractive to educators involved in second-language teaching. The second-language learners they taught were not Chomsky's ideal native speaker/hearer. Instead, these language users approximated to varying degrees—typically without fully acquiring—the linguistic and sociolinguistic rules of the language they were learning.

The notion of communicative competence was given great impetus in the early 1980s by the work of Canale and Swain (1980), who proposed that strategic competence (i.e. the ability to use strategies to compensate for deficiencies in linguistic or sociolinguistic knowledge) was also a necessary part of communicative competence. A few years later, Canale (1983) further refined his earlier collaboration with Swain to include discourse competence (i.e. the ability to produce coherent oral and/or written messages that are more than one sentence in length). This four-component framework of Canale and Swain has persisted and has been applied pedagogically in a number of settings (e.g. Hoekje and Williams 1992).

There have been other proposed models of communicative competence (e.g. Bachman 1990, and Bachman and Palmer; in press), but these are hierarchical, discrete-competency models that have been developed for the purpose of doing research in language assessment rather than for pedagogical application in language teaching. For pedagogical purposes, the Canale and Swain model has had and still exerts the greatest influence.

Proposal for an elaborated model of communicative competence. Starting with Canale's 1983 proposal as outlined in Figure 2, I would like to suggest an elaboration that starts by maintaining three of his components, which I list and redefine as follows:

Figure 2. Elaborations of sociolinguistic competence

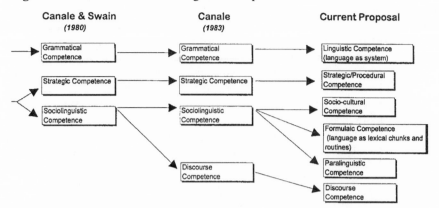

- Linguistic competence (language as system) comprises the basic elements of communication: the sentence patterns and types, the constituent structures, the morphological inflections, and the lexical resources, as well as the phonological and orthographic systems needed to realize communication as speech or writing.
- Strategic competence comprises the strategies and procedures relevant to language learning, language processing, and language production (e.g. Levelt 1989). It activates the knowledge of other competencies and helps language users compensate for gaps or deficiencies in knowledge when they communicate.
- Discourse competence concerns the selection, sequencing, and arrangement of words, structures, sentences, and utterances to achieve a unified spoken or written text. The top-down features of communicative intent, background knowledge, and formal schemata intersect with the bottom-up lexico-grammatical resources and cohesive devices; if the interaction of top-down and bottom-up resources is successful, the speaker/writer is able to express messages, attitudes, and to create coherent text.

I now propose a division of Canale's one remaining component, sociolinguistic competence, into three distinct components: sociocultural competence, formulaic competence, and paralinguistic competence. These I list and define as follows:

- Sociocultural competence refers to the speaker's knowledge of how to express messages appropriately within the overall social and cultural context of communication, in accordance with the pragmatic factors related to variation in language use—factors which reflect that a language is not simply a coding system but also an integral part of any individual's identity and the most important channel of social organization in the culture of the communities where that language is used. Participant variables, situational variables, conventions of face and politeness, and styles related to formality level or to field-specific registers are all part of this component.

- Formulaic competence captures the fact that language use consists of activating lexical chunks and prefabricated routines as much as (if not more than) activating discrete structures and words (Pawley and Syder 1983; Pawley 1992). This competency is a necessary counterpoint to linguistic/grammatical competence; it includes all collocations including fixed multiword expressions, idioms, and cliches, as well as lexical phrases associated with direct and indirect speech acts and other pragmatic functions.

- Paralinguistic competence includes primarily those nonverbal aspects of oral face-to-face communication such as body language (e.g. intake of breath, tensing the body and leaning forward to indicate interest and comprehension, facial expressions, gestures, and eye contact and movement).[4] It is also concerned with the speakers' use of space (physical distance between interlocutors), conventions regarding touch, affectively-loaded nonlinguistic sounds such as grunts and hisses, and conventions regarding silence.[5]

I now propose to move beyond listing my components of communicative competence because, in the model I am proposing, these six competencies have important interrelationships (see Figure 3 below). The core competence is discourse competence, not because it is "generative" in the sense that syntax is for Chomsky, but because this is where the other components all come together

---

[4] During the conference several participants made strong arguments to the effect that written language also has paralinguistic-like features such as quotation marks, use of the "[sic]" convention, use of smiley faces, etc. These proposals deserve further consideration. Nevertheless, whatever paralinguistic information we may be able to convey through the written mode is very minor compared with what we are able to convey through oral face-to-face interaction.

[5] I personally became aware of the importance of paralinguistic competence at the JALT conference (Japan Association of Language Teachers) in 1991. I had given a talk about the interconnections between grammar and discourse in oral communication. Then one American teacher asked me about everything else people do in oral communication (the eye gaze, the bowing or not bowing, etc). His point was that all the grammar and discourse in the world won't help very much if these other behaviors are left unanalyzed and untreated and are thus potentially used in ways that are completely out of sync with the language being spoken. I had to agree.

Figure 3. Interactions among components of communicative competence

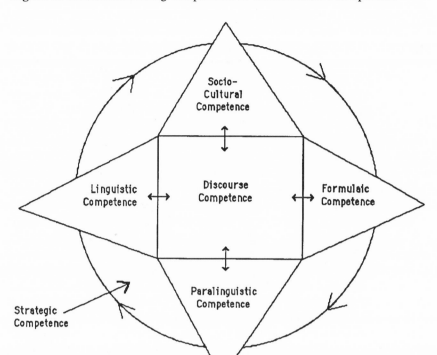

and manifest themselves both individually and interactionally.

Sociocultural competence, the top facet in the four-pointed diamond that overlays the discourse competence core, represents the speaker/listener's background knowledge of the target community. This component operates at both very specific levels (e.g. understanding an instance of communication in terms of the participants and the situation) and also at very general levels (e.g. understanding—but not necessarily adopting—the beliefs, values, conventions, taboos, etc. of the target community). It makes informed comprehension and communication possible. Then the two facets on the left and right sides of the diamond (linguistic/grammatical competence and formulaic competence) complement each other and allow the user to draw upon the system and forms of the language to express original and creative messages or—perhaps even more frequently—to draw upon prepackaged and routinized mundane messages. The bottom-most facet (paralinguistic competence) applies mainly to face-to-face oral interaction (but see footnote 5) and captures the fact that expert interlocutors use conventions of eye gaze, body posture, gesture, etc. that support and enhance the ongoing oral communication.[6] The sixth competency underlying all the other five is strategic competence, which activates, monitors, and corrects or compensates for any problems in form, meaning, communication, or appropriacy.

It should be emphasized that the interactions and overlaps schematically represented in Figure 3 are integral aspects of the proposed model of communicative competence. It is not sufficient simply to list all the components as was done in Figure 2; it is important to show the potential overlaps, interrelations and interactions, and to realize that discourse is where all the competencies most obviously reveal themselves. Discourse thus is the component in which (or through which) all the other competencies must be studied—and ultimately assessed—if one is concerned with communicative competence, which is not a hierarchical system of discrete competencies or abilities but a dynamic, interactive construct.

Also, it should be pointed out that apart from linguistic and formulaic competence, native speakers—much like nonnative speakers (though to a lesser degree)—may have gaps in the other components that make up communicative competence. With respect to sociocultural competence, we know that many native speakers have a low level of cultural literacy (Hirsch 1987). If we consider discourse competence, it is clear that many native speakers have problems with basic writing. Strategic/procedural competence is compromised in certain native speakers who suffer from language disorders such as dyslexia or aphasia that limit or undermine their use of procedures and strategies. Finally, the impaired paralinguistic competence of native speakers who are severely cross-eyed, painfully shy, or who have other social or physiological problems makes one-on-one communication awkward with all interlocutors other than those well habituated to such individual speakers.[7]

Implications for teaching. Perhaps the most important thing to ask about the proposed model is how it relates, if at all, to research in applied linguistics

---

[6] When paralinguistic support is not present, there are often communication problems. For example, the Chair of my Department recently told me about a discussion he had with one of our female Japanese graduate students. He asked her a question and she replied "Yes" but showed no reaction or comprehension; in fact her wide-open eyes seemed to indicate she had not understood. My chairperson then tried to rephrase the question using simpler language, and he still got the same response. At that point, he decided to abandon the conversation.

[7] People who do not provide appropriate paralinguistic support are not always nonnative speakers. When I was an undergraduate student, I can remember having an instructor, a native speaker of American English, who always looked out of the windows along the side of the room while lecturing instead of looking at the class. I found it extremely difficult to pay attention to and comprehend her lectures; and I found myself frequently looking out of the windows trying to figure out what the instructor found so interesting.

and trends in language teaching. There should be a close connection and a good fit if the model is reasonable. I believe such a connection can be made between the proposed model and trends in our discipline.

Without making any claims about causality, we can consider each component (in order of historical appearance) and see what its past and current connections are with research in applied linguistics and with trends in language teaching. Let us begin with the four competencies discussed in Canale (1983).

Linguistic or grammatical competence has been and still is a research issue in second-language acquisition whether one does error analysis, interlanguage analysis, morpheme-acquisition studies, or UG-oriented acquisition research. Approaches to language teaching that have focused on this competency include grammar-translation, audiolingualism, and cognitive code. The current interest in grammatical consciousness-raising (cf. Rutherford and Sharwood Smith 1985; Ellis 1993; Schmidt 1990) is further evidence that interest in this component of communicative competence persists in language pedagogy.

Hymes's sociolinguistic competence had its parallels in applied linguistic research on politeness (or rudeness),[8] register, speech acts, and language functions. The pedagogical counterparts of this research were the notional-functional syllabus (Wilkins 1976) and the principles and practices of early communicative language teaching (e.g. Savignon 1983; Widdowson 1978).

Strategic competence parallels applied linguistic research on cognitive, meta-cognitive, and communicative language-learning strategies in the work of researchers such as O'Malley and Chamot (1990), Bialystok (1990), and Wenden and Rubin (1987). The pedagogical counterpart has been the teaching of learner strategies (Rubin and Thompson 1994), learner autonomy (Wenden 1991), and a general emphasis on learner introspection and self-awareness.

Discourse competence has had its manifestations in applied linguistics where a keen interest in discourse analysis has developed, including specific focus on coherence (de Beaugrand 1980), cohesion (Halliday and Hasan 1976), genre analysis (Swales 1990), and conversation analysis (Sacks, Schegloff, and Jefferson 1974). This has had a variety of pedagogical counterparts in the emphasis on using authentic materials and tasks (Andersen 1987; Rings 1986), whole language (Newman 1985), language for specific purposes (Johns 1991), and content-based language teaching (Brinton, Snow, and Wesche 1989).

The three newly proposed competencies also correspond to developments in applied linguistics and language teaching:

---

[8] See the paper on rudeness by Leslie Beebe in this volume.

- Formulaic competence is reflected in research on corpus linguistics (Sinclair 1987), lexical phrases and routines (Nattinger and DeCarrico, 1990; Hoey 1991), and collocations (Benson, Benson, and Ilson 1986). The pedagogical counterpart of this has been renewed interest in teaching vocabulary—especially the collocations, lexical phrases, routines, and prefabs needed for specific functions and purposes.

- Paralinguistic competence is a more recent concern in applied linguistics; however, the work of communications researchers such as Goodwin (1994), Streeck (1993), and Tanenhaus (1995) show us how the eye gaze and gestures of the speaker and listener can be crucial in face-to-face oral communication. Their research, as well as the work of applied linguists such as Kellerman (1992), alerts us to the importance of this component and helps us realize that we can no longer ignore it. Teaching English through drama (Via 1976) and the use of dramatic techniques such as simulation and role-play (Stern 1991) are current pedagogical practices which incorporate paralinguistic competence into the language classroom.

Sociocultural competence (a part of Hymes's original sociolinguistic competence) is reflected in applied-linguistic research that is ethnographically informed, which can include social and cultural aspects of language acquisition (Schumann 1986) and language socialization/acculturation (Ochs and Schieffelin 1995) as well as all the studies on attitude and motivation that have been done in applied linguistics (see Snow with Shapira 1991 for an overview). The pedagogical counterpart of this research is found in situated and interactive language-teaching practices—e.g. dialog journals (Kreeft-Peyton 1987), guided observation and analysis, and learn-by-doing types of apprenticeships that teachers can create in the classroom using approaches such as project work (Fried-Booth 1986).

See the summary of all of these interconnections in Table 1 below, but also consider a few caveats. Undoubtedly further components of communicative competence and perhaps even other models of communicative competence will be proposed in the future. I hold no illusions about having the final word on this topic. Furthermore, any theoretical model of communicative competence is relative, rather than absolute, since communicative competence can have different meanings depending on the learners and the learning objectives in a given context (McGroarty 1984). Some components of the proposed model may thus be assigned more or less importance in some teaching situations than in others.

Table 1. How current model relates to applied linguistics and language teaching.

Model of Components (in order of appearance)	Research in Applied Linguistics	Language Teaching Approaches and Trends
• Linguistic/grammatical competence	Error/interlanguage analysis SLA morpheme acquisition studies	Audiolingualism Cognitive Code consciousness-raising
• Sociolinguistic competence	Research on politeness, register, speech acts, language functions	Notional-functional syllabus Early communicative language teaching
• Strategic competence	Research on cognitive, meta-cognitive, and communicative language-learning strategies	Teaching learner strategies, learner autonomy, and introspection/self-awareness
• Discourse competence	Discourse analysis: cohesion, coherence; genre analysis; conversation analysis	Authentic materials and tasks; whole language; content-based instruction
• Formulaic competence	Corpus linguistics: lexical phrases, routines, collocations	Teaching vocabulary, i.e. lexical phrases, routines, and prefabs needed for specific functions and purposes
• Paralinguistic competence	Research on eye gaze, gesture, and body posture/movement in oral communication	Dramatization, simulation, role play
• (Sociocultural competence)	Ethnographically-informed approaches; language acquisition as socialization/acculturation; attitude and motivation studies	Situated and interactive language practice (dialogue journals, guided observation/analysis, apprenticeship/project work)

Conclusion. Interestingly, Chomsky's notion of linguistic competence, which goes back to 1957, still persists in the current model of communicative competence, but only as one component in an intricate and dynamic social and cultural system. Hymes's early and quite complex notion of sociolinguistic competence has been reconfigured into five competencies in the current model: strategic competence, discourse competence, formulaic competence, paralinguistic competence, and sociocultural competence.

Using the theme of this conference as an organizing principle, it appears that strategic/procedural competence is essentially psycholinguistic, that socio-cultural competence and paralinguistic competence are essentially ethnolinguistic, and that formulaic competence is sociolinguistic. Grammatical competence remains essentially linguistic, while discourse competence is unique in that it is central and potentially embodies all four of these "linguistics."

The challenge of educating language teachers is that somehow we must include in their preparation an awareness and knowledge of all of these perspectives—linguistic, psycholinguistic, sociolinguistic, and ethnolinguistic—not merely one or two of them. We must meet this challenge if we hope to give prospective second language teachers a broad background that will enable them to understand communicative competence in all its complexity and to respond with appropriate pedagogies to a variety of language learners, learning contexts, and purposes for learning second languages.[9]

REFERENCES

Andersen, Roger W. "The real McCoy: A model for an authentic text-based language curriculum." Report to the National Security Agency, Cooperative Agreement No. MDA904-86-H-011 with the University of California, Los Angeles.
Bachman, Lyle. 1990. *Fundamental considerations in language testing*. Oxford: Oxford University Press.
Bachman, Lyle and Adrian Palmer. (in press). *Language testing in practice*. Oxford: Oxford University Press.
Benson, Morton, Evelyn Benson, and Robert Ilson. 1986. *The BBI combinatory dictionary of English: A guide to word combination*. Amsterdam: John Benjamins.
Bialystok, Ellen. 1990. *Communication strategies*. Oxford: Blackwell.

---

[9] The challenge is even more pronounced when teacher educators are nonnative speakers training language teachers who are also nonnative speakers. In such cases, presenting relevant information, providing opportunities for practice and guidance, providing native-speaker input via various media, and serving as good models seem to be appropriate practices. Ideally, one would have had rich and extended contact with native speakers of the target language prior to undertaking work as a teacher educator.

Brinton, Donna, M. Ann Snow, and Marjorie Wesche. 1989. *Content-based second language instruction*. Boston: Heinle and Heinle.

Canale, Michael. 1983. "From communicative competence to communicative language pedagogy." In Jack C. Richards and Richard W. Schmidt (eds.), *Language and communication*. London: Longman.

Canale, Michael and Merrill Swain. 1980. "Theoretical bases of communicative approaches to second langauge teaching and testing." *Applied linguistics*. 1(1): 1–47.

Celce-Murcia, Marianne, Zoltán Dörnyei, and Sarah Thurrell. 1994. "Communicative competence: A pedagogically-motivated model with content specifications." Unpublished manuscript, University of California, Los Angeles.

Chomsky, Noam. 1957. *Syntactic structures*. The Hague: Mouton.

Chomsky, Noam. 1965. *Aspects of the theory of syntax*. Cambridge, Massachusetts: MIT Press.

de Beaugrand, Robert. 1980. *Text, discourse, and process*. Hillsdale, N.J.: Lawrence Erlbaum.

Ellis, Rod. 1993. "The Structural syllabus and second language acquisition." *TESOL Quarterly* 27(1): 91–113.

Eubank, Lynn. 1995. "Generative research on second language acquisition" In William Grabe (ed.), *Annual Review of Applied Linguistics* 15: 93–107. New York: Cambridge University Press.

Flynn, Suzanne. 1991. "The relevance of linguistic theory to language pedagogy: Debunking the myths." In *Georgetown University Round Table on Languages and Linguistics 1991*. Washington, D.C.: Georgetown University Press. 547–554.

Fried-Booth, Diana L. 1986. *Project work*. Oxford: Oxford University Press.

Goodwin, Charles. 1994. "Co-constructing meaning in conversations with an aphasic man." Paper presented in the colloquium on co-construction at the Annual Meeting of the American Association for Applied Linguistics, Baltimore, March 6, 1994.

Halliday, M.A.K and Ruqaiya Hasan. 1976. *Cohesion in English*. London: Longman.

Hirsch, Edward D. 1987. *Cultural literacy: What every American needs to know*. Boston: Houghton Mifflin.

Hoekje, Barbara and Jessica Williams. 1992. "Communicative competence and the dilemma of international teaching assistant education." *TESOL Quarterly* 26(2): 243–269.

Hoey, Michael. 1991. *Patterns of lexis in text*. Oxford: Oxford University Press.

Hymes, Dell. 1967. "Models of the interaction of language and social setting." *Journal of Social Issues* 23(1): 8–38.

Hymes, Dell. 1972. "On communicative competence." In J.B. Pride and J. Holmes (eds.), *Sociolinguistics: Selected readings*. Harmondsworth, U.K.: Penguin.

Johns, Ann. 1991. "English for specific purposes (ESP): Its history and contributions" in Marianne Celce-Murcia (ed.), *Teaching English as a second or foreign language*. Boston: Heinle and Heinle. 67–77.

Kellerman, Susan. 1992. "I see what you mean: The role of kinesic behavior in in listening and implications for foreign and second language learning." *Applied Linguistics* 13: 239–258.

Kreeft-Peyton, Joy. 1987. "Dialog journal writing with limited English proficient students" (Educational Report 7). Los Angeles: Center for Language Education and Research, University of California, Los Angeles.

Levelt, Willem J. M. 1989. *Speaking from intention to articulation*. Cambridge, Massachusetts: MIT Press.

McGroarty, Mary. 1984. "Some meanings of communicative competence for second language students" *TESOL Quarterly* 18(2): 257–272.

Nattinger, James and Jeanette DeCarrico. 1992. *Lexical phrases and language teaching*. Oxford: Oxford University Press.

Newman, Judith M. (ed.) 1985. *Whole language: Theory and use*. Portsmouth, N.H.: Heinemann Educational Books.

Ochs, Elinor and Bambi Schieffelin. 1995. "The impact of language socialization on grammatical development." In Paul Fletcher and Brian MacWhinney (eds.), *Handbook of child language.* Oxford: Blackwell. 73–94.

O'Malley, Michael and Anna Uhl Chamot. 1990. *Learning stategies in second language acquisition.* Cambridge, U.K.: Cambridge University Press.

Pawley, Andrew. 1992. "Formulaic speech." In William Bright (ed.), *International encyclopedia of linguistics, Volume 2.* New York: Oxford University Press.

Pawley, Andrew and Francis H. Syder. 1983. "Two puzzles for linguistic theory: Nativelike selection and nativelike fluency." In Jack C. Richards and Richard W. Schmidt (eds.), *Language and communication.* London: Longman.

Rings, Louise. 1986. "Authentic language and authentic conversational texts." *Foreign Language Annals* 21: 467–478.

Rubin, Joan and Irene Thompson. 1994. *How to be a more successful language learner.* Boston: Heinle and Heinle.

Rutherford, William and Michael Sharwood Smith. 1985. "Consciousness-raising and universal grammar." *Applied Linguistics* 6: 274–282.

Sachs, Harvey, Emanuel Schegloff, and Gail Jefferson. 1974. "A simplest systematics for the organization of turn-taking for conversation." *Language* 50: 696–735.

Savignon, Sandra J. 1983. *Communicative competence: Theory and classroom practice.* Reading, Massachusetts: Addison-Wesley.

Schmidt, Richard. 1990. "The role of consciousness in second language learning." *Applied Linguistics* 11: 129–158.

Schumann, John H. 1986. "Research on the acculturation model for second-language acquisition." *Journal of Multicultural Education* 7(5): 379–392.

Sinclair, John McHenry (ed.). 1987. *Collins COBUILD English language dictionary.* London: Longman.

Snow, M. Ann with Rina G. Shapira. 1985. "The role of social-psychological factors in second language learning." In Marianne Celce-Murcia (ed.), *Beyond basics: Issues and research in TESOL.* Boston: Heinle and Heinle (Newbury House). 3–15.

Stern, Susan L. 1991. "An integrated approach to literature in ESL/EFL." In Marianne Celce-Murcia (ed), *Teaching English as a second or foreign language.* Boston: Heinle and Heinle. 328–346.

Streeck, Jürgen. 1993. "Gesture as communication I: Its coordination with gaze and speech." *Communication Monographs* 60: 275–299.

Swales, John M. 1990. *Genre analysis: English in academic and research settings.* New York: Cambridge University Press.

Tanenhaus, Michael K. 1995. "Using eye-movements to investigate spoken language comprehension." Lecture presented at the University of Southern California, Department of Linguistics, March 21, 1995.

Via, Richard A. 1976. *English in three acts.* Honolulu: University of Hawaii Press.

Wenden, Anita. 1991. *Learner strategies in language learning.* New York: Prentice-Hall International.

Wenden, Anita and Joan Rubin. 1987. *Learner strategies in language learning.* Englewood Cliffs, N.J.: Prentice-Hall International.

White, Lydia. 1991. "Adverb placement in second langauge acquisition: Some effects of position and negative evidence." *Second Language Research* 7(2): 133–166.

Widdowson, Henry G. 1978. *Teaching language as communication.* Oxford: Oxford University Press.

Wilkins, David A. 1976. *Notional syllabuses.* Oxford: Oxford University Press.

On the changing role of linguistics in the education of second-language teachers: Past, present, and future[1]

Diane Larsen-Freeman
School for International Training

Introduction. Three observations can be made upon examining the development of the fields of linguistics, language pedagogy, and language-teacher education over the last half-century. First, in the past, linguistics has had a dominant influence on language-teaching pedagogy. This has been true not only in its obvious role in contributing to the conceptualization of the subject matter, i.e. language, but also in its view of the language-learning, and even the language-teaching, processes. It follows, then, that linguistics has been featured prominently in language-teacher education (LTE) curricula.

Second, within the last decade or so, the dominance of "mainstream"[2] linguistics has declined significantly to the point where its influence on contemporary pedagogy is not easily discernible, at least as it is discussed in the literature.[3] Thus, third, while LTE curricula have been slow to respond to the declining influence of linguistics on language-teaching pedagogy, a future place for linguistics in LTE is by no means certain. With the recent suggestion that we examine teaching in order to establish the content of language-teacher-education programs (rather than just assuming that disciplinary knowledge like linguistics is isomorphic with teaching knowledge) (Freeman 1994), it is not difficult to imagine a point in the future where some language-teacher educators will question the place of any linguistics in their curricula.

I will begin the paper by attempting to show how the diminished role of linguistics has come to be. Next, I will argue that the latest influences on language teaching have come from outside of the field although they have current analogs in linguistics. In charting the antecedents of modern

---

[1] I am grateful for discussions I have had with my colleague Francis Bailey pertaining to the central premise of this paper.

[2] Following Fairclough (1989), I use "mainstream" linguistics to refer to "linguistics proper," that is, the study of phonology, morphology, syntax, and semantics.

[3] What transpires in classrooms might be an entirely different matter.

methodological practice I will be drawing on Bowen, Madsen and Hilferty (1985), Howatt (1984), Prator (1991), and Stern (1983), as well as my own experience. Due to the limitations of the latter, my comments on language-teaching methods relate most directly to ESL within the United States. Thus when I discuss language pedagogy, I am thinking mainly of English although I believe that many of my remarks will be applicable to other foreign languages as well. Finally, while I think that mainstream linguistics best serves language pedagogy in a circumscribed role, I think its elimination from language-teacher education would be a mistake. I will, therefore, conclude by saying what I believe the role of linguistics in LTE should be.

The waning role of linguistics. According to Prator (1991), the first large-scale attempt to directly apply linguistics to English-language teaching was made at the University of Michigan, accompanying and following the appearance of Charles Fries' *Teaching and learning English as a foreign language* in 1945. The Michigan method, later termed the oral-aural approach or the audiolingual method (ALM), called for the inculcation of sentence patterns through the training of good foreign-language speech habits. The training consisted of the use of repetition drills and pattern practice; however, according to Fries, more important than specific language-teaching practices in accounting for the success of the ALM was the "scientific" nature of the linguistic description employed. Fries wrote:

> For at least ten years some of us have been trying to explain that the fundamental feature of the new approach to language learning is not a greater allotment of time, is not smaller classes, is not even a greater emphasis on oral practice, although many of us believe these to be highly desirable. The fundamental feature of this new approach consists in a scientific descriptive analysis as the basis upon which to build the teaching materials. (Fries 1949, in Bowen et al. 1985: 36)

Whatever the reasons for its success, the imprint of Fries' structural/descriptive-linguistic approach was impressive. Howatt (1984) indicates that the teaching of English in America before 1940 was a minor activity; throughout the 1940s and 1950s, however, English-language teaching attracted high-level institutional support. The stimulus of the Michigan Institute prompted the publication of many significant descriptive and applied-linguistic studies. The strong influence of structural linguistics persisted to the end of the decade. For example, in the summer of 1959 twelve summer institutes for foreign-language teachers were held offering courses such as "Instruction in Linguistic Analysis and its Application in Language Teaching." Furthermore, the newly established Center for Applied Linguistics in Washington, D.C. was contracted by the

Table 1. Evolution of views on language, language learning, and language teaching for the past fifty years, and the disciplines which informed them.

DISCIPLINE	LANGUAGE	LANGUAGE LEARNING	LANGUAGE TEACHING
Linguistics: Descriptive/Structural	Patterns	Habit-formation	Audiolingualism: Repetition drills Pattern practice
Linguistics: (a) Transformational-generative	Rules	Rule-formation	Cognitive-code Approach: Inductive/Deductive exercises
(b) Government-binding	Principles/Parameters	Resetting the Parameters	Grammatical consciousness-raising activities
Linguistics: Sociolinguistics	Functions	Interactionism	Communicative Approach: Role plays Information exchanges
Linguistics: Discourse/Functional Corpus	Texts	———	Authentic texts In context

Table 1 (continued).

DISCIPLINE	LANGUAGE	LANGUAGE LEARNING	LANGUAGE TEACHING
Education: General	Unanalyzed whole	Engagement	Whole Language Approach
		Developing learner autonomy	Learning-strategy instruction
	Medium of learning	Experiential	Content-based Approach Language across the curriculum Cooperative Learning Task-based Approach
L1 Acquisition/ Literary Criticism: Social Constructivism	Meaning-making activity	Co-construction	Process Approach
Education: Critical Pedagogy	Instrument of power	Empowerment	Participatory Approach

U.S. Government to produce contrastive studies of English and the main European languages. These studies would, it was hoped, constitute a major step in bringing modern linguistic science to bear on the teaching of foreign languages (Howatt 1984: 268–269).

It should be acknowledged that the first row in Table 1 records the linguistic antecedents to modern English-teaching practice in the United States. Concurrent with this activity in the United States was a different tradition developing in Britain, where the linguistic approach of John Rupert Firth was very influential. Halliday, McIntosh, and Strevens elaborated and systematized the theoretical concepts originally suggested by Firth and offered them as a linguistic basis for language teaching in *Linguistic sciences and language teaching* (1964). These three authors

> regarded adequate language descriptions as the principle contribution that linguistics could make to language teaching. But descriptions, based on structuralism, in their view were unsatisfactory largely because of their neglect of contextual meaning and their inability to present an integrated picture of language as a whole. (Stern 1983: 164)

With the advantage of hindsight, we can readily see that the British and the American view of language would later converge.

But meanwhile, back in America, structural linguistics was also being attacked by Chomsky and his transformational-generative grammar (TG). "The publication in 1957 of Noam Chomsky's work electrified the linguistic community with its dramatic and powerful challenge to structural linguistics" (Bowen et al. 1985: 37). Rather than language being seen as a set of habits, Chomsky saw language as rule-governed. Thus language acquisition was a creative process of rule formation requiring considerable learner initiative rather than mere mechanical manipulation.

While the application of structural linguistics to language pedagogy was direct and its influence powerful (and still is; Tagmemics, for instance, has contributed greatly in this regard),

> the influence of transformational generative grammar, on the other hand, was of a different kind. Admittedly, "transformations" and "rules" began to appear in some language courses and a few textbook authors made serious attempts ... to devise teaching programmes which embodied insights from transformational generative grammar. (Stern 1983: 168)

In the main, however, TG did not contribute a methodology to the same extent that structural linguistics had. In fact, Chomsky explicitly rejected such a role. Thus the Cognitive-code Approach of the 1960s, involving deductive and inductive grammar exercises, did not emerge as a direct contribution of linguists, but rather from an acknowledgement that language acquisition should be viewed as a more rational than a solely empirical process (Diller 1971).

During the current incarnation of Chomskyan linguistics (Government and Binding, or GB, theory), which is receiving attention in linguistic and second-language-acquisition (SLA) circles these days, a set of abstract and linguistically significant principles are seen to underlie all natural languages and to comprise the essential faculty for language with which all individuals are in general uniformly and equally endowed. Acquisition proceeds when, given exposure to the target language, the parameters of these universal principles get fixed in a certain way. As Chomsky puts it "experience is required to set the switches; once they are set, the system functions" (Chomsky 1984: 25). Interesting questions are being asked from this perspective in SLA these days having to do with whether or not the principles and parameters of universal grammar are still accessible to the adult language learner or if the parameters that have been set in the first language need to be reset or readjusted for second-language acquisition. The pedagogical implications are far from being fully articulated at the moment. One could imagine looking to GB theory to provide guidance in selecting possible grammatical candidates for instruction. For those that are selected, one could foresee building a series of grammatical consciousness-raising activities (Rutherford and Sharwood Smith 1985) around them.

While we can appreciate once again the two-fold Chomskyan contribution of both a theory of language and an explanation for language learning, it should be noted that Chomsky's theory is self-acknowledged to be a theory of grammar, not communication, and thus a theory of grammar acquisition, not total-language acquisition. Moreover, as we have seen, any pedagogical implications have more to do with syllabus construction than with actual pedagogical practice.

Interestingly, despite its revolutionary approach and tremendous impact on linguistics, Chomsky's approach was conservative in perpetuating the focus on grammatical structures. Not surprisingly, this focus was to be challenged in turn. Believing that what was crucial was "not so much a better understanding of how language is structured, but a better understanding of how language is used, Hymes and [sociolinguistic] colleagues sounded a new note in American linguistics" (Howatt 1984: 271), a note consonant with many of the ideas and aims of British applied linguistics which had grown out of the Firthian tradition during the previous decade. Indeed, "after 1970 British and American work shared common themes" (Howatt 1984: 272).

Writing in 1972 on his notion of "communicative competence" Hymes asserts that "besides mastering linguistic forms, we need to know when, how and to whom it is appropriate to use these forms" (Bowen et al. 1985: 49). Hymes analyzed the message as a speech act or function (a request, compliment, directive), embedded in a speech activity such as a conversation, a lecture, or a joke, which occurs as part of a speech situation. British applied linguist Wilkins (1976) observed that such language functions had been overlooked in language-teaching pedagogy in favor of synthetic syllabi which featured linguistic forms. This observation encouraged teachers and materials writers to expand their goal from teaching the language system to teaching the language as communication.

In order to address this broadened goal, language educators embraced the Communicative Approach, among whose basic techniques were role plays and information exchanges. To my knowledge, the Communicative Approach makes no formal claim to having a companion theory of language learning. A tacit assumption seems to be held though, and that is that one learns to communicate by communicating. It is through interactionism, that is, students and teachers and students and students interacting, that language as communication is acquired. Notice the shift from an assumption that a focus on language forms prepares students to use language communicatively to an assumption that students learn to communicate by communicating.

Notice also for my purposes that linguists contributed neither an explanation for learning nor any elements of language pedagogy to the Communicative Approach. This is not meant to be a criticism of linguists for it is not their responsibility to prescribe practice to educators. The point is simply that by the 1970s the influence of linguists had waned. At the zenith of their influence in the 1940s and 1950s, linguists supplied a definition of the subject matter, a learning theory (with influence from behavioral psychology), and a language-teaching methodology. By the 1960s linguists were only looked to for a definition of the subject matter and a learning theory. And as we have just seen, by the 1970s they were relied on exclusively for providing an expanded definition of the subject matter.

In keeping with the circumscribed role of helping to define the subject matter, the final two schools of linguistics which could be said to have any bearing, however indirect, on modern language teaching is discourse or functional linguistics and corpus linguistics. Linguists such as Halliday, van Dijk, Thompson, and Givón are interested in language as text, not just written texts, as work by conversational analysts attests. Important insights into the nature of grammar and discourse can be gleaned from the work of these linguists. Drawing upon these insights, applied linguist Celce-Murcia (1993) has called for language teachers to adopt a discourse perspective in the explanations they offer language learners. She has also recommended the use of authentic texts for teaching language forms in context. The contribution of corpus linguistics has been in generating text-based descriptions of language usage upon which materials developers have drawn.

The rising influence of other disciplines. More recently, the allied disciplines to which language educators have turned have not been linguistics, but rather education, first-language acquisition, and literary criticism. Tracing the geneology of ideas which are new to the field is tricky. One reason for this is because ideas rarely have single pedigrees. The ideational bases for the trends which are featured in the bottom half of Table 1 are ubiquitous. Another reason for the risky nature in stating anything definitive about modern trends is that the trends overlap considerably, making it difficult to specify precisely what is distinctive about each. Doubtless at some future point, some of the trends I list separately will disappear; others will coalesce. Time will sort them out. Nevertheless, despite the considerable overlap among them, I think it is worth treating them distinctly at present because it is too premature to know which will be enduring and which fleeting. Doing so, however, will force a cursory treatment. One thing is certain: Although there are linguistic analogs among the trends I am about to discuss, and I will call attention to them, it is not linguists who have introduced them to the language-teaching field.

Significantly, this is true even for the origin of the modern conceptions of language. Closely aligned with discourse analysis, although not its direct descendant (in my reading of the literature at any rate) is the Whole Language Approach, the first of several modern-day trends that one can attribute to the field of general education. Whole Language advocates see language as "whole" and resist any attempt to analyze it into its component parts. Furthermore, the language is uncontrived: Teachers utilize complete texts in communicative situations. Finally, the language that students learn is language that relates to their own lives and cultures. In this way, individuals learn naturally when there is purposeful engagement, i.e. they become active in their own learning by being engaged in activities whose themes and issues are meaningful to them. (Edelsky, Altwerger and Flores 1991).

Another modern trend in the language-teaching field is devoted to encouraging and supporting learner autonomy. In fact, it really has more to do with what Wenden (1985) refers to as *learner* training than with *language* training. As such, no independent conception of language for this trend exists to my knowledge. Nonetheless, a great deal of importance has been placed on helping language learners expand their repertoires of techniques or devices with which they can achieve success in second-language acquisition.

As far as I can ascertain, Joan Rubin (1975) was the first to to introduce the notion of learning strategies to the language-teaching field. Although it does not seem to be what prompted Rubin to undertake her research, in her article on good language learners, Rubin mentions the work of educator Jerome Bruner. Bruner, in his seminal *Beyond the information given* (1973), has argued that "schooling cannot prepare students for all contingencies in a constantly changing world. Therefore the best currriculum is not one that is based on a static body of knowledge, but one which teaches students to cope with change—which focuses on the process of learning rather than its product" (Stern 1992: 258). This perspective certainly seems to underlie much of the calls for learning-strategy training as it has been applied to language teaching.

Contrasted with learning-strategy activities is content-centered language learning where a unitary focus on learning language is expressly eschewed in favor of one which integrates academic content with language instruction. Following Crandall's (1994) classification, one program model which belongs to this approach is content-based language instruction. In this model, teachers use instructional materials from academic content areas as the vehicle for developing language, content, cognitive, and study skills. The second language is used as the medium of instruction for academic subjects such as mathematics, science, and social studies. The language and content teachers, or a combination of the two, usually provide the instruction. Other program models which belong in this category, according to Crandall, are sheltered subject-matter teaching, theme-based teaching, the sheltered instruction of immersion programs, the adjunct model, and the language-across-the-curriculum model. The language-across-the-curriculum model is the name given to content-centered instruction that involves a conscious effort to integrate language instruction into all other curricular offerings.

There are a variety of strategies and techniques used in content-centered second-language instruction. One that has not been previously discussed is cooperative learning, where students of different linguistic and educational backgrounds and different skill levels work together on common tasks for a common goal in either the language or the content classroom. While cooperative learning focuses on the students, proponents of task-based learning deal less with specific student configurations than with the linguistic benefits students might derive by carrying out specific tasks or projects.

I turn next to disciplines other than education: First-language acquisition and literary criticism. It seems to me the ideas from these disciplines, although sharing certain philosphical perspectives with ones previously discussed, warrant their own unique place in Table 1. In second-language teaching, these ideas are perhaps best appreciated in the Process Approach. The Process Approach seeks not only to honor the process nature of writing, but also to underscore the need for the student to produce reader-based prose by having the student respond to teacher and peer feedback on successive drafts of a composition. The effect is that second-language writing becomes a process of co-construction, that is, the feedback and queries from one's teachers or classmates aids the student in creating prose that conveys a clear message to the writer's intended audience. It is not as though writers come into a situation with fully formed ideas—rather through an iterative process of writing and revising based on feedback from others, writers come to make meaning, or as Zamel (1982) puts it, "discover meaning."

As far as I can tell, these ideas in second-language teaching were stimulated by L1 acquisition researchers such as Emig, Shaughnessy, and Murray. However, the idea that knowledge is essentially socially-derived is evident also in the fields of literary criticism with the work of social constructivist Bakhtin, in child development with the work of Bakhtin's contemporary, Vygotsky, in the philosophy of science by Kuhn, and in anthropology by Geertz. As for the analog in linguistics, at the 1992 Georgetown University Round Table on Languages and Linguistics, Michael Halliday reprised on a familar theme by asserting that language is an act of meaning and the act of meaning is a social act. Thus the act of meaning is not the coding and transmitting of some pre-existing information or a state of mind of an individual but a critical component in a complex process of reality co-construction.

Similarly, with the last row of Table 1, it is not difficult to find a linguistic analog. The linguist who comes to mind because of recency is Norman Fairclough, who wrote in his book *Language and power,* "Mainstream linguistics is an asocial way of studying language, which has nothing to say about relationships between language and power and ideology" (1989: 7). Nothwithstanding Fairclough's indictment, for introducing the view of language as an instrument of power to the second-language-teaching field I think we have to credit individuals other than linguists—perhaps social theorists Foucault and Habermas, and certainly educator Friere, and more recently, Giroux.

An example of the way this view is applied to the L2 field is the Participatory Approach of language educators Wallerstein and Auerbach. Basing the principles of their approach explicitly on the work of Friere, Wallerstein and Auerbach call for students to learn language through empowerment by engaging in consciousness-raising activities around issues of disproportionate power allocation. Auerbach and McGrail put it this way: "As educators we must constantly connect what happens inside the classroom with what happens outside the classroom, and work with students to make literacy a tool for impacting their lives" (1990: 96).

While these latest two trends in our field may have themes which resonate with certain linguists, I believe the ideas which influenced language teaching and therefore LTE originated with disciplines other than linguistics. Thus, to recapitulate to this point: First, where at one time linguistics was dominant in language teaching, defining language, language learning, and language-teaching practices, it has undergone a diminution of influence; second, its influence in present practice has waned to the point that one could argue that linguistics has not been looked to even for a definition of the subject matter, i.e. language. Of course, descriptions of language abound in linguistics, many more than the mainstream ones I have listed here; it is just that no single theory has captured the attention of the language-teaching field the way that previous theories did or the way that other disciplines have today.

Reasons for the declining influence of linguistics. Let me now attempt to answer the question why the influence of linguistics has declined. There are four reasons, I believe. First, linguistic theories have become increasingly abstract over the years—at a level far removed from apparent classroom application. Then, too, due to the abstractness, the theories are often inaccessible without considerable expenditure of time and energy.

Second, much of mainstream linguistics deals with the formal properties of language abstracted from context, not the meaningful use of language, which is the preoccupation of most language teachers and learners.

The third reason has to do with the perceived character of linguistic knowledge[4] as contrasted with the nature of language teaching. Linguistic knowledge is perceived to be static and self-contained. Although actually tentative and incomplete, linguistic "facts" are presented categorically. They appear in the form of fully intact, rigid rules—when there are behavioral deviations from these rules, the departures are termed exceptions connoting aberration rather than variation. But the reality of language teaching is anything but absolute. Teaching and learning are dynamic and open-ended. Teachers deal with the messy, complex, and contingent nature of the classroom. Little wonder that there is a mismatch between elegant theories of language and the realities of second-language teaching.

Fourth, where the notion of language undergoes periodic redefinition by linguists, teachers need to entertain competing views of language simultaneously. Teachers need not be concerned with methodological purism. They cannot afford to subscribe to one theory of language. They are eclectic out of necessity. Their eclecticism stems not from capriciousness, but rather from the self-evident (to teachers) observation that language is a set of patterns. But it is also rule-governed, functional, textual, and communicative. Moreover, it is whole, it is a medium of learning, it is a meaning-making activity, and it is an instrument of power. In short, teachers need to accept the validity of every conception of language in Table 1. Thus teachers will be impatient with any linguistic theorist who attempts to tell them that only one of these is true of language. Teachers believe that descriptions of language are incomplete if they are not multifaceted, with each facet allowing a different glimpse of linguistic reality.

In sum, due to their properties, linguistic theories are seen by teachers as too divergent from language teaching to be of real utility in language teaching. Moreover, while I would endorse Freeman's (1994) suggestion that we establish a knowledge base of second-language teaching by examining teaching itself, and not depend on a priori prescriptions from other disciplines, I believe we need to draw upon disciplinary knowledge to support teachers' understanding of the

---

[4] I call it the *perceived* character of linguistic knowledge because I think that what is perceived to be true and what is actually true is quite different.

subject matter they have chosen to teach.[5] The question then for me becomes, How can I help teachers move from seeing linguistics as something outside themselves (an etic perspective) to something they own (an emic perspective)?

A new role for linguistics in language-teacher education? Rather than reject linguistics (and other disciplines) outright, I think it is incumbent upon language-teacher educators to help teachers (and I include teacher trainees) alter the nature of their relationship with linguistics and other disciplines. This process will be assisted in three ways. First of all, teachers must learn to see linguistics as a resource to be drawn on, but not the purveyor of all facts germane to the content of their teaching. Furthermore, teachers are not mere recipients of "received wisdom" from linguists. The relationship between teachers and linguists should be construed as a lateral, nonhierarchial one. Of course, merely saying this does not make it so. One way in which this attitude can be encouraged is to expose teachers to a variety of different linguistic approaches and to play the doubting and believing games with each (Larsen-Freeman 1983a). In this way the relative strengths and weaknesses of the different approaches will become apparent. Teachers need to cultivate a consumer mentality. We need not be dictated to by others.

Second, language-teacher educators need to recognize that what linguistics has to offer lies at least as much in the areas of awareness and attitude as it does in knowledge (Larsen-Freeman 1983b). This seems especially true of the hyphenated linguistics of ethno-, socio-, and psycholinguistics, but is no less true of what I am calling mainstream linguistics. I have found that questions work best to raise teachers' awareness and to encourage them to examine their attitudes in the context of linguistics: What does it mean to communicate? What is a language and how does it differ from a dialect? What is a word? What are the components of language and how do they interact? What does it mean to be a native speaker? How does the way language is used among native speakers vary? What does grammatical mean? What does appropriate mean? How is appropriateness determined, i.e. by whose standards? These questions and others help teacher trainees reach beyond the limits of their own experience and attitudes and begin to see that definitions are not givens in language itself, but are reflective of society's views, including issues of who in society wields the power.

Third, and finally, teachers have to be encouraged to cultivate a new attitude towards linguistics with regard to its perceived finiteness and absolutism. I no longer expect my teacher trainees to retain all the linguistic "facts" where

---

[5] Freeman, of course, does not say that we should not look to applied linguistics in this regard. He merely suggests that we should not rely on prescriptions from disciplines outside our field in order to define teaching. I heartily agree with this (see Larsen-Freeman 1990).

they exist. My teaching of linguistics has evolved to the point where it is less and less knowledge-driven. Instead, trainees work with frameworks to construct their own understanding beyond what any linguistic theory can provide (Larsen-Freeman 1992). I am not talking about issues of making linguistic insights accessible; I am talking about altering the form of social participation through which teachers' understanding is constructed. In addition, I do believe trainees need to be socialized into the discourse of the linguistic community to the extent that they need to learn how to label linguistic structures according to conventional metalanguage. By being able to do this, trainees have abundant linguistic resources available to them.

I should make explicit another assumption underlying these three measures. Knowledge transmission as a vehicle does not work well. It is not only the form that linguistic theories are in that keeps them etic; it is also the way that participation with them is invited—or is not. If teacher educators lecture about linguistic theory and facts, the information may remain external as a reified body of information whose relevance is seen to have little bearing on the teachers' practice.

Thus what we are left with as language-teacher educators is the responsibility not to reject the contributions of linguistics outright, but rather to do a better job of not only researching teachers' knowledge bases, but also of helping teachers develop their own relationship to disciplines which might expand or contribute to this knowledge base.

Conclusion. In conclusion, it seems to me, as Stern has indicated, our attitude towards linguistics has undergone a very significant shift from "applying linguistics directly to treating linguistics as a resource to be drawn on for the benefit of pedagogy" (Stern 1983: 174).

Thus clearly the role of linguistics in language teaching is more circumscribed than in the past. Rather than lamenting this fact, however, we should recognize linguistics for what it rightfully contributes—awareness of language and attitudes regarding language issues, and a source of insights which is indispensable as teachers construct their own understanding of teaching, learning, and language.

REFERENCES

Auerbach, Elsa and Loren McGrail. 1990. "Rosa's challenge: Connecting classroom and community contexts." In Sara Benesch (ed.), *ESL in America: Myths and possibilities*. Portsmouth, N.H.: Heinemann, Boyton/Cook. 96–111.
Bowen, J. Donald, Harold Madsen, and Ann Hilferty. 1985. *TESOL techniques and procedures*. Rowley, Massachusetts: Newbury House.
Bruner, Jerome. 1973. *Beyond the information given*. Allen and Unwin.

Celce-Murcia, Marianne. 1993. "A nonhierarchical relationship between grammar and communication. Part II: Insights from discourse analysis." In James E. Alatis (ed.), *Georgetown University Round Table on Languages and Linguistics 1992*. Washington, D.C.: Georgetown University Press. 166–173.

Chomsky, Noam. 1984. "Changing perspectives on knowledge and use of language." Unpublished manuscript.

Crandall, JoAnn. 1994. "Content-centered language learning." *ERIC Digest,* January 1994.

Diller, Karl C. 1971. *Generative grammar, structural linguistics, and language teaching.* Rowley, Massachusetts: Newbury House.

Edelsky, Carole, Bess Altweger, and Barbara Flores. 1991. *Whole language: What's the difference?* Portsmouth, N.H.: Heinemann.

Fairclough, Norman. 1989. *Language and power.* London: Longman.

Freeman, Donald. 1994. "Educational linguistics and the knowledge-base of language teaching." In James E. Alatis (ed.), *Georgetown University Round Table on Languages and Linguistics 1994.* Washington, D.C.: Georgetown University Press. 180–196.

Halliday, M.A.K. 1993. "The act of meaning." In James E. Alatis (ed.), *The Georgetown University Round Table on Languages and Linguistics 1992.* Washington, D.C.: Georgetown University Press. 7–21.

Halliday, M.A.K. 1964. Angus McIntosh, and Peter Strevens. *The linguistic sciences and language teaching.* London: Longman.

Howatt, A.P.R. 1984. *A history of English language teaching.* Oxford: Oxford University Press.

Larsen-Freeman, Diane. 1983a. "Training teachers or educating a teacher?" In James E. Alatis, H.H. Stern, and Peter Strevens (eds.), *Georgetown University Round Table on Languages and Linguistics 1983.* Washington, D.C.: Georgetown University Press. 264–274.

Larsen-Freeman, Diane. 1983b. "Second language acquisition: Getting the whole picture." In Kathleen Bailey, Michael Long, and Sabrina Peck (eds.), *Second language acquisition studies.* Rowley, Massachusetts: Newbury House. 3–22.

Larsen-Freeman, Diane. 1990. "Towards a theory of second language teaching." In James E. Alatis (ed.), *Georgetown University Round Table on Languages and Linguistics 1990.* Washington, D.C.: Georgetown University Press. 261–270.

Larsen-Freeman, Diane. 1992. "Punctuation in teacher education." In John Flowerdew, Mark Brock, and Sophie Hsia (eds.), *Perspectives on second language teacher education.* Hong Kong: City Polytechnic of Hong Kong. 309–318.

Prator, Clifford H. 1991. "Cornerstones of method and names for the profession." In Marianne Celce-Murcia (ed.), *Teaching English as a second or foreign language, Second edition.* New York: Newbury House. 11–22.

Rubin, Joan. 1975. "What the 'good language learner' can teach us." *TESOL Quarterly* 9(1): 41–51.

Rutherford, William and Michael Sharwood Smith. 1985. "Consciousness raising and universal grammar." *Applied Linguistics* 6(3): 274–282.

Stern, H.H. 1983. *Fundamental concepts of language teaching.* Oxford: Oxford University Press.

Stern, H.H. 1992. *Issues and options in language teaching.* Edited by Patrick Allen and Birgit Harley. Oxford: Oxford University Press.

Wenden, Anita. 1985. "Learner strategies." *TESOL Newsletter* 19(1): 4–5, 7.

Wilkins, David. 1976. *Notional syllabuses.* Oxford: Oxford University Press.

Zamel, Vivian. 1982. "Writing: The process of discovering meaning." *TESOL Quarterly* 16(2): 195–209.